Fatal Charm

By the same author:

The Celluloid Sacrifice: Aspects of Sex in the Movies
Stardom: The Hollywood Phenomenon
Stanley Kubrick Directs
Hollywood, England: The British Film Industry in the Sixties
Rudolph Valentino
Double Takes: Notes and Afterthoughts on the Movies
Superstars
The Shattered Silents: How the Talkies Came to Stay
Garbo
Peter Sellers: The Authorized Biography
Joan Crawford
Dietrich
No Bells on Sunday: The Journals of Rachel Roberts (Edited with a Documentary
    Biography)
National Heroes: British Cinema in the Seventies and Eighties
Bette Davis
Vivien: The Life of Vivien Leigh
'It's Only a Movie, Ingrid': Encounters On and Off Screen
Elizabeth: The Life of Elizabeth Taylor
Woody Allen: Beyond Words (trans. Robert Benayoun)
Zinnemann: An Autobiography (collaboration Fred Zinnemann)

Alexander Walker

FATAL CHARM

The Life of
Rex Harrison

St. Martin's Press
New York

Library of Congress Cataloging-in-Publication Data

Walker, Alexander.
    Fatal charm : the life of Rex Harrison /
Alexander Walker.
        p.   cm.
    ISBN 0-312-09284-9
    1. Harrison, Rex.   2. Actors—Great Britain—
Biography.
I. Title.
PN2598.H336W34   1993
792'.028'092—dc20
[B]   93-19055
                                              CIP

First published in Great Britain by Weidenfeld &
Nicolson.

First U.S. Edition: August 1993
10 9 8 7 6 5 4 3 2 1

For Jojo,
Francesca and Andrew Grima

Contents

Part Four: Kay

Part Five: Rachel

Part Six: Elizabeth

Part Seven: Mercia

Epilogue

Illustrations

Rex's school photograph, 1917 (Edward Hutchins Collection)

Rex, the 'juvenile lead' (Arthur Barbosa)

Rex, Arthur Barbosa and others dressed as the tsar's imperial court (Arthur Barbosa)

In *French Without Tears*, 1936 (Mander & Mitchenson Theatre Collection)

With Collette Thomas, his first wife (Private Collection)

In *Men Are Not Gods* (British Film Institute)

With Vivien Leigh in *Storm in a Teacup* (British Film Institute)

With Kaaren Verne in *Ten Days in Paris* (British Film Institute)

In *Night Train to Munich* (British Film Institute)

With Robert Morley in *Major Barbara* (British Film Institute)

With Constance Cummings and Kay Hammond in *Blithe Spirit* (British Film Institute)

In RAF uniform on the day of his marriage to Lilli Palmer, his second wife (Mander & Mitchenson Theatre Collection)

With Lilli in *The Rake's Progress* (British Film Institute)

At home with Lilli (British Film Institute)

With Lilli and their son Carey, *c.* autumn 1945 (British Film Institute)

Rex in 1945 (Mander & Mitchenson Theatre Collection)

Rex in Los Angeles (British Film Institute)

In *Anna and the King of Siam* (British Film Institute)

In *The Foxes of Harrow* (Weidenfeld and Nicolson Archives)

With Gene Tierney in *The Ghost and Mrs Muir* (British Film Institute)

With Carole Landis and Arthur Barbosa in London (Arthur Barbosa)

With Linda Darnell in *Unfaithfully Yours* (British Film Institute)

With Lilli in London, 1948 (Topham Picture Library)

As Henry VIII in *Anne of the Thousand Days* (Mander & Mitchenson Theatre Collection)

With Lilli Palmer in *The Four-Poster* (British Film Institute)

With Lilli in *The Four-Poster* (British Film Institute)

With Lilli in *The Four-Poster* (British Film Institute)

With Kay Kendall in *The Reluctant Debutante* (Hulton Deutsch Collection)

With Kay, November 1957 (Topham Picture Library)

Sunbathing with Kay Kendall, his third wife (Arthur Barbosa)

Rex directing Kay in *The Bright One* (Topham Picture Library)

With Kay in Portofino, 1958 (Topham Picture Library)

Rex with his sons Carey and Noel, and Noel's wife, at Kay Kendall's memorial service (Hulton Deutsch Collection)

Collette Harrison (Weidenfeld and Nicolson Archives)

Rex with Tammy Grimes (Pictorial Press)

With Rachel Roberts in *Platonov* (John Timbers)

With Rachel Roberts, his fourth wife, at Villa San Genesio, Portofino (Pictorial Press)

With Rachel at Villa San Genesio (Pictorial Press)

With Rachel on his cabin cruiser, *Henry* (Camera Press)

With Rachel, Arthur Barbosa and Robert Bolt in Portofino (Nancy Holmes)

On the set of *My Fair Lady* with Wilfrid Hyde-White and Audrey Hepburn (British Film Institute)

With Audrey Hepburn in *My Fair Lady* (British Film Institute)

Cartoon of *My Fair Lady* by Hirschfeld (British Film Institute)

In *Doctor Dolittle* (British Film Institute)

Being taught by choreographer Lee Theodore for *The Honey Pot* (British Film Institute)

With Richard Burton in *Staircase* (British Film Institute)

With Elizabeth Harris, his fifth wife, and her children (Terry O'Neill)

As Don Quixote (Scope Features)

With Julie Harris in *In Praise of Love* (Martha Swope)

With Mercia Tinker, his sixth wife, on their wedding day (Private Collection)

With Mercia and the insignia of his knighthood, 1989 (Topham Picture Library)

'He had no idea he was being so intolerant. It was his right. His right to behave as his name implied, as "the King".'

Stanley Donen

Fatal Charm

Preface and Acknowledgements

To write the life of a man who lived (and continued working) for over eighty years requires more than the usual amount of co-operation, and luck. I had both in more measure than I hoped when I began my research shortly before Rex's death in June 1990. I also had the advantage of knowing Rex.

I still smile when I recall the first words he spoke to me, rapped out at staccato speed from the ammunition clip he always carried on his person in case of ambush from his enemies in the media: 'Well, what are you in this for, the money?' One warms to people who have the courage to show the other side of themselves in a business which deals with concealing the true self to the advantage of the manufactured image. Rex showed both sides with the confidence, indeed the arrogance, of knowing that he owed the fear as well as the affection in which he was held to no one but himself. To people he wished to love him Rex was an incomparable charmer; to others he was a killer. That he was a great star, incomparably the best high-comedy actor of his own generation and indeed the following one (or two), there is no dispute. But there was always another side to the man which ensured that some people would remember him not by the love they bore him, but by the scars he inflicted. It says something, of course, for the legends surrounding him that they were often proud to strip their sleeve and show the scars and retail the story of how they got them. There are a good many such stories in the following pages. It may be that the injured will not like Rex any better when they reach the end of the book, but I hope they will understand him a lot better, and maybe in a forgiving way. The rest who read about his extraordinary life will not, I trust, lose their admiration for the great stylist they saw in action on stage and screen. Both Rexes were real, but one could not have been made without the contribution of the other – and a great incompleteness would result if any biographer went in for sympathetic subtraction. Rex certainly would not have wished it.

Since I owed him nothing – indeed, I had come to see him at his urgent request because I had been engaged to prepare for publication the journals of one of his wives, the tragic Rachel Roberts, and he had a well-justified anxiety to know their contents – I responded to his opening shot with the rejoinder, 'Well, what are *you* in it for, the money too? Of course, but you do it for more than money, I hope.' He then unsheathed the cold steel. 'Well, your friends will never speak to you again.' I am afraid that the idea was so manifestly absurd as well as unexpected that I laughed: 'I don't know who you think my friends are, Mr Harrison, but I doubt if they're as well brought up as yours. I hardly see them crossing the street to avoid meeting me because of a book.' After which, we fenced a little more lightly and respectfully with each other before getting down to business. And for the next few hours, Rex talked and talked and talked about his late wife, which is really to say that he talked about himself. The insights I gained then I have used here, supplemented, of course, by many more observations from those who knew Rex for far longer than I did.

When it was time to leave him, he found the butler had left – at the end of his working day, I suppose – and he was obliged to show me out himself. At the hall door he paused, screwed up his eyes – I knew how poor his sight had become – and said, 'Haven't we met before?' In fact, we had met several times before, but I knew the one time he remembered without being willing to admit it, since the circumstances again had not been of his own choice. 'Yes, in Tehran, a few years ago. We had supper together for a week.'

I was treated to a groan so eloquent that it would surely have upstaged any line of mine had we been appearing together in a play. I had the wit not to take on Rex on his own ground, but leave.

As well as Rex himself, those I have to thank for making it possible for me to write this book include three members of his immediate family: his sister Sylvia Countess De La Warr DBE, Noel Harrison, his son by Collette Thomas, and Carey Harrison, his son by his marriage to Lilli Palmer. All three were wonderfully detailed and graphic witnesses to the gifts and frailties of Rex as brother and father, man and artist. I am deeply in their debt.

Two people who knew Rex intimately, one of them his oldest friend and the other his long-time agent and adviser, helped me understand the many aspects of Rex – and, indeed, of the Reggie there had been before Rex – which it would otherwise have been hard to discover except by hearsay: they are Arthur Barbosa and Lawrence Evans. Listening to them, I felt a lot of my work being done for me.

Nearly all the above names were interviewed by me several times over. In addition, I interviewed specifically for this book the following people whose work and memories touched Rex's life: Luisa, Lady Abrahams; Lindsay Anderson; Frith Banbury; Isabel Barbosa; Peter Brook; Joan Buckmaster (Mrs Robert Morley); Sir Isaiah Berlin OM; Christopher Cazenove; Diana Churchill; Joseph Connolly; Lady Donaldson (biographer Frances Donaldson); Stanley Donen; The Hon. William Douglas Home; Dominick Dunne; Mary Evans; Richard Fleischer; Robert Flemyng; Angela Fox; Edward Fox; Bryan Forbes; Harold French; Margaret Gardner; Patrick Garland; Sidney Gilliat; Tammy Grimes; The Hon. Elizabeth Harris (Rex's fifth wife); Jones Harris; Sir Anthony Havelock-Allan Bt; Charlton Heston; Richard Huggett; Julie Harris; Gayle Hunnicutt; Jane, Duchess of Somerset; Richard Kershaw; Deborah Kerr; Robert Morley; Sheridan Morley; Joseph L. Mankiewicz; Rosemary Mankiewicz; John Mortimer; Ronald Neame; Darren Ramirez; Ronald Shedlo; Ned Sherrin; Richard Usborne; Peter Ustinov; Elisabeth Welch; Peter Yates; and Virginia Yates.

I have also drawn upon notes (in some cases unpublished) made during interviews I conducted while editing Rachel Roberts's journals with those who had known her and Rex. I express my gratitude for the double duty they have done in contributing to the present account to: Lionel Bart; Athol Fugard; Nancy Holmes; Edith Jackson (Rex's personal assistant); Lionel Jeffries; Pamela Mason; Dame Anna Neagle; Karel Reisz; Tony Randall; and Emlyn Williams.

Researching a life involves much paperwork in archives and libraries. To the following individuals, companies and institutions, I remain grateful for access given me to their invaluable records or for providing me with information:

At the University of Southern California, Los Angeles: Leith Adams and Ned Comstock of the Cinema-Television Library, who, once again, not only provided me with all the files I requested from their special collections, but pointed me to documents and memoranda about Rex I did not know existed.

At the Academy of Motion Picture Arts and Sciences: the head librarian and staff of the Margaret Herrick Library; and, in particular, Sanda Archer, who prepared documentary material for me and helped me arrange interviews.

At Fox Inc., and Twentieth Century–Fox Film Corporation Inc: Barry Diller, chairman and chief executive officer of Fox Inc. at the time of research, who received my request for information about Rex's post-war years at Fox with sympathy and practical help; Lorrayne Jurist, senior director in charge of basic properties at the film studio, who furnished me with details of Rex's contracts and employment; and Richard Handelman of the studio legal department, who was a most useful contact.

Also in Los Angeles: Charles Champlin, former entertainments editor of the *Los Angeles Times*, who gave me valuable introductions; the Los Angeles Police Department; and the Los Angeles County Museum of Art film department.

In New York: The Museum of Television and Broadcasting, with particular thanks for the rare film of Rex performing part of *Anne of the Thousand Days*; the Billy Rose Collection at the New York Public Library, Lincoln Center; and the New York Public Library, Fifth Avenue.

In Washington DC: The Office of the Postmaster-General, for information about delivery schedules, 1948.

In Boston: Dr Howard Gotlieb, University of Boston's special collections department, for information about the Rex Harrison acting scholarship.

In London: Mark Shivas, head of drama, BBC Television, for making available a recording of Rex Harrison in the BBC Television production of *The Adventures of Don Quixote*.

Jackie Morris of the British Film Institute's viewing services, who arranged screenings of Rex Harrison's films; the Information Library at the British Film Institute; and the National Film Archive's stills department for providing many illustrations of films made by Rex Harrison.

Dr Christopher Dowling of the Imperial War Museum, for providing information and contacts about Rex Harrison's wartime activities in the RAF.

The British Library and British Museum Reading Room staff; the London Library; and the head librarian and staff of Associated Newspapers.

In Liverpool: The Liverpool *Daily Post* and *Echo* Ltd for Rex Harrison material in the newspaper archives.

For the successful efforts they put into helping me trace hard-to-find material or individuals, I thank: Dianne Jeffrey; Edward Hutchins, who went to great lengths to track down details of Rex Harrison's First World War days at Birkdale School, and provided the enchanting period photograph of the class of 1917; Andrew Kyle of the British Council, Paris; Alvaro of La Famiglia, for help with translations relating to enquiries in Portofino; John Higgins, obituaries editor of *The Times*; Rose Tobias Shaw; Philip French, for information on Liverpool; and David Day, for information about the Rex Harrison auction.

All writers will appreciate the especial debt of gratitude I owe to two individuals who unselfishly made available to me research and programme material of their own: Richard Huggett, biographer of Binkie Beaumont, who let me use unpublished interview notes; and Richard Kershaw, who arranged a screening of the Rex Harrison film he made

4

for BBC Television and allowed me access to out-takes and audio overmatter of untransmitted material.

I acknowledge the kindness of the following individuals for allowing me to quote from plays and diaries referred to in the text:

Mrs Valerie Eliot and the T. S. Eliot estate for permission to quote from *The Cocktail Party*; Peter Carter-Ruck and the Terence Rattigan estate for permission to quote from *French Without Tears* and *In Praise of Love*; Mrs Sally Burton and Melvyn Bragg for permission to quote from Richard Burton's diaries as printed in the latter's biography, *Rich*; Darren Ramirez for permission to quote from Rachel Roberts's journals as printed in *No Bells on Sunday*, as well as to refer to passages hitherto unpublished.

A full list of other books which have yielded references or quotations contained in the text is to be found in the Bibliography, and I express my gratitude to their authors and publishers.

In order to simplify the section of source notes, the first quotation from any individual interviewed for this book is referred to by name, place and date. All other quotations, unless specifically noted, come from this (or these) interview(s). The present tense ('he/she says') is used to distinguish such quotations from those from other sources appearing elsewhere in the text.

I thank my agent, Carol Smith, for her support, advice and patience. And at my publishers, I thank Allegra Huston, Alex MacCormick and Elizabeth Blumer.

Lastly, I still remember the comfort and facilities given me by the managements of the Hotel Schweizerhof, Davos (and especially its director, Paul Heeb), and of the Hotel Miramare, Santa Margherita, where sections of this book were drafted and, in the latter hotel, supplemented by those among the staff who knew Rex in the days when he was the lord and master of the Villa San Genesio.

Alexander Walker
London, May 1992

Prologue

1: The Property of a Gentleman

He did his best, as so many other stars had attempted to do before him, to combine an undoubted liking for his own celebrity with a defensive reticence where his private life was concerned. But after death, one has no choice in the matter. A bare six months after he died, aged eighty-two, the curious world or at least the part of it within easy reach of the William Doyle Galleries at 175 East 87th Street, New York, was able to inspect the life, reputation and property that had belonged, uniquely, to Rex Harrison.

Doyle's was a good address for a man who had paid particular attention to such things while alive. Along with Sotheby's and Christie's, it is one of the city's leading auction houses. The sale scheduled for 13 December 1990 would attract a respectable crowd and hopefully a gratifying range of prices, even though 'crowds' and 'prices' were things that Rex disdained to linger over if he met them at the stage door or on the sales tag of the more desirable things in life. This sale was, of course, not a forced one: not one rendered necessary by the poverty of the deceased's estate. The value of Rex's fortune remains a secret, as well protected from posthumous disclosure as it was from the tax collectors of the many countries in which he worked, but where he also took care not to bank the income he accumulated through shrewd and wholly legitimate manipulation of the tax-avoidance laws. But his worldly estate was huge: the royalties alone from his recordings of the *My Fair Lady* lyrics added up to millions of dollars. Well, no one begrudged him that. Few stars had worked harder or more seriously: 'damned seriously', as he would have characterized the deceptively easy-looking business of practising the subtle, complex and ultimately mysterious craft of high comedy.

Dame Maggie Smith had spoken at his memorial service, held that June at the Little Church Around the Corner, not far from where the more solid sorts of memorabilia were now open to inspection at Doyle's. She recalled Edmund Kean's words to a young admirer who was visiting the great nineteenth-century actor on his deathbed. The youth was tongue-tied in the presence of the expiring celebrity and stammered out that, 'Dying must be difficult.'

'Oh, no,' Kean is said to have answered. 'Dying is easy ... It's comedy that is difficult.' Rex would have taken the same view.

Doyle's auction sale was for a good cause: to fund a Rex Harrison drama scholarship at Boston University. Rex, of course, had never been to drama school; nor had he shown much regard for those who graduated by yearly examination into the business that he had had to pick up from watching and emulating the great Edwardian actor-managers like Charles Hawtrey and Gerald du Maurier, or brilliant farceurs like Ronald Squire, Ralph Lynn, Tom Walls and A. E. Matthews. They still held the stage and captivated the town when Rex was a sixteen-year-old, £3.00-a-week juvenile in a provincial repertory company. But Boston University had honoured him with a Doctor of Humane Letters degree; no reason why Rex's property should not, in some small measure, enrich it in return.

As early as a month before the sale, the New York tabloids had begun speculating about 'what he might fetch'. 'Garbo sells, but does Rex?' asked the New York *Post*.¹ This was just the sort of impertinence Rex would not have wasted words replying to – well, maybe a four-letter one had anyone said it to his face. Garbo had died the year before. Besides their fame as film stars, Rex and she had something else in common. They had both spent their final years – though 'final', by Garbo's definition, connoted more than half a lifetime passed in reclusive retirement – at the same Manhattan apartment house on the East River and 52nd Street. The world had been astonished when her personal effects came up for auction and exposed a life-style far removed from convent austerity: rich period furnishings, valuable paintings, jewellery and other *objets*. A costly hoard, but impersonal too. Rex's belongings were in a different class, valued not for their intrinsic worth but for sentimental associations. Garbo's sale had brought in $20.7 million. Rex's sale was unlikely to match that, but would be much more popular. No Renoirs, maybe, but more homely. Brian Smith of the Doyle Galleries was disarmingly frank on this point. Evaluations of the 150-odd assorted items had been made as if Rex Harrison were an unknown, for it was impossible to say how much the celebrity factor would push up the prices. *Rex Harrison an unknown!* Of course there had to be a time when he was, but few people now alive could remember it. 'I go back to Methuselah,' Rex himself told a *Time* magazine interviewer five years before his death, unconsciously quoting the title of the play by George Bernard Shaw, the dramatist to whom he owed the role that, however indirectly, had set Rex's public image for his lifetime and ensured that his fame would long outlive him – *My Fair Lady*'s Professor Higgins.[2]

It was as much Henry Higgins as Rex Harrison that the crowds had come to Doyle's to see. Death had rendered the two of them even more inseparable. And indeed there they were. The first thing a visitor's eye fell on was a dominating black-and-white blow-up of Rex as Higgins, three feet by two and a half, resting with imperturbable authority against the artist's easel that Rex had used in later years when he had taken up painting as a spare-time occupation and, to his own delight and surprise, found a talent in himself 'at least as good as Churchill's', according to the young theatre director Patrick Garland, who had introduced Rex and his paint-box to the rugged beauty of Corsica.[3] In Doyle's photograph of him, he was wearing the best-known suit and hat in the world: the narrow-brimmed, high-crowned tweed hat from the London shop of Herbert Johnson and the matching tweed coat and vest that confirmed Rex's air of casual aristocracy – as well, it must be admitted, as his hollow-chested torso and the sloping shoulders that proved such a trial to the costume designer when he played Caesar in the *Cleopatra* film. Perhaps his French cuffs protruded a little more from the jacket sleeves than a Savile Row tailor would have thought fit. But when did a gentleman take orders from his tailor? Like Higgins, Rex was no respecter of rules – except the ones he made himself.

The face beneath the hat usually struck people as an essentially English one. But, if so, it was the kind of Englishness that is bred in few people today outside of families that are very sure of their place in the world and, even so, take care to hide their arrogance better than Rex did. His eyes had a hooded imperiousness that looked out at life and did not hesitate to judge it. Judgment was usually delivered on a tongue whose cadences were equally useful for coercion or courtship. A marvellous instrument of offence or charm. His nose was strong, a characteristic associated with masculine sexiness. *That* word – 'sexiness'. How he had hated it ever since a bitchy English actress way back in the 1930s had rhymed 'sexy' with 'Rexy' and turned it into an ironic jibe for not returning her affections. 'It annoys me,' he used to say, 'because I'm a more serious person than that vaudevillian label suggests.'[4] 'Sexy Rexy', indeed! Just because he had had six wives, like that 'Tudor bugger', as he habitually called King Henry VIII, though he spoke with a certain sympathetic understanding of the monarch whose carnal appetite for women was as vital to his well-being as the food he scoffed at the banquet table. Rex was also fond of recalling his own performance as King Henry in Maxwell Anderson's play *Anne of the Thousand Days*, a piece of acting rated by peers such as Robert Morley as 'among the greatest he ever did'.[5] And he had had to do it with the memory all too fresh in his mind of the woman who had taken her own life for love of him 3,000 miles away in Hollywood.

The mouth in the photograph was as unmistakable as the much imitated voice which issued from it. No disguising those love-thirsty lips, except when Hollywood unwisely tried to graft on its own artificial glamour by giving him a Ronald Colman-type moustache. It was the mouth of a sensualist: full and ripe, slightly wicked. Rex could be enormously kind to the women he adored, but some of those women also found the bully in him to be attractive, too.

For all its Englishness, this was a face which might have been set in a foreign mould. Over the years it had given rise to persistent surmises about Rex's own origins or distant ancestors. One was that he enjoyed the secret advantages of Jewish blood in his restless quest for what was new and challenging. That was untrue. Another *canard* had him as an offspring of a family which had had connections with English or German royalty in its distant past. It could not be proved, of course, said the green-room gossips, but didn't he behave like royalty? A remark not intended to be complimentary or loyal.

It was true, however, that Rex did not quite 'fit into' his century. Four hundred years earlier the Elizabethans might have accepted more easily someone of his full-blooded temperament. Their society, with its astonishing alloy of sensitivity and callousness, bred men like Rex, 'men of passionate parts', who never drew back from a confrontation and were ruthless in following up an advantage. They could seduce a woman without regard for consequences, love her and abandon her in order to seek fresh proof of their prowess, and the wonder was that she would forgive the experience. Such men did not leave enemies behind them when the affair had run its term: they made friends of their women. Even the most dissolute Elizabethan 'blood' might write exquisite poetry. Rex was never dissolute and could not write poetry, though he could manage a ribald parody of the song he had made famous, the one in which he confessed he had 'grown accustomed to her face'. Yet Rex spoke words with the sensitivity of a man who created art through speech. He handled words and sentences in ways that revealed the hidden poetry of the prosaic.

To the crowds in the auction rooms, passing Rex's portrait, he seemed rather aloof, but distinguished and urbane – though 'urbane' was another of his detested words. He regarded it as a belittling virtue, not in keeping with a man of his temper. If he could have turned round, however, and seen what was gong on behind his back, he would have been anything but urbane and his temper would have been famously exercised.

On display were dozens and dozens of his most intimate possessions, heaped higgledy-piggledy, being pawed over by sightseers in search of the vicarious thrills relayed by the touch of celebrity. These people did more than touch. Many made directly for the coat-stand on which hung half a dozen Professor Higgins hats in various checks, tweeds and plain materials. Now and then a man would snatch one off and ram it on his head and strike a pose while his wife or girlfriend worked the Polaroid. The grey silk Ascot top hat was ignored. Only the Higgins headgear held the magic. It had literally capped Rex's career. How annoyed he had been to learn that one American ambassador in London had had the gall to order a replica from the hatter's. Now at Doyle's it was up for grabs.

Nearby stood Rex's divan-style bed with its slightly faded padded headboard and its smooth silk coverlet in a tiny mulberry pattern, exactly as it had looked when *Architectural Journal* had featured it in a photo-spread of the New York apartment. Only then a pair of the master's gold monogrammed velvet slippers had been placed in waiting at the foot. No such sense of order now prevailed – and how Rex loved, *needed* order in his life! Over the bed was scattered a job lot of worn and torn parasols, vestiges perhaps of days in the hot Italian sun at the marvellous villa he had once owned high up in the hills above Portofino. And tumbling off the bed, in a slippery shoal of Cellophane and cling-film bags, were dozens of the long-sleeved cardigans with the pockets – 'Cheltenham coats', to give them their trade name – like the one he had worn in *My Fair Lady* and then adopted for his days off stage too. For Rex, acting and tailoring sometimes seemed cut from the same length of cloth. The cardigans came in a range of hues from oatmeal to butterscotch, but all were in cashmere. Women, he used to explain, liked the slightly slinky texture of the material as they took his arm. Clothes make the man, the advertisements of Rex's youth had told him. He discovered for himself how they could attract the women.

There were racks of Savile Row suits, made (like him) to last, yet now disconcertingly shrunken-looking without his six-foot two-inch frame to fill them and show off the bespoke tailoring of Huntsman or Sullivan, Woolley. Grey chalk-stripes, windowpane checks, country tweeds, a smoking jacket confection in navy velvet, blazers galore – 'Always blue round the waist,' he joked, but meant it – tails for evening wear, a white tuxedo, the same morning coat that had been made for him by Sullivan Williams in May 1958, and which he had worn to Buckingham Palace in July 1990, when the Queen dubbed him 'Sir Rex', and then, with a sovereign show of concern for her newest and by now very frail knight, enquired, 'Is it very hard work, the theatre?'[6]

Not so long before, he might have lost his temper at such a well-meant banality. Now all he said was, 'Yes, ma'am, it is.' He had less than a year to live.

Doyle's had assembled so much of Rex's haberdashery that it risked looking like a branch of Brooks Brothers, the Madison Avenue clothing emporium. There were Turnbull & Asser shirts by the boxful; bins of Hermès ties; shoes in scuffed condition but everlasting shape from the craftsmen at Trickers or New & Lingwood; dressing-gowns and bathrobes looking slightly soiled from the dust that had settled into the folds since their owner's death had condemned them to disuse. There was one exotic 'outsider': a velvet evening cape from the *atelier* of Pierre Cardin. Surely it had been made for the stage. It was too showy a garment for Rex's latterday tastes, though, if he had been able to afford it, it might conceivably have partnered the monocle he sported in his dandyfied youth.

There was a large bowl of assorted magnifying glasses, including examples from Hermès and Asprey. They puzzled people who did not know of the successful fight he had put up against blindness in his declining years. But even in earlier times, his vanity had dissuaded him from wearing spectacles in public, to the extent that he would drive out of the gates of his home in the South of France without his glasses on lest one of the ever-lurking *paparazzi* snapped him. Then seeing the coast was clear, he would shift over from the driving seat of his Rolls-Royce and yield the wheel to his wife. He did not like being driven by a woman, but what was the option if one did not wear glasses? One kind of vanity had its price in another kind. A bizarre rumour kept on pursuing Rex down the years: that he had only one eye. 'One *good* one, that's what I meant,' he would explode on finding himself once again erroneously included in a list of 'The Ten Best-Known One-Eyed Persons in the World' along with Lord Nelson and the Israeli general Moshe Dayan.

Naturally enough, there were plenty of tokens on show of Rex's success and esteem, and his 'incomparable contribution to excellence in the theatre and motion pictures'. This last encomium was written by ex-President Richard Nixon on the fly-leaf of his book *The Real War*, a title that, on second thoughts, was not inappropriate for Rex's involvement in the sphere of show-business operations. He and Nixon had got on well. Both men believed in 'hanging tough' and defending the primacy of the star role to the bitter end. There were framed gold discs for the sales achieved by albums of Rex's 'talk-songs' from *My Fair Lady* and *Doctor Dolittle*; a box of postcard-size fan photos, mostly still unsigned, for Rex's notorious indecisiveness extended even to his autograph; scrolls of honour; award plaques; a photo of Rex from the film *The Honey Pot* inscribed by its director, Joseph L. Mankiewicz, 'with grateful remembrance, really, NY, 1990, Joe.' That 'really' caused those who knew the trouble Rex's niggling, perfectionist nature occasioned to raise a knowing eyebrow.

Other mementos were more idiosyncratic, the kind that royalty is always having thrust upon it while touring remoter territories of the world. There was a shaving mug inscribed 'Rex' from The Mug Makers of Hollywood. The National Cap and Cloth Hat Institute commemorated Rex's continuing loyalty to their product by making him two awards in 1959, both gold-plated brass, though, not tweed. A more arcane plaque had the McVitie Highland Games, San Francisco, 1971, as its provenance. An impenetrable connection, since Rex abhorred organized exercise of any kind. The Aborigines of Australia had sent him a canoe paddle: perhaps a subtle Aboriginal comment on his one and only visit to their country when he toured it with *Aren't We All?* in 1986 and found that, except for Sydney, it was not yet ready for Frederick Lonsdale. If he had to go there again, he resolved, he would go 'as a civilian and enjoy it, and not have to act'.[7]

There were over a dozen framed stage-bills going back as far as *No Time for Comedy* in 1941, when the 'evening' show had to end at 7.30 pm, because of air raids on London, including *The Cocktail Party*, *The Emperor Henry IV*, *In Praise of Love*, *Bell, Book and Candle*, *Heartbreak House*, *Venus Observed* and coming right up to the present with Somerset Maugham's *The Circle* in which Rex was playing up to three weeks before his death.

An inscribed silver salver deserved its prominent place among the stage memorabilia: it marked his appearance in Terence Rattigan's *French Without Tears* in 1936. That play, more than any other, made Rex a star.

Oddly enough, some thought, there was scant evidence to be seen of the forty-four films he had made. Not a still from *The Rake's Progress* (or *Notorious Gentleman*, as it had to be retitled for America, where the original suggested a gardening interest), *The Reluctant Debutante, Anna and the King of Siam, The Constant Husband* or even *Cleopatra*. But then Rex came from the last generation of English actors that held the cinema in lower esteem than the stage. The theatre was his only true home, even though it was haunted by his own fears and anxieties. He confessed he never made an entrance without a sickening feeling of nervousness, though so well concealed that only fellow players and those waiting in the wings were aware of it. The live audience was something he loved, feared and needed: it constantly regenerated him. Like exercise, or marriage, it felt good after one had been through it. Hollywood was another country: they did things differently there. Some of the worst events in his life had happened in Hollywood.

Rex's paintings on the walls of Doyle's Galleries showed the well-travelled routes of the international set: views of Corsica, Barbados and Mustique, glimpses of forest, sugar-cane plantations, palm-topped islands and a cooler stretch of stud farm in Co. Kildare. Landscapes done in bold, vivid colours of the Fauves school: next to no figure studies, not even a self-portrait. That might have been asking too much of himself. The brilliant caricatures of him by Al Hirschfeld, sharp, taut, quizzical, equine-looking, eyes like slit trenches, brows in flight, mouth ready to snap on a line as if it were a mouse in a trap, these were mirror enough for him.

The big surprise was the books. Even his friends did not suppose Rex spent much time on reading outside the necessary lines in a script, and even these he tended to reduce arbitrarily – frequently incorporating other players' dialogue in the self-sacrifice – since he believed, usually correctly, that he could always do more with less. But dozens of cardboard boxes filled with books (*Ex libris* Rex Harrison) gave the lie to an unlettered existence. It is true that most of them had to do with work in the theatre or cinema, background for his roles. Even so, the range of interest they demonstrated was enormous, in some cases esoteric. There was one peculiarity. Most of them had had their dust jackets removed, in keeping with the snobbish English upper-class opinion that a book is not fit for a gentleman's library until it has been stripped of its commercial wrapping. Copies of Shaw's three-volume collection of reviews, *Our Theatre in the Nineties*, were prominent. They had provided Rex with the material for his well-received one-man show at the 1977 Edinburgh Festival, reading the playwright-critic's pungent opinions of his contemporaries – who were, in some cases, the models for Rex's style and behaviour. Though Rex met Shaw twice only – on the sets or locations of *Major Barbara* – both men, despite the age gap, felt a temperamental affinity with each other. When Shaw or Rex had made up his mind, there was no room for a second opinion. Both of them also hated Shakespeare. The pages of the Shaw volumes were roughly turned down, creased right down the centre, to mark the place where Rex had encountered some Shavian onslaught out of which he could squeeze, ever so exquisitely, the acid of abuse.

Then there were piles of art books, biographies of Victorian and Edwardian actor-managers, gifts from writers like Coward, Rattigan and Garson Kanin, who sent him a copy of *Remembering Mr Maugham* along with a letter hoping he would spot the dramatic nuggets in the often disgraceful life of the old man of letters and perhaps agree to play Maugham on stage. There was Elizabeth Jane Howard's *The Lovers' Companion: The Pleasures, Joys and Anguish of Love*; Rex's own anthology of amorous poetry and prose entitled, a little less certainly, *If Love Be Love*;

Winston Churchill's *The Island Race*; H.V. Morton's *In Search of England*; Osbert Sitwell's *Tales My Father Taught Me*; *The Café Royal Story*; Neville Shute's *The Rainbow and the Rose*; a collection of Guy de Maupassant's short stories; Cole Lesley's *Time Remembered*; Jane Austen's *Sense and Sensibility*; Arthur Bryant's biography of Charles II, a role Rex coveted throughout his life, but never found the chance to play; Sacheverell Sitwell's *Monks, Nuns and Monasteries*; Margaret Peter's *Mrs Pat*, a life of Shaw's platonic muse Mrs Patrick Campbell; Bryan Forbes's *Ned's Girl*, a life of Edith Evans, who had caused Rex one of his rare theatrical disasters; the 1966 Grove Press edition of the pornographic Victorian masterpiece *My Secret Life*. Two of the books had especially intimate connections with Rex. One was *Freud: A Novel* by his own son, the writer Carey Harrison, and a copy of T. S. Eliot's play *The Cocktail Party*, bearing the inscription 'Mercia. Calcutta. 1950.' Lady (Mercia) Harrison was Rex's widow. This last item, not strictly *ex libris* Rex Harrison, might have alerted one to the curiously missing dimension in what was literally the sale of a lifetime. There was no other hint, no evidence in letter or photograph, nothing at all to show that the owner of it all had been marrried not once, not twice, but six times. Rex's love life, in whatever form it may have been preserved, was not for sale – not even on show.

Collette Thomas, Lilli Palmer, Kay Kendall, Rachel Roberts, Elizabeth Harris, Mercia Tinker – all of them at one time or another had been 'Mrs Rex Harrison', had shared his affections, borne with his tantrums, basked in his fame, been admitted to the marvellous world he created for himself by his talents and his will. But none of them was visible here as an object of remembrance, regret or some sharper emotion. As in life, so in death Rex was the only star ... the king. His consorts did not enter the picture.

If one looked carefully, one could spot the king's throne. Few did, though, for it did not resemble the usual uncomfortable encumbrances of sovereignty. Here, as in most things, Rex pampered himself. It was a provincial Louis XVI-style armchair in fruitwood and polished leather with an oval back and a swivel base. On its wide seat Rex sat to put on his make-up for every performance as Henry Higgins. Next to it was his make-up box, looking as dingy as most much-travelled 'actors' requisites' come to be. But now its pastes and pencils were dry and cracked: the greasepaint, like Rex's own final transfiguration, was falling into dust. And this was not all. There in the centre of the table, on a tiny stand, imparting to all the inanimate objects around it an unsettling sense of a human relic, was a strange, flat, flexible piece of material. In its owner's heyday, it had been one of his best-guarded secrets: Rex's hairpiece. Even that was up for sale.

Part One

Reggie and Rex

2: Applause, Please

When he had settled his father and mother and his two sisters on chairs in the drawing-room, and maybe a grandparent and a few family friends as well, he would retire behind the plush velvet curtains drawn across the big bow window. He was then six or seven years old. They all waited. Then the drapes were pulled back by strings wound round his fists. To polite applause, he advanced a step or two and took a curtain call ... then another. More applause. At the third bow, he retired. The curtains rattled closed on their rods and the Harrison family waited for the show to begin, whatever it might be: a recitation, a joke he had remembered the sea-front entertainers telling on family holidays in North Wales, perhaps even a snatch of Gilbert and Sullivan. The Harrisons never missed Sir Henry Lytton whenever the star came to their native Liverpool with the D'Oyly Carte Opera. The curtains jerked apart again; and the young entertainer took three more bows – and retired.

Sylvia, his younger sister, then about ten, giggled. Marjorie, the eldest of the three children just into her teens in 1914, caught her mother's eye. As her only son prepared to take the third curtain call of the evening, Edith Harrison said patiently, but firmly, 'Reggie dear, it's not enough to show yourself, you know. That's not what's meant by acting. You've got to *do* something. You've got to be worth clapping."

He knew that, of course. He had been taken often enough to the Liverpool Repertory Theatre and once had laughed so helplessly at Seymour Hicks in *The Man in Dress Clothes* that the ushers had had to ask the Harrisons to take their son outside until he had recovered. Years later, he would insist in interviews that he had never known a moment in childhood when he did not want to act. 'That was evident at a very early age,' says his sister Sylvia today, 'much earlier than is usually documented. Around the age of four or five, he'd amuse us by turning a table upside down and standing in between the upright legs, waving his tiny arms and shouting.' But the trouble was, what sort of actor did he want to be? What sort of thing should he do? The applause he had heard when the star came on – the 'reception round' was the tradition then – was only exceeded by the roars of devotion as the cast took their curtain calls in ascending order of celebrity. But what one did to earn such love was still a mystery to him. Some people seemed to do nothing at all – just be themselves. Yet they were the best loved of all.

He was not called 'Rex' Harrison then. He'd been born on 5 March 1908, and baptized Reginald (for his father, a man more casually known as Bill) and Carey (a family name of his mother's). Where the 'Rex' came from was something he was always vague about, perhaps deliberately, for his early childhood held enough uncomfortable memories to make him acutely suspicious of even the most innocent questions of probing interviewers. He used to say that he asked his family to call him Rex when he was about ten. Since that is when he would have begun his struggles with schoolboy Latin, he may well have taken a fancy to the regal connotation of the word, though he never offered this up as an explanation. 'My father said, "You only call a dog Rex,"' Sylvia remembers, herself surprised that he did not go on and later change his name completely, since 'Harrison was not a very actorish sounding name, for those days anyhow.'

His birth had been a difficult one and Edith was advised not to have more children. For some time Rex (as he shall be called) stayed a puny-looking, sickly child. Croup, the build-up of phlegm in the thorax and lungs, caused a few early morning panics and an urgent resort to the steaming kitchen kettle which aerated the baby's breathing passages. Later, the distinctively throaty rasp in Rex's voice, as if the words were being propelled through the rifling in the barrel of a gun, each one precisely aimed on target, would be attributed to this successful battle against infantile congestion. To other people, though, the voice had simply the coercive petulance of a child who had been given his own way too early and too often. 'We called him "Baby",' says Sylvia. And for a time, he called himself 'Ba', finding the plaintive diminutive brought him attention and, perhaps, protection if his sisters tried ordering him around.

The house in which Rex was born, a double-fronted dwelling imposing enough to carry the name of Derry House, was in Tarbock Road, in what was at that time the semi-rural suburb of Huyton, about eight miles east of the great port of Liverpool. It had a large front lawn and a laburnum tree at the gate. A typical middle-middle-class place: comfortable and secure. But there was 'terror' in Rex the day his mother took him up the lane running past their home and put him into a kindergarten that was part of Huyton College, a girls' school which accepted village children in the infant forms.[2] Attempting to get his own way with the other pupils, mainly small girls, Rex found they ganged up against him and bullied him quite hard. His two sisters appeared a safer bet. Even so, he was a little afraid, and even slightly in awe of the tomboyish Sylvia. 'I've always liked spirited, funny women who know how to enjoy themselves,' he admitted later.[3] And he would say of his sister, half warily, half admiringly, 'I play lords and earls on the stage, but Sylvia marries them.'[4]

He declined to join his sisters in their games, preferring to be, as he put it, 'alone in my imagination'.[5] Not quite alone though. Around the age of six, he began playing truant from kindergarten, slipping across the road to satisfy his 'first romantic urge'[6] with a girl called Sheila Brunner, a skinny infant like himself and black-haired too. Both of them romped in the swampy pastureland, sometimes stark naked, splashing through the tadpole-infested pools. Watching his nude playmate, both of them damp and slimy, but enveloped in the satisfaction of breaking the rules, Rex felt like the runaway and his girl. In later life, when the 'romantic urge' had settled into a passionate pursuit of women for companionship or marriage, Rex's keenest satisfaction was often derived from the truant thrill of ignoring conventions. His parents and Sheila's found out, of course, and hauled their children off home. But behaving in a way that scandalized the grown-ups had given Rex a precocious taste for the illicit pleasures that life held well beyond the usual temptations of smoking or robbing apple orchards. He was punished by being locked up and forbidden to see Sheila, whereupon he hit himself on the head with a hammer, hard, and discovered the gratifying fuss that is made of him who throws a fit – the value of being a nuisance.

On the family's annual seaside holiday, taken with a multitude of cousins in North Wales, Rex would sometimes run ahead of his mother and sisters, hide in the hillside bracken and leap out, making horrible faces and uttering cannibalistic howls. So of course did – and do – plenty of other children who want to call attention to themselves without necessarily exhibiting the dramatic stirrings of a born actor. But there were other tensions in the Harrison household which were influencing Rex's career and character.

Edith Harrison was the dominant figure in the family. She came from a Baptist background: her grandfather had once tried converting the heathen in India. Her father had made commerce his business, not Christianity, and had become a successful industrial chemist. Edith had inherited his work ethic and was to pass it on to her son. Photographs show a self-confident woman with strong brows, eyes that are almond-shaped and heavily lidded, lips of quite unusual thickness and, one might think, sensuousness. These, too, were features that her only son inherited. Her mother, one Mary Jane Picard, is thought to have had French

Huguenot blood, which may help account for Rex's later propensity towards Continental nonconformity as well as the assertive nature of his Englishness, which he carried off with a dash that an Anglophile foreigner might have affected. Later in life he would be compared, for the 'Englishness' of his looks at least, to Leslie Howard; it is worth remembering that Howard originally came from Hungary.

Edith put up with no contradiction when it came to running things. She was a born manager: the only daughter in a family of four who had nursed her own mother through painful illness and then played hostess at Rex's grandmother's house, Belle Vale Hall, a large Georgian-style property within a mile of her own family home. It had its own cricket pitch and pavilion, tennis courts, and enough stable boys and gardeners to field a cricket eleven captained by Rex's father and his five brothers. The place gave Rex an early and abiding liking for the English country house that was to feature so often in the plays he did on stage. He remembered Belle Vale Hall's great staircase, gun room, huge dining-room, the views across fields and orchards, the stables that were themselves like a small mansion, where he climbed into the works of the clock in the tower, waiting with his hands over his ears for the hour to sound.

How the Harrisons had made their money is still rather obscure: marine insurance, maybe, though some reports say that a branch of the family took a lucrative hand in the slave trade of the eighteenth and early nineteenth centuries. Liverpool was then one of the departure points for the slave boats plying between Africa and America. By Rex's time, in the 1910s, the family may have developed investment links with Germany. Rex's father had been to Harrow at the same time as Winston Churchill and John Galsworthy, later one of his son's favourite novelists and playwrights, but he trained as a mechanical engineer at Hanover University, since Oxford and Cambridge had no faculties of that kind at the time. In the lay-off of the merchant fleets following the First World War, the Harrisons' income declined suddenly. 'We were never poor, but had to make do with a great deal less money,' Sylvia says. Belle Vale Hall was sold. Rex recalled his grandmother, now in a motorized wheelchair, chanting like a mantra an old North-of-England children's rhyme: 'Have to eat hash/Have to eat stew/No money, no money, no money.' Seeing how money could vanish, quite quickly unless held on to, was one of the lessons Rex learned early and well.

His father was no great example of industriousness. 'The sweetest man, but hadn't Mother's drive,' says Sylvia. 'A potterer and tinkerer. Rex probably got his love of cars and boats from him. I remember that poor dear Father used to get these wheezes that didn't quite work out, like making fire bricks out of coal dust. All his brothers were successful in business and quite rich, but not Father.'

Harrison *père* had been good at sports – cricket, in particular, and running – but the athlete turned into an easy-going man with marriage. His 'delicate' son was to grow up resembling him physically. He was a handsome six-footer with a very straight back, was dandyish and partial to Norfolk jackets with a cornflower (emblem of Harrow, he said) in his buttonhole. He had a moustache that he kept well clipped, a small forest of walking canes and a larger stock of bawdy jokes that earned a 'tut, tut' from his wife. And that was really all he amounted to. He remained kindly, but detached, always 'something of an enigma' to his son because 'for some reason or another, he didn't seem to want to *do* anything'.[7] One reason may have been his shyness. 'He found it very difficult to express his feelings, even to talk to strangers,' says Sylvia. It was always difficult for Rex, too, to show affection directly to his own sons, who doubted at times if he were capable of it at all. The vague gestures of 'fatherliness' that he made were probably the most he himself ever received from his own diffident parent. He even remained unsure about what kind of job his father did: he was 'something' on the Liverpool Stock Exchange, indeed 'something of an enigma'.

There were sometimes sharp words, if not rows, between the parents. Rex often heard his father reproached for 'just sitting around', whereupon Bill Harrison would select a cane and go walking. He thought his wife indulged Rex and would have preferred to see him sent to boarding school, not kept at home because of his 'delicateness'. Rex remembered his father quietly taking his bed pillow after one of these rows and retreating to his son's room, while the little boy climbed into the place beside his mother that his father had occupied.

In many ways Rex was the spoiled child of the family. To one of the women he later married, he once confessed that he thought his father had resented the way his mother fussed over her son. One of his earliest traumas, or so he claimed, was of his father trying to choke the small child. Whether or not this inexpressibly painful episode actually happened or was simply fabricated by an adult Rex as a self-exonerating reason for the coolness between father and son, it is, of course, impossible to say. There is no doubt, though, that relations with his father were strained in small ways as well. He used to recall his parent gazing in a melancholy fashion out of the windows of the living-room, looking at nothing in particular, for minutes on end. The waste of time this represented irritated the boy. Rex was always looking for something to do and hated the inactivity that came from not finding it. The fear of being ruled by a strong woman, as his father was in their household, goes a long way to explaining the lifelong mistrust that Rex preserved towards womankind in general; while at the same time the little boy in him that many women felt they detected and found immensely attractive was always seeking a woman who could be beautiful, companionable – and motherly. An antithesis was set up from early childhood between his need for a woman and his fear of being dependent on her.

His mother innocently awakened the boy's other senses. When she came to tuck him up at night, he observed her figure in the lamplight with pleasure – those wide hips, that generous bosom. When he later referred in his memoirs to such feelings, he felt obliged to add, in exculpatory parenthesis, that he was sure all small boys felt the same way – something by no means certain. This small boy, though, used to bellow down from his bedroom while his parents were giving a dinner party and then Edith would leave the table and come up to see what the matter was. On such occasions, when she kissed him goodnight again, he smelled the Bordeaux on her lips or the whiff of men's cigar smoke in her hair. Good living, for Rex, always had its maternal associations.

Unsurprisingly, therefore, Rex took after his mother. If he had admiration for any man at this time, it wasn't his father. It was the elder brother of his playmate Sheila Brunner, a youth called Godfrey, who enlisted immediately the First World War broke out during the Harrisons' August holidays in 1914.

All his life Rex remembered Godfrey leaving home, swept along in the initial rip-tide of jingoism, wearing well-pressed khakis and the red shoulder tabs and hatband of a newly commissioned lieutenant, looking immensely glamorous, a ready-made hero. A few months later he was told that Godfrey had fallen in action. At the same time, he heard his father declaring firmly that *he* was not going to put on uniform to get killed. The remark sparked off a fresh round of domestic discord. Edith told her spouse that if he would not fight for his country, then he should work for it, get himself a 'war effort' job. Bill Harrison dilly-dallied over this, as he did most disagreeable decisions. Rex was being taught chess at the time by his father. He found himself overturning the board, 'by accident', when the game reached a critical point so as not to incur the indignity of defeat by a man who would not fight for king and country.

Eventually Bill Harrison could no longer stand the nagging of his wife – and perhaps the ill-concealed partisanship of his son – and he took a job designing armour plating for battleships at a steel firm in Sheffield owned by a friend, a 'Mr Rigby', who had been with him in pre-war Hanover.

So, late in 1915 or early the next year, the family moved across the

Pennines and into a rented house in a community called Sharrow Bottom, not far from the Rigby steel mills.

However, if Rex's pubescent sense of patriotism was satisfied by his father's engagement in the war effort, a more seductive example of how to serve one's country and enjoy oneself at the same time was soon standing on the Harrisons' new doorstep in the shape of Uncle Vivian, on leave from the Canadian Expeditionary Force, unwashed, unshaven and lice-ridden, but in high spirits and even a little bit drunk. Bill immediately took his brother off to a Turkish bath – the quickest way of delousing the warrior. This relative, who had gone to Canada or been sent there for obscure reasons before Rex was born, quickly became the recipient of the boy's hero worship. Uncle Viv was a happy-go-lucky, rakish fellow. 'As so often happens,' Rex later said, 'the ne'er-do-well turned up trumps in our hour of need.'[8] 'Need' was perhaps pitching it a bit strong, despite a few Zeppelin raids on Sheffield that sent the Harrisons scuttling into their cellar. Uncle Viv took it all in a very relaxed manner. If he drank a bit too much, it only made his tongue wag more merrily, telling his young nephew of the chances that even war offered a man who could look out for himself. He was a crack shot and not unduly troubled about sportsmanship. The best way of dealing with the enemy, Rex was told, was shooting him while he was stationary, preferably while he was having a shit. 'Keep yourself on the move,' Uncle Viv recommended, before he, too, was moved back to the front line. He never reappears in Rex's reminiscences, but he had done his work well in sowing the seeds of unsentimental self-survival. The 'rake' had indeed served his purpose. The pupil would make steady progress.

When Rex was about eight, he was sent as a day boy to Birkdale Preparatory School, one of about sixty pupils. The school records have no mention of him, save in a poem composed by an unnamed member of the staff for a Christmas concert in 1917. School was a simpler experience then. One may imagine the pride that a boy of nine might feel by being included in the piece of doggerel verse composed by a teacher who had to include the name of every boy in the school. 'JOHNS together with the HOWES,/ Whom he came by chance to meet/Walking slowly down the street,/ Now declares with solemn vows/That to see a picture play/He will take them straight away./HARRISON is walking with/BESCOBY, and BUCK with SMITH./SPACIE, BALFOUR now are seen/With a victim in between ...' and so on, for pages.[9]

Rex always called himself a backward boy, though without much sense of shame. Lack of intelligence was not the cause of lack of distinction. He simply hated the method of being taught things by rote, just as, years later, he would approach the first reading of any new play he was in with an attitude of resigned necessity. 'Like having treacle poured over your face,' he called it:[10] it smothered initiative. It held everyone to the same pace.

He had a physical drawback, too. He caught measles soon after the move to Sheffield and it affected one of his eyes, though he seldom complained. And as he was later notoriously 'choosy' in acknowledging people he did not particularly like, his impaired sight was a help in pushing them out of vision.

Misconduct did not figure in his school reports: all that one of his form mates can recall about him is his neatness. He liked to know where things were.

The war over, the Harrisons settled for a time in modest lodgings in Southport, presumably to get their reduced finances sorted out, before returning to Liverpool, where they took a smaller house at 5 Lancaster Avenue, Sefton Park, an area where the nineteenth-century shipping families had built mansions for themselves. Rex's father resumed his light duties as a produce broker and Rex, aged eleven, was enrolled at Liverpool College for what he later described as 'a hugely and hideously unsuccessful education'.[11]

'I suppose the only real efforts I made at school were at cricket,' he said.[12] 'Father was mad keen on the game,' recalls his sister, 'and for a time he got closer to Rex than he ever had by coaching him, but eventually, I'm afraid, my brother was frustrated by being told how it *must* be played. Rex was allowed to be a left-handed bowler, but Father insisted he play a right-handed bat. Very irritating!' Much of the aggressiveness Rex could not express towards his parent went into his bowling style: an exceptionally long run up to the crease and then a snort as he sent the ball down, all designed to make himself look a fearsome threat. But the run-up was better than the delivery. Though he made the First Eleven team, 'Reggie' (or 'Bobby', as he was sometimes inexplicably known at college) did not exert himself much after that. To his father's utter disappointment, the school magazine noted: 'R. C. Harrison. The disappointment of the season. His bowling has possibilities, but owing to his temperament he has only "come off" once.' He liked dressing up in his prized cricket blazer better than the hard sweat that practice required; this he found repetitive.

As if to prove he was no 'mother's boy', he joined the school's Officer Training Corps, but hated the after-class square-bashing for the same reason. Interestingly, he found the manoeuvres gave him no trouble: he appeared to have a natural sense of timing.

'Rex liked doing things with his hands,' Sylvia recalls, 'it took his mind off other things. He could be a very pessimistic little boy, either up or down in the dumps. But he enjoyed taking me into the school laboratory and tinkering around with the crystal set – one of the "cat's whiskers" wirelesses – trying to receive the early radio broadcasts.'

And then he discovered what he really wanted to do. It was acting in school plays that brought Rex formidable compensation 'for being made to seem inadequate in almost everything else I did'.[5] He joined the junior dramatic society, run by a 'kind and gentle' Mr Wilkinson, and made his first appearance on a public stage when it presented two performances of *A Midsummer Night's Dream* at Crane Hall, Liverpool, in May 1922. Rex played two roles, Flute and Thisbe, and, since the college was not co-educational and boys had to take the female parts, Mrs Harrison fashioned a blond wig for her son. 'A sort of basin thing, made of straw,' he remembered, adding with an enthusiasm undiminished by more than half a century under other, more sophisticated hairpieces, that he had endowed himself with 'rather large breasts and hips' modelled on his mother's figure.'[3]

He wore a frock and pronounced his lines with a lisp, a notion that had occurred to him as he uttered the name 'Thisbe'. This bit of 'business', the first recorded example in Rex's large repertoire of self-serving additions to the author's text, was rewarded by appreciative laughter as he spoke the lines, 'O Wall, full well hath thou heard my moanth/For parting my fair Pyramuth and me./My cherry lipth have often kith'd thy stoneth ...' He also developed a crush on the boy playing Titania, though 'her' attractiveness disappeared the minute costume and make-up came off. Rex's reminiscences of his schooldays contain no other allusion to the transient passions that boys develop for each other at that age. In adult life, he showed more concern over what he called 'the male female', and was wont to add a 'thank God' for the fact that 'she' had not come into fashion when he was a boy growing up.

Another part he played was that of The Cat in Maeterlinck's *The Blue Bird*. For this, his mother made him a cat's suit in clinging black velvet, which had a hood with ears on it, whiskers made from waxed pipe-cleaners and an enormous tail. Still worrying over the part years later, he regretted that at that age he had not yet mastered the art of tripping on his tail: it would have won him more laughs. As it was, he managed quite nicely with the opening line of 'Miaow-are-you?'

Playing The Dog in the same production was Rex's best friend, a boy called Derek Mills-Roberts. Rex admired Derek's effrontery: the way he acted on impulse without the slightest regard for consequence. One day he witnessed Derek being sent off the field in a rugby match. The scrum had unexpectedly parted, disclosing his chum happily slamming another player most efficiently in the guts. Mills-Roberts was among the first commandos ashore in the D-Day landings on the Normandy beaches some twenty years later. Physical courage came to mean a lot to Rex, who had once been thought too delicate a child to display much of it. What appealed even more to him was recklessness.

Acting, he had found, was not at all like being at school. It had extracurricular rewards as well. A blonde tomboy called Cynthia Miles (or Myles), who lived near the Harrisons, saw his performances and complimented him. The approval of this funny, active, high-spirited girl gave him an early taste of a new power, one he could exert off stage, too, just by using the persona – not that *that* word would have occurred to him then – which had helped create the part on stage. In short, he felt the first heady beat of 'stardom'. The two of them bicycled furiously around the country lanes in Sefton Park, Rex screaming out his 'Miaow-are-you?' entrance line for Sylvia's delectation and she greeting every repetition of it with shrieks of delight. As he overtook her on his bike, he marvelled at the shapeliness of her figure, which surpassed even the treasured memory of Sheila Brunner's naked form. Sheila was to grow up, become a teacher, then a school principal, and never marry. Cynthia would fade out of his life as well, though never out of his recollections. Both girls were forerunners of the type that Rex was destined, and sometimes doomed, to pursue down the highways and byways of his life.

In 1925, when he was seventeen, his sister Sylvia, who, he had noted with interest, had a string of male admirers, decided to marry a young Scottish lawyer called David Maxwell Fyfe.

The wedding was probably made the more memorable for Rex because his parents took him and his sister Marjorie off to a theatre in the West End once they had bidden farewell to the honeymooners. It was a C. B. Cochran revue they saw, *On With the Dance*, starring Alice Delysia and two wonderful exponents of ballroom dancing, Terry and Pat Kendall. The evening left Rex entranced. The gratification he had felt appearing on the amateur stage was now raised to the pitch of professional excitement and envious enchantment. In retrospect, Cochran's spectacular show contained other omens of minor and major significance in his life. One day he would find himself on the same stage as Alice Delysia. And stranger still, the male partner in the brother-and-sister dance act whose apparently effortless inflections had so captivated him would one day soon become the father of the girl who was to be Rex's best-known and most tragic wife, Kay Kendall.

3: 'That Noisy Harrison Boy'

To Rex's alarm, David Maxwell Fyfe, his new brother-in-law, suggested he might go into the law when he left school. 'He needn't have worried,' Rex's sister says, 'he hadn't the brains for it.' Anyhow, Rex had already made up his mind. He wanted to be an actor; he even had a leaning to musical comedy. Were his parents shocked? 'No, Mother encouraged him,' says his sister, 'and she had the say-so in the family. She was very liberal-minded for those times – she even let me work for a bit in an art studio. Mother may have felt a bit thwarted herself, as she had artistic leanings and had studied music at Stuttgart.'

Bill Harrison knew someone on the board of directors at the Liverpool Repertory Theatre, the city's principal playhouse, founded about thirteen years previously. So Rex put on a 'natty suit'[1] and presented himself before William Armstrong, a dour Scot, who looked at him with distaste. Rex was gangling, nervous and, in addition, spotty. The theatre took on about ten pupils a year, using them in bit parts, as understudies and general factotums until, if they showed promise, a vacancy occurred in the resident company. The hours were long, from 10.30 am until after the curtain. The petty tyrannies and entrenched privileges of a stock company could easily kill what ambition tedium had not already extinguished. Armstrong may have calculated that Rex would not stay the course. No harm would be done, then, in humouring his father's 'connection' with the theatre. He would keep him in mind, he said, and, as Rex recalled, added with Scots precision that the starting pay would be thirty shillings a week. This is almost certainly incorrect. An absolute beginner at the Rep in those days would be lucky to rate half that. However, Rex 'took a small curtain call' and left satisfied.[2]

'Please attend rehearsals 10.30 am, 30 May 1925 [signed] William Armstrong,' said the eventual summons.[3] The relaxed groups of people, all older than he and chatting away convivially, did not help put him at his ease when he sauntered self-consciously across the stage to join them. The stage manager immediately pulled him away from the resident members of the company he had inadvertently infiltrated and put him where he belonged, with the nervous new recruits.

Training at the Rep was largely left to the observation of the trainee. Instruction in acting did not come into it – not yet, at least. Rex had hardly found his clothes hook in the communal dressing-room when the theatre closed while the company took their ten-week (unpaid) summer break. Many of them joined seaside shows. He did not report back until September. Luckily, gaps had opened in the residents' ranks and the tempo of his 'training' accelerated. One of the one-act 'curtain-raisers', a playlet called *Thirty Minutes in a Street*, required all hands to turn out on stage and play a variety of passers-by on foot or bicycle, tradesmen, military types, professional people, policemen, etc., fleeting cameos with a line or two and whatever 'business' could be invented. Rex was cast as 'The Husband', though 'The Father-to-be' would have fitted the bill better, as he had to run across stage in a panicky, dishevelled state crying out, 'Fetch a doctor ... it's a baby.'

On the opening night, with his parents out front, he did his mercy dash, but called out midway across the boards, 'Fetch a baby ...,' paused, realized something was not quite as it should be and added lamely, '... doctor.' In the hurly-burly of incidents and utterances, few of the audience probably noticed the slip-up. But, Rex recalled, he stood in the wings, hot, nervous, 'degraded and debased. In my own eyes, I was a wash-out. Here I was making my first entrance ever, messing it up, likely never to be allowed back in the company.'[4] He did not sleep that night. But the next day, with Armstrong silent – 'what he thought was another matter'[5] – Rex's self-confidence returned and he was soon regaling his friends with his 'blob'. But it had been 'the most fearful shock to my nervous system.'[6] The shock, or the anticipation of it, was to go on reverberating throughout his career. There was hardly a moment before he went on stage when Rex Harrison was not in a state of nerves.

He frequently recounted this incident in later interviews, embroidering on it, so that, 'Fetch a baby ... doctor,' became, 'It's a doctor ... fetch a baby' – a solecism that Armstrong could hardly have ignored. It was as if by indulging his gauche beginnings, Rex Harrison could lower the safety curtain between them and his later pre-eminence.

Sometimes other people did the work of exaggeration for him. In another bit part he played soon afterwards, that of a native boy in Eugene O'Neill's *Gold*, he had to black up and, wearing only a loincloth, shin up the trunk of a palm tree which was still wet from the flame-proof chemical sprayed on to it. His body make-up rubbed off and he came down again a piebald aboriginal. This contretemps was not thought embarrassing enough by Twentieth Century–Fox when it signed up Rex some years later, for it put out a publicity hand-out relating how 'the loincloth caught on a prop twig and I came as near to public nudity as I have since my diaper days.'[7] Rex was furious over this fiction. All right for him to poke gentle fun at himself, but this was holding him up to ridicule. The incident helped ingrain his mistrust of the media, even the public relations people.

Another on-stage embarrassment had a more encouraging outcome. He was playing a young footman in the 1926–7 season's production of John Galsworthy's *Old English*, waiting behind the old aristocrat played by Herbert Lomas and responding with the port decanter every time this veteran star of the Rep cried, 'Fill up, fill up,' in his richly fruity voice. Lost in Lomas's performance, however, he missed his cue and had to be prompted – this time to a ripple of laughter from the audience savouring the drollness of the old buffer not getting his glass replenished. Rex's negligence was turned into a bit of business by Lomas, who quite relished milking the inconsequential line of dialogue for its comic potential.

Rex told this story against himself. It is evidence, however, of how absorbed he was in studying, at close range, the marvellous naturalness of Lomas's acting, the casual ease of his by-play with port, cigars and Galsworthy's dialogue. Rex observed what he would never have seen from the stalls – how the player's performance was tuned up to give an impression of total naturalness. It was almost tangible, he recalled. 'Rex was a great observer, though you might not have thought so from his self-centred manner,' says his sister. 'He interpreted what he saw very exactly.' He did impersonations of Lomas around the Harrison house until his parents prayed for *Old English* to be taken out of repertory.

He was cast as a Messenger in John Drinkwater's *Abraham Lincoln* – another Lomas vehicle, revived as the actor's 'retirement piece' early in 1927 – and proceeded to screw himself up to the pitch of 'naturalness' by standing in the wings at rehearsal and evacuating his lungs of air so that he would arrive on stage gasping for the breath to utter his few lines.

'Harrison, are you all right?' came Armstrong's voice from the stalls, sharp with alarm.

'Yes, Mr Armstrong.'

'Then what are you *doing*, Harrison?'

'Acting, sir.'[8]

Presumably, he eventually got the balance right between exhaustion and exhalation, for the *Liverpool Post* noted that 'Mr Harrison's dumb show [*sic*] as the messenger from Fort Sumter was finely effective.' Earlier, he had been commended for a minor role – unspecified – in Edward Knoblock's *Milestones*: 'Mr Rex Harrison was nicely in the picture.'

33

This was probably the first time 'Rex' appeared in a theatre notice.

Armstrong kept casting Rex in bit parts, often requiring him to remain silent. Perhaps he was trying to tell him something, or simply hoping he would be bored and go away. If so, he completely misread Rex's character. Underemployed he may have been, but 'the theatre' was all around him, giving a purpose to the day and supplying the kind of ambition his father's existence so signally lacked. Rex had a chameleon side to him. He was particularly drawn to people who stood out from their background, as the older generation of Rep actors did. Off stage, too, Herbert Lomas retained the authority that went with his particular brand of character acting which he could modulate so well on stage. He was promising material for study, particularly as Lomas cultivated an indifference to convention. So, for that matter, did another of Rex's colourful uncles, this time Stanley Harrison, who owned and trained racehorses and had ridden in the Grand National, falling off, breaking his collar-bone, remounting and finishing a respectable sixth. Rex liked his sort of dash.

Uncle Stanley didn't sound his Gs (as in 'huntin'' and 'fishin''), and he had a red face and a dimpled chin that made him attractive to women. His wife was an Irish woman who wore a monocle. All this seemed to Rex the quintessence of chic. They should be on the stage, he told his uncle and aunt.

He noted with approval the perfectionism that other actors brought to their roles. Hugh Williams, for instance, always insisted on having his umbrella rolled afresh for each night he brought it on stage. Rex performed this chore for the compliments it brought him. Details like this appealed to the boy who was remembered at school only for being neat and tidy.

He soon formed friendships with boys his own age, who shared his zest for life and had the energy to get rid of it after work. There was Basil Moss, a junior member of the company; Christopher Thomas, an apprentice at the Leverhulme soap works at Port Sunlight and later a War Office civil servant; and there was Arthur Barbosa ...

Barbosa, an engaging and lanky young Anglo-Portuguese, became Rex's confidant and remained one of the few friends in life whom he did not lose or alienate.

Always called 'Art' by Rex, whom he in turn addressed a little sardonically as 'Sir', Barbosa is the best witness to Rex's formative years. 'There was still a lot of "Reggie" in him then,' he says today. 'For a couple of years after we met, Rex pretended he'd been educated at Uppingham, a school that was a bit of a cut above Liverpool College. He was already turning himself into a "gent", but not assembling the pieces any too well. But he made up for it by the tremendous self-confidence he displayed, at least in public.'[9]

Arthur was not an actor: he was at art college. The boys' friendship had been assisted by the fact that their homes were on the same No. 15 tram route, which made it easy for Rex to drop in on Arthur. 'He never announced himself. My mother used to say, "That noisy Harrison boy, no manners at all." He'd simply walk past the maid as soon as she opened the door – or open it himself if it were unlocked – and stand at the foot of the stairs and shout up them, "Art! ... Art!" Mother took a dim view of him. If he was ever aware of it, it didn't worry him.'

The Liverpool that the two boys spent their days and nights in was a rough, bustling, exuberant city with a tidal current of post-war youth flooding through it with a power that was not to be matched until the fame of the Beatles revived it forty years later. In spite of the economic depression, a freebooting air hung over the eleven miles of waterfront quays, docks and shipyards. Pony traps and horse-drawn delivery vans jostled motor traffic in streets that Irish navvies were perpetually digging up for the new electric cables. Rattling, rocking, swaying tramcars were the commonest public transport and an hour's journey on the top deck was popularly believed to effect any miscarriage that was desired. The novelist Nicholas Monsarrat, who had been to the same good public school in Cheshire as Barbosa, described the typical Liverpool sky as 'putting a lowering lead umbrella over the whole city'.[10] Everyone wrapped up warmly, summer as well as winter, against 'a ferocious draught that seemed to have come straight off the Irish Sea'.[11] In spite of his mother's childhood anxieties, Rex's health was to remain robust throughout most of his life. After Liverpool, perhaps, he was well proofed against the most inclement cities whose theatres he would play in.

The dance halls were where Rex, Art and their pals spent time between matinees and evening performances, buying sixpenny tickets in long rolls and choosing their partners from the girls sitting in 'the pen'. Rex apparently believed that his roll of tickets gave him the right to monopolize the girl of his choice for the whole afternoon. 'He'd turned into a young swell,' Barbosa remembers, 'rather more brash than actually smart.' Rex himself looked back fondly on 'my own lovely beige Oxford bags', the broad-legged trousers then affected by college undergraduates.[12] Sportier clothes he begged or borrowed from Uncle Stanley, particularly his racecourse tweeds. For a few years, he wore his hair greased to a patent-leather shine and parted down the middle. He sometimes wore a monocle, saying it compensated for his 'bad' eye. 'To be fair to him,' Barbosa says, 'monocles were all the rage then with young men-about-town. I wore one myself.'

Liverpool's leading hotel, the Adelphi, had opened a new dance hall for the younger set, the Bear Pit, where jazz was played. Rex first gained his lifelong love of that music from nights spent listening to Blues and early New Orleans jazz played by what Barbosa calls 'a washboard-type band'. Sometimes, at rowdier events in smaller halls, the two of them would take turns conducting. Barbosa remembers Rex wearing plus-fours and doing an energetic Charleston. And along with Basil Moss, he formed a ukelele duo, the pair of them twanging away on the strings after the curtain had come down at the Rep, filling the Sandown Club, the city's meeting-place for 'arty' types, with the transAtlantic rhythms of 'When the red, red robin' or 'There's a rainbow round my shoulder'. The 1920s were the era of parties – and arrogance. Any excuse served young people of Rex's age who had escaped the death toll of the war and were out to enjoy themselves almost in reaction to family bereavements. If reproached for being too cocky or callous, the snappy come-back phrase that Rex was heard to use was, 'I didn't ask to be born.' 'Since we were here, without having been give the choice,' Nicholas Monsarrat put it, 'we felt that we were owed a living, and that it ought to be a good one.'[3]

Rex took to the social side of drinking enthusiastically. 'Bung ho, troops!' was his rallying cry to his pals at the bar. He was rather less definite about what to drink. 'He dithered, even then,' Barbosa says, 'for he knew next to nothing about wine and rarely had the money for spirits. Generally, he ended up with beer.' His drinking companions noticed another early trait. Was it forgetfulness or really stinginess that forced others to nudge him to stand his round? 'Your shout, Harrison,' was a cry that often went up.

He did not hang back, however, when it came to what his mother would have called 'language'. Rex swore freely, with a relish for particular expletives. Barbosa recalls that when Rex, himself and their pals were out in a roadster they had maybe borrowed from a local garage, 'one of those open-to-the-breezes sports cars', and went over a bump in the road, Rex's monocle would sometimes jump out of his eye. 'Then he'd yell at me, "Where is it, you cunt?"' 'Cunt' was perhaps his favourite swear word – short, percussive and applied to animal, vegetable or mineral. He was not fussy. He used this invective freely in front of women and, like his wardrobe, it expanded. Both were useful ways of catching their attention.

He had already made the discovery that girls were fun. Now that he was frequently absent from his parents' home, he found out just how much fun. He flirted promiscuously. There were not many women employed in the Rep and few of them were young, so Rex plucked a girl away from a young actor in Sybil Thorndike's touring company when it visited Liverpool to play Shakespeare and Shaw. The actor in question was Carol Reed, the future film director, for whom Rex would eventually star in *Night Train to Munich*. But he had not much say in what Harrison did on this occasion, which was to take his girlfriend, Primrose, out to dinner, then home to meet his parents 'for a drink'. By the time they reached the Harrisons' place, the household had retired for the night. Rex put Primrose up in the spare room and broke the news of her presence at breakfast time. 'Mother was very tolerant,' says Sylvia, 'Rex could turn the charm on her.' By now it was evident to his family just how much charm he possessed for women. 'It came almost too easily to him, I think,' is his sister's opinion. 'Girls liked his deliberateness, so to speak: his strong opinions about anything and everything. There was a feeling it reflected a very precocious sex drive.'

'He became fairly nomadic early on,' says Barbosa. 'It was usually left to me to bring his family news of him, particularly when he went on tour. Rex was never a boy for letters home. In fact, writing letters gave him difficulty, not with putting words together, but with putting his feelings down on paper. He was like his father in that respect. A show of affection was difficult for Rex. From time to time, I'd call in at the Harrisons' and let them know what their son was up to – within limits.'

These limits presumably excluded news of Rex's developing taste for audacious encounters with the sort of girls one did not bring home. Like every seaport in the world, Liverpool had a large and well-established trade in prostitution. Every sort and shade of desire was served. The exuberant night-life of the city centre, plus the new tramways, drew the more mobile prostitutes away from their old haunts in docklands into the smarter streets. Rex patronized a few 'regular' girls, like any 'fast' young man of the time, but conceived a special fondness for black ones. He liked to be with women who were 'fun', even perhaps a bit theatrical in their behaviour, and the Afro-Caribbean girls provided him with more ribald amusement than their white sisters. More often than not, his preference ran to the voyeuristic. Watching was more 'fun' than doing: it had elements of the stage show, only now *he* could be the audience, amused, aroused and experiencing no attack of pre-curtain nerves. He would pay his money and then vanish into the back room, while Arthur Barbosa waited for him outside and played jazz records.

Another friend of both boys was Stuart Jeans, one of whose uncles, Ronnie Jeans, wrote sketches for C. B. Cochran's revues, while another, Frank Jeans, was a notable Liverpool surgeon happiest spending his after-work hours with theatre folk. It was at the parties Frank threw in his house in Rodney Street, where all the doctors seemed to live, that

Rex met many a London star who was touring the provinces – Binnie Hale, Ronald Squire, Jack Buchanan – as well as a sprinkling of West End managers on talent-trawling expeditions: 'If the light was burning in the big round cornice window high up in the Rodney Street house, that usually meant there was a party in progress, and you were made welcome,' says Barbosa. 'The connections Rex made there certainly helped him later.'

In the 1920s the distinction between the metropolitan West End theatre and the provinces was not as severely drawn as it later became. London stars were not only expected to tour but also found it very rewarding to do so. It secured them work between their last West End show and the next. The multiplicity of provincial theatres attracting touring companies from the capital was a vital part of the nation's entertainment and there was no stigma attached to 'going on tour'.

Rex stayed about two and a half years with the Liverpool Rep; though of the four dozen or so plays staged in his time there, he only appeared in 'perhaps six of them, in tiny parts'.[4] But he absorbed what he saw and heard, and even the plays he did not appear in influenced the sort of actor he was bent on becoming. By the late 1920s, the theatre had largely dispensed with the aura of imperious authority assiduously cultivated by the great actor-managers of the nineteenth and early twentieth centuries: Irving, Alexander, Tree ... One by one they had fallen back, exhausted by their rule, eroded by the incessant obligation to keep the public entertained. But they had created a theatrical tradition that still needed stars. The play was *not* the thing – or, at least, not the first thing. Audiences were attracted by actors who imposed their personalities and styles on the production. Plays were put on as showcases for the stars' talents, not the playwrights' skills, though they could coincide memorably on occasion.

Whenever he could, Rex would rush down to London to enjoy the stars of the West End: Celia Johnson, Gladys Cooper, Ronnie Squire, the American import Tallulah Bankhead and, of course, Gerald du Maurier, then actor-manager of the St James's Theatre. The capital's theatres were booming, thanks in part to American business methods introduced in the previous decade, but also to the strong public demand to be amused, stimulated, but not overly taxed by a serious theme or text. Shakespeare was still performed by Lilian Baylis at the Old Vic (then at the Lyric, Hammersmith) and by Sybil Thorndike and her husband Lewis Casson, but few West End managements risked putting on 'the classics'.

The post-war vogue for things American had popularized musicals like *Hit the Deck* and *The Girl Friend*; revues were in; so were the Ben

Travers–Ralph Lynn farces. 'It was the dawn of the superlative age,' Daphne du Maurier said, writing of her father Gerald, 'and the vogue of the emphasized adjective: the word "darling" rose too easily to the lips, and "marvellous", "wonderful" and "divine" described the colour of a new lipstick or the texture of a silk stocking.'[15]

Of all the actors whom Rex watched on his sorties into the West End, there was one he yearned to emulate with his own developing talent. Gerald du Maurier's great claim to fame, according to Frances Donaldson in her study of the actor-managers, was 'the development of the naturalistic manner' which had killed off the overemphatic nineteenth-century melodrama and facilitated the presentation of new kinds of popular plays.[16] It was harder than it looked. 'A lot of people copied [du Maurier],' Edith Evans was to say later. 'All he did was to throw away, but *they* didn't throw anything away, d'you see?'[17] Certainly Rex *saw*. Being an actor himself, albeit hardly tested, he was filled with admiration for this fellow professional who could conceal so immaculately the enormous difficulties inherent in looking, sounding, acting 'normal'.

Du Maurier at this time was the cleverest comedian on the English stage: a reputation, it has to be admitted, acquired in the imported Broadway 'crook' plays, as they were called, like *Raffles, The Gentleman Cracksman, Alias Jimmy Valentine* and *Arsène Lupin*, as well as the often revived *Brewster's Millions*. Daphne du Maurier's account of what her father contributed to roles that were shallow and flat in the printed script conveys an eerie intimation of how Rex was later to approach some of his parts. '[It] was personal and unique – a suggestion of extreme tension marked by a casual gaiety – making of Raffles someone highly strung, nervous, and finely drawn, yet fearless, full of a reckless and rather desperate indifference, someone who by the force of high spirits developed a kink in his nature.'[18]

Watching du Maurier and other 'personality players ... relaxed ... elegant ... men who thought nothing of balancing a cup of tea in one hand and a duchess in the other'[19] provided Rex, albeit lanky not relaxed, high-spirited but uncontrolled, flashy rather than elegant, with models to emulate.

To perfect their technique, however, it was necessary to aspire to the manner. These actors looked as if they were playing themselves. Rex's manner at that time was pretty uncouth. It could not easily be grafted on to the understated casualness of people who looked, he said later, as if they had merely dropped into the theatre on their way to the gentleman's club in St James's. As well as professional adulation, there was personal envy in Rex's view of them. For someone like himself, without formal training, practising to become proficient in the apparently untrained manner of these men was the best method available to him.

To make the effort would require an enormous amount of social assurance. His own unpolished identity would have to acquire a sheen to go with his professional reflection of contemporary manners. The wit and urbanity, elegance of dress and persuasive worldliness implicit in the du Maurier manner were attributes he longed to bring on stage with him and then, when the curtain came down, leave the theatre wearing as if they were part of his street clothes and day-to-day persona.

In some ways, Rex at this stage of his life resembled another actor from an English provincial city, Bristol this time, who had been born just four years before him. The name had been Archibald Alexander Leach until, working in the medium of film, he had invented a character for himself, a sophisticated man of the world he called Cary Grant, and then, as he confessed afterwards, 'found that I grew to like me'.

4: Chasing Girls and Jobs

Rex, just turned nineteen, came to London some time at the end of June 1927 to look for work – and his mother came too. Edith saw her son settled into her widowed sister's maisonette in Paddington before he did the rounds of the West End agents. He had been over two years at the Liverpool Rep, and sensed that he was being tolerated by William Armstrong, but not advanced. Armstrong sent him off with a bleak bit of advice. The theatrical profession was overcrowded. 'I do beg you to give it up, Harrison. You have to have *some* talent, you know.'[1] Rex left with no regrets – and those years held no nostalgia for him. He was to write in his memoirs, with a realistic shrug of the shoulders at the fates that befell his fellow actors at the Rep: 'None of them did anything much of note with their lives.'[2]

His Aunt Evelyn lived in leafy Leinster Gardens. She had several daughters. Once again, Rex found himself being mothered by women. He already knew and enjoyed the carnal side of their sex, but their maternal comforts were a need that was fixed in him early and stayed with him throughout life; even when he cursed his dependence on women, he had to have their 'companionship', their 'understanding', their 'intuitive' knowledge of what a chap wanted without his having to tell them. Rex never went out of his way to fit into a woman's life. Perhaps only a mother could have fulfilled the role perfectly and forgivingly.

The country's economic slump was at its worst: even 'respectable' jobs were hard to come by, never mind an acting role. Yet he felt the metropolitan tingle as he and Edith walked down Shaftesbury Avenue and saw famous names on the marquees: du Maurier (at the St James's), Gladys Cooper (at the Playhouse), Ralph Lynn, Tom Walls, Robertson Hare (the troika of low farce, at the Aldwych). As they passed the playbills for *The Garden of Eden*, he nudged his mother. There was the name of Hugh Williams, whose umbrella he had rolled nightly at the Rep – a star now. Why not ask him for help, Mrs Harrison suggested. Rex demurred: he was not up to troubling an important man. That attitude, too, persisted when he himself became 'important'. He expected younger players to defer to him, not importune him for an introduction. Eventually he ran into Jack Minster, a chum from the Rep, who hung out with other hopefuls in a bar off Leicester Square, circulating news of parts in forthcoming productions. Feeling she could do no more, Mrs Harrison returned home, but every week, unfailingly, she sent him a ten-shilling note. Rex opened a post office savings account. He had visiting cards made up, simply his name and 'The Liverpool Repertory Company' in the top corner. He found the theatre's name carried more weight than his. Actors of Rex's lowly status were not then represented by a single agent who did his best to advance their careers (and pay). They went the rounds of what were really casting agents, who would send several hopefuls off for the same part. Management waiting-rooms, he found, were as crowded as a platform at Lime Street Station, Liverpool.

He secured his first role on the strength of his appearance, not his experience. He looked like a young gentleman to the somewhat older gentleman he was sent to see by an agent casting a touring version of *Charley's Aunt*. Jeavon Brandon Thomas, whose father had written the celebrated farce of cross-dressing and high jinks, was exactly as Rex envisaged a leading man: tall, cultivated, in easy control of the interview – hardly even that, more like a chat between two clubmen. A butler stood by, just as on the stage. The play had made the Brandon Thomas family rich, and snobbish. *Charley's Aunt* was a mildly titillating farce about a couple of Oxford undergraduates scheming to inveigle a pair of politely reared girls into their rooms by the ruse of dressing up one of their male chums as a chaperone, Charley's aunt from Brazil, where – in the play's single line of catch-phrase popularity – 'the nuts come from'. It could be played as risqué as one wished, or dared, but the Brandon Thomases liked its behind-the-back flirtatiousness, bottom-pinching and boulevard complications to be played by a well-bred cast, or people who could pass for such. Hence Rex's warm welcome: he looked like one of the varsity sprigs. He left the house with the part in the pocket of his one good suit, where it was soon joined by eight pounds a week salary – very good money.

The opening taught him a lesson that money was not everything: health came first. The troupe, which was managed (and chaperoned) by Mrs Brandon Thomas, opened in Hull on 25 July 1927, and Rex had caught a cold. He was not easily audible as the girl-crazy undergraduate Jack Chesney. Fortunately, he was ably supported by Michael Shepley, himself just down from Cambridge, who played Charley Wickham, the one with the 'aunt'. But it taught Rex that poor health made for poor control and contributed to a fussiness of diet and creature comforts that he worked up into a minor production of his own in later years.

The two girls in the play were either too ladylike for his taste or else too well guarded, but he found available company in the dance halls of most of the seaside towns they played that summer and, in Whitby, partnered a buxom barmaid to win himself the title of 'Best Fox-Trotter on the East Coast'.

Farce, of course, was not the best graduation course to the subtleties of high comedy, but Rex learned the basics: to pitch his voice to the volume of the theatre, to distinguish a relaxed audience (one ready to laugh) from a challenging house (one determined not to) and to tolerate the tedium of repeating the play eight times a week or more. The older types varied this by a little subversive pantomime, like the old fellow playing Charley's stern guardian, who, with his back to the audience, would try to 'corpse' or break up the cast by letting his false teeth fall into his top hat and grinning at them with toothless gums. Rex was tempted into a bit of horseplay himself: he found it relaxed his nerves. He became a bit too relaxed, started giggling and wound up being reprimanded by Jeavon Brandon Thomas: any more of that and he would have to go, a threat which left him badly rattled. Control – that magic word – had to be mastered. He discovered that the trick lay in never letting the effort he was making show. But this was terribly hard work. Hard, not satisfying. Though farce was a good apprenticeship, requiring physical fitness and a variety of tempo, there was too much to it for his liking. 'High comedy is a form of truth,' he wrote later, 'and farce takes it beyond truth into a form of idiocy.'[3] Still, just as quantity at some point turns into quality, playing farce taught Rex the elements of comedy that were within his reach, if not yet his grasp.

Plays usually toured the provinces for sixteen weeks, then the cast broke up back in London to find another West End hit that could spin off an out-of-town company. The comforts of touring were variable. Rex received about £4.00 to £6.00 a week, which easily covered digs and meals at a theatrical landlady's – more, if she were a motherly type – and left him with thirty shillings a week for entertainment. He managed to save £20 or so a tour, which went into his post office acount with Edith's weekly ten-bob note. Travel was a bind: by train and on Sunday, the day when, it was said, only fish and actors travel. Loneliness was even worse. The company generally mixed only amongst themselves. The mystique of the stage had not yet been dissipated by the talking pictures and the peripatetic life left only time for transient relationships, though Rex's pursuit of pleasure gave him a closer acquaintance with some of the more notorious locals. But even when he became famous, he disliked permanent relationships – his marriages not excepted.

Depending on the company he was in, time between shows was either 'great fun' or intolerably 'boring'.[4] His mother occasionally joined him when the play passed within travelling distance of Liverpool, or if Arthur Barbosa had reported back that her son's spirits were low. 'I still had no real conviction that I was going to succeed in any way,' Rex recollected. 'But at nineteen, everything is fun.'[5]

Well, not quite. The company he was in was playing at Reading one week and Rex had gone canoeing on the Thames between shows. A passing motor-launch capsized his craft. He would have drowned but for the quickness of a local workman, who just managed to snare Rex in his gardening rake and pull him into shallow water. Rex told the story frequently, inevitably punning on the word 'rake'. But it seems to have given him a shock. 'He told me that he had felt himself on the very edge of death,' says Anthony Havelock-Allan, the producer of some of Rex's films.[6] At an age when most able-bodied teenagers think they will live forever (if they think about it at all), Rex had an early brush with mortality. 'I think it unconsciously influenced the excessive care, which others besides myself found so infuriating, not to get out of his depth in any project he was involved in. He always liked to feel firm ground beneath his feet. Even when he was out in his yacht, he'd anchor it in a cove and go swimming in the shallows.'

The *Charley's Aunt* tour ended in mid-October 1927, and he took a room at a raffish 'theatricals' hotel in St Martin's Lane, London, reflecting that his mother would be shocked to see the seedy types who also put up there.

Rex's own appearance at this time was in the tradition of hard-up actors posing as carefree young men-about-town in the belief that work was easier to come by if you looked as though you did not need it. A camel-hair coat had been his first expensive present to himself, though his sister suspects their mother slipped him the occasional windfall, for 'her estate was much less at her death than we expected'. A cigarette-holder and gold-plated lighter were other suave accessories. But the effect was not very 'finished'. He had the faint air of a stage juvenile in a *Punch* cartoon of the time. He made out he had more *savoir faire* than the society pages and gossip columns entitled him to claim. He was impatient to imitate life on that level, but the only opportunity that presented itself came with his next play, *Potiphar's Wife*, set in a world of wealth, titles and upper-class conventions. It was a society melodrama about a countess, bored with her older husband, who attempts to seduce her chauffeur and, failing, accuses the man of assaulting her. Rex played the Hon. Maurice Worthington, a dissolute hanger-on. Though minor, the role required playing with style and Rex gained a lot of satisfaction seeing how far he could go in playing a worthless character and keeping him interesting, not to say attractive.

He spent almost all of 1928 touring the country from Glasgow to the Channel resorts. He also fell in love.

Grace Underwood was a seventeen-year-old who acted under the name of Christine Barry and played another of the countess's titled set. Rex began an affair with her and was serious enough about it to take her home and introduce her to his parents. Once again the bed in the spare room was made up. Compared with Rex, one of his cousins said, Christine was a most attractive person. In the second half of 1928, however, news reached Rex in a roundabout way that a girl he had flirted with in a Midlands town was pregnant and blaming the baby on him. *Potiphar's Wife* required him to spend much of the third act in a witness box undergoing a grilling about the countess's degenerate habits. At this time he developed a phobia about being sick on stage: he used to stuff himself with anti-seasick pills before coming on. It was a stressful time. However, in both cases his fears proved groundless, but the prospect of involuntary paternity may have put him off incurring family obligations to Christine Barry, at least temporarily.

They continued to act together, though, in Agatha Christie's mystery *Alibi*, based on her book *The Murder of Roger Ackroyd*. Neither was willing to give up work for marriage. In both love and marriage, Rex could be callously direct. Already, at an age and in a profession where most people with their careers still to make take care whom they offend and prudently pull together like good troupers, Rex had no regard for whose feelings he hurt.

When he and Christine were in Glasgow, his girlfriend shared digs with an attractive seventeen-year-old who was in another company. Angela Worthington made no secret of the fact that she thought Rex 'a complete phoney. He needed pretty people falling at his feet, for he was enormously unattractive, or so I thought then,' she says today. 'He had no clothes worth speaking about, wore a pair of scuffed suedes, a monocle, a broad-brimmed hat – far too stagey, one of those "actor lads". And he had a terrible complexion."[7] One day she found a note that her roommate had carelessly left lying around: 'Christine, get rid of that little Worthington girl, or I shall leave you. She's driving me mad.'[8]

In truth, Angela Worthington, who later married one of Rex's agents, Robin Fox, was a very clever girl – too clever by half for Rex's comfort. But he might have altered his opinion of her had he known who she really was.

Angela Worthington was a love child of one of Rex's most admired playwrights. Her real father was Frederick Lonsdale, author of some of the best light comedies ever written, including *On Approval, Aren't We All?* and *The Last of Mrs Cheyney*. His brittle, disillusioned, worldly wit attracted the leading actors of the day, Gerald du Maurier and Charles Hawtrey among them, whom Rex sought to emulate.

'He was very, very insecure at this time in his life,' Angela Fox recalls. 'His womanizing I put down, at least in part, to this. Even if he wasn't going to have a great acting career, he thought he'd be a hit with the girls.' Rex himself seems to have approached romance with theatrical expectations. 'I had a friend with a wicked sense of fun,' says Angela Fox. 'We arranged to play a prank on Rex and got him up to her room on the pretence that she was expecting an amorous call. We hid in one of the closets while she stretched out on a sofa bed like Mme Récamier. Rex came in and immediately we heard him say, "Low lights ... a pretty woman ... what about a kiss?" Who could have imagined that out of that corny chrysalis there'd come a smart, laconic actor?'

But was he a good lover? 'Of course not. Rex was and remained an *actor*. He always had this romantic image in his head. But the only men who are any good in bed are those who get down to the practical business and don't fantasize about it. Rex wasn't that kind.'

Christine Barry had at least one ameliorating effect on Rex: his wardrobe improved. His sister Sylvia, whose husband David was now a barrister on circuit in Manchester, invited Rex and Christine out to lunch when their play arrived there. 'We went to pick them up at their digs. It was a ghastly lodging house, but they both looked the smartest folk in town.'

The Midlands and northern audiences were hard to play to, but those Rex hated most were the ones in south London, in Brixton, Woolwich and Stratford East. Boisterous and physically intimidating, they criticized not only performances, but class, race and character. *The Chinese Bungalow*, a huge West End hit for Matheson Lang, began its tour in June 1929 with Rex in a sola topee as a rubber planter who rescues his fiancée from the clutches of a no-good Chinaman, who has already murdered his English wife. By the time this rich stew was ladled out to south London audiences, in districts where the Chinese had settled since the nineteenth century, their execration of the villain had turned ugly. To Rex's astonishment, the actor playing the Chinese dropped his 'chelly brossom accent', as Rex described it, and give his detractors a sound telling off.[9] Touring prepared Rex for anything, though only once, he insisted, did *he* stop the play to 'Shhussh!' an unruly house. After which, he could not think of his next line and had to suffer the taunting of those he had just rebuked until the prompter came to his aid.

He was beginning to make his mark and be noticed on the touring circuits. Occasionally now he received a 'reception round' as he made his entrance. Second best he might be, compared to the West End stars who created the roles he played, but being recognized by playgoers was the first step to gaining their respect, then their love.

Robert Morley, almost Rex's exact contemporary and also touring the provincial halls, says: 'Rex learned, as I did, to play the audience rather than the play. We were never allowed the luxury of being unaware of the audience in the provinces; much more so than in the West End where a general level of sophistication kept them respectful. At this time the touring companies did the same play twice nightly for the better part of a year and we actors had nothing to practise on except the changing nature of the audiences. I suppose Rex did what I did, what we all did. Face front. Do a rough count of the house. Take its temperature. Get on with the play.'[10]

But one has to ask, was Rex not impatient to break into the West End? Why did he put up with nearly ten years on tour in the provinces? Rex himself never supplied an answer, because the question did not occur to him. For anyone in steady employment, as he was by now, with few weeks that were not spoken for in the theatrical calendar, rather like a dance card, that he had printed up at the beginning of every year, touring was well paid and secure. He was earning about £15 to £20 a week – excellent money. Then, too, Rex was a worrier. His basic insecurity about himself counted more than his willingness to risk an uncertain gamble in the West End. 'In those days,' Robert Morley says, 'you didn't go to the West End until, as it were, you'd been hatched. And if you did go, successful or not, you didn't leave it again very willingly. As you tried for work in London, you became acutely aware of the lucrative career you'd thrown away in the provinces. But you couldn't return. Someone else was now on the agents' books and filling the roles you thought you'd patented out of town. Unless you succeeded in the West End, the future could be grim – very.'

One thing Rex did in the metropolis between tours was film acting. He appeared in a couple of cheap 'quota quickies' in May 1930 and July 1931. He was at the bottom of the cast in Paramount's budget-conscious production of *The School for Scandal*; and he played a character called George in the Gaumont-British comedy *The Great Game*, about a small-time soccer team's uphill battle to win the Cup Final. Insipid and boring was how he remembered them. His mind was on his new possession, a second-hand car called an Airedale with a mascot of the hunting dog in question on the bonnet, a symbol of its master's own pursuit of 'game' in the shape of easily winged girls.

But then a few lean months at the end of 1930 forced him to do what he had avoided up to now: Shakespeare. For him, the bard conjured up the daunting thoughts of student courses in drama. He was always acutely conscious of this blank in his education. Almost alone of all the great actors of his generation, Rex Harrison received no formal training. Unlike Olivier, Gielgud, Richardson and others who made their reputations in the classics, Rex made his in the middle-class melodramas and boulevard comedies. He was self-taught. He spoke colloquial prose, not verse, wore suits, not costumes. It was not high art, but it was hard work. 'A damned serious business,' he would affirm with some heat, all his life.[11]

But fear overcame any feelings of inferiority when unemployment threatened, and he snapped up a role as Second Messenger in Baliol Holloway's production of *Richard III*, which Bernard Miles had occupied before gaining promotion to First Messenger. He had only two bits to say, both in battle scenes and both 'as unintelligible to me as Welsh'.[12] His only previous brush with Shakespeare had been in the school performances of *A Midsummer Night's Dream*. But he felt it required an extrovert style, whereas he bent all his efforts to making his own style fit comfortably 'indoors'. Olivier, he came to think, was the only Shakespearean actor able to introduce twentieth-century mannerisms convincingly into a classical text. Rex's first line in *Richard III* was the answer to the question, 'What is't o'clock?' and he said afterwards in the pub that he had been tempted to roll up the sleeve of his chain mail and look at his watch before replying, 'Upon the stroke of four.' In fact, he delivered it so conversationally that his 'speech' was taken away from him and assigned to another player. That left him with only one line. When Richmond asked him, 'Where is Lord Stanley quartered, do you know?' he replied, 'His regiment lies half a mile at least/South from the mighty power of the king.' Trust me to draw a Shakespearean tongue-twister, Rex thought. On opening night, he confused history by an amendment alluding to 'the mighty power of the King of France'. On the second night, dead scared, he lurked behind the scenery. The audience did not notice the absence of Second Messenger, and another actor, quick on the uptake, delivered his reply – which confirmed Rex's suspicion that audiences only half-listened to Shakespeare. On the third night he got out his two bits' worth, but it was the last time he tackled Shakespeare on stage. He was paid only £3 a week, quite a come-down from his salary on tour, although, *pro rata* and per line, quite high pay.

Thankfully, he reverted to racier speech and retrieved his status playing a reluctant heir to a modern dukedom in something called *Getting George Married*.

But his run of bad luck held. Though he got a break playing a Second

Detective in a crime thriller called *The Ninth Man,* and invented some amusing business with a hat and a police notebook, the critic who noted 'a new face, a new personality' had forgotten his name. Rex never forgave James Agate.

As the talking pictures were rapidly eroding the entertainment empires of the provincial touring companies and tours were being cut in half, Rex signed up for a season at Cardiff Repertory Theatre, doing half-a-dozen plays in six months.

Then his luck changed. He took the road again in a John Van Druten play, *After All,* in a role created by Laurence Olivier. He kept distinguished company: Violet Vanbrugh played his mother; her own daughter, Prudence, was his sister. He played a rebellious son who quits home to lead a life of frenzied night-clubbing and comes to miss the peace and security he abandoned. He felt it was the first time he had really hit his stride, for the part contained quite a lot of his own feelings, bar the repentance. Evidence that his nerves were still jangling, however, is suggested by the gratitude he expressed – by no means a trait of Rex's character – to Violet Vanbrugh for her hints on how to overcome a lack of confidence about how to use his hands. 'Make a gesture,' she told him, and, having made it, 'just take the use out of the limb and let it return to its normal position.'[13] He found the advice calmed him down whilst acknowledging that, if taken to excess, it would look like a minor seizure. The critic of the *Birmingham Post* praised his 'impertinence' in the part, which was as touching as his pathos – and, Rex found, more fun.

Another young actor, Robert Flemyng, was then in twice-weekly rep at Teignmouth – 'for £2.7s.0d a week' – and looked in on a matinée of *After All* in nearby Torquay. 'I'd vaguely heard of Rex,' Flemyng says today. 'He walked on stage and immediately it was obvious he was someone to watch. The timing was there already, and the sort of relaxation that actors only attain after a great deal of concentration, or if they're very confident. Rex wasn't trying too hard – it was only a matinée at Torquay, for God's sake! – but he got the laughs. He was playing a slightly louche character, but what charm – already!'[14]

A while later Flemyng found himself playing at Rex's old repertory theatre in Liverpool. 'Oh, God, yes, Rex Harrison,' said William Armstrong to him when he mentioned the name. 'Very remarkable man. Never did much with him here, I'm afraid.'

In 1932 he gained his first chance to sing on stage, a duet in a farce called *For the Love of Mike,* and showed he had a pleasant light tenor voice.

His basic instinct for self-preservation had been put to the test and proved right when he led a revolt against doing too many shows a week –

twice nightly and three times on Saturdays. None of the other protesters backed him up. The slump was biting hard. Rex found himself out of work for seven months. Sticking up for others was a fool's game.

To cut costs he left his St Martin's Lane hotel and moved into a tiny flat in Hertford Street, Mayfair, rented by another actor called Tom Macaulay. 'He was a great one for living second hand,' Macaulay later commented a shade drily, like a man whose hospitality has been used and maybe abused. Rex was forced to sell the Airedale, but he always knew a girl with a car of her own. 'And when he was through with one of his bus-stop affairs,' said Macaulay, 'he would shrug and say, "I've always got the job." '5

Occasionally, though, the job was threatened by 'double booking' – keeping a girlfriend and a play going at the same time.

In Bristol one afternoon, pleasantly relaxed after a lunch-hour assignation and confident it was a Tuesday, he was extremely discomposed to discover on a post-tumescent stroll past the theatre where he was doing a play that it was a Wednesday and that he should be on stage in the matinée performance. He had to apologize to cast and understudy.

The out-of-town tour of a musical comedy, *Mother of Pearl*, put on in the last four months of 1933, cast him opposite Alice Delysia, the French star he had seen on the evening of his sister Sylvia's wedding day. But she was no longer the sylph of boyhood memory. He was now the object of desire when she cornered him in her suite and began pressing rose petals between his lips. He murmured something about meeting his mother and escaped. Much more worrisome than being cornered by a fat lady was being upstaged by a clever actor. Robert Coote was playing a gentleman-cricketer in this A. P. Herbert show and stole the thunder from Rex, cast as Lord Amber, a society gossip writer, by keeping the house in continuous fits of laughter during the last act by his timing and expressions. All actors are wary of this eventuality. But Rex was to become jealously obsessed. When he gained power as well as reputation, he was alert from the first rehearsal to the last curtain call to any performer who threatened his primacy; and he did not scruple to cut lines, truncate scenes or even have the ambitious fellow replaced. Coote, who played Colonel Pickering in *My Fair Lady*, was made to suffer in a way that suggests Rex still resented his scene-stealing twenty years before. Rex considered he was defending himself; to others, it looked like bullying. And he was to devise ever slyer strategies for guarding his own invincibility. With Rex, power was never tempered by humanity: only glory counted.

He and Christine Barry had now ended their engagement. Though Rex was ambitious, Christine had caught the eye of the same Seymour

Hicks who had once knocked Rex 'off my seat with laughter' when his parents took him to the theatre in Liverpool. Hicks took Christine into his West End company. However, she eventually married the Cockney actor Gordon Harker, 'which shows, I think, how little she was taken with Rex,' says Angela Fox. But by now, it was not Rex's habit to tolerate life for long without a woman to love, honour and, when both of them tired of that, disobey each other. Attraction and repulsion, one comes to recognize, were built into Rex's expectation of a fulfilling existence and in matching the one to the other lay a great part of the adventure, as he was now to find out. He needed the order of a well-run home; he also wanted the stimulus of an unpredictable mate. As Christine Barry left, Noel Marjorie Collette Thomas entered his life and seemed to fit the bill – for a while anyhow.

Part Two
Collette

5: Breakdown on Broadway

Rex met the woman who was to be his first wife at a party sometime in 1933, obtained her telephone number and then thought no more about her until his current girlfriend stood him up one night and, on impulse, he telephoned Collette to come round. It was a casual beginning to an affair that, in retrospect, should never have happened. Collette was pretty in the way that Rex always found attractive. She was blonde, bright and had a temper. She was then living with a family friend, a Mrs Manley, in Mayfair, not far from the flat Rex shared with Tom Macaulay. She worked part time teaching young men French; she also did spare-time work, quite profitably, as an occasional fashion model-cum-salesgirl for the Rhavis sisters, a pair of *couturières*, who did not rank with Worth, Stiebel or Molyneux in the London rag trade, but were well enough established to provide Collette with an ever-changing clientele of fashionable women with moneyed husbands or men friends. 'Collette was rather alluring in a way – "roguish", I think, is the word,' says Robert Morley. She carried herself well, liked a good time and could hold her own with any man on the party circuit. Her family lived near Bude, in Cornwall. Her father was an ex-Indian Army major, who saw through Rex immediately he was invited down. However, like Rex's own father, he let his wife take the decisions in life, including those to do with a prospective son-in-law who was an actor.

'Can't you get a *job*?' was her discouraging enquiry to Rex. 'When the subject of marriage came up,' says a friend, 'Jessie Thomas ran around like a chicken that's lost its head, while her husband beat a retreat into the back garden like a man who has lost the battle for supremacy many years before and is terrified of the gunfire." Rex's family were equally unexcited. 'I really didn't think either was suited to the other, because they were in many ways so alike,' says Rex's sister. 'He needed stability at this point in his career, someone with a different set of values.' But there was no stopping them.

They were married at the beginning of 1934 and, if Rex had any twinge of conscience about the Thomases losing their daughter to a touring player of uncertain prospects – and it's unlikely he did – it may have been eased when he learned soon afterwards that another of the girls in the family married a future Duke of Somerset.

Arthur Barbosa always held that Rex's marrying into a family with good social connections was part of 'his developing snobbishness'. Still, he and Collette got on well – at first. They lived like many young people at the time who had a taste for fast living without quite possessing the means to support it. They rented a small flat above an automobile repair shop in Bruton Mews, Mayfair, carried their supper drinks across from the pub opposite and made do with one-course meals that could be quickly cooked by Collette before they went out on the town ... to night-clubs like the Florida, just round the corner in Berkeley Square, where telephones on the tables connected the patrons to each other, or the Café Anglais in Leicester Square, or occasional trips over to Chez Ennui in Long Acre, where Hutch sang and they played Rex's favourite Louis Armstrong and Duke Ellington records.

Unsurprisingly, money problems arrived early in their marriage. Some-times Rex found, to his surprise, that the grocery bills had not been paid and this aroused a disproportionate amount of irritation in a man who liked to have someone to keep his life in order. That was definitely not Collette's strong point. She had a more easy-going attitude to money. Both of them drank more than they should, though Rex did not like drinking all *that* much. He could become plastered, but generally he knew his limits and kept to them.

In strength of temper, he and his new wife were well matched. Neither yielded to the other, so that a domestic tit-for-tat often escalated into a loud argy-bargy, as in a West End play, and crockery got smashed. A sex drive was perhaps the strongest thing they shared.

Arthur Barbosa was now establishing himself as a designer in London and was still Rex's closest friend. He recalls riding back in a taxi one night with Rex and Collette to their flat. A row had begun and the young marrieds quarrelled loudly and incessantly all the way, with Rex occasionally shoving Collette off the taxi seat on to the floor and she, just as determinedly, scrambling back up again on to it. Eventually Collette said, 'I'm going home with you, Arthur, not *him*' – and she accompanied Barbosa back to his flat in Chelsea. They were having a drink when the phone rang. It was Rex. '"What are you doing with my wife?" he bellowed at me,' says Barbosa. '"Nothing," I said. There was an irritable pause, then he snapped, "Well, you must be doing *something*."' How could a man be alone with a woman, he implied, and not be thinking of sex.

Securing work became even more pressing for Rex when, within a few months of their marriage, Collette became pregnant. He took a couple of ill-paid small parts in one or two 'quota quickie' movies and then, for not much more money, but mainly to catch a West End manager's eye, appeared in a series of short-run plays put on at a theatre which catered to actors temporarily between better paid jobs. Here, he scored a success with St John Ervine's *Anthony and Anna*. The critic of *The Stage*, viewing with approval his 'glib impudence and self-confidence', hazarded the opinion that the character he played 'would have been quite at home in a Shavian extravaganza'.[2] It is probably the first linking of Rex with Shaw, the playwright who was indirectly to make him world famous. He did not impress St John Ervine, however. That touchy author insisted on replacing him with a better known West End name before the play transferred.

On 25 January 1935, Collette gave birth to a son, who was christened Noel, one of the Thomases' family names. Barely staying to drink the baby's health and fortune, Rex entrained for Glasgow and a pre-London production of an 'amnesia drama', *Man of Yesterday*, in which Leslie Banks, playing a financier whose loss of memory transports him back to his wild young self, stole the notices.

Rex seemed doomed never to find the leading role in the hit play that, according to Robert Morley, preoccupied his thoughts at the time. Yet he went on trying to find his style and assuming off stage, too, many of the characteristics he was developing in the roles he did secure: wilful, reckless, smart, supercilious, handsome and superficially elegant, quick-tempered, with an even quicker tongue for an oath or a petulant reply to people who put him on edge with what he suspected to be superior *savoir faire*. He had acquired a metropolitan veneer without any real sophistication, but he had 'presence' and ruthlessness, and these saw him a long way. He was, of course, sexy looking with just enough devilry in his callow features to take them out of the matinée idol class. He had at this time the sort of personality that signified he liked women and could be kind to them, but appealed even more strongly to women who liked him to be a bit cruel first. In short, he had the brand of charm that was described, sometimes with reluctant fascination, as 'caddish'. Once Rex acquired the celebrity to go with such a personality, the impact would indeed be formidable. He kept on searching.

As well as a son, Rex had also acquired a new car – at least a new second-hand one, a Chrysler brought with £20 borrowed from his mother. This new toy gave him more hours of pleasure than his family responsibilities. Little Noel often sat in the pram 'amid the petrol fumes of the mews,' as Rex unrepentantly said later, while his father and the mechanic who owned the automobile repair shop beneath the flat tinkered with the Chrysler.[3]

Then, midway through 1935, his luck changed. Robert Morley had written a play, *Short Story*, for Marie Tempest. In addition to the grandest of West End *grandes dames*, the first-rate cast included A. E. Matthews, Sybil Thorndike, Margaret Rutherford and Isabel Jeans. The role of a theatrical agent remained to be filled. 'As written,' says Morley, 'it was that of a middle-aged American. But Binkie Beaumont' – Hugh Beaumont, the rising power-broker of H. M. Tennent, the most influential London theatrical management – 'said to me, "There's no one in the play under fifty. I really think we ought to get a young man, even if it's not the part you've written." So Tyrone Guthrie, who was directing it, thought of Rex.'

Guthrie could be a man of monastic severity. He threw an already nervous Rex further off balance when the latter turned up for the audition in his Chrysler. A car, Guthrie implied, was a luxury for an actor still with his reputation to make and ranking very low among the present eminences.

Rex noted enviously how the eccentricities of the stars were tolerated, even indulged. A. E. Matthews showed up riding a bicycle, which he brought on stage and propped against the bare rear wall. Marie Tempest sailed in regally with a martinet's anticipation of displeasure in her imperious gaze. 'She was the one who made trouble then, not Rex. He wouldn't have dared,' says Morley. 'She used to have her chair nailed to the floor, up stage centre, so that no one would move it and destroy her dominating relationship with the rest of the cast.' From this despotic woman, Rex perhaps learned more than technique – but this he certainly did. His main scene had him and Margaret Rutherford jousting with each other for possession of the telephone. As the go-getting agent, Rex wanted to put a call through to Hollywood – international calls were still quite an event in that period of telecommunications. Rutherford was equally insistent on using the phone to ring up the vicar about a fête. Guthrie realized Rex's telephone manner needed to be more assertive, and, perhaps sardonically, suggested Marie Tempest give him some tips. The result was a quite savage tussle between him and Rutherford, verbal and eventually physical, which several critics mentioned with relish in their reviews.

Rex also had a short scene with Marie Tempest in which he tried persuading her to go to Hollywood. It ended with their exiting through a French window. As the theatrical dame did so on the first night, she clapped her hands – starting applause among the audience, who did not divine the source of this one-woman claque, but thought it was people in the stalls. Rex at first thought it was a joke, until it occurred at every performance. He digested that lesson well: his ego was being expanded as well as his expertise.

Rex felt himself being brought up to pitch with the distinctive acting styles that now surrounded him. This was 'personality acting' to a high finish. He particularly admired A. E. Matthews, a natural eccentric in the mould of the later Ralph Richardson: nearly anything he did endowed his role with a sense of independent life. Rex observed him forever inventing fresh bits of 'business', trying out this and that, prolific enough to discard what had already raised a laugh in order to test the audience (and surprise his fellow players) with an alternative innovation. Guthrie tended to give Matthews his head. Rex always admired actors with 'a touch of madness about them, and who could get it into their parts'.[4] Matthews rarely smiled off stage, never on it. Playing it straight, he would say, was the difference between a dry and a sweet wine. Rex also preferred to be a 'dry' player. That way, he reasoned, an audience enjoyed the compliment of identifying the vintage from the performance itself and not from the label put around it.

His *Short Story* role had only one serious drawback as far as he was concerned: the 'terrible American accent' he had to put on, derived from Hollywood movies and none the better because he seldom went to the cinema.[5] So at first he thought Guthrie was being sarcastic when the director asked him, early in the run of the play, if he would like to go to New York. In fact, he was being offered his next job.

Joyce Carey, the actress daughter of Lillian Braithwaite, had written a play under the pen name 'Jay Mallory'. *Sweet Aloes* had done well in London and was now bound for Broadway under Guthrie's direction. Rex said yes before he had even finished his drink. Collette was not so enthusiastic. She had recently begun an affair with what Rex called 'a rather bad actor of the period' who used to get her to go out with him dressed as a Red Cross nurse.[6] This was, in fact, Guy Middleton who, outwardly anyhow, had something of Rex's own buccaneering attractiveness to women. Collette's love affair with Rex had been hectic, their marriage impulsive, and now both were coming to an end. But she eventually agreed to accompany him to New York and stay for the opening. So Noel was packed off to his grandparents in Cornwall, while his father and mother crossed the Atlantic on the *Majestic* with two tickets provided by Binkie Beaumont, who had also secured Rex's release from the London run of *Short Story*. Beaumont was an unrivalled talent-spotter, and was obviously consolidating his association with Rex.

Sweet Aloes opened in Washington, three weeks after they arrived in America, to encouraging but not enthusiastic notices. A stagehands' strike coincided with its move to New York and Rex had his first taste of the *grandeurs et misères* that the city imposed on its celebrities when he had to help Guthrie push a handcart with their props piled on it from the Broadway theatre where they were forbidden to rehearse up Seventh Avenue to a hastily rented (and cold) hall on the West Side.

Rex felt miserable. His rehearsal pay was barely $60 a week. Collette had gone haring off by herself to explore this exciting city, leaving him to fend for himself. He lived mainly on cups of hot milk and baked potatoes at an Automat. In New York's wintry winds his London wardrobe was as useful as tissue paper in keeping him warm. The only congenial atmosphere he found was in Harlem night spots, where he could nurse a drink and hear the best jazz of the day played by Count Basie, Fats Waller, Louis Armstrong ... the real stuff at last! But to a combination of homesickness, hunger and worry over Collette was added a localized neurosis – fear of heights. 'Have you got a room on the second floor, because I can't stand being higher up?' he asked his hotel. A room at that level was cheaper too. All the same, he had to seek a loan from Joyce Carey to pay his bill when the hotel locked him out for failing to settle punctually.

The star of *Sweet Aloes* was Evelyn Laye, who had won the affections of American playgoers six years earlier in *Bitter Sweet*. She and her husband, Frank Lawton, did what they could to feed Rex with dinners in their duplex apartment, and also tried to get him to relax by exercises consisting of lying on his back on the floor and individually loosening every muscle and joint. Sometimes he would fall asleep for hours in this position and wake up to find his hosts peering concernedly down at him.

The only other place where he could find blessed, if temporary, unconsciousness was rather more painful. This was at a dentist's on 34th Street, where he went for fillings. Rex's bad teeth gave him trouble throughout his life and he was often to curse his vanity for not having them extracted. Patients in those days were fed a whiff of gas every time the drilling started. Rex used to suck it in greedily, just to drift out of his troubles for a few minutes. He seems, in short, to have been undergoing a minor but debilitating nervous breakdown, most likely linked to the collapse of his marriage. He could not see any real hope for it. How would he cope with fatherhood without a wife? Why had Collette found other men more desirable? He sucked on the gas like a baby at the nipple and mercifully drifted off ...

It did not add to his comfort that he was in a play whose message was that mental health depends on facing up to the memory of unpleasant experiences.

Rex was cast as a brilliant and omniscient young novelist called Tubbs

Barrow, who applies his mind to the problems of surrogate motherhood when a woman friend (Laye) sins with the son of the local baronet. She has sold the baby to the man, who is married to a barren wife, and now repents of it. It was basically a Victorian weepie slickly updated by wit, wisecracks and a fashionable interest in psychiatry. The Broadway critics were amused, but patronizing, finding 'the American epilogue to the English indiscretion ... difficult to tell without coincidence and effort, and Miss Carey writes as if she were breathless,' Brooks Atkinson said in the *New York Times*.[7] And the tone of other reviewers was not as charitable. Yet all agreed on one thing: Rex was a discovery. Virtually every notice said good things about him. 'The play could not get along without him' – Brooklyn *Daily News*.[8] 'He has the most attractive part in this play, or, at any rate, gives that impression, for he plays it with ingratiating animation' – *New York Times*.[9] 'A newcomer from London who is both clever and amusing' – New York *Evening Journal*.[10] 'The ebullient Rex Harrison' – New York *Evening Post*.[11] 'The inestimable Tubbs Barrow is done in a rollicking falsetto by Rex Harrison. It is capital to hear him address the comedienne osteopath as "Bones",' – New York *World Telegram*.[12] And the New York *Daily Mirror* ran Rex's picture above Robert Coleman's notice: 'And now a word about a young man who is making his debut on the American stage, Rex Harrison. Recently [*sic*] discovered in the English provinces, Mr Harrison, with his ingratiating manner and fine sense of comedy, is indeed welcome to Broadway. You will go for him in a big way.'[13] Unfortunately, however, only for a short time. Despite Rex's personal triumph, *Sweet Aloes* closed within three weeks, adding frustration to his misery. A longer run might have established him as a star and transformed his immediate future. And this was not the only disappointment. He had a double blow to his professional hopes, for, had things gone better, he would in all likelihood have begun his film career in America.

The weeks before *Sweet Aloes* opened had been filled with persistent and at last successful attempts by Warner Bros. to get Rex to sign a long-term contract. It would have guaranteed him, subject to Warners' picking up the option, a six-picture deal over five years. It was to start with $1,000 a week – four weeks minimum – for repeating his *Sweet Aloes* role in the film which Warners planned to produce after the play, in which the studio had a financial stake, ended what was expected to be its successful run. Thereafter, Rex's salary would have risen each year until he would have been on $2,500 a week for two films a year. It was an attractive offer, even if the power to renew or cancel it rested with the studio, which was commonplace in Hollywood then.

Rex was represented in New York by the powerful Louis B. Hayward agency – probably Binkie Beaumont arranged this – whose negotiator, a Mr Streger, kept the Warners man 'running around after him until I was weary ... I can well understand his attitude. He was tying Harrison up without receiving anything [in the way of a percentage], and many times he threw that up to me.'[4] This dyspeptic comment seems to confirm it was a deal done as a favour to someone else – Beaumont? – though no doubt a favour that would be called in some time in the future.

But Rex's attitude to the deal is worth notice, for it was to be the same throughout the rest of his career when he had to make up his mind about whether he did this, that or nothing at all. Indecisiveness overtook him, eventually chronic indecisiveness that he began to use as a power base in the negotiations, or encouraging his agent to use it as such until he, too, driven to distraction by his client's prevarication, would beg Rex to close the deal or forget it.

On this occasion, Rex's refusal to make up his mind at least had a rational basis. He dug his heels in over the stipulation that he would not appear on stage during the time each year when he was to shoot the two films. If shooting was completed early, why should he not do a play? The Warners man wearily acceded to this bit of contractual grafting which 'was weazled out of me'.[5]

But everything still hinged on Rex's making a successful screen test. For the consideration of 'one dollar ($1.00) to me in hand paid,' as the letter of intent dated 14 February 1936 put it, Rex agreed to 'act, pose, sing, speak or otherwise appear and perform as directed' at Warner Bros.' New York studio within seven days of the opening of *Sweet Aloes*.[6]

Rex nominated 9 March for his test. By 6 March, however, Collette had left New York. His bitterness at being left in the lurch was still apparent when he said, nearly forty years later, that 'she returned, steerage, to join her son, she said'.[7]

Disorientated and depressed despite the good personal notices he had received, feeling rejected and humiliated by his wife's walking out on him when he most needed her, Rex presented himself for the test in what was hardly a propitious mood. The test no longer exists, but it was apparently so disappointing that Warners decided not to pick up the option. *Sweet Aloes* was later filmed under the title *Give Me Your Heart* with Roland Young in Rex's old role stealing the notices just as Rex had done on Broadway.

His first-class ticket and a batch of favourable press notices were all he salvaged from the experience. When he got off the liner at Southampton, his mother was waiting. There was no sign of Collette.

Anthony Havelock-Allan feels that Rex's 'increasingly cavalier attitude to women' dates from the wounds that his vanity and sense of security suffered at this time. 'It killed his sympathy for women without extinguishing his need for them.' Any romantic illusions he had had of the female sex were badly shaken by the break-up with Collette. She had left him and Rex could not handle that then or ever. In the opinion of those who knew him best, he took the view that, while he would enjoy the favours of any women who fell in love with him by their own choice or his encouragement, they would be the ones who took the risk and it would be just too bad for them if things did not work out. They had asked for it.

In all probability he soon came to see his aborted film career as a reprieve, not a set-back. He felt far more at home on the West End stage than on a Hollywood sound set. Collette was still living with him, but, as he put it with undisguised contempt for the things some men will do, 'working in a hat shop run by fancy male designers'.[18] Her work seemed to keep her out till all hours of the night.

Noel, now eighteen months old, was left in the care of an Irish daily, who once told Rex that, if she won the Irish Sweepstake, her vow would be never to see another baby in her life. Rex told Collette this, and the girl was sent packing. They still shared some sense of family responsibilities, it seems.

However, Rex had put it around how well he had been received on Broadway and a good part soon came his way in a most unlikely play. Set in a grand hotel on the periphery of the Arctic Circle, *Heroes Don't Care* concerned a cowardly member of a Polar expedition who gets moral cold feet at the last moment and decides the only way to back out of the enterprise is to seduce its leader's far from unwilling wife. Rex played the seducer. It was one of the best roles he had had to date and, significantly, one in which he would use all the characteristics he had acquired in a variety of earlier parts – as well as what was coming to be recognized as his own set manner.

The anti-hero who does all kinds of caddish things without forfeiting the audience's enjoyment of his bounderish conduct was still a fairly novel figure in the mid-1930s. Heroes were, well, heroes still – and, though often dull roles, they were fit for leading men. A man who put his own skin before group loyalty and seduced a brave explorer's wife could not have counted on the laughter of playgoers in an earlier decade. As Rex put it, 'imagine poking fun at a Captain Scott'.[19]

Lady (Frances) Donaldson, Frederick Lonsdale's legitimate daughter and the half-sister of Angela Fox, wrote in her biography of her father that, 'The great discovery of the 1920s was that honour and respectability are not necessarily synonymous.'[20] In other words, the most useless specimens of humanity could often show a streak of witty and even elegant effrontery. Lonsdale's plays had helped create and popularize this type of disreputable but amusing bounder. Rex admired Lonsdale's work enormously. He was later to meet him and become friendly with him and even adopt many of the playwright's opinions, poses and mannerisms, but he had not had the good fortune to act in a Lonsdale play. *Heroes Don't Care*, a very Lonsdale-like title, was the nearest he had yet come to it. For although, improbably, its authors were two middle-aged Australian ladies, the play and its characters resembled a pastiche of Lonsdale's amused attitude to adultery as well as the aristocratic assumptions of privilege by those who fancied themselves born to lead. It was a reasonably witty and subversive work which backed the unconventional or downright reckless act with caddish *bons mots* that would have got a fellow drummed out of polite society not so long before. Without the benefit of Lonsdale's sparkling dialogue, Rex gave the unsportsmanlike but amusing cad the benefit of the Lonsdale polish he himself was acquiring.

Histrionics, in this case, neatly coincided with historical events. All over Europe, Britain included, the policy of appeasement was compelling statesmen, more or less humiliatingly, to make their peace with Hitler and hope for the best. Pacifism had become respectable, for the moment anyhow. The generation that was due to answer the call-up in a few years' time was still bent on demonstrating its independence of its parents' 'mistakes' by rejecting any notion of a 'duty' to fight for king and country. In a minor way, in a play of passing interest, Rex represented the anti-heroic stance of this generation. A man of tactical honour and only notional patriotism, with no liking for self-sacrifice evident in him, he nevertheless appeared a sympathetic chap compared to Felix Aylmer's fossilized blimp leading the expedition. It was the making of the play – and of Rex.

Generally he headed the notices it received, including the one in *Theatre World*, whose critic declared: 'Rex Harrison proves himself one of the best light comedians on the English stage with his study of a timorous yet resourceful youth, warring with circumstances beyond his control or seeking.' He concluded: 'I am very much afraid the film magnates will be after Mr Harrison in a clamorous body.'[21] The last sentence actually required no great powers of prophecy. Alexander Korda, the Hungarian-born film magnate who had just opened his ambitious new studio a month before at Denham, made a practice of arriving early at the dressing-room door of the star who had been 'discovered' the night before. Korda was the first to clamour for Rex's services.

6: Breakthrough in London

Two thousand five hundred pounds a year was Korda's offer. Not a fortune; but fifty years ago, it was an attractive sum and brought Rex timely relief from his debts, even if it gave Korda the right to take a percentage of anything else he earned on stage or in loan-out arrangements to other film-makers. Moreover, Korda had a film role ready and waiting for Rex to fill. This was unusual. Korda often signed up talent, then caused dismay and frustration by not having a picture available in which he could employ what his peculiar book-keeping methods termed the 'company assets'. Like many a connoisseur of the rare and fine, Korda looked upon each acquisition he made as representing current value and future profit, and marked it up accordingly. Things did not always turn out that way, but he had not yet overreached himself. His financial backers, the Prudential Assurance Co., were still happy to be paying for the tunes of glory piped by this ebullient and enterprising, if extravagant film-maker. And Rex, accordingly, felt his status enhanced by being put under contract to him.

Before the end of September 1936 Rex was playing a newspaper reporter in *Men Are Not Gods*, a marital entanglement in which a loyal secretary (Miriam Hopkins) strives to prevent her actor-lover (Sebastian Shaw) from killing his actress-wife (Gertrude Lawrence) during a performance of *Othello*. Rex took fourth billing. His was not a large role, but he was unhappy in it. The trouble was the style imposed on him by the German-born director Walter Reisch, one of the émigré talents who had fled from the Axis powers in Europe to seek work in Hollywood, Paris or London – where Korda used them to apply an international sheen to British and American stars and stories. But Reisch insisted on a quick-paced, emphatic delivery that was the opposite of Rex's throwaway colloquial style. A light comedy was turned into an overly emotional drama. Moreover, Rex still felt incompletely relaxed in front of a camera he could hear running softly and, it seemed to him, threateningly. Despite this, he used his long, lanky body effectively to express his light-hearted attitude to his work as the obituary writer who is always after more space in the paper. He admitted later that with Reisch demanding, 'Quicker ... quicker, Mr Harrison,' 'I gabbled my head off, and really hardly knew what I was doing." His self-confidence was not helped by that old scene-stealer A. E. Matthews, playing the paper's theatre critic. It was a relief to Rex to return to the cast of *Heroes Don't Care* in the evenings after his day's work in the studio. On stage he felt at home, in charge.

The play which was to transform his fortunes so dramatically that year had already been written, but was having trouble getting farther than the office desk of the impresario who had bought it 'on spec' the previous summer. It was then entitled *Going Away*. Anxious at the lack of activity in putting it into production, its young author, Terence Rattigan, sought the opinion of a chum, Robert Flemyng, the actor who had been so impressed seeing Rex in the Van Druten play, *After All*, in Torquay a few years earlier. Flemyng himself was now established in the West End, playing across the road from Rex in an Yvonne Arnaud comedy, *Tread Softly*. As he recalls it, '*Going Away* was a very light, funny, frothy comedy about a bunch of English chaps trying to learn French at a crammer's academy in provincial France, and what happens when a *femme fatale*, who's the sister of one of them, descends on them unexpectedly and plays them off against each other – all except a cynical young fellow who's being groomed for the diplomatic service and sees through her tricks. Johnny Gielgud, who was a friend of Terry's, thought it wonderful; so did I. But nothing was happening.'

Then another play came off abruptly at the Criterion Theatre and the manager, Bronson Albery, had to find a substitute at short notice. At Gielgud's prompting, he fished out *Going Away* and for £1,500 capitalized a breakneck production and began casting at once with the help of its director Harold French. Kay Hammond was the man-eating blonde, and others included Trevor Howard, Roland Culver, Robert Flemyng and Jessica Tandy. Though this sounds resplendent enough today, only Hammond and Tandy were established 'draws' at the time.

The most difficult bit of casting – because everything depended on getting it right – was the role of the Hon. Alan Howard, the cynic-in-waiting. Albery suggested to Harold French that he go and see Rex in *Heroes Don't Care*, then nearing the end of its successful run.

'I took Kay Hammond with me,' French recalls today, 'since it was useful to have her approval. After all, she was to be the heart-breaker. She'd never heard of Rex. When he came on, he was wearing a monocle, which suited his role, but Kay said immediately, "Oh, darling, he's so common." I thought he did chew up the scenery a bit that night – probably the overconfidence of an actor knowing the run is nearing its end. But then he did a bit of business, packing a suitcase full of lady's clothes including her underwear – and, without playing broadly at all, he got the laughs. "Oh, darling, he's wonderful," Kay said to me, when she heard the applause. That settled it.' Later on, French took Rex aside, ' "Look, chum," I said to him, "is the monocle really necessary?" – "Well," he said, "I'm a bit weak in one eye, but I don't need it on the stage." – "Then drop it," I advised, "You all look a bit old already for students." '[2]

Rex demanded £30 a week, but did not get it, and settled for £25 with five percent of the house take, most of which went to Korda.

Dry-lipped and nervous, he attended the first reading of the play at Albery's office on the evening of 15 October 1936. It was satisfactory, but flat – everyone was on edge and Rex mumbled. He hated readings, anyhow. Then rehearsals began. It was not long before it was evident that one of the cast was not coping too well with the role of a rakish Englishman complete with moustache, sports car and an eye for the girls. He was quickly and quietly dropped and replaced – by Guy Middleton. Thus Rex found himself sharing rehearsals with the man who was currently sharing his wife's affections.

'Everybody said, "Well, it's too bad if Rex is being cuckolded, but we need Guy," ' Flemying recalls. 'The two of them didn't exactly go out together during the run, but they seem to have called some kind of truce.' In fact, it was a very raw relationship. Only Rex's thought of the figure he would cut in court as a cuckold saved Guy Middleton from being cited in a divorce suit. As it was, Rex had to endure Collette's hearing his lines in the evenings at home, aware that she was reading her lover's lines, too, from the text in front of her.

By this time he and Collette had agreed on what would later be called an 'open marriage'. Rex was further deterred from taking action against Middleton by his own *amours*. He was pursuing an actress who was well known for having a rather exotic talent. Not only could she keep several lovers going at the same time, but she possessed the particular curiosity of a *vulva agitans* whose coital vibrations were a source of curiosity and pleasure. Rex was later somewhat indiscreet about his enjoyment of this special charm and had to keep a wary look-out for the lady's angry husband.

'We had only about ten days to get the play ready,' Harold French says, 'and we had to open cold, too, not having time for even one or two out-of-town previews. The dress rehearsal was a disaster.'

In his memoirs, *I Never Thought I Could*, Harold French vividly recalls that ragged spectacle. 'Trevor Howard "dried" on his second line; Rex Harrison played as though he were constipated and didn't care who knew it; Roland Culver put in more "... ers" than he had done at the reading; Jessica Tandy was so slow she might have been on a modern strike; Percy Walsh forgot he was playing [the French head of the crammer's school] and every now and then lapsed into an Oxford accent; and only Guy Middleton and Kay Hammond knew what it was all about.'[3] An irate French ordered a second rehearsal in fifteen minutes' time. Meanwhile, the show's three backers, shaken by what they had seen and heard, tried to sell their shares in it to any friend who could be persuaded to buy through an agitated phone call. (If anyone had, he would subsequently have made a fortune.) Even Ralph Lynn, the Aldwych *farceur*, who had been present, advised Albery that opening the play would be a complete waste of time. The second rehearsal was, well, satisfactory; but everyone left the theatre at ten o'clock that night apprehensive about what would happen on opening night.

The curtain rose ... and to French's horror, a nerve-ridden cast began racing through the play until, mercifully, 'Roland Culver put on the brake, slowed the thing down, got the timing right, and gave the rest their cue to do the same.'[4]

Only a few days before, Rattigan had changed the name of the play. Under its new title *French Without Tears*, it became the best-known comedy of the decade, made its author's reputation as a gilt-edged playwright for the next twenty years or so, and established Rex in the front rank of West End players.

His part was singled out by the critics for special praise and attention not just because of his drily adroit, throw-away style, but because his character, alone of all the students squabbling over the love and favours of the manhunter in their midst, offered insights into the attitudes of young men of the time – such as not being ashamed to say 'No' to your country's call to fight, but, when the hour of crisis struck, yielding to more basic needs and instincts, and taking up arms in her defence. It sounds like sophistry, a case of tactical morality, a means of having it both ways. But on Rex's lips, the speech of the Hon. Alan Howard attained a tender gravitas: 'In a hundred years' time, men may be able to live up to our ideals even if they cannot live up to their own.'[5] This contemporary gloss on the question of the day – to fight or not to fight if Germany makes war – gave the audiences who flocked to *French Without Tears* for amusement a salutary and flattering pause for thought and allowed Rex to step outside the frothy comedy for a moment and deploy his incisive tones to serious effect.

It was, so to speak, the end of his 'monocle' days. He had at last tasted the pleasure of expressing deeper feelings than the run of recycled West End comedies had provided for him over the last ten years.

Rattigan's words were like a suit from an altogether better class of tailor, and he felt the difference even as he tried them on. He had been able to modulate his talent so that it went without a jolt from the exuberance of ensemble playing to the sobriety of single-minded commentary on life. Timing, tone and language were henceforth the instruments of his art and not simply the props of his character. He had come into his own.

There was more to it than that, though. Robert Flemyng insists that, although *French Without Tears* has often been revived, no one has ever equalled Rex in the role. 'He was phenomenal. The part had really found the man.' True, but one wonders if it would not be just as true to say that the man subsumed the part. Anthony Havelock-Allan feels so. 'Rex was playing a part that had all the characteristics he admired and wanted to acquire: a man of the world, someone who never lost control of himself except, perhaps, when faced with an infuriating sort of woman, able to cope with any situation, possessing a natural superiority. This was the ideal. In practice, of course, Rex fell far short of it.'

All the same, a lot of the characteristics of the Hon. Alan Howard in Rattigan's play overlap with Rex's prejudices and predilections. There is the mistrust of women, amounting to misogyny. 'You can't judge women by our standards of right and wrong,' one of his fellow students says to Howard. He answers, 'They have none of their own, so how can you judge them?'[6] Women are adorable creatures, but totally unreliable and make men do things that it is not in their interest, as men, to do because basically women are conniving bitches. 'You'd like anything that gave you a chance to come down to breakfast in a bathing dress,' Howard says to the temptress who's turned his companions' heads. She offers to go and dress. Sarcastically, he answers, 'No. There's no point in that. You've made one successful entrance. Don't spoil it by making another.'[7] There is a theatrical heartlessness in such responses that suited Rex's delivery admirably, but there is also an ill-concealed chauvinism that wouldn't be acceptable today, but was then, in that era when a certain caddishness was still an entrenched part of the male ego. A whole genre, such as that of the Hollywood screwball comedies, depended on the ritual humiliation of women by men who didn't dare let their defences down and surrender in the way that the romantic heroes of a previous era had done. Rex sympathized with that view whether or not he admitted it to himself. At one point in the play, Howard sketches his ideal woman. Rex could have been quoted in much the same terms at any later period of his life, except, of course, that his innate antipathy to being quoted at all would have forestalled it. 'First of all, she must not be a cow. Secondly, she will be able to converse freely and intelligently with me on all subjects ... Thirdly, she will have all the masculine virtues and none of the feminine vices. Fourthly, she will be physically unattractive enough to keep her faithful to me, and attractive enough to make me desire her. Fifthly, she will be in love with me. That's all, I think.'[8]

Rattigan's creation, a character based in many ways on his own idealized self, codified Rex's own experience of women – with one important omission. Rattigan, a homosexual, had never been involved with the desire and pursuit of women in the way that Rex had been and was. Nevertheless, both men manifested a self-defensive wariness of the fair sex and the havoc they could wreak. The play ends with a coda of exactly this premonitory kind as Alan Howard makes a hasty exit pursued by the women he has jousted with all through. 'It isn't funny. It's a bloody tragedy,' he cries, as the others laugh even louder and the curtain falls.[9] That last line may have echoed in Rex's ears plenty of times in the years ahead.

The pace of Rex's life accelerated with the triumph of *French Without Tears*. Barely a month after its opening, Korda rushed him into *Storm in a Teacup* opposite another of his recently signed artists, twenty-four-year-old Vivien Leigh, her third Korda film and her first major comedy role. A sense of humour was not Vivien's forte, but the lack of it was used to advantage in playing a haughty young lady who is at first humiliated and then humanized by a plain-spoken and personable man of the people, a newspaper reporter played by Rex. Under a congenial director, Victor Saville, Rex became more relaxed and his voice took on the familiar muscular petulance that suggests there is an abrasive reality behind the personable manner. He and Vivien make unexpectedly good 'chemistry'. His flippant sarcasms at her expense – 'Finished being "finished"?' he asks this spoilt girl when first they meet – are deflected by her debutantelike disdain for this pushy fellow until their repartee turns into true love in the screwball tradition. Some reviews suggested that Rex and Vivien should become a screen pair, like William Powell and Myrna Loy. It was also Rex's first film as a lover. When romance finally breaks through the class barrier and Vivien's face dimples into a sparkling smile, bewitching in its unexpected and impish warmth, the romantic kindling bathes Rex in a warm humanity as well.

In all likelihood, Rex wanted to follow up the affair off screen, too, and would have done so had Vivien not been head over heels in love with another of Korda's newly signed stars, Laurence Olivier. Both of them were then married to others: Olivier to Jill Esmond and Vivien to a barrister, Leigh Holman. Her talk off the set had one topic only – Larry. For once, Rex respected the strength of another man's claim on a woman; or was perhaps rebuffed by this particular woman's love for another man. Either way, she reminded him of his hopeless crush on his childhood sweetheart Sheila Brunner – 'and with Vivien, alas, no chance of swimming in a pond among the tadpoles'.[10]

An affair would have been hard – though, for Rex, not impossible to slot into his life just then. He was working an eighteen-hour day, up at 6 am to drive to Denham Studios, home by 5.30 pm for a hurried meal, off to the Criterion for the evening performance of *French Without Tears* – he was excused matinées when filming – and even after the curtain fell he did not turn in. His restless nature thrived on a routine that would have made most people drop with fatigue. He loved the romance of work. People put on evening dress for the pre-war theatre and Rex recalls gazing over the footlights at a sea of white ties and tailcoats, evening gowns, socialites and even an occasional Royal like the Duke and Duchess of Kent. Rattigan's play had social cachet as well as hit status.

After the show, Rex himself donned a dinner jacket to stroll through the West End, from the all-night coffee stalls in Charing Cross Road, past the Leicester Square buskers, exchanging banter with the scores of prostitutes who then worked Piccadilly and Mayfair (paying their fines in court with dutiful regularity) and enjoying a more active, but less arduous, night life than he once had hanging around Sandy's Bar in St Martin's Lane to pick up tips about where work was to be found. Now fun was to be had with Rosa Cavendish, the 'Duchess of Duke Street', at the old Cavendish Hotel, with Ma Merrick at her 32 Club or at Millie Howe's Bag o' Nails night-club. No longer, he found, did he need relaxing exercises. 'Rex adored parties then,' Harold French says, 'he was never in any hurry to get home.' Indeed, with Collette leading her own life, home was where he was loneliest.

'He loved it best when it was a fancy-dress party,' says French. Arthur Barbosa shared this taste and it was Arthur, with his talent for costume and design, who used to arrange one of the year's most exotic and exclusive events in Whistler's old artist's studio in Tite Street, Chelsea. This took the form of an elaborate entertainment called an 'Imperial Court'. It was generally held round about Arthur's and Rex's birthdays, 4 and 5 March respectively. 'It was a sort of Chelsea Arts Ball in miniature, only with stricter rules,' says Barbosa. 'I was the ruling monarch, Rex was one of my *aides de camp*, the cartoonist Nicholas Bentley was the court chamberlain, actors and actresses came on from their West End shows to make up the courtiers. We all took German titles – my old friend was Rex von Hartenstein, since the family "estate" was in Hartington Road, Sefton Park, and I remember Christine Barry attending court. She was Rex's "wife", a morganatic marriage, I suppose, and used the title Gräfin Maria-Christina von Hartenstein und Bahre. I hired the Ruritania-style uniforms from a theatrical costumier's. Rex looked terrific in the frogged and braided military uniform of an imperial count, his chest covered in medals and ribbons I'd also designed. Every detail had to be correct. Rex loved that.'

The affairs went on all night. 'The rule was that all the women had to wear white, so as not to clash with the gorgeous uniforms of us menfolk. I discouraged the men wearing wigs or covering their mugs with false fuzz. The idea was to be transfigured, not disguised.

'We used to hire a new-fangled radiogram, load it with swing records and dance the night away. Half-way through, there'd be a slide show of what we'd got up to since the last "Imperial Court". Rex, I remember, appeared on one slide wearing a Red Indian chieftain's full-feathered head-dress. He loved dressing up. Years later, when he did the wireless programme *Desert Island Discs*, it was actually I who chose the eight records he said he'd pick to pass the time in solitude that, in fact, he couldn't have tolerated for half an hour. The discs were all ones we'd played at the "Imperial Courts" in the 1930s.'

Despite his success in *Storm in a Teacup*, Rex now began to experience the frustration felt by quite a few of Korda's contract artists: lack of available work. The mogul's creditors were already pressing him to economize. Projects were announced, then shelved. Two musicals with parts in them for Rex were cancelled in 1937; and he did not appear as Sir Percy Blakeney in Korda's planned sequel to *The Scarlet Pimpernel*, his 1935 success which had starred Leslie Howard as the laconic, deceptively effete English nobleman who leads a double life as an adventurer saving French 'aristos' from the guillotine. The reason is interesting and suggests Rex's limitations. It was not that he did not look the part in period periwig and knee breeches or lacked the talent to assume a foppish manner. What was missing, in Korda's view, was romantic conviction. He was not cut out to be a Leslie Howard type of lover. Where Howard was reactive, Rex was assertive. There was a hardness in his heart: threat, rather than trust in his attitude to women.

Rex himself seems to have accepted with equanimity his unsuitability for romantic leads – in costume, anyhow. He could not really understand the thought processes of eighteenth-century noblemen, he said. Other actors might have laughed off the need to do so. Not Rex. Where a character was outside his experience, he used to work hard and long to repair the gap in his knowledge. He had the industriousness of the self-taught, and some of the humourlessness too.

This aspect was always a surprise to those who imagined that working with so accomplished a comedian would be a ball of fun. It showed up early in his career. Having no film ready for him, Korda lent him out to another producer making a comedy called *School for Husbands*. His role had a distant kinship to the one he was still playing nightly in *French Without Tears*. It was that of a cynical and successful novelist whose views on women are as blunt as his manipulation of them is smooth. Basically, they are deceitful creatures. He helps two husbands (Henry Kendall and Romney Brent) revenge themselves on their unfaithful wives (Diana Churchill and June Clyde). The wives, needless to say, have been taken in by Rex.

His performance is a cut above the others. Whereas the husbands tend to play the farce 'not only booted but hobnailed', as the *New York Times* said, Rex played it in town pumps, suave, and slightly dangerous."[11] It also takes on an edge because, for all his ironic instruction in *School for Husbands* in how to keep a wife in happy submission, he himself was currently flunking the examination off screen.

According to Diana Churchill, a playful on-set mood prevailed until Rex arrived to shoot his scenes. 'Then it was like a splash of cold water,' she recalls. 'He didn't relax. It was all work to him. It may have been quite simply nerves, but he made it clear he didn't consider film-making a barrel of laughs. No fun to be with at all – and very pernickety."[12]

Rex's insecurity made him a suspicious man. Harold French says: 'When he suspected anyone of putting one over on him, or of pulling his leg, then his little eyes darted towards you and he could look very threatening. I used to stare him out, then he'd waver and laugh. Others who stood their ground weren't so lucky.' Robert Morley agrees. 'It's wrong to say that Rex didn't suffer fools gladly. The truth is, he didn't suffer anyone gladly. He didn't make any distinction between fools and those who made him feel insecure, or ignorant or who, quite simply, bored him.' Co-stars found him unbending. With friends he unbent all right, but he had few friends. Even in these early days, when he was earning the respect of his profession, he was forfeiting its affection.

The split in his working life – sound stage by day, theatre stage by night – made for ambivalent feelings. He already felt stage acting more satisfying: it had many more levels to it. In film acting everything had to be naturalistic, but this required greater concentration and control. 'Trying to do [films and theatre] at once is simply desperate,' he said at this time. 'All day in the studio, I am trying to learn from Merle, who can express everything with her eyes in a way one never learns on stage ... Then at night I have to unlearn it all."[13]

The 'Merle' referred to was Merle Oberon, Korda's mistress, with whom Rex made his next film. And an unhappy experience it was to play second fiddle to the boss's beloved. *Over the Moon* was being shot in the still novel Technicolor process, because Korda wanted Merle to look at her best; it took a horrendously protracted seventeen weeks. So long that even Korda, who had sacked one director he considered incompetent, himself lost interest in directing it and delegated the balance of the script to a third director. The 'balance' was largely Merle's part and, to economize on time, Rex's character was dropped from the story for long stretches. This is a pity, for he was playing a genial country doctor whose poor but beguiling fiancée suddenly inherits £18 million. Will her money sap his ambition, he wonders, or, worse, his manhood, as her ascent into high society involves him in an effete round of activities like cocktail parties, dances, bridge and fashion shows by primping male *couturiers*? The early scenes give Rex plenty of chances for what was now his characteristic manner: a kind of sexual jousting with a woman, in which his coercive tones could be wonderfully astringent or petulant and then, when their emotional gears engaged, ingratiating and considerate.

Later, when he protested at the way his part was being truncated, Korda waved him airily away: 'Rex, you worry too much.'[4] The dismal experience had one effect: it hardened his resolve to do his damnedest to prevent others doing their damnedest to him − and to do it first. He would very soon be pushing his contract to the limits to see how far he could bend the rules without suffering the consequences.

Korda did not believe in making overnight stars. He preferred the slow build-up. He put his contract artists in as many films as possible, playing much the same character as the one that had made a hit the first time: the Hollywood system, though without the Hollywood hype. So again Rex found himself out on loan, to the Charles Laughton–Erich Pommer film company, making *St Martin's Lane*, whose star was not Rex, but Charles Laughton. When he possessed the clout in later years, Rex insisted on approving his leading lady. He had no such seigneurial rights yet, but he did his best to have Vivien Leigh, who was playing the London street busker with whom Laughton's old musical-hall 'ham' is hopelessly infatuated, replaced by Diana Churchill. ' "I'm going to talk to Alex [Korda]," he told me when we were making *School for Husbands*,' Diana Churchill says, ' "because I like working with you rather than having to make another picture with that Leigh girl who can't act." ' Korda had other ideas: they did not include offending Vivien or Olivier, whom he was secretly trying to encourage to make the break with their respective spouses and form a romantic couple in law as well as cinema. Laughton was as ruthless as Rex. He had expelled his own wife, Elsa Lanchester, from the role when Korda offered to finance the film if Vivien were cast in it.

At first Rex turned down the role. He knew that Laughton would hog the love interest just as surely as his physical bulk would make it a tight squeeze to share the screen with him. His apprehension was well justified. Clemence Dane, the playwright, had created a character specially for Rex, a talented man-about-town and composer-showman who stages the Ivor Novello-type musicals that take Vivien from the gutter musicians to West End stardom. It was an odd forecast of the *My Fair Lady* theme. But Rex's romance with Vivien was cut on Laughton's orders lest it distract from his own gluttonous enjoyment of being scorned by her. Laughton masochistically enjoyed his own ugliness.

Laurence Olivier showed up several times during shooting to keep an eye on Vivien and Rex. The future Oliviers would then vanish into Vivien's dressing-room. It would be very hard to get her back to work. Rex ground his teeth at the wait – and, possibly, at the fact that no similar opportunity for rest and recreation was available to him. Later on he would sternly disapprove of mixing sex with work, but just now it would have been welcome.

His marriage, though on the rocks, had not yet broken up. He and Collette reminded one of a screen couple whose togetherness is maintained by the regularity with which their tempers go off. Surface tension prevents the bubble bursting. Many years later, their son Noel recalled how, as an infant, his own instinctive intervention in his parents' rows helped defuse the immediate crisis. 'I used to hear them shouting, "Shut up!" – "Shut up yourself" at each other,' says Noel today. 'And I suppose that phrase must have stuck in my mind. I was told that when I'd toddle towards them to get a hug, I'd call out, "Shut up! Shut up!" without, of course, knowing what it meant, which made them laugh.'[15]

Rex's tiredness increased all through the spring of 1938, but when he expressed fears for his health to Korda, he was assigned the role of an opportunistic society doctor in A. J. Cronin's indictment of the higher ranks of medicine, *The Citadel*. It was yet another cameo, but at least he had the film's best joke and delivered it with a throw-away grace that Gerald du Maurier would have applauded. Asked by a Harley Street colleague how his patient's chest is doing, he answers gleefully, 'It's a treasure chest.' An actor's career is sometimes irrationally but immeasurably advanced if a wisecrack like this becomes a catch-phrase at large. 'It's a treasure chest,' he heard everyone repeating, mimicking his accent. Even his own doctors did so: his hypochondria now kept several medical men on the go prescribing him pills and powders he did not really need and often forgot to take. The simple joke brought Rex a popularity akin to that enjoyed by the actors a generation or so later who found their celebrity enhanced by 'an offer he can't refuse' or 'lunch is for wimps'.

7: Casualty of War

French Without Tears was still drawing packed houses, but Rex was restless and irritable. He had made five films during the run and appeared on stage almost every night for eighteen months. He wanted a change: he wanted out.

When the play had to transfer to a different theatre, his agent, Vere Barker, seized on a contract technicality to secure his client's release. Albery reluctantly granted it. Rex was growing accustomed to getting his own way.

He and Collette were going through one of their periods of reconciliation. They had moved into a larger flat at 93 Sloane Street, in the Chelsea area. Now they shoved their bags into a second-hand Bentley he had bought in part-exchange for his clapped-out Chrysler and set off for France along with Harold French and his wife Phyl. They headed for St Tropez, still a small fishing port, and then went on along the Côte d'azur to Ste Maxime for two or three nights. Taking a meal with Rex, Harold French noted, now had elements of unconscious comedy in it. 'He had become so picky about what he ate – indeed what other people ate too.' Rex made out that it was to do with his health. French felt it had more to do with acquiring a sophistication that could dovetail on stage into a comedy of upper-class manners. 'We were all having dinner one night and Rex took it on himself to order the wine. When the bottle was presented, he made great play of sniffing the cork, tasting the contents, rolling it round his tongue, and so forth, and then he turned to the rest of us who were hanging on his verdict like the defendants at a trial and said, "Not bad, not bad at all. Grown on the wrong side of the hill, but quite presentable." Most of Rex's drinking up to then had been confined to night-club stuff or Guinness. But he always held that you didn't have to know anything, unless it was to your advantage. Let the other chaps do the spadework. To his dying day, I think, whenever he wrote to me from France, the letter always came addressed to "Angletaire". He never learnt a word of French, save what he needed for *French Without Tears* – and that came with the job. At least he never skimped on that. But off stage, "languages" were things foreigners spoke.'

At Ste Maxime, Rex and Harold French got into a spot of fisticuffs. 'Rex, as we all knew, was keen on jazz. So was I. He had brought a wind-up horn gramophone with him in the Bentley. It was between midnight and one o'clock and the brandy was flowing. Rex kept playing Hutch. I wanted Bix Beiderbecke. Our tempers rose. "Beiderbecke, atrocious music," Rex snorted. I came back with, "Don't say that ... Don't dare say that." He lowered his head and charged me, butting me in the stomach. We wrestled each other to the carpet and rolled over and over until we eventually collided with the gramophone, which put an end to the entertainment that and every other night. When you look back on it, it was just like a scene from *French Without Tears*: young to middle-aged men behaving like schoolboys in France.'

They drove on to Lyons. There were rumours of imminent war all the way, so reluctantly they abandoned the rest of their holiday and headed for the safety of the Channel ports. French recalls Rex saying, 'It's the army for me.' He had not long turned thirty-one. But the Munich summit between Hitler and Chamberlain spared him what would have been a bout of superannuated duty, for the time being at least.

Once home, he was cast in a revival of Noël Coward's *Design for Living* with Diana Wynyard and Anton Walbrook – 'not, in my opinion, God's gift to the comedy stage', Rex said of the Austrian-born actor.' He was suspicious and perhaps a little envious of Walbrook's famous charm. The latter had had a passing affair with Coral Browne, the tart-tongued actress from *Heroes Don't Care*, who had laughed off Rex's advances with the nickname 'Sexy Rexy'. This is almost certainly the origin of Rex's dislike of the epithet although, between friends, he would sometimes refer to it with wry affection and was not above signing dinner menus for his intimates with 'Rexualis Harrison', as near as could be to 'sexualis'. Rex played jazz (and his beloved Hutch) in his dressing-room before curtain-up, well aware that the tastes of Walbrook next door ran to the heavier German composers.

Binkie Beaumont produced the Coward play and Harold French again directed Rex. Reviews were generally enthusiastic, though James Agate wrote, 'Rex Harrison tries hard, but not hard enough,' which pained Rex, as by now he made every effort to conceal how hard he tried. He could scarcely make his efforts more visible in order to please Agate, the critic who had even forgotten his name seven years before.

Korda, meantime, kept Rex's nose to the grindstone. *Design for Living* had barely opened at the end of December 1938 at the Theatre Royal, Haymarket, Rex's favourite London playhouse, when he was cast in a film called *The Silent Battle* as an espionage agent known as 'the Chinese Fish'. Set on the Orient Express, during an assassination attempt on a Balkan head of state, it gained an urgent topicality from the Munich crisis. The producer was Anthony Havelock-Allan, who married the leading lady, Valerie Hobson, soon after filming ended. It was the first time he had worked with Rex, 'though I'd had my eye on him since I'd spotted this young man, attractive, an Etonian type, I thought, carrying himself rather well in a £6,000 British "quota quickie" some years earlier. He reminded me of Jack Buchanan. Same kind of charm.' By now, though, Rex's reputation for being 'difficult' had put 'charm' some-what further down the list of things that potential employers had in mind. 'But to everyone's surprise, and my relief, he was very co-operative,' Havelock-Allan remembers, 'even when he almost had to hang upside down on the outside of an apparently speeding train with a wind machine blowing in his face and threatening his toupée – yes, he was wearing a small hairpiece by then, and it was a worry to him.'

'Rex Harrison is outstandingly good,' said a British critic at the time. 'He gives a polished and effective performance ... and dominates every scene in which he appears.'[2]

The Silent Battle finished shooting early in 1939. Korda gave Rex no rest. Deep in financial trouble, owing £1 million to his backers, Korda bought respite, if not solvency, by assigning his stars to work on a series of films that Columbia Pictures undertook to produce at Denham. Rex struck lucky. *Ten Days in Paris* is seldom mentioned among his memorable movies, yet it is easily the best of those he made before the war. Directed by an American, Tim Wheelan, with a Lubitsch-like touch for narrative shorthand and sophisticated comedy, it shows Rex coming into his prime. His timing is flawless. He plays a character who at first seems to be a well-connected playboy suffering memory loss in Paris. Gradually, he learns he has been a counter-espionage agent frustrating an enemy plot to penetrate the French defence system of the Maginot Line and blow it up. (To avoid distribution difficulties in the then uncommitted United States, Germany is not named as the villain.) Rex trades easily and effectively on what were by now a more than passable set of well-bred responses to the world of grand hotels, *concierges* and cocktail bars. He cuts an elegant figure too. By 1939 he was already runner-up to Anthony Eden, the former Foreign Secretary, in a poll of Britain's best-dressed men. Keeping audiences in the dark as much as Rex, the film turns its espionage plot into the social comedy of an amnesiac feeling his way into the routines above and below stairs of the heroine's château near Paris and making the discovery that he is supposed to be the chauffeur-

cum-manservant. Man-about-town or butler to the French nobility, Rex
fits both roles as perfectly as his tailcoat fits him.

His long apprenticeship in provincial farces pays off handsomely. He
handles the haughty instructions of his aristocratic employer – played by
Kaaren Verne, a Continental star who later went to Hollywood and
married Peter Lorre – to erect a picnic tent with deft slapstick, ham-
handedly carrying out her crisp commands, enveloping himself in the
flapping canvas, tugging on a recalcitrant guy rope and finally pre-
cipitating both of them backwards into a country stream.

They have to change behind a tree, from which Rex emerges clad in
several irregularly draped towels that reveal a pair of skinny legs ending
in black socks and garters.

Not by a hair does Rex misjudge the reaction that physical or verbal
comedy demands of him. He is already a merciless dispenser of the
'respectful' put-down that makes his social betters do a double take,
doubtful if their servant is cheeking them. He is no respecter of womankind either. By now he has patented a slightly flip, challenging approach
to the opposite sex that forces the woman to accept him at his own
estimate or fight him for supremacy. His self-esteem has a punitive reach.
Women who give him an initial brush-off are put on his agenda for later
rebuke. His attitude is not quite misogynistic, but it is an assertion of
superiority in the battle of the sexes that makes the heroine come to him
on his terms and, as the last line has it, 'kiss her butler'. 'We don't care
that the supporting performances are less than perfect,' said the *New York
Times* critic, when the film was shown in America two years later,
'because Rex Harrison is ... [He] cuts through the adventure with rapier
lightness.'[3]

Oddly enough, the holiday he took in France after finishing his role
and gaining leave from *Design for Living*, which had settled into a
comfortable run, seemed to be an extension of the scenario he had just
been shooting.

Unaccompanied by Collette, he motored down to the Côte d'azur
alone, this time in yet another second-hand car, a Brough Superior sports
two-seater that ran off the road as he was returning. He backed it on
again, saw steam rising from the radiator and unscrewed the cap. A jet
of pressurized water hit him in the face. He received emergency treatment
from a local pharmacist, then checked into hospital on reaching Paris.
There he lay in bed for a day or so looking like the character he played
at the start of *Ten Days in Paris*, except that his face was swathed in
liniment-coated bandages to stop the skin peeling, leaving only slits for
his eyes.

Still partially bandaged, he rested up in a hotel. It was late July and rumours of impending war filled the newspapers. When Rex felt well enough to make the rounds of the night-clubs, he looked like a casualty case. 'Has the war started?' gasped a French girl he met. He did not say yes, but he did not say no either. He used his 'wounds' to strike up sympathetic acquaintance with her. 'Oh, *mon brave*,' she said.[4]

A few weeks later, bandages off, he sat alone in his Sloane Street flat in a mood of profound depression and listened to the Prime Minister declare the country at war with Germany. He was convinced this was the end of his career as an actor, but he was far from sure what role his country would want him to play.

Desperately in need of company and advice, he hopped in his car immediately the broadcast was over to drive down to Hurstpierpoint and seek the opinion of his sister Sylvia and her husband, who was by now a Member of Parliament. Hardly had he left London than an air-raid alert sounded and he took refuge in a small tobacconist's, 'convinced this was the end of me'.[5]

But after ten minutes lying low, his impatience got the better of his prudence and on he drove. He later learned that 'some ass had been in Le Touquet, gambling, and had come back a bit late in a private aeroplane, and set the entire alarm system going all over the south of England. It was hysterical.'[6]

He remembered his father's rather detached attitude to the First World War and the spirit of defiance his mother had shown. He resolved not to let king, country and mother down, but to get into uniform as soon as possible. He did not call his agent; this was not playacting. But his agent called him. 'Rex, where have you been? I've been holding a place open for you in the Inns of Court cavalry regiment. Get in a taxi right away. Come down here. The Colonel wants to see you.'[7] This was more like it. He telephoned Collette, who had taken Noel down to her parents' in Cornwall. Then she intended to join the Red Cross. Rex took what he thought might well be his last look at Sloane Street. With the alacrity that distinguishes the born role-player from the undifferentiated rest of humanity, he already saw himself in officers' uniform. 'Kissing my old self goodbye,' he hopped in a taxi, 'just as I stood, knowing the army would provide me with all the necessities to fight a war.'[8] An hour later he was back in the flat. He had not landed the role.

The Colonel told him there were no vacancies. Had there been, Rex Harrison's life as well as his career might well have been cut short, for the Inns of Court regiment, one of those inter-war groupings of reserve officers from a similar background or profession, was thrown into the early rounds of battle until better trained conscripts could be mustered. They lost a lot of lives. Rex was spared.

But he felt rudderless. He had no theatre to go to. All London's playhouses had been ordered to close until further notice. The ban lasted a short time, but it cut off many an actor's sense of existence, besides the despondent Rex's. 'He had always been a great pessimist,' says his sister. 'Everyone in the family was more optimistic than Rex.' He didn't want to go to Bucks, his gentleman's club, where chaps were already appearing in uniform with newly minted commissions. In any case, Rex was not a natural clubman. 'He was a superb stage aristocrat,' says Robert Morley, whose father-in-law, Herbert Buckmaster, had founded Bucks, 'but not so good among the real dukes. Like all actors who want to be gents, and silly things like that, Rex never got it *quite* right. He finished up more of a snob than a gent.' Morley had put him up for membership of Bucks with slight misgivings. 'The chairman said to me, "I don't have anything against him personally, but I'm afraid of the menagerie he may bring in with him." So I wrote him a reference that said: "The smartest little juvenile in the business" – it was what we used to write as a reference for a stage role – "dresses well on and off and has natural bad manners which will endear him to the members."'

His favourite restaurants were deserted; even the Mayfair prostitutes were unusually reticent. Rex cleared out of town to the West Country – he had a cousin called Buster Tonge who lived near Bath. Because of his age, it was unlikely his call-up papers would arrive in the early post, but it never occurred to him – Rex did not have a good mind for connecting cause and effect – that by moving to this temporary address he might not receive them at all. They were, in fact, sent to his Sloane Street flat and then, after the regimental Colonel received no reply, a duplicate set went to him care of the House of Commons and his brother-in-law. By the time these made their way down to the west of England, the Inns of Court Cavalry Regiment had begun its war. Rex had missed his cue. He moped around Buster Tonge's estate, shooting rabbits and discovering he had a good aim, fractious, constipated and nervous about the future. He was still on salary. H.M.Tennent kept its artists on full pay, knowing it would repay them to be able to field a full stage company quickly whenever the ban on theatre performances was lifted – which it was before long, and one of the greatest boom times of the West End ground into wartime gear.

At first theatres only opened in officially designated 'safe areas', which meant the provinces, so Rex set out on tour again with the reassembled cast of *Design for Living*. After playing Southport, Leicester, Oxford and Cardiff, they arrived at the Theatre Royal, Birmingham, at the beginning of November. It happened that the city's other principal theatre, the Alexandra, was occupied by another hastily reconstituted touring company, who were doing a comedy called *You of All People*. Their cast had been squeezed into the same hotel as Rex and his fellow players. When Rex entered the dining-room one evening, he saw the leading lady of *You of All People* having an early supper with Rex's fellow Liverpudlian, the actor Leslie Banks. Apparently, Rex still carried his monocle for social occasions, if not for stage wear, for the elegant, poised and confident girl who looked up and saw him scrutinizing her remembers that it lent him 'an air of authority'. Leslie Banks introduced him to her – 'Lilli Palmer.'

Part Three

Lilli

8: Assignations and Alarms

Lilli Palmer had already seen Rex on the London stage and recalled 'he was that rare combination: a born comedian who looked like a leading man.'[1] Lilli associated· the 'authority' she now sensed in Rex's attitude to her with that of her father, a surgeon in Berlin, but a native of Posen in a part of Germany annexed by Poland after the First World War. Her recollections of 'this unchallengeable man' recall many aspects of the other man who was to make her his second wife.[2] Her father had been a notably impatient man. He had a temper: his voice could become alarming. He had 'serious, sometimes threatening eyes'.[3] She learned later from her mother that he had also been unfaithful and had had an affair with one of the nurses at the hospital where he was a consultant. But such lapses, her mother had taught her, were a male prerogative, only to be expected; one must forgive them.

Lilli was the second of three daughters and at the time Rex met her she had the status of a resident alien in Britain, with a little film work behind her including Hitchcock's *Secret Agent* and a Carol Reed film, *A Girl Must Live*. She had appeared in several stage plays. She might have crossed Rex's path even earlier, for Korda tested her just after he had signed up Vivien Leigh. But either Lilli could not then get the work permit a foreigner needed or, more probably, Korda realized she was too similar to Vivien in personality and did not exert himself to wangle a permit for her. She had been taken under the Myron Selznick agency's wing and was offered a contract at £35 a week with the British arm of one of the Hollywood companies which cannily renewed her application for a work permit week by week. This allowed her to be employed, though scarcely made her feel secure.

Lilli had, like Rex, an insistent need to control events around her. Her father had said that he, as a surgeon working with the terminally ill, had to have the control of an actor. He passed that on to his second child. Young Lilli was 'insanely ambitious' about succeeding, largely to please a schoolmistress on whom she had developed a crush. She did not often allude to her Jewish ancestry. Her father, a relaxed man in matters of religious practice, believed that the future of the Jewish people lay in assimilation. Lilli was a mixture of contradictions. She desperately wanted to belong, yet to be outstanding; to feel secure, yet to consider herself independent. As a child, she had wished to be baptized a Christian in order to take the role of the Virgin Mary in a school nativity play. Like Rex, she had suffered agonies of insecurity after beginning her stage career in 1932. When substituting for a soprano in the operetta *The Student Prince* in Berlin, she suddenly discovered she could not make herself heard above the orchestra. Coincidentally, Rex was to suffer exactly the same fear when he began the dress rehearsals for *My Fair Lady*. Professional rebuffs only hardened Lilli's will-power. When she left Berlin for Paris, because the Stormtroopers had begun invading the performances at theatres employing Jewish players, her father warned her, 'You'll need a steel corset, *mein Fraulein.*'[4]

Lilli, it seems, had an affair in either Berlin or Paris with the British heir to a grocery fortune, whose family was then helping prominent German Jews get out of the Reich and make their way to Paris, London or New York. Her resolution was immediately tested by discovering how few people in London, where her love affair had taken her, understood why Jews in Germany feared for their jobs or their lives.

Even Rex asked her, soon after they met in Birmingham, why she had not gone home to her family in Germany when things got tough in England. And later, when the Allied bombing raids had begun on Germany, Rex was amazed to hear Lilli crowing with jubilation. She tried telling him to imagine his feelings if he had had to leave a Fascist Britain and take refuge in France. 'Oh, I wouldn't have gone to France,' he replied, 'I can't make it with the lingo.'[5]

One of the strongest characteristics she and Rex shared was that both were workaholics. They did not mind how long they spent, or at what cost to other people's patience or skills, to perfect whatever they were doing. Rex was entirely self-trained. Lilli was taught by one woman, a Frau Schreiber, like herself a refugee in London, who made a modest living out of coaching players for screen tests, theatre auditions and then rehearsing them in private when they had won the part. More of a director than an actress, though with great insight into the problems of performers, Elsa Schreiber had shown Lilli how to make a negligible part worth something. As described by her years later, the technique she used closely resembled the one Rex had devised for himself: 'Work on every single sentence, turning it inside out if necessary, always looking for the simple, and at the same time, original solution.'[6] 'Don't compromise,' Lilli was told. That was Rex's way too.

Shortly before the war, Elsa Schreiber quit England to continue her work in Hollywood. She left behind for Lilli an *aide-mémoire* listing her strengths and defects. It began: 'Remember, you have no charm,' and ended, 'Courage – above all, courage.' The first indictment was the one which Lilli stuck into her make-up box. She had overcome it by the time she met Rex, though those who came to know her professionally sensed the discipline to which she submitted herself in order to retain an outlook of apparent confidence – and charm. Few people recall a totally relaxed Lilli Palmer. Rex could understand this. He, too, hid the emotions he suspected might make him vulnerable. Lilli used poise, efficiency and authority to make an impression; Rex, when he wanted to, used charm, authority and threats to get his own way. Together, they were to make a powerful couple.

Lilli's will-power had shown up early in work, in the matter of reconciling appetite with diet. She would gorge on milk chocolate, then immediately dose herself with a laxative, or else hold a rich truffle in her mouth to get the taste of it before spitting it out. That way she obtained the sensation without the calories. She kept her trim figure, though at the price of a certain surface tenseness.

She also parted from an early boyfriend because he was set on the Bohemian life of a painter. Lilli, on the other hand, was driven, like Rex, by a compulsion to work inside the system.

Lilli spoke fluent English, but retained a slight, attractive foreign intonation. Understandably sensitive to anti-German feeling, she some-times claimed to have been born in Austria. She also changed her name to 'Palmer' from Lilli-Maria Peiser. She was a born organizer: life made her an opportunist and survivor.

Shortly before she ran into Rex, her film contract had been abruptly terminated – 'war as a *force majeure*' – but she quickly found refuge in the new play, *You of All People,* that was about to go on tour.[7] In spite of being in work, the war and the ancient fear of the displaced person down the ages, who is forced to be continually moving from one temporary place of safety to another, made her feel that 'everything one did seemed pointless'.[8] This was the mood she was in when Rex met her.

The morning after their encounter, Rex accompanied Lilli on an invitation she had to see the Earl of Dudley's private zoo, the largest of its kind in Europe. Rex was impressed that Lilli already knew the Earl, but curious and suspicious too.

Dudley had been one of the 'overlords' appointed by the Government in the first weeks of war to exercise vague powers of command over sectors of the country in case invasion cut off Whitehall from the rest of it. As the 'phoney war' dragged on, he and the others in Midland

Command grew bored and welcomed any diversion, especially if it was an elegant and amusing one like Lilli. Lord Dudley was not at all pleased, however, to see her turn up accompanied by a 'self-invited actor fellow'.[9] Dudley squired Lilli and Rex round the cages, and then suddenly plucked a large snake out of its lair in the reptile house and draped it round Rex's shoulders. It was harmless, but who (save Dudley) was to know that? Rex kept admirably cool. Indeed he even managed a few words of conversation with it as the reptile explored the interior of his topcoat. It was a dry run for *Doctor Dolittle*, had he but known. Lilli laughed and felt even more attracted to this amusing Englishman. The Earl scowled.

Later, over a powdered egg omelette at a country pub, Rex opened up and told her what a bad state his marriage was in. The trial separation from Collette had not worked. He had no sense of a stable home life for his little boy. Indeed, he felt that he himself had no home to go back to. Collette was now in the Red Cross, wearing a uniform tailored for her by Victor Stiebel. In any case, he said, Collette had not known how to run a household. Lilli told him enough about herself to convince him she was the opposite of Collette in many ways: reliable, orderly, steadfast of purpose, even if she was rather short on a sense of humour. Her ex-boyfriend, Rex learned later, had nicknamed her 'the Girl Guide'.

In its essentials, this was to be a scene repeated frequently over the next fifty years as Rex's deteriorating relationship with the woman to whom he was currently married impelled him to confess his loneliness to a woman whom he had only just met and invite her sympathy in one practical form or another. Sometimes it worked, sometimes it did not; but towards women in whom Rex discerned a long-term advantage for himself, as well as an amorous relationship, he manifested a *need* rather than a desire. By representing himself as a helpless case, in need of care and attention, he greatly added to the magnetism of his other attributes. In this case, two mutual needs were being satisfied: companionship and stability on Rex's part, security and glamour on Lilli's. They were more than good friends by the time their respective plays moved from Birmingham to Liverpool. Rex took Lilli up to his home town in his Bentley and, again for her sake, put up with her snappish Sealyham dog, eventually dumping it on Arthur Barbosa, who had to share the back seat with this small hell-hound. By the time their plays went on separate routes, Rex and Lilli were enough in love to look for a play to do together in London.

'When I met Lilli,' says Rex's sister Sylvia, 'it was obvious to me she was very different from my brother in some ways. Their sense of humour, for instance, very prep-school in Rex's case, much soberer in Lilli's – the "German thing", I expect. But it was obvious to us that she was equipped to sort him out, and his affairs were then in a terrible muddle. In that respect she was a bit like Mother. He was always looking for things to be arranged for him without any trouble – the "motherly" touch. Lilli had that. You could see she was very intelligent and would probably broaden Rex's mind. With Lilli, he grew up. He would never have grown up with Collette.'

When Rex got back to London, they started seeing each other almost daily throughout the winter of early 1940. Collette was not around much. She had been posted to a base outside London and was finding service life to her liking. She found even more interests when the first American servicemen began arriving. 'If she'd been free to marry,' says Robert Morley's wife, Joan Buckmaster, who became a friend of Collette, 'she wouldn't have escaped becoming a "war bride". She looked very glamorous. People who saw Rex and Collette, but didn't know they'd broken up, would have said, "Don't let that one get away, you won't find her like again easily." '[10] But he had already found her successor.

Rex's *Design for Living* had opened at the Savoy after returning to London; Lilli's *You of All People* was at the Apollo. It was easy for them to see each other. Arthur Barbosa played *poste restante*, if need be, to ensure that letters from Lilli to Rex did not fall into Collette's hands, for Rex was notoriously careless with correspondence. 'You'd take infinite pains to convey a love letter to him,' says Barbosa, 'and after he'd given it a read, he'd stick it behind the clock on the mantlepiece for his wife to find.'

Over the next few months, Rex drove Lilli around the countryside near London as far as gasoline rationing allowed: they lunched in rural pubs, where he drank beer and scoffed cheese and pickle sandwiches, indulging his taste for solid English fare when there was no need to demonstrate his discernment over a menu at the Ivy or the Savoy. Lilli did not care for it much, but pretended she did. Together they listened to Churchill's first broadcast as Prime Minister. Again and again Rex lamented he was not in uniform – except, that is, in the film he was currently making.

While he was playing *Design for Living* in Newcastle at the end of December 1939, Carol Reed, whose girlfriend he had once pinched and who was now a film-maker of growing reputation, offered him the star role in a movie tentatively called *Gestapo*. It was one of Twentieth Century–Fox's British productions, made at the small Shepherd's Bush studios of Gaumont-British, and intended to score propaganda points for freedom and democracy when distributed in the still officially neutral USA. But for Rex, the attraction lay as much in the material on his back as in the stuff from which the script had been fashioned.

'Rex just loved that uniform,' says Sidney Gilliat, who co-authored the screenplay with Frank Launder.[11] He meant the German officer's disguise that Rex wears to penetrate security in the Berlin War Office. Monocled, and even fitting a ceremonial sword under the tail of his military greatcoat, he assures the guards who challenge him, 'I only left the Siegfried Line last Tuesday.' He goes on to fool the Nazi High Command into believing that he and Margaret Lockwood, playing the daughter of a German scientist, have enjoyed a romance years before and he can employ gentler means than the Gestapo to discover the whereabouts of her scientist father. Some of the dialogue was rather too near the truth about Rex, though it is unlikely he saw it this way. 'If a woman loved you like you loved yourself,' Lockwood tells him, 'it would be one of the wonders of history.'

Since he impersonated a German for much of the film, he was forced to disguise his voice and rely on a series of snappish barks. It showed how much of his persona depended on the by now familiar and effective Harrison querulousness. The more recognizable Rex is present, however, earlier in the story as a British Intelligence man masquerading as a seaside sheet-music hustler in a bow tie and straw boater – an act Rex must have seen dozens of times as he toured the coast resorts. He sings, too, rendering 'Only love can lead the way' in a pleasant and confident light tenor.

'I really did enjoy the film,' he recalled. 'By this time I was growing easy with the camera and Carol was already a chum.'[12] In this amiable mood, probably assisted by his current love affair with Lilli, he even agreed to Carol Reed's discreet suggestion that he 'blow' a few lines of dialogue in order to help an elderly and once distinguished English actor who was playing a bit part as a German admiral and fluffing his lines to recover some of his confidence. But then Rex nearly always showed consideration to the elderly men he met throughout life. Perhaps it was penitence for the gap he had allowed to open between himself and his father.

Night Train to Munich played in New York for fifteen weeks from the end of December 1940 under the title *Night Train*, and won enthusiastic reviews not uninfluenced by the critics' sympathy for beleaguered Britain's war effort. Rex said the thing he liked best about the film was its assertion that the secret weapon of the English was an impertinent sense of humour which could impose itself on people and events. He cultivated it, too, he said hopefully. Many recognized the impertinence, but were hard put to find the humour in his relationships.

When filming finished in June 1940, the Battle of Britain was at its fiercest. On Sunday walks through the Denham countryside, Rex and

Lilli watched the dogfights beteen the RAF and the Luftwaffe, and he sighed again about not being in uniform. The day after the Dunkirk débacle that same month, he got his wish – up to a point. He joined the Chelsea Home Guard, which was commanded by a beribboned retired general who had fought in India and now found himself guarding Chelsea Bridge. Rex had a platoon under him, but was nervous at issuing orders and, as Lilli giggled through the railings of Chelsea Barracks, tried putting on the voice of authority which had got him so easily into the Berlin War Office. After a few weeks of this, he gave up the unequal struggle with reality and went back to work in illusion. He started filming George Bernard Shaw's play *Major Barbara*.

It was not as simple as that, however. For a few weeks after quitting the Home Guard, he hung around London at a loose end and in a bad temper, soothed only by periodic visits to Lilli who shared a modest flat with her mother in Parsifal Road, Hampstead. But Rex was now very self-conscious about wearing civilian clothes when so many men his age were in the services. It did not ease his discomfort when the Government announced that 'key actors' could best serve their country on stage or screen, rather than on the battlefield. Who were the 'key actors', he asked at an Equity union meeting. It is typical of Rex's egocentric nature that he should see nothing improper in asking Whitehall to pick out the stars in the profession for exemption from national service. He was told, curtly, to pipe down. A bit chastened and perplexed, he left the Drury Lane meeting feeling he had been unfairly picked on. From this impasse the offer of a role in *Major Barbara* rescued him. Maybe he did not appreciate the irony that it would put him in Salvation Army uniform.

However, Rex was not the obvious or even the first choice for the role of Adolphus Cusins, the dreamy academic who follows Wendy Hiller's eponymous heroine out of love and bangs a big drum for God's army. The part had first been offered to Leslie Howard in the hope of repeating the pairing of him and Hiller, who had played Eliza Doolittle in the film of Shaw's *Pygmalion* two years earlier. But Howard, who could be as obstinate as Rex when off screen, wanted to co-direct – as he had done on *Pygmalion* with Anthony Asquith. This was unacceptable to Gabriel Pascal, the Hungarian émigré whose conman's charm had weaseled the film rights to Shaw's works out of the hitherto reluctant playwright. It was already taking all Gaby Pascal's wiliness just to keep in with Shaw, who fretted if even a line of his text was cut to make the play more 'cinematic'. After Howard declined it, Pascal offered the part to Andrew Osborn, whom he selected from the pages of *Spotlight*, the casting directory, and filming began in late spring 1940 on location in the West Country.

'It was always raining,' says Robert Morley, who was cast as Barbara's father, Andrew Undershaft, the imperturbable plutocrat and armaments king who asserts that poverty and injustice can be eliminated more effectively by worldly power than religious faith. 'Gaby Pascal, who had a lot of talent for deal-making, but none at all for directing, got frustrated by the rotten weather and vented his annoyance on poor Andrew. He was a rather nice but inexperienced boy. After several days of this, I said to him, "Andy, you're the star of the show. Don't let Gaby bully you. Try answering him back for a change." That very morning, during an appalling downpour, Pascal started on him and said, "Andy, when you speak your lines like that, it's all grey – like the damn sky outside." Andy smiled sweetly and said, "Oh, I happen to think grey's a most attractive colour." I think that was the last thing he said. He was out of the film.'

Present in Devon was Harold French. Pascal had engaged him as dialogue director, though in fact he directed quite a few scenes of the film while Pascal's energies were absorbed by keeping Shaw happy – or at least in ignorance – about the changes he was making to his play.

'Gaby was in what you could call a devil's dilemma about replacing Osborn,' French says. '"What about Rex Harrison?" I asked – "Oh, he's too lightweight." – "I think you're absolutely wrong. Get him in. Try him out."' Rex got the part. His fee, which was £10,000, mostly went to Korda, to whom he was still under contract.

Before he began filming, early in July 1940, Rex was asked by Pascal to move out of his London flat – the director did not want to hazard one of his stars in the London air-raids. He rented a cottage near Denham Studios, and Lilli moved in with him. While working on the film, Rex was trying to work out the terms of a divorce from Collette. Both the film and the divorce were maddeningly protracted affairs. *Major Barbara* had originally a ten-week shooting schedule. It took more than six months to complete.

From the start Rex did not take to Pascal. 'He couldn't stand him,' says Morley. But Pascal soon recognized the astringent quality Rex was giving the role. 'It's difficult to avoid making Cusins a prig,' says Morley, 'and it's difficult to make Shaw's dialogue amusing. The Cusins role requires a great deal of acting that mustn't show. Rex had the pitch, the tempo and the voice to perfection. He was soon Gaby's blue-eyed boy.' Pascal believed he had discovered another Leslie Howard. And indeed, at the start of the film, when Cusins falls under Barbara's spell as she drums up recruits for God from her Salvation Army soapbox, he removes his spectacles and his face assumes a dreamy look, part love, part worship, that for a moment or two turns Rex Harrison into a near look-alike Leslie Howard. Pascal openly exulted in his 'find'. 'Rex has the face of a tortured Christ,' he remarked to Morley. David Lean, who was editing the film, but who would also direct some of its scenes, happened to overhear this. 'Yes, but tortured by shoes that are too tight,' he said drily.[3]

Shaw visited the production on 26 July, his eighty-fourth birthday, and met Rex when he was doing a huge crowd scene on location at the Albert Hall. The two men got on well from the first handshake. Rex was awed by Shaw's age and eminence, and recognized the Bohemian side of him. The Irish delight that derived from contradictory conduct and downright mischief-making was akin to his own refusal to suffer fools or permit other people to dictate to him. And the resemblance between Shaw and Rex did not stop there.

Both men had a similar attitude to the female sex. They adored the idea of women, but held them inferior to their own sex, exceptions being made for women who could behave like a man and fight a spirited fight or be intellectual playmates (for Shaw) and frolicsome companions (for Rex).

Shaw's fascination with phonetics soon told him that Rex's voice was the perfect instrument for orchestrating the lengthy paragraphs of abrasively expressed paradox in his own plays. Shaw had a musician's ear; Rex had a musician's timing. Both knew the 'score', the words and music of debate that Shaw could write and Rex could make sound entertaining. Shaw told Rex he should be very grateful to be in such an important play, since up to now he had wasted his talent on West End frivolities. Coming from anyone else, this would have incensed Rex. Coming from Shaw, whose egotism Rex regarded as the imprimatur of genius, it led him to react almost meekly.

Shaw pushed his self-conceit to the limits. If Rex should ever be fortunate enough to appear in other plays by him, he would soon discover Shaw was superior to Shakespeare. As Rex hated Shakespeare, he readily agreed. Verse speaking was anathema to him, he said. A mistake. Shaw suddenly suspected that an actor was setting himself above the sacrosanctness of the author's words. Rex must respect the playwright's voice, he thundered, not diminish it. Rex was at least quite ready to respect Shaw's voice – well, his temper anyhow. Later, Shaw sent Pascal a memorandum: '[Rex Harrison] thinks that when an actor is unfortunate enough to have to speak old-fashioned verse, he should be as colloquial as possible, so as to make it sound like cup-and-saucer small-talk. This, of course, only throws the verse away. When I write verse, it must be deliberately declaimed as such – I mentioned this to Rex.'[14]

Notwithstanding this *contretemps*, Rex always regarded meeting Shaw as a seminal event in his career. He soon fancied he saw a lot of himself in the man's erect figure and dominating stare, as well as in his style of dress. For although Rex dressed in a classic fashion, Shaw's eccentric garb of Norfolk jacket, knickerbockers, long grey stockings and brogues displayed the same sort of self-assurance as the bespoke tailoring that Rex now carried like a part of himself.

Shaw made a second visit to the film, this time to let the camera record him delivering a pithy preface directed at American audiences who, he hoped, would see his play as a fair return for the war matériel which the United States was sending Britain under the 'Lend Lease' policy. This time Rex noted, with approval, Shaw's actorish vanity. When the camera ran out of film, flustering Shaw and forcing him to halt his spiel until it was reloaded, Rex was amused to see that this great man of letters 'fumbled and mumbled and dried up like any novice actor'.[15] If Pascal was the man whom Shaw had quixotically chosen to film his plays, Rex came close to being the official interpreter of his written words. Rex felt that Shaw delegated an almost palpable authority to him to maintain the integrity of his text. In the years ahead Shaw would have no stauncher defender.

When Shaw later met Lilli, he took to her as well. Here was a woman with a man's mind: a self-compliment, of course, but also an accurate assessment of the woman who was by then Rex's wife. Rex could not accompany Lilli on that occasion because of a promise he had made to visit his son Noel at boarding school. Rex could see his son anytime, Shaw replied testily, 'but he may never see me again'.[16] Shaw was then a man of ninety-three. The annoyance was almost paternal.

Rex's own vanity grew with his power. 'Oh, the endless discussions we had about that hairpiece,' says Ronald Neame, the film's director of photography. 'And not just it ... He was also choosy about which profile he showed the camera. He thought one side was better looking than the other. This wasn't hard to cope with, except when he was playing a scene with Wendy Hiller, who also had a "good" and a "bad" side and, although attractive looking whichever side she showed, had to be photographed carefully. A scene with her and Rex rendered one or other vulnerable. I believed it didn't matter too much if a man looked a little bit "off" for a few seconds, but that a woman's beauty had to be sustained. Rex couldn't see it that way. He sensed that Wendy was being favoured, which added to his insecurity ... which increased his willingness to be difficult.'[17] Some of the cast referred to him as 'the Liverpool virus'.

Progress on the film was painfully slow. Not all the delays could be laid at Rex's door. The Luftwaffe played its part too. Although no bombs were dropped on Denham Studios, each time the sirens went off, everyone rushed for the shelters. The electricians up on the sound stage gantries slid down ropes as quickly as they could. 'One day Rex and Wendy were doing a love scene,' Neame remembers. 'Suddenly the alarm bell went off for an imminent air-raid. Everyone froze. When we got our power of movement back, we all dashed for cover so fast that the camera was left running. It went on recording the scene. We looked at the rushes the next day. There were Rex and Wendy staring in surprise as people ran into the scene past them and the "sparks" slid down their ropes like a tribe of Tarzans. Rex looks around, slowly coming out of character. Then the need for self-protection strikes him and he suddenly turns tail and without a single word to Wendy takes off for the air-raid shelter. It turned out that Wendy had been away from the studio when people had been told the drill. She just sat on there, bewildered by Rex's precipitate desertion of her. "Well, old boy," Rex said, when we taxed him with it, "I'd been told to run, and run I bloody well did." That was Rex in a nutshell. Self first, the rest nowhere.'

Neame, Lean and the others who came to know him well are convinced that much of Rex's belligerent attitude came from a fear of public embarrassment. He hated being put at a disadvantage. The feeling was not confined to work. On Saturday nights fellow actors and friends that he and Lilli had made would gather in their house at Denham: Neame, Lean, Anthony Havelock-Allan and his wife Valerie Hobson, John Mills and his novelist wife Mary Hayley Bell. 'We men would play poker,' Neame recalls. 'It surprised me to find Rex wasn't very good at it. In fact, he was quite nervous. When he made a call that didn't work, he'd look flustered and say, "What have I done? Have I made a booboo?"' The actor's old fear of fluffing his lines was deeply imbedded even when he was not on stage or in shot. Among his friends' memories, there are few that conjure up a completely relaxed Rex.

Yet to the few friends he made – and the fewer still he kept – Rex could exhibit a very practical loyalty. One day Gabriel Pascal and Harold French had a severe falling out. French quit on the spot.

'When Rex arrived and asked, "Where's Harold?" they told him I'd resigned. Rex threw a fit. I was enjoying lunch at the Savoy and congratulating myself on seeing the back of Pascal when the phone call came to return at once. Rex had absolutely insisted on it – refused to go on or even be made up until he saw me again. If I say it was a most unexpected gesture from him, I don't mean to knock it.'

The protracted shooting schedule of the film – it did not finish until December 1940 – meant that Lilli more or less took up permanent residence with Rex.

Arthur Barbosa was not unhappy to see her established under his roof. In the early days of the romance Barbosa and his wife had lent the couple their flat in Chesil Court, Chelsea, for their assignations, which could not take place in the Hampstead home that Lilli shared with her mother. 'But to tell the truth, I didn't take much to Lilli,' says Barbosa. 'I found her "Germanness" off-putting. She pretended she came from Vienna, but she was a Kraut all right. However, as Rex was my friend, I helped him go along with the romance and my wife acted as a "Mrs Mop", clearing up after them. Lilli was a great one for stuffing fruit into herself – God knows how many plum stones we picked up. Sometimes, after she'd gone, I'd come back and find Rex in deep depression and wondering what would become of his life. I'd make him an omelette – he liked "eggy" things – and surprise him by my culinary skill. Rex was very unculinary.'

Rex grew more and more impatient to be free to marry Lilli, and now Robert Morley played his part. He and his wife Joan had just moved into a duplex apartment in the luxury block called Arlington House in Piccadilly, overlooking Green Park – 'all for ten pounds a week then,' says Joan Buckmaster. 'Rex rang us up. He and Collette wanted to have a serious talk about divorce. Could we put them up for the night? Robert hadn't got back from filming *Major Barbara* when I opened the door to this gorgeous looking girl in Red Cross uniform – you know how that adds glamour. She wore it like a fashion model. I couldn't believe Rex would want to cut himself loose from this. But by the time they left the next day, they'd had their talk and she'd agreed to give him a divorce.'

English divorces in those days – and for many years afterwards – were not quickly procured; all kinds of legal hypocrisies had to be undergone or a too obviously 'arranged' divorce might be deemed to have broken the law. It was to be almost two more years before Collette's divorce suit came to court, charging Rex with adultery and cohabitation, and citing Lilli as co-respondent.

9: Rex's War

Immediately Rex finished shooting his role in *Major Barbara*, Binkie Beaumont had a play waiting for him. It was S. N. Behrman's *No Time for Comedy*. He was to be the philandering playwright who dashes off light comedies, but yearns to write serious dramas. Rex made one condition: Lilli had to play his girlfriend. Rex's was a role that he could have tucked easily and elegantly into his breast pocket and he wore it that way too, deceptively casual but not a fold out of place. For Lilli, it was an important step. It helped make her accepted by a public still suspicious of the presence of aliens in wartime Britain; and it promoted her to the ranks of notable stage players, amongst whom was Rex's leading lady on this occasion, Diana Wynyard.

Also in the cast, playing the household's sassy maid, was Elisabeth Welch, who was later to make her name as a singer of distinction. As she recalls the pre-London tour, it was a disturbing time for everyone. Whilst the company was in Blackpool, Lilli was detained by the police. An alien had to report every change of address and Lilli had failed to inform the authorities she was now living with an actor called Rex Harrison. The play opened with her understudy. 'Rex was furious,' Elisabeth Welch recalls, 'but apart from giving off over the phone to Binkie, there was nothing he could do.' Anyhow, he was terribly nervous, afraid the Blackpool folk wouldn't appreciate the sophistication of a play that, in spite of being Anglicized in parts, was still basically an American situation comedy. One of my clearest memories of this time is of him pacing around the wings, waiting to go on, repeating his lines and taking swigs from a tumbler of bicarbonate to settle his stomach. His back hurt too. He calmed down when Lilli got back. Maybe she had a gift of massaging his tensions away. She always kept herself under control – nerves of steel, never flustered, never unsociable, but not mixing easily. We called her "the pussy cat", she had an air of walking alone. She told me she wrote to her mother every day. I knew Collette: she had plenty of spirit. But Lilli had ambition. She set out to be a star. Very definitely.'

Rex was put out by several incidents that happened on the tour. While they were playing at the Theatre Royal, Nottingham, Lilli and Diana Wynyard received a letter backstage. Two Army officers who had seen the show wanted the 'girls' to have supper with them. With servicemen dying for their country, social formalities had become noticeably relaxed and the actresses felt they should be polite and accept. 'Rex threw a fit,' says Elisabeth Welch. 'He may have felt a tad guilty, not being in uniform himself.' When he and Welch entered the dining-room of the Black Boy Hotel, where the cast were staying, the 'girls' and their hosts were already eating. Rex limited himself to a surly look. 'We were served cold salmon, which I thought looked good, but Rex picked the plate up, put it under his nose and sniffed loudly. "Don't eat it, Elisabeth, it's off. I can smell it."' This was a habit of Rex's. 'He was a great "smeller". He used to smell the wine, which is understandable, but also the food he'd ordered before he put it in his mouth. He even used to smell the bread roll he'd broken to see if it was fresh. It reflected his "Don't trust anyone" mood, I think. This time, the food was the first thing he could vent his annoyance on.

'He called over the *maître d'hôtel*, who was Italian, and barked, "This fish is off. Take it away." The man stood his ground. "Is a'right ... is fresh." – "I tell you it's not. Send for the chef." – "Is too busy to come out." – "This is intolerable. Bring me the manager." – "Is gone home."'

Rex flung the plate of fish across the table and it skidded on to the carpet. The *maître d'hôtel* lifted his hand and cuffed Rex behind the ear. 'Rex scrambled to his feet in fighting mood. But his chair caught the back of the seat behind, which put him off his stroke and he almost fell. The waiters rallied round the *maître d'hôtel*. All conversation had stopped and I could see Lilli and Diana looking transfixed.'

Rex roared, 'How dare you ... you fucking Italian,' screwed his napkin up and strode out to get the manager – who *was* off duty. 'We couldn't go back into the restaurant,' says Elisabeth Welch, 'we couldn't find anywhere else open in Nottingham at that time. We went to bed hungry.' Worse followed in the morning. 'Lilli crept round to my room and said, "Pack your things ... we've been kicked out."' A good *maître d'hôtel*, the manager had decided, was more valuable in wartime than customers who were choosy about the fish. They all struggled with their cases across town to the only other hotel that could accommodate them for the rest of the run. It was a very cramped place and Lilli and Diana had to double up – to Rex's fury. And to Diana Wynyard's, too, since she was in the middle of her affair with Carol Reed and accustomed to calling him after the show and talking for hours.

The incident showed what a jealous man Rex could be when his pride was hurt by what he perceived as a threat to 'his' woman. Irrational and in this case baseless, it none the less triggered a reflex reaction that in the future brought him to blows with people who carried even more clout than a head waiter.

Elisabeth Welch also noted the early onset of another characteristic. 'He arrived at rehearsal with his lines already learnt, more or less word perfect. It was almost impossible to get him to alter his performance unless a better notion occurred to him. He used rehearsals to try out the variations he'd thought of in his own part, which was infuriating to the rest of us following the director. It's true, he often improved things – but for himself.' Another feature was that, like many an actor who arrives word perfect, Rex was the first to start forgetting his words. He was to be seen reciting his part like a church litany before curtain up.

If an air-raid alert was sounded during the performance on tour, it was Rex's duty to halt the proceedings, step up to the footlights and tell people where the nearest shelter was, which he had ascertained in advance. But he soon found that few of those who had already paid wanted to leave. So the play resumed, rather shakily, with the cast keeping one ear cocked for approaching aircraft or explosions. 'It was all slightly unreal,' he recalled. 'People had only half their attention concentrated on the actors and we were only half concentrating on our lines.'[2] In the circumstances, a few fluffed lines passed unnoticed.

No Time for Comedy was a great success and a personal triumph for Rex, 'Long-limbed and magnetic,' Ivor Brown called him in the *Observer*, '[he] puts a gleam of charm on the dull surface of a boor's behaviour.'[3]

They played mornings and afternoons only: no evening performances due to air-raids. At night Rex did fire-watch duty twice a week in the theatre and on the roof. Though he took this minor chore seriously, his ache to serve in a wider theatre of war had not diminished. Though the play ran for nearly 350 performances and could have gone on indefinitely, he fretted to be out of it. Ralph Richardson, six years his senior, was serving with the Fleet Air Arm. Laurence Olivier, almost exactly Rex's contemporary, had returned from America in 1940 with Vivien Leigh and from April 1941 was taking flying instruction – though his unacceptable score in crashing planes limited him to ground duties. John Mills, who was Rex's age, was in the Royal Engineers. If these people were not 'key actors' and therefore excused war service, Rex asked himself, then who was?

It did not cheer him up to learn that Collette, having agreed to a divorce, was now bent on making him, the guilty party, pay for it with heavy alimony.

However, April 1941 was a good month for Rex. *Major Barbara* had its première with Prime Minister Winston Churchill in attendance.

Although not as popular as the film of *Pygmalion*, it was given a respectful welcome. The critics mainly carped about the liberties taken with Shaw's play. It would seem that the shorter version of the film was the one chosen for the occasion. This lasted 121 minutes, against two and a half hours of the full version, and it is an inferior work. The cut version was due to the exigencies of wartime politics; and it is amusing in retrospect to note how Pascal's blind allegiance to Shaw led him into the production of a film so out of tune with what the collective leadership of the free world was then thinking or at least saying. The parts that had to be cut included Undershaft's gospel of freedom backed by a machine-gun, the munitions tycoon's cynical pragmatism about arms dealing, his imperious advocacy of war, and his delight at the thought of trying out new and improved explosives on overpopulated nations like China, which was then fighting on the Allies' side.

Rex's performance is brilliant – and prophetic. His Adolphus Cusins, the collector of religions, who agrees to follow Christ in order to keep in step with Wendy Hiller's spirited Salvation Army lass, might be a first cousin to Henry Higgins, the collector of accents, whom he was to play fifteen years later. The sense of a time-slip is reinforced by the brief appearance of a genial policeman, stomach pushed majestically out, played by Stanley Holloway – later Doolittle, the dustman, in *My Fair Lady*.

As Rex was the first to realize, Shaw left the love scenes between himself and Wendy Hiller underdeveloped. But Rex is less harmed by this than his co-star, whose enraptured style of playing does not wear well. The very look of Rex in the film sets up a strange tension. His academic aura is a disquieting contrast with his sensual features. He is both scholar and satyr, a latent menace where the latter is concerned, of course, but present all the same in temperament, if not text. The fact that the film remains essentially a piece of theatre is no handicap to a man of the theatre like Rex, but his marvellously nuanced performance is a superb piece of cinema. He toes the line between farce and comedy with perfect balance. Indeed when he does get drunk in Undershaft's Byzantinely luxurious apartment, having attempted to cool his mouth with two goblets of claret after innocently gulping down a glass of vodka, he lets his long body stiffen as if suddenly freeze-dried before falling flat on the carpet. Chaplin could not have done it better.

Without pause, in the middle of one of his own lines, Rex repeats a trick he must often have used when he was in the touring farces. He plucks an overly neat hanky out of its folds in the breast pocket of Undershaft's prissy son, thus giving the prim young man a suddenly rakish appearance.

But his best scenes are the ones with Robert Morley as Undershaft. Together, these two consummately sly players deliver Shaw's lines like a couple of musicians capable of playing every instrument in the orchestra and in no need of Gabriel Pascal's negligible direction. They play in flawless unison, each with a hard-edged wiliness of mind and nimbleness of tongue that signifies their quicksilver wits and makes Cusins a plausible heir to Undershaft's armaments empire. The pleasure does not come from watching rival performers manoeuvring for advantage, but two players driving a bargain together – a contest of self-confident equals. It is one of the greatest acting duos in British films and it is a shame that these scenes are the very ones not included when the shorter version of *Major Barbara* is shown, as is most often the case today.

'To call [*Major Barbara*] a manifest triumph would be arrant stinginess with words,' Bosley Crowther wrote in the *New York Times* and, warming to his theme, he continued: '[it is] a lasting memorial to the devotion of artists working under fire, a permanent proof to posterity that it takes more than bombs to squelch the English wit.'[4]

Sometime between the end of December 1941 and mid-January 1942, without informing even his agent or H. M. Tennent's management, Rex made his bid to join the RAF. The high-ranking officers on the selection board expressed mild surprise. Did he not know he was exempt? He was unapologetic: 'I'd rather not be, sir.'[5] They wished him good luck and told him he would never regret it. It appears he never did.

By February he was doing rifle drill in bitterly cold weather on a barracks square in Uxbridge, Middlesex, as part of a six-week officers' training course and sleeping in a hut with forty or so men who ran through a repertoire of snores, grunts, farts and other not so easily defined noises whose variety, scope and amplification surprised him. Yet he found the drill and assault courses made him fitter than he had felt for years. The daily routine was a bit like the discipline demanded by a long-running play, and he was able to sneak out on early evening passes for supper with Lilli, who continued to live in the cottage at Denham, while appearing in films like *Thunder Rock* and *The Gentle Sex*. Lilli was as impatient as Rex for his divorce to come through. She still felt an alien and believed only marriage to an Englishman could legitimize her status. That her fears were not groundless is proven by the fine of ten shillings levied on her and her mother by a court in Slough in February 1942 for offences against the Aliens Act – failing to notify the local police of her mother's arrival to spend Christmas with her and Rex. 'The police said they were Germans,' averred the news report, adding solicitously, though inaccurately, that they were Austrians.[6]

From Uxbridge Rex was posted to an air reconnaissance unit near

Oxford, a little too far from London to see Lilli regularly. Here he had a nasty shock. His commanding officer was Hugh Wakefield, a West End actor already well known to Rex before the war. That was not too bad. What worried Rex was an article he had had published in January 1942 in the newish, pocket-sized 'men's magazine' *Lilliput.* As it is the only known piece of journalism to which Rex – who was even then a fervent hater of journalists – put his name and apparently wrote himself during fire-watching sessions at the Theatre Royal, Haymarket, it repays study, quite apart from the disconcerting implications it held for him at his new posting.

He was one of five contributors who each described 'The Foulest Christmas I Ever Had'. Rex by this time was well known, though possibly not as eminent as *Lilliput* made out when it described him as 'a descendant of Edmund Kean'.[7] His co-writers were certainly distinguished.

Arthur Koestler wrote about sharing a stone cold bed with a Russian novelist on Christmas Eve in Kiev in 1941; Lord Berners, the art dealer, on a certain 'Herr Schickelgruber', a vile amateur artist as the future Führer was then, demanding space in an exhibition in Vienna; the actress Beatrix Lehman on an uneasy Christmas spent with a pro-Nazi family in pre-war Berlin; and the Red Dean of Canterbury, so called because he was a Communist fellow traveller, on the vilification he had suffered following Stalin's signing a non-aggression pact with Hitler. Rex wrote about driving into a duck pond when his old Chrysler's lights failed as he was on his way to spend Christmas with a duchess. He emerged with 'my beautiful tweeds covered with green slime'.[8] The unnamed aristocrat (actually Constance, Duchess of Westminster) gave him the feeling that 'she quite expected an actor to be covered in green slime, anyhow'.[9] But what worried him now was a reference he had made to the 'rather pompous actor friend'[10] who had salvaged his personal effects and got him to the Duchess. He was Hugh Wakefield.

Rex blessed himself for not naming Wakefield in the article, but hoped he had not read about the exploit in *Lilliput.* It was a lesson to him: putting things down in print did a fellow no good.

If he had, Wakefield did not hold it against Rex, who performed his duties well. Life was not too onerous. Although he was in the RAF, it was the voluntary reserve, and his age gave him a privileged seniority, if not youthful glamour. And when he was sent on for training as a flying control liaison officer, it was to the very same country estate belonging to his cousin, Buster Tonge, where he had cooled his heels in the early days of the war. His training taught him to guide returning bombers safely home to their bases if they had sustained damage or to send an air-sea rescue team to them if they had to ditch before regaining land.

It was all ground duties. His limited eyesight ruled out flying.

When he was finally posted to control HQ, it was back to Uxbridge – and Lilli. Every night an elevator took him hundreds of feet down into an oval operations room, where he entered a glass-fronted booth high up on one side and followed on his headset the progress of his 'babies', the 'wounded' bombers, while down below him girls with croupier-style rakes charted their touch-and-go progress home on maps of south-east England. Rex sometimes nursed up to twenty damaged aircraft. He was shouting intructions into half-a-dozen telephones, contacting emergency landing strips, getting coastal beacons illuminated, directing pilots to the nearest available field, if they were in dire straits ... and then feeling sick and helpless as communications ceased abruptly and he knew another crippled plane had not made it home. It was like being producer, director and actor in a play that would only last for a night and then would have to be set up all over again – only this time the 'reviews', based on the stream of instructions logged by an attendant WAAF as Rex issued them, were matters of real life and death. No place here for temper tantrums. And, strangely, he never experienced the nerves that habitually went with play acting. Rex was already an actor who worked on any role he played with great and diligent – if occasionally selfish – thoroughness. It is likely his RAF experience intensified his concern for detail, for working out the hundreds of things on which the job depended, doing them in the right order and forgetting none of them – or, if he did, not panicking, but picking up the fault and rectifying it. The concentration this required was enormous.

He was utterly oblivious to anything but the job in hand. If his concentration was broken by someone else falling down on it, Rex's reprimand was merciless. The report he filed was untempered by any concern for other people's feelings.

Rex's war service was processed in time into an even more demanding approach to acting: stamina, concentration, detail, a disregard of every-one's feelings, since he was the one who would get the glory or carry the can.

Terence Rattigan, who was now an air gunner in Coastal Command, found that his experience broke the prolonged spell of writer's block he had suffered from immediately after *French Without Tears*. He began writing his next enormously successful play, *Flare Path*, about life on an RAF base in the long intervals between flying missions. In the same way, Rex made a highly stimulating connection between his own art as an actor and the exhausting, yet transcending, human drama he took part in nightly for the better part of two years. By that time a sufficient supply of officers trained in the same duties was available and Rex was honourably discharged and posted back to civilian duties. He had done his job quietly and well.

He had also got married again. Some time in July 1942 he made Lilli a formal proposal – by telephone from his RAF base. The decree *nisi* had come through: in six months he could make her Mrs Rex Harrison. And almost six months to the day, on 25 January 1943, they were wed at Caxton Hall Register Office. Arthur Barbosa, then an officer in the Pay Corps, was best man. Rex was extremely nervous. 'You don't think the papers will find out?' he kept asking.[11] Apart from the £6,000 a year alimony he had been ordered to pay, it dismayed him to think he had hurt his family, especially his mother, by having to admit his adultery in public ('Oh, damn the press!'). When he and Lilli had gone to Caxton Hall to buy the marriage licence, he looked furtively around as if expecting the *Daily Mail*'s man to step from behind a pillar and confront him with his sins. 'Er, I'm in rather a hurry,' he confided to an official, 'can you tell me where I go?'[12] The man indicated a corridor. At the end of it, Rex and Lilli came face to face with the door to the gentlemen's lavatory. When he finally reached the registrar's office, there was another hitch. 'The thing costs £2.10s.0d,' he said, reappearing suddenly, 'and I've come away without my wallet.' Lilli paid for her own marriage licence.[13]

They spent their honeymoon at home – all five days' leave of it – with only Lilli's white Sealyham dog for company. By May she was expecting a baby, but still working. Her film fees and Rex's RAF pay were virtually their only income, but these were the happiest months of their life together: Rex's RAF duties gave him a settled purpose; Lilli's marriage gave her security. A son, Carey, was born on 19 February 1944 and came into the world looking the way Rex had done – uglier than most newborn babies. 'Rex sat down on the bed,' according to Lilli, 'and said, "Darling, he's ours, and we'll love him. But don't let's show him to anybody, please." '[14]

Even before his discharge from the RAF Voluntary Service in the spring of 1944, patriotism and self-esteem satisfied, Rex had accepted the leading role Noël Coward offered him in the film version of *Blithe Spirit*, which David Lean was to direct at Pinewood. The Harrisons rented a larger house in Buckinghamshire, not far from the studios. But work on *Blithe Spirit* was not to be an experience that anyone remembered with pleasure.

10: Wraiths and Rakes

Over two years' absence from stage and screen had left Rex feeling rusty. Moreover, he did not jump at the prospect of filming *Blithe Spirit*. One would have thought that he and Coward had much in common. The very opposite was the case. Rex hated playing Coward – and, towards the end of his life, was not inhibited about saying what he thought of the Master himself. But at this time his objection was principally an actor's one. Every line of Coward, he felt, had been written for the author himself to speak. It was very difficult for anyone else to deviate from Coward's style. Rex did not like imitating *anyone*, even the influential popular playwright of the day.

In addition, David Lean was going to direct him, and Lean admitted that he did not much appreciate Coward's brittle and, he felt, attenuated sense of humour. It was a bleak outlook for a play dependent on the rapid swapping of barbed witticisms, not to mention the use of funny-sounding names – for this, after all, was the play that contained the classic line 'And what's the matter with Budleigh Salterton?' as well as the revelation of Captain Bracegirdle's golf-course assignation.

The story has been often told of Rex's rehearsing some joke of this kind and hearing Lean turn to his director of photography, Ronnie Neame, and say, 'That doesn't sound funny to me. Does it to you?'[1] Lean at this early stage in his directing career was not a man who gave confidence to the insecure; he got on best with players like Trevor Howard, Celia Johnson or Coward himself, performers very sure of themselves. 'Rex needed constant encouragement, compliments by the score,' says Neame, 'and *especially* not to have his comic talents questioned by David. He felt that if he wasn't getting David's praise, he wasn't doing it right.' In future years mention of *Blithe Spirit* in interviews or conversations with Rex always drew the same countercharge: Lean did not have a shred of humour in his body. But it went deeper than that, says Neame. 'David loved technicians above actors. He would refer a shot he'd just done – perhaps some bit of business that Rex had sweated over for hours – to me or someone else in the crew. I'd hear him in the cutting-room later – he was happiest there, putting together the film he'd just shot – viewing a take of *Blithe Spirit* and swearing at someone in it, "You silly bugger," or, "You silly bitch, why did you do *that*?" '

Blithe Spirit should have presented Rex with few difficulties. It was Coward's biggest success to date: it ran for nearly 2,000 West End performances, not closing until a year after the war ended, and the film was therefore in production while it was still on the stage. It was the story of a man's first wife who is summoned back from the dead by a séance that goes wrong and who stays around the house as a mischievous sprite, teasing and tormenting him and his present wife. In Charles Condomine, Rex seemed to have a part made to measure. Charles, though married, is essentially a bachelor by inclination who finds women irresistible, but bothersome once they threaten to take over his life. Like Rex, work comes first for him. Women are the disturbers of a man's peace and quiet. Even the grave cannot hold them. And two women at the same time is sheer hell. There is already more than a hint of Henry Higgins in Rex's interpretation of the part. Charles's most comfortable moment in the film is one whose cosiness Rex puts over feelingly. It is when his second wife, played by Constance Cummings, has been killed in a car crash malevolently engineered by the ghost of his first, played by Kay Hammond. Thinking himself happily free of both spouses, Rex settles himself before the fire with his slippers, his cigar and a book – ah, blessed bereavement!

Why, then, was *Blithe Spirit* not funnier? Coward had departed on a tour of the Far East – he was bored by the time spent waiting around in film-making – with the warning to Lean not to change a line of it, but 'just photograph it, dear boy'. Lean did his technical best, though inexperienced in high comedy and liking it no better for confining his story and stars within four walls. When Coward returned and saw the finished film, his judgment was blunt: 'My dear, you've just fucked up the best thing I ever wrote.'[2]

But Anthony Havelock-Allan, the producer of the film, has a more satisfactory explanation for what went wrong. 'The first mistake that Noël, David and I made was agreeing that Rex should play Charles Condomine.

'The role, you see, was written for a middle-aged actor – Cecil Parker, who was in his late forties then, was playing it on stage. A great deal of the fun comes from Charles's embarrassment when he has to think himself back to the days when he was the young husband of a wife whose premature death has kept her forever youthful. But to enhance the film's box-office appeal, it was decided that Charles himself should be played by a youngish chap: hence Rex, who was in his mid-thirties, but looked ten years younger. He was like some fellow who's just got married for the first time, not at all like an ageing buffer who's let himself go to seed and huffs and puffs and pants with anxiety and regret at being reminded by his spirit wife's flirtatious approach of the youngster he was when the sap was rising.'

There was another irreversible mistake. This involved Kay Hammond as Elvira, the troublesome spirit. She did not photograph easily and needed a lot of attention from Neame. Even then, in her chartreuse green body make-up, carmine lips and nails to match and accompanied by a green spotlight, she hardly looked a seductive figure, more like a she-devil. 'We began filming the scene of Elvira's return from the dead,' says Havelock-Allan, 'largely to see how the make-up and lighting would look on screen. In the scene Constance Cummings as Rex's second wife makes an entry in her nightgown, looking quite ravishing and unaware of Elvira's ghostly presence, to tell her husband to come to bed. At this point in the rehearsal, I heard one of the crew saying – and I'm pretty sure Rex heard it, too – "What's this bloke doing wasting his time with the other harpy when he's got this bit waiting for him upstairs in bed?" We knew then we were in trouble.'

It was not surprising if all this chipped away at Rex's self-confidence. But, though unhappy, it was one occasion when he could not do anything about it. 'He felt intimidated by the three of us, Noël, David and me,' says Havelock-Allan, 'he was outgunned. David was Noël's blue-eyed boy – up to the time he saw the film, at least – and was slated to direct *Brief Encounter* immediately after the film. Moreover, *Blithe Spirit* was Noël's greatest stage success and Rex did not want anyone telling Noël that he was causing such trouble on the set that it was harming the way the Master wanted it filmed.'

The result is an oddly unsatisfying compromise of a movie. Rex is technically perfect. It is a pleasure to catch even the minor things he does, and how well co-ordinated he is despite his 'nerves'. Things like throwing his braces over his shoulders when dressing for dinner – like a child with a skipping rope – and then, when commenting on his first wife's 'extreme acidity when she doesn't get her own way', knotting his shoelaces with a vicious tug as he utters the last three words – like a professional garotter.

It has to be admitted that the film gains through retrospective irony. It is amusing to see Rex characterizing a man who is haunted, inconveniently and often distressingly, by the memory or palpable presence of women he has married. *Blithe Spirit* is one of the earliest Rex Harrison films in which art seems to be forecasting life. This thought often relieves its ponderousness.

Though out of uniform, Rex did not forget his wartime obligations. Sundays would find him and Lilli – and often other players like his two leading ladies – making the rounds of service bases in the neighbourhood to entertain the men and women there. Lilli sang and danced. Rex did sketches, like the one entitled 'Father and Son' by Herbert Farjeon, the revue writer, in which an embarrassed father, played by Michael Shepley, tries in vain to put his boy wise to the facts of life. It was fun, but it did not bring in the money. This is why Rex speedily accepted a rather slim role – 'just a fraction fatter than a supporting role' – in a romantic comedy about London in wartime entitled *I Live in Grosvenor Square*.[3]

Herbert Wilcox, the producer whose patriotic cavalcades like *Victoria the Great* had won him a large popular audience, was making the film – retitled for the United States as *A Yank in London* – mainly as a vehicle for its star (and his wife) Anna Neagle. Rex's role was that of an RAF officer (and Parliamentary candidate) who is engaged to Anna, a duke's daughter, until an American GI, played by Dean Jagger, blows into town with the confidence of a man who knows the US box-office is backing him. Rex took the role for the fee (not much) and the appealing presence of Robert Morley as the duke. For both it was money easily earned for assuming, respectively, urbanity and dottiness designed to flatter transAtlantic perceptions of the English. Rex's performance is simply a recap of the elegant nonchalance and easy one-upmanship which had served him well a dozen times already. Jagger, by contrast, was no palpitating juvenile lead. The result was the same ill-balanced romantic equation that had dulled the edge of *Blithe Spirit*. One wondered why on earth Anna should bother with this awkward GI when she was obviously in for a better time with Rex's sly charmer. Both Rex and Jagger wore hairpieces. According to Morley's wife Joan Buckmaster, Dean Jagger used to come into their room at the location hotel in the West Country, asking them to check that his toupée defied detection before he went down to dinner. Then Rex would come in, too, on the same mission, since Lilli was away making a film of her own. Two men, anxious about receding hairlines, amused the Morleys. But another source of amusement which they had to conceal even more carefully was the fact that Rex had been left by Lilli holding the baby, even though Carey, then about nine months old, also had a woman looking after him. 'Lilli hadn't been able to engage a permanent nanny – who were in short supply in wartime – so, typical of her methodical way, she hired a rather grim-looking trained nurse from a hospital,' Joan Buckmaster recalls. 'Rex had to take his meals with this formidable woman and the baby.' He was not the picture of charm or patience seated apart from the rest of the cast at the Château Bellevue Hotel, Totnes.

Rex's attitude to his infant son fluctuated between excessive concern and apparent disregard. He was clearly not turning into a family man. When his paternal obligations were pointed out to him by the nurse, he took them almost like directions in a play, did his best to carry them out, and then, feeling he had done so, forgot about them. The baby was not sleeping well. Joan Buckmaster suggested the nurse might not be giving him the right sedatives. 'That created such a furore! A great ringing up of Lilli by Rex. Urgent interrogation of the nurse. Then the scene was over – on to the next.'

Anna Neagle came to the rescue by putting the fractious child into a good humour so effectively that the nurse confided that, 'Miss Neagle would love to have a baby of her own.'

'Why doesn't she,' snapped Rex, 'she's married to Mr Wilcox, isn't she?'

'But it's not very likely now, is it?' was the reply. 'She's past forty.'

This was news to Rex and everyone else, as Anna was playing a girl in the film who was barely past twenty. 'It was not a very romantic atmosphere, making that film,' says Joan Buckmaster.

Herbert Wilcox, however, had his heart on deals, if not heirs. Rex reminded him of Jack Buchanan – as he had reminded Anthony Havelock-Allan – in whose chorus line Anna Neagle had started her dancing career.

Seeing how well Rex partnered his wife, Wilcox tried to sign him up to a new motion picture contract – his one with Korda was nearing its end. The terms were attractive: freedom to do plays and accept outside film offers. And as a sweetener, Wilcox threw in a farmhouse he then owned, offering to sell it to Rex at a very favourable price. It would be a good investment, he told his star, as well as a present that Lilli would love, for she believed in fresh air and was ahead of her time in serving organically grown food at mealtimes. Rex assented to the deal and, though nothing was signed, a search for suitable properties for Anna and him began. Rex and Lilli, meanwhile, pooled their earnings and bought the first home they actually owned, not rented, a contemporary-style, light-filled villa just beside the sixth green on Denham golf course called unimaginatively, but aptly, The Little House. They appeared to have sunk roots at last. So Lilli hoped. Rex was not so sure. He wanted order, but not necessarily domestic permanence.

Anyway, he had scant sense of permanence at the moment, for he went from the Anna Neagle film, almost without a day's rest, into one that would prove the most popular of all he made in these years: *The Rake's Progress.*

It was the first film conceived expressly for Rex by the screenwriting team of Frank Launder and Sidney Gilliat, who had worked on *Night Train to Munich*. And because it used the public image that Rex had by now gained of a sexy leading man of enormous and rather dangerous charm, the film has acquired over the years the character of a surrogate autobiography. The impression is strengthened by the fact that the eponymous hero – or anti-hero – makes a deal to marry a Jewish girl who is desperate to escape from Germany and the Nazi threat. The character is played by Lilli, the Jewish exile from Nazi Germany, who had recently married Rex. Because of this close parallel, and the way in which the role later became ingrained in Rex's reputation, it is worth stressing that he was *not* the model for the film's playboy ne'er-do-well, Vivian Kenway. 'By no means,' says Sidney Gilliat today, with the force of one who has denied this *canard* for too many years.[4] 'It was another man entirely who suggested aspects of the character to our story writer Val Valentine. I won't name him, for he may still be alive, but he was very well known between the wars at one of the most fashionable London clubs. He was a gifted musician, both jazz and classical, but by all accounts the original absolute bounder. The last I heard of him was that he had married a girl in the South Seas with a rich father, who paid off his debts bit by bit on condition that he stayed on the island, thus rendering him a virtual prisoner. In other respects, though, where his social background was concerned, he was not a role model for our Rake.' Quite a number of well-known people, Gilliat adds, naming an actor or two, had features in common with Vivian Kenway: it was a composite picture, not a portrait of Rex.

This is unchallengeable, yet the fact that Vivian should have so many aspects of Rex's character is no accident either, for Rex had more or less consciously modelled his public and private persona, as well as his acting craft, on a type of individual whom he must have observed and met frequently between the wars. The wild young playboy, as one has seen, had a great attractiveness to the personable but insecure young Harrison; there was no scarcity of role models for him. If further evidence for this is needed, it is provided by the novelist John Masters, whose memoirs, *Bugles and a Tiger*, published in 1956, contain the following observation: 'It gave me an odd feeling to recognize many of my RMC [Royal Military College, Sandhurst] acquaintances blended into the principal character of a picture called *The Rake's Progress* ... a masterpiece in the way it summarized the archetype of our between-the-wars generation. Of that type, some had money and some none, but all were as wild as hawks. They seemed unable to find either happiness or release in peacetime, but came into into their own and showed quite unexpected qualities of generosity – most of them had courage, anyway – when war concentrated their unstable energies in suitably destructive channels.'[5]

Rex, just out of the services, had already felt the patriotic compensation that came from subsuming some of his own 'unstable energies' in the responsibilities of his RAF duties. He had met the type in air-force blue, he understood it; in certain very real ways, he *was* it even before a 270-page screenplay arrived from Launder and Gilliat. They subsequently reduced it by a hundred pages or so, though Rex was already so enthusiastic that he begged them to put parts of it back. This was the best role he had ever had.

As for the character Lilli Palmer played, Gilliat is equally adamant that it was not based on her either. 'I tested four or five actresses for the part – without mentioning it to Rex – at the old Riverside Studios while the flying bombs were landing all around us. None of them pleased me. Finally someone said, "What about Lilli Palmer?" Rex said, "I'll put it up to her, but it's a bit near home." Lilli showed no resistance. Why should she? It was a very sympathetic part, the trusting girl who marries a cad and finds him unfaithful and tries to kill herself.

'Rex was a great help in directing her, for Lilli needed to work on a part, hard, before she got it right. But she had that Teutonic thoroughness, and of course Rex was a great taskmaster. He took her through the post-suicide speech about thirty or forty times – she'd done it a bit glibly at first. Rex relaxed her, brought out the grief. My wife cried every time she saw it. One of the salesmen for the company that distributed *The Rake's Progress* in America said to Frank [Launder] and me, "You've got a moneymaker here. The women will be in love with Rex, but they'll feel for Lilli." '

To demonstrate the feat Rex accomplished by charm and force of personality, and which undoubtedly confirms this strictly commercial estimate of a hugely successful film, it is necessary to remember the catalogue of narcissistic, self-centred disloyalties and downright mean-nesses that his character accumulates in the film. He is born into wealth, but decides debt is more convenient; he throws away a privileged education at college as well as stealing a friend's girl; he gets sacked from every job his father's influence secures him; he seduces his best friend's wife; he marries a Jewish girl for what he believes will be her money; he drives her to attempt suicide by his infidelities; he kills his father while driving drunk; he proposes marriage to his late father's secretary, then walks out on her leaving the bill for her wedding dress unpaid; he declines into selling second-hand cars – a fate, incidentally, Noël Coward said would have been Rex's, if he had not been the best light comedy actor in the world – and partnering lonely women at *thés dansants*; and he is saved from total ruin only by the war, in which he shows a foolhardy courage and makes amends for some of the misdeeds he has done in this world by blowing himself (and, admittedly, the men under his command) into the next one.

To make this inventory of conscienceless selfishness into a coherent and comprehensible character is Rex's sizeable achievement. To make him appear forgivable is something that lies beyond artifice and resides in the nature of Rex himself. As Rex was to do more and more in the years ahead, Vivian Kenway follows his own interests as naturally and thoughtlessly as he puts the parting in his hair. He relies on charm to pull him out of a mess. He occasionally performs some act of friendship or shows some unexpected loyalty that is to his credit, but generally makes it a by-product of his refusal to take anything seriously except his own survival. His saving grace is that he never makes excuses for himself. He knows he behaves like a rotter at times, but he lives life to the full as if he also knows what a shortening fuse he is on and is determined to get the most out of life while there is still time. There is enough overlap betwen Rex and the part to explain why he felt particularly at home with it and insisted on getting it dead right – even to the extent of usurping the director's prerogative to call 'Cut'. 'That's no good,' he'd cry at Sidney Gilliat, breaking off a scene he was playing. 'You can't see yourself, and you don't know,' Gilliat would answer from behind the camera but he added afterwards, 'He knew ... we both knew ... and we knew when he did it again and got it right.'

He showed 'unexpected guts', according to Gilliat, 'doing things other actors would leave to their stand-ins'. In one scene he and Griffith Jones, as the husband Rex has cuckolded, have a fight in the flower shop at Harrod's that sends Rex crashing backwards into tiers of blooms in buckets and vases. Rex insisted, as if on a point of honour, that he do it himself. Word spread. Crews from other films shooting at the Gainsborough Studios, Shepherd's Bush, gathered to see Rex for once on the receiving end of someone else's temper. 'He was perfect,' says Gilliat. 'He didn't flinch in anticipation, which can ruin a take like that, but did a backward fall that could have been quite dangerous and sent the whole wooden structure of flowers and vases crashing down round him. But when they did it again and Griffith Jones, by accident or not, hit him a bit too hard for his liking, Rex called a halt and proceeded to instruct his fellow actor on how to fake a punch. Then, with the other's guard down, he socked him on the jaw, very hard, with a gleam of satisfied retribution in his eye.'

How well Rex and Lilli could now play together is apparent in the scene where Vivian has no money to pay the bill in his plush Vienna hotel and is taking his customary way out of a tight spot by legging it over the balcony. As he hangs there, he spies the table being laid for a breakfast he has not ordered. Enter Lilli, chicly dressed, with a tiny cap like a yarmulka to emphasize her Continental (i.e. Jewish) background. Rex creeps back, then tucks into the food while she puts her business proposition to him – offering to pay his debts if he will marry her. Rex drives a hard bargain, exaggerating the sum he says he owes, while Lilli asks touchingly, like someone hesitating to request something to which she realizes she is not really entitled, 'Could you love me just a little?'

Only a player with Rex's self-absorption could play such a scene and still remain sympathetic. For Vivian, as for Rex, love is a matter of opportunity and marriage a matter of attention span.

The Rake's Progress cost between £216,000 and £229,000, and proved exceedingly profitable. It opened in London in the middle of December 1945, a fortnight after *Brief Encounter*. The critics' spirits had been raised by the 'truthfulness' of the Lean film and most of them were in a mood to enjoy the 'candour' of the Launder–Gilliat one. Even so, it came as a gratifying shock to many to discover the extent to which a film could have a cad as its 'hero'. For most, Rex's charm mitigated his misconduct; the recklessness that made such a mess of Vivian's life was turned to his credit when he sacrificed himself in battle. 'What we always meant to convey was nothing of the kind,' says Gilliat today. 'We were simply making the ironical point that war suits such people.' A few of the English critics, though, took a harder look at the thesis that Rex's sins in the film are forgivable because of his heredity and his upbringing in the 1930s – roughly what John Masters felt too. C. A. Lejeune in the *Observer* wrote a cutting and durable opinion. 'Putting on a generation and a class a weakness that is inherent in the individual is a mean and paltry device,' she said.[6] She called Rex's character 'a brilliant study of a social parasite', but added, 'up to a point'. There was truth in this indictment: it had worried Launder and Gilliat too, and even exercised the film censor, who recommended that the line which had originally blamed character 'on what we inherit and the circumstances around us' be altered (as it was) to *'partly* by what ...'. 'In other words,' says Gilliat drily, 'we had to leave room for the Almighty.' The philosophical nicety, rather understandably, tended to be overlooked by audiences enjoying Rex playing what James Agate called 'one of those irresistibly forgivable and seductive top-drawer skunks'.[7]

Those who worked closely with Lilli at the time noticed how marriage had begun to change her. She often spoke now as if she were making the decision for the two of them, for herself and Rex. She was still charming and self-assured, but a few wondered how much of the real Lilli this concealed. After *The Rake's Progress* finished shooting, a party was given for the children of the crew, and the stars came along too. Among them was Guy Middleton, who had played Rex's best friend in the film – an ironic, perhaps not too accidental bit of casting, considering his affair with Collette. He suggested a game: let the children tell the adults what they really think of them. One child confronted Lilli and said, 'Well, anyone can see you're an actress – you're acting all the time.' Lilli did not think it at all amusing.[8]

It was generally wondered how she could put up with her husband's self-centredness. But this was to misjudge her. She was as 'serious' about acting as Rex – rather better organized too – and took his restless, earnest self-interrogation about how he should speak, look or move in a role as a symptom of his dedication. Lilli herself was never to give a bad performance in her life and always collected a personally good notice, however poor the part or indifferent the movie. 'But she was a calculator,' was the opinion of a close acquaintance. 'She calculated how useful people could be to her and graded her friendships accordingly.'[9] Sidney Gilliat veers to that opinion. 'She creamed me,' he says, meaning that she was flattering and compliant until she had got what she wanted; then, her object achieved, 'she got back on her pedestal'.

Gilliat allowed her a day off while they were shooting on location in Cornwall – she wanted to return to London to see Carey. She came back a day late and made no apologies. There was a row. 'Give her an inch, and she'd take a furlong,' says her director. He sent for Rex, whom he had always found 'totally honest', who gave him Lilli's account of what had happened. Gilliat said quietly, 'What you've been told is not true.'

'Rex looked very uncomfortable,' says Gilliat, 'and then asked, "Would it help if I stayed here until you've finished the shots with Lilli?"'

Little by little, Lilli began to organize Rex, making the decisions he would have endlessly postponed, running the home, bringing up Carey, to whom she was devoted, and keeping an eye constantly open for any young woman in Rex's vicinity. 'She made it clear she didn't really take to me,' says Arthur Barbosa. 'She suspected – and she was right, of course – that I was on Rex's side whenever he had something going with a girl. What she forgot is that I'd done the same for her when she started her affair with Rex.' Opinion was that Lilli was 'a very determined woman – determined not to lose him'.[10]

Very shortly after Rex completed *The Rake's Progress*, he found himself being offered a Hollywood contract. One of the first people to hear of it was Herbert Wilcox, who thought he already had Rex's agreement to a series of co-starring roles with Anna Neagle.

'"What about our deal?" I asked. – "Nothing signed," [Rex] replied. –

"But we agreed on a deal – and I sold you my house." – "This is my first Hollywood nibble, Herbert, and I must take it. You can easily get rid of your farm," he told me."[10]

And that was that. Vivian Kenway could scarcely have brushed off an obligation with more charm or less conscience.

11: Royal Bloomers

Rex had never expected to hear from Hollywood. Indeed, his view of the place was downright dismissive. Ronald Neame, who had been sent there immediately after *Blithe Spirit* to study studio and labour union organization, recalls Rex saying on his return: "Doesn't seem right to me, the way they're behaving [in Hollywood] with the war still on."

Rex himself, in the opinion of Anna Neagle, had not behaved any too well when both of them, accompanied by Roland Culver, toured several recently liberated parts of the Continent presenting *French Without Tears* for the Entertainments National Service Association (ENSA) in the last few months of the war. Neagle played the Kay Hammond role – and at the time still thought of Rex and herself as a future film 'couple'.

'As soon as Rex and Roland got to Holland, they took out their golf clubs and looked for a handy course – this in the middle of all the war damage and food shortages." Neagle was invited to a rehabilitation centre for concentration camp victims and asked the others to accompany her. 'Rex said he hated visiting hospitals. Other people's illnesses depressed him. Besides, he said, he'd been cooped up in a film studio and needed fresh air.' By the time they reached Paris, he was tired of the play and threatened to kill Anna if she proposed extending the tour into Germany. In the event that was forestalled by Roland Culver suddenly accepting a contract to go to Hollywood for a film, *To Each His Own*, with Olivia De Havilland. Rex was furious. It was bad enough to be deprived of his golf partner and drinking chum, worse to have to suffer his understudy in the play, but going to *Hollywood* – that was the bloody limit! 'If I may say so, dear boy, your atitude is that of the shit which you undoubtedly are ... What do you want to go to Hollywood for? It's finished, old man; last legs, dear boy. You are making a big mistake. Hollywood's had it ...'²

Yet on 11 October 1945 Rex and Lilli found themselves waiting on a quay at Southampton to board the *Queen Mary*, which was still in her wartime role as a troopship, along with 12,000 returning GIs crowded into what had been accommodation for 2,500 passengers in peacetime.

He had returned from the ENSA tour to find Twentieth Century–Fox offering him a contract. *Night Train to Munich* had performed well in America. On the basis of this, Fox wanted to sign him up for seven years, with annual options, at a starting salary of $4,500 a week rising to $10,000 in its last year, a huge sum at the time. Unusually, the first film he would make was named in the contract, suggesting anxiety on Fox's part to secure his services. It was to be *Anna and the King of Siam*, the highly romanticized story of the mid-nineteenth-century monarch, King Mongkut, who was tamed, civilized and won over to a grudging admiration, if not exactly affection, for most things Western, including the English governess who came to his Bangkok court to instruct his numerous wives and his sixty-seven children.

Rex asked the agent from the Music Corporation of America (MCA) to get him a script. 'They were courting me. I was very much on my guard.'[3] His guard dropped when he saw the length and prominence of his part, though he thought the film would be even better if retitled *The King of Siam and Anna*. Years later, when the same story was made into a musical, Rex's suggestion was (almost) adopted as *The King and I*, though he certainly would not have liked the 'Anna' of the story to be given the prominence of the first person pronoun.

'It was a very big decision,' he said afterwards, 'on the other hand, it was a very big amount of money.'[4] Lilli was apprehensive. She had thought herself settled permanently at last with a husband, a baby, a home for which she had just finished sewing curtains, and a career of her own which she was pursuing with success. But she and Rex were heavily in debt. They owed back taxes and future mortgage payments, not to mention Rex's alimony. But the fear they both shared, if they went to Hollywood, was being separated by work and distance from appearing on the stage. Movies were a well-paid occupation for now and then. The theatre was its own world: the pay might be less, but the satisfactions were infinitely more fulfilling. Rex was dead set against putting himself in someone else's power for seven years, then the standard term of a Hollywood contract (and legally banned a few years later as a form of peonage akin to the serfdom of California's Mexican labourers). He ordered MCA to renegotiate. His agent reflected that he was already behaving like an Oriental despot before he had succeeded to the throne. Finally Fox gave in. A contract was signed to take effect from 26 October 1945 to run for three years, with a year off to do a play, and then for another three years firm. Evidently Fox wanted him badly.

And so they set off on the crowded liner with only a suitcase each, Rex's despatch case and Lilli's handbag. Never again would either cross the Atlantic with so little luggage. 'If anyone ever suggests this trip to you,' Rex said to Arthur Barbosa, 'decline with thanks. Only two things happened of any note. I saw my first whale, and I caught a bloody dreadful cold.'[5] He lived on whisky – as the 12,000 GIS also seemed to do, for by the end of the trip their slightly bored air of obedience had given way to boisterous and then boozy high spirits. The ship arrived in New York under a collective hangover, Rex included. Three nights and two days later he and Lilli disembarked from the Super Chief at the Pasadena railroad station, which stars arriving in Hollywood preferred to the proletarian bustle of Los Angeles. A man from Fox was waiting with the usual back-up of flashlight photographers – 'As if you needed more light,' Rex reflected, screwing his eyes against the sun. Perhaps his slit-eyed appearance accounts for the earnest sincerity of the welcome: 'Gee, you're just like the King of Siam.'[6] As the king had been barely five feet six inches, bandy-legged and bald, Rex was left wondering why on earth Fox had made such efforts to get *him*.

The truth was that Fox wanted a leading man who could carry a film, but not be associated by the mass of filmgoers with any already established star. He must appear unfamiliar enough to personify a foreigner – a *royal* one, too, which, to Fox's way of thinking, meant an English actor with the 'class' which that country's exports had traditionally contributed to the film colony. (Not that this was the opinion of the film's director, John Cromwell, who had pushed strongly to get William Powell.) As the journalist Pete Martin later wrote, 'In importing Harrison, Twentieth Century–Fox gambled on bringing a composite Ronald Colman, Cary Grant and Trevor Howard across the Atlantic.'[7] Yet this is to oversimplify things. Whenever a new actor has to be introduced to the American public and is explained in terms of established stars, people grope for comparisons of this kind because the new man or woman has some quality of his or her own that is not yet readily definable. Rex was by no means a natural progression of the English-born actor who becomes a Hollywood star. For one thing, he was nearly forty, and his personality was already set in his way. He was not young enough or malleable enough to fit the designer shape that a great Hollywood studio could fashion in pre-war times once it had snared its catch in the invitingly baited seven-year contract. He was already a self-made star of English stage and screen when he came to Fox, not given to compromise or easily amenable to discipline, as the studio was to find out.

The studio's publicists had difficulty in defining Rex's screen appeal. 'Ty Power with a broad "A" ... Boyer with an Oxford accent,' was one attempt. The strain showed. A fan magazine attempted a peppier analysis, which made Rex wince with distaste when he read it: 'If you're a bobby-soxer, he makes you want to grow up fast. If you're just forty, he makes you want to forget you are.'[8] It was the American way of saying 'Sexy Rexy'.

Rex's initial reaction to Hollywood was one of suspicious unease. He feared he might be 'seduced by its ease and richness and laziness, and lose my drive'.[9] Moreover, coming straight from an austerity Britain, he could not easily come to terms with this flamboyant and colourful world where his casual tweeds and reserved manner made him feel, in Pete Martin's words, 'as if he had been set down suddenly in the middle of a huge impromptu costume party'.[10]

Fortunately, Lilli had secured a Warner Bros. contract, though her starting fee of $2,000 a week was well below Rex's. She would be co-starring with Gary Cooper in her first film, *Cloak and Dagger*. Her German origins were even more heavily concealed than they had been in England. 'Miss Palmer is the daughter of a London doctor and an English actress,' Louella Parsons said confidently, if a trifle vaguely.[11] They stayed for a few days at the Beverly Hills Hotel and then, when this ritual welcome of a new star had been completed by the presentation of the bill, they rented Clifton Webb's home in Bel Air – Webb had played Rex's role in *Blithe Spirit*. Lilli immediately began rearranging the furniture, vetting the maid, subscribing to New York magazines and waiting for Carey to be brought over by his nanny. But her most immediate concern was coping with Rex's massive attack of nerves.

He had been only a few hours in their Beverly Hills bungalow when his impatience took him to the studio to discuss his role. He had expected John Cromwell to be a Harold French figure: a director who would also offer him guidance, support, approval. But Cromwell, probably nursing a grievance over losing William Powell, kept his ideas to himself, if he had any. And the producer, Louis Lighton, who did have some, could not easily articulate them and tell Rex how he, a six-foot Caucasian, was expected to play a Siamese nearly a foot shorter. Rex soon learned that Darryl F. Zanuck, the studio head, was more comfortable with his polo-playing cronies than advising an actor on Oriental manners. After a warm greeting, Rex scarcely saw Zanuck again. His attempts to make an appointment to discuss his role were politely cancelled. Of course Fox's researchers had done their work well, but their plethora of information about the Thai monarchies did not help Rex in playing his first character role, a role for which he could not simply extend his own personality into the part. He paced the garden in Bel Air, script in hand, trying out accents and gradually losing his nerve. 'Relax,' Cromwell had told him, 'that sort of stuff will come from you quite naturally, you know, when you're in your costume.'[12] But he could not relax, even when he wasn't 'at work'. He was overawed by the stars he met socially. He still saw them as the magnified images dominating cinema screens back home and felt crushed and insignificant, unable at first to muster courage to make conversation and then disconcertingly discovering that the Coopers, Tracys, Grants and Stewarts did not want to talk about work at all, but only about their ranches, oil wells or hunting pursuits. Rex was soon quite ready to break his contract and rush back to England rather than make a fool of himself.

In this crisis Lilli came to the rescue. She sent for a 'witch doctor', her old drama coach Elsa Schreiber, who had steadied Lilli's nerves in the past and was now teaching privately in Los Angeles. Ordinarily Rex would have disdained such help, fearing it would encroach on how he saw the part. But now, as he could not see the part at all, he grasped at any clue. Cautiously at first, he quizzed Schreiber about the man's likely walk, demeanour, and so on. From plausible speculation about the Oriental potentate's accent ('staccato and high-pitched, a bit like birds twittering') and the way Easterners laughed ('inaudibly, almost convulsively'), she drew Rex imaginatively into assembling the monarch's persona.[13] Her methods closely resembled the recommendations of the great Russian film and theatre director V. I. Pudovkin, whose book *Film Technique and Film Acting*, published in English in 1929, would have been a very unlikely addition to Rex's dressing-room. But now, working under Elsa Schreiber for several weeks, he was transformed from an actor thinking about a role – and becoming paralysed by so much anxious meditation – into a man acting it. 'Rex depended very heavily on Elsa,' says Anthony Havelock-Allan, who visited him and Lilli at this time, being driven up to the Harrison home by a young MCA agent called Swifty Lazar and seated next to Ernst Lubitsch, who talked of Rex doing a film with him.

It was an altogether more confident Rex who reported to Fox for costumes and make-up. Make-up was not extensive. They browned his face – though the film was being shot in black and white – and patched a glossy black toupée into his own thinning stuff. But Rex's eyes and eyelids had a naturally narrow look: this was one of the features that gave his face its expression (when he wished) of insolent menace. When the fan magazine writers closed in on him briefly, for he soon barred them, they usually began with his eyes. 'He looked at me – or should I say *into* me – intensely, probingly,' one began. 'Under his drilling gaze, I was having a difficult time keeping my wits about me. *Ye gods*, I thought, *is my soul showing?*' Fanzine gush, of course, yet remember it was Rex's 'cold-looking' face that had originally caused Lilli to stare back across the dining-room of the Birmingham hotel and ask for an introduction to him.[14]

Apart from concealing the upper fold of the eyelid, Ben Nye's make-up skills were not stretched. Then the wardrobe department moved in, wrapping him in shimmering silk jackets, sashes covered in medals – Richard Lyon, Bebe Daniel's son, playing the governess's small boy, offered Rex his own 'Honorary G-man's badge' to add to the show on his chest; it was coldly declined – and finally, as Hedda Hopper reported, 'handed him those green things which in Siam are called *panungs*, but which any woman's wear department would put in the bloomer barrel.'[15] It was these Oriental trousers ('oversized, droopy-diaper kind of pants,' as the uncivilized sections of the American press insisted on terming them), out of which Rex's skinny legs protruded, bare from the calf down, that helped give a prowling, predatory, semi-barbaric feeling to his walk. And as he often had to squat, cross-legged, on throne or stool, his long-limbed king looked coiled, serpentlike, ready to strike.

The simmering mistrust between him and Cromwell broke out when, at the first take, he began speaking in the high-pitched tones evolved by him and Elsa Schreiber. 'What in the world do you think you're doing, Rex? Why don't you speak normally?' Rex replied, stiffly, that he was speaking like King Mongkut of Siam. 'Out of the question. We hired Rex Harrison, not a bird imitator.'[16] Rex stood – or, rather, sat – his ground. The rushes were screened for Zanuck next morning and Cromwell confidently waited for Rex to be reprimanded. Instead, Zanuck sided with the King's English. Thereafter, Rex and Cromwell communicated through third parties and the star continued to perform as directed – by Elsa Schreiber.

It has to be admitted that the film does not wear well. A flatly directed, story-led succession of stiffly enacted scenes, it is so uninventively photographed that even its much vaunted $300,000 worth of oriental décor (publicists' valuation) looks like a tawdry antique shop. Irene Dunne's governess is testimony to the tenacity of American women in getting their own way, but otherwise is shrill and unnuanced. Rex is what preserves the interest. It is partly because he is giving a theatrical performance, very physical, unpredictable from moment to moment, filled with tiny pauses suggesting a primitive but cunning mind being made up, and then the owner acting impulsively on his decision. Rex's accent is not markedly oriental. But its pitch is high, its rhythm clipped, its tenor admonitory and he uses his head, arms, hands, eyes and accusing forefinger with kinetic impact. He is quite unlike any other star then appearing on the American screen. Most important of all, Rex raises the role to his own well-practised level of high comedy. Without relaxing his dignity, he slyly and even touchingly plays against it. This king wants so strongly to prove himself educated in the ways of the West that, although the hand-made dinner napkins are late in arriving, he personally distributes them to his English guests and his own courtiers long after they have finished the banquet. Rex gives the solecism a solemn ceremonious flourish. The *New Yorker* critic said, 'Even when he stoops, he towers. His nervous strut and his overenunciated chatter express the quirkiness that can grow in autocratic isolation.'[7]

He was an immense help to a film that had to have no sex in it – Hollywood's morality code strictly prohibited interracial love, however historical or royal the precedent. The most intimate moment between the King and the pedagogue comes when they share a bowl of soup. But their relationship has an erotic charge that is always threatening to explode, and much of this is due to Rex's palpable virility. He looks as if he could be a potent force in his well-stocked harem. Indeed, the role became the man so well that when a reference was made to King Mongkut's sixty-five children, Rex interrupted the take to correct the actor and point out that he had sixty-seven. Trust Rex to feel self-protective about a fellow's manhood; two fewer infants would have made little difference to history, but it mattered to the character Rex was playing.

In the wake of the Pacific War, the film revived the East as the land of exoticism and mystery. It was timely. Audiences wanted to forget the harshness of war so long as General MacArthur was imposing, like Anna, western values on a barbaric people. It did well at the box-office; and for Rex it was a triumph.

His future looked secure. So it might have been, had Hollywood been about to turn the clock back ten years to the mid-1930s. But the loss of the European market during the war had compelled the studios to find more stridently American subjects than the international stories which profited from English-born stars. Rex had arrived just a little too late. New stars were about to appear who were cast in a more rugged American mould, with an appeal to returning GIs and their womenfolk. They wanted screen heroes with less of the studio groomed look, more of the self-confident, aggressive qualities that had won the war: Burt Lancaster with *The Killers* (1946) and *Brute Force* (1947), Kirk Douglas with *Champion* (1949), Robert Mitchum with *The Story of GI Joe* (1945) were about to redefine the screen image of a leading man. Frank Sinatra was showing the box-office value of stars with appeal to the new, moneyed and rather terrifying generation of wartime bobby-soxers who wished to put their own icons in place of the ones their parents venerated. The change was to the disadvantage of talents like Rex. He would find this out quickly, though perhaps not so brutally as English-born stars like Granger, Mason and Wilding, who followed him to Hollywood slightly later.

In short, there was little of the incentive there would have been in the pre-war era to build up a name like Rex and make him a major box-office attraction. He was a prestigious name on the studio roster and, in the right picture, a money-maker. The problem was going to be to find the right picture. During the six months after completing *Anna and the King of Siam*, he did nought but turn down scripts.

Zanuck showed remarkable patience as his new star found nothing to his liking. He rejected a remake of *Berkeley Square*, a big Leslie Howard hit, because he did not want to be 'a second Leslie Howard'; a film of the novel *Britannia Mews* ('too squalid'); another of *Forever Amber* ('period ... and costume doesn't suit me'). Just as well that Zanuck was an Anglophile, half overawed by Rex's tailoring, half by his English accent, or so the studio gossips had it.

Nor did Rex do himself any good with the interviewers. 'A Fisherman Out of Water' was the *New York Times*'s headline – and it was not a newspaper usually given to sardonic type – when 'the angular English actor', as Thomas M. Pryor called him in an article of increasing asperity, talked animatedly about fishing when he came to town to publicize *Anna and the King of Siam*.[18] Pryor had made the mistake of ordering scallops, in Rex's opinion a solecism for mid-day lunch. When the talk was towed back to Hollywood, he animatedly attacked columnists who had hinted that he and Lilli were going to apply for American citizenship, which he made clear he considered inferior to the one they already possessed. Hollywood's 'intellectual insularity and factionalism' were next on his hate agenda.[19] 'It is rather astonishing to me,' Rex pontificated, 'that we in England have only two political parties and we don't use the term "Fascist" as loosely as you do here.' Dangerous talk from a film star, sure to be carried back to a company town where 'Fascist' was a term used by those below for those above.

Rex's first brush with Hedda Hopper harmed him considerably, at least later on. Hopper herself could hardly have been more fulsome. 'With his crisp accent, the smiling crinkle of his eyes, his gracious manners, he was charm incorporated.'[20] But why had Rex come to Hollywood? Unwarily, he replied: 'Taxes ... If I have no residence there and no property in England for a tax year, I only pay taxes here.'[21] Rex was less than fully informed, and did not appreciate the difference between being 'resident' in a country and being 'domiciled' there. But the distinction was quite clear to the British Treasury official who, at that time, was on the staff of the British Embassy in Washington expressly to check on the earnings of Britons in the United States. He filed the column away for future reference when the Inland Revenue back home caught up with Rex's US earnings. Rex and Lilli were not even resident in America yet; they needed to leave the country every nine months until residence was granted them, and then obtain a quota number to re-enter. Usually this simply meant slipping over the Mexican frontier for a long weekend, while the studio arranged with Immigration to see that their stars did not have to become 'wetbacks' and swim the Rio Grande to return to work.

Again and again it was left to Lilli to salve the feelings of columnists who had been rubbed up the wrong way by Rex's short temper. When the day of reckoning came, he had no capital of goodwill to draw on.

Finally, at the end of the summer of 1946, Rex found a script he liked: *The Ghost and Mrs Muir*. Ironically enough, for an actor with his reputation for sexiness, there is no fleshly contact at all between the lovers in it. In the same way as the taboo on miscegenation prevented a romance in *Anna and the King of Siam*, the affair between the widowed Mrs Muir and the spectre of the sea captain who haunts her villa remains unconsummated. The appeal of the film – the point that touched Rex – was the pathetic fallacy that is found in books, plays and films in wartime or in the aftermath of war: the belief that death is not the end, love transcends it and the other world provides an inviolate haven for reunited lovers. Joseph L. Mankiewicz was set to direct it. He and Rex were men with a love of words and took to each other at the drop of a syllable. Rex would make three more films with Mankiewicz and the latter always referred to him as 'my Stradivarius'.[22]

'English actors have a special way with words that Americans seldom possess,' says Mankiewicz today. For him, Rex was 'a siren voice. The lines never wilted on his lips. Always fresh and crisp. He had a way of *slapping* people with a line of dialogue.'[23] Others, too, noted that Rex seldom played *with* an actor – one of the reasons why other actors, while grudgingly admitting his brilliance, often accused him of lacking generosity.

Rex adopted a crustier manner and a gruffer voice than usual for the spectre mariner. He is allowed a belt buckle of macho proportions to hint at what lies below the belt, as well as a few 'be hangeds' and 'blasts' as befits an old salt. He plays on a note of insistent masculinity that convincingly reawakens the libido that Gene Tierney's widow retired with her bereavement. Though he is absent from the story's last third – the caddish George Sanders taking his place in the widow's affections – it is a tribute to how strongly his male presence has permeated the story that he can take command of the short, final sequence so movingly and pull the spirit of the young Mrs Muir out of the deceased husk of the older woman with a gentle but firm promise, 'And now you'll never be tired again.' There is a touching hint here of the notion of 'guardianship' – of one divinely appointed person keeping watch and ward over another – that later made such a profound impression on Rex when he appeared on stage in *The Cocktail Party*.

He modelled the fierce, whiskered captain on his boomingly opinionated old friend Bernard Shaw. (Mankiewicz was a great Shavian fan, too, and later on seized the chance in *Cleopatra* to rework the modernistic romance of Shaw's *Caesar and Cleopatra*.) Rex's way with dialogue in *The Ghost and Mrs Muir*, a masculine force breaking over a feminine object like salty sea-spray, adds a vigour to the romance that GBS would have relished.

The theme of the film struck most critics as novel enough to make them forgive such lapses as its heavy-handed whimsy, though *Time* called it 'a bit of ectoplasm left over from *Blithe Spirit*'.[24]

The enjoyment of working with Mankiewicz did not, however, last long enough for Rex. His choosiness over film scripts meant that he had more time on his hands than most stars. He took his work so seriously, picked holes so assiduously in the properties that Fox presented to him and his agents at MCA, that the studio was hard put to find any plausible reason for suspending him from work without pay. For the first time in his life, he began to feel rich. Back in rural Buckinghamshire, he had spent the leisure time he had 'beating about the hedgerows in an old banger', as he put it in a Hollywood interview that must have been baffling to a few residents.[25] Now he had the means to buy a brand new banger – a bright red convertible – and go to work in his shirt sleeves, with the smell of orange blossom scenting his route. Economically minded Lilli, however, discovered that paying $1,000 a month in rent for their Bel Air mansion, and an extra $1,000 in housekeeping and staff, was an extravagance. They moved to a house closer to the Roland Culvers – and a golf course – in Pacific Palisades.

Rex later claimed that this was the beginning of his ruin. It infiltrated his defence and encouraged the English hedonist to come out and play – California-style. Soon he and Lilli were well and truly caught on the endless treadmill of social pleasures, playing golf, going to the beach, sailing round Catalina Island, weekending in Palm Springs, giving parties and going to them, meeting the same old faces whose famous owners no longer intimidated him, but did little to enliven life either as the men and women at the evening's reception automatically drifted into separate groups by gender as if there were an invisible fence between them. Rex confessed he was 'impatient and desperate and saying "Yup" too often to everything except work.'[26] In his boredom, waiting for work and still being paid in large weekly cheques for not working, he began to do what was tempting to a man of Rex's nature – he started looking at the women on the other side of the fence.

12: The Fatal Affair

If Rex considered that lazing around doing nothing was dangerous for a man possessing a strong commitment to work, then the objects of his contemplation were soon to prove fatal. Beautiful women, of course, had long been an occupational hazard of life in Hollywood. Lubitsch had described the place memorably as a village full of professionals lacking an audience. Almost every day Rex and Lilli received telegrams inviting them to someone's party. Lilli noticed her husband was beginning to drink quite heavily – for him, anyhow. On one occasion, he crashed through Sam Goldwyn's entrance gates as he was driving himself and Lilli home. The ironwork portals were still draped over the bonnet when they got to their house in Mandeville Canyon: they had not dared go back and explain. Rex sent them back with a jereboam of champagne as an apology. Goldwyn did not think it funny. Another time, Rex insisted on driving home on the left side of the highway. That is how English gentlemen drove, he said. Fortunately for them, not too many American gentlemen were on the road at 5 am. Thereafter, Lilli took the wheel. She disliked drinking; alcohol did not agree with her. The intellectual level of the average Beverly Hills party bored her to distraction. Rex, though, seemed to want to stay on until the place emptied. 'When you've got a Scotch in your hand,' he told her, 'even the dumbest conversation becomes fascinating.'¹ A female never appeared alone at a Hollywood party, there was always an escort; but as the guests tended to congregate by gender, the unconventional male could usually find a temporarily unaccompanied female and Lilli noted her husband, glass of Scotch in hand, having a conversation with quite a few women, not dumb ones either. When taxed, Rex laughed it off: 'Mustn't be stuffy; they don't know good manners here.'² Their broadmindedness, was also in question, as was shown by an incident in the summer of 1946.

Rex's son Noel arrived to spend the school holidays with his father, and Collette came too. Despite their divorce, Rex kept on good terms with her, which was to be the pattern in almost every one of his subsequent marriages. He liked to think his ex-wives should be acceptable to his current one – he and the King of Siam had that in common, at least. Collette and Lilli managed to be companionable enough with each other not to make Rex feel that he was reliving scenes from *Blithe Spirit* with a more material emanation of his first spouse.

After Collette and Noel had stayed two weeks at the Beverly Hills Hotel – then the permissible duration since accommodation was under pressure in post-war Hollywood – they moved in with Rex and Lilli, and the two women accompanied Rex, one on each arm, to the first available Saturday night party: it happened to be Norma Shearer's. They caused an unvoiced apprehension. Scandal still had the power to blight careers by inciting the various 'decency leagues' to call for a boycott of the films made by some star who had been named – or maybe not even named, but hinted at by his or her initials – in the gossip columns on grounds of 'immoral' behaviour, which often simply meant unconventional conduct. Rex appearing in public with two women, 'ex' and 'current', was certainly grounds for disapproval in that self-protective little community; and those who tolerated such 'offenders' might find themselves reprimanded as well. Norma did not find it funny.

Collette enjoyed herself in Hollywood. She was a natural party-goer in a town that threw one nightly. She persuaded Lilli to come out with her on the town while Rex was absent dubbing some dialogue for a scene in one of his films. After dinner and several glasses of wine and brandy at Romanoff's, the two Mrs Harrisons made it home, at the cost of Lilli colliding with a pillar in their garage, before collapsing together on the double bed in the master suite. When Rex found them on his return, he let them sleep it off and retreated in disgust to his dressing-room, cursing the inconvenience. Actually, it suited him to be able to feel, for once, smugly superior to Lilli and see her both hung-over the next morning and guilty at her act of self-betrayal where alcohol was concerned. It felt good, after a suitable period of reproach, to extend his self-righteous forgiveness to her. Speaking to a friend some years later, Rex summed up his approach to women in general and such circumstances in particular: 'Women ... always leave them beholden.'[3]

The incident, however, put a slight damper on Rex's warmth towards his ex-wife. It brought back some of the disorder he felt she had caused when they were married. Collette and Noel returned to England in due course, and soon afterwards, feeling that she was making out well enough by herself, Rex let the alimony payments tail off. It was an injudicious decision he was soon to regret.

Meanwhile, a script called *The Foxes of Harrow* was presented to him even before he had finished shooting *The Ghost and Mrs Muir*. He had just turned down a film called *13 Rue Madeleine*, a spy thriller which had also been offered to Jimmy Cagney. Rex commented that, 'If Cagney can play it – I can't.'[4] He decided, for once, not to push his luck with Zanuck too far, and accepted *The Foxes of Harrow* and the role of an illegitimate Irish immigrant who makes a fortune as a Mississippi riverboat gambler and incubates a dynasty with the help of a proud redhead, who was to be played by Maureen O'Hara. At least he would be wearing trousers and could look forward to a clinch with O'Hara in his arms. So far, he had not even laid a hand on a woman in the two Hollywood films he had made, being an untouchable oriental in one and a ghost in the other.

In assigning him this role, Fox were clearly bent on trying on the Errol Flynn image. With it went the Errol Flynn moustache, though Rex's Anglophilia made him determined to think of it as the Ronald Colman moustache. Either way, it signified an active life with wine, women and physical virility to the fore. Half-a-dozen instructors were drafted in to teach him the other arts necessary for the role: fencing, horse-jumping, dancing, singing and wrestling. He took to card-sharping so well that the expert was surprised. 'Very simple,' Rex said, 'I merely practised three times as long as you told me to.'[5]

However long he practised, through, he made no headway with Maureen O'Hara. Unwilling to accept he was lacking in attraction for her, he convinced himself that her Irish nationalism was aggrieved by the idea of an Englishman playing the role of one of her compatriots. But vanity, not national identity, probably came into it. In one of the waltz sequences, Rex insisted on turning to the right, thus bringing what he considered his 'best angle' to the attention of the camera, thereby leaving O'Hara presenting the back of her head to the lens. Nothing would induce him to favour her. 'English actors in general were wary of being in films,' Joseph L. Mankiewicz says, 'and Rex was no exception. He was always a little jittery about knowing where the camera was. He said to me at one time, "If you can't see the lens, the bugger's not looking at you."'

Considering the stars' relationship on *The Foxes of Harrow*, there was some irony in the request of Eric Johnson, the Ratings Code Administrator, who supervised screen morality, that Fox reshoot the scene where Rex breaks down the door of O'Hara's bedroom. The expression on Rex's face was 'suggestive'. Rex replied stiffly, 'It was not passion, it was pain,' and explained more colloquially to his friends, 'Imagine hurting my shoulder to get at that bloody woman.'[6]

His venture in costume romance met with a bad press everywhere. 'Dull ... pompous ... faked,' said the *New York Times*, 'and the performances, even of good actors, embarrassingly attitudinized,' although

Rex's 'grim and somewhat testy air' was 'mildly sardonic and intriguing'.[7] For Rex's countrymen and women back in England, however, even these compensations were invisible. He caught it from the flails with which English critics were now beating the hides of English stars who had gone to Hollywood. C. A. Lejeune, who had been so immune to Rex's playboy charms in *The Rake's Progress*, showed no more mercy to him this time round: 'Illegitimate son of a noble Irish household, [he] is for years nurtured at the knout's end by a Galway-born foster father and emerges with the clear Knightsbridge accent which is later to make him such a splendid success in New Orleans. Mr Victor McLaglen (a genuine Irishman) appears in two brief sequences, through which he stampedes with the gusto of a brogue elephant. Mr Harrison appears in almost every sequence and behaves more like a white one.'[8]

Rex communicated with Arthur Barbosa at this time, leaving his old friend in no doubt that 'these two endless years in this fucking terrifying country' was more than he could stand. He had been disappointed by the English critics' reception of *The Ghost and Mrs Muir*, which he had thought '*very* good'. And he felt 'they' were determined to keep him in a dinner jacket and firmly in the drawing-room, yet they would decry him as being completely out of date if he were still doing that kind of movie. Since they had dismissed *The Ghost and Mrs Muir* in three lines, then *The Foxes of Harrow* would probably reduce them to a single line only. Fortunately, the American public would love it – he thought – 'so although I'm losing endless fans at home, I am building up a far greater number here. So the thing will probably work itself out in the long run.'[9]

'He ended up asking me, "How is the night life and the fucking?" and addressed me as "you old Liverpudlian cunt",' says Barbosa. 'He was still the old Rex.'

That was part of the trouble. He simply could not – or would not – adopt Hollywood standards. His publicists had virtually given up on him. He refused to fit in with any saleable image, which meant that they had to fall back on guying his Englishness, sometimes in extremely strained ways. Thus he was set to do a playlet on Eve Arden's radio show posing as 'Bugsy', an American hoodlum with an English accent. He treated the project so contemptuously that he did not even bother to read the script before turning up at the broadcasting station; only when half-way through the rehearsal did he discover that he had a line comparing George VI of England to a retired American radio magnate, Atwater Kent, who was famous for throwing lavish garden parties at which many of those invited never met their host and a fair number did not even know who he was. Rex flared up at what he considered a slur on his king – and walked out, adding that the role could be done by *any* English actor. (It was swiftly rewritten for a female comedian and played by the then popular Vera Vague.)

Perhaps because he lacked a sense of humour, it was agony for Rex to be required to send himself up in public. Yet this seemed to be the only idea in their heads. His appearance on *The Louella Parsons Show* was hardly more rewarding. He had refused to be interviewed by Parsons, so Bebe Daniels took over and explained that, since she had lived in England with her husband Ben Lyon, 'Louella feels I may understand your problems as an Englishman living in America.'[10] Rex, though wincing audibly, managed to declare that 'he was too low-brow for Hollywood and not elegant enough'. In case the irony was lost on Louella's loyal listeners, Bebe continued: 'You can't get away with that. Why, practically the basis for your outstanding success – aside from your great acting ability – has been, um, how shall I say, the manner in which you wear your dinner jacket.' Gamely, Rex got out the fact that he was a jazz fan and was himself 'quite a carpet beater'. Bebe used her experience of English life to translate that into 'rug cutter' in American. Then she asked, 'Who's boss in the Harrison home?' This was a dangerous bit of carpet (or rug) and, fearing it might be pulled from under him, Rex ended the interview there and then with a 'Goodbye, Bebe.'

Rex's touchiness about England and things English was not simply a way of expressing his loathing of all things Hollywood without bluntly insulting those who were paying him now at the rate of $207,000 a year, a sum that would have to be multiplied forty times at least to bring it into line with the purchasing power of money today. He genuinely missed London, being able to lead an unsupervised life, the weather, his friends. He had a twinge of guilt at not being in Britain to share the austerities under a Labour Government, despite being very glad of escaping their draconian taxes – or so he still believed. He and Lilli used to despatch food parcels home once a fortnight to leaven the harshness of the food rationing that was still in force. Most of all, Rex missed the excitement of the West End stage. He knew that Olivier and Vivien Leigh were most prominent among those revitalizing the post-war theatre and he hankered to be part of it, not stuck out here in 'the village', playing Irish ne'er-do-wells and being asked to insult his monarch on the radio.

To add to his frustration, Lilli seemed to be adjusting better than himself to Hollywood life. Her career was flourishing, some would say better than his. After a fairly routine tale of an immigrant girl, *My Girl Tisa*, she had co-starred as John Garfield's sophisticated European girlfriend in the Robert Rosen–Abraham Polonsky boxing exposé, *Body and Soul*, which followed the débacle of Rex's *The Foxes of Harrow* by two months and emphasized how Lilli, working inside a much more vigorous and hard-hitting film-making tradition, had caught the powerful new current of American social conscience movies, while Rex was still drifting in a backwater aboard some very old-fashioned craft. He had refused Elsa Schreiber's help for *The Foxes of Harrow*; Lilli had sought it for *Body and Soul*.

The best hope that Rex could see for himself around the middle of 1947 was finding a film that would get him out of Hollywood and back to England. After endless nagging, he had persuaded Fox to vary the terms of his contract yet again, so that one of the three films he had to make after *Anna and the King of Siam* would be shot in England, provided a suitable property could be found.

But he had another reason for wishing to be back home by the late summer of 1947, a reason he did not declare to anyone in Hollywood and only hinted at to Arthur Barbosa, when he alluded to a life he was leading in Hollywood that was 'extremely interesting and full of adventure despite the press and the village-like atmosphere'." The truth, which he did not yet dare breathe even to his old friend, was that Rex had a mistress, a woman he had begun seeing quite regularly and who was now scheduled to make two films in England herself. Her companionship would be an additional attraction, if only he could get back home to be with her.

Rex said later that he did not know Carole Landis until they met by accident one weekend in Palm Springs. Accompanied by some friends, she walked into the bar of the Racquet Club, where Rex and the club's owner, the former film star Charles Farrell, were passing the evening with Lucille Ball.

This is not correct. Before her 'official' entry into his story, he had secretly been meeting the twenty-eight-year-old actress at several quiet rendezvous outside Los Angeles. An affair had begun almost at once. Carole was what a later generation would have called 'a liberated woman' and Hollywood at that time knew by less flattering names – or at least the community made up of Hollywood wives did. To some of their menfolk, she was 'a good sport': in other words, she was available and dependable. This in turn meant that, although she expected professional favours in return for her companionship, she was not going to jeopardize their status or her own place in the hierarchy of the film colony by indiscretion or blackmail. Carole Landis played by the rules, although, like most things in Hollywood, these were made by men for the advantage of men. On the other hand, there was much in her background that would have made a man like Rex pause, had he been of a prudent nature, which of course Rex was not. An impulsive nature, that was his; and that was Carole's too.

Carole Landis, who had been born Frances Ridste, came from a broken home – not that this was unusual among Hollywood stars then or now. Stardom itself is an aspect of an unbalanced personality, part or parts of which have caught the public's attention and led to a fascination with the owner. Her father, a Navy mechanic, had left their Wisconsin home when she was three. She had got herself married one Saturday at the age of fifteen after running away from school and had been dragged back to class on the Monday by her mother, who had had her marriage annulled. Though Carole was stubborn enough to remarry her beau a while later, it lasted only twenty-three days. Rex's meeting with her took place when she was Mrs Horace Schmidlapp, the wife of a wealthy businessman and sometime backer of Broadway plays, although she was about to separate from him or had already done so and would be suing for divorce. Schmidlapp lived mostly on the East Coast. Carole Landis did not let bad experiences stay with her long. That was part of her attractiveness – to the men in her life anyhow. She could laugh them away, or so they thought. Later events were to reveal a different story: one of hidden heartbreak, repeated disillusionment and embittered cynicism at the treatment she had received from the male sex almost all her life.

Her early career had been as a song-and-hula dancer with club orchestras in southern California before she set out for Hollywood with $100 in her purse and, with good luck or shrewd management, had caught the eye of Busby Berkeley when the director-choreographer was casting a musical. Considering her small-town origins and professional background, Carole had gained a wider experience of the world than many of her kind in post-war Hollywood. She had gone overseas to entertain the GIs in England and North Africa during the war, and had written up her experiences in a book, *Four Jills in a Jeep*, which was later filmed; her travelling companions had been Martha Raye, Mitzi Mayfair and Kay Francis. The easy, comradely way she had with men, while probably part of her basic nature, was no doubt expanded by this kind of overseas trip. She was a cuter, cuddlier, all-American version of the *femme fatale* which Marlene Dietrich embodied on her wartime visits to the battle lines. Carole's post-war relationships benefited from dealing directly with men, and enjoying it. She reminded Rex of Collette: both women had zest, a sense of humour and could match a man drink for drink without falling under the table.

Her Hollywood career had not prospered. Girls who indulged in sex in the afternoons with their bosses – as Carole did at Fox and Warner

Bros. – rarely got the chance to excel on the screen. They were kept on the payroll, put into parts that kept them busy – but not too busy, although in one year alone, 1940, Carole had had six films on the go – and, until age or a change in the studio management caused them to 'retire', were given moderate attention by the publicity department, which usually advertised in a softer, more generalized way the same attributes that had made them welcome on an executive's office couch. Thus, in her nine years and twenty-four movies, Carole Landis had been publicized successively as 'The Ping Girl' (because, illogically perhaps, 'she makes you purr'), 'The Zipper Girl', 'The Sweater Girl', 'The Garter Girl', and 'The Girl You'd Like to be Marooned with on a Desert Island'. On one occasion, a news agency reported she had been voted among the best undressed girls on the screen by a fashion expert whose ratings went: 'Lana Turner, prettiest in a slip; Rita Hayworth, most languorous in a negligée; Carole Landis, liveliest in a nightgown.' Carole threatened a lawsuit, alleging this suggested she was promiscuous. The agency backed down and blamed a typographical error: the word should have been 'loveliest'.

Like many such starlets, she thought herself more demeaned by her career than elevated and felt she deserved more respectful treatment. A couple of her ex-husbands had been well off, and their income, separation allowances or alimony made it possible for her to live in reasonable comfort, dress in Don Lopert's movie-star fashions created for people who were not quite movie stars, and be seen around, though never in the best drawing-rooms and rarely at the top tables. Like her later abused and doomed counterpart, Marilyn Monroe, her upbeat outlook and underlying pathos invited male protectiveness which was sometimes hard to tell apart from exploitation. Like Monroe, too, she could generate a line of snappy repartee that got her quoted and kept her name in print. Asked what was keeping her and Mr Schmidlapp apart, she quipped succinctly, 'Distance.'

She wore four wedding bands, one for each of her failed marriages. She said they were better than tying a piece of string around her finger to remind her of something. Asked what, she replied, 'Not to get married again.'

Also like Marilyn Monroe, she had aspirations to be considered a serious actress. An attempt to start a stage career in New York, backed by Schmidlapp, had come to nothing, but she was reading Freud and, when Rex met her, attempting to change her image. It is all too likely that she saw this civilized and urbane actor, and, for all she knew, a sincere and passionate lover, as part of that change. She had asked Fox to release her from her contract, believing that a studio which put her in movies as bad as her last one, all too aptly named *It Shouldn't Happen to a Dog*, was not plotting her career with any zeal. Zanuck freed her, probably with relief, and filled the role she had occupied in his office between 3.30 pm and 4 pm most days of the week without much trouble with other talent from the casting department.

She was not a girl without resource, however, and, given a more humane set-up in a less manipulative community, she might have found a modest but satisfying level as a character actress-cum-comedienne. 'I thought her a rather bright girl,' says Anthony Havelock-Allan. 'She was courageous and ahead of her time in the way she was prepared to risk scandal by doing her own thing. I suspect it was this daring side of her that attracted Rex. When he was bent on something – or someone – he rarely gave much thought to consequences. He relished the sort of Feydeauesque thrill that went with an illicit affair – the secrecy and the risk of being discovered.' Feydeau, though, did not end in tragedy.

As Rex was at odds with Fox as well, Carole's 'independence' was an additional bond between them. Lilli's contract with Warner Bros. originally stated that she would not be expected to work when Rex was not making a film, but the unrealistic nature of this clause soon became apparent when it started losing her roles. It was quietly dropped. While she was working almost daily on *Body and Soul* and Rex had finished his role in *The Foxes of Harrow*, he could relax with Carole in reasonable security; and he always had the excuse of a wife to pick up at her studio when his afternoon trysts with Carole were over. His friends Tyrone Power and Cary Grant occasionally lent their homes, or a bungalow was rented for the day at the Beverly Hills Hotel, or they would meet on the beach at Malibu, or sometimes they would play in mixed doubles on someone's tennis court. Openness like this added to the thrill of it all for Rex.

His compulsive risk-taking in liaisons of this kind caused affectionate amusement among his men friends. A few months before he had started seeing Carole Landis regularly, some of them had hired a couple of actresses from Central Casting, a ravishing girl and a more mature woman, and 'placed' them at one of the Hollywood parties where Rex would be likely to run across them. He did. Posing as mother and daughter, they soon had him accepting an invitation to come over to where the mother said she lived, a good address on one of the more hidden canyon roads, and take afternoon tea. The story goes that, when Rex arrived, the mother had been called away on an errand and her daughter was waiting alone to entertain Rex: a not displeasing prospect. In the middle of a more intimate relationship than the conventions of afternoon tea usually allowed, the other woman suddenly made her return and caught Rex nearly naked. He panicked as the mother went into a loud tirade of threat and lamentation about her daughter's damaged virtue. Professional ruin, blackmail, perhaps even criminal charges were chasing through his mind as he struggled to get his trousers back on when he looked through the picture window to see Ty Power, David Niven and his own particular chum, the actor Jack Merivale, as well as other male cronies who had been let into the secret, killing themselves with laughter. Both actresses then stepped out of their roles, and a good time was had by all. Rex later admitted it had scared the hell out of him.

He had continual cause for unease, wondering if the gossip columnists or their spies among the servants in the stars' community were keeping tabs on his assignations with Carole. They were; but they, too, observed the convention of the place, which was not to break a good story until the time was ripe. Rex was a valuable asset to his studio, and Hopper, Parsons and the other 'vultures' depended on the good will of the studios for their daily access to the contract stars and were not yet ready to dish the dirt on anyone until it was indicated to them that the payload had already been extracted from the star's career. They preferred to operate by hints and innuendoes rather than risking a head-on confrontation with names. But they had had their eye on Rex well before he began his affair.

What had crystallized opinion about Rex's randy nature and his underlying vulnerability was the film he had made two years earlier, *The Rake's Progress*. It did not open in America until November 1946, a full year after he had become a member of the Hollywood colony, when people were still trying to decide what sort of person he was. Up to then he had been presented as belonging to the rather whimsical English tradition of Leslie Howard, tetchy at times like Howard, but gentlemanly underneath it and endearingly vague. Many of the stories printed about him at the time had emphasized his supposedly absent-minded eccentricities. When he played tennis at Sam Goldwyn's, it was reported, he had had to be reminded when it was his turn to serve. Then again Lilli had had to return an armful of trousers belonging to Douglas Fairbanks Jr which Rex had thoughtlessly pulled on at various times, thinking they were his own, after the two of them had taken a steam bath. And there was the time when Lilli bought him a gold cigarette case inscribed 'With love', which he promptly lost; so she bought him another inscribed 'Once more, with love', which he lost too.

Then *The Rake's Progress* was shown and widely written about, and the attitude to Rex changed and hardened. The characteristics he brought to the role of Vivian Kenway, as well as those aspects of the character that rubbed off on him, began to follow Rex around Hollywood. The movie was not all Rex, as one knows, but there was enough of him in it to make his performance look as if it were nearer the real man than the roles he had played to date in the couple of films he had made or was making in Hollywood. It defined him as an incorrigible cad who pursued his pleasures selfishly and did not think twice about the tragedies he brought to others. In a very real sense, and not just on the screen, character became destiny on the day he met and became infatuated with Carole Landis.

13: Unfaithfully Hers

Carole Landis was trying to pick up her career where the termination of her Fox contract had left it. It looked flat on the ground. As she was now a freelance actress, she was open to offers from any producer or studio. Few came in. Gamely, she took up the best of them: a deal for two low-budget movies to be shot in England back to back – that is to say, using the same crew on each and with scarcely an interval between them – for the Eagle-Lion company, the overseas distribution arm of British Lion. It believed there was enough drawing power left in her name to justify the stingy budgets of the two films. Once Rex heard that Carole would be working in England for the best part of six months in 1947–8, he began pressuring Zanuck to let him make *his* next film there too. As usual, he got his way. It was a movie appropriately named *Escape*.

Rex had been hoping to film this story for quite a few years. It had sentimental links for him. Based on John Galsworthy's play, it had already seen service in 1930 as the first talkie to star his old stage idol Gerald du Maurier. Du Maurier was then near the end of his career. Having to rough it on location in bad weather with endless waits between takes depressed Rex immeasurably. Not a good omen, maybe, but he felt the role would strengthen the kinship he felt with the great du Maurier. Besides, there would be Carole...

It suited Fox to buy the movie rights. They were not expensive. Moreover, agreement had recently been reached between the American and British governments resolving a dispute over the levy which Britain proposed charging on Hollywood films in order to protect her own film-makers. The levy was dropped in return for an American promise to invest in British-made films. *Escape* was to be the first under the new scheme. Thus even trade aided Rex's devotion to art and his desire to keep Carole near him.

With Lilli and Carey, now three years old, he sailed for England, arriving at Southampton on 21 August 1947. 'Try to give us a welcome,' he told Arthur Barbosa, 'and get well and truly pissed."

Carole Landis was to follow a short while later to make *The Brass*

Monkey and *Noose*. The second film would keep her there for a little after Rex's return to Hollywood, but being together in a country that was strange to both her and Rex – for, as he said, a lot of things had changed since he had left – gave their illicit romance a piquancy. At last they were away from the Hollywood 'village'. Arthur Barbosa would act as go-between.

Escape was being directed by Joseph L. Mankiewicz, who, as has been noted, got on well with Rex. It was not perhaps the sort of film to bring out the best in Mankiewicz. Set between the wars, it was a manhunt story with Rex as an ex-officer and gentleman sent to prison for taking a prostitute's part in Hyde Park and accidentally killing an officious plainclothes policeman who was harassing her. Escaping, he is pursued across Dartmoor, where everyone he meets adopts a moral or social stance, aiding and abetting his flight, or else trying to capture and turn him in. It was essentially a dated piece of liberal pleading against class prejudice and social injustice. Shooting began on location in September. In spite of Carole Landis being kept busy on her films in London, she and Rex contrived to meet almost every weekend in Plymouth. Mankiewicz soon guessed at the affair. When Rex returned to London, he had to take more byzantine measures to conceal it. Sometimes, the plot got a little beyond him.

Mankiewicz recalls: 'We were all staying in the Savoy Hotel – not Carole Landis, of course. One Sunday morning, the rain was pouring down, absolutely pissing, and I encountered Rex coming down the corridor from the suite he and Lilli had with this huge bag of golf clubs over his shoulder. The clubs were his alibi. He was actually on his way to meet Carole. "Rex," I said, "have you looked out of the window and seen what kind of day it is? You're not going to tell me you're off to play golf in weather like this?" He jumped a bit, looked startled when he saw the rain, put the bag of clubs in a laundry room and said, "Can't tell you how grateful I am to you, Joe." '

Apart from his clandestine liaisons, Rex did not much enjoy making *Escape*. The English film unions were at their most truculent, perpetually ready to go on strike, conceding no privileges to stars like Rex or his leading lady, Peggy Cummins, but insisting they stand in line for lunch and even demanding 'fog money' to compensate for the inconvenience to their breathing they claimed was caused by the fog-making machines. Rex was tempted to lose his temper almost daily. Only his more sanguine director restrained him. Even the finished film provided scant compensation. 'Grimness and a sense of social injustice are not the natural companions of Mr Harrison's talent,' said *The Times*.[2] It was true: he was badly miscast. British critics in particular refused to accept him as a martyr, having lauded him not so long ago as a rake.

Rex and his family returned to America in the *Queen Mary* early in the new year, 1948, accompanied by 500 jazz and swing records – he could now indulge his youthful passion – and an individual described on the passenger list as 'valet to Mr Harrison'. Old Cunard hands were reminded of Edwardian travellers, when no gentleman left home without his 'gentleman's gentleman'.

Waiting for him in New York, he found a screenplay that had been air-expressed to the hotel by its author, the writer-director Preston Sturges. Its title was *Unfaithfully Yours*. Fox were going to distribute the film. Sturges, a once famously reliable money-maker and still reckoned to be a comedy talent second only to Lubitsch, had struck lucky with Zanuck after a string of flops. He offered Rex the leading role. When Rex had finished reading it, he threw down the script with a whoop of delight and cabled Sturges enthusiastically: 'Part better than Hamlet Stop Longer Stop And much funnier Stop Thanks Rex'. To Zanuck, he wired acceptance, adding, 'Shall need time to learn all the lines and gather new strength.'[3]

Considering Rex's continuing affair with Carole Landis, who was following him back to Hollywood in a few weeks, *Unfaithfully Yours* was an ironic choice. It was the story of a monstrous egoist, a temperamental English orchestra conductor, who suspects his wife of infidelity with his young assistant. While conducting three concert pieces, each in a different mood, he fantasizes three different revenge sequences. In the first he murders his wife and frames her lover; in the second he humbles and shames both lovers with a show of resignation; in the third he challenges the lover to a fatal game of Russian roulette. It was the Othello complex given a screwball twist: a black rage extruded into a black comedy.

He began work on it just as Carole returned at the beginning of February and they resumed their liaison. An unfaithful husband in real life playing a jealous husband most of the day, the one thing Rex never saw himself as was a guilty husband. Then as always, he was able to convince himself that infidelity was essential to the life a man lived, and invigorating, provided it did not interfere with the more ordered existence offered by a faithful wife. He believed that Lilli still knew nothing of the affair. He hoped so. The thought of a wife prepared to put up with her husband's amorous escapades made him uneasy. Fine, if she were simply showing broadmindedness, but what if it were indifference? That was the time to worry.

The gossip columnists knew about it, of course, but still feared to strike. They confined themselves to titillatingly coded innuendoes: 'Which actors with initials beginning "H" and "L" are co-starring in their own productions?'⁴ If she saw this sort of thing, Lilli was either ignorant of the identities hinted at or else did not care to ask. She, too, was putting in a long day's filming, making a Lewis Milestone movie called *No Minor Vices*, about a wife who lets a young artist (Louis Jourdan) come and paint her, and then finds he has fallen for the woman in the flesh rather than the one on the canvas. After work, when Lilli came home from playing a love scene with Jourdan over at MGM and Rex from running the gamut of rage as a jealous husband at Fox, the last thing either of them wished to discuss was the state of their marriage.

It seems, in retrospect, that what Rex tragically underestimated was how seriously Carole Landis took the affair. She knew him as a lover, yes, but also as a means of renewing her career. Just before they met, she had dyed her blonde hair a shade of brunette, since she thought that blondes were never taken seriously. A change of image, she thought, might promote her to a better class of picture. Then along came Rex, a sophisticated Englishman, whose knowledge of the world and reputation as an actor could be an entrée to the kind of life from which she fancied herself unfairly excluded. Rex was still able to assess her capabilities more dispassionately than her charms. 'I don't say she was a talented actress,' he wrote later in his memoirs, 'but she was a beautiful girl, and full of life, and could certainly have fitted many parts.'⁵

One part she tried to fit, on returning to Hollywood, was the title role in a stage production of Elmer Rice's *Dream Girl*, which Ross Hunter, a resourceful young actor soon to become a much more successful movie producer, was putting on in a tent in north Hollywood. Rex had coached Carole for the audition, but Hunter soon discovered she could not take direction because her mind was not on the play. 'She was absolutely head-over-heels in love with him,' he recalled.⁶ He replaced her, wisely refusing comment when an indignant Rex called to demand why. Privately Hunter concluded that a girl who could not say the line, 'I'm a virgin,' without bringing the house down was, to say the least, miscast.

A despondent Carole fell back on Rex for consolation and advice about her future. He listened patiently to her monologues while tucking into the food that her cook-cum-housekeeper prepared for him whenever he appeared on the doorstep of the house in Capri Drive, not far from the Roland Culvers' home in Napoli Drive. Her living-room was decorated with informal photos of them both, for developing and printing her own snapshots was a skill Carole had learnt on her wartime entertainment tours. Sometimes he found her in bed, suffering from the malarial virus she had contracted on her travels. Around her lay an assortment of prescription medicines and sleeping pills.

Unfaithfully Yours consumed most of the waking time he did not spend with his wife or his mistress.

Like Rex, Preston Sturges made up his own rules and enjoyed breaking other people's. In contrast to the factory floor atmosphere of most film studios, the *Los Angeles Times* reported, 'his sound stage resembles a circus'.[7] Friends dropped by, were welcomed, joined in crowd scenes. Sturges's own restaurant, The Players, catered to the cast and crew, who sat at long tables without any places reserved for the stars. Rex, though, usually ate in his dressing-room, listening to jazz, often joined by Sturges. Their views coincided on other things besides music. Sturges was just emerging from a long and costly divorce from his third wife. *Unfaithfully Yours* bears marks of its maker's increasing misogyny.

And then, around the middle of March, when they had about a month's shooting still to do, Rex's affair went public. Walter Winchell broke the news in his New York column. 'Carole Landis's next and fifth husband, when she becomes available, will be Rex Harrison,' he wrote.[8] He went on to imply that the two of them, as Rex put it more bluntly, 'had been screwing our heads off' while filming in England.[9] Within hours the story was reprinted in all the major American papers. What happened next, Rex later described to Arthur Barbosa as 'hair-raising and not very funny. The only thing that has saved my poor old nut has been Preston Sturges.'[10]

Having to concentrate on the movie he was currently shooting may have saved Rex's sanity, but it was not enough to save his skin. Reporters and photographers were after him in hordes. His employers were furious and apprehensive. 'What is called in this fucking, barbaric, puerile and infantile country "a scoop" really set the balls rolling,' Rex raged to Arthur Barbosa and added, 'Mine went solid for a moment or two.'[11]

No trouble now about making an appointment to see Zanuck. The studio boss summoned Rex straight from the set to a conference with the lawyers. He was warned that his misconduct, if such it proved to be, might be cause for breach of contract, since such agreements then had a 'moral turpitude' clause written into them. Zanuck pointed out that the Sturges film was already over budget; if public pressure groups boycotted it because of Rex's alleged adultery, he might be held liable for losses. Furthermore, Carole Landis had filed for divorce from her husband. If Winchell's story were true, Rex might be cited by him and sued for damages. 'What do I do?' Rex asked, by now thoroughly alarmed. The reply was immediate and blunt: 'Deny everything.' Which is what all parties now did, vigorously.[12]

The hardest part of Zanuck's reprimand, where Rex was concerned, was his disclosure of Carole's lengthy history of promiscuousness. She was 'booked continuously', she had had 'everyone on the lot', he told his nervous leading man.[13] Rex emerged from the interview feeling, as he later put it, 'in a bugger's muddle'.[14] He was going to have to decide one way or the other: the very worst position to be in, or so he felt. He loathed Hollywood, but he knew that Lilli liked it better than she pretended. At the same time, he did not look forward to divorce; he hated changing what he called his 'background', that is to say a wife and family. And if the truth be told – as he supposed it had to be, now – he was not a little afraid of embarking on an unknown adventure with a woman whose feelings were as unrestrained as his own. Yet, if denied it, he would miss the excitement and have to settle for the conformity of the cabbage-patch with Lilli – 'probably with the odd eroticisms on the side', as he said to Barbosa.[15] Maybe he should just go off by himself.

It would appear that Rex's relationship with Lilli had become difficult just prior to Winchell's 'scoop', for Rex had left their home in Mandeville Canyon and gone to stay with the Roland Culvers. But luckily he had moved back to his own place just before the Winchell story broke. 'Lilli and I fought it together,' he told Barbosa, 'so we were able to deny all the rumours and stop a complete shambles. I must say she has been magnificent.'[16] And so, he added, was 'Suzie', the name Rex took the precaution of using whenever he referred to Carole. By 'denying our heads off', Rex, Lilli and Carole Landis managed to get the gossip-mongers to lay off, at least for the time being, so that Rex was able to complete the film in peace. But, in spite of this scare, he still went on seeing Carole. Danger seemed to sharpen his appetite for romance.

Of course, the story complicated Carole's divorce from her husband. Her chances of alimony were seriously diminished. 'She's flat on the cheeks of her well-rounded ass,' Rex said, 'but it doesn't seem to worry her a bit because she is one hell of a girl.'[17] As for the risk of being cited by Mr Schmidlapp, his luck held here too. Carole Landis had employed a private detective to obtain what she regarded as evidence of her husband's misconduct; he was unlikely to risk a public scandal, she assured Rex. He was in the clear there too. Like the rake he had played on the screen, Rex looked set to come out of it all virtually undamaged.

But what of the immediate future? He was determined to go on seeing Carole, but, according to a letter he wrote at the time, much as he loved her, he simply could not face up to marrying her: it would be far too unsettling. He thought this was Carole's view also. Rex's argument at the time seems to be that he remain married for the moment to Lilli until he found out exactly what he wanted to do and with whom he wanted to do it. Lilli, according to him, was ready to stay in Hollywood with Carey, while he 'buggered off' to London, say, where he had plans to set up his own production company – or, if not London, then anywhere other than Hollywood, a place which had almost made him forget what living humanely was like. Thank God, Lilli could be relied on – up to a point anyway. Arthur Barbosa gained the impression from what Rex told him that this point might be passed if Rex 'buggered off' to Portugal in Carole Landis's company – Carole was very keen on a holiday in Lisbon. That might prove too much for even Lilli's loyalty. What if she turned ugly and cited Carole?

The truth was, in the aftershock of the Winchell story, Rex did not know what to do – but was not ready to stop what he had been doing. It was a selfish and unrealistic attitude.

Carole's attitude was less confused, yet potentially more dangerous. She was not about to give Rex up; indeed she was determined, if possible, to have that holiday in Lisbon with him in May. By that time her divorce suit should be through. But Carole clearly hoped that Lilli would sue for divorce from Rex – in a quiet way, of course, so as not to cause embarrassment. 'It's impossible to know whether she will or won't,' she told Barbosa, but then added, 'We hope.'[18] *We* hope. This opinion was expressed in March. By April, it had ceased to be Rex's view, if it ever was. He wanted his wife to stand by him and not make a move until his own mind was made up. Yet Carole was banking on Rex and her going on from Lisbon to London in June and staying there while he tried to line up a film. She asked Barbosa's help, when the time came, in finding a flat for them both.

Lilli would have had to be made of truly angelic fibre to have tolerated such an arrangement as Carole was envisaging for her husband.

Rex finished the last shot of *Unfaithfully Yours* on 20 April. Barely a month later Lilli left their Mandeville Canyon home and flew to New York to stay with her married sister, Hilde. She left Carey behind in the care of his nanny. While thus conserving her dignity, Lilli also judged the situation astutely. Rex now found himself with nothing to do all day except spend it in the company of his mistress. What had been a titillating situation, running two women together, began to lose the savour of risk. He was neither willing to make the break with Lilli, whom he kept calling daily, nor was he able to see far into the future with Carole. The rake's progress had run into a temporary dead end.

Now real danger arose. In Hollywood terms a wife's withdrawal from the battlefield usually meant that she had forfeited her claim on her man. Carole probably saw it thus, but Rex did not. And an event occurred that was to prove decisive. He received an offer from his other love, his first love: the theatre. Some time, probably in mid-June, his agent Leland Hayward brought him the typescript of a new play by

Maxwell Anderson. *Anne of the Thousand Days* was a drama in verse about the fatal relationship between Henry VIII and Anne Boleyn. Hayward intended producing it in New York and wanted Rex to play the Tudor king. As Rex read the text, he confessed later, his head seemed to clear. Except for the brief ENSA tour in liberated Europe, he had been away from the stage for almost seven years, and now he had the opportunity for a comeback in a play that, though tricky for an actor like himself, with no liking for period costume and no experience of speaking verse, could establish his reputation in the one place he had not yet conquered – Broadway. 'I read this play and loved it,' he recalled.[19] Not only was it a 'marvellous change of pace' but it also represented a chance to get away from hated Hollywood.[17] But he wished he had a drama coach by his side in the way he had done when playing an oriental king had perplexed and almost defeated him. He might again need the assistance of Elsa Schreiber. A love affair of the kind in which he now found himself would be no help to the concentration he knew he would need. In order to transform himself successfully into the ample monarch, he had to find the place where passion and brutality met in Henry's complex character.

He asked Carole to read the play, hopeful that she would recognize the marvellous opportunity it offered him. Of course it would mean leaving her in Hollywood, which would be sad for them both, but then, as he had told Arthur Barbosa, she was 'one hell of a girl' – she would get over it.

On the afternoon of 4 July 1948, Independence Day, Carole Landis had some friends up to lunch and they relaxed around the pool. Probably none of the guests knew that the $100,000 Spanish-style house on the hilltop, overlooking the Riviera Country Club golf course, was up for sale or that Carole's finances were now so low that she had dismissed her cook-housekeeper and relied on a daily maid, Fanny Mae Bolden, to help about the house. Whatever else she expected from the divorce suit she had filed on 22 March, it would not be a handsome alimony. 'Marry a rich man – then support yourself,' she had said to her mother, revealing an unwonted bitterness.[20] Her life, career and any happiness it might bring her now seemed to depend on turning her affair with Rex into a stable relationship.

When Rex arrived around 6 pm at 1463 Capri Drive in his red convertible, he found Carole dressed in casual evening wear: a frilly blouse, a black striped bouffant skirt and gold leather sling-back sandals. She wore no stockings and for once, as if declaring herself free from all previous commitments, she had removed the four wedding bands from her fingers. She served them both cold roast chicken and a salad, and placed a lemon chiffon pie she had cooked in front of Rex. He ate with his usual healthy appetite. Neither of them drank much: a pre-dinner Scotch for him, then a glass or two of white wine for both of them. The maid, of course, had the day off; it was a Sunday as well as a public holiday. As they talked, a phonograph played softly in the background: it was a recording of one of their favourites, 'Warm Kiss, Cold Heart'.

Rex did most of the talking, discussing the Maxwell Anderson play, turning his part inside out, probing with his mistress the motives of a king who could command his wife's execution on the grounds of her suspected infidelity.

Later, he would say that they had discussed Carole's future too and he had promised to help her find work, perhaps making a film in England.

There is no way of knowing what actually ensued as the hours went by; but it is reasonable, in view of later events, to conjecture that Rex left Carole Landis without having been able to convince her that their coming separation – on which he was determined – was in the best interests of both of them. They had reached the end of the affair – which was all it ever had been, or so he later swore to his intimates – and he would do everything in his power to help her financially and professionally.

He said that he left the house around 9 pm, but, instead of returning to his own house, where he had no company since Lilli was still in New York and Pat, the nanny, would have put Carey to bed, he drove the short distance to the Culvers' house at 750 Napoli Drive. The place actually belonged to Gladys Cooper; they were renting it from her, while she was in a smaller house next door. Assuming that what Rex said is true, he spent four hours there – discussing the play, he asserted – and did not leave until 1.30 am. It was 3 am before he was in his own bed at 1928 Mandeville Canyon.

Fannie Mae Bolden got off the bus at the Riviera Country Club at about 9 am later the same day, 5 July, and walked to the Landis residence to begin her day's work. There was no sound in the house, but the maid knew that the hardest job of the day, sometimes, was waking her employer. The sleeping pills that Carole took made her tetchy if shaken into wakefulness, and the maid judged it better to let her sleep on. The first phone call of the day was from Atwater Kent, the millionaire whose comparison to George VI on the radio show had caused Rex to stage his walk-out; it was no surprise to find he was giving a party and wanted to ask Carole. At about 11 am Rex called, to be told Carole was not yet out of bed. He called again a few minutes later. Would Fannie Mae tell her mistress that he would be a little late for lunch. He was calling from

Malibu, where he had driven with Leland Hayward and Swifty Lazar to discuss Maxwell Anderson's play with the author, who lived there with his large family. He wanted desperately to do it and only hoped Fox would agree to let him.

They all picnicked on the beach and at about 2.30 pm Rex called Carole's house again. He was told she still had not come downstairs. This may have caused the first twinge of alarm.

The maid first realized Rex was in the house when she looked up from some chore she was doing in her work room and saw him standing just outside the doorway. He had come in through the back entrance. He looked awkward and stiff, she said later, not like his usual self – though with Englishmen it was hard to tell. When he spoke, his voice was dry, not a bit like the sharp bark with which he ordinarily addressed her. Had she been up to Miss Landis's room, he asked. No, she had not. 'Well,' said Rex in a whisper that gave the maid the impression that he was almost speaking to himself, 'I think she's dead.'[21]

14: A Hollywood Death

Rex and the maid went upstairs. Carole Landis's bed had not been slept in, but there was a depression on it, as if someone had recently been lying down. Carole was lying on the bathroom floor, curled up in a foetal position. She was wearing the same clothes as the night before, when she had dined with Rex, and had clearly not retired for the night. Her head rested below the medicine cupboard on what appeared to be her jewel box. In her left hand she held a satin ribbon lettered with the Lord's Prayer; in her right was a crumpled envelope that was later stated to have contained pills – one was left in it. There was a half-filled water glass, marked with lipstick, on the rim of the wash-basin.

Fannie Mae watched as Rex fell on his knees and listened for a heartbeat. Then he spotted a letter propped up on the actress's dressing-table. It was addressed to Carole's mother, but Rex ripped it open and read it. 'Oh no, my darling,' the maid later testified she heard him say, 'why did you do it?'[1]

The letter said:

Dearest Mommie,
    Am sorry to put you through this. But there is no way to avoid it.
    I love you, darling. You have been the most wonderful ma ever and that applies to all our family. I love each and every one of them, darling.
    Everything goes to you. Look in the files and there is a will bequeathing everything.
    Goodbye, my angel.
    Pray for me.[2]

Then, in the same pencil scrawl as the rest of her suicide note, she wrote, not her name, but 'Your baby'.

Later, in a deposition made at his lawyer's, Rex stated: 'I felt her pulse. It must have been partly my imagination, but I thought there was a little beat.'[3] If this is so, then Rex's behaviour over the next hour is not only inexplicable – it seems inexcusable.

Given the possibility of Carole's life not being totally extinct, one would imagine his first thought would have been to call a hospital. But this meant making the affair immediately public. Instead, Rex tried to find Carole's address book containing the name and number of her own doctor. (Fannie Mae, being a relatively new employee, did not know it.) Rex knew she consulted several doctors, but could not remember the name of any of them. 'By looking from A to Z,' he later stated, 'I hoped to find a name I could identify as a doctor's.'[4]

Going through anyone's address book takes time. Even when one is in haste, with maybe a human life at risk, searching a book with presumably the names of half of Hollywood in it is an irresponsible waste of vital minutes. Failing in his search, Rex still did not call the paramedics. To the maid's astonishment, he left the house by the back door, exited through the rear gate and roared off in his car. It was left to Fannie Mae to seek help, which she did by attracting the attention of a neighbour swimming in his pool. It was this (unidentified) man who called the police and the coroner's office.

Meanwhile, Rex had returned home intending, he said later, to call his own doctor. Since it is unlikely he had forgotten the name of his physician and could have consulted a directory in the Landis house if he did not remember the number, why he rushed home to make the call is a mystery. It must be supposed he desperately wanted privacy to make other calls, not necessarily all medical. As it happened, his doctor was still out of town on the Independence Day holiday and it would take his assistant half an hour at least to reach the Landis house. (What Rex told the assistant, if he actually spoke to him, was never revealed.)

Rex said he then called Roland Culver. This is not strictly true. Culver was out playing golf. He spoke to Culver's wife, Nan, who told him to do what should have occurred to him at the start – to call the authorities. The better part of half an hour must have elapsed since he had found Carole's body. Only now did he telephone St John's Hospital, Santa Monica. Whether he gave his own name is unrecorded, but the hospital, after noting the call, told him to phone the police. 'The idea hadn't entered my head before,' he was quoted later. 'I just hadn't thought of police. So I called them.'[5] The call book at the West Los Angeles precinct station recorded the call at 4.10 pm. Well over an hour had now elapsed. This time his head was clear enough not to give his name. He said he was 'someone calling for the maid'.[6] He was recorded in the police ledger by the officer who took the call simply as 'a male voice'.[7] Captain Emmett Jones, Lieutenants John Layman and H. W. Brittingham went straight to Capri Drive. There they found Rex, who had returned and, much to his dismay and alarm, discovered the place crawling with newsmen alerted by a police or hospital tip-off.

Rex was accompanied by Nan Culver, whom he had called again to report what he had done, and an actress friend of the Culvers, Judith Fellows. His state of mind can easily be guessed at. His actions all testify to near panic. He knew very well that the worst construction would be put on his liaison with Carole, which was already public knowledge; Fannie Mae would testify they had dined together every night the previous week. The account of that moment contained in his auto-biography, published twenty-six years later, gives the impression of a desire to distance himself from things as far as possible. 'I asked the police inspector in charge what had happened, if there was any hope of resuscitating her – I still hoped she could be saved ... the body had already been taken to the morgue, I never saw her again.'[8]

Lilli was still in New York. He had spoken to her that morning, to tell her he was set on doing the Maxwell Anderson play and, perhaps, to express contrition for what had led to their separation. When he finally left the Landis house, after making a statement to the police, he called Leland Hayward and begged him to come over. The producer found Rex's house under siege from reporters and cameramen, and its owner, grim and pale, behind drawn curtains. Hayward called Lilli, said that Rex had something to tell her and put her husband on the line. 'Something terrible has happened. Carole has killed herself. Can you come at once?'[9]

This is how Lilli remembers things. Rex gives a different account. According to him, Lilli first read of Carole's suicide in the New York press, which would have been the next day's papers, 6 July. But, since Lilli arrived at Los Angeles airport on an overnight flight at 6.30 am on 6 July, her version is the likelier one. She told waiting reporters, 'I love Rex. I love him very much. We are very happy.'[10]

Rex himself had already undergone reluctant interrogation by newsmen at the crowded Landis house. In his nerve-ridden haste to deny an allegation even before one had been made, he only succeeded in raising his questioners' suspicions. 'I had dinner with Miss Landis, who was strictly a good friend, on Sunday night ... I was astonished [by her suicide]. I cannot understand why she did it. We were good friends.'[11] This was just the sort of declaration most likely to raise laughter from the cynical men in rolled-up shirt sleeves at the news desks.

In the same edition of the paper that announced on its front page 'Carole Landis Suicide: Rex Harrison Finds Body', a staff columnist, Dorothy Manners, was already confiding to readers that she knew why Carole had done it. 'They say the shocking suicide of beautiful blonde Carole Landis was induced by malaria ... But knowing the gay laughing girl well and seeing her frequently at Hollywood parties, I believe she died of a broken heart and loneliness and the sudden reversal in her career and fortunes ..."[12] This did not directly involve Rex. But then the columnist put in the knife. 'And she had been deeply in love with a man who was forced to tell her that nothing would ever come of their romance.'[13] Hollywood, reading this at its breakfast table, did not need to rack its brains to put a name to the man.

From this moment on, Carole Landis ceased to be simply one more small-time actress of failed ambitions and dubious reputation: she became a martyr in a film colony that did not like to dwell on how 'the system' drove even talented people to extremes like suicide, but preferred to pin the blame for a tragedy like Carole's on someone else – in this case on a man who had not endeared himself to the place. Carole Landis suddenly became that stereotype, the betrayed woman, who deserved the sympathy of the very society which had looked down its nose at her while she was alive and whose womenfolk had kept a tighter grip on their men if she were present.

Rex was all the more easily identifiable as 'the guilty party' because this was exactly what was to be expected of the star of *The Rake's Progress*. Had he not driven a girl to attempt suicide in that film as well? Even in Hollywood, image and reality can be accepted as the same when local prejudice decides so.

So Carole was promptly depicted 'as one of the best scouts in Hollywood ... adored by the workers on her set ... knew the funniest and newest jokes ... had the gift of telling them on herself ... was the first to interrupt her career [when the war began] ... not only sang and danced for the boys overseas ... had long talks with them about the folks at home.'[14] And now she lay dead on her bathroom floor, victim of an English playboy's heartlessness.

Not all the heartlessness was Rex's, though Dorothy Manners could not have known this. Roland Culver did not hear the news until he had finished playing golf. Then, as was his custom, he walked off the course into his own house, which abutted it, and looked for his wife, who usually had afternoon tea waiting for him. The house was empty. So he walked into the garden and found Gladys Cooper at the swimming pool, exhausted by the efforts she had been making to get through on the telephone to Lilli in New York, and keep her up to date with events. 'Where's my tea?' Culver asked. 'There's been a terrible accident,' Gladys Cooper said. 'Carole Landis is dead. She's killed herself.'[15]

Culver took this in and then said, 'Selfish bitch.'

When Lilli arrived at the airport, Leland Hayward was waiting and whisked her into a private room to warn her of the press reporters barricading her home. The English butler had been repelling doorsteppers all night long. He had left Rex sleeping; a doctor had had to sedate him. Policemen were guarding the gateway to the single-storey, white-shuttered building. Lawyers from Rex's studio (Fox) and Lilli's (Warner) would be coming round at mid-day. Nothing must be said until they arrived.

When she reached the house, she was surprised to see smoke rising from the chimney on that warm July morning. Later she learned why. Rex had been saved from even more excruciating embarrassment and perhaps ruin by the fortuitous discovery of all the letters he had sent to Carole, and all the snapshots she had taken of them both, which Carole had made into a package after he had left. She had deposited this reproachful bundle in the mailbox at the Culvers' front gate and left Rex's portfolio beside it. As it happened, the front entrance was rarely used by the Culvers and their guests, who used the side gateway with its generous parking space. Nan Culver found the bundle and portfolio on the evening of 5 July and realized their damning nature at a glance. Leland Hayward had brought them over to Rex under cover of darkness, and he had burnt the letters there and then. Now he was destroying the slower-burning photograph albums, page by page, in the living-room fireplace.

The Fox lawyers arrived with studio bodyguards and raised a new fear for Rex. He could be criminally implicated in Carole's death if a grand jury were satisfied that he had contributed, by threat or persuasion, to her killing herself. Then the lawyers from Warner Bros., not knowing what the fall-out might be, warned Lilli to take no chances. She and Rex must appear to be a connubially supportive couple.

Why, it must be asked, did Lilli bother to return and stand by Rex, considering all the grief and humiliation to which his affair had exposed her? Carey Harrison, their son, says today: 'As well as feeling she owed Rex some debt for giving her a nationality at a difficult moment in her career – indeed her life – my mother was always a one-man woman. She had three men in her life: a boyfriend she met in her youth, Rex, and her last husband, all of them notorious womanizers. And she was faithful to all of them. I always felt there was a huge amount of passionate fire in Lilli, but she preferred to keep it banked down, see herself as a good girl and, if need be, a victim rather than the tempestuous woman she really was deep down. I think if you are determined to keep the rage to live confined inside you, as Lilli did, then the answer is to marry someone who will do it for you and give you the vicarious satisfaction without the guilty hangover.'[16] Carey, who was later to become a noted novelist and playwright, has no clear memory of the Landis affair: 'I never dared ask my father, and I was only four at the time.' Moreover, the Culvers had taken the child and his nanny into their house away from the scene in Mandeville Canyon.

The reporters were now frantic for an interview, so, at their lawyers' urging, Rex and Lilli stepped out on the patio to practise 'connubial support'.

Once more Rex denied that he had noticed any unhappiness in Carole when they dined together. What had they talked about? 'We talked of our plans, of going to Britain and making a picture there ... I told her I knew producers there, and might be able to help her.'[7] This explanation was greeted with audible scepticism. Rex tightened his lips. 'Is that *all* you talked about – for *two hours*?' Rex lost his temper. 'No further comment,' he snapped, turned to walk inside, but halted when a reporter called out, 'Is it true that you and your wife are on the point of separation?' – 'That's not true, we are very happy.' – 'Was Carole Landis in love with you?' – 'Absolutely not,' he lied manfully.[8]

The butler then called him to the telephone. Ten minutes later, the lawyers having decided that the story needed repeating, they reappeared to reiterate their distress and unalterable attachment to each other. Then Lilli let slip a precious bit of hard news: they intended flying to New York the next day, perhaps to go on to England. Almost certainly this was on the advice of both lawyers, but before they could even buy the tickets, the Los Angeles coroner's office got wind of the plan and ordered Rex not to leave town, at least until the pathologist's report was delivered.

While Carole's body reposed in the Wilshire Funeral Home, Santa Monica, the Los Angeles county toxicologist was analysing tissue samples from her stomach, digestive tract, kidneys and brain. He soon established she was not suffering from any incurable disease and had probably died from an overdose of 'red devils', Seconal capsules procured on pre-scription in New York. Pathetically – almost parenthetically – he also reported that she was incapable of bearing children.

This fact intensified the protective sympathy Hollywood was now expressing for a woman who, while she was alive, had barely aroused anything more demonstrative than a knowingly arched eyebrow. It pushed opinion even more fiercely against Rex. The Hearst press at that time, represented locally by the Los Angeles *Examiner*, was virulently anti-British – all the more reason for taking the side of a deceased all-American girl like Carole and venting its anger on Rex, the callous foreigner.

Rex received formal notification to hold himself for questioning. The studio told him it would support him as far and as long as possible, but better get his own lawyer up to date with the facts, just in case. It sounded very sinister.

Meanwhile, a search of Carole's effects had turned up no will – none was ever found – though it revealed she had been receiving counselling from Carroll Righter, the astrologist.

It also turned up something in Rex's favour: a past history of suicidal depression and previous attempts to kill herself. Lupe Velez, the Mexican star who also killed herself, had drawn an admission from Carole at the time that she, too, had thought of taking her own life. And one of her close friends told reporters that she had actually overdosed on several occasions in the past, but had always managed to telephone her in time for a doctor to be called. Later Rex and his friends concluded that by depositing his love letters, photos, etc., at the Culvers' house, where she guessed he had gone after leaving her, Carole had been trying to signal that their affair had reached a dangerous crisis – and he would come charging back penitently to see her. But of course he had used the other gate and missed the signal. Moreover, no mail was delivered on the Monday, since it was then the custom in the Los Angeles postal area not to make deliveries on the day following a public holiday, if the latter fell on a Sunday. Therefore no one went to the Culvers' postbox to collect the mail (and discover the memorabilia) until it was too late to save Carole. If Rex's calculation was right, if life was not quite extinct when he found the body around 3 pm, it would suggest the fatal overdose was taken on the Monday morning, around the time that people would usually have been opening their mailboxes. Since no one did so in the Culver household, the alarm signal was not sounded, and Rex did not turn up in time to revive Carole.

Her funeral, fixed for 8 July, was postponed while the pathology tests went on. But by 8 July a sensational new development was banner-headlined on the front pages. 'Did Carole Landis write the real reason for her suicide ... in a second note?' asked the *Examiner*,[19] not letting up the pressure on Rex. A second note had allegedly been found on Carole's body. The paper's star reporter, Harry Lang, disclosed that, according to Fannie Mae, 'after the police had arrived, a woman friend of Miss Landis came into the kitchen and said, "Fannie Mae, you must remember that Miss Carole said in the note she left that you must not talk about this to anyone." The maid added, "I knew there was nothing like that in the note that Miss Landis left for her mother." '[20] The inference Lang drew from this was clear and potentially damning to Rex. If a second note existed, it was quite likely addressed to him and could contain the reason why the star had taken her life. 'Does Harrison know anything else, as yet untold, that may solve the mystery?' Lang thundered.[21]

The real mystery, however, is this second note. From this point on, it comes and goes in the affair, its contents established and then contradicted, its importance emphasized and then dismissed, until eventually it inexplicably vanishes from the case, though not quite from history.

The 'woman friend' was soon identified as Mrs Florence Wasson, the wife of the professional at the Riviera Country Club, a close friend of the deceased: she had been her stand-in at various times at Fox studios. She had been telephoned by the maid and had come rushing over. But she testified at the coroner's enquiry that the second note did not contain any confession of unrequited love for Rex. All it said, Mrs Wasson stated, was simply an instruction to the maid to take the cat to the vet, as its paw needed attention. This was certainly an anticlimax. Yet it raised more questions than it answered. If a second note existed, why had Rex not seen it? Who found it? Where was it now? Mrs Wasson said that 'someone' handed it to her. She read it, then told the maid not to be making any statements at the moment: things were too confused. This and her subsequent replies to the coroner were reported by Harry Lang in a manner that captures the brisk proceedings at what the papers characterized as an 'informal enquiry'.

She [Mrs Wasson] didn't know [who handed it to her] because 'there were so many men there and confusion and everything'.[7] She read [the note], handed it back to the same man and still doesn't remember who he could have been. She didn't remember a single thing in the note – not even a signature – except some business about sending Carole's cat to the veterinarian. 'It had a sore paw,' she said. [Mrs Wasson] big-eyed the coroner and stuck to her story. If in that last note, just before Miss Landis ended the glamorous life she loved so much, Carole had thought to write anything else, anything more important – maybe the reason for doing it – well, sorry, but Florence Wasson couldn't for the life of her remember.... she didn't wait long; she tripped quickly off the stand and out the door, parried newsmen's questions with, 'You're going to get me a quick divorce from my husband if you don't go away.'[22]

Where the note was now, why it was never produced – such questions were never asked. Mrs Wasson was not even asked if anything had passed between her and Rex when she revealed what must have been frightening news to him, that a second note of Carole's was in her possession. She remained unwavering and uninformative. She was dropped as if too hot to handle by the inquest officials whose handling of the informal hearing, while sticking to the rules, betrayed extreme reluctance to press any of the principal witnesses.

Rex continued to be surrounded by an impenetrable legal screen of advisers. He even pre-empted the coroner's enquiry on 8 July by appearing with a typed set of answers to questions that had not yet been put to him by court officials. Arriving at the Hall of Justice, accompanied by his lawyer, well after the 2.30 pm hour set for the hearing, '[he looked] pale, wet his lips nervously and said nothing,' according to the press.[23] His lawyer spoke for him. The deposition Rex had made under oath in his office answered 'all the questions in the papers'.[24] In other words, it was a public relations statement as much as personal testimony. Anything Rex had left out, his lawyer added graciously, he had agreed to answer under oath. Even the coroner was startled at the way his guns had been spiked. ' "Taking that deposition yourself wasn't my idea," he snapped. "No, it was mine," blandly replied the lawyer.'[25] It was read into the record by the deputy coroner, a courtesy that verged on the subservient. It simply summarized what Rex had already said.

When the reading was concluded, Rex, dressed in a Prince of Wales check suit and black tie, took the oath.

'[He] was nervous,' according to a court report. 'His eyes were never still. His tongue wet his lips again and again ... [but] he spoke with the crisp, sharp enunciation of the well-educated Briton.'[26] Rex could not think of any motive for the suicide. Could it have been her career? 'I think she'd have got a lot of work in England and here,' he said,[27] then, clearly realizing this lacked conviction, added lamely, 'I don't think she was entirely happy about her career.'[28] Well, then, could it have been her impending divorce? 'I don't think that is so.' Well, then ...? 'Sorry, I can't give you any explanation for it at all.'[29]

He denied all knowledge of a second note. At this point the court officials simply gave up. They had gone through the obligations of their office with little zeal. They appeared anxious to get it over with. The hearing was simply to establish the cause and motive of death. An overdose of Seconal was the cause; the motive would apparently never be established. As was customary, the Los Angeles coroner's office was not empowered to query facts not pertinent to these points, even though such facts might have been highly relevant to any police enquiry. But the District Attorney made no move. As for the police, they seemed happy to let bygones be bygones. Unless the coroner advised otherwise, the case would be officially closed on the police blotter.

Rex was excused and stepped down. Then, for the very first time amidst the reams of reports and speculation printed in the Los Angeles papers since the discovery of Carole Landis's corpse, a name cropped up. It was a name that had been so conspicuously absent up to now that it was as if a blanket request for invisibility had gone out to the papers in the early hours of the drama and been honoured by all of them. It was the name of Rex's current employer: the studio that had him under contract and stood to be harmed by any unpleasant developments such as a grand jury hearing or a subsequent trial. Yet although it had not been mentioned, it is impossible to read the day-to-day reports without sensing its presence in protecting the reputation of its unfortunate star.

Harry Lang of the *Examiner* suggested this to be the case. He was the only newsman who conveyed, in the closing words of his report, the close order studio security enveloping the film star. 'Harrison nimbly stepped off the stand,' he wrote. 'A man from Twentieth Century–Fox studios, where he is under contract, stepped in front of him. His lawyer stepped behind him. They practically lock-stepped out of the room together, down the hall, out ...'[30]

The rake's luck had held. But it might not have done so had the elusive 'second note' been discovered and produced.

Lilli Palmer's memoirs record a curious event she says occurred just before Rex was due to give evidence. According to her, a policeman came to their house, saying he had found a second note, screwed up in Carole's clenched hand, and had kept it. 'It contained something highly compromising. So he'd rather turn it over to us than to ... the authorities ... or, well, the press. Of course it would cost something.'[31] Lilli says she and Rex refused to pay the $500 suggested, but their lawyers did. The note turned out to be instructions about taking the cat to the vet. However, if this is true, and the lawyers had the note, why did they not make it available to the authorities ... or, well, the press? It would have been a help to Rex.

A former Los Angeles policeman, an officer long retired from the force, is sceptical about the truth of this story. He says he recalls seeing the note and it was a three-line lover's farewell to Rex Harrison. He has no idea what happened to it.[32]

Carole's cat, incidentally, had nothing wrong with its paw.

So Rex was let off the hook – the criminal one, anyhow. But he still remained impaled on the disapproval of his Hollywood peers. In the absence of a motive, a scapegoat had to be found.

At least Rex showed bravado in attending Carole Landis's funeral on 10 July. More than 1,500 people filed past the open coffin in which she lay, on a sloping panel, wearing a turquoise blue dress with blue and white sequins and beads chosen by Mrs Wasson from the rack of gowns in the actress's wardrobe. She held an orchid between her hands. The pallbearers were Cesar Romero, Pat O'Brien, Willard Parker, a wavy-haired leading man of the time, Ben Nye, the make-up artist, and Lou Wasson, husband of the lady with the bad memory. Lilli, ever concerned with doing the right thing, wondered what she should wear for the church service at the Forest Lawn 'grounds of rest'. She consulted Doug Fairbanks Jr's wife. Was black suitable? Oh, no, Mary Lee Fairbanks told her, not black. Dark blue would be more appropriate on this occasion. You should never wear black to the funeral of your husband's mistress.

Rex and Lilli left after the service and before the half-couch coffin had been closed. Three days later, the amount of Carole Landis's estate was published. It added up to less than $30,000 – or would have, but for her husband Horace, whom she was divorcing when she died. Although he had been contesting the property settlement, he now agreed to honour it and pay over another $30,000 to Carole's mother. Hollywood opinion held that Mr Schmidlapp had behaved somewhat better than Mr Harrison.

15: The Comeback

A few days after Carole Landis's funeral, Rex was playing golf on the Monterey peninsula while Lilli did the rounds of the antique shops with Nan Culver. 'I think the change did them both good,' Rex's golfing partner, Roland Culver, wrote later.[1]

Rex was not seriously worried by the risk that Fox might terminate his contract. He wanted out of Hollywood in any case. If Zanuck hesitated, it was not because of decency, but corporate caution. What if Rex's last film, *Unfaithfully Yours*, turned out a box-office hit and Fox had sent the star packing, perhaps for some other studio to snap up and so gain the value of Fox's investment in him? Meanwhile, the film's première was postponed until the scandal had subsided.

However, Zanuck underestimated Hollywood's hostility to Rex. The columnists kept up the attack, particularly Louella Parsons in the Hearst press, thus denying Rex any refuge in the shortness of the public's memory. He was glad to have a cast-iron excuse for leaving town – the Maxwell Anderson play was due on Broadway in November.

He and Lilli boarded the TWA flight for New York on 12 August 1948 still denying an 'impending separation'.[2] If he had intended going on to London, he changed his mind. Collette was currently suing him there for alleged unpaid alimony of £7,000 – and asking for another £1,000 to be added to the £6,000 already awarded her annually. Her barrister estimated that Rex had £17,000 left after paying taxes, 'making allowance for his life on a most luxurious scale'.[3] He was warned that, if he appeared in London, he stood a good chance of being arrested and brought to court to explain why he had flouted the alimony order. Even prison was not ruled out and, like Hogarth's Rake, he might end up with some 2,000 others then behind bars for similar offences.

Rex and Lilli flew on to Paris, giving the gossip writers a chance to tarnish him further as an 'alimony dodger'. Lilli was to film *Hans le Marin* in Marseilles with Jean-Pierre Aumont. She had got out of her Warner contract by using the clause she had insisted on including in it which gave her the right to end it if her husband's domicile changed. Three

days after they left Hollywood, the contents of their house were advertised
for sale.

While Lilli was filming, Rex toured the Paris night spots with Aumont's
brother-in-law, who did his best to make him forget the recent past. A
round of eating places was not the sole remedy, nor the most successful.
A feature of Rex's personality, rarely commented on, was his susceptibility
to taking on board the ideas and opinions current in the company he
kept. Friends would hear him come out with some thought or saying,
as if it were his own, that he had just picked up from some supper table
where the talk went into areas of life and art with which he had little
familiarity. Existentialism was then at fever pitch in Paris. Some of Rex's
excursions through the Left bank cafés and *boîtes* introduced him – albeit
superficially and hence more attractively – to a philosophy that sanctioned
the impulses of the ego without incurring the penalty of guilt. In his own
way, by osmosis and imitation, Rex had invented himself quite as much
as those who obeyed Sartre's imperative to 'choose and be yourself'. His
introduction to the French attitude to life and love, as he noted, was
'gloriously alien' to the anxiety-ridden morality of his own middle-class
upbringing.[4] He had a need to soothe the guilt of Carole's suicide. Sartre
was his unlikely salve.

But comfort of another, more familiar kind came from the relationship
he quickly formed with a young French starlet while Lilli was away
shooting her film in Marseilles. Claude Dauphin, then one of the French
cinema's elegant leading men, rather a Gallic version of Rex, had
introduced him to a girl who, Dauphin said rather condescendingly, was
a pretty little thing, but destined more for a *soubrette*, than for stardom.
Her name was Martine Carol. In later years, Rex always said – to his
intimates, anyhow – that she had helped save his reason at that desperate
time when he very nearly went under, as he put it, so acute was his
misery at losing Carole. He gave Martine the code name of 'Moustache'
when he entrusted Arthur Barbosa with being their go-between. It
referred, one must suppose, to charms that were not apparent on her
upper lip. The English actor David Tomlinson, who found himself in
Paris at this time, has cause to recall the stealth with which Rex pursued
the liaison with Martine Carol. 'I remember Rex asking me to meet this
French girl at the Crillon and keep her entertained until he could pick
her up. It was a pleasure, of course, until Rex came in and immediately
pushed the bill for our accumulated refreshments in my direction. That
evening we went on to the Crazy Horse Saloon or some such "in" place,
with me acting as Rex's cover, I suppose. When the time came to settle
the *compte*, Rex found he had to go to the loo. Still, it was easy to
understand Martine's fascination for him. Dauphin couldn't have been

more wrong about her. The very next year, in a film called *Les Amants de Verone*, she was one of the biggest stars in France.'[5] Rex made assignations with her in the Hotel Meurice, always taking care to call Lilli in Marseilles before he met his new mistress. 'It's going to be tough going with Lilli,' he said to Barbosa, 'but I'll do my best to make a go of it.'[6] Such conduct is inexcusable, yet explicable. No sooner were the consequences of tragedy apparent to him than Rex sought to distance himself from them by some new distraction which, very often, resembled the one which had brought him catastrophe and sorrow in the first place. The cure for love in his case was not infrequently a homeopathic one.

He was in good humour when he and Lilli returned to New York at the end of September, he to rehearse *Anne of the Thousand Days* and Lilli to do a play called *My Name Is Aquillon*, which Aumont had translated and would co-star in. Aumont radiated the Gallic equivalent of the charm which many women found irresistible in Rex. But the French star treated Rex with benign amusement, seeing him 'as more a little boy, often stammering, throwing tantrums, and hiding in corners so that he can do what has been forbidden.'[7]

As Lilli had a week or two to put in before starting rehearsals, she flew to Hollywood to reclaim Carey from the Culvers and to sell their house, which she did with difficulty – the scandal had not helped – for around $85,000. The gossips did not let up even then. 'I don't believe Lilli need worry about [returning to] Hollywood,' wrote Louella Parsons, 'because it's very doubtful if Rex's option will be picked up by Twentieth Century–Fox.'[8]

Suddenly Lilli and Rex had many more worries than where they would sleep if work brought them to the West Coast again. They were hit by brutal news from their accountants. The $85,000 would be decimated by a mortgage that still had to be repaid. They owed unpaid American taxes of $35,000. Then the British tax people, who had filed away Rex's crow of triumph about avoiding their bills by moving to America, presented him with one for $17,000, the difference between British and American income tax levels. It was to take him years to pay this off in instalments deducted from current income.

On top of this, his Fox contract was terminated 'by mutual agreement', in the usual phrase. The truth was that *Unfaithfully Yours* had opened in early November to mixed reviews and downright bad business. It is possible to blame this on Rex's poor publicity, but this ignores the fact that Preston Sturges's comic judgment was in serious decline by this time. It is the work of a man who has fallen in love with speeches, not dialogue; it frequently feels like the product of a windbag. A man in love with the power of words, Sturges was infatuated with Rex's delivery of everything he wrote for him, enjoyed his own work a fatal bit too much, and frequently allowed expansiveness to ruin a joke that would have gained by conciseness. The repetition of the theme three times in fantasy and then once in reality, as a coda, made cutting virtually impossible, though Zanuck must have been tempted. Playing the ruthless egoist was by now second nature to Rex, but so many of his lines were written to be delivered in a tone of relentless sarcasm that eventually it grows wearisome. Very soon it is the jealousy of a maniac that he is exhibiting, and madness was not Rex's preferred method of comic revelation. Rex makes a splendid conductor on the podium and thoroughly deserves the 'Harrison Fanfare' that the studio orchestra wrote for him for mastering the three classical works he conducts; but he proves himself only an indifferent performer in the marathon of comic slapstick he has to undertake when trying to execute the final murder set-up. The comedy of recalcitrant things is no substitute for that of well-aimed lines.

The movie's sizeable flop has been blamed by later critics on its being out of step with a period in which black comedy was unfashionable. Maybe so, though whether one would ever find fun in the notion of a man slashing his wife to death with a cut-throat razor, as Rex does to Linda Darnell, is arguable. In the context of Sturges's costly divorce, it seems an intrusion from another kind of film and more in line with the writer-director's own murderous feelings after meeting the lawyers' bills and facing the alimony.

'There is only one good thing that has happened,' Rex told Arthur Barbosa at the time, in mid-November, when he was in Philadelphia with the pre-Broadway try-out of his play.[9] 'I'm out of my Hollywood contract and only have to do three films for Fox in Europe. One a year over the next three years.' He would make them for his own company, thus reducing taxes.

It may seem strange that, with his sizeable salary from Fox, Rex was so hard up all of a sudden. Unexpected revenue claims are only part of the story. He always took care to get paid what he considered he was worth, but throughout his life he hated keeping track of where the money went in either earnings or expenses. English royalty never carried cash. After a certain point in his career, Rex also ceased carrying money on his person. His fame was his guarantor, he thought, and very often it was. Fame, however, did not pay tax bills and his accountants used to plead for an itemized list of his expenses to set against his liabilities. He would promise to do his best. One day his accountant received a scrap of paper. On it was written: 'Taxi $1.50; tip 25 cents; miscellaneous $83.00.' An attitude like this led to frequent charges of being stingy. No doubt he was. He presumed on friendships to provide things he would have had to pay for heavily if a contractor had undertaken them, but he took it as his due that others paid. His main satisfaction was not simply what he saved – he did not really keep account of that – but keeping himself at a distance from the everyday frustrations of getting and spending. It was a very lordly view, but then ...

It is possible the shock of Carole Landis's death was delayed and only really caught up with him in these weeks before he opened on Broadway, for he seems to have suffered something like a minor collapse in Philadelphia. Admittedly the complications of the set for the play would have contributed to anyone's distress. The revolving stage occasionally hooked people's costumes as it turned; chairs that were intended to project the actors forward towards the audience for their intimate monologues before retracting them back into the main action sometimes would not budge. Eventually Jo Mielziner's overly complicated sets were reduced to more or less a simple proscenium with staircase and curtains. However, Anderson was doing a great deal of rewriting – 'as I thought', Rex told Barbosa. On top of all this, his stomach finally collapsed from nerves and general strain and he had to be x-rayed for a suspected ulcer. He was ordered to give up smoking and drinking – 'so life's an absolute hell on earth and not worth living', he said to his old friend. 'I'm about as low as I can get.'[10]

Playing Henry VIII presented its special problems, the main one of which was shape. Rex worried most about this. How could a tall and spindly chap like himself play a monarch built like a traffic bollard? Plaster casts had to be taken of his torso, legs and even his head – which was like being buried alive, he noted – and then a foam-rubber shell moulded round him to suggest a regal girth. Then his head had somehow to be made to match it, otherwise the King would be a pin-head. A velvet hat, copied from Holbein's portrait, avoided the problem of a wig, and a beard that squared off his oblong face was placed over cheeks inflated with invisible foam-rubber strips. He felt at times like a Thanksgiving turkey. But Rex's greatest achievement was not the physical load he carried: it was the imaginative bulk he suggested. He created the illusion of being many pounds heavier by slowing down his gait. He realized Henry was not a *fat* man, but a heavyweight – a burly athlete. He dropped his voice. Now it appeared to well up from the depths rather than take off from Rex's tongue like the customary lightweight lines that winged, dartlike, onto their target.

'In my opinion, it was his best bit of acting – ever,' says Anthony Havelock-Allan, who caught the opening night in Philadelphia. 'One reason was the total absence of Rex's familiar physique. This was a bull of a man, and a raging bull at that.' Robert Morley, who saw him on

Broadway, agrees: 'The best performance apart from *My Fair Lady*. You accepted this Rex as being a very *large* man when demonstrably he was not. His authority was wonderful. Make-up apart, the role suited him in an *interior* way. He had all the arrogance natural to royalty and accepted the fact – very easily – that he was a superior person.'

Robert Flemyng also saw the Broadway opening. 'There's no denying it, Rex was a marvel. We suddenly saw how far he was capable of stretching himself – physically, vocally, intellectually. Well that's how it appeared. Rex was no intellectual, but he had an instinctual guile that's sometimes more serviceable if you're an actor. That's what he used as the King. He wasn't gross or cunning, the way Laughton was in the Korda film, but he convincingly simulated the quick-wittedness that went with physical weight. There was, of course, a lot of Rex himself in the part and the royal role gave him, as it were, a divine right to display it.'

'It was the most wonderful performance I shall ever live to see,' says Angela Fox. 'I always recall him down-stage, at a *prie-dieu*, his robes spread out around him, praying as Anne Boleyn is executed. Rex wasn't just a good actor. At that moment, he became a great one.'

A fragment of Rex's performance has been preserved in a recording he and Lilli Palmer made for the very first edition of the *Omnibus* show on CBS television, broadcast on 9 November 1952. It amply confirms these views. It is the sequence where Henry, against his will, is impelled by his old passion to defend his Queen against her accusers. Lilli replaced Joyce Redman in the role. Rex indeed presents a complex human figure, not just a royal figurehead. What is most striking is the collision between sensuality and intelligence: the thick lips making light work of the words, his eyelids emphasizing each jealous beat of the heart, the head-strong and violent nature of the man modulating into a pathetic sense of loss as he imagines the Queen's execution and then, guilt-stricken, prays that memories will wear out, as Anderson puts it, 'like a path nobody walks on'. Coming in the immediate aftermath of Carole's suicide, some lines must have had a chilling relevance for Rex as he uttered them nightly: 'Death is a thing the coroner can see: I'll stick to that,' and, 'It might have been easier to forget you living/Than to forget you dead.'

Rex's verse speaking is so natural that one can credit many who saw the play believed it was in prose: he had found the way into formalism without losing his colloquial confidence. His self-discovery was soon to serve him well in another verse drama which also reached painfully into his own past.

Anne of the Thousand Days ran for 288 performances in New York and, early in 1949, won him an Antoinette Perry Award (a 'Tony') for the

'Best Leading Actor' on the stage in 1948. And who should have come all the way from Hollywood to present it but his old persecutor Hedda Hopper, obviously aware that Rex was a strong candidate, but hoping against hope to be spared the humiliation of lauding a man whose career she had said was as moribund as a dead mackerel. No mercy. She called out Rex's name – sections of the audience who had perhaps suffered the Hopper lash too cried out for her to repeat it – and up he ran, like a pole-vaulter measuring his leap and scaling the victory bar. 'Congratulations, Rex,' Hopper said weakly. He condescended to give her a nod and later confided to Lilli: 'It was better than a beheading.'

Rex's triumphs to some extent eased the cold reception that even sophisticated New Yorkers had given him when he had first arrived to do the play. 'I wanted to ask Rex to dinner, go to a restaurant perhaps,' Angela Fox recalls, 'but my other guests said, "Impossible!" because he was so unpopular at the time of the Carole Landis suicide. So we ate in their apartment. He never referred to it, and never complained about being cold-shouldered. Rex, I remember thinking, had complete mastery of himself from the feet up. As he left, he said he was going to England, and added, "I dread it." But I think he was relieved to leave New York; there were people there who would get up and leave if they saw him enter a party.'

There was no doubt about it, however; success, like a new love affair, was a great healer. He had the satisfaction of seeing Hollywood acquaintances who had kept their distance from him a year before now crowding the corridor outside his dressing-room. 'They're all constantly up my arse,' he told Arthur Barbosa.[11] But now he was entertaining on his own ground and saw only those he pleased. What would have happened to him, though, if the play had failed? 'God help me!' he told his old friend; it didn't bear thinking about.[12] Stage acting was a great relief from film-making – and oh! the joy of being free from his Fox contract. 'God is wonderful!'[13] Though he was financially strapped, his life had become much more settled, like the old days in the London theatre before the war, when he could get up late and go to bed even later. Some nights when the curtain had come down, he would unburden himself of his royal appurtenances and walk across Central Park, feeling the cool air of midnight on a face that had been swaddled in Henry's beard and cheek padding; and then he would take a cab up to Harlem, where he had contacted a very sweet coloured girl who ran a discreet brothel. He tried to keep the memory of Carole Landis under control, though it took very little to bring the nightmare back. Early on in the run of the play, he was at one of the weekly luncheons held in the theatre's basement dining-room. There were more than a dozen round the long table, enough for the visiting English writer not to have spotted him when Rex heard him ask his companion, Joan Buckmaster, what the truth was about Carole Landis and Rex Harrison. Why did he not ask Rex himself, was the reply, he is sitting almost beside you. Evelyn Waugh caught sight of Rex's face and decided not to play the inquisitor.

It was the practice then to close Broadway shows, even the most successful, for a few weeks in the hot, humid summer, since air-conditioned theatres were still a rarity. So, in June 1949, Rex, Lilli, Jack Merivale – Gladys Cooper's son by the actor Philip Merivale and one of Rex's intimates – and Jack's half-sister took off for a vacation in Europe. Though together again, Rex and Lilli were no longer the devoted couple they had once been. Lilli's public display of loyalty and devotion weakened as his remorse for the death he had caused began to be dissolved by work and success – or so it appeared, though inside, out of sight and beyond his power of confession, his guilt persisted. His egotism got the better of his gratitude to Lilli: he was made uncomfortable by the indebtedness he felt to her.

After crossing to England by liner, they took a flying boat to Genoa and on to the Miramare Hotel at Santa Margherita on the Ligurian Sea, just where the Italian Riviera bends round towards Monaco and France. A few days there, then the Harrisons would go on to Rome, where Anthony Havelock-Allan was trying to set up a film, the first for Rex's newly formed company, based on a Suso Cecchi d'Amico story about the discovery and subsequent violation of a statesman's tomb in the Etruscan era. 'The project fell through,' the producer recalls, 'Rex wasn't well enough established with Italian audiences for me to raise the co-production cash. It led to a temporary coolness between us.'

Rex and Lilli spent most afternoons cruising along the beautiful coast in a motor-boat piloted by an ex-prisoner of war called Alberto. And it was from the sea, as Alberto throttled down to glide into the narrow, wedge-shaped harbour of Portofino, a few kilometres south-west, that they saw the place which was to become the nearest thing to a home that Rex would ever possess.

Portofino as yet showed no sign of becoming the ultra-smart watering place for the *dolce vita* set that it would start to become a few years later. No boutiques bearing names like Rodier, Hermès and Vuitton lined the precipitous cobbled streets that ran down to a waterfront not more than a couple of hundred metres in width, with two jetties on each side. Tall houses in plain washes of colour, the occasional café, a bar and restaurant that was soon to count many a famous name amongst the guests who dropped in off their own yachts rose in steep terraces broken by tiny church piazzas and bits of private greenery. All of it was backed by an abrupt-looking hillside with a grand hotel, the Splendido, half-way up and a few well-off villas below the line of pines that spiked the crest. Portofino was a small place then and still is today, though wealth and tourism now jam its streets and cause the traffic along its single approach road to move in stop-start relays. Today, its rich residents, if they are wise, arrive in their own helicopters.

But in the summer of 1949 the place was still a Mediterranean toy town. Rex fell in love with it at first sight. He felt completely removed from his current worries. For a man temperamentally disinclined to take decisions, here was the perfect way of opting out. He and Lilli pushed on up the hillside, turned and looked down on the port, along the Ligurian gulf, right down to La Spezia, with the Appenines behind it and villages like spilled white crystals of salt in the crevices of the breathtaking coastline. What a wonderful place to build a villa! Impossible, they were told, Portofino was part of Italy's architectural patrimony, an officially listed 'Picturesque Monument': no new building was permitted except – and there is usually an 'exception' in Italian regulations – where one has stood before.

The occupying Germans, who had once threatened to blow up this coastal jewel in reprisal for Italy's switch of allegiance in the later stages of the war, had placed a gun-site on the hill where a villa had formerly been. A doctor from Santa Margherita, hearing of *gli Inglesi* and their enquiries in Portofino, recognized Rex from *The Rake's Progress*, which he had seen in England whilst a prisoner of war, and now urged the star's case for becoming a resident of Portofino and building his home on the former gun emplacement.

The Countess Besozzi, who owned the land, sold it to them and was to supervise the building of the villa when they returned to Broadway. Lilli was anxious. How could they afford it, given the state of their finances? 'But she assented eventually,' says Rex's sister, 'she felt that having a home would steady their shaky marriage.'

To pay for it, they grabbed whatever offer came along, which happened to be the worst film they ever made together. *The Long Dark Hall*, backed by Huntington Hartford, the American millionaire who wanted to 'get into' films, cost £95,000 and looked no better than a British pre-war 'quota quickie'. It was a downbeat tale of a suburban husband (Rex) falsely convicted of a London chorus girl's murder and only saved from hanging by Parliament abolishing the death penalty on the eve of his execution. Lilli played the loyal wife; and the film, by awful irony, was produced by Eagle-Lion, the same company that had signed up Carole Landis in the months before her death.

'To my shame,' Rex said later, 'I hardly asked to see the script.' But the £23,000 he and Lilli picked up in fees, while well below what he had been getting in Hollywood, was enough for them to dynamite the old German gun-site and, before they returned to Broadway, to see the plans for their villa start to take shape.

Back on Broadway there was bad news. Closing down *Anne of the Thousand Days* had taken the edge off the public's appetite to see it; it shut down for good after four months. Rex quickly did a tour of the Mid-West and Canada to pick up ready cash for the bills which would soon be coming in from Portofino. Lilli plunged into a well-received production of Shaw's *Caesar and Cleopatra* opposite Cedric Hardwicke.

When Rex returned to New York, he did what for him was an extraordinary thing: he consulted a psychiatrist. In fact, he consulted several. Carole's suicide still troubled him deeply. Not that he had a guilt complex, or so he said; he just wanted to understand what had driven her to take her life.

Such a quest, of course, never arrives at a solution, however many analysts' offices one passes through. In any event, it would be a poor psychiatrist who would offer a ready-made one to a patient not prepared to work through to his own catharsis – and Rex resolutely held back from that. What he was perhaps attempting to do was to construct a picture of his late mistress that was different from the one he had had of her when they were together and in love. Despite his protestations, it is evident he shared a responsibility for the tragedy and he approached it, in retrospect, like an actor wondering if the outcome would have turned out differently if he had understood things better – if he had had a keener awareness of how a seemingly normal girl could push herself to such a horrifying fate.

By seeking 'the truth' about Carole, Rex was avoiding (as he usually did) facing the truth about himself. He later told Terence Rattigan that some of the things he had heard from half a dozen analysts over as many months had been very useful to him 'in terms of theatre'.[4] This, Rattigan concluded, was the nearest he would get to feeling guilt or making atonement.

However, it is also possible that Rex's quest was connected with a project he had been offered while touring with *Anne of the Thousand Days*: to do T. S. Eliot's verse drama, *The Cocktail Party*, in London the following May, and play the psychiatrist Sir Henry Harcourt-Reilly, whom Alec Guinness was playing on Broadway.

He turned down a chance to play his old role of King Mongkut in the musical *The King and I*, which Rodgers and Hammerstein had based on *Anna and the King of Siam*, feeling confident it would be a success, but not wanting to be trapped in it for years. Yul Brynner got the part. As

The Cocktail Party was to be a limited run of three months, Rex could do it and then make *The Long Dark Hall* – and pay the bills with both.

Rex went to see Guinness in the Eliot play, which he found fascinating but, to be frank, frequently beyond his understanding. Nevertheless, in his present mood, perplexed by what had caused Carole Landis to take her own life, Eliot's play connected with his feelings, if not his comprehension. It was more than prestigious: it was 'interesting',[15] as he admitted later, which was the farthest he ever went in describing his role – that of a man who plays God. *The Cocktail Party* represented the spiritual transfiguration of the conventional drawing-room comedy that Rex cut his teeth on during his early career. The customary quartet of husband, wife, mistress and lover were all present; so, too, was the Unidentified Guest, a Harley Street psychiatrist who helps the husband and wife square up to the truth about themselves. Through him, they recognize that they are incapable of loving or inspiring love – and the recognition becomes the bond which binds them together. The mistress, on the other hand, is to be called to a higher vocation, which she discovers when Sir Henry urges her to choose, to abandon doubt and embrace fulfilment. She does so, and finds sainthood in a savage martyrdom.

To Rex, Eliot's Catholicism was austere, to say the least: 'like sitting for several hours in a tepid bath,' he wrote.[16] But the theme of the play offered him a certain comfort. The idea of a beautiful and desirable woman, someone's mistress, dying a painful death that she could be said to have willed on herself had a welcome ring to a man who had gone through a similar tragedy. It did not explain it – but then Eliot never did 'explain' anything – but it suggested to Rex a more transcendental motive than a self-centred lover who had refused to follow through with a marriage proposal.

The psychiatrist Rex was to play does not see the mistress's death as a horrifying event, but simply as a predestined fate. And, best of all, he does not blame himself:

If we were all judged according to the consequences
Of all our words and deeds, beyond the intention
And beyond our limited understanding
Of ourselves and others, we should all be condemned....
You will have to live with these memories and make them
Into something new. Only by acceptance
Of the past will you alter its meaning.[17]

16: Up at the Villa, Down in the City

An unwelcome discovery awaited Rex when he arrived in London in March 1950 for *The Cocktail Party*. He discovered Eliot's play had already been performed for a week at the Edinburgh Festival in August 1949 with Alec Guinness in 'his' part. It shows how out of touch he was with other theatre people. He had thought Guinness was safely tucked away on Broadway. His antennae told him that some of the London critics would have been in Edinburgh and were certain to make a tiresome comparison between the two of them. And so it proved.

New York and London productions had the same director, E. Martin Browne, but each was shaped by the style and bias of its leading man.

Guinness, as befitted a deeply committed Roman Catholic, saw it primarily as Eliot's quest for spiritual transfiguration which only the very 'fortunate', in terms of suffering transcended, would be able to achieve. Guinness's *Party* had a sacerdotal austerity: the actor's voice resonated with priestly authority. Rex's, by comparison, was a social affair, warmer, wittier; in Harold Hobson's phrase, he was a 'man-of-the-world, not a man-of-another-world'.[1] He could not repress the amused and quizzical charm that gave Sir Henry Harcourt-Reilly his professional veneer. Guinness was like an altar candle burning pure and serene; Rex shed a smarter illumination. Guinness gave the part gravitas; Rex was worldlier by far, not so much the stern arbiter of salvation as a glossy social worker who, as the *Daily Telegraph* put it, 'has formed certain members of his London acquaintance into [a] sort of underground movement for bringing unhappy people out of their troubles'.[2]

Rex confessed to Browne that he never *quite* grasped what certain of his lines meant. Do not worry, he was told, neither do the audience. The sound of the words, heightened by Rex's precise diction, would convey the mystery, possibly enigmatic, but elevating. Yet of the rightness and wisdom of Eliot's central theme, Rex had no doubt. Had he not already experienced a sort of 'martyrdom' in America? '[Eliot] points up how people in great mental anguish will find "guardians",' he wrote later, 'those who have already been through the fire and endured, to help them over bad times. I believe [this] is absolutely true ... I have had guardians and been a guardian.'³

Rex had, as usual, committed himself to learning his part in advance. He found Eliot's poetic metre hard going: 'very abstract', he said in a rare interview, after the earthy Rabelaisian drama of Maxwell Anderson.⁴ But Browne did not see him simply as the 'smart' actor who 'charms his way along', as T. C. Worsley accused him of doing.⁵ The distinction between 'smart' and 'serious' was to nag at Rex all his life and found its way defensively into the title of his book on acting: *A Damned Serious Business*. His success with the verse showed him to be quite capable of working within a rigorous discipline; he should not have been terrified of Shakespeare.

However, one characteristic of Rex's which was to gain ascendancy later on showed itself for the first time when he did this play. This is his compulsion to ingratiate himself with playgoers and so keep their attention securely and flatteringly focused on him. Rex tried to invent bits of 'business' for those moments in the play when Eliot leaves his character with no dialogue, no stage directions, with nothing very obviously to *do*. Rex hated such occasions: it meant yielding the interest of what was going on to others and broke the tie he had established with the audience. He was to become more and more autocratic about this, making directors feel they had less to lose by falling in with his 'business' than falling out with him. But on this occasion, T. S. Eliot objected to what Rex got up to during one such moment early on. Rex decided to benefit from the temporary absence from the drawing-room of the few other characters to help himself to another shot of gin, only to be caught off guard by their return and forced to put the bottle back quickly before his intention was spotted. It was the kind of brief moment of *en passant* comedy relished by West End playgoers, but Eliot pointed out that it falsified the character. It gave the impression that this arranger of other people's destinies had a demeaning frailty of his own – he was a secret tippler. It was gently explained to Rex that Sir Henry Harcourt-Reilly's drinking habits had been introduced into the play only to make a thematic link between his behaviour and that of the miracle-working Heracles in Euripides's *Alcestis*. Rex, looking a bit miffed and totally mystified, agreed to abandon a comedy turn that would not have been out of place in *Charley's Aunt*.

For good measure, Eliot begged Browne to make sure that Rex kept his arms down at a crucial point to forty-five degrees 'and avoid the crucifixion suggestion'.⁶

Rex found himself more at ease, though, in the Eliot play than he had imagined. Once he got the hang of the blank verse, he found it cunningly reproduced the naturalistic cadences he was so good at simulating in the well-made plays of Rattigan and the drawing-room comedies of an earlier era. He was not far wrong. Martin Browne had pained Eliot by asking him to reduce the amount of religious symbolism in his play. Eliot had replied that every step he took in simplifying *The Cocktail Party*'s meaning 'brings me nearer to Frederick Lonsdale' – and, of course, to Rex's ideal.[7]

He and Lilli could hardly wait to finish filming their potboiler, *The Long Dark Hall*, the shooting of which overlapped several weeks in July with the Eliot play, so that once more he was working day and night, before rushing down to Portofino to see how their villa was coming along. To their delight, it was half built: they would be able to occupy it in summer of 1951. How would they keep themselves occupied until then? To Lilli, in particular, this was a worry. Their marriage was holding up, but she dreaded Rex not having anything to do. An idle Rex was a roving Rex.

It was Lilli who found the answer. She opened 'a fat envelope' addressed to her at Santa Margherita and found a play called *Bell, Book and Candle* within. Since the author, John Van Druten, had given Rex an early taste of stardom in *After All*, nearly twenty years before, he read it too. It was a modern light comedy sending up witchcraft in much the same way that Coward had sent up spiritualism. Lilli was offered the role of an alluring witch, living in Manhattan, who casts a spell over a handsome publisher, only to make the mistake of falling in love with him, losing her witching powers and turning herself into a mortal – a no less desirable woman, but a safer one to be with. It was not a 'natural' role for her. She was unversed in light comedy. Indeed, as she read it, she was not quite sure it was comedy. Her logical intelligence told her it was silly stuff: witches, spells, furry feline 'familiars', so insubstantial even Elsa Schreiber's coaching would be a waste. Rex did not approach it logically, but instinctively. The bewitched lover's role was thin, but he could infuse it with comedy 'business' – and there was no T. S. Eliot to rein him in this time. It is more than likely his reaction was what the producer, Irene Mayer Selznick, had hoped for when she sent the play to Lilli, but intended it to catch Rex. Rex's enthusiasm persuaded Lilli to say yes. Typically, he did not – yet, at any rate – but, using caution and cunning, he grafted on to the offer his own demands. But Irene Selznick knew a trick or two herself. She told Van Druten to enlarge his role: 'It's going to get so good, Rex might agree to play it.'[8] Marking the laughs on each revised page that arrived by courier, hearing them with his inner ear, Rex finally did so.

Lilli confessed that she needed a hearing aid to pick up the comedy that Rex was listening to in his head, but, if it put a roof on the villa

Class of 1917, Birkdale Preparatory School, near Sheffield: Rex, aged nine, is the boy with the wide Eton-type collar seated just in front of the second master from the right in back row.

below left: The 'juvenile lead', with centre parting and monocle: social graces were required as the plays got more sophisticated.

below right: At one of the 'court balls' which Arthur Barbosa, enthroned, organized for friends and theatre folk in Chelsea during the 1930s. Rex, bemedalled and besashed, is on the extreme right. The lady on Barbosa's left is his first wife; the one being presented, Mrs Walter Goetz. Also in the group are the Jeans boys from Liverpool, whose theatrical connections were invaluable to the young Rex.

In the West End success, Terence Rattigan's *French Without Tears*, 1936, with Kay Hammond, Roland Culver and Robert Flemyng.

With his first wife, Collette Thomas: 'Shut up!' was soon the most frequent exchange in a stormy marriage.

Cub days: Rex, as the happy-go-lucky newspaper reporter (with colleague) in *Men Are Not Gods*, covers his inexperience on the screen by a little bit of business with a stage cigarette.

With Vivien Leigh in *Storm in a Teacup*: tipped as the English William Powell and Myrna Loy.

In the spy comedy *Ten Days in Paris* with Kaaren Verne; playing the butler, in and out of uniform, Rex showed he already had the physical and verbal timing of a superb comedy actor.

Rex's love of uniform was put to good use in *Night Train to Munich*, in which he played a British spy masquerading as a German officer 'just back from the war front' (with ceremonial sword, of course). It was one of his favourite movies.

Unhappy trio: an ethereal Kay Hammond comes between Constance Cummings and Rex in *Blithe Spirit*. It forecast the shades of wives to come in Rex's married life off-screen, too.

In *Major Barbara*, with Robert Morley, playing a perfect duet to a theme by Shaw.

In Royal Air Force uniform on the day of his marriage to Lilli Palmer in 1943.

The fatal charm at work: Rex in *The Rake's Progress* puts away a good meal while Lilli Palmer, his wife at the time as well as his co-star, pleads for him to marry her.

Angry husband Griffith Jones floors Rex in *The Rake's Progress*. The star won admiration for the aplomb with which he performed his own stunt.

Rex and Lilli study the script in their home at Denham.

An informal shot of the Harrison family, *circa* autumn 1945: Rex, Lilli, son Carey and Lilli's Sealyham outside their home at Denham.

A studio portrait of the well-groomed Englishman, probably taken just before his departure for Hollywood in 1945.

and a foundation under their marriage, she was game.

Irene Selznick changed the image of Rex and Lilli. Hitherto they had been best known as individual performers. Now they became a husband-and-wife team, one of those peculiar stage assets, doubling the audience each of them had won by establishing an intangible but potent link between themselves. Audiences now felt taken into their confidence, shown how their private relationship was inspiring their stage one. Audiences were dead wrong, of course, but the illusion was a powerful one. The Oliviers and the Lunts had cast the same sort of spell over theatregoers in London and New York. Rex and Lilli never generated synergy of this kind; they were never known as 'the Harrisons'. But a married couple starring in Van Druten's play gave it a marital cohesion and added relish to the magical entrapment.

Rehearsals began in September. Rex was unusually 'difficult'. He was so clear how he wanted to play the role that he intimidated people. Irene Selznick describes a routine that eroded the patience or resistance of many a theatre director or producer in years to come. '[He] groped around as if he had never read the play ... He would worry a single line over and over, writhing and shuddering, oblivious to everything else, until he got it just right. It was the purest concentration I had ever seen.'[9] It was also sheer hell for the rest of the cast. But 'the results were brilliant'.

The real trouble was not Rex, but Lilli. Basically a dramatic actress, she was unused to the lightness of situation comedy. She could not hold her own against Rex. And he was a merciless taskmaster and pitiless tutor. As he 'ticked over like a time bomb', she struggled to 'hear' the pause that was a comic caesura in a one-liner, or get the half-octave note needed for a verbal double take.[10] During the New Haven try-out, her voice cracked, she went into spasm. Van Druten wrote and rewrote lines for Lilli, which Rex made her repeat so often they became meaningless.

The big problem was the second act curtain, when Rex storms out of the witch's apartment, leaving Lilli to play a big emotional climax by herself. She could not do it. After Rex had kept Irene Selznick up all night, twisting the play this way and that, she was finally vouchsafed the solution as she tossed in a fever of dawn sleeplessness – a bit of business that, she remembers, had Rex whooping. He spent hours rehearsing the new manoeuvre, which involved stage machinery and split-second timing. At the first night, on 14 November 1950, playgoers watching Rex leave Lilli's apartment in a fury, apparently beyond even her power to hold him in thrall, saw him raise his arm to hail an off-stage cab, freeze, then be instantaneously pulled backwards in to the apartment by an invisible but irresistible force. A shameless sight gag – but it worked. He loved it. It put him in total command of the theatre. And it had the added advantage of completely eliminating the dramatic solo that had defeated Lilli.

She was a realist. She showed gratitude, not resentment. Together, they played up to the public image of themselves as 'the junior Lunts',[11] their on-stage love scenes generating, in the words of one critic, 'such meat-and-potatoes jobs of kissing that it is reassuring to know they are married in real life'.[12]

Their sparring matches kept the play going well into the new year, 1952, until the summer heat again closed the theatres.

Their off-stage life, if not so spectacular, had at least stabilized. Carey, now seven, had been enrolled in New York's Lycée Français. A governess and a maid were part of an Upper East Side apartment decorated with an art collection that they had been able to save from the claims of the tax authorities. A Vlaminck windmill hung over the fireplace, a Utrillo and a Derain in their bedroom; in Rex's den a Grandma Moses. He had settled his alimony payments to Collette; money was coming in again. Lilli started doing a fifteen-minute television show each Thursday, a kind of mini-*Omnibus* produced by her brother-in-law, which tapped into middle-brow viewers with its wide range of items on drama, music, the arts and literature. Rex rather resented her intellectual celebrity. 'What in God's name do you want to bore them with for fifteen minutes?' he demanded. – 'With all the things that don't bore me,' she replied coolly.[13]

Their Portofino home was now finished. In the shape of a wide 'V', with its point facing south-east towards La Spezia, it consisted mainly of two large wings. The left-hand one was simply a tall, airy sunhouse with huge floor-to-roof windows, the shutters of which could be rolled up. Above were bedrooms with window walls. A swimming pool was planned for the other wing, where the dining and living quarters were situated and Rex had his study. The house had been built with stone from the rocky hillside, so it toned into the surroundings and matched the walls and vineyard terracing of the smallholders' farms. A cook and gardener were hired locally; a Sardinian caretaker was soon added. Labour was cheap: there were no worrisome outgoings. Rex had a flagpole erected and signalled he was 'in residence' by running up the red cross on a white field that was the standard of St George. Throughout his entire sojourn in Portofino, he never mustered enough Italian to hold a reasonable conversation with the locals, but his insularity stopped short of giving the place an English name; that might have been a bit too common. In fact, the house remained unnamed until the day he visited

Max Beerbohm. The Edwardian man-of-letters lived in retirement in nearby Rapallo. He suggested it would be appropriate for Rex, an actor, to name his house after the profession's patron saint, San Genesio. The Villa San Genesio it became.

There was only one drawback in Eden, but one that should have been forseen in as introverted a place as Portofino, where land rights were as complex as jigsaw puzzles and often required the services of well-compensated lawyers, never mind tactful pay-offs to neighbours, in order to fit them together. The pathway up to the villa was at that time scarcely more than a mule track, with a horrendously steep drop on one side. Rex bought an old US Army Jeep that happened to be there – no one quite knew how or why – whose gears and horsepower were equal to the steep haul up the hillside once the metalled road ended at the Hotel Splendido a few hundred metres below the house. But the Jeep was not permitted to cross the property of an automobile-hating neighbour. So the transfer from visitors' cars to the Jeep for the last stage of the journey to the villa had to be made on foot, a hundred yards or so of rough going that taxed even the athletic. However, at the end of the five-minute slog lay paradise, and for the moment that was enough.

It is impossible to pinpoint exactly when Rex met the man whose work so influenced his style and indeed his own character. Undoubtedly, he had seen Freddy Lonsdale in London before the war, but probably had not approached this testy luminary of the Green Room Club. Yet he later referred to him as a 'magnificent' man whom he loved dearly and called him one of the most amusing people he had ever had to stay with him at Portofino.[14] Probably he ran into him in New York during the success of *Anne of the Thousand Days*. Lonsdale's wartime views, which initially seemed pro-German, had made him unpopular at the end of the war and somewhat neglected. Rex took to him like a long-lost father.

The resemblances between the two men were indeed uncanny, as the excellent biography of her father by Frances Donaldson reveals. Like Rex, Lonsdale had limited formal education, but quickly acquired a taste for upper-class life aided by his talent for both mocking it in his plays and aping it in his manners. He reinforced everything that Rex had acquired by the same route. Both men were wilful, ruthless, disrespectful – except when they wished to turn on the charm, which they nevertheless accompanied by 'a kind of negligent conviction of superiority'.[15] They were easily bored by their own thoughts. They recognized in each other someone who was always happiest when on the move, always compelling change to happen – change of place, change of role, change of wife even. The only thing constant in such a restless life was the affection of the stage audience – for Lonsdale's plays, for Rex's performances. Both men were apprehensive when they encountered ruthlessness in others – Binkie Beaumont was always held in awe by Rex – and therefore behaved badly, rather than good-naturedly out of self-protection.

Frances Donaldson might have been writing of Rex when she said of Lonsdale: '[He] knew that, on the whole, people loathe the humiliation of a row and will not provoke someone who is fearlessly willing to cause one. And so [Freddy] built for himself a terrifying personality, one far better never scratched.'[16] The two shared an aggressive masculinity. Lonsdale did not even put talc on his face after shaving and believed – and Rex shared his assumption – that anyone, like an actor, who painted his face nightly must be a son of a bitch. They had instinctual rather than meditative natures. They hated the press of their day for rather similar reasons – the unconventional nature of their married lives, Lonsdale supporting two families only a few miles from each other in different towns and Rex maintaining a continuous flow of new lovers. Both were unerring in their knowledge of high comedy and found they agreed that it was 'the disciplined avoidance of intensity' which could make the most ordinary line sound funny when pronounced.[17] Lonsdale directed his own plays by a process of elimination so fastidious it drove performers to distraction; Rex, when he got power, likewise steadily refined his own performance by throwing out things which did not work and gradually extended it to encompass the other performances around him, sometimes to the point of throwing out an actor or actress he did not like.

The irony was that Lonsdale never wrote a play for Rex. He came to Portofino about two years before his death, in 1954, with a newly written work, but Rex felt he had lost his gift by that time. In any case, Rex hated being read to and was uncomfortably reminded of the great falling out between Lonsdale and Gerald du Maurier, when the actor fell asleep as Lonsdale was giving him a post-prandial reading of his new play.

Lonsdale had a physical tic which became apparent whenever he was pondering where self-interest lay in some opportunity he was being offered. He would, according to his biographer, 'place the four fingers of his right hand vertically along the bridge of his nose and the thumb between the nostrils'.[18] All who knew Rex recall that this was precisely what he did too. The disciple learned his trade well from this mocking old devil.

Rex and Lilli never thought they would be back in Hollywood, of all places, until Stanley Kramer made them an offer. He wanted to film Jan de Hartog's play *The Four-Poster*, and remembering the emphasis given in newspaper interviews at the time of *Bell, Book and Candle* to the appeal of a husband-and-wife team, he believed that having a married couple starring in the story of forty years' togetherness, from honeymoon through childbirth to bereavement and spiritual reunion, would assist the illusion. It would also be a sop to the film censors, still worrying at that period about anyone who was in proximity to a bed.

When news of the casting broke in Hollywood, however, the old howls of indignation were heard afresh. 'I don't see a very cordial welcome for sexy Rexy and Lilli,' said Hedda Hopper.[19]

Rex refused point blank to publish an apology for the things he had said about the place. Kramer agreed to bite the bullet, reassured that Columbia Pictures did not give a damn about bad feeling in the neighbourhood so long as there was profit in the picture.

Actually, when they returned to the scene of Rex's tribulations at the end of August 1951, feeling like immigrants at an unfriendly frontier, no one turned them away. The venom of the 'reptiles', as Rex called Hedda, Louella and the rest, had been drawn by the alternative publicity outlet of television; the prurient revelations of the past were now being challenged by the slipping of moral standards all round. Moreover, they returned trailing their Broadway successes and Rex's award for *Anne of the Thousand Days*: no longer residents expected to conform to the hypocritical community norm, but celebrities passing through.

They were even on the cover of *Life* magazine, though the photograph was a formal medallion shot of two left profiles. Since Rex and Lilli both had the same 'good' profile, neither of them had wanted *Life* to show him or her at a disadvantage. Actually, it made them look quite regal, like iconic images on a coin of the realm.

Rex soon demonstrated his flair for breaching convention. Since they had been away, Danny Kaye had shot to international prominence as the most inspired comic in America. The easy-going comedian found himself sitting on a sofa next to Rex at Sam Goldwyn's. Rex was drinking gin and tonic. 'To everyone's amazement,' says Jones Harris, son of the Broadway producer Jed Harris and a witness, 'Rex raised his glass above Danny's head and poured the gin and tonic on to his pompadour. Kaye looked amazed. "Why the hell did you do that?" he blurted out. "Well," said Rex, "I hear you're a funny man, so I wondered what you'd do if I tipped my drink over you. Go on, be funny." '[20]

It was at this time that the future changed for Lilli. She was at a party in Jack Warner's home when Rex approached her with a long-limbed, handsome young man in tow. He introduced him as Carlos Thompson and said he had something he wanted to tell Lilli. Introductions made, Rex then went off in pursuit of other companions. Thompson, then in his mid-thirties, had been born in Buenos Aires, but was of German descent like Lilli – his family name was Mundanschaffer. A sometime novelist turned stage and screen actor in Argentina, he had been blacklisted by the Perón dictatorship. But good luck, good looks and good connections got him a Hollywood contract. He now told Lilli he had fallen in love with her after seeing *Body and Soul*. This and much else rolled off the young man's tongue during supper with a fluency and charm that prompted Rex, later on, to give Carlos Thompson the nickname of 'Coverboy'.

By the time Rex rejoined Lilli, indicating it was time for her to drive him home, her usually reliable sobriety had been shaken. Not in a way that affected her driving; but in a way that was to affect her marriage.

Unknown to Rex, Lilli was to conduct her affair with Carlos Thompson, off and on, over the next five years or so without a twinge of guilt, but also without experiencing any compulsion to break up her marriage. Rex had drawn – overdrawn, she later felt – on her loyalty in time of crisis a few years earlier, and he had been unfaithful since. But she recognized that his infidelity was more a character reflex than a marital crisis. 'One adjusts ... to the life-style of the stronger partner,' she later wrote in explanation of why she maintained the status quo.[21]

They were the only players in *The Four-Poster*. The film's minimalism intrigued, but also challenged them. The cut-price shooting schedule – three weeks instead of six – meant that Rex had no chance to point the comic nuances for Lilli or nudge along her tempo as he had done in the early stages of *Bell, Book and Candle*. Though they had three weeks of rehearsals, it was paradoxically too long: at the end of it, they had forgotten most of the subtleties they had elaborated at the start of it. Oh, for a supporting cast – even a dog!

But such conditions brought out all their technical proficiency. On her bridal night in the film, Lilli had to do a shy undressing scene, jettisoning corsets, chemises, petticoats, a ten-minute take-off on camera. Rex insisted they bring home her bridal gown and underwear, and he timed her with a stop-watch as she stripped off the twelve items. He had his own worries: how his skinny legs would look in a period nightgown. He decreed the garment must be ankle-length. He won that battle, but lost the one about his nightcap. Ever afterwards, when a film required him to wear unusual headgear, he approached it with reluctance and suspicion, be it a nightcap or a papal mitre. It is a tribute to both players that the film does not show its haste. It contains one of Rex's most touching scenes: a grace note of pathos as he moves around the familiar bedroom at the end, an arthritic widower, reliving his life in memory and waiting for the moment when the spirit of his wife will come to fetch and guide him into the other world: a coda suggesting *The Ghost and Mrs Muir* in reverse.

While Rex had been briefly in London over the summer, Laurence Olivier had invited him to take the role he was then playing in Christopher Fry's *Venus Observed* to Broadway for the next season. Rex was still wary of verse drama, but his experience with Eliot had convinced him he did not need to understand the poet's mind to persuade an audience that he was making sense. His vocal authority was enough. Fry's play was a modern comedy of Eros, flamboyantly yet at the same time feyly versified, about a ducal amorist and amateur astronomer whose observation of the celestial bodies is matched by his enjoyment of the earthly ones. He finds his own son a rival for one of his mistresses – played by Lilli. As Olivier was alternating in 'the two Cleopatras' (Shaw's and Shakespeare's) on Broadway at the same time as Rex was rehearsing Fry, he could not give the latter the attention he thought he should have. Rex was not sorry. The two stars did not really like each other. 'Rex used to refer to Olivier when talking to me as "your friend" in a tone that made it clear he wasn't his,' says Patrick Garland. 'Larry was more direct about him. The genius of each man didn't make him very pliable to the other's direction.' To Rex, Olivier meant Shakespeare. 'I suppose it's too late for me to think of playing *Hamlet*,' Rex sniffed in a rare interview at this time, 'but I could some day at least take a crack at Malvolio.'[22]

Words always fascinated Rex, though he was a terrible speller, and Fry pandered to the lover of strange words, though Rex privately confessed the denseness of the verse made him feel a bit constipated. His favourite line, interestingly, was one that applied to the duke's adventures with a multiplicity of partners. His son enquires if he has loved them equally. '"Equally" is a mortuary word,' Rex replies. He trimmed the character of the Duke to fit a more flattering view of himself, managing to 'knock' Olivier in the process: 'I played him a bit younger than Larry [did in London] because I felt a man in his late forties isn't really considered old any more.'[23] Rex at this time was forty-four.

The play opened on 13 February 1952, and closed less than twelve weeks later. It was Rex's first major flop. The huge theatre it was in did not help the intimate delivery of verse, but the vogue for Fry had benefited from the way the poet's full-blown style reflected the renewed sense of national pride which the 1951 Festival of Britain had promoted. That cultural exhalation had not wafted much trade in Broadway's direction. The reviews were courteous, but, like the audiences, puzzled. Rex put a good face on the failure. 'It's always so much more fun and stays more interesting than the usual sort of thing [Lilli and I] get to do.'[24] As Fry might have put it, 'interesting' is a mortuary word. At least it left them free for their beloved San Genesio.

They were early birds in a whole flock of celebrated summer migrants. Word of 'Rex's place' had spread, to the commercial benefit of Portofino – at first, anyhow. Their powerful terrace telescope spied more private yachts anchored in the harbour than ever before. The *Sister Ann* was chartered by the Duke and Duchess of Windsor. Rex and Lilli had met them in New York. By sentiment and, indeed, his own family origins, the former King Edward VIII was much attracted by Lilli's German side and looked forward to his 'German lesson', as he called the cosy chats between the two of them in a corner of the villa's living-room, while Rex, excluded from what he dubbed 'the language course',[25] had to make do with the Duchess. A charmless woman, he found her. It baffled him what the king had seen in Wallis Simpson to make him give up the throne. The snob in Rex was flattered by having the ex-King of England under his roof, but the Duke's retentive grip on royal protocol and the courtesies he expected made social life uneasy. Quite simply, there was not room enough in San Genesio for two kings. Rex had to cede the head of the table to the Duke, stand up when he did, give the ducking nod that was the required greeting of a British subject to the Royals: in short, behave in ways that made him feel a stranger in his own house. 'The little twerp', as he privately referred to the Duke,[26] irritated him further by relieving him of the host's task of passing round the canapés as they sat on the terrace over their pre-dinner *apéritifs*. It made Rex, who had walked out of a radio production because of a tasteless remark about royalty, feel that his gesture had been in vain if a man who had been King was prepared to act like a servant. Rex confided to friends that he came close to commiting an act of *lèse majesté*: it was as intolerable as seeing a guest-star role precede one's own on the credits.

More welcome was Greta Garbo, who arrived on a yacht chartered by George Schlee, her lover as well as the husband of the New York *couturière* Valentina. Rex was once asked what Garbo was really like. In a phrase that unconsciously recalled Coward summing up and simultaneously cutting down some great entity such as Norfolk ('very flat') or China ('very big'), he snapped, 'Very depressed.'[27]

It was not the whole truth. Rex and Garbo shared a taste for strenuous hikes. They indulged in these together along the hilltops, Garbo's piston-shaft legs pacing Rex's lanky shanks. They fed apples into the contentedly crunching mouth of a black donkey Rex adopted on a nearby peasant's allotment. They drank coarse red wine in a tumble-down hostelry on a track that led up to Olmi on the hilltop. They negotiated with goatlike nimbleness the long, rocky, narrow, zig-zagging descent down to the tiny bay where the thirteenth-century Abbey of San Fruttuoso stood at the water's edge. This was Rex's favourite walk. Carey sometimes took it too, tethered to the waist of his Swiss governess, a woman with a passion for Alpine climbing.

Other guests at San Genesio that summer were John Mills and his wife Mary, Jean-Pierre Aumont, and the Culvers.

Rex had already established his own routine, which diverged from Lilli's. She liked entertaining and being entertained by their neighbours. Rex hated it. He had 'no intention of mixing with the stuffy Italian bourgeoisie'.[28] Lilli ran the villa punctiliously, kept the servants on the go, made sure Rex had everything he needed (or thought he did), and for all this he was grateful. But he was happiest in the company of his own chums: chief among them Jack Merivale and Roland Culver. He found conversation with some of Lilli's 'intellectual' friends, well, 'difficult', though he made an exception for the philosopher and Oxford don Isaiah Berlin, who used to stick halved corks round his tennis shoes so that he could bury his nose in a book as he walked and not worry if he stubbed his toe. Rex loved such idiosyncrasies. With his own chums, conversation was hardly necessary at all: they all shared the same unspoken view of 'the natives' and were 'fairly riotous'[29] on their excursions into town, before driving crazily home again skirting the sheer drop by inches in the Jeep with the brake plate strapped on by sticky tape. And he loved eating *al fresco*, not just because of the Anglo-Saxons' fondness for the warm south, but because it helped draw the line between the civilized pleasures of his world, as he saw them, and the locals, who ate in their own gloomy interiors and thought 'only peasants eat outside'.[30] He did very little to endear himself to the people on whom he depended for his comforts and security. This Eden had its serpents too.

Portofino helped Rex to store up all the important energy for the next round. This happened to be a production in New York of Peter Ustinov's satirical comedy of national stereotypes, *The Love of Four Colonels*, the first play to be directed by Rex himself. Ustinov, wisely, did not involve himself in it: 'It would have been like telling someone how to bring up one's baby by correspondence course,' he recalls.[31] Rex played the Devil and four other roles with mixed-to-favourable reviews. Early in the run, in February 1953, he received news that his mother had died; he had already lost his father shortly after the Carole Landis scandal. 'He was terribly hurt,' says his sister, 'she probably meant more to him than any other woman.' He commemorated her by a highly uncharacteristic act of self-denial: he gave up cigarettes. (He had temporarily stopped smoking when he had his collapse in Philadelphia, but took it up again.) His mother had died from a smoking-related illness. It was also, for him, a break with the theatrical tradition in which he had learned his craft: the 'cigarette play', the mannered comedies where the artifices of lighting, holding and puffing the cigarette solved the dilemma of what to do with one's hands. Rex had conquered that problem. Now he conquered cigarettes.

There was a great deal of activity in the early 1950s, caused by the rising expenses of educating Carey – he was enrolled at an English boarding school because Rex wanted his son to have an Englishman's education, though Lilli found it heart-wrenching – and planning new vineyards for San Genesio. He and Lilli did not turn down as many offers as they used to. It was a pity they did not. Rex did American television in a series of plays distinguished only by their capacity to produce cheques. And he returned to Hollywood at the end of November 1953 to make *King Richard and the Crusaders*, a movie which has since become a camp classic that gave the world – or the part of it which plays Trivial Pursuit – such lines as those addressed to King Richard: 'War, war, that's all you think of, Dick Plantagenet.'

Following the success of MGM's *Ivanhoe*, Jack Warner had hastened to fit his stars with suits of armour: George Sanders as Richard the Lion-Hearted, Laurence Harvey as a Scottish Knight, Virginia Mayo as the Lady Edith, and Rex as a Moorish physician complete with beard, enough jewellery to deck a Christmas tree and costumes weighing over forty pounds. Still, he was being paid $65,000. Mentally he rearranged the money in vine terraces.

He scarcely cared that the British critics ate him alive.

'As he airily [in his guise as a doctor] prescribes cures for the sick Richard, the tent in the Holy Land becomes the consulting room of a fashionable Harley Street specialist,' wrote *The Times*.[32] 'A character who appears to have dropped in from one of the minor works of Noël Coward,' said Dilys Powell in the *Sunday Times*.[33] The American critics tended to dwell on the mixed ancestry Rex's impersonation suggested. 'Harrison plays the Saracen in the old Japanese manner, all hisses and bows,' said Philip Hamburger in the *New Yorker*,[34] while Howard Thompson, in the *New York Times*, opted for Anglo-Irish ancestry and cited 'a greased Mr Harrison' as a 'composite of Uriah Heep and the *Finian's Rainbow* leprechaun'.[35]

While filming, he and Lilli rented Errol Flynn's house on Mulholland Drive, noting with interest its two-way mirrors and concealed tape recorders. Perhaps the ambience was responsible for Rex having another outbreak of randiness with various starlets. Yet neither he nor Lilli was willing to force the breaking point. He always came back from a flirtatious excursion and was content to tie up in the safe anchorage of their marriage. An interview he gave the *Los Angeles Times* at this time shamelessly – and unconsciously – articulated his chauvinism. 'The husband's career must always come first ... Lilli is first a wife and mother, a very good one, I might add, and then the artist ... Marriage between two persons in the same line of work can and should be ideal, if the wife never forgets that her career is secondary to the marriage. Lilli and I have a perfect understanding on this matter, so there's no reason why we shouldn't go on being happily married until we're tottering into senility.'[36]

All too soon, after this choice piece of hubris, some listening god decided it was time to furnish Rex with a reason long before senility or any other infirmity prevented him from pursuing it. The 'reason' came with the next film he made. Her name was Kay Kendall.

Part Four

Kay

17: 'Ravished over Cold Beef'

Sidney Gilliat, the co-producer of *The Rake's Progress*, had written to Rex while he was in Hollywood proposing a new film. *Marriage à la Mode* it was to be called, though lest it be thought a French film, the title became *The Constant Husband*. It was again the story of a rake, but this time an involuntary one: an amnesiac who only gradually discovers what he has got up to, which is acquiring six wives. The notion delighted Rex. He committed right away – with two provisos: the film must be made in the three months he was permitted to stay in England without incurring tax liabilities, and he must have a say in the casting. Believing that casting half a dozen women would be additional bait, Gilliat and his partner Frank Launder readily agreed, though they informed him that one of the 'wives' had already been filled by Kay Kendall, whose natural talent as a comedienne had recently surfaced in the film *Genevieve*. The impromptu boogie-woogie she blew on a trumpet in a night-club recalled those deliciously scatty heroines in the screwball comedies of pre-war Hollywood.

Kay Kendall, in the spring of 1954, had just turned twenty-eight and described herself as 'a freak, an oddity – face too narrow, nose too long'.[1] At five feet nine-and-a-half inches, she might have added that she was also too tall for the comfort of cameramen and co-stars. Self-disparagement was one of the tactics Kay used to diminish her chronic insecurity and enhance the tomboyish frankness that appealed to women as much as men. In fact, although no conventional beauty, each of her features added individuality to a temperament that was volatile, but could pass for being simply vivacious. Her nose did take an odd little turn, but it was the kind deemed 'sweet'. The truth was that she had injured it in a car accident and had it rebuilt by the well-known plastic surgeon Archie McIndoe. The operation robbed her of her sense of smell, but this also added to her 'wacky' temperament, since on occasion it returned and then she would rush around the house or hotel suite burying her face in everything from flowers to garlic.

Yes, her mouth was slightly too large for her chin, but then her lips were never at rest. Her face was constantly animated. She was indeed taller than the average girl, but her slim legs seemed to end where her arms began, giving her boyish figure the look of an exclamation mark in constant motion. Her eyes were a deep amber: some said the colour symbolized her indecisiveness, caught between the green of 'Go' and the red of 'Stop'. 'Take care,' it said. Kay herself took very little care in life. She was part-Irish and wholly impulsive. She had been born, like Rex, in the north of England, but on the east coast, near Hull, in a seaside resort called Withernsea, but, as one interviewer shrewdly remarked, her spiritual home was London and her pedigree stretched through chorus line and music hall and intimate revue and figures like Gertrude Lawrence, Anna Neagle and Jessie Matthews. Her family were show-business: her grandmother, Marie Kendall, had topped the variety bill with Marie Lloyd. Her father Terry and his sister, Pat, had formed the dancing team that Rex had watched as an entranced teenager in the Cochran musical. A convent-educated girl, Kay took to her liberation into the outside world with extra zest. She compared herself to a bottle of champagne. Working on and off from the age of eleven, then touring with her sister Kim in a dance act when she was fourteen, she developed a natural scattiness of temperament partly to hide her lack of education. She soon picked up the playful, girlish manners that helped keep her safe from the wrong sort of men by encouraging them to treat her as someone in need of protection, rather than as someone inciting lust. Some men, of course, found her need for protection was itself seductive. One of her tricks was to invite any admirer who happened to be there when she was putting on her make-up to decide where the beauty spot should go, and apply it to her upturned cheek.

By the time she met Rex, her friends were well used to her habit of using diminutives like 'housey-wousey' or calling people (of both sexes) 'wifey', or giving nicknames to those she liked so as to tie them to her in private knots of affection.

All this might have been considered irritating to unbearable affectation but for her broad and unforced sense of fun. She had a natural talent for carrying off an attention-getting bit of misbehaviour or a self-consciously coarse remark with a poise and instinctive timing that added up to 'style'. One of the typically 'scandalous' things Kay used to get up to at parties was to treat her equally tall sister as if she were a lamp-post and, falling on all fours, go around sniffing her – 'The rest of the act can be imagined,' says someone who saw it.

When one came to know Kay Kendall, however, the same coltish nervousness that kept her a lively companion began to assume a slightly more disturbed character. Like Rex, she had been made restless by an adolescence spent touring and in cheap lodgings, and by doing the rounds of army camps. Like Rex, too, she had had her share of early rebuffs. 'You're too tall. You can't be photographed. You have no talent. The best thing to do is go off and get married.'

Her break came when she was picked by the Rank Organization for the film musical *London Town*, designed to prove the British could turn out musicals as good as Hollywood's. It proved just the opposite, and put a jinx on everyone associated with it. For four years, Kay could not find a worthy bit of work and went back to touring, where her craft was planed smooth by the abrasiveness of all kinds and conditions of audiences – just like Rex's. Launder and Gilliat put her into *Lady Godiva Rides Again* and then she raised the trumpet to her lips in *Genevieve* and the walls of the film world came tumbling down.

Before she met Rex, she had been escorted around by the likes of Billy Wallace, a member of the 'Princess Margaret set', the Marquess of Milford Haven and the Maharajah of Cooch Behar. But marriage remained something wished for rather than pursued. In restaurants sometimes, when a waiter asked her what she wished to order, she would quip, 'One husband, two children, three Boxer puppies.'[2] Companionship meant more to her than courtship and held less dangers. Dirk Bogarde, a fellow Rank artist, met her around this time and he and his friend and manager, Tony Forwood, invited her down for the day to their country home. Using playful wiles and wistful hints, she proposed moving in with the boys, promising to help out with the drinks and do the mending for them as a form of rent. Bogarde has recorded how she took over the front double bedroom a week later, along with the ox-blood pills she said she needed for her anaemia and a white rug like a security blanket, and she stayed, off and on, over the weekends for the next five years – a girl about the house, platonically sharing the fun with the two bachelors.

Beneath an easily bruised sensitivity, however, she stored up a wilful determination. As Bogarde later wrote, 'Kay made her own decisions.'[3]

Rex first met Kay in the studio commissary about a week before shooting began on *The Constant Husband*. Like the witch his wife had played in *Bell, Book and Candle*, Kay cast an irresistible spell over him with her informality, high spirits and zany, inconsequential way of hopping, skipping and jumping through their conversation. 'Rakish' was the word he later said she suggested: she seemed to embody the same impertinent free will, unattached to any of life's more boring responsibilities, that he had impersonated in *The Rake's Progress*. 'I left the table in that drab old studio dining-room about fifteen feet in the air. I had been ravished over cold beef.'[4]

Lilli had left for Munich with her mother to make a German film called *Feuerwerk*, the first time she had set foot in her homeland in twenty years. But her misgivings about the country which had forced her into self-exile were soon overcome by seeing old friends, speaking her native tongue and by her pragmatic acceptance that things had changed and she had to change with them. This was important in subsequent dealings with Rex. She went to Munich feeling an Englishwoman; she came back accepting the fact that she was still German in spirit and artistry. Thus, at the very moment Rex was being bewitched by his new girl, Lilli was rediscovering the old enchantment of her native land.

Sidney Gilliat soon spotted there was 'something' going on between Rex and Kay. 'Rex's driver began complaining about the late hours he was having to keep after the day's shooting when Rex had him pick up Kay and take them out for the night. That was always a sure sign there was a romance on the set.' In the film, Kay played a society photographer, a career girl with a mind (and income) of her own. She thinks she's learnt all there is to know about men from one unhappy divorce – until she meets Rex and marries him. Kay's wicked sense of fun revealed itself when she and Rex were shooting the scene where she shows him home movies of their wedding day, in the hope this will jolt him out of his amnesia and also arouse his passion. According to Rex, he suddenly felt her hand fall on his crotch – below the camera frame, of course – and there certainly is a moment of completely off-guard surprise on his face. This was the mood of amorous mischief quickly established between them and consummated in a flat near the one where Rex and Collette had lived in Sloane Street.

Rex also took her on a round of night spots, accompanied by her sister, Kim, who soon guessed this was not just a passing romance. He was annoyed that Kay had so few scenes in the picture with him. And when she went off to Paris for weekends – she had another admirer there – he was frustrated and jealous. 'It was frightening,' he wrote later, 'that somebody I knew only superficially should have such a violent effect on me.'[5] In the film, Rex was put in a similar fix, a chap unable to cope with his own sex appeal. He had to play his role in a continual dither of bewilderment and alarm as each new 'wife' makes her appearance in his search for his own identity. He very skilfully rings the changes on this narrow band of emotions, letting the fatal charm come into view now and again. Though no more closely based on Rex's life than *The Rake's Progress* had been, the story develops in a way that is very close to his character and indeed the life that lay ahead of him. The main problem his character has to face is not really that of a man who insists on taking a new wife every few years: it is that of a man who, for some reason he cannot fathom, is compelled every few years to desert the woman he has married and forget about her. He is an unconscious polygamist, his caddishness redeemed by his having no memory of it. What each of Rex's own wives would agree on is his reluctance to refer to any of his marriages before their own – as if he had put them completely out of mind, several of them said. Nor did his much-married status ever throw a shade of doubt over each new liaison. As Margaret Leighton, playing the lawyer defending him in the film on a charge of multiple bigamy, remarks to him, 'For some strange reason [women] appear to find you irresistible.' Soon after this rebuke, she herself melts and seeks his sympathy with a hard-luck story of the misogynist judges who are always summing up against her in court. Like all of Rex's own wives, the females in the film are willing to forgive him many things, including his leaving them to marry someone else. At the end, the 'wives' all declare they would take him back, if given a chance. Granted a strong streak of female masochism in the comedy, the outcome confirms what Rex's closest friends came to think as they watched his progress from marriage to marriage: that here was no ruthless predator, but a fellow who was vulnerable in the extreme to the emotions that his appearance and personality aroused in women, a fellow who could never completely understand the sexuality that drew them to him.

The Constant Husband finished shooting well before Lilli's German film and Rex was plunged into despair by the thought that his idyll with Kay was over and he had to rejoin his wife in West Germany. 'Total agony,' he wrote.[6] Of course he communicated with Kay by telephone almost daily and, once he and Lilli had gone to San Genesio for the summer, he volunteered to go back to London to collect Carey from his boarding school – a chore he usually left to Lilli. He met Kay at the London flat where she was staying that week. She changed London addresses with bewildering rapidity, claiming she was extremely sensitive to her surroundings. Friends suspected it was her intermittent difficulty in paying the rent. Kay spent all she earned without thought or conscience – another of the things about her adored by Rex, who was of the same mind. When Rex telephoned Lilli from London, her suspicion that there was 'someone else' – exactly who, she did not yet know – hardened into near certainty. She could tell he was lying from his voice. In marital matters, Rex was always an unconvincing actor. His finesse totally deserted him.

Late that August he and Lilli were playing host to the Windsors, the Oliviers, Jean-Pierre Aumont and other San Genesio guests at a restaurant called Pitisforo, which projected over the western side of the harbour like the glassed-in verandah grill of an ocean liner. Binkie

Beaumont was there too, congratulating himself on signing up Rex and Lilli for the London production of *Bell, Book and Candle* that coming autumn.

A waiter handed Rex a note, and the next minute he was on his feet stammering out excuses. 'Er, er, the press fellows ... want to know who's here ... better step out and tell them ... not have them invade us.'[7] And he was gone. He met Kay waiting about a hundred yards way, astonished and elated to see her here, but apprehensive too, and looking back at Pitisforo as if he expected to see Lilli's silhouette at the window. There was time only for a quick drink and a promise to meet her the next morning; she was staying at the Hotel Eden in Santa Margherita. Then he rushed back, collecting some curious glances from his guests who had not been aware that Rex truckled to press demands for an interview with such alacrity.

Kay had arrived with a friend, Carol Saroyan, who had been married to the writer William Saroyan and was soon to become the wife of Walter Matthau. Though aware of what might be in the wind, Carol Saroyan maintained an embarrassed neutrality.

Elated by the theatricality of his illicit affair – it was like a scene from *The Constant Husband* – Rex took his Jeep over to Kay's hotel the next day and that afternoon she and Carol showed up as guests of the Earl of Warwick aboard his yacht, where the Harrisons happened to be also. Rex immediately invited all of them up to the villa for supper. At last, as Lilli later recorded, '[It was] in the open, as clear as daylight.'[8]

Kay was in mischievous mood, enjoying every minute of the tense situation she had precipitated. Lilli said later that she felt a cold pain in her stomach, as if she had swallowed all the ice cubes on the drinks tray. Over supper, Kay was pulling Rex's leg a lot and not only that, but resting her hand again affectionately on his crotch. The dining-table was glass-topped and her gestures were visible. He had to keep continually moving his supper plate to give some solid cover to what was going on underneath it. Lilli took it badly. Her sense of decorum was offended by this brazen flirtation in front of their guests. Binkie Beaumont was also upset. He saw a risk of the husband-and-wife team for *Bell, Book and Candle* breaking up before the play opened. In fact, Lilli asked to be released from her contract. Beaumont sympathized, but was inflexible.

The crunch came when one of the Saroyan children accompanying Carol went down with appendicitis and had to be hospitalized. Rex paid the medical bills. Kay travelled with Carol to her sister's house in Geneva. From there she called Rex. Propelled by the momentum of events and his own emotions, Rex rose before the rest of the household, got in the Jeep, changed into his Jaguar and with one suit of clothes drove as if on automatic pilot to meet Kay in Milan. They spent the next week together, driving through Appenine passes, dropping down to Genoa, roaming at will, travellers without maps, letting their hearts guide them.

When he returned to the villa, Rex found only Carey. Lilli had gone to London. Reluctant to encounter her before he was to begin directing her in the Van Druten play, he invited himself to spend a week or so at Jean-Pierre Aumont's house at Malmaison, near Paris, and there Kay called him, demanding to know what he was doing in 'a bad house', as Aumont's French housekeeper had translated 'Malmaison' for her benefit. Such daffy confusion, he felt, rendered his mistress more adorable than ever. They spent time together in Paris.

Binkie Beaumont had to confess he took a sadistic pleasure watching Rex prepare to direct the wife he was cheating on in a role which gave her power over the love life of the character he was playing. Rex was angry, as the guilty frequently are.

'Lilli's got a lot of qualities,' he told a woman friend at the time, 'but I'm afraid that lightness in adversity isn't one of them.'

'Rex,' replied this friend, 'you're an absolute pig.'

'Well,' he answered, grinning like a schoolboy, 'perhaps I am.'

'With all his faults,' said the woman years later, 'you couldn't help feeling a bit sorry for him.'[9]

Lilli had her allies too. One was Noël Coward, in whom she had confided. 'Rex Harrison has fallen in love with Kay Kendall,' Coward entered in his journal on 12 September 1954, 'and is breaking Lilli Palmer's heart.'[10]

But despite the rows that employees heard frequently going on in the suite where Rex and Lilli were staying at the Connaught Hotel, they did not separate – not yet. They were yoked together professionally in the play. Kay met Rex almost daily, waiting for his rehearsals to break for lunch, so that he could join her at The White Tower, a restaurant close – but not too close – to the Phoenix Theatre. Soon, however, she had to leave for Dublin, where she was playing Elvira, the tormenting ghost, in a revival of *Blithe Spirit*. Ironic casting.

Bell, Book and Candle opened on schedule, despite the acrimony of its stars, on 5 October 1954 to enthusiastic reviews for Rex and Lilli. A few critics remarked on their first-night edginess; a comment maybe inspired by inside knowledge of their off-stage relationship. Even when tempers cooled, the temporary state of grace was fragile. One who witnessed this was Laurence Evans, whose agency, International Creative Management, had 'inherited' Rex from MCA, when the American conglomerate decided to let its 'talent' go and retain its film-making facilities after the Hollywood studios had to rid themselves of their monopolistic practices in the 1950s.

Evans was to become London's most influential agent, representing not only Rex but many of the greatest players of the time, including Olivier and Gielgud.

'I was with Rex in his dressing-room and Lilli, as it happened, was there, too,' he recalls today. 'The phone rang. I answered it. "Is Rex there?" It was Kay. I saw Lilli prick up her ears. "Yes ..." I said cautiously. – "Can I speak to him, Laurie?" – "No ..." Lilli, of course, knew what was going on. But Rex didn't dare take the call in her presence.'[11]

Rex regarded his affair as a dalliance within marriage rather than a prelude to divorce. The Carole Landis pattern was repeating itself. But this time Lilli acted first.

Binkie Beaumont was awakend by a call from Rex at 2 am, after the first night of *Bell, Book and Candle*. Where the hell is Lilli, Rex demanded. Beaumont replied how the hell would he know – was not she with Rex? The truth was that Lilli had moved out of the Connaught into Jack Buchanan's apartment, further down Mount Street, on which she had taken a short lease. Rex was not amused. He had suggested to her that maybe she should 'take a lover'.[12] She recorded that he meant it kindly, but that is precisely what she did, and probably would have done without her husband giving her the cue. Carlos Thompson, the film star from the Argentine, whom she had met in Hollywood, had been shooting a picture in Madrid. A mutual friend, knowing of Lilli's unhappiness, persuaded him to come to London. He walked into her dressing-room – and back into her life.

The 'desertion' of his wife left Rex confused; it was calculated to force him to do what he hated doing – make up his mind between her and Kay. Kay was persistently urging him to marry her. Now they had rows, though they were 'theatrical' rows, more aphrodisiac than alienating, resolved by bouts of love-making. The fiercer the argy-bargy, the sweeter the reconciliation.

Diana Dors, then the British film industry's 'sex star', recalled the two of them coming for lunch with her and her husband at the Riverside Inn, a fashionable restaurant on the banks of the Thames at Cookham. Driving there in the Dors Cadillac, Kay kept talking to Rex, whom she called her 'boyfriend', in a wheedling tone, frequently mentioning marriage, which seemed to be the last thing he had in mind. 'Oh, for God's sake, Mousey, don't let's start all that bloody nonsense again.'[13] When she persisted, he suddenly clouted her on the ear, quite hard. The row continued over lunch. After it, when they were going down river in the Dors cabin cruiser, with Rex sinking into a silent, sullen temper, Kay suddenly jumped over the side. Rex was compelled to leap into the water after her. He finished the day's outing, surly as hell, drying out in a towel and bathrobe while his clothes steamed on the radiator.

The truth was that his self-esteem had been badly wounded by Carlos Thompson's reappearance. One day, when he was visiting Lilli in her flat, he idly opened a drawer, his mind on something else, and saw a man's jockstrap in it. Carlos was an exercise freak, but it symbolized for Rex his wife's intimate relationship with young 'Coverboy'. He more than ever missed Lilli's orderly touch. Kay's charms were of the unpredictable, zany kind. Fun, yes – in a mistress. But in a wife ...? Rex's sister always felt he enjoyed the energy they each put into the relationship, but was quite unsuited to settling down together for a long run. 'In my opinion, so many of the women my brother met pushed *him* into marriage; which was sad for both of them.'

Eventually, the nightly strain of appearing together in the play, and running love affairs with others by day as well, took its toll on Rex and Lilli.

'They couldn't stand being on stage together and hating each other more and more,' says Laurie Evans, 'and asked me to get them out. So I called Binkie. "I've got a doctor's certificate," I told him, "saying that Rex is exhausted and unable to perform. I have a statement saying much the same from Lilli's doctor." Binkie said, in that cold and steely voice of his, "Then keep them locked up in your desk drawer, my dear Lol, and don't show them to me, ever." '

18: Tyrannosaurus Rex

The show that was to make Rex's name world famous was not at first called *My Fair Lady*. The title that Alan J. Lerner and Frederick Loewe had in mind for their musical version of Shaw's *Pygmalion* was *Lady Liza*. That put Rex on guard immediately. Later on he said he had been unaware there were such things as 'male' and 'female' titles in show-business. He was being disingenuous. All his instincts told him that putting a female title on a show indicated it was a vehicle for a female star. Rex was not going to abdicate what he considered male supremacy, never mind star status, however successful it might turn out. Not until Lerner and Loewe revised the title, and restored a sense of masculine possessiveness with the pronoun 'My,' did Rex accept to star with *any* Fair Lady.

Although Rex now seems, in retrospect, the only possible choice for Henry Higgins, he was not the first choice of Lerner and Loewe. Noël Coward was. According to Sheridan Morley, an executor of the Coward estate, the actor-playwright did not need convincing that *Lady Liza*, as it was still called at the time, would be a huge hit. 'But he couldn't face up to spending a year or two in a hit show consisting of someone else's music and lyrics,' says Morley. 'He declined.' The way was open for Rex.[1]

When they arrived in London in January 1955, Lerner and Loewe and their prospective producer, Herman Levin, begged an interview with Rex, who was in the middle of marital troubles which (according to Lerner) 'were covered in a cloak of secrecy so large it could be seen for ten miles'.[2] The three Americans had already made up their minds: they must have Rex playing Henry Higgins. A run-through of a verse of 'Molly Malone' on the piano after dinner at Claridge's removed any lingering shred of doubt: he had a tenor voice that, though restricted in range, would be heard above an orchestra. Rex then listened to the composer and lyricist performing two of Higgins's songs. In contrast to his non-commital attitude over the larger question of doing the show, his response to the lyrics was immediate. 'I hate them,' he snapped.[3]

Those three words were to prove more creative than dismissive. For he pitched his snap judgment in a tone of voice that made Lerner instantly revise the view of the character. He took Rex's egotistic rasp and made it the key-note of the character. From then on Rex *was* Henry Higgins – he and the character had become interchangeable. Over the following months, Lerner would be writing not so much for Rex as about him. Had Rex taken a liking to the Henry Higgins who had been mellowed for the stage musical, perhaps it would never have enjoyed its phenomenal success.

Significantly, the two songs he rejected both dealt with Higgins's attitude to women: 'Please don't marry me' and then 'Lady Liza' in which Higgins lets slip his affection for the urchin flower girl he has wagered he can transform into a simulacrum of a duchess. Since Rex was still being badgered by Kay to marry her, the first lyric was particularly ill-timed; and the second reminded Rex of who the star of the show was intended to be (at that time) and lacked the egocentric quality that almost every song subsequently written for Higgins had built into it.

But Rex still did not commit himself. He confided his doubts to Sir Malcolm Sargent, the fashionable orchestra conductor, who said, 'If you do this version of *Pygmalion* with music, you'll be making the mistake of your career.'[4] He also feared comparison with Leslie Howard's performance in the film version. Howard had not sung, of course, but he had put such a strong imprimatur on the part that Rex could not see it being played any other way. It took Alan Lerner to arrange a screening of the film before he saw he could create a far less benevolent Higgins than Howard had dared do. Hardly had this doubt been set at rest, however, than a new one arose. Would it mean sacrificing too much of Shaw? Rex felt himself an unofficial trustee for the late playwright, a guardian of his text, and self-interest came into it too. If he could not quite cope with a musical to the standard of perfection he set himself, he could at least triumph as an actor who had no peer when it came to Shavian comedy.

No, said Lerner and Loewe, they had had to promise the Shaw estate they would treat the play with respect. Well, said Rex, he would think about it ... and they did not hear from him for a few weeks.

It is Dirk Bogarde who claims to have brought matters to the sticking point, just when Lerner and Loewe were getting desperate, by suggesting they come down to his country home at the weekend. Rex would be visiting 'the lodger', Kay Kendall, and they could angle for his interest by playing him the songs on Bogarde's spinet, the only kind of piano he owned. Lerner accepted – but Rex again avoided commiting himself.

One wonders whether Kay Kendall at this time ever fancied herself as Eliza Doolittle. Impossible to answer with certainty, of course, but not improbable. After all, she was a singer, a dancer, a music-hall artiste; she had the looks and was not so old at twenty-nine that stage make-up could not have plausibly subtracted a few years. And Rex himself recalled that 'she had grown up in the area of Covent Garden and knew every lane and byway of that warren'.[5] Moreover, she would have no trouble speaking Cockney, a difficult art which would prove to be the making or breaking of many a hopeful Eliza who tested for future productions of the show.

It was not until mid-February that Rex took Lerner and Loewe for a brisk two-hour walk around Hyde Park and, just when the more compact Americans were ready to drop, stopped short and said he would do it. 'I don't know why, but I have faith in you.'[6]

Exultant, Lerner and Loewe returned to America – Levin, a shorter-tempered man, had already left. And Rex got on with playing *Bell, Book and Candle*, though he and Lilli hardly spoke to each other except on stage. When Rex was in a dilemma – such as the one with Lilli and Kay – he invariably overworked, which is one reason why he agreed to continue in the play and simultaneously direct Edith Evans in an H. M. Tennent production of André Roussin's play *Nina*. This was against his better judgment. A few years earlier, David Niven had appeared in the same play with Gloria Swanson and, fearing all was not going well, had wired Rex and Lilli to come down to Philadelphia to see the try-out and offer advice. In his memoirs, Niven recalled he asked over supper, 'Well, what do you suggest?' ' "Get out of it," said Rex.'[7] Now it was Rex's turn, and he soon realized he should never have become involved in it, for Edith Evans collapsed, had to be replaced by Coral Browne, and for all the sweat and tears he and the cast lavished on this tale of a husband, a wife and a lover – a replication of Rex's own marital mix-up – the play came off within the month.

Instead of showing gratitude for his brave try by agreeing to release him from *Bell, Book and Candle*, the inflexible Binkie Beaumont let Lilli depart – for a film in Germany – and kept Rex on.

What Rex did not realize was the extent to which he had become a pawn in a manoeuvre that would make millions for H. M. Tennent.

As Richard Huggett, Binkie Beaumont's biographer, told the story, Beaumont said he could not dream of closing *Bell, Book and Candle* so long as business was going up – with the Americans in London for the summer tourist season. He was even taking bookings for Christmas and the New Year. Lerner and Loewe panicked. They had been counting on starting rehearsals with Rex in December. Herman Levin arrived back in London and hastily invited Binkie to lunch. Binkie had only one card to play, but it was enough: it was the one with Rex's face on it. It was agreed that he would close his play in November; Rex would be bought out of the remaining term of his contract for £25,000 – the equivalent of over £150,000 today – and H. M. Tennent would acquire the English and Continental rights to *My Fair Lady*, plus 1.5 percent of its Broadway and touring grosses. Rex had never been worth so much – or personally made so little out of it. Yet, as Huggett says, 'Binkie made possible the greatest triumph of Harrison's career.'[8]

He flew to New York in December to start rehearsals. Kay had looked forward to going with him, but Binkie had other plans. He did not want anything or anyone breaking Rex's concentration on the musical, so he offered her the co-starring role beside Robert Flemyng in the touring production of *Bell, Book and Candle* (which immediately became known as *Bell, Book and Kendall*).

'Everyone thought Binkie did it because he liked Kay,' says Flemyng. 'The truth is, he did it because he didn't want Kay following Rex to New York and fucking things up. I told Binkie, "I don't want Kay Kendall, she can't act." When she showed up, I'd say: "Take two paces to the right and then turn." She'd ask if Lilli had done that and I'd say, "I suppose she did." After a few days of this agony, a letter arrived from Binkie enclosing one from Rex. It was fairly blunt: "All this fucking about with Kay must stop." She collapsed in tears when I showed her the letter and said, "What's this?" "I'm so unhappy about Rex that I don't know what I'm doing." She wanted him to marry her, and he wouldn't. From that time, we became good friends. The play was a success, because everyone said, "Oh, there's the girl who was in *Genevieve*," and came to see it.'

Tyrone Power had lent Rex his Manhattan apartment: it was small but pretty, and overlooked the city. As soon as he arrived, Lerner and Loewe played him the last number for Higgins: 'I've grown accustomed to her face'. Rex was thrilled. Here was a lyric that could use all his acting nuances, yet had been adroitly written within the musical range of his singing voice, about three notes that is.

During the previous few months Rex had gone to a *bel canto* expert to see what he could do to increase his range. By mutual agreement, the attempt was soon abandoned. Alan Lerner finally put him on to the man who gave him the clue. Bill Low had had to cope with singers (and non-singers) of all sorts and conditions from his redoubt in the pit at the London Coliseum, where he conducted the orchestra. He told Rex to reverse the procedure, let the orchestra follow *him*. And don't try to sing the words, just speak them – but on pitch.

Actually, this was an old English music-hall technique much used by comedians who wanted their jokes to terminate in a patriotic song, but who did not have voices that were up to the quality of the sentiments. Instead, they recited the words on pitch with the orchestra, so to speak, clipping them on the heels. Rex's sense of timing had been helped by his love of jazz and swing. It was an exhausting technique, but effective. Sometimes, after *My Fair Lady* had become a tremendous hit, he would relax on a Saturday night and actually *sing* the numbers: it was much less fatiguing than continuously hitting the pitch.

At rehearsals Rex worried his way through every line of the book as well as the lyrics, questioning this and that interminably. Occasionally, he would suspect Shaw had been 'got at', and then he would call out, 'Where's my Penguin?' and check the script against the text printed in the Penguin edition of the play. This ritual became so familiar that Lerner bought a stuffed penguin from a taxidermist, mounted it on wheels, and had it brought on stage at Rex's next outburst.

Rex, to tell the truth, was glad of a rest from Kay. He did not pine for her that much. He said to Lerner, '[It] isn't how much I will miss Kay that bothers me. But what will I do for fun?'[9]

He found Lerner's own misogyny very much to his taste. The lyricist had almost exactly the same attitude to women as Rex. He put into words what Rex already had in his head. It is a curious irony that *My Fair Lady*, for all its eponymous gallantry, is a continuous demeaning of the fair sex. Lerner had the advantage over Shaw: his multiple marriages had allowed him to test practice against theory and speak with rueful conviction. 'The commitment to marriage can frequently arouse some rather peculiar behaviour, in men and women alike,' he wrote in his memoirs, 'but the bizarre notion that one can change the character of one's mate seems to occur more often to women than to men.'[10] One marriage down, and one tottering, were bringing Rex round to that point of view too. Towards the end of his life, Alan J. Lerner remarked to the actor, 'It's a melancholy fact, Rex, that between us we have supported more women than Playtex.'[11]

The melody and wit of the women-mocking lyrics fortunately reduced the offensiveness, just as the shared misogyny of Rex, Lerner and Bernard Shaw gave a seamlessness rare in musicals then or since. Unsurprisingly, though, constant rehearsal and repetition reinforced Rex's own misogyny. There were outbursts that, even for him, seem excessive, as if the anthem to male superiority stayed on his lips long after he had stopped moving them on pitch. Over supper at the try-out in Philadelphia, Lerner's wife Nancy had a mild difference of opinion with her husband and remarked,

'No, I don't think so.' Rex instantly roared, 'You bitch! Who are you to disagree with him?'[12]

Julie Andrews had been cast as Eliza. She had perfect pitch and she could sing – none of which endeared her to the suspicious man who could muster only three notes. The price of stardom being eternal vigilance, Rex watched so carefully to see that the centre of power did not shift from Higgins to Eliza that Moss Hart, who was directing, finally rehearsed Julie Andrews alone.

Rex also threw his weight around over his colleague Robert Coote, who was playing Colonel Pickering and had developed a bit of business, telephoning a friend called Boosie at the Foreign Office, into a model of well-timed comedy. But Rex was concerned that Higgins had no musical 'spot' between Eliza's triumph at the diplomatic ball and his own plaintive admission that he'd grown accustomed to her face. Nancy Lerner came up with the sort of notion that contributed to the male bonding of her husband and Rex – namely, that a woman does not know what she wants. This became the lyric 'Why can't a woman be more like a man' – and Rex suggested the perfect 'home' for it. Bring Higgins on and off stage, working his way through the lyric with exasperated energy, while Pickering is making that phone call. The result was a gratifying switch in the audience's attention from Coote to Rex. 'Bobby Coote was a prickly old pro,' says Robert Flemyng. 'He never forgave Rex for having his telephone act cut to the bone and robbing him of the laughs he'd worked so hard for.'

Another strained relationship was Rex's with Stanley Holloway, playing Doolittle the dustman. Holloway was a robust character with music-hall soil still clinging to his hobnails and he particularly disliked what he regarded as 'side': an overbearing attitude combined with an assumed superiority. Rex, in turn, hated what he regarded as Holloway's 'stage manner'. He complained to Moss Hart that Holloway was always playing to the audience, not to his fellow actors. There was some truth in this. But Holloway's hackles were raised by Rex's condescension. Though thorough professionals on stage, the two seldom exchanged a social word.

Rex's relationship with Cecil Beaton, who was doing the costumes, was strained by both men's perfectionism. Rex endlessly questioned the niceties of a gentleman's wardrobe in the Edwardian era, a period that Beaton almost considered his own invention. All Rex's tweedy suits and cardigans were tailored or bought in London. Professor Higgins's soft tweed hat was made for him by Herbert Johnson, the Bond Street hatters. It became so much Rex's 'trademark', too, that he wore one like it for the rest of his life and was extremely irritated to learn that the shop had supplied an identical one to William S. Paley, the American broadcasting magnate. Beaton could be a tyrant himself. In Rex, he met his match. 'Very tiresome,' he recorded in his diaries.[3] A sigh of understatement.

But tiresome or not, Rex had to be tolerated, indulged, flattered ... 'Tyrannosaurus Rex,' as he came to be labelled, was hatched in these days.

One man who stood up to him was Moss Hart, particularly when they clashed over Eliza's number 'Without you', a paean of feminine triumphalism in which she exults over Higgins after winning the wager for him at the ball: 'Without your pushing them, the clouds roll by/ If they can do without you, ducky, so can I.' Rex refused to stand passively by and take everything his leading lady could throw at him. The *Cocktail Party* itch to invent a bit of business and hold the audience was still strong. Hart met him head on and told him he could walk off the stage if he liked while Julie Andrews was singing and return when she finished, but 'you'll look the biggest horse's ass in the history of the theatre'.[4] They arrived at a compromise: a shameless transfer of the credit from Eliza to her mentor. The instant Julie Andrews finished, before her last note had died away, Rex shot in with a crow of, 'By George, I really did it/ I did it, I did it/ I said I'd made a woman. And indeed I did.'

He came in on cue so quickly that the audience would have no time to applaud Julie Andrews. (Exactly the same routine occurs in the film.) Diverting his co-star's moment of victory to his own credit shows why Rex, like many a Caesar, always kept a wary eye on his cohorts. Every night could be an ides of March.

He also alarmed Lerner and Loewe, and made them wonder for a moment if they had made a horrible mistake in casting him. At the first rehearsals in New York Rex sounded, well, *hammy*. He was over-emphasising things. He did not seem capable of speaking the lyrics on pitch except in a manner that was far too dramatic. Their nervousness increased until, gradually and then quite quickly, Rex went into reverse, toned down his act, began to get everything beautifully right. What he had been doing was blocking it all out in his mind and taking the measure of his co-stars, all of them musical pros, himself the only 'amateur'. Frankly, they had terrified him.

The first preview was to be held in New Haven, Connecticut: opening on a Saturday, then doing a week's performances from Monday. This was when Rex got his biggest fright. Up to then he had been rehearsing with a stage piano. Now he discovered he could not hear the melody amidst the competitive fervour of the orchestral accompaniment. And that was not all. One of his most artful dodges became useless – the pause. Harold French claims he taught Rex this trick. 'Rex in the early days used to copy the mannerisms I had. The pause was one of them.

A very difficult thing to pause *effectively* – but he was soon a master.' However, with a thirty-two-piece orchestra on one's tail, a pause was impossible. He had to keep on following the melody, singing through the laughs, at least until he got the hang of it and insisted the orchestra take its timing from him. At first, it was like crossing a high wire without a balancing pole: one had to take it at the run or perish.

Once he discovered this, Rex issued an ultimatum: he could not possibly open on Saturday; he would need all Sunday to rehearse with the orchestra; even Monday was in doubt.

His behaviour fed the company's latent *schadenfreude*. Some were appalled at seeing the star in a state of funk; others were half-delighted at what they felt to be a well-merited come-uppance. The management tried to dissuade ticket-holders from turning up on the Saturday by announcing the postponement, 'for technical reasons', on the local radio every half hour; and it began to snow. But from late afternoon the line of people formed: those who had not heard or did not heed the news. Rex remained locked in his dressing-room, never before or since so frightened. Moss Hart, Herman Levin, and his New York agent all took turns pounding at the door, begging, cajoling, ordering him to come out. It was useless. Then things turned ugly. Robert Morley tells, with relish, how the impasse was resolved. 'The manager or a representative of the chain of theatres arrived, wrote a message on a sheet of paper, slipped it under the door. Five minutes later the door opened, Rex appeared in make-up and costume, shot a glance of mingled self-sacrifice and murder at everyone and agreed to be ready for curtain-up. "What did you say?" they asked the miracle worker. "Nothing," he is said to have replied, "I just wrote down the figure we were going to sue him for." '[5]

Apocryphal or not, the story had a happy ending. The curtain rose late, at 8.30 pm, and fell even later, at 12.45 am; but, when the last hurrahs had subsided, the audience knew it had not just seen a show – it had witnessed a tremendous piece of theatrical history.

Rex began very shakily. He did not recover his nerve until the tremendous applause that greeted 'Why can't the English'. By the time of 'The rain in Spain', he was rampant again. When he finished 'Grown accustomed to her face', he was triumphant, as confident of his success as Higgins was of his.

Throughout the week, his dressing-room held many times its own volume of people congratulating him. One night, as the well-wishers dwindled, a woman entered: Lilli. Financing her flight to America by an appearance on the Perry Como Show, she had come to plead for a divorce. Rex would not hear of it. She would make a fool of herself, he told her, marrying a much younger man. Besides, what would happen to Carey? It was plain to Lilli that 'What would happen to Rex?' was at the heart of his reluctance to face up to the situation. Marriage to Lilli, however strained or even estranged it might be, was the best excuse he could make to Kay when she kept on begging him to make her his wife. Rex liked variety, but hated change – most of all the change that a new wife brought. They talked until the early hours of the morning, then walked back through the snow to the hotel – to lead separate lives, but stay husband and wife. Lilli returned to Europe, to Carlos and another film in Germany. Rex went on to Broadway, to Kay and to his greatest success.

The police barriers went up early on the day of 15 March 1956, mounted officers on patient horses marshalling the crowds behind them. It seemed every celebrity in New York without a show of his or her own was in the Mark Hellinger auditorium.

Time magazine later described Rex's entrance with a precision and clarity that few of the other reviews, despite or perhaps because of their unbridled enthusiasm, managed to do:

Out from behind a pillar [of the Covent Garden set] pops a man – lean and lank, cave-chested, middle-aged, his head stooped forward as if he were perpetually peering over invisible glasses. His accent is meticulously English, his habitual mood one of irascible impatience. His face scrooches up into a demoniacal, teeth-baring grimace that makes him look like a dissipated Walt Disney wolf, or falls into sagging folds reminiscent of a despondent bloodhound. He is insulting and invincible and indifferently cruel. The audience sees his charm and falls into a trance. He raps out songs in a voice that would insult a blue jay, but when he croaks a gruff admission of love for the little flower girl ... there is a lump in many a throat.[16]

For Rex, that night just ten days after his forty-eighth birthday was the most memorable of his career. Had he played no other role thereafter, he would still have been safe in legend – and not only legend. As news and reviews of his performance were disseminated far and wide throughout the world, 'Professor Higgins' passed into the demotic speech of people who would never see Rex. 'Are you a Professor Higgins type?' this writer recalls a black Nubian guide at the pyramids in Giza asking an Englishman sweltering in his cardigan and tweedy hat. The gap between the human being and the perceived image of him, which is where stardom is formed, closed that first night and sealed Rex in with his creation for the rest of his life. The vast majority of mankind could not tell the difference between them – or did not want to.

Marilyn Monroe, Charles Laughton, Cole Porter, Louis Armstrong, Spencer Tracy arriving with Frank Sinatra and saying – rather sweetly,

Change of scene: Rex, now signed up by Twentieth Century-Fox, leaves their rented home in Beverly Hills for the morning drive to work.

Living up to his name: Rex in *Anna and the King of Siam*, a role that suited his regal disposition and, in lieu of love scenes, brought out all his coercive charm.

In *The Foxes of Harrow*: an ill-fated attempt to turn Rex into a carbon-copy Errol Flynn, complete with moustache, hell-raiser shirt and bull whip.

With Gene Tierney in *The Ghost and Mrs Muir*: a very macho spectre, but, alas, no touching allowed.

Assignation in London: Rex seized the chance of making *Escape* to see his mistress, Carole Landis, with a little help from his old friend Arthur Barbosa.

Jealous husband plots murder: with Linda Darnell in *Unfaithfully Yours*.

Rex and Lilli board the boat train in 1948, after his English film *Escape*. Lilli probably suspected his infidelity; Rex never expected the tragedy it would bring in a few months.

As Henry VIII in *Anne of the Thousand Days*, accounted one of his greatest stage performances. After the show, he headed for the jazz clubs and bordellos of Harlem.

A life in one room: Rex and Lilli in *The Four-Poster*. *Clockwise from below*: as newly-weds; in mid-marriage crisis; when love outlasts old age.

The stars (and the newly-weds) in their prime in *The Reluctant Debutante*: Rex's marriage to Kay Kendall, third wife, matched his triumph in *My Fair Lady*. Privately, he had to endure the secret of her fatal illness

above right: More like pals than a married couple: Rex and Kay enjoying every moment of life together.

Rex, in his underwear, relaxes with Kay in the sunshine soon after their marriage.

Rex directs Kay in the ill-fated *The Bright One*: a 'dreadful little play,' said Noël Coward, 'in which she was enchanting.'

Their last weeks together in Portofino: despite the smiles for the camera, the handclasp has a hint of desperation. A month later, Kay died from leukemia.

Rex with his two sons leaving Kay Kendall's memorial service at St Martin-in-the-Fields, London, in September 1959. Noel Harrison (with his wife) is on the left: Carey Harrison is on Rex's right.

Collette Harrison in the early 1960s: Rex's first wife was soon to take up work for church charities.

Rex thought – that he had 'made the little Wop cry': these were a few of the talented and famous who felt a talismanic need to go round after the show and fête Rex. Even T. S. Eliot allowed that Shaw had been greatly improved by the music. They were, Rex recalled, compliments from giants but now they were also tributes from equals.

The reviews put his ascension beyond doubt. Only one theatregoer is on record as coming away unimpressed. 'I thought it was the dullest, lousiest show I had ever seen. Even as *Pygmalion* without Harrison it was pretty bad; with Rex Harrison it is awful. I had always considered Professor Higgins the most loathsome of all stage characters, but I never realized how loathsome he could be until I saw Sexy Rexy playing him."[7] Thus P. G. Wodehouse, as unyielding as he had been when he saw Rex and Lilli in *Venus Observed* and tried to go to sleep. Frances Donaldson, his biographer, concedes that 'Plum' Wodehouse was a bad critic; and Joseph Connolly, another Wodehouse scholar, adds that he nourished a lifelong grudge against anything 'smart'. Perhaps Rex had played too many Wodehouse-type characters in his salad days on tour and made no secret of his opinion of them.

Rex now rented an out-of-town place within easy reach, a seafront cottage on the Long Island estate of Michael Phipps, the international polo player – Wodehouse country, all right, if he had cared to admit it. He had moved into the house by the time he had to endure an inquisition by *Time*, which was preparing to put him on its 23 July cover. He recalled it as being like a Feydeau farce, since Kay Kendall, who had moved in with him, had to keep tip-toeing from room to room, a step ahead of *Time*'s team, lest they caught sight of her and hinted that 'Professor Higgins' was keeping a mistress. It was not yet the Swinging Sixties.

Kay had arrived in April, at the end of her *Bell, Book and Candle* tour, when Rex was safely on the other side of *My Fair Lady*'s opening. These were the happiest months of Rex's life. He socialized with the 'Old Money' Americans represented by the summer migrants to Long Island; took long walks around the Long Island shore with Kay; went sailing on the Sound with her; and six nights a week played to full houses. Even visiting VIPs had to beg management to let them sit on a chair in the wings. It particularly pleased Rex to see the rich and famous endure such discomfort for the contiguous privilege of seeing him. Kay would often stand in the wings while he sang 'Grown accustomed to her face' looking in her direction. If Rex's performance drooped a little from weariness or sheer repetition, Moss Hart had only to drop the name of a celebrity who would be coming that night, and Rex became miraculously refreshed. When he was out of the show with mild throat trouble, the ticket touts sent him a message to get well and come back as soon as he could: their business was being disastrously affected.

Rex and Kay had their rows, of course. 'When she spoke her mind, boy did she get it all said!' says Jones Harris, adding, 'That was the Irish side of her.' Her high spirits struck sparks when they clashed with Rex's ingrained stubbornness. But some days, Rex noticed, she looked unusually listless, while on others, she had enough energy for two – or three. Had he been more attentive, he might also have noticed how feverish some of her pranks had become. One day, she pulled a black bin liner over herself and hid in the garbage tip while her house-guests searched for her. Another time, she left what purported to be a ransom demand from her kidnappers. Rex was already calling the local police when she jumped out from behind a curtain. In his relief, he hit her, as one might smack a naughty child who has innocently done something dangerous. 'You bugger!' she cried and burst into tears. He soothed her until she had forgiven him in the sort of baby-talk that betokened a child's need for affection. 'I's sorry, Miss Scarlett,' was one of her favourite ways of showing contrition, by mimicking Scarlett O'Hara's cute but helpless child-servant played by Butterfly McQueen in *Gone With the Wind*. Then Rex found it impossible not to kiss and fuss over her. He might have speculated, though he did not, why she so often resorted to antics designed to get people's attention and consideration for her well-being. But he did not do so. He put her tiredness down to the anaemia she said she had had from childhood, and he just loved her high spirits.

In the autumn, they both checked into hospital: Rex for a routine examination as the new Broadway season got under way, Kay because she had had some mild headaches which kept recurring.

Their New York physician was a Dr Atchley, who was later to be described by Rex in terms that strongly recall his own role as the omnipotent psychiatrist in *The Cocktail Party*. This 'dedicated and priestlike old man of good intentions' recalled Kay for some extra blood tests.[18] Rex recorded the doctor calling him at the theatre shortly before Christmas and asking to see him. What Dr Atchley said on that occasion has never been divulged, but Rex made an appointment for after the holidays.

Dirk Bogarde and Tony Forwood were their house-guests for what Kay called an old-fashioned English-style American Christmas, which is to say one considerably more American than most folk in England nowadays stage: holly wreaths, scarlet ribbons, ivy-covered boughs, Christmas carols on the record-player, a huge tree plastered in lights and bedecked with bows. Bogarde noted that, 'Sometimes in the hurry and rush there came a little pause. Suddenly tired, [Kay] would crumple into a huge armchair ... "Oh, wifey," she would sob happily, but tired, "I'm getting to be an old, old woman." "[9]

Rex may have been more alarmed than he let on by these spells of tiredness. There is a strong probability he had an inkling that more was wrong with Kay than he or she had been told. Nothing is more disconcerting than a doctor who is unusually reticent. Kay was to leave for Hollywood immediately after Christmas to make a film, *Les Girls*, directed by George Cukor. Later, Rex told his few intimate friends that he had been unwilling to hear what the doctor had to tell him until Kay had left for the Coast – a decision open to the interpretation that he either distrusted his own ability to conceal it, should it be bad news, or was unwilling to accept the responsibility of telling her.

He could not go with her to the airport, for he had a matinée, but Bogarde and Forwood saw her off, a picture of misery bundled up in her black mink with Gladys Cooper's corgi for company. That evening, according to a friend, Bogarde or Forwood stood in the wings while Rex sang his tender ballad to 'her face'.

When Rex kept his appointment with Dr Atchley is not known, but it was probably at the very end of the year; for he immediately sent an express letter to Lilli, who was ski-ing with Carey in the Austrian Tyrol. 'I remember it very clearly,' says Carey today. 'We were in Kitzbuhel when the letter arrived. I recall her being in tears, in the bathroom, and then having a terrible scene with me because I couldn't respond to her distress. I was aged twelve and she couldn't explain why she was so upset. She probably felt it all too complicated for a child to understand.'

Lilli flew to New York at the turn of the year, leaving Carey with his aunt in London, and she and Rex saw Dr Atchley on 2 January 1957. Rex never referred to this later meeting. His memoirs give the impression that there was only one meeting with Dr Atchley – his own – and he took all the decisions following it. Lilli's memoirs, published eighteen years later, describe the later appointment. 'Although in general matters,' says Carey Harrison, 'my mother was not always a trustworthy witness, I would go along with her account of this occasion. It was typical of Rex to "censor her out" of many events in his life, particularly one as sensitive as Kay's future with him.'

The interview must be one of the most bizarre in medical history. Dr Atchley, in Lilli's account, comes across as a man with an in-built sense of theatre quite as much as an unorthodox attitude to medical etiquette. In brief, he repeated to both of them what he must already have told Rex: that Kay had an incurable illness, myeloid leukemia, and possibly had no more than three years to live. Nothing could be done. He was aware, he said, that he was informing the husband in the presence of his wife about a death sentence that fate had passed on his mistress. Kay wanted to marry Rex, he said: she had told him so. Were Rex and Lilli willing to divorce, so that he could do so and look after her for the time she had left? If not, she would have to be told and helped to bear the future as well as she could.

19: The Masquerade

Lilli says she immediately assured Dr Atchley that Rex would stand by his moral obligations: he would marry Kay and take care of her for as long as she had left to live. Sounding even more like Eliot's God-like Sir Henry Harcourt-Reilly, though in flatter prose, the physician followed up his prognosis with his blessing: 'You are both good Christian people.'¹ Lilli, a Jewess, says she let that pass, understandably in these charged circumstances.

If this account is accurate, Rex must have left the doctor's suite alarmed and enraged. Alarmed at Dr Atchley's finite diagnosis: the disease was untreatable. Enraged that Lilli had usurped his right of decision by making up his mind for him. His self-esteem had been as badly wounded as his love for his stricken mistress. He felt morally blackmailed.

Lilli describes how she argued the case for her divorcing Rex and him marrying Kay as she and her husband walked back to his apartment. Rex resisted her logic. She leaves the impression that his concern was not simply with Kay's early demise, but with the loneliness that would be his as a widower. Perhaps Lilli saw this tragic turn of events as the opportunity she needed to cut herself free of Rex – after two years' separation – in order to marry Carlos Thompson. It is quite probable. As for Rex, he was now well and truly trapped between self-interest and compassion. According to Lilli, he did not know what to do. But by the time his memoirs came out eighteen years later, his mind had cleared and, by his account, he was quite sure what he had to do: 'I would marry her because I loved her.'² Lilli, in turn, was to dismiss this picture of a conscience-stricken Rex as 'a fairy tale'.³ She remembers his saying, after anguished reflection, 'I could marry [Kay] if you promised to come back to me when – when it's all over.'⁴

It is only fair to Rex to recall that, when Lilli attributed this remarkable proposal to him, she herself had become a best-selling novelist in her native Germany. However, assuming she is a reliable witness to her own self-interest, she was naturally hesitant about falling in with this plan.

But, as Rex pursued the argument for remarriage to Lilli after Kay's demise, he became increasingly convinced of its good sense, and began to talk more calmly and reasonably. This rings true. It shows Rex repositioning himself at the centre of the drama. Finally, Lilli says, she agreed, feeling she had no right to her own happiness while Rex was about to enter into the most painful relationship of his life and, incidentally, his most protracted performance – nursing a dying woman without letting her know she was dying. Lilli pledged herself to return to him when the time came. She admitted to herself that, in so saying, she was lying.

Thus everyone – except poor Kay – could claim (and later did) to have acted with the noblest of motives; and even Lilli's false promise, in these tragic circumstances, would seem a forgivable deceit. It was an extraordinary situation they had got themselves into, the sort that playwrights invent. The battle of the moral self against the superficial self deserved Eliot; instead, eighteen years later, it was to get Rattigan.

'I will never let a woman in my life,' Rex was singing nightly. Now he went on stage knowing he had to devote the next few years of his life to a woman who must not know how little time she had left to her to live her own. This meant he must go on behaving to Kay the way he usually did. He was genuinely heartbroken to think of this beautiful woman having a stern term set to her existence. It quickened his love for her, having a part to play. He would have to take care not to show unusual solicitude and anxiety if she suffered one of the bouts of fatigue she put down to simple anaemia. Kay had a telepathic sensitivity. What Rex had to fear most was that she might intuit the truth about herself. No fussing, then; it would still have to be, 'Fetch my slippers, Eliza,' and brace himself for her flinging them at him.

Immediately she left New York, Lilli started work on her divorce. She filed the suit in Juarez, Mexico, on 4 February 1957. As well as saving time, a 'quickie divorce' in Mexico assisted secrecy. A large number of similar petitions were routinely processed daily. Lilli used her family name of 'Peiser' and cited 'Reginald' in place of the more famous 'Rex'. As there was no opposition, simply a formal declaration of incompatibility and irreconcilable differences, the application was granted and Lilli won custody of Carey and a half share in the Villa San Genesio.

Her move was soon uncovered by the media, but the change in her manner, when she was interviewed while passing through London on 6 February, might have alerted the press even earlier. Hitherto she had always deflected questions about a reconciliation with Rex; not any longer. 'Let's face it,' she said, 'Englishmen don't like women, at least not in the way that Italians or Frenchmen do. Englishmen don't ever really look at a woman. The greatest compliment Rex could pay me was to say that being with me was as good as being with a pal.'⁵ She referred to him now as 'Harrisburg' and 'the youngest blimp'.⁶

While Lilli chilled the prospects of reconciliation, the husband whom she was secretly divorcing was arriving in Hollywood on two weeks' leave from *My Fair Lady* to be at Kay's side. She had been running on her energy since starting *Les Girls*. Occasionally it failed her, and then Cukor had to shoot round her wan countenance. Studios required stars to take a medical examination for insurance purposes, but a blood test was not part of this. As any sign of illness had, as likely as not, disappeared the next day, MGM had no cause to suspect they had a dying star in their film. Rex later said he went resolved to tell Kay the truth, but, when he saw her, she looked so ravishing he could not bring himself to do so.

His dilemma continued as Kay dragged him to all the Hollywood parties, when he knew she should be home in bed, but dared not say that to her lest it arouse her suspicion. At producer Charles Feldman's home he caught her chatting to Frank Sinatra in the chill midnight air of the terrace. 'Come home,' he snapped, 'you bloody well know it's past your bedtime.' Kay was aware of Rex's jealousy if a wife or girlfriend spent too much time with another man, however famous, and took this to be the Rex she knew, loved and fought with – as he had intended. 'But I'm admiring Frank's shirt, wifey,' she teased. 'Don't you think it's beautiful?'

'I don't give a fuck about Frank's shirt,' Rex said, seizing her arm, 'come home.'

Sinatra then looked directly at Rex and said, 'Yes, it's just an old shirt, Rex, a bit off-white, sort of *yellow*.'⁷ Whether intended or not, Sinatra's emphasis on the word 'yellow' caused Rex to recall the taunt made at the time of his hasty exit from the film colony over Carole Landis's death. He slapped Sinatra on the face.

Fortunately for Rex, perhaps, Sinatra did not answer him in kind, but simply repeated, 'It's still *yellow*.' Rex hit him again. Kay screamed an oath at Rex and ran off. Terence Rattigan, who was in Hollywood writing his script for *Separate Tables*, pulled Rex away. Sinatra calmly walked back into the drawing-room. The two men later made things up when Bing Crosby brought them together at Palm Springs.

On 17 February Rex learned that Lilli's Mexican petition had been granted. The next day he and Kay celebrated their engagement over a snack of hamburgers and malteds in her MGM dressing-room. They still had to wait for the divorce to be finalized under American law.

When she finished shooting, Kay moved with Rex into the annex, called The Boathouse, of Jock Whitney's magnificent Long Island mansion.

Rex's sister came to see him that spring. She had another object in mind besides enjoying his Professor Higgins. 'I really didn't think Rex and Kay were suited to each other and I wanted to dissuade him. He half confessed to me that he had a moral obligation to marry her. "She gets in such a state if I suggest our not marrying," he added.' Sylvia left without persuading her brother to her viewpoint – or, indeed, without Rex having made his mind up.

His nerves were continually stretched. The least flare-up of Kay's nervous agitation, or signs of tiredness, compelled him to keep her under close observation that day, all the time concealing his concern. He would telephone Lilli, wherever she was, and report on his 'watch and ward' agony. From time to time he was able to have Kay's health monitored more accurately by taking her for a medical check-up under the pretence of keeping tabs on her anaemia. By June her condition had worsened slightly; then the phone calls to Lilli grew panic-stricken. He settled the wedding date as soon as he could. On 23 June 1957, after the show in which an extremely nervous Rex had fluffed some of his lines, they exchanged vows around midnight – anything to avoid press attention – at the Universalist Church of the Divine Paternity on Central Park West, a place much favoured by Broadway players who knew it by its more convenient label of The Little Church Around the Corner. The chapel was kept open for the late-night ceremony, at which Rex's lawyer, Aaron Frosch, and Kay's sister Kim, who was now living on Long Island with her banker husband, were witnesses. Kay was a little woosy from medication she had taken for her nerves and got a fit of the giggles, which drew the minister's soft reproof. Rex had had a few stiff drinks and was highly nervous. Their wedding 'breakfast' was at Orsini's, well after midnight. To console Kay for the lack of a romantic ambience, a second ceremony was held soon afterwards on a warm afternoon at the agent Leland Hayward's house on Long Island. Rex then wrote a heart-rending letter to Lilli to repeat, like a dutiful son, that he had kept his part of the bargain. 'But my brother was still terribly hurt by what he called Lilli's "defection",' says Sylvia. 'His self-esteem was injured. One did not mistreat that with impunity.'

By agreement, Rex and Lilli now used the Villa San Genesio in turn. There was a scare *en route* when Rex and Kay went there that autumn. As he drove them from Genoa along the beautiful coast road, the russet hill slopes rising steeply on their right, the emerald sea on the left, nothing seemingly changed since the day he had landed in Portofino's harbour, Rex's for once tranquil thoughts were broken by Kay saying, 'What rubbish they print.'[8] She had been puzzling her way through a mass-circulation Italian magazine. 'It says here I've got leukemia.'

'Obviously they mean anaemia,' Rex said as evenly as he could. But it was a shock to know Kay's real illness was a matter of international gossip.

The incident only entrenched the opinions he held about the press. 'Is it possible,' he said to Aaron Frosch, 'to imagine the depravity of a man who will write a magazine article without caring whether or not Kay knew the truth? If anything proves how right I am to give the whole fucking press wide berth, it's this. You only suck up to them if you're a cabbage or a crook.'[9]

The masquerade, besides taking its toll on Rex's nerves, also began to affect his performance as Higgins. He found himself dwelling on Kay's condition as he did the numbers. Then he had a couple of horrifying experiences when he suddenly forgot the words. For safety's sake, he took to repeating the lyrics to himself all the way through before every show, excluding everyone from his dressing-room, even Kay. He ran other risks, too, not to do with loss of memory, but on one occasion coming close to loss of life. A forty-foot beam suddenly broke away, falling behind the curtain in front of which he was performing. The curtain billowed out with the force of the crash. The audience jumped. The orchestra stopped. Rex recovered from the shock first, called for a clarinet to give him the melody, and resumed. He had not quite finished before the whole house, unable to restrain its admiration for his coolness, broke into a storm of applause. Another time, the reaction was less flattering. A chandelier being hoisted up to the flies caught on his hairpiece and took it aloft too. To his credit, he carried on just as coolly as he had when he had come within an ace of being crushed, not scalped.

Finally, on 2 December 1957, he played his last show. Kay played it with him, anonymously, having changed places with the Queen of Transylvania in Act One and then Mrs Higgins's maid in Act Two.

They stepped off the *Queen Mary* at Cherbourg, not Southampton, so that Rex would not jeopardize his tax-free status by setting foot on English soil after two years' absence. What was he going to do, asked the inescapable reporter on the quay. 'Rest, rest, rest,' he snapped. But he knew it was an untruth. He and Kay had already agreed to play Lord and Lady Broadbent, an international banker and his disarmingly scatty wife, in the film of William Douglas Home's successful play *The Reluctant Debutante*, which Vincente Minnelli was to direct in Paris – again to help Rex's tax status. He had dismissed the script when first sent it. It had been vulgarly Americanized. Minnelli promised revisions and a return to aristocratic British folkways. While this was being done, Rex and Kay went to Switzerland, calling first at Vevey-sur-Corsaire to see

Charlie Chaplin, whose wife Oona had been one of Kay's pals when Charlie Chaplin's son Sidney used to date her. Chaplin tried interesting Rex in appearing in his next film, a shipboard comedy about a British ambassador who mistakes a high-class prostitute for a titled English-woman. (It was later made, disastrously, as *A Countess from Hong Kong* with Marlon Brando and Sophia Loren). Rex listened politely, demurred and later said to Kay, with an entirely accurate forecast of what eventually happened: 'Charlie's brilliant, but he wants everyone to act in his style.'[10]

They went on to St Moritz, where Rex had taken a chalet at £100 a week. 'Good God,' cried his old friend, the Earl of Warwick, 'do you have to pay for food and servants on top of that?'[11] A room at the Palace Hotel could then be had for £5 a night. Rex was thought to be living very extravagantly, but then his immediate neighbours were Opel, the car magnate, and Springer, the publishing tycoon. They had hardly settled in before Kay's temperature soared to 103°F and Rex, thinking the end had come for her even sooner that Dr Atchley had forecast, called in an English physician and told him the truth. He also told Terence Rattigan, who was a house-guest. The blood tests on Kay proved so alarming that she was put in a clinic and there she might have languished or expired but for a Zurich doctor who prescribed pills of his own recipe, which he claimed retarded the spread of the cancer cells. Kay rallied and was back in her snow boots in about three weeks, still unaware of her true condition, and treated by Rex with his customary mix of adoration and snappishness.

Revisions for *The Reluctant Debutante* arrived by special delivery every other day. He rejected them all. 'We wouldn't play one word of your lousy script,'[12] he telephoned the American producer, Pandro S. Berman. Privately, Rex wanted to do the film, if only to keep Kay occupied. Professionally, he knew the longer he temporized the more power he would have. 'He told me, "Widdle it around a bit,"' says his London agent, Laurie Evans.

Noel Harrison was with his mother in Klosters, where Collette had established a successful boutique, when Rex telephoned. 'He sounded so concerned about Kay that I immediately joined him in St Moritz,' says Noel. 'It was then that father told me the truth about her condition. I saw what a burden he'd been carrying since his divorce from Lilli and remarriage. He wondered if she could stand up to the film schedule, if they did *The Reluctant Debutante* in Paris. At the time he was arranging for his Rolls-Royce to be driven from the ski resort to France. "Dad, I'll drive it," I volunteered, and he *must* have been upset, for he let me do it. I later made a brief appearance as an extra in a ballroom scene in the film.'

At the end of the holiday in St Moritz, Rex, Kay and Noel made a short visit to see Collette at Klosters. Ever the tomboy, Kay took to tobogganing, cracking her pelvis. Now two deceptions had to be maintained. When they arrived in Paris, she did all her pre-production press interviews without letting anyone know of her disability, which made standing painful, by lying on a *chaise-longue*. This courtesan-like posture only added to her allure. To Rex's satisfaction and relief, she was passed fit for the film without her pelvic crack or her leukemia being discovered. The screenplay, however, was not yet fit. Rex's deliberate delay in signing a contract produced a production crisis, for he had less than four weeks for the film before reporting for the London production of *My Fair Lady*. So the Hon. William Douglas Home was rushed across to Paris and given a long weekend to bring the screenplay back to something Rex would accept. This he did by bringing much of it back to his original stage play, confident that Hollywood would be so grateful for a 'Yes' from Rex that it would not complain and, indeed, might not even notice. This is precisely what happened.

Some of Rex's objections showed his pernickety nature had not grown any less. 'He took exception to a scene where a young Guards officer arranges an assignation with his girlfriend,' says William Douglas Home.[13] 'He tells her that, if his horse raises its tail as he and his fellow officers ride past, he'll take her out to tea. Rex exploded when he read this. "Do you think a horse with a mechanical tail is funny?" he asked. "Because I damn well don't."' Out went the scene, tail and all.

'Rex was still in a bad temper when he and Kay and myself got together for dinner in Paris,' says Douglas Home. ' "You've sold yourself to the Americans," he barked at me. Kay made to hit him over the head with the wine bottle. The next day, as I slaved away at the script, a scarlet azalea arrived, so big it could barely enter the door of my suite at the Lancaster. The card from Rex said, "Sorry you were there when I saw red." So he could apologise when in the right mood, though ordinarily he didn't give a damn who he offended. We played golf later that same day and he put a ball through the window of the very smart French club house, and laughed it off. They didn't seem to mind, either, though: one of those eccentric things the English do now and then.'

Since his work went quickly, Douglas Home had time to see Rex and Kay socially. It never crossed his mind that Kay was seriously ill. Just the reverse: she seemed in a continuous mood of endearing unpredictability – and would do anything for a joke.

'One night, Rex and she asked my wife and myself to have a drink before dinner in their hotel suite. Rex was wrestling the cork out of the champagne in the kitchen when the phone rang in the sitting-room. "Answer it, Kay," he called. Imagine the captivating bit of eccentricity we witnessed when Kay, responding to her master's voice, emerged from the bathroom with only a hand towel for cover – and that she wore wrapped round her hair.

'She walked past us, unconcerned that she was totally naked, and picked up the phone. It was Sir Gladyn Jebb, then the British Ambassador, asking her and Rex out to dinner. Still standing in the nude, she said sweetly but very firmly, "Rex and I work very hard during the week, Jebby." He must have suggested the weekend. "Well, you see, Rex and I like to dip our fingers in the gin bottle on Saturday nights, Jebby," and she added roguishly, ". . . if you know what I mean." She put down the phone, shrugged her bare shoulders at us, gave us an airy little wave – all as if she were standing there fully dressed – and walked back into the bathroom. The coolest bit of impudence I'd ever seen.'

It was Kay's way of doing what she delighted to do most – shocking the company, but carrying it off like a lady.

Together, she and Rex give the most felicitous performances imaginable in *The Reluctant Debutante*. He was now in his comic prime, buoyed up by the biggest success of his life. Kay, as if converting the fever of illness into the high temperature of controlled comedy, partnered him to perfection. For all the lessons in high comedy it contains, the film should figure permanently on the curriculum of acting schools. The best way of conveying its multiplicity of comic inflections and impeccably timed and mutually dependent nuances of verbal and physical wit is by itemizing the details of their performances. Each of them acts so freshly and patly that the bond between them transcends the merely professional and becomes a deeper kind of union.

Rex is in his aristocratic element as the titled banker. He can act with the whites of his eyes. The crisp, raspy, semi-querulous voice is as neatly in place as the hairpiece. The intonation is a gift to the lines. 'Potato salad,' he declaims, as if announcing someone's title. 'How well do you know Staines?' he is asked by the silly-ass Guardsman who bores everyone by describing how he avoids traffic jams and who sounds like a road map. Rex's reply, 'Not intimately,' is inflected in a manner that would have turned Coward emerald with envy. The very pupils of his eyes seem to be able to harden on command like snipers in two slit trenches whenever he is bored. He has a hundred expressions that would make a playwright cancel out a page of dialogue if only to encourage him to employ one of them. Thus he scavenges among the bottles for anything at all drinkable at one of the endless debutantes' balls he is doomed to attend through the London season, and lights on a triangular shaped one containing an odd blue fluid. He stares at it suspiciously: it is as if the bottle has just propositioned him.

Kay embodies the feminine spirit of comedy, floating in clouds of grey marabou at the balls or carrying off the drawing-room repartee unfazed by the fact that her tomato-red Balmain gown is exactly matched to the colour of the lampshades. Her ski-tip nose gives a pert inflection to her exquisitely boned face. She excels as the fluttery wife who can carry on a telephone conversation while feeling compelled to straighten the ornaments around her, remove a dead flower from the table arrangment and generally demonstrate that her mind is all over the place – at the same time giving an an impression of vulnerability that cries out for protection. Though Rex deploys his Higginsish look of migrained exas-peration, he is part and parcel of their double act. Never, one feels, was he to put himself on such an equal footing with his co-star, deferring to her without fear, rolling with her punches – or doing the opposite when, loaded with drink and swaying dangerously as the National Anthem breaks out in the ballroom, he is tilted upright again by a dig in the ribs from Kay. The two excel at *tête-à-tête* exchanges, she letting her scatty logic blow around like dandelion seeds, he doing a marvellous job just keeping track of it with many a sharply accented 'Eh?' or 'What's that?' He makes expert use of mute double takes and simple gestures that suggest he is trying to translate her words for the benefit of the deaf, then eventually gives up on the sense they may carry even to ears that can hear and suddenly declaims, 'The whole thing is fundamentally insane.' As Kay proposes some particularly hare-brained manoeuvre in the match-making game, he collapses back on to the sofa like a puppet whose strings have been cut, closing his eyes to indicate there is nothing – absolutely *nothing* – more to be said. Douglas Home's comedy is made so much Rex's and Kay's that it is hard to believe anyone else will ever have the impertinence to play it.

None of this, of course, however effortless it may look, was achieved without hours of private rehearsal by the stars. And the old, selfish Rex was not sleeping either. Minnelli's memoirs afford a glimpse of the players off the set. Knowing more than Minnelli obviously did at the time about Rex's chronic self-protectiveness, one can sense how every bit of the script was reconnoitred in advance for its hidden landmines. The director recalls opening the door of his Hotel Georges v suite to a couple of unexpected callers: Rex in an angry, sulky mood and Kay looking very concerned. They apologized for disturbing him, but there was an emergency. They had been looking over the pages of the script they had just received for the next few days and Kay had discovered that, while she had yards of dialogue to speak, Rex had hardly a line. Moreover, the 'silly-ass' young actor who shared the scene with them also went on and on. Kay demanded where Rex's part was. Should there not be another rewrite? Rex said little, but Minnelli guessed he had put Kay up to this *démarche*. Patiently he explained that the wife in the film gabbled ninety to the dozen and the young man in the scene was a prize bore. ' "I assure you," I told Rex and Kay, "that Rex's actions will be so hilarious that it will be his scene. It all plays off Rex." '[4] This is indeed what happens in the film. But a script that did not clearly designate Rex's share of the scene had rung a distant alarm bell in his mind. He was not so green that he could not have anticipated what Minnelli told him. The visit was probably meant as a professional *caveat* to Minnelli that Rex, like time and tide, waited around for no man or woman, especially when playing a scene with them.

The film collected mixed reviews. Critics said it was still a stage play. Thank goodness, this is true. It provides an invaluable permanent record of English high-comedy acting in its prime, dependent for its pitch and subtlety on the players getting enough continuous screen time to create their characters for the camera, not just the cutting-room. It is theatrical, but not 'stagey'.

One of the most perceptive critics, A. H. Weiler of the *New York Times*, paid tribute to Rex for the generous way he partnered Kay. 'She garbles phone numbers, conversations, scandals, and people with blithe abandon. Small talk becomes a minor art as she voices it. As her patient spouse, Mr Harrison is a perfect catcher for the benign inanities she pitches at him.'[5] Not only as an invalid was Kay guarded by Rex over the brief span of their marriage: he sustained her talent as well as her stamina. Weiler also noted the change in the two stars since they had made *The Constant Husband* a few years earlier and had met and fallen in love. 'Although they last appeared together in a film ... some years ago,' Weiler wrote, 'they behave [in *The Reluctant Debutante*] as if they have been frolicking about regularly as a happily married couple.'[6] They did and, of course, that is what they now were. If one wishes to see what life together was like for Rex and Kay when both were in their best temper, he charmingly wry and she adorably scatterbrained, co-habiting a world that only peripherally touched what saner, more settled and infinitely duller mortals called real life, master and mistress of their own egotism, living to the beat of the complex moment as if the heart would never fail, then this is the film that catches the reflection of it.

20: Circle of Deception

Rex was very nearly not in the London production of *My Fair Lady*. His own arrogance was to blame. He arrived in London on 4 April 1958 in a foul temper, physically tired, and tired, too, if truth be told, of Henry Higgins. It would be a tremendous success, he had no doubt of that. Its production cost of £85,000, a huge sum in those days, had been well covered by advance bookings of £132,000 in the four months since tickets (at £1.5s.0d) went on sale. By the time it opened, the Drury Lane Theatre was sold out until January 1960. But Rex dreaded long runs: he knew he would have to fight tooth and nail for his release at the end of the year to which he had agreed. Still, all went well at the read-through, until Moss Hart dismissed the cast, telling them to be back the next day at 10 am prompt for rehearsals. Rex said, 'You won't be needing me, will you? I'll be seeing you in a fortnight or so.'[1]

'But I do need you, Rex,' Hart replied. Rex insisted he knew 'every word and move in the show'.[2] Hart held firm. Rex's irritation turned into irascibility. 'Well, you *won't* be seeing me tomorrow and that's that,' he barked, and out he strode.[3]

The ensuing ructions have been chronicled with the detail and fatefulness of a title fight by Richard Huggett in his Binkie Beaumont biography. Binkie called all parties to a crisis meeting at his home that same evening. Rex insisted ever more stubbornly that the last place he would be found the next morning was the stage of Drury Lane. Beaumont knew that the only argument he had to win with a star of this magnitude and obduracy was the first one, otherwise the war was lost. 'Rex, my dear,' Huggett reports him as saying, 'I'm warning you that if you don't [appear at rehearsals], I will replace you. And I am not bluffing.'[4] Screams and curses followed this ultimatum, climaxing in Rex shouting, 'You Jewish cunt,' at Moss Hart. But Binkie Beaumont was *not* bluffing. As soon as he had heard of Rex's defection, he had called Laurence Olivier, who, Alan J. Lerner revealed later, had indicated an interest in the part before Rex had been cast. Binkie hinted it might be on the market again. Olivier's attitude has not been made public, but Binkie subsequently played his hand with confidence.

After two hours or more of bitter argument, Rex gave up the struggle. Having won the battle, Hart ensured Rex would not regroup for a guerrilla raid. 'Rex, please don't try any tricks, don't pull any fast ones with me ... I know all the tricks and even a few you don't know.'[5]

At 9.55 am the next day Rex's silver-grey Rolls-Royce accelerated past the fans already on duty at the stage door, almost colliding with one of them. Rex was out and inside the theatre without pause or smile. Later that week, with Kay, he went to a Berkeley Square car dealer and bought a new sand-and-sable Rolls-Royce, £6,000-worth of automobile in those days, saying that the grey one was an unlucky car. His status thus reaffirmed, he settled down to work hard and smoothly. Beaumont prudently added his own balm to the hurt feelings by engaging Arthur Barbosa to redecorate the star's dressing-room, which he did over in dark green and damask, correctly believing it corresponded to Rex's penchant for the style of the Edwardian actor-manager.

On 30 April 1958 over 2,000 sightseers blocked the Strand, which had to be closed temporarily. Black-market tickets were fetching 200 times their face value. It was a social, political and diplomatic occasion that even seasoned first-nighters were to compare with Coronation night. In fact, the Queen graced the performance five days later and most of the other Royals in the weeks following. Sylvia witnessed her brother's ecstatic reception: 'I had never seen him so happy.'

Other friends of Rex's sensed a change, too, but of a different kind. 'He developed a sort of remoteness which was a bit discouraging,' Anthony Havelock-Allan says. 'I found myself walking behind him on the street one day. I wondered whether to approach him. Somehow, it seemed to me now that he might resent being tapped on the shoulder. One felt he had become a very private person, as if he had retreated farther into himself, or into Higgins.'

Boredom was one of his worries. The challenge was still there every time the call-boy cried his name; so was tedium. 'It's like a housewife having to cook the same meal every night − and then having to eat it,' he told an interviewer.[6]

Another thing on his mind was money: not earning it, but keeping it. He was being paid over £1,200 a week (the equivalent of £15,000 nowadays) plus various percentages of the house take. He enjoyed the tax status of a non-resident. But after six months he would start to pay British taxes. Out of some £60,000 earned in the year, one-third would be regarded as legitimate expenses, but tax and surtax on the remaining £40,000 would amount to £28,141, leaving him with just £11,859 for his labours. His own company, Transglobal Ltd, registered abroad, would protect him from the worst of this, but every pound Sterling he 'imported' into Britain for living expenses was taxable, which was another reason for not extending his contract beyond the year.

And then there was the endless worry of Kay's health. She had been house-hunting, after a falling-out with their old friend the Earl of Warwick compelled them to leave his house in Swan Walk. She found one in Cheyne Row, Chelsea. Every night she sat in the wings at the end of the show, but something would have to be found to keep her busy, Rex felt. By this time, he had engaged a secretary to keep his own affairs in order. Edith Jackson was introduced to him by his agent, Laurie Evans, and for more than ten years she was to bear the brunt of his shortening temper and dictatorial nature. She stayed on out of fascination for the way he conducted his affairs – in every sense of that word – and developed a talent for giving as good as she got, which was the only way to stand up to Rex.

Kay's health now fluctuated unpredictably. The pills she had been put on in Switzerland were losing their effectiveness. Edith Jackson was told of her true condition by Terence Rattigan's secretary, but she was still ignorant of it when the papers began calling over reports of Kay's collapse, blood transfusion in a London hospital, and then rapid recovery and departure with Rex, who had been given leave from the show, for, a long weekend holiday on the Cote d'azur with Prince Bertil and Princess Lilian of Sweden. No, Edith told a reporter, she had not heard that Miss Kendall had leukemia or even a bad cold. She was playing golf at that very moment with Mr Harrison at St Tropez, 'and Miss Kendall is undoubtedly carrying his clubs', she added.[7]

'Kay's madcap behaviour sometimes got everyone into scrapes,' says Joan Buckmaster. 'Peter Bull once invited her and Rex to dinner. He lived in awful clutter in a flat over the Chelsea Cinema in the King's Road, sort of Greek people selling tee-shirts on the ground floor and sixty stairs to climb through a rather grotty bit of the building. They had plenty to drink, I suppose, for Kay started doing imitations of her mother's music-hall act, and had Rex joining in the dancing with her. When it came time for them to go, about 1.30 am, they found they could hardly get down the staircase because all the plaster had fallen off the ceiling what with Rex and Kay jigging about. The next day, Rex sent Peter this huge bouquet of flowers and Kay gave him a beautiful *faience* salad bowl, so he didn't care. Peter bought armfuls of daffodils for the people who owned the place, and the flowers stimulated the landlord's old desire to paint and he took his flower paintings to St James's Park and sold them off the railings – so he didn't care. That was Kay all over. She somehow touched everyone's life.'

By now, the number of those who 'knew' about Kay was increasing. Lilli told Noël Coward when he stayed with her in Portofino that August. He came away thinking, 'The poor dear [Kay] may have behaved badly in the first place when she went bald-headed after Rex, but having got her own way she is certainly paying a ghastly price for it.'[8] Lilli also showed Coward Rex's letters, which now arrived every week or so, detailing the anguish he said he was enduring and looking forward, with a mixture of dread and relief, to the day when death freed Kay from her mortal illness and left him free for remarriage to Lilli. As yet, Lilli had not told Carlos Thompson, whom she had married shortly after her divorce, of the 'arrangement' between herself and Rex. She felt, with some reason, that he might think he was being manipulated. Coward asked her what she would do when the day came and she had to break her promise to Rex. Lilli's memoirs record her answer: 'I shall let a bit of time pass, and then I'll write a letter to Rex. The last one.'[9] No wonder Coward noted in his journals his feeling that the Villa San Genesio 'reeked of deceit'.[10] It was a strange circle of deception: Rex keeping Kay's illness from her; Lilli concealing her bargain with Rex from her husband; and Rex expecting to remarry Lilli, while she had her mind made up to remain Mrs Carlos Thompson.

Kay's restlessness, meantime, had to be catered to quite as much as her illness. She wanted to do a play that would keep her busy at nights while Rex was on stage. *The Bright One*, a whimsical comedy about a schoolteacher on a Greek islands cruise who is turned into a classical nymph, appealed to her. Rex was not so sure, thinking it very thin; but, along with Jack Minster, his Liverpool Rep friend and now a London impresario, he agreed to part-finance and direct it himself. It meant carrying a double burden, but Kay grew hysterical when he suggested other names to direct it. He added Gladys Cooper to the cast as reinsurance. It closed after ten days, on three of which Kay had been absent through illness. Rex lost £5,000 – and his friendship with Minster, who had not the same sentimental need as Rex to subsidize Kay. The letters to Lilli became more and more self-pitying.

The existence of Rex's letters to his ex-wife, and his assumption that she would remarry him, has sometimes been questioned. None of them has ever appeared in print or even been quoted from; but his sister Sylvia declares she saw them later, at Lilli's insistence, and that 'Rex wrote to her in terms that left no doubt that he fully expected her to live up to her promise and become Mrs Rex Harrison again one day. I have absolutely no doubt that an agreement had been reached between them, hingeing on Kay. Lilli had been a mother-figure to Rex. Kay was a sweet and lovable girl, but totally incapable of looking after Rex's needs. I may be wrong, of course, but I don't think Rex's marriage to Kay would have lasted if Kay hadn't had a fatal illness. Neither of them was temperamentally suited to settling down with the other in the long run. From day to day, it was all right: they had rows, of course, but they struck me as acting out the life of a temperamental married couple. Much would be said at the tops of their voices, then just as soon forgotten, leaving nothing even to forgive. But the play's run would have ended one day and the make-up would have had to come off. They really couldn't have gone on at that pitch for ever.'

Rex celebrated the start of 1959 by tacking up a calendar in his dressing-room and ticking off the days until the date he won release from *My Fair Lady*: 30 March. Three and a quarter years was long enough to have grown tired of even 'her face'.

Kay, meanwhile, fretted in idleness and confessed she hated 'that show' for robbing her of Rex for the best years of her marriage. She had drawn closer to two other actresses suffering from misfortunes of their own. One was Vivien Leigh, whose husband, Laurence Olivier, was steeling himself to ask for a divorce, since he could no longer take the strain of her bouts of manic-depression and had fallen in love with Joan Plowright. The other was Lauren Bacall, whose husband, Humphrey Bogart, had recently died of cancer caused by smoking. Vivien infected Kay with a touch of the radical politics she had developed, some thought as a symptom of her manic phase, and Rex suddenly found himself being dragooned into a London students' parade under a banner which read 'Education Has No Colour Bar', his wife and son Noel on either side of him. He escaped after a hundred yards and took a taxi to the Savoy, where he waited for Kay in the grill room bar, the only kind of 'bar' which he cared about. It is his sole recorded political 'act'.

Lauren Bacall accompanied Kay to the last night of *My Fair Lady* at the end of March, the former wearing white, the latter black, in a graceful tribute to Beaton's two-toned 'Ascot Gavotte'. 'Eliza, bring me my slippers,' Rex commanded for the last time. Bacall growled out, 'Speech ... speech.' None was forthcoming. 'What could I have said out there?' Rex asked, sipping whisky backstage from a cut-glass tumbler engraved with the date: a present from the stage hands. 'You know what I want?' he continued. 'A civilized drink at a civilized hour and not having to go to bed with a supper hanging heavily on my stomach.'' Even when liberated from Henry Higgins, Rex continued to sound like him.

He had deliberately made no plans. Dr Goldman, his London physician, believed Kay's illness was nearing crisis point. A hospital cot had been moved into one of the small guest rooms in their rented Cheyne Row house and there she had blood transfusions from time to time, avoiding the risk of hospital visits and her illness becoming public with all the damage that would do to her career. Being a 'patient' at home, however, brought her and Rex almost unbearably close. No escape into *My Fair Lady* was possible now. Night and day, his total concern was Kay.

Where some of her friends were concerned, Kay's illness was a *very* well kept secret. 'Archie McIndoe, the plastic surgeon who "did" Kay's nose, had become a very good friend of hers,' says Angela Fox. 'He was dining with her and Rex and me. Kay looked ravishing. She was wearing a Balmain gown and was at her most vivacious. Rex asked her, "Have you taken your pills, Kay?" He insisted that she leave the table and go upstairs immediately and take them. When she was gone, McIndoe said, "For God's sake, Rex, you'll turn that girl into a hypochondriac. Anyone would think she was ill." A few months later, she was dead.'

Ironically, it was she who seized the chance to go to work, perhaps as proof of her stamina. Stanley Donen, the film director, offered her the female lead opposite Yul Brynner in his new comedy *Once More, With Feeling*. In deference to his stars' tax-avoidance needs, he agreed to shoot it in Paris. Rex consulted Dr Goldman. Well, said the physician, dissuading Kay from doing the film carried more risk – not least that of revealing the gravity of her illness – than permitting her to work for five or six weeks in the French capital under careful supervision.

Kay had gone to Paris herself in early March to discuss the film with Donen. An anxious Rex, still in the closing weeks of the musical, insisted she call him between the acts. Donen relates: 'Kay and I were having dinner one night in one of those huge Paris places – Le Dôme, it may have been – along with hundreds of other diners. Kay excused herself to call Rex; there was a phone outside the main dining-room. I heard her yelling at the top of her voice, "Rexy!" I guess that Rex, sitting in his dressing-room, screamed something down the line like, "Kay ... I can't hear you. What's all the din? Where are you?" Quick as a card sharp, Kay screamed into the phone, "Darling, I'm in a Christian Science reading-room." '[12]

Rex said later that he never let Kay be examined independently by any doctor who was not in the know. This is not true. Even Rex had to bow before the insurance companies' insistence on the stars of a film having a pre-production check-up. But here, too, luck was with him. The day before Kay was due to report for hers, Donen was called. Was the story true that she had leukemia? A blood test would be necessary.

Kay was startled when a sample was taken. She called Rex. In a state of great alarm, Rex called Donen. 'What the hell's going on?' Up to then, Rex had sustained himself with the belief that only a few people were in on the secret. Actually, the reverse was becoming true: the nature of Kay's illness was now the subject of accurate speculation in London show-business circles. Whether Kay's own ravishing looks played a part is unknown, but the medical judgment was that she was fit enough for the film. Great care was taken of her by Donen. She was kept away from other players when not actually shooting. They noted she was unnaturally quiet for *her*, but things went ahead. Rex played golf at St Cloud, rather than witness the strain he knew she was enduring, and preoccupied himself further by laying plans for an Anouilh play which Irene Selznick wanted him to do in New York. They still had rows. 'They reminded me of the couple in *Who's Afraid of Virginia Woolf?* at times,' says Donen. 'In one of the worst, Rex threw Kay's clothes out of her hotel suite, then locked the door on her.' But by now his reasoning that, if he had done less, she would have guessed the truth begins to sound a bit disingenuous. The greater likelihood is that his own nerves were shot to pieces. 'Kay could be infuriating at times,' Donen says, 'overstrung by her illness, I guess. But it wasn't part of Rex's nature to treat any woman considerately all the time. I expect he yielded to his temperament quite as much as Kay did to her temper.'

A week or two into the shooting Kay came down with a debilitating fever. Production was suspended for a couple of days. She was by now extremely vulnerable to any virus that her weakened immune system could not fight. Blood transfusions became necessary. They were carried out at the American Hospital in Paris. Understandably, treatment of this nature was reported to the insurance company and, when Donen's film had to shut down for a second time within a month, the enquiries about what was 'going on' began to multiply. 'But they continued to pay the bills and we continued with Kay,' says the director. However Columbia Pictures paid an enhanced insurance premium once the nature of Kay's illness and her prospects were determined, for they were confident the film would be a winner and the extra costs soon absorbed in the profits due. 'She was very brave,' says Donen, 'but it was poignant to watch her. Everything was now an effort. You could see her fragility getting more and more pronounced as we screened each day's set of rushes. I think she knew her state of health was serious, perhaps worse than that, for she said to me one day, "Can we shoot all we can today, for I simply don't know if I'll be here tomorrow." She perspired a lot. We couldn't turn the lights up above a certain intensity, so that the photography in the film is a minor miracle of make do. Her bouffant hair-do took three hours' work and wilted quickly, she was losing so much water.'

For Rex there was a grim irony about the film Kay was fighting a battle with her life to complete. *Once More, With Feeling* was a screwball comedy about a pompous, egotistic, eloquently abusive orchestra conductor, played by Brynner, who browbeats his wife and is only discovered to have lovable qualities when the couple are on the point of divorce. The character strongly resembled the one Rex had played in *Unfaithfully Yours*, just before Carole Landis's suicide. He confided to Rattigan that he could not sleep he felt so much caught up in a time warp.

When Kay collapsed for the third time, he took the blame, saying he had passed on a cold to his delicate wife. But one look at Kay told another story: this was no cold.

Dr Goldman decided on an immediate return to London. No charter plane was available at such short notice, so a painful overland journey by train and ferry boat was taken in stages. A white-faced woman, looking not just pale but eroded, clutched Rex for support as he guided her out of the Golden Arrow at Victoria Station the next morning. Then the London Clinic swallowed her up – and the obituary writers on Sunday and weekday papers were put on stand-by.

Rex spent the next week commuting between the Connaught Hotel and Kay's sick room, still denying the rumours, but adding to the suspicions by saying Kay had one ailment (bronchial congestion) while hospital spokespersons said she had another (anaemia). The word 'leukemia', mercifully, never appeared in the editions of the papers that Rex ripped open and scanned before allowing Kay to see them. Miraculously, she recovered enough to be back in Paris before the week was quite over and at work on the film again. 'How we got her through the rest of it, I don't know,' Donen says, 'but we did it, or rather she did it.' It was clear, though, they had a dying woman in front of the cameras.

Dr Goldman now had to fly over and give her injections to stimulate her heart and provide her with the energy necessary for a role that demanded a lot of physical slapstick between her and Brynner as she broke up the furnishings on the set – Rex closed his eyes, wincing at the memory of the similar scenes Preston Sturges had put *him* through.

Release came at last, and they entrained for Portofino, only to find Lilli in residence when they climbed the hill. She still had her half-share in their former home and the letter Rex had sent her had failed to arrive before they did. Had she not seen how Kay's state had deteriorated and known the truth of the matter, it might have been the subject of a Lonsdale or Rattigan comedy. Lilli obligingly left, realizing her own 'moment of truth' with Rex was not far away.

But the heat that summer in the Gulf of Spezia was overwhelming, more than 100°F. Kay could not stand it, so they left for St Moritz. It was a bad refuge. The newspaper people kept what Rex called 'a death watch' on them,[13] so back they dragged to Portofino, where the long toil up the hill at least reduced the number of reporters, though they had to erect screens around themselves in order to eat lunch outdoors for fear of *paparazzi* with long lenses snapping them from the hilltop *castello* on the other side of the little harbour.

It was from the Villa San Genesio that Kay Kendall, at the end of August, set off on the last journey of her life. Taken suddenly ill, she was rushed to hospital in Rapallo. The faithful Dr Goldman insisted she be transferred to the London Clinic and he accompanied Rex on the seemingly endless train journey across Europe, while Kay lay on the bed in their sleeping compartment, having her face sprayed with water. When they got to Dover, she was so weak that two seamen had to link arms and provide a human chair to transfer her from the ferry to the train. Customs formalities were waived. Rex carried her to the car at Victoria, his strong arms locked around her waist, one of her shoes falling off as he got her across the forecourt. Looking back, it is difficult to credit that an ambulance was not waiting at Dover, but this was all part of the masquerade in which the two of them seemed inextricably trapped. Neither could (or would) admit that Kay's condition was terminal. 'I'm only here for a couple of days,' Kay managed to say on the threshold of the London Clinic.[14]

At first, it seemed likely. She rallied strongly. Though weak, she insisted on sitting up in bed in her fourth-floor, thirty-guinea-a-week room, planning a television spectacular she was to make in New York in December. Rex again kept vigil as she was given blood transfusions. Then her vitality suddenly deserted her. Rex moved from the Connaught into an adjoining room. The Queen's personal physician, Dr Bradley Scott, was called in to consult with Dr Goldman.

Yet Rex still assured Kay's family – her father, sister and grandmother – that things were not as bad as the damned papers were making out. Only he was present as Kay's life ebbed away. It was feared that anything like a family reunion around her bed would be tantamount to sounding a death knell for her.

Rex's agent, Laurie Evans, recalls the end: 'When Kay was near to death, she said to Rex, "Mousey, you wouldn't tell me that I'm not going to die, if I were, would you?" Rex snapped, "Of course not, you silly little fool. See you tomorrow." Those were the last words he spoke while she was still conscious.'

She sank into a coma around midnight on 5 September 1959 and the hospital bulletin issued the next morning at 11.30 am admitted for the first time that she was 'gravely ill'. An hour or so later, at 12.30 pm, without regaining consciousness, she died. She was thirty-two. Rex embraced the loyal Dr Goldman who had done so much to prolong his wife's life, then he slipped back to the Connaught. For several hours that long afternoon no one could find him. Years later, to one of his closest friends, he explained where he had gone – 'to that church across the street'.[5] Presumably, he meant Farm Street, the Roman Catholic Jesuit Chapel. 'To pray for Kay?' his friend asked. 'No, just sitting,' was the answer, 'she would have laughed at the thought of anyone praying for her, especially me.'

Lilli, by melancholy coincidence, was in London at this time, caring for her dying mother. Rex wrote a letter to her on London Clinic writing paper after packing Kay's few personal effects and before returning to the Connaught. It was reported that Edith Jackson took it personally to Lilli by taxi. This is not so, she says. It went the normal way, by post. But either way, Lilli must have been expecting its arrival and hardly needed to open it to guess what Rex had written. It cannot have been any comfort to her to know that she must now break the vow she had made Rex and disillusion him about the prospects of their remarriage. Too often in her life Lilli had seen her world fall to pieces. Now all she wanted to do was keep it together. For an embittered Rex, the task he faced was going to be one of reassembling his world, and in matters like that he possessed far fewer resources than Lilli. In the months ahead of him, he was to go about it in the only way he knew how – with the help of women.

21: The Reluctant Widower

There were only thirty-three mourners, just family and close friends, many of them famous but all subdued, and without the crowds of photographers and autograph hunters usually drawn to 'celebrity funerals'. The eighteenth-century parish church of St John, Hampstead, in north London, did not seem a place made for headlines or masses of spectators. The dozen policemen stationed discreetly in the narrow, tree-lined street were scarcely needed. Housewives out shopping were the main onlookers, their view obscured by sheets of canvas hung over the railings next to the site of the grave under the evergreen trees. There were some 40 wreaths. 'To Pussycat – from Carey', said one. 'Darling girl, my love – Cootie', said another from Robert Coote, also echoing Kay's childish love of nicknames. But it had been requested that donations be made to a cancer research fund, so most of the affection had been expressed in cheques, not flowers. There was no funeral cortège. Mourners simply walked into church as they arrived, singly or in friendly groups. The oak coffin was unadorned save for a bouquet of six dozen red roses and a card reading 'For my beloved – Rex'. The brass plate on it struck a few of those who passed it, pausing or with bowed heads, as slightly unfamiliar: 'Kay Harrison', was the name; totally accurate, yet strangely alien to a bright spirit who had always been known to them as 'Kendall'. Rex slipped in by a side door with Carey and Noel. He had asked for one of Kay's favourite hymns, 'Jesu joy of man's desiring'. The service lasted less than ten minutes. After the Twenty-Third Psalm had been recited and the vicar had read the lesson from St Paul's Epistle to the Thessalonians – 'to sorrow moderately for the dead' – four ushers and a church verger with a black and silver staff led everyone across the road to the 'actors' corner' of the graveyard where, between gravestones to Herbert Beerbohm Tree and George du Maurier and his son Gerald du Maurier, Rex's mentor and model, the coffin was lowered into a grave whose headstone said simply, 'Kay Kendall Harrison. Deeply Loved Wife of Rex.' In years to come a single rose would twine itself round the grey slate headstone: the rose was called 'Mermaid'.

Among those round the tiny plot of land were the Oliviers, Gladys Cooper, Lauren Bacall, John Gregson (co-star in *Genevieve*), Jack Hawkins, George Cukor and tireless Dr Carl Goldman. Rex's sons held his hands as he stood for a few seconds with bowed head; then he walked away and got into his car. Within the week he was hard at work preparing for a new play.

Rex had left his hotel the day after Kay's death. He moved across town to Westminster. He wanted to be with 'family' for a few days. Sylvia's husband, David Maxwell Fyfe, had made a brilliant political career for himself in the Conservative Government, becoming Home Secretary and now Lord Chancellor, responsible for the judiciary, with the title Earl of Kilmuir. It was into the Kilmuirs' official residence that Rex moved, an apartment high up under the roof of the House of Lords. It was a novel refuge for intimate grief, not that he really found himself comfortable there for all its aristocratic elevation. 'He never really adjusted,' says his sister. 'My husband would be up and at his desk by 8.30 am, and Rex wouldn't bestir himself until 10.30 am, and then appear in his dressing-gown like the first act of a play and be eating his breakfast with all the House of Lords messengers buzzing in and out on business.'

After the funeral, Harold French and his wife gave him what comfort they could in their home. Then he moved to Sunningdale to be with Terence Rattigan, although the work of raising his spirits was best done by a round of golf with Rattigan and the actor Michael Gough. Rex took to Gough's sombre and forceful personality. He saw him as a 'guardian' in the T. S. Eliot sense of someone who has 'the gift' of helping people through bad times. It was probably Gough who got Rex over the bad news which eventually reached him when Lilli wrote and said that she had to renege on the promise she had made to him: there would be no remarriage. He reportedly sank into the deepest depression in which his friends had ever seen him. In a very real sense he had lost two 'wives' within days of each other: one by death, the other by deceit. Work, he decided, was the only sure antidote to grief. He pulled himself together and got to grips with the Anouilh play, *Hurluberlu*, now retitled in English as *The Fighting Cock*, which Peter Brook was to direct on Broadway in October.

The immediate reaction of the media to Kay's death had been to praise Rex for bearing the double burden of her illness and of keeping her in merciful ignorance of it. It rendered the tragedy all the more poignant, Rex's conduct all the more gallant. Perhaps this is so, but equally it may not have been this simple at all. There is a weight of evidence which suggests that Kay was aware her illness was serious –

more serious than anaemia, anyhow – and then fatal, but that she chose not to acknowledge the fact. Kay approached life with an air of innocence which was very engaging, but it was a mock innocence. She knew very well what it was all about. Dirk Bogarde drops a hint in his memoirs that there was an intimation of mortality hanging over her even before she met Rex. A friend of his, a woman of insight and sympathy, chided him for losing his temper with Kay on one occasion, saying, 'Be kind to that little one, she hasn't very long here, my dear.'' Of course this is not to say that *Kay* knew her days were numbered, but as her leukemia began to take savage toll of health, strength and looks she would have needed to be very, very stupid not to be alarmed. And she was not stupid. The journalist Jon Bradshaw, interviewing Rex in 1972, quotes an unnamed woman friend of Rex who says about Kay's death, 'How long do you go on believing the excuse of anaemia, bronchitis or mononucleosis? She must have known. And knowing, I believe she allowed Rex to keep his secret to himself, because it was more important to him than to her.'²

Jones Harris, who knew both of them well, also believes Kay 'played the game' where her illness was concerned. 'It was a sort of "actorish" thing to dissemble, not to own up to reality.' Stanley Donen, the last person to work with Kay professionally, privately thought that she knew she had not long to live, 'but pretending to ignore this was, to her, like acting a part. It was easier than facing up to reality and its consequences.' Rex's sister agrees. 'Like Rex, she had a great capacity for putting what she didn't want to know completely out of her mind. It was one reason why they were so well suited to each other, in the short run, anyhow. Either she didn't want to know – to admit it to herself – or, more likely, she didn't want her knowledge to show and attract the thing that she and Rex hated above all else: other people's pity. Rex always took care not to let the man he really was show. It went back to the era he was born in. Children then didn't like their parents to know what they were really thinking and talking about. It would have wounded Rex deeply if people had found out he was married to a dying wife. He accepted the "father role", looking after her, but preferred to continue to appear the loving if occasionally temperamental husband.'

Carey Harrison also finds it incredible that Kay did not know she had a terminal illness. Of his father's willingness to conceal *his* knowledge, he says: 'Rex possessed no meditative side to his nature. He saw everything around him, everything that was happening to him, in terms of drama – of theatre. Concealing Kay's illness, even though he may have known that *she* knew, was a very theatrical thing to do. It gave him a role. I don't mean he was insincere. Perhaps he was even more sincere because he was playing the part for effect, and it had to be perfectly played to succeed with an audience of one, with someone as hypersensitive as Kay.'

Noel Harrison also feels that both his father and Kay knew the truth, but continued to act out a somewhat more bearable deception – 'certainly over the last months of her illness,' says Noel.

Others, of course, will have none of this. Anthony Havelock-Allan thinks 'Rex never gave her an inkling of what was really wrong with her'. Laurence Evans concurs. But perhaps Robert Flemyng read the inadmissible evidence correctly on Rex's lips when they met after Kay's death and Flemying reproached Rex with not telling him the truth. 'He said to me, "Well, it helps to make up for Carole."' Where so much is necessarily speculative, caution is advisable. But had Rex told Kay what he knew, even though he suspected she was aware of it already, his 'guardianship' of her would have lacked the sense of expiation implicit in his remark to Flemyng. Directly or indirectly, he had made one woman take her own life. With Kay, he was given a chance to see another woman through to the end of *her* life; and because neither admitted to the other the finite nature of his self-appointed task, he was able to make moral restitution for the earlier tragedy.

Some such tantalizing questions must also have been in Terence Rattigan's mind. He refused to send any flowers when Kay died. She would have hated it, he said. When he and Rex took a brief holiday in Cannes at the end of September, Rattigan broached the idea of writing a play about a husband who conceals his wife's terminal illness from her by treating her in the same bloody awful way as he usually did. Kay had known she was dying of leukemia, Rattigan began to say, but Rex cut him short in mid-speech. His reaction to the notion of a play was decidedly negative. 'When the press got wind of the possibility,' write Rattigan's biographers, Michael Darlow and Gillian Hodson, '[Rattigan] put out a strongly worded denial, saying that he was not at the moment, nor would be in the forseeable future, engaged on such a project.'[3] A prudent response, maybe, given Rex's feelings at the time, but Rattigan seldom wasted a germinal idea supplied by his friends' complex and, at times, highly dramatic lives. He always believed that Kay was giving Rex strength by refusing to acknowledge that her illness was terminal. She and Rex, in his opinion, knew how to play that kind of scene together. They were both of them keeping reality at bay. Just as they made the unreality of stage and screen a way of earning their living, it was also the way they faced the prospect of Kay's dying – or so Rattigan persuaded himself. He put the project on hold, however, in deference to Rex. Fifteen years later he revived it, when Rex could face the past and relive the strangest of all his marital tragedies.

Rex certainly said nothing to anyone about the humiliation and betrayal he felt Lilli had heaped upon him. 'There was, of course, no reply,' she noted, after sending 'that letter' to him.[4] It took her another year before she told her husband of 'the arrangement', ' "You did well not to tell me then," [Carlos Thompson] said quietly. This was the end of my nightmare ...'[5] But Rex continued to be haunted. In 1974, when he was making a BBC Television film in Portofino, and Richard Kershaw asked him about his second marriage, he could not bring himself to reply. The unedited version of the tape reveals the resistance he put up to mentioning even Lilli's name. All he said for the record was, yes, he had been married to her.

This was a time of endings and beginnings for Rex. His dedication to living for tomorrow almost deserted him, so insistent was the pull of the past. A bit of it showed up, unexpectedly, when he was seen off at London airport, *en route* to New York, by his first wife, Collette, now devoted to a Canadair test pilot, but not immune to the Rex's charm. 'It's nice to know that he was my husband once,' she said, 'otherwise I might feel that I'd like to be married to him now, if I met him for the first time.'[6]

The Fighting Cock relied heavily on Rex's pulling power, for, on the face of it, this satire on De Gaulle, the 'General' or the eponymous 'fighting cock', a quixotic figure shaped by a romanticized past, had little obvious appeal to Broadway audiences. But there were Shavian echoes in it – the General's great rage against democracy characterized as 'the greatest good of so many fools' – and he was as much an egotist as Professor Higgins, even though he finished with his illusions shattered rather than his prejudices softened. But it depended on Rex to be amusing, if misguided, otherwise the argument could seem reactionary, if not actually Fascist. It was not to be a success. It fact, it administered a severe jolt to Rex, whose self-confidence in other matters had already been so badly shaken.

One reason for its failure became clear to Laurie Evans at the first night in Philadelphia in November 1959. 'The curtain went up and there was Rex, sitting on a tin trunk, very heavily made up, large nose, drooping mosutache. *And no one recognised him!* He sat there waiting for the reception round of applause that never came, and then had to start cold. It was an awful set-back. He took the moustache off the next night and little by little the rest of the make-up went too, or was thinned out enough to let the familiar face be seen. Not that it saved the play.'

The director, Peter Brook, says today: 'Rex did brilliant sketches at rehearsal, but never managed to assemble them into a solid performance.

He was doing something that was novel and dangerous for a star like himself: he was attempting character acting, and when he appeared in his make-up a chill settled on the audience. We had a front cloth in the tricolour bands and a fairly austere set and Rex felt exposed and, because of his character make-up, also concealed. It was all too new an experience, for him and the audience. But I'd not call it a failure. A semi-success, yes.'[7]

There had been other strains and stresses not so visible to the audience, but very characteristic of Rex recuperating from his wounded self-esteem. 'He had a say-so over the casting of his leading lady, and it became plain he wanted a girl whom it would be fun to be with over the anticipated lengthy run,' says Brook. 'He was immediately hooked by a very poised and charming foreign actress who showed up at the auditions, superby dressed, beautiful, seeming not to care if she landed the part or not. The right attitude to Rex. He thought her entrancing. But whatever happened in the interval, his attitude had changed by the time of the first rehearsal. He called me early in the morning and said, 'Do you think she'll be all right?' This was trouble. In the days following he turned against her, undermining her confidence as only an upper-class Englishman can, unsettling her with throw-away remarks like 'You'll be all right after a bit more rehearsal,' or 'Can you do this, do you think?' Nothing full frontal, no attack like that, but destroying her confidence. After five days of this, her English, which had been quite competent and attractive, became almost incomprehensible. Rex had created an impossible situation. 'Think you can get Natasha?' he asked me, meaning Natasha Parry, to whom I was then married. It meant buying her out of two films for which she'd signed up. Anouilh and I had known from the start that Natasha was ideal for the role, but Rex had engineered this impossible situation because, well, that was his nature.'

The play closed after only eighty-seven performances and Rex, rather than be stranded with nothing to do, grasped at an unlikely project: a film thriller entitled *Midnight Lace*, starring Doris Day, a trite melodrama set in a London fog, where a rich American wife is going in fear of her life from an anonymous and disembodied voice.

Several of the *Fighting Cock* cast – Natasha Parry, Roddy McDowall – had been signed by producer Ross Hunter, taking advantage of the play's premature closure. Rex followed them to Hollywood, much to Hunter's gratified surprise. He was in a miserable mood. One might have thought Doris Day would not have helped. In fact, they got on well together. Both were thorough professionals, and more: Day was a Christian Scientist who shared Rex's non-denominational refusal to look back on life, repenting of errors or grieving too long. Moreover, Doris Day's attitude to work was identical to Rex's. What she (or her amanuensis A. E. Hotchner) wrote in her memoirs, Rex could have written very easily in his own without altering a word: 'It has been my good fortune that at those times in my life when tragedy has struck, I have had to work ... Life must go on, and it is only through the society of the living that one can overcome the despair that a death inflicts.'[8]

This was exactly his mood. Improbable though it seems, Doris Day succeeded in lifting a lot of Rex's depression. He drew the line, though, at joining in the Christian Science sessions held on the sound stage before a shot, when the director invoked the Lord and assured true believers that 'God is in the studio ... God is on the set.'[9] Perhaps the invocation of God made Rex feel unusually humble. He even thanked Ross Hunter for his solicitude for furnishing his dressing-room with towels bearing the monogram 'RH'. Hunter, wisely, did not tell him they had been left behind by the last occupant, Rock Hudson.

While still in Hollywood, he ran into the last person he wanted to meet, yet also the first person he needed to heal his wound: Lilli. She was filming *The Pleasure of His Company*. He again appealed to her. She was obdurate. 'Lilly always saw herself as superior to Kay Kendall – that showgirl, that bimbo, as we would say today – and was totally impervious to the charms that Rex and, to be honest, I, too, at the age of fourteen, detected so easily in her,' says Carey Harrison. Her refusal to take Rex back was barely concealed punishment for his taste in women quite as much as for his infidelity.

'We are still friends,' she said in an interview at the time, 'but [it's difficult] whenever formerly married people meet in Hollywood ... Noël Coward can write such scenes for the stage, but it's much harder in real life.'[10]

How much harder, only she and Rex knew; and only Rex now cared. It was in this directionless mood that he renewed a friendship he had begun at the end of 1959 – this time with the hope that it would provide him with the thing he needed most: a new love and, perhaps, a new wife.

In each new marriage, it is said, there is something of the old one. Looking at Tammy Grimes, one can see the truth of this. She had a self-confident poise, an opinionated disposition inherited from her New England ancestry, and, 'so I've been told, a nose and brow very like Kay Kendall's. When Rex began his affair with me, I was also coincidentally wearing my hair the way Kay used to do. Strange, when one looks back,' she says today.[11] She had just turned twenty-five and was separated from her husband, the Canadian actor Christopher Plummer, by whom she had had a daughter, when she met Rex at a dinner party on Long

Island. It was not their first encounter, though. 'That happened when I was thirteen, when he and Lilli were touring in *The Four-Poster*, and came to my father's country club to play golf. 'That's Rex Harrison,' I gasped at father. 'I know, dear,' he said quietly but firmly, 'and I don't want you to do anything about it.' But I hung around the doorway and smiled at him, and he smiled back, and from that moment I was in love with him, and dreamed of taking the Greyhound bus to California when I heard he was doing a film there.'

Twelve years later she met a man in mourning, and Rex, as was his custom, found a woman willing and able to give him comfort and companionship – with a view to marriage, at least on his part. There can be little doubt he wanted 'another Kay Kendall'. Tammy Grimes, besides looks, shared Kay's outgoing nature, unpredictability and mischievousness, but she also knew when a man in an emotionally bruised state needed tenderness. 'We used to take long walks around the Central Park reservoir until my hands were freezing that cold November. He'd stride on, not saying much: his mind and heart were with Kay. I was just a friend, a companion – no problem.'

Certainly no problem, but in Rex's bleak moments Tammy Grimes was formidable consolation. Together they went all over New York, back to the places he had been with Kay. Gradually, she saw him begin to enjoy himself again. And she felt the way his charm was made palpable: 'in the very clothes he wore, the yellow cashmere sweater, the Tattersall checked shirts, the hound's-tooth jackets. Just running a hand over him was sexy. Walking down the street with him made you feel you were the most important couple ever. When you are in the company of a person like that, it's irresistible. I don't think there was one person who passed us without saying, "There's Rex Harrison," although I can't recall any of them asking for his autograph. They sensed he wasn't a man who welcomed the recognition of strangers. He didn't like to be "crowded", he used to say, or "invaded". It made him all the more special to be yours.'

As they became closer than friends, another aspect of Rex appeared: his possessiveness. 'He could be very short-tempered with people who paid me attention when we were together. Suddenly he turned into another man with a killer's temper. And one of my failings he didn't tolerate – my unpunctuality. If I were late for a dinner party he was giving in the house he was staying in with Michael Gough, in Sutton Place, when he was doing the Anouilh play, he'd bark at me, 'Get out! You're fifteen minutes late. Get out of here!' But he was always quick to make up.'

Their relationship gradually turned into a courtship. 'The first thing he gave me was a coral ring from Buccellati.' Rex first slipped it on one of his own long, thin fingers, beside the two rings he wore: one a gold Cartier band bought for him in New York by Kay, which said 'Rex, with all my love' on the inside, and the other a signet ring that his father had had made up with the motto '*Courage sans peur*'. The coral ring was followed by one that Tammy Grimes herself chose, gold with a peridot and diamonds. 'Then, one day, a messenger from a Madison Avenue art gallery buzzed my door with a package. When I opened it, there was the Renoir pastel I'd admired so often as we passed the window, a woman in her bath. No message. Not even a card. That was Rex's way, doing things out of the blue.'

When Rex flew to California to make *Midnight Lace*, he continued the affair by nightly telephone calls and letters – 'he wrote very romantic ones, always remembering to mention my child, Amanda.' On his return to New York, he persuaded her to follow him back to London. They took separate suites at the Connaught. 'He gave me a Cartier watch, 'Now you can always be on time.' He put his blue Bentley at her disposal, 'which, I regret to say, I used to visit another actor I was dating. Then came the proposal of marriage.'

Now it was Rex who was a little late. A proposition had already been made to Tammy Grimes – to star in a new musical, *The Unsinkable Molly Brown* – 'and I told him I was going to do it. He was absolutely shattered. "I know what's going to happen to you, Tammy," he said. 'You don't want to be *just* a star – you want to be a *sta-a-a-ar*.' But I can't live like that. You must be with me, Tammy. You must commit yourself to living with me – and working with me. I can't have you living in New York and doing a musical." Sure, it would have been wonderful to have done a play with him and then another and another ... and perhaps a film in between. But it wouldn't have worked out that way, as I sensed. He was very depressed again, but drove me to the airport.'

Soon he was over in New York. 'The courtship continued. He drew me one day when I was sleeping on a couch and at the bottom of the pencil sketch he wrote just one word, 'Because ...' He asked me again to marry him, promising me the Sutton Place house he was living in. He came with me when I was asked to hear the score of *The Unsinkable Molly Brown* for the first time. We went to the composer Meredith Wilson's apartment. Dore Schary was there and about everyone on Broadway who mattered, the whole gang, and in I walked with Rex Harrison. Well, I really did feel a *sta-a-a-ar*. After listening to the music, I really had no choice. "Rex," I said, "this is really awful, but I can't marry you. I love you too much." Came the opening night of *Molly Brown*, and three dozen yellow roses arrived for me. No card, just as before. But I knew who'd sent them.

'Later on, I went to California and took the Renoir pastel with me. But because it would be in the sun, and nobody knew what it was, I sold it and bought a Ferrari – they all knew the price of that. Wasn't I silly? And later still, when I was in Rome and had probably broken up with someone, I felt a rekindled thing for Rex, and called him in Spain. "I was just thinking of you, Rex, and missing you," I said. And he said, not unkindly and not in any slangy way, "Actually, Tammy, I've found another bird." It was beautiful while it lasted, but it would have been folly to make it permanent.'

Rex returned to London more than a little downcast after Tammy Grimes's second rejection of his marriage proposal. He was without a wife, an unusual and disorientating experience for him. It seemed, too, that he had also been dispossessed of his home. That 'home', in normal times, would have been the West End theatre and the 'well-made play' by his friends Terry Rattigan and William Douglas Home. But he had been cocooned so securely in the success of *My Fair Lady* on two continents that he had failed to note the radical changes that were sweeping over the London theatre scene. The year that *My Fair Lady* opened on Broadway was also the year when John Osborne's *Look Back in Anger* was produced at the Royal Court Theatre by the new English Stage Company, a loose association of left-wing playwrights, directors and actors, commited enemies of the theatrical establishment to which Rex belonged. When he arrived to do his musical in London, the anger of youth, as the press labelled its most saleable if not generally applicable characteristic, had turned into a theatrical revolution which was threatening his own and even more ancient thrones. To his mind, it was an example of 'grudge' theatre. At first he had been amused as well as irritated by the mutual jealousy rather than general anger which its leaders demonstrated – jealousy, he felt, at the kind of success he represented. But now, after seeing how suddenly and steeply his own career could go into decline after the phenomenal success of *My Fair Lady*, Rex was far from sure what kind of success he continued to represent.

His nerve was further shaken when, in July 1960, he attended the first night of a new musical, *Joie de Vivre*, written by Terence Rattigan or, rather, a musical version of an old play, *French Without Tears*, which had successfully launched both Rattigan and himself on their dazzling careers nearly twenty-five years earlier. Rex heard the show go down in a storm of booing. It closed after four performances. The débacle was the beginning of Rattigan's loss of confidence in his talent and his audience: no stage play came from him for ten years.

Rex, likewise, was unsure which way to turn. He felt depleted in professional and private life. He had no chance of remarrying Lilli

Palmer. He had been turned down by Tammy Grimes. He had not made a success of *The Fighting Cock* and he had been obliged to accept a co-starring role with Doris Day.

But once more he showed that desperation, if viewed from a certain angle, can look remarkably like fearlessness. The family motto, 'Courage sans peur', decided him and with a certain swagger he entered the enemy camp. He went into a play at the Royal Court. A gentleman come to judgment, indeed!

Yet it was not quite such a foolhardy gesture as it would once have seemed, for if Rex felt he could do with a transfusion of new blood, the English Stage Company had by now discovered that it would benefit from the brighter aura of the star actor. Peggy Ashcroft had led the way by appearing in the Court's production of Brecht's *The Good Woman of Setzuan* in October 1956; and Olivier, undergoing a Pauline conversion by making a second visit to *Look Back in Anger,* had then been reborn when John Osborne invited him to incarnate Archie Rice, the stand-up comic emblematic of run-down Britain, in *The Entertainer* in 1957. 'I was instantly,' Olivier recorded, 'put in touch with a new, vitally changed, entirely unfamiliar *Me*.'[12] Now it was Rex's turn to seek the miracle cure for a failing career. In July 1960 George Devine, the theatre's artistic director, asked him to appear in one of Chekhov's earliest and almost entirely forgotten plays, *Platonov.*

He took the play with him to Portofino that summer and, for once, stuck to his first instinct. He would do it. A play about a desperate man had found an actor who was in the same straits. For the role might have been tailored to Rex's measurements as faultlessly as his own suits. Platonov is a high-tempered egotist with a talent for insulting and belittling what he feels is a world of fools. He is in the middle of a broken marriage precipitated by his drinking, but also by his misogyny. Women are his means of revenge against the lesser sort of mankind. And, despite his rough treatment of them, he retains a hypnotic fascination for them, especially for Anna Petrovna, a general's widow who lusts after him physically.

Actually, being offered the leading role was a closer thing than Rex knew. Ian Bannen had been the original Platonov when Lindsay Anderson was going to direct the play, but Royal Court politics removed Anderson from the play and switched him to direct a new Christopher Logue offering, *Antigone,* and George Devine took over and plumped for Rex. But Devine kept the actress who had been Anderson's choice for Anna Petrovna. She was a thirty-three-year-old Welsh woman. Her name was Rachel Roberts. Before too long, she was going to become the fourth Mrs Rex Harrison.

Part Five

Rachel

22: The Enchanter's Castle

Rachel Roberts was not pleasantly surprised when told she would be playing opposite Rex in *Platonov*. 'Outrage' was the feeling she recorded in a journal she started keeping haphazardly some years afterwards.[1] 'Unfair.' Rex Harrison's international renown would overshadow hers, she felt. Indeed, her first reactions carried the same hint of mistrust and apprehension that Rex habitually manifested when opening the bargaining for a new role. Her second thoughts were more womanly. Was she attractive enough for a man she knew was a formidable womanizer?

He liked women with small noses, she had heard. Would he like hers? By coincidence, she had had it reduced in size by the removal of cartilage not so long before in the very room at the London Clinic where Kay had recently lain ill and dying.

She sought reassurance from a fellow Welshwoman, Donald Houston's wife Brenda, who told her not to worry, she had other charms. To boulster her courage further, she played Rachel the *My Fair Lady* recording that Rex had made. After hearing it, she felt he might grow accustomed to her nose as well as her face, but immediately they met, all hesitancy vanished. It was a *coup de foudre*. 'Rex crackled,' Rachel wrote. 'He seemed charged with electricity. Tall and hooded looking, dressed in blue dog's-tooth tweeds, and a blue cashmere sweater, thin and suspicious, lithe as an electric eel.'[2] He gave her 'a guarded look of approval'.[3] Within a few days, Rachel had fallen for him.

Many of the elements that would combine in Rex's stormiest marriage were already present in this extraordinarily gifted and ultimately tragic woman. Rex himself sensed and liked the raw energy that concealed her profound feeling of insecurity, even inferiority. She asserted herself more than she needed to. A lot of what Rex stood for Rachel had been brought up to spurn. 'Being a Celt,' says Lindsay Anderson, who got to know Rachel better than most, 'she had a love-hate relationship with "the bloody English", as her Welsh ancestors saw them, and Rex was the most challenging example of High Englishness she had met.'[4] Socially and politically, they seemed on opposite sides of a divide. Rachel was the neglected younger child in a Welsh Baptist minister's family. At school, she had turned into a bit of a wild child. On her Welsh university campus, where she took a degree in English, she adopted left-wing attitudes. She ran away from a teaching job – that ultimate goal of the Welsh education system – and enrolled at the Royal Academy of Dramatic Art. But a strong pull was exerted by night-clubs, where she worked as a cloakroom girl between terms, and even by the circus, which she joined as a *soubrette* in the vacation. She played around with quite a few men. Then, to steady herself, she married Alan Dobie, a good actor, but a mite sober for a girl who desired the glamour of stardom, its status and wealth, yet despised herself for betraying the puritan nature of her countryfolk.

Despite her ebullient, outgoing nature, Rachel had a low level of self-esteem which no amount of praise, prize-winning or professional counselling would be able to alter significantly. She was very skilful at manipulating people; she had learnt this out of self-defence as early as her days in the school playground. She was terribly vulnerable to the allure of celebrity, but achieving it gave her no sense of self-confidence; it was overwhelmed, sooner or later, by a return to a self-lacerating depression. Her sexual fantasies were usually ones connected with degradation. She described them in her journals. She imagined herself being auctioned off to imaginary slave-drivers who fondled her breasts to make them swell and ordered her to stand with her legs wide apart. When she was in her penitent mood, she clung to men who were passive sympathizers and good comforters; when she swung to the other extreme, she found men who enjoyed the wild Welsh side of her while giving her a rough time.

Rex and Rachel perfectly illustrate how opposites can powerfully attract and reinforce each other. It was like new blood meeting old money. There must be a strong supposition, too, that Rex deliberately manipulated her sympathy for him in his bereavement as well as his physical attraction for her. Edith Jackson, his secretary, who had seen through him by this time, maintains that this was the basis of most of his affairs. There was a consciously self-serving element in them. In Rachel he saw aspects of his last three wives: Collette's raucous enjoyment of life, Lilli's intelligence, Kay's disregard of decorum and easy surrender to unladylike fun. Tammy Grimes, who had noticed her own physical resemblance to Kay Kendall, later looked at Rachel and saw she had her mouth. 'I then realized that, where Rex's wives were concerned, I had been the "intermediate" face – *eerie*.'

When she met Rex, Rachel had just finished her first starring role in a film, *Saturday Night and Sunday Morning*. She played Albert Finney's mistress, a carnal yet half-fearful woman whose working-class atittude to sex had a fleshly candour rarely seen in British film actresses before the proletarian realism which a new generation of directors like Karel Reisz, Lindsay Anderson and Tony Richardson had brought to their native cinema. The movie had yet to open, but if Rex's future attitude to Rachel's 'grubby roles', as he called them, was anything to go by, he would have hated it. Like the new playwrights, the new film-makers threatened his own well-mannered, upper-class style. Now, however, taking her out to lunch every day between rehearsals to a small French restaurant beside the Royal Court, he 'cut a dash' for her. 'He was acclaimed, looked up to. *And he had chosen me!*' she recalled.[5] She felt swept off her feet ... pampered ... paid attention to. It was heady. As Angela Fox says, 'A man who's famous and powerful – if he shows you a minute's kindness, he has you for life. That was Rex's secret.'

While rehearsing, Rex lived in the Oliviers' flat in Eaton Square. Olivier was in New York preparing to do *Becket*; Vivien Leigh, separated but not yet divorced from him, was touring Europe with her lover (and Rex's old chum) Jack Merivale. Rachel often went to the flat after rehearsals to cook Rex his supper. Instead of Vivien's elegant French *cuisine*, the supper table now more often saw a bacon and eggs fry-up, or sausage and mash, or a roast joint – the good, stolid fare that Rex had liked from childhood and been fed in hundreds of theatrical 'digs'. He found Rachel's mothering much to his taste. She had no nonsense about her. That, too, appealed in his present mood. He began to perk up and remember how bossy Lilli had been in her too well-drilled Prussian way. Rachel was relaxed, warm, earthy, humorous. She caught Rex on the rebound from the cosmopolitan life with Lilli and Kay. Perhaps the novel experience of working in the 'real' theatre, the Royal Court instead of Binkie Beaumont's West End, predisposed him even more to the charms of a woman who could let her hair down in the pub next door after the show. Rex felt as if Eliza had already brought him his slippers – the physical relationship was bound to follow.

'He looked at me with fondness for that simplicity, that naiveté, that sweetness, that warmth (for which I'm famous) – the opposite of the "society" world,' she wrote.[6] And if that sounds slightly bitter, remember it was written looking back.

The encounter released Rachel's energies and recharged Rex's. He told her she had given him back his youth. She was still a married woman, of course, with a husband living in their tenth-floor council flat in Bayswater. Rachel had referred to 'poor Alan', until Karel Reisz, tired of her harping on the point as he directed her in *Saturday Night and Sunday*

Morning, said: 'Rachel, has it ever occured to you that "poor Alan" might be relieved to see you go?'[7] A joke, maybe, but it hit the mark. It offered her encouragement when Rex appeared on the scene.

Platonov only ran an agreed forty-four performances, every one of them a virtual sell-out. This vote of confidence in his drawing power was just the tonic Rex needed. He was praised extravagantly. He brought his comic talents to a playwright, Chekhov, not usually regarded as comic by his English admirers. He converted a study of self-destruction into the destructive mischievousness of a hell-raiser. He made a play about despair into a black comedy by the intonation and tempo that his tongue imposed on lines that another actor might have regarded as too full of hopelessness to be even bearable. The kind of attrition to which Rex submitted the text during the rehearsal period paid dividends: he tumbled to the anti-hero's satyrlike nature faster even than his director George Devine did. And Devine showed good sense in letting the play be turned into a star vehicle when he saw the hit that Rex was making of it.

Rex was in a buoyant mood. He was going down Burlington Arcade one day when he met Robert Morley walking up, accompanied by his son Sheridan. It happened that Robert had recently been inveigled on to the *This Is Your Life* television show. It had gone out the night before, and Rex had seen it. 'My God, Robert, you are a brave fellow,' he said, with a shudder of apprehension. 'I wouldn't have put up with five minutes of that. An absolute nightmare.' He squinted at Morley. 'You know,' he added, 'compared with me, you do lead a very sheltered life. Very stable, I'd say, Robert. One wife, one house ... and, come to think of it, one performance too.' He then walked on, chuckling. The unfairness of the remark was self-evident, but what stunned both Morleys was its unexpected sharpness, coming from a man not known for his wit so much as his invective.

As soon as the play closed, at the end of November 1960, Rex swept Rachel off to Portofino for Christmas. It was her first taste of an extravagantly lush place and a luxurious existence that left its dangerously seductive aftertaste on her lips for the rest of her life. Nothing else was ever to seem so fulfilling a fantasy as the one Rex had made reality.

The Golden Arrow, the *de luxe* boat-train, still ran from Victoria to Dover in those days. 'And *de luxe* it was,' Rachel wrote in her journals. 'A *coupé* was reserved for us, mahogany and gleaming. The table was laid with white linen and crystal, attentive friendly stewards serving chilled champagne and a perfect English breakfast. Oh, the "Sirring" and "Madaming" that went on, and oh! didn't all the participants enjoy it.' The Lancaster Hotel in Paris ... the sleeping car on the Rome Express ... the descent at Santa Margherita Ligure ... 'The deference to Signor Harrison, the villa with Mario, Giuseppe and Pina waiting in the doorway ... Ease entered my life. Rex took all the decisions. I had nothing to do but live for him.'[8]

Saint Genesio's power to watch over the lives and compatibility of actors was to be severely tested in the years ahead, but Rex had calculated exactly the impression that this 'waking dream' would make on Rachel.

She found the 'Bismarck touch' that Lilli had given it stiff and uncomfortable, and set about changing it. And Rex for his part was glad to see the traces of a woman he had damned for her betrayal yielding to Rachel's less chic, but eminently sensible importations. She put in a small oven of her own to cook his steak-and-kidney puddings or, slightly up the scale, the sole *véronique* he loved. She added a Welsh dresser that Lilli would have thought the worst kind of provincial gaucheness. Rex found her an energetic companion on their walks through the olive groves; or drinking Black Velvet at La Gritta, the bar on the port; or making love in the firelit bedroom while the rain drummed on the windows and Ray Charles records played softly in the background. At fifty-two he could still leap like a goat from rock to rock on the epic descent to San Fruttuoso, with Rachel screaming in mock fear, but following just as surely. It looked like what it was, a grand romance. Rachel's journals show she was drugged by the experience and prayed that her happiness would never end. The Villa San Genesio had the effect of an enchanter's castle on her. Later, she would see the ominous side. For the moment, though, it was paradise enough.

An unsettling interruption was the arrival over the Christmas period of Rita Hayworth and the film producer James Hill, her fifth spouse. Despite *Platonov's* success, Rex's anxieties about where his career was going had revived. He was impatient to find a play or a film that would restore his *popularity* with audiences far and wide. It was proving difficult. Agents saw him as Henry Higgins, and there were not many parts like that around. Thus, when Hill's own production company offered to star him with Rita Hayworth in a comedy called *The Happy Thieves* and were ready to meet his price to play a gentleman thief involved in murder, he winced a little, but listened to his agent who told him to get the money while he could. At least he would be playing opposite glamorous Rita Hayworth, he told himself; he remembered her from *Gilda*. But *Gilda* was made way back in 1946 and Rex, like many film stars, did not often go to the movies. ('Why should I go?' he used to ask testily, 'Don't I make 'em?'[9]) Then he saw Rita when she arrived and was badly shaken. She sat on the sofa, a picture of failing health and faded looks with bland, drugged eyes from the medication she was taking for her alcohol problem. No longer the Love Goddess, but an automaton. He realized he was going to have to make the film with a disintegrating leading lady.

When he and Rachel arrived in Madrid in February 1961, he became more despondent still. Rita simply went through the motions. Perhaps she was feeling the early onset of the Alzheimer's disease that was to rob her of even the memory of what she had been. The only thing that lifted Rex's spirits were the bouts of love-making with Rachel in an apartment they had rented in a palace in the old quarter of Madrid: they had hardly waited for the estate agent to quit the place before throwing themselves on each other.

A somewhat more pathetic scene of love-making was played out when Rex opened the apartment door one evening to find Rita Hayworth outside, alone. Of course he invited her in. Rachel was in the kitchen preparing supper. She had just washed her hair and had it wrapped in a towel while she busied herself over the sausages and mash which she and Rex had decided on. Rachel spied Rita as she entered; up to that minute they had never encountered each other. Rachel had an attack of her old inadequacy feelings over the prospect of meeting Rita who, although badly 'failed', as already mentioned, seemed to have regained something of her old glamour for this unannounced visit. Therefore, while his mistress stayed in the kitchen, Rex was left to entertain his guest. Rita's growing intimacies left him in no doubt that she had come over in the hope of seducing him. Her progress was interrupted by Rachel bringing in the 'bangers and mash', planting them on the table and then, smoothing her apron down, turning to greet Rita. The sex symbol seated close to Rex paid her absolutely no attention and it took Rachel only a few seconds to realize that Rita had mistaken her for the cook. Rex made mumbling introductions. Whatever else the *faux-pas* did, it certainly killed romance that night, to Rex's relief for once.

Missing Rex while he was filming, Rachel welcomed the daily chore of packing a picnic lunch for him and, along with the two kittens, Don Pedro and Don Paco, that she had bought in Madrid, joining him on location. She sat opposite Rex on the grass, her legs apart, as he ate his food and mischievously stroked the long wineglass with his fingers in the secret sign they had evolved to intimate that sex was in his thoughts. But then, in the middle of their nightly love-making, Rex would suddenly call her Kate, the nickname he had given Kay. That shook Rachel. At such moments, the 'waking dream' she was in suddenly turned into a bad one.

She left him for a few days and flew back to London to accept two prizes: the Clarence Derwent award for *Platonov* and a British Film Academy award for her role in *Saturday Night and Sunday Morning*. She returned to find Rex in a black mood, resentful of her leaving him, and, even more disturbing, resentful of her success. She did not know how insecure he was then, or how lonely – Dr Goldman only told her later – or how he must have felt, low in spirits and despairing of the film, as he saw the young optimistic woman glowing with pride in her awards. She took her success so joyfully. Rex felt he would never know success again. In exasperation he slapped her face. Now Rachel began to fear she would lose him.

Some comfort was to be had from James Hill, who was in an even bleaker mood than Rex. He was to divorce Rita the following year. When he confided his troubles to Rex, the two men got to talking about what both of them would do if they were without women. Hill vowed that if he ever found himself single again, he would make sure he stayed that way. He later recalled, 'Rex said: "A word of advice ... Women are like gilt-edged stocks. The more you have, the greater the dividends." ' [10]

When the film mercifully reached its end, Rex and Rachel fled to Portofino; but again he had forgotten it was Lilli's turn, and they were obliged to ask Richard and Sybil Burton if they could borrow their chalet, Pays de Galles, at Celigny, in Switzerland. There, to Rex's alarm, Alan Dobie found them and took Rachel off to talk things over. Now it was Rex's turn to fear he would lose her. But back she came; a few hours away and already she missed the glamour, the charm, the stares she attracted when Rex had her on his arm. By nightfall they were together again and the Dobie marriage was over, bar the divorce.

Rex showed his gratitude. He bought her an otter coat in a fur shop in Lausanne. Rachel hugged the sleek symbol of luxury around her; then her Welsh puritanism rebounded on her. She threw it back at Rex, and shouted that she did not want to be bought.

But there was no going back now. Rex invited Rachel's elderly parents to stay at the villa. The Rev. Roberts reminded him of his own diffident father, and he was uncharacteristically kind to the old man. He was also amused by his untainted simplicity. Offered a choice between *cappucino* and *espresso*, the Baptist minister considered carefully, then, obviously confused, said, 'A little of both, I think.' He also treated the prospect of Rex becoming his future son-in-law with an endearing mix of tolerance (where morality was concerned) and naiveté (where the press was concerned). He told reporters on his return to England: 'I would not be surprised if there was a match between them.' [11]

At the end of July 1961 Rex and Rachel arrived back in London and moved into the Oliviers' flat again. But it was not quite the same free-and-easy co-habitation they had enjoyed before. Edith Jackson was frequently present. And Carey, now in his late teens, came to tea. The boy was familiar enough with Rex's world to be able to view his father with an objectivity that had been lacking when he was younger and Rex was married to Kay. 'I adored Kay,' he recalls, 'her gaiety and sweetness to me. Just like a big sister. I think this was very painful to my mother, because I didn't conceal it terribly well from Lilli. But then Lilli brought me up very "correctly". I was barely out of babyhood when she told an interviewer, "I will give him the marvellous childhood, so long as he obeys me in everything I tell him to do." Well, "correctness" and "obedience" were never words you'd find Kay or Rachel using, which probably accounts for a lot of their appeal to my father – and myself. Of course, I never witnesed Kay's ferocity or the self-destructive side of her or any of the rows and scratches she and father gave each other. When Rachel entered his life, I was older and more alert to things, which made Rex a bit cautious, for he felt I was now capable of judging him. With my half-brother, Noel, who was less serious than I, he felt more at ease, he could be himself. But Rachel, I found fun. She liked me, too, and stood up to Rex, whom she didn't mind provoking. I remember that a few years later I came back from a midnight swim – Rex was filming in the Caribbean – to find my Dad waiting up for me, furious. Rachel had been reading him parts of the diary I'd been keeping, probably to taunt him. He roared at me, "You unwanted spawn of a woman who bored me shitless twenty years ago." Not bad, unless he'd rehearsed it; bloody good for spontaneity. It has the rotundity of his dialogue as Henry VIII in *Anne of the Thousand Days*.'

Rachel was aware that Rex's reputation for outbursts like these was not confined to the family circle. His high-handedness with employees was apparent when she stepped into the Rolls-Royce he was hiring and the chauffeur asked if she was 'the new one'. She concluded he meant 'secretary'. 'I was told how much "they" hated him and how, when a call came [for a car] for Rex Harrison, they tried to avoid going.'[12] There was never any money in it, and a lot of abuse. But Rachel had also seen the weak, lonely, defenceless side of Rex; she pardoned his bullying.

He had no worries now about money. As well as being one of the highest earners in show-business – most of it untaxed, due to the judicious use of off-shore fiscal havens – he was receiving huge royalties from his recording of *My Fair Lady*: £103,000 was paid him at this time from the Columbia disc alone. What was in short supply was work.

This is why he went back to the Royal Court to do a play by the novelist Nigel Dennis.

His instinct should perhaps have warned him off *August for the People*, but he no longer trusted his instinct the way he once did. It had the superficial feel of a Shavian satire. The hero was a high-tempered earl, a misanthrope who detests the common man and 'that disgusting thing' democracy. It had a part for Rachel as the man's mistress. But the satirical tone wavered uncertainly and the politics of the piece were unattractive. Ordinarily Rex would have performed his usual strong-armed tactics on the work and had it – or, at least, his role in it – comprehensively revised in rehearsal. Dennis, however, fought for his play's integrity until Rex said he would not attend rehearsals if the author were present; and by the time the play reached Newcastle on the try-out before the Royal Court opening on 12 September, Dennis had given up the unequal struggle. But no one profited from what John Osborne, the English Stage Company's leading playwright and Royal Court director, called a 'fractious' mood. It was due to go on to the Edinburgh Festival, but even before it closed in Newcastle Kenneth Tynan described it as a dead duck. Rex exploded, denouncing everyone as a 'fucking amateur'. Blessed with the richness of his talent, Osborne reported, the company had 'squandered it like a spendthrift slut'.[13]

The angry and uneasy star leapt into a waiting limousine at Edinburgh's Waverley Station, leaving Rachel to run down the platform like a cat in a maze, as she was to recall, and join him later in their hotel. They were still denying rumours of a romance. Rex had a suite; Rachel a mousehole of a room. She felt the silence between them and resorted again to the sort of voyeuristic love-making which she had found engaged the attention of a man who, despite his reputation, did not overexert himself in bed and sometimes preferred just to watch. Rachel's own sexual fantasies were of the masochistic kind. This fitted in well with Rex's predilections: he usually gained amusement from watching Rachel re-enact some of the 'acts' at which he had been a curious spectator in his Liverpool youth. But when the aphrodisiac effect of Rachel's tricks wore off, he fell back into self-pity and developed a sore throat. Rachel the exhibitionist became Rachel the mother-figure: 'I wrapped a sock around his neck and comforted him.'[14]

Rex should not have been in low spirits for, while he was still in Newcastle, Laurie Evans arrived with an offer that, as Rachel remembered, made him 'gleam again'.[15]

Twentieth Century-Fox's multi-million dollar production of *Cleopatra* had just had to shut down at Pinewood Studios, where the frosts of an English winter had blackened the palm fronds imported daily from Egypt. Elizabeth Taylor, its star, had succumbed to a near-fatal bout of pneumonia and, in the hiatus, the film changed director, studio and stars. Joseph L. Mankiewicz, who had made *The Ghost and Mrs Muir* and *Escape* with Rex, succeeded Rouben Mamoulian. The Pinewood sets were abandoned and work was begun on new ones at the Cinecitta Studios, Rome. Stephen Boyd surrendered Mark Antony's role to Richard

Burton, and now Rex was being hired in place of Peter Finch as Caesar, but he had to begin shooting in the middle of next month. Fox would buy him out of his Royal Court contract.

He accepted. *Cleopatra* would put him back above the title in a major film – this time, unlike *My Fair Lady*, he did not raise objection to the fact that the title had been pre-empted by a female. And he already sensed in his bones that *August for the People* was not going to run many calendar months at the Royal Court.

Of course, this was not how the Royal Court saw things. Its management was appalled at his bad faith. Without him, the play had little hope of survival, none of a West End transfer. Up to Newcastle came Laurence Olivier, despatched on a mercy errand to appeal to his decency in vain. 'The cupidity of rich actors,' John Osborne wrote in his memoirs thirty years later, 'is usually tinged with self-righteousness, but Harrison was too stylish to apologize for claiming his portion of the greed and disloyalty the peaks of his profession may bestow.'[16]

The only sign Rex gave of a bad conscience was an admission to Rachel: 'I don't think I behaved frightfully well.'[17] The gloom had descended on him again with the lukewarm welcome the play received in Edinburgh. To lighten it, she played up to him: 'You did what anyone would have done.'[18] Well, not anyone perhaps, but Rex certainly.

He appeared in the play for twelve days when it opened in London, then withdrew, and the rest of the cast were handed five weeks' compensation out of the sum that Fox paid the English Stage Company to buy Rex out of his contract. As frequently happens in film-making, the extravagance was needless. It proved a case of 'hurry up and wait'. Laurie Evans, who scrupulously checked out his client's commitments before Rex appeared in person to fulfil them, arrived in Rome to discover that the impressive table-top model of the sites in ancient Rome where Rex would render Caesar's lines was still only knee-high in the studio. 'It would be a month or more before he was required. He could have finished his run in the play.' A bad omen. Rex flew to Rome on 25 September 1961 and moved into a suite at the Grand Hotel. Rachel joined him a few days later by train. He was still jittery about the *paparazzi* and, when she ran down the platform towards him at Rome Terminal, in one of the new outfits she had bought at Simpson's, he looked furtively right and left before embracing her.

Rex was on $10,000 a week, expenses of $500 a week, had the use of a twenty-three-hour chauffeured Cadillac and a guarantee of star billing in screen credits and advertising. In short, all was ready – except the film. 'That's when the drinking began,' says Laurie Evans.

Rex was bad at waiting, though he conscientiously put in the time reading widely about Caesar and his era. It was on occasions like this that Rex made up for his lack of formal education. If the reading had a purpose, he had no trouble doing his homework, but Rachel now found him an unresponsive lover. That, too, happened as he put himself into 'training' for a movie. They both of them consumed more drink than he certainly would have done when working, but he could hold it, she could not. Alcohol probably began to gain its grip on Rachel's life during this spell of anxious inactivity, when she had broken with Alan Dobie, but now knew periods of doubt and even of despair for the future as Rex entered his customary period of indecision which preceded commitment to marriage. She would come out of a vodka-induced stupor to find Rex slapping her into wakefulness and snapping, 'For God's sake, stop screaming. You'll have the concierge here.'[19] – 'What was I screaming?' – 'You were fucking well screaming, "Alan ... Alan,"' he said resentfully, meaning Alan Dobie, to whom she was still legally bound as the divorce went slowly through the courts. Rex considered Rachel's involuntary cry an insult to him. Whenever he called her Kay in the middle of love-making, he put it down to forgetfulness.

When filming began, they moved into a villa on the Via Appia Antica. Elizabeth Taylor and her then husband, Eddie Fisher, were not far away and invited them to a party. Whereupon Rachel suffered an attack of her old inferiority complex: she was among the stars, but not one of them. She could not match Elizabeth's legendary beauty. She would not go. Reg, as she persisted in calling Rex, almost to remind herself that he, too, had once been an ordinary mortal called Reginald, turned into a cold-eyed Rex Harrison and she felt 'the world was not finding me up to it'.[20] He went alone. The next day, to his surprise, she appeared in his dressing-room at the studio and proposed they make love there and then. Curtly, Rex dismissed her: could she not see he was working? She left feeling desperate. He, in turn, was irritated by her demanding sex at a time when he was concentrating on art. As he had told James Hill, he liked women to be beholden to him, not *vice versa*.

Rachel served to give him confidence in other respects. She had a good knowledge of the Latin classics and prepared background notes for him on Caesar's expeditions. She did the rounds of Rome's museums by herself, then advised him on which ones to visit in order to study Roman statuary. She persuaded the costume department to take Rex out of the red velvet in which they had dressed him for Caesar and put him into robes dyed in the imperial purple of the murex shell. She soothed him when he returned one day, shaking and chastened, and confessed how he had 'blobbed' a particularly tricky passage of Mankiewicz's dialogue again and again and again in front of what seemed to be half the national theatre of England, who had been brought out by Fox at great expense to play noble Romans. With no special cause to love Rex, their very presence behind him in the Senate was enough to put him off his stroke until the photographer, Leon Shamroy, with Mankiewicz's sympathetic approval, pretended the light was no longer right and the scene was postponed until the next day. 'He didn't really complete it until six months later,' says Mankiewicz, 'since we hadn't yet built the rest of the huge set containing the people he was supposed to be facing.'

He had flare-ups with Fox executives over what he considered slights to him – he resented the pampering of Elizabeth Taylor that went on. One day his nonappearance forced the studio to go looking for him. He returned in the car they had sent to the villa still wearing his dressing-gown, insisting they had slipped up by not reminding him he was needed and should pay more attention to him. They took the hint. Rex used time as his weapon to get his way. Time wasted was money wasted.

Despite this, filming his scenes with Elizabeth went smoothly. Joe Mankiewicz revelled in hearing and seeing how Rex turned Caesar into a pragmatic leader and lover, making him seem capable of great acts of war and statesmanship yet at the same time – as a few of Rex's own women friends could confirm – using his fame like an aphrodisiac to make a woman feel more important to him than any other event on the empire's agenda that day or night. His shaping of the kittenish queen into a consort fit for himself and the people of Rome has the Shavian echo of Henry Higgins transforming a flower girl into his social equal and surrogate wife. The passion of Rex's emperor, as in his Edwardian phonetician, springs from the way he can make an insult sound like a male chauvinist endearment. 'You product of a generation of incestuous mental defectives,' he snaps at Cleopatra – and promptly his lips are pressed to hers.

Rex's wonderful voice made Caesar into a figure who was both colloquial and commanding. He did not seem to read his lines, but to live them in every step, look or gesture. Beside him, Elizabeth sounded girlishly shrill and flat rather than sharp and feline, yet Rex brought to Mankiewicz's screenplay his own scenario, many times played out in life, of the older man whose tutelage of a young girl supplies him with a sexual confidence before he reaches the desired point of sexual consummation. *Cleopatra*, the reviews were to decide a year or so later, belonged to him, if anyone.

Then, towards the end of January 1962, Taylor and Burton played their first scene together; and within the week the star-crossed lovers of the script had become reality and the scene was set for what Burton called drily '*le scandale*', and what the world's tabloids proclaimed as 'the most public adultery in history'.

In it Rex played next to no part. He was rather glad of the attention being deflected from Rachel's less sensational, but still potentially embarrassing adultery with him. In one respect only was he affected by the way that Burton and Taylor were feeding their own headstrong passions into the historic figures they were playing with, alas, only a pale approximation of reality. As their romance made the arrangements for filming them more and more erratic, Rex's scenes were kept in reserve. He could be relied on. It would be useful to hold him over 'as cover', in case love stopped play the way rain stops cricket where the other two stars were concerned. So instead of being in Rome a matter of weeks, he was kept on the film, earning huge extra fees in 'overage' for many months: 'a stop-gap who could be called in to work, so that they need not close the studios'.[21]

During this time Rachel made a film in England, *This Sporting Life*, which was Lindsay Anderson's feature debut. Rex had yielded ungraciously to her now obsessive need to work again. Partly, he resented being left alone. Partly, he detested the role she was offered: a working-class woman, a widow who will not accept the pleasure of releasing her dammed up sexuality when a lonely, inarticulate but virile lodger, played by Richard Harris, becomes her frustrated lover. Rex slipped over to London on a few days' leave and, according to Karel Reisz, who was producing, 'made it plain to us that appearing in dirty clothes pretending to be working class wasn't what show-business stars did.[22] The "little twits", as he called Lindsay and me, were making his kind redundant.' Anderson angered him more when Rex suggested that the many scenes of rough and indeed 'dirty' Rugby in the film would require the use of stunt doubles. 'No,' Anderson replied, 'the actors will have to rough it on the field. Do them good to get a few hard knocks in life.' Rex flared up. 'He became unreasonably furious. "Little man," he said, looming above me, "if you were the last film director in the world, I wouldn't work with you."' Anderson later figured out that Rex had thought he was implying that actors were an unmasculine tribe who had things easy and could do with some honest dirt on their faces, and not just make-up. Rachel ran after Rex, concerned at the possibility of losing her role or even her man.

She returned to Rome from the film a 'free' woman, legally able to marry Rex and so 'puffed up with the pride of thinking I'll soon be Mrs Rex Harrison' that she neglected to go through Customs at the airport, but ran straight towards Rex.[23] After a heated exchange with officials, both were arrested. Fox had to spare a moment from the Burton–Taylor romance to sort out the Harrison–Roberts brouhaha. The inactivity caused by filming his part while Mankiewicz wrote and shot the scenes between Antony and Cleopatra eventually overcame Rex's inertia where his own future was concerned. Rachel's nagging about marriage also stirred him to action, though his signs of reluctance were not lost on his secretary. But complying with the rules for marriage in a country like Italy while simultaneously trying to escape press attention landed Rex in situations that would have made a comedy in themselves. When he went over to the British consulate, a stencilled form was thrust into his hand after he had stood in line and he was told to fill it in 'in ink', pay the equivalent of £3 and then take his place again with all the other glum Brits seeking help over lost passports or picked pockets. He wanted to get married in Portofino – to have the bolt-hole of the villa to hand. Impossible, he was told. It would have to be solemnized in Genoa.

For all his publicity-shy tactics, the names of 'Reginald Carey Harrison' and 'Rachel Dobie' of Via San Sebastian 13, Roma, were spotted when they appeared on the green baise board in Genoa's town hall beside the notice of the impending marriage of an English typist.

On 21 March it seemed to Rex that the entire international press had taken a day off from Burton–Taylor-watching in Rome to cover his nuptials in Genoa. He had been so nervous that he turned up a day early – an extreme case of getting to the church on time. His nerves were no better on the right day. 'We both drank a considerable amount,' Rachel recalled. 'Rex drank whisky. I had Fernet-Branca. He was frightened. I was jittery.'[24] He glared at the mêlée of *paparazzi* at the town hall and threatened to call the whole thing off. Rachel promptly made as if to faint. Those close to him were later of the opinion that Rex had last-minute cold feet and was preparing to make the unruly media an excuse for not going through with the marriage and that Rachel pretended to faint to forestall his announcement, and then revived and made him proceed with it. The aptly named Dr Machiavelli, who combined the duties of marriage registrar and budget assessor, called out above the pandemonium that a 'state of emergency' existed. This formal declaration allowed the doors to be closed against the mob and, after a few *paparazzi* who seemed to have slipped under them were ejected, the ceremony got under way, the groom in grey checks and carrying a Henry Higgins hat, his bride in a tailored chocolate silk suit. Dr Machiavelli reminded them that, under Italian law, Rex was head of the family and Rachel was obliged to contribute to her husband's maintenance, should he lack sufficient means. Rex was asked if he understood this. He had no difficulty replying that he did. They were declared husband and wife.

Then it was a race back to Portofino, pursued by a convoy of shouting, gesticulating, threatening and cajoling cameramen and reporters. Up the hill they sped, a quick transfer into the old Jeep and at last, thankfully, the gates of the Villa San Genesio locked the two of them into the relative peace and safety that the patron saint had so often been invoked to supply down the ages.

23: 'By George, I've Got It!'

'Before I married Rex, if God had said to me, "Rachel, what do you want to be, apart from a great actress?" I would have said a dazzling courtesan,' Rachel said to an English interviewer. 'Not a whore, not a hooker, but a lovely lady whom men adored. But after meeting Rex, all I wanted to be was the best, the most brilliant *wife* in the world.'¹ For the moment, anyhow, they were content – with themselves and with each other. But it was not in the nature of Rex or Rachel to be content for long.

They honeymooned for a few days only. Love for Rex did not mean the same thing as it did for Rachel. For him, it was a tranquillizer; for her, an aphrodisiac. For him, it translated into creature comforts; for her, into sexual satisfaction. If Rex had listened a little more carefully to what his new wife said in interviews, he would have sensed how she was damping down her passion for pursuing her own career. Instead of stoking herself up on the artistry that fed her, she was radiating a cosy domestic warmth for his comfort. But Rex never listened...

However, he noted with some concern how Rachel was continuing to drink too much for her own good. The actress Jean Marsh, an old friend of Rachel's, witnessed Rex's jumpiness when she turned up at the couple's rented villa in Rome to be asked immediately by Rachel: 'Want a vodka, Jean?'² It was only 10 am. The hope was that, if Jean accepted, Rex would not object to Rachel having one too. Tempers were occasionally lost and drink was usually to blame. The two women were enjoying a friendly argument on some topic of English politics – 'both of us had pug noses, both of us were a little radical,' says Jean Marsh – when Rex turned on them and called them 'a couple of Left-wing cunts'.³ Rachel immediately whipped off her shoe and hit him over the head with the heel. 'I was terrified lest the sharp end would dent him, or worse,' Marsh recalls.

But Rex may be forgiven if his temper was even shorter than usual. He had a major worry on his mind. Jack L. Warner had bought the rights to *My Fair Lady* from CBS, which now owned the property, for the then unheard of sum of $5.5 million. By agreement with the Shaw estate – which received five percent of the net profit – he would not release the film before December 1964. But by the summer of 1962, when it was apparent the Broadway run was coming to an end after five and a half years, it was prudent to think of casting the film version. Rex was desperate to play the Henry Higgins role he had created. 'It was the one film role he actively coveted and went all out to get,' says Laurie Evans, so well used to his client's chronic procrastination or feigned uninterest in a part. Rex had staked his claim as early as 1960, when he said in a rare interview: 'When *My Fair Lady* is brought to the screen, as I am sure it will be some day, I would like very much to be in it.'[4] Now this looked increasingly remote. By early summer 1962, while still working in fits and starts on *Cleopatra*, he became aware that he was not the automatic choice. Jack Warner thought him too old now. Moreover, the film's huge budget made it essential to cover all risks. One unnecessary risk, in Warner's opinion, was using a Broadway name like Rex with no reputation of being bankable in films when a star like Cary Grant was available. Though almost four years older than Rex, Grant's screen persona, an impression of charm with a hard centre, had worn well with the years and the public. However, though available, he was not willing. 'Not only will I not play Higgins,' he told Warner, 'but if you don't use Rex Harrison, I won't even go to the film.'[5]

But there was a dark horse – or, rather, a bright hope – who did not take the same view of Rex's prior claim on the role. Peter O'Toole, just turned thirty in 1962, had pole-vaulted to stardom in *Lawrence of Arabia*. He possessed something of Rex's imperious attitude and bullying charm, as well as the talent to turn the Shavian rasp of selfishness into an air of slightly besotted surprise at falling in love with the fair lady he had created. O'Toole, in short, was a formidable contender. For the first time in his life, Rex felt threatened by a fellow actor.

He was unusually restive at Portofino that summer and joined Rachel in her drinking, though he stopped well short of her score. Rachel was now the mistress of San Genesio in the domestic sense of the word, yet all around her she was aware of the past. 'Lilli and Rex' – she often heard the names coupled in the remarks of villagers and even the gathering numbers of tourists. The bartender at their favourite watering hole conjured up another ghost and the *Blithe Spirit* scene restaged itself. 'Sorry, signora,' he told Rachel in Rex's hearing, 'the most beautiful woman in the world, with the exception of Ava Gardner, was Kay Kendall.'[6] Rex took the man outside and slapped his face. But the gesture seemed more to do with Rex's fractious disposition than innate gallantry.

He was constantly on the telephone to London – no easy feat in those days in that part of Italy – to ask Laurie Evans for the latest news about his chances of getting the part. One day an English newspaper which Rachel bought in Santa Margherita carried a columnist's firm prediction that O'Toole was about to be cast. Rachel hid the paper from Rex and went down on her knees to pray that it was not true. Warner had indeed opened negotiations with Keep Films, the company jointly owned by O'Toole and his producer partner, Jules Buck. George Cukor, who had already been signed to direct the film, cabled Alan J. Lerner from Istanbul on 17 September 1962, asking Lerner to meet O'Toole and Jules Buck, who were then in New York. Lerner had not the power to say who should play the role, but he possessed a contractual right almost as good – to say who should not. When Cukor reached Noël Coward's home in Switzerland, on his way back to America, he wrote to Warner's right-hand man, Steve Trilling, observing that Lerner had seen O'Toole and Buck on 24 September and he added, 'I hope O'Toole was liked – I think he is our man.[7] I agree with you [about the film], it should be made in California. If not, I'd do it in London.'

Meanwhile, Rex sweated it out in Portofino, where Coward had passed a few days trying to persuade him to play the Prince Regent in a musical version of Rattigan's play *The Sleeping Prince*, which had been filmed as *The Prince and the Showgirl* with Olivier and Monroe. Though tempted, Rex dared not commit himself until he knew who had got the Henry Higgins part. He had almost abandoned hope when he went to Paris, along with Rachel, to record some dialogue tracks for *Cleopatra*. While there, he bought one of the new Polaroid cameras – 'to take pictures *à la Playboy* of me, to put it delicately', Rachel confided to her journals.[8] Back again in Portofino, he was swimming off the coast from his Criscraft cabin cruiser, which he called *Henry* for obvious reasons, when Rachel used the camera to take 'a few silly snaps of him, thin, balding, naked'.[9] Cukor had suggested, he hoped tactfully, that Rex come over to Hollywood for a screen test – a proposal that enraged and rather frightened Rex, since he knew it was for one purpose only, to see how he had aged. Rachel now cheekily suggested sending Cukor the Polaroids she had just taken as Rex's 'photo opportunity'. He did so. It was the act of a man making his last bet with a kind of gay disdain for the way fate would decide things. It was also a humorously defiant way of snapping his fingers at George Cukor.

His nervousness grew as he heard that Warner would be making the casting decision any day now. His unease would have been increased had he known that Steve Trilling, at Warner Bros, was agreeing with Cukor over Peter O'Toole's suitability as Professor Higgins. On 2 October 1962 Trilling cabled Buck to say that Warner Bros would pay O'Toole

$200,000 for the picture. No screen test would be needed, which was flattering. On the other hand, there would be no participation in profits, gross or net, simply a flat fee for the duration of the filming. This was disappointing. Keep Films had proposed that O'Toole be paid $400,000 for twenty weeks services and then overage, plus a ten percent profits participation. Either O'Toole and Buck overplayed their hand or else Alan J. Lerner kept faith with Rex and rejected each and every actor proposed, including O'Toole, until the election fell on Rex.

One day in late October the tiny post office in Portofino sent a messenger boy puffing up the hill to deliver a telegram to the villa. (The telephone was undergoing one of its not infrequent break-downs. Genesio was clearly not the patron saint of communications.) The housekeeper carried it out to Rex, who was lounging in a sunchair on the terrace. He opened it with his face betraying nothing of the way his heart was beating. Then, as he read it, every furrow and wrinkle on him converged into a huge grin of triumph. Without getting to his feet, according to one eye-witness, he flung his arms aloft and wide open in a victory gesture. The same fierce crow of self-congratulation that he had uttered as Higgins when Eliza Doolittle finally mastered her elocution lesson broke from Rex's lips. 'By George, I've got it!' he whooped.[10]

They broke out the champagne and sat in the sun, happily drinking. Then Rex's face clouded over. His eyes narrowed like a man trying to pick out the hazards of a distant but difficult landscape. 'You know,' he said, 'I really wonder if George Cukor is the right director for this picture.'[11]

Work on *My Fair Lady* was not due to start before August 1963. How to keep himself busy until then? With no regret, he turned down the Rattigan musical. It was put on, as *The Girl Who Came to Supper*, in New York the following year with José Ferrer in what might have been Rex's part and fared poorly. Then, prompted by Rachel and boredom, he did what he had sworn never to do: Shakespeare. In January 1963 he made a recording in London of *Much Ado About Nothing*, playing Benedick to Rachel's Beatrice with an all-British cast directed by the young American playwright Howard Sackler. 'It's fascinating to hear my father,' says Carey Harrison. 'Extraordinary swooping rhythms ... vocal acrobatics ... flowery and fiery at the same time ... rococo is the only word for it. Oh, Rex, why hadn't you the nerve to do it on stage!'

By now, Rex owned the whole of the Villa San Genesio. He had asked Lilli to sell him her half of it. Perhaps nagged by residual guilt over the deception she had practised on him, she agreed. Another reason why Lilli parted with her share of the villa was that she could not afford to contribute to its upkeep. She and Carlos had their own home in

Switzerland and, although Lilli was earning a good salary from film acting, the royalties from her books would not begin flowing in until much later in life. Rex really had no fixed home, therefore fewer expenses, and much of his living expenses were paid for by the companies for whom he made his films. But it was Rachel, anxious to possess fully the dream of San Genesio, who harped on at him until he sat down and wrote to Lilli offering to buy her out.

He gloried in being its sole master. These few weeks at the turn of the year, with Higgins safely in his pocket, brought Rex total contentment: 'It seemed like the world before the Fall,' Rachel wrote.[12] The garden was exquisite. The vineyard Rex had planted was now producing a hundred or so bottles of very drinkable wine. Every day they ate off the glass table on the terrace. 'Dad loved the elements,' says Carey. 'He loved standing erect in his Criscraft as it bucked and bounced across the bay and feeling the wind buffet him – the same when he was behind the wheel of his open Rolls-Royce with the breeze whipping through what hair he had left. He was never a man you could call contented, but submitting himself to the elements gave him real joy. Perhaps facing into the wind suited his abrasive nature. It upset others, but refreshed him. I recall him standing in the window of the first-floor living-room at San Genesio watching a fierce electrical storm raging over the bay and occasionally calling out to the lightning, "Well hit, God!"'

About the middle of February he was recalled by Fox. The Battle of Pharsalia would have to be reshot to give the opening of *Cleopatra* more epic impressiveness. The version shot on a hastily imposed economy budget the year before would not cut together very spectacularly. It meant going down to Almeria in south-east Spain. Still feeling grateful to God (if not to Cukor), Rex agreed to work for expenses only. After he had finished location work, he and Rachel motored back via Madrid and he tried to get into the Ritz Hotel there, knowing full well that after one celebrated actress had behaved with spectacular vulgarity in the dining-room, the place had banned all people with show-business connections. Unfortunately the manager penetrated his 'Reginald Carey' disguise and Mr Rex Harrison and wife were refused accommodation and had to move to another hotel. Still smarting, he and Rachel took themselves off to see Hitchcock's *Psycho*, which was playing in its original English version. Walking back to their second-best hotel, they ignored a street sign saying (in Spanish) 'Pedestrians Don't Walk'. Rachel knew what it meant; Rex, short-sighted and still in a huff, did not see it or pretended not to and then refused to pay the equivalent of a twenty-five cent fine summarily levied on him by a policeman. They were arrested and jailed, and held until 4 am, by which time the manager of his hotel, alarmed by his failure to return, had located him and stumped up the fine. Apologies poured in along with fruit and sherry from the Mayor of Madrid. Rex was unmollified. They would never again set foot in Spain. Home they went to Portofino. An ignominious end to Caesar's rule.

As the time for them to leave for California approached, Rachel began suffering inadequacy symptoms again. She knew that there she would not be regarded as a star in her own right, simply as Rex's consort, enjoying the privileges of life by courtesy of his status and feeling she was there under false pretences. Rex also began withdrawing from her the way he had done in the weeks preceding *Cleopatra*, becoming wrapped up in his film commitment, reading and rereading the words of his songs, oblivious to the sense of deprivation which Rachel was manifesting by increasingly heavy drinking. Even the luxurious ambience of their state room aboard one of the Queens, the best table in the Verandah Grill, the bowing and scraping did not excite her the way it used to do. Rex caught her sitting alone on deck and photographed her with the famous Polaroid. Now it showed up her own miserable state. 'I was looking like I felt,' she later wrote. 'He laughed and said I looked like an early immigrant. I suppose I was.'[13]

Rex had ordered his Rolls-Royce, which had accompanied him on the liner, to be driven across the States and made ready to meet him when he and Rachel arrived at Los Angeles airport. Meanwhile, in New York, he got himself in the mood for doing battle by taking on Fox, who had had the temerity to exclude his face from the poster advertising *Cleopatra* in Times Square. In a ploy to publicize the film by reference to the Taylor–Burton affair, it depicted them only, she reclining, he brooding over her. A suit filed by Rex in the Superior Court soon ended this 'twosome', though whether it was to his advantage is doubtful, for Caesar now appeared in a little 'window' behind the adulterous couple. 'Hell, he looks more like Peeping Tom,' said one passing New Yorker polled for his opinion.[14]

On 24 May they arrived at the airport and Rex's spirits were restored by the comfort of the resplendent automobile awaiting him. Rachel's drooped even more. To her, it was a perfect example of the effortless way Rex dominated his world. 'Elegant and guarded, sophisticated and famous,' she later recorded, '[he] drove his Rolls-Royce to Warner Bros to star in the film of the play that made him world famous. Rex lived up to his myth – and the myth shut me out.'[15]

When Rachel was looking after 'her man', she was in her element, but now that he had turned into 'the star' again, she felt herself becoming a 'Hollywood wife', a non-being. She yearned to be back in Portofino, where she had adapted so easily to the local life, where her serviceable

Italian made her better liked than Rex, who had remained a rather remote celebrity, feared for his temper, but endured for the *cachet* he gave the place and the hard cash he put in the town's tills from tourists who came hoping to see '*il professore 'iggins*' at the local bar.

Now the hierarchies of Hollywood made her feel incompetent to organize Rex's life the way he liked. After a few weeks at the Bel Air Hotel, she had rented a house for them in Coldwater Canyon that seemed suitable for Rex's style and status – and regretted it once they moved in. 'A terrible little faggot house', owned by two interior decorators, everything about it was made to impress.[6] He constantly cast its pretentiousness up to her. As Rachel did not drive, she was immobilized for much of the day. The hired servants patronized her, well aware who was the star of this household. The meals they prepared displeased Rex, who missed the trencherman food she used to cook in the small oven at the villa. She reacted to her own inadequacy by increasing her intake of alcohol. She became 'noisy' and embarrassed him when they went out to parties. Rex's mind became more and more fixed on his *Fair Lady* as a relief from his wife.

Jack Warner, knowing how desperately Rex wanted to play his old role, had driven a hard bargain. One aspect of it especially hurt Rex's self-esteem: the fee. Warner Bros were to 'borrow' his services from Voltiguer SA of Chur, Switzerland, one of his tax-avoidance companies, for $200,000 – much, much less than he thought his due. He had been inclined to haggle angrily over it, but Laurie Evans begged him not to. 'Take it, Rex, and take it quick,' he urged. It would be paid in $10,000 instalments each weekend for the first twelve weeks, then in a further sum of $80,000 on 15 January 1964. If his services were used over the twenty weeks guaranteed minimum, he would draw overage at $10,000 a week until his role was declared complete. During filming, he would draw $500 weekly in expenses, have 'first star' dressing-room, retain a chauffeured car on twenty-four-hour call for use instead of – or in addition to – his own Rolls-Royce, which Warner Bros agreed to have shipped to New York and back. (It cost £169. 10s. on the outward voyage, as it turned out.) Rex protested at the studio not meeting the onward cost of the car's being driven to Los Angeles. Warner was firm. It pleased him to be stubborn over details: he knew these were often the thorns in a star's proud flesh. Rex had no participation whatsoever, gross or net, in the film's profits, though his royalties from the record of the sound-track would subsequently prove munificent and, along with his stage recording of the show, provide him with a huge annual income for the rest of his life.

What he gained in the long run, therefore, might have consoled him were it not for what he knew Audrey Hepburn was being paid in the short term. Her deal left no doubt that she was the one who carried the money on the screen. By an agreement made on 20 October 1962, she was to receive guaranteed compensation of $1 million – five times what Rex got – payable in seven annual instalments of $142,957.15 between 1 July 1963 and 1 July 1969, thus greatly reducing the huge bite that tax would have taken out of one lump sum payment. She was to be paid overage, if necessary, at $41,666.67 a week or *pro rata*. Even allowing that she, too, had no profit participation – and would not share in the recording royalties, since her singing voice was to be dubbed by Marni Nixon – Rex was incensed by what he regarded as the inequitable treatment meted out to him, who had been the *making* of the stage show. Even Cukor was being paid more than himself: $300,000.

An additional anxiety: Cukor had a well-deserved reputation as a 'woman's director'. He had achieved some of his most notable successes with actresses like Garbo, Katharine Hepburn and Norma Shearer. Now he was to direct an actress whose fee vastly exceeded Rex's in a version of the musical in which Rex had taken every ruthless step possible to 'protect' himself, even to the extent of having its title changed. He feared his role would now be secondary and it took a lot of reassuring talk from Cukor to disabuse him. Even then, an annoyed Rex was a niggling Rex – even more than usual.

On 24 June, one week after he began rehearsals (for which he was not being paid at all), he had Edith Jackson send in his first bill to Warner Bros: an itemized invoice for his and Rachel's transportation to Los Angeles: 'Car from Portofino to Santa Margherita, £10; round-trip first-class train sleeper from there to Paris, £122.00; round-trip first-class Paris–Cherbourg–New York on Queen Elizabeth, £970. 16s. od; round-trip drawing-room New York–Los Angeles, $230.00.'[7] Not much, maybe, to a major film studio, but a warning shot from a star who meant to watch over his own interest every minute, inch and cent of the way.

His main worry as he went through the nine weeks of rehearsals before principal photography began was one of 'reduction'. He had learnt how to project the Higgins role to hit the back wall of the theatre. Now he had to go only as far as the camera lens, or it would become stagey. But he was a quick learner. 'Rex is surprisingly good,' wrote Cecil Beaton to his secretary in England after watching the first week's rushes. 'He has learnt how to project on the screen.'[18]

Another concern went deeper and was not so easily mastered. Rex was well aware that he acted the lyrics as much as he 'sang' them: he needed to feel the emotion coming from his own particular kind of *parlando* or 'pitch speaking'. But it was the general practice when making

Hollywood musicals to pre-record the numbers and then have the artists mime the expression to go with the songs on the sound-stage playback system. Rex insisted that any pre-recording he did would be 'flat'. Deprived of the spontaneous edge of a live performance, his matching of visual image to pre-recorded words would be dulled. As he seldom did a number exactly the same way in each take, dubbing would be a nightmare. In short, he had do the lyrics live on camera. 'Six years later [after the stage show], his nerves are worse,' Beaton wrote in his diary.[19] True, but his will was unshakeable. Cukor accommodated him, using one of the tiny radio microphones then coming into use where more mobility was needed than the sound boom could provide. Thus it was Rex who called the shots – literally. Cukor used two cameras for Rex's numbers, for long shots and close-ups. It would be 'theatrical', but that did not disturb a director who had come from the theatre originally and entered Hollywood as a dialogue director. It was Cukor's ability to work 'out front' with his stars, physically as well as mentally, which gave his films their notable sense of performance, rather than technique.

Despite all this, Rex found his final number defeating him. One reason why he resisted doing the 'Grown accustomed to her face' number, if asked for it at private parties or his rare appearance for charity, was because he could not start it 'cold' – he needed the 'motor' of Higgins's earlier, if undeclared, love for Eliza that has been ticking over in his bachelor head during the previous scenes.

Realizing Rex needed not to be at anyone's beck and call in this number, which was additionally charged with other associations like Kay Kendall's presence in the wings, Cukor told Rex to do whatever he felt – 'felt' being the key word – and the cameras would follow him, the way the stage musicians had done. They did, faultlessly. And as he walked up to the front door of Higgins's house, one camera left running but unmanned picked him up as he entered the shot until he closed the door. 'I imagined it was Kay,' he told Rachel later.[20]

No one felt Rex's insistence on things being done his way more keenly than Cecil Beaton, himself no corner-cutter on all the grand details of the work in hand. All Higgins's outerwear, Rex decreed, must come from England – from tailors, hatters and shoe-makers whom he used to furnish his own wardrobe. He loved the endless confabs over details that are reflected in Beaton's correspondence with London retailers.

No ordinary top hat would do for Higgins to wear to the ball with Eliza: only a silk one supplied by Mr Glazier of Herbert Johnson which was of pre-war vintage – 'they are now rather scarce' – with a crown exactly $6\frac{1}{2}$ inches deep. The same Mr Glazier forwarded patterns of 'tweedy material, speckled, etc., for Mr Harrison's inspection' and the famous Henry Higgins hat, instead of being entrusted to Hollywood, was made up in London. Beaton, however, scored a notable victory by persuading Rex to have the brim made a half-inch wider than the one he had worn on the stage – 'and he deemed it an improvement', Beaton recorded, no doubt with relief.[21] Trickers, where Rex had his shoes made, obligingly forwarded their catalogue, marking 'the footwear already supplied Mr Harrison, so that you can reorder if necessary'.[22] Rex's seven suits were tailored for him by Sullivan Williams of London; his figure hardly ever varied, so no new measurements were needed. Higgins's shirts for day and night wear did not have an American stitch in them: all were made to order in the London work rooms of Washington Tremlett, whose 'Mr Woodhead understands what is needed and will forward ... three day shirts in lighter weight material with collars; one cardigan as before; a selection of knitted ties in the colour range required.'

The bills for all this survive in Warner's archives and make illuminating reading, if only to show how inflation has entered the gentleman's wardrobe. Washington Tremlett's account, for instance, ran to: (1 Cheltenham jacket (cardigan) £8. 15s. od; three knitted silk ties, £4. 4s. od; three further ditto, £5. 6s. 6d; three collar-attached shirts, £17. 17s. od.'

The one garment that Rex permitted the studio to make up for him was a double-breasted waistcoat, which had to be carefully made if Rex was not to look stout in it.

Not strictly a garment, but essential outerwear, was the hairpiece that Rex habitually wore for his roles and for formal public appearances, though he was not vain enough to wear it permanently – the Henry Higgins hat covered that problem. The honour of making up this item fell to Max Factor, but it caused more trouble than anything else Rex wore. Argument raged over where precisely the parting should come. Rex seemed to use this inoffensive, if essential, little piece of artificial hair as a test of other people's competence. Perhaps it also reflected his disquiet at the irresistible advance of age. On the increasingly rare occasions he saw his sons, he resisted being photographed with them; their grown-up appearance unsettled him.

Rex's relationship with Audrey Hepburn was wary at first, but it warmed into helpful understanding of her difficulty in coming 'cold' to the show. He saw he had the upper hand in ensuring it would be his own performance that drove the film.

The movie finished shooting inside four months – surprisingly quick and a tribute to Cukor's thoroughness in rehearsal. Rex saw a rough cut early in 1964 in the company of Jack Warner and George Cukor. When it ended, there was the usual indeterminate silence. All eyes turned not to Rex, but to Warner. The studio head said nothing. He simply got up and, turning to Rex, made a deep bow from the waist. That said it all. In the car taking them home, Rex told Rachel that it was the happiest experience he had ever known. He had seen his performance given permanent form. Henry Higgins would be his for life – and after.

24: Agony and a Little Ecstasy

When Rex was acting, not much else engaged his attention. One exception was a dog, the other a new but short-lived affair with a woman. Of the two, the former probably held more of his true affections. While in Hollywood at this time, he was greatly taken with a basset hound belonging to his neighbours. Touched by the animal's liking for him — not an emotion he had met with often on four legs or two — he set about acquiring one of the same breed. So Homer entered his life, a pedigree puppy from a litter in the San Fernando Valley. This 'man's dog', surely the very breed that Higgins would have picked to bring him his slippers before Eliza appeared to perform that chore, was to accompany Rex everywhere he went, though in England the strict anti-rabies law required six months' quarantine. Dog owners are said to grow into passable likenesses of their pets: in Homer's case, the reverse was true. The hound quickly assumed a lot of his master's characteristics: a refusal to obey anyone except Rex or do anything that did not please him were soon apparent to people who met Homer — or Rex. The dog also appeared to have an uncanny knack for getting in the way of people Rex did not particularly like at that moment. Rachel found herself frequently tripped up by the growing dog's propensity to shift itself into her path after she and Rex had had a spat. Later on, Rex would be torn by his customary indecision over whether to dedicate his memoirs to his wife or his dog. And Rachel, for her part, was inspired to produce a birthday present for Rex consisting of a small, privately printed book entitled *Odyssey to Homer.* She preferred the company of her cat, Alice, whom Homer fortunately ignored as if she did not exist. Alice was now the only company Rachel had after Rex departed for the studios and she 'wept and woke up to the emptiness and the dog'.[1]

Rex pleaded the concentration his work required. True, but only up to a point. She soon sensed that he was running a new affair from the alertness he manifested every time Romy Schneider, the Austrian film star, was included in the weekend parties they went to at the David Selznicks'. 'Rex would leap up at her bidding,' she recalled.[2] However,

Rex's affair ended abruptly when he made a late afternoon call on Romy Schneider as he returned from the day's filming on *My Fair Lady* and found her in a drugged state on the sofa. It was not a suicide attempt, simply an accidental and minor overdose of cocaine, but the shock of walking in again and discovering what, for a moment, he took to be another corpse like that of Carole Landis's caused Rex to back out of the affair in haste and some alarm. Thereafter, he was not nearly so alert to Romy Schneider's demands on him at parties. Drugs terrified Rex: he belonged to a generation that believed stimulants came out of a bottle, not from the dealer.

Meanwhile, Rachel's sense of her own worthlessness grew. Not knowing how to integrate herself into Hollywood life at her husband's elevated level, she tried filling her day with tennis lessons, singing lessons and driving lessons, and even appeared in a television play with Richard Kiley in an effort to stop the rust growing on her unused talent. Her frustration was increased when the film she had made in England, *This Sporting Life*, opened in New York to sensational reviews. The boom in all things British, which included the James Bond movies and soon the Beatles, helped focus attention on this raw and powerful study of the sexual bleakness of working-class life in the provinces.

Rachel would have returned to work in England, where Hollywood money was funding the new generation of indigenous filmmakers, but Rex could not because of taxes. So she stayed put in California, turning down even as tempting a role as Dylan Thomas's wife in the play *Dylan* with Alec Guinness. 'I ignored it loftily. I wanted the easy life,' she rationalized.[3]

Life was not easy, however. On the money earned from her television play, she rented a Malibu beach house for herself and Rex to try to warm their relationship back into a reassuring glow, but Rex just drank, patted Homer, gazed out to sea. Rachel drank and turned 'bright and breezy, but not in control'.[4] Her salvation was David Selznick. She got on with him famously, for she was well read and could keep up with the producer's manic disquisitions on great books he wanted to bring to the screen, as well as pace him drink for drink. Rex was jealous and showed his disapproval, both of excess in liquor and literature, by long silences once they got home. It took a visit from her parents to bring his genuine affection to the surface. The Rev. Rees Roberts was dying from cancer, but enjoying temporary remission. 'Reverend,' said Rex, 'you've just got to make a comeback.'[5] It was like one actor talking to another. Rachel's father did indeed manage to preach a few sermons full of his old fiery *hwyl* before he died the following year, with Rex by his bed holding his hand. Having been absent when his own father died, Rex felt the loss of someone who was the opposite of himself in his frail but trusting attitude to life.

The truth was he was 'bored shitless' by his marriage, but couldn't see any way out of it and was rather apprehensive of what Rachel might do to herself. In such straits, he took the old escape route – work. Before he even finished *My Fair Lady*, he had signed up for his next film, *The Agony and the Ecstasy*, based on a popularized life of Michelangelo. Charlton Heston would be the artist. Rex, for a consideration of $250,000 and the assurance that the film would be shot in tax-free conditions in Rome, agreed to impersonate Pope Julius, the pontiff who commissioned the great painting on the ceiling of the Sistine Chapel. Rex plunged into his 'homework', swotting up on the period with every book he could borrow from the Los Angeles city libraries. It did not help Rachel's hope of rekindling their love when her husband spent hours worrying over whether the papal mitre would look as tall on his head as it did in ecclesiastical illustrations of Pope Julius. Agonizing went on, but little ecstasy resulted.

In New York, before they boarded the *ss Leonardo da Vinci* for Genoa, Rex ran into Carol Reed, who was to direct the film, and began immediate talks about how he saw the Pope. Reed had been a long time without a successful film and Rex came away with the impression that Heston would enjoy the director's patronage the way Michelangelo had the Pope's, but for worldlier reasons. Reed needed a hit and knew which star was box-office. *My Fair Lady*, remember, had not yet been seen.

He sailed with Rachel, Homer and Alice the cat, feeling apprehensive. It did not help to have Rachel referring to his new film as 'your pope opera'.[6] At such moments, Homer was indeed a support.

However, he got to Portofino to discover that the advance word among those in the film community who had had a preview screening of *My Fair Lady* had made him, as it were, 'hot'. Offers were already coming in for his next but one picture His agents forwarded a script with particular interest for him. Written by Terence Rattigan and to be directed for MGM by Anthony Asquith, it was called *The Yellow Rolls-Royce* and was to start shooting in England almost at once. It told three stories all revolving around the ownership, happy or tragic, of the eponymous vehicle. Rex was offered a role in the first segment, that of an aristocratic politican who discovers his wife *in flagrante* with his secretary in the back seat of the car during Ascot races. The combination of a luxury automobile, an illicit romance and a fashionable occasion all appealed to Rex's snobbery. So did the $150,000 fee he was able to wring out of MGM for a few weeks' work. The short shooting schedule made it possible to be in and out of England without incurring tax obligations. Rattigan,

Asquith and the producer, Anatole de Grunwald, were friends and people of taste. He felt safe with them. They were also a little in awe of him. He could be his own master and, if need be, theirs as well.

On Rachel, however, the demands for Rex's services acted like a depressant. Now she saw him signed up for two films that would keep him active over the rest of 1964. She had nothing lined up. Realistically, she might have hoped for a role in *The Yellow Rolls-Royce*, perhaps the society bitch who breaks the news of his wife's infidelity to Rex. But Moira Lister got that part and played it bitingly well, perhaps incited by the ruthlessness with which Rex reduced the amount of dialogue she had in her scenes with him. *The Agony and the Ecstasy* was virtually an all-male coupling.

Just before Rex started on the Rattigan film, news came that he and Rachel had both been nominated for Oscars: he for his role in *Cleopatra*, she for hers in *This Sporting Life*. It was the first time since Alfred Lunt and Lynn Fontanne in 1932 that a husband and wife had received Academy Award nominations, and, as Rachel pointed out with emphasis, 'the Lunts acted *together*'.[7] Here she was, Oscar material and not an offer in sight. She began to ponder even more wretchedly whether being Mrs Rex Harrison, the one role she had craved, was going to exclude her from every other role she might play.

Rex was in his element when *The Yellow Rolls-Royce* started shooting at MGM's Borehamwood studios in March 1964. In the words of Richard Huggett, the biographer and actor, who had a minor role as 'Sir Somebody Something', he was 'aloof and disdainful, never speaking to anyone except the other stars in his episode, Jeanne Moreau and Alan Badel, and not much even to them.'[8] The only people he obviously wanted to be agreeable to were 'the girls among the extras whom he invited to lunch at his table in the restaurant in groups of three or four. Very pretty they looked surrounding Rex in their long 1930s-style Ascot dresses, floppy hats and white gloves. He kept them in stitches of laughter.' Huggett decided that, although Rex enjoyed the female audience, he was using beauty as a barrier, so that he would not be forced into talking to strangers, that is to say people not of his rank. Huggett broke through the *incommunicado* fence, however, with a compliment on how well Rex wore his topper and morning coat, and asked who was his tailor. Someone in Savile Row? 'Actually, no,' Rex said, recovering his aplomb after this extra had ignored protocol and spoken to him, 'he's a little chappie in Conduit Street ... I've forgotten the name, but you can ring up my agent.' The lofty politeness indicated that a gentleman does not remember the name of his tailor; he leaves that to his agent.

But Huggett saw the 'killer instinct' at work too. It happened that an

MGM executive objected to Alan Badel, playing Rex's private secretary at the Foreign Office and his wife's lover at the races. He looked 'faggoty'. Asquith defended Badel, asking, 'Anyhow, where can you find a man who's more attractive to women than Rex?'[9] In vain. Badel was out. Edmund Purdom was brought in without anyone bothering to tell Rex. He did not find out until Purdom's hunk of handsome manhood began saying the lines that had been Badel's. 'Then I heard Rex scream at Asquith at the top of his voice, "You didn't have the decency to tell me, let alone ask my view ... I consider myself grievously insulted," and so on, for ten minutes or more. That was Rex militant, all right. The row only ended when he'd beaten everyone into the ground, but, unable to reverse the recasting, had to return to the set, sulkily, and redo Badel's scene with Purdom, to whom he was civil, but nothing more.'

The *contretemps* may have had its unanticipated bonus in enabling Rex to muster even more mortified feelings of being deceived when he comes across the lovers in the back of the car. With his triumph over his horse winning the Ascot Gold Cup turning to ashes along with his marriage, he orders his chauffeur to take the Rolls-Royce back to the showrooms: 'It no longer pleases me.' Five words, but Rex uses them to sum up the stifled cry from the heart of a man who has treated his wife as just another prized possession and now prefers to sacrifice the car rather than suffer the constant reminder of what his neglect has allowed to happen. The episode shows what large emotion Rex could manifest, even when it was writ small.

There was, of course, an irony in Rex playing the role of a man whose neglect of his wife causes her to turn to another for comfort when, at the same time, he was neglecting Rachel for his own work. But his consent in allowing her to appear in a new London musical had less to do with the benign influence of *The Yellow Rolls-Royce* than his fear of how Rachel's interference was increasing, as well as her temper. It was plain even to him that she could not keep her will to work bottled up, so to speak, very much longer. Lionel Bart had written a musical called *Maggie May*, set in Liverpool's docklands, about a prostitute who incarnates the life force of the place. It was inspired, in a lay mode, by the story of Christ and the Magdalen. Georgia Brown turned it down: 'Didn't want to play second fiddle to Christ,' Bart said acidly.[10] It was offered to Rachel. It meant she would not be with Rex when shooting began on *The Agony and the Ecstasy* in Rome that June, but Rachel had had enough of being Rex's 'ideal' – i.e. non-working – 'wife'. She flew off to London and he was left alone in a studio-rented villa which contained a Christian crypt that had to be kept open and available to visiting archaeologists. Not a place to raise the spirits – Rex's kind, anyhow.

In playing his papal role, he had decided to go against the ecclesiastical grain of the man and instead emphasize his belligerent nature as a warrior-pope. There was good historical basis for this, but it was a favourite ploy of Rex's to play against expectations, which had worked well in *Cleopatra*, where he had decided Caesar's aphrodisiac would be work, not love, as indeed it was Rex's. He also cut down Julius's set speeches to church and laity. Rex hated doing crowd scenes: he knew there were too many actors present who wished to see him embarrassed by a fluff or a fit of forgetfulness. The hardest part of *Cleopatra*, he admitted, had been Caesar's oratory: 'Here an actor has to become an after-dinner speaker and actors are notoriously bad at that.'[11]

He needed little rehearsing for the Pope's scenes with Michelangelo. Almost all of them were fiercely argumentative. One culminates in the irascible churchman striking the painter with the rod on his desk which he has used to refer to the ceiling designs. Heston was impressed – to the point of impatience – by Rex's pernicketiness. 'He was very, very anxious to know where exactly the rod would be lying on the table when he seized it. "Picky" in the extreme.'[12] He was also very protective of his appearance. According to Heston, he refused to be seen wearing the papal crown. Just as it descends on to Rex's head, the scene ends. And for all his fastidious attention to historical detail, Rex refused to accommodate the feature of Pope Julius that was widely remarked on at the time: he was the first Holy Father in hundreds of years to wear a beard and moustache. Rex plays a clean-shaven pontiff. Maybe his vanity still rankled after the audience failed to recognize his heavily disguised General in *The Fighting Cock*.

As with his Caesar, Rex gives a very modern interpretation of the role. He often said he could never really think himself into the distant past. Here he takes history and mentally rewrites it in order to fit the world he inhabits. Meddlesome, crafty, testy, autocratic, unfeeling: his pontiff resembles a movie producer forever at odds with his director (Heston) and the slow progress of the production and constantly sneaking in to see how the picture is coming on, interfering at all levels, measuring his concept against the evidence of the rushes and raging on about the amount of schedule still awaiting completion.

While Heston labours literally and impressively with the physicality of his role, Rex goes about lightening his by a dazzling display of hyperactivity and egomania. It does not save a ponderous yet simplistic film, but relieves it, which is some achievement at least.

Rex took no chances. The story goes that he had 'lifts' put in his boots to bring him up to Heston's eye-level, which was an inch or so higher than even Rex's six-foot plus. Then he found his fellow player mysteriously rising in height and managing still to out-top him. Did he do it by 'lifts' or by will-power? Heston has always refused to divulge which it was, but in his journals, published in 1978, he notes courteously that 'Rex has the temperament of a thoroughbred racehorse ... highly strung with a tendency to snort and rear and kick at the starting gate.'[13] Rex was perhaps a shade less complimentary than he could have afforded to be about Heston: 'Thinks the world is his supporting cast.'[14] Perhaps he still saw him with the eyes of a producer.

Without Rachel and in Rome, a city he hated only a little less than Hollywood, seeing it as having 'an air of evil hanging over it', he brooded on his problems.[15] Chief among them was Rachel's mental health. He feared she was exhibiting something akin to the manic depression that had been putting Vivien Leigh into electro-convulsive shock therapy. The basis of Rachel's illness was different, a doctor had informed Rex: it resided in her own quite unfounded but compulsive sense of worthlessness. She had incredibly low self-esteem and reverted to flamboyant behaviour to conceal it as well as heavy drinking to deaden it. The drink made it difficult to reach and alleviate the disorder.

Rex had already suffered some of Rachel's alarming 'fugues'. Once in Portofino, when he was using crab bait for fishing off his boat, she had suddenly tipped the bowl of bait into the sea with screams of, 'Fish murderer ... crab murderer!' at the top of her voice, followed by a menacing growl. 'When I heard that spoiling-for-a-fight sound,' says Nancy Holmes, the American photo-journalist who happened to be aboard, 'I knew it was time to get the hell out of the way.'[16]

Her drinking might have precipitated occasional misbehaviour, but with Rachel the conduct that followed a glass of white wine too many had an extravagant, manic aspect. One evening in '21', the New York restaurant, Rex saw his anxiety spill over into public embarrassment. 'Rachel was lowering the Pouilly Fuissé we'd ordered,' says Nancy Holmes, 'really knocking it back to Rex's concern. She'd refused the soft-shell crabs we'd ordered. "I'm not having anything like that!" Instead, she commanded the waiter to bring her an uncooked egg.'[17] She was wearing a beautiful white dress with a scooped-out neckline. As Rex watched with a darkening countenance, she cracked the egg at one end and tried to suck the raw yolk out of the shell. 'Of course,' Nancy Holmes recalls, 'the sticky, messy stuff ran down her chin, down her bosom and on to her white dress. Rex ordered her to stop. But she shouted at the waiter, "Bring me another egg." Eventually, we jollied her out of it. But she demanded a separate check – for the egg – and said that all she'd wanted to find out was how much '21' charged for a raw egg.'[18] Rachel screamed with laughter. Rex looked grim.

She began her *Maggie May* rehearsals in London in July 1964 and 'was good but difficult', according to Lionel Bart.[19] When Rex was not on call for *The Agony and the Ecstasy*, he flew over. But his attempt to take a hand in the rehearsals in Manchester – 'I wouldn't do that, if I were you,' said his voice from the gloom of the dress circle – met with justified resistance from the director, Ted Kotcheff, and he flew back to Rome in a temper, missing the first night. As always when he had problems, Rex walked. The motion itself seemed to bring him relief. 'Never be a sitting target,' was one of his rules of combat. He would order his chauffeur to set him down in some out-of-the-way part of Rome with instructions to return in an hour or so's time, and then he would roam the hilly neighbourhoods of the capital, recognized by some, but warding off any approaches with one of his deadly looks. Occasionally he would drop into one of the hundreds of side street bars and sit there, brooding, his back to the other customers, one of the most famous stars in the world, alone and lonely and depressed.

'Rachel got pissed out of her mind one night,' Lionel Bart recalls, 'forgot to put her girdle on and came in from the wrong side for one of the duets.'[20] When he went round after the show, she asked defiantly, 'Do you think I'm drunk?' He shoved a roll of bank notes at her and said, 'Darling, I tripped over the empties outside. Here – run after the audience and offer them their money back.' Around 2 am Bart's telephone shrilled continuously until he got up to answer it, still feeling 'very choked'. It was Rex calling from Rome, blazing angry after Rachel's report of the incident. ' "I hear you've been bloody rude to my wife," he said to me. "What did you say to her, you little homosexual runt?" I wasn't standing for that. "Here," I shouted back down the phone, "who're you calling little?" ' Rex went on even longer walks by himself.

At last, even Rachel yielded to her problem. Taking advantage of a six-month 'break' clause, she gave in her notice and returned almost at once – Georgia Brown took over from her – to the villa at Portofino. There she tried to resume her role 'as a proper full-time wife'.[21] In an interview at the time, she talked of Rex and her adopting 'a Welsh baby ... a boy who will come and live with us in our villa here'. Adoption was constantly in her head and in the interviews she gave over the following months. She usually spoke of giving a home to 'a plain child', such as she was told she had been. It was noticeable that Rex spoke with much less enthusiasm. Transforming a child's life did not bring out the Pygmalion side of him at all. His own future was once again unsettled.

Since filming ended on *The Agony and the Ecstasy*, and with it, thank

God, his sojourn in Rome, he had been turning down projects right and left. A musical of *Don Quixote*, which interested him keenly until W. H. Auden, who was writing the lyrics, got fired. Then a musical remake of *Goodbye, Mr Chips*, which Peter O'Toole ultimately accepted. Rex invited Robert Bolt down to Portofino and tried without success to interest the author of *A Man for All Seasons* in writing a play about Charles II for him. There were also on-and-off talks with Olivier about appearing at the National Theatre in *Much Ado About Nothing*, for which Rex had already made his recorded 'practice piece'. But now that his nerve was steady for Shakespeare, Rachel's reliability was in doubt. Olivier blenched at the thought of another woman with a mental instability like Vivien Leigh's.

Indeed, fitting Rachel into his own far from definite plans taxed Rex's patience to the limit. The petulance of Henry Higgins, rasping out, 'Why can't a woman be a *chum?*' is apparent in a *Daily Mail* interview: 'What I need in a wife is a companion, someone who understands my work ... During the day you're preparing mentally for the night's performance. You need [someone] who shares that time with you, stays up for dinner after the theatre. I suppose that's why I marry actresses.'[22] But having a 'wife who is a companion' presupposes a wife who is sober and obedient. Rachel was neither much of the time now. She would spend hours away from him, down at the port, and he wondered – justifiably, as it turned out – if she did not have a relationship with some of the handsome Italians who admired her outgoing, demonstrative personality. He used to try to follow her progress through the market-place with the telescope on the villa terrace.

However, April 1965 proved the kindest month. At long last he had the satisfaction of hearing his name read out when the envelope was opened at the Academy Awards and having the gold statuette of the Oscar presented to him by his co-star Audrey Hepburn for the 'Best Actor' performance as Professor Higgins. It was a popular win: no one could quarrel with it. Whatever the sins of the man, the actor could deliver the goods. Hollywood understood that.

One honour seemed to attract others. He served as a juror at the Cannes Film Festival the following month, protested at Sidney Lumet's film *The Hill*, whose depiction of the brutalities in a British Army prison camp he considered a slur on his country, and voted (successfully) for Richard Lester's *The Knack*, 'a charming, kooky comedy' about a youth with power over women, and British too.

Noël Coward had passed through Cannes with a shiver of distaste and noted in his diary that Rachel was 'noisier than ever'.[23] Partly it was due to booze, but her underlying instability also fuelled her now unpredictable public behaviour. Rex recalled how Kay and he could have rows in public, but she had always some reserve of poise, some unexpected turn of phrase that defused the situation. Rachel, in contrast, was just rowdy. He remembered how Emlyn Williams had told him that if he married her, she would 'pull you down'.[24] Rachel had one way of getting attention when, as Rex put it, 'the fit was on her' which made him grit his teeth particularly hard.[25] Though she adored cats and collected strays everywhere she went to nurse for a day or two, she had a party act which consisted of falling down on all fours and barking. 'I'm pretending to be a Welsh corgi,' she told baffled and uneasy guests as she nipped their ankles or chewed at their trouser legs under the supper table. Rex himself was perfectly capable of knocking over the table if the occasion demanded it, but that was what a chap did who was upset. Rachel's conduct was highly unconventional and an embarrassment to him on grand occasions.

When *My Fair Lady* was invited to the Moscow Film Festival for a non-competitive gala screening in the Kremlin, Rachel got some of her own back. The Soviet Union was one of the few places in the world where she was better known than her husband. Her social-realist films, *Saturday Night and Sunday Morning* and *This Sporting Life* had been seen there and her performances had earned her high praise, if not immediate recognition when their aircraft touched down. The delegation of waiting Russians rushed a bouquet into the arms of Nancy Holmes, who was covering the trip with them; they mistook Rachel for Nancy's 'maid'. As Rex watched frozen-faced and ignored, Rachel flounced in between Nancy Holmes and the bowing Russians and screamed, 'How dare you give flowers to the woman who is living with my husband.'[26] The Russians were probably not of a mind to enjoy such a joke, if indeed they understood it. And nor was Rex. 'Rachel, this is Russia,' he hissed, 'you'll get us all shot.'[27]

Once Rachel had identified herself, she was followed everywhere in Moscow by photographers who, out of courtesy, squeezed off a few pictures of her husband – a situation that recalled Rex's fury some years earlier when, in Carey's hearing, a hotel employee had called him Mr Kendall. 'I didn't even dare look at Dad,' his son remembers.

The vodka added its own chill to the relations between Rex and Rachel. One evening she left their table and began crawling on her stomach around the dining-room of the National Hotel, barking like a dog. Rex's eyes narrowed. Suddenly Rachel screamed, 'Nancy, I've found a cat,' and rushed out pursuing the thoroughly frightened animal.[28] Rex went to bed. At 5 am he called Nancy Holmes and asked if she knew where Rachel was. 'Isn't she with you?' she asked. Whoever she was with, she did not get back until after breakfast and Rex discovered she was not wearing her wedding ring. An unidentified Englishman returned it to her later in the day. Rex realized that physical fidelity did not count for much when his wife was not sober. It did not matter much to him that his own shortcomings ran along fairly similar lines even when sober. His sense of decorum had been affronted. Life was being made uncomfortably unpredictable by what he now called her 'mad' bouts.

He quickly became adept at sensing the tremors caused by Rachel's eccentricities before the social earthquake happened, but the anxiety was never far from his thoughts. Even when asleep, it appeared to haunt his dreams. From Sicily that summer, after he had accepted a Davide di Donatello award in the Greco-Roman arena during the Taormina Film Festival, he sailed with Rachel for Corsica aboard a yacht chartered by some English friends. Returning from supper in the port of Ajaccio, Rex was in a very good mood. Rachel was tipsy. He turned in. Rachel went for a walk along the jetty and came across a stray cat, which she scooped up, despite its angry protests. 'Poor thing,' she assured the animal, as it glared fiercely at everyone, 'I'll put you in our cabin.'[29] Rex's heavy snoring could be heard as she opened the door. She tossed the cat gently on the bed beside him, where it let out a series of ear-splitting yowls. Without waking up, Rex said in a voice of infinite weariness, 'Is that you, Rachel?'[30]

25: Animal Crackers

'I know money, McFly, there's never enough of it.' Rex could sympathize with that. The Oscar was still warm in his hand, yet here he was considering making a movie about a man whose view of life, love and, of course, money coincided remarkably closely with his own. No reason to be surprised. Joseph L. Mankiewicz, who had brought the screenplay of *The Honey Pot* to the St Regis Hotel, New York, and tipped it out of a suitcase still in its original manuscript, had known Rex for twenty years and three films. If any writer-director knew what would attract him, it was Mankiewicz. His film was well named: it was an up-dated and fairly free version of Ben Jonson's *Volpone*, a satire on human greed and gullibility. Universal vices, of course, but particularly endemic in the world of film-making. After the traumas of *Cleopatra*, was it any wonder that Mankiewicz's next film should have had an air of remedial therapy and, as some critics later said, of revenge?

Mankiewicz created the character of Cecil Fox seeing and hearing Rex in the role. This eccentric, charming and tyrannical millionaire is supposedly dying in his opulent Venetian *palazzo* and summons the three women with whom he has enjoyed the best years of his life to his bedside for what each of them hopes will be the biggest portion of his estate. All are duped. Fox is a mountebank living like a movie mogul on the illusion of wealth, his *palazzo*'s rich furnishings rented from the Cinecittà studios, his secretary, a young American called McFly (Jonson's original Mosca), in on his master's duplicity and improvising the action like a screenwriter, so as to assist this bitingly cruel revenger's comedy. Time, the mortal enemy of all people who make films and see the passing of the hours in terms of money spent, is a recurring element in the plot and Ponchielli's 'The Dance of the Hours' is the music of time to which even Cecil Fox must literally dance.

As Mankiewicz read and probably enacted the scenes, Rex became so enthusiastic that the two men cancelled their dinner together and talked animatedly about the film into the small hours.

Mankiewicz said he had, or was about to secure, promises from Susan

Hayward, Capucine and Edie Adams for the roles of the three deluded gold-diggers – in whom reviewers would later see similarities to some of the more monstrous stars with whom the director had worked in the past.

Originally called by several titles, including *Anyone for Venice?* and still known in some versions as *Mr Fox of Venice, The Honey Pot* was a most ambitious and off-beat project. What made it even more unusual was a Pirandello-like device that intermittently distanced the cast from the action. They would be heard on the sound track, arguing over the credibility of a scene they are shown enacting; memos from an unseen 'front office' would criticise the plot and call for changes; and sometimes a censor's edict would forbid certain things to be shown or said under pain of infringing the still repressive Hollywood morality code. It all had a not too distant echo of the trials and tribulations that Mankiewicz had suffered during the two and a half years he spent directing *Cleopatra* and discovering how reality continually screws up the artist.

Almost all of this unconventional structure eventually had to be abandoned when the producers, United Artists, took fright at the prospect of having to turn an *auteur* movie into a money-making one and to this day Mankiewicz laments the opportunity for an *avant-garde* piece of film-making that was denied him by the very same reactionary forces that his film was written to ridicule. But in the form which Rex read it, *The Honey Pot* was attractive enough for him to say yes. For all its self-referential sub-text on movie-making, Rex saw it mainly in terms of elegant drawing-room comedy – well, *palazzo*-comedy – of which he knew himself to be a total master. He already preferred Jonsonian to Shakespearian analysis of human folly, since it was more within his own reach and sympathy. He had just won the Oscar, he could afford to risk an off-beat role. In any event, he strongly identified with Cecil Fox, as Mankiewicz knew he would. 'Cecil Fox was the portrait of a man who is dependent on women, yet takes advantage of them. And that meant a lot to Rex,' Mankiewicz recalls. Indeed a line in the film – 'It isn't easy for a man when a woman needs him more than he needs her' – kept on cropping up in Rex's conversation and reflections over the next few decades as justification for what had already happened to him and was likely to happen to him again. There is a huge element of conscious or covert autobiography in *The Honey Pot*. Even when the producers forced Mankiewicz to tone down the 'satirical-metaphysical' angle in favour of the more saleable 'comedy-mystery' one, Rex's enthusiasm did not wane. Considerable consolations remained, particularly the Shavian cynicism of Fox's dialogue. 'On other films,' Mankiewicz says, looking back on his star's career. 'I'm told Rex would sometimes wish out loud that Joe Mankiewicz could be there to write for him.'

However, as the date for the start of shooting drew near in Rome, both men discovered that time, the agent of change in the film, had not left their own relationship unaffected. Mankiewicz was 'far less relaxed' than Rex remembered him on their earlier films, which was hardly surprising in view of what he had suffered on *Cleopatra.*' Rex, for his part, had become far more difficult, which somewhat understates the reality. The continuing troubles with Rachel, who had taken it very hard that Maggie Smith and not she was to play Cecil Fox's nurse, the only sane and wholesome character in the film, and the emotional challenge with which each project now confronted him, all put Rex into an intractable state of defensive belligerence. His initial nervousness, always present when he undertook a role, had now, as he had grown older, increased to paralysing proportions.

'I shall never forget that first day on *The Honey Pot*,' says Laurie Evans, who had made it a practice to be present when Rex started work on a film. 'When I got to Rome airport, I was told Rex was waiting for me in his villa. He was pacing up and down, looking furious. "Shouldn't you be at the studio?" I asked. – "I'm not going near the fucking place until *he* sorts this mess out." It appeared that his big scenes were to be shot "back to back," one after the other, that is, thus saving time and money, and he wasn't having any of that. Rex's objections had some validity: he wrought himself up to such a pitch in every scene, though none of it showed, that he would soon have been exhausted, and that *might* have shown. But the strength of his resistance suggested a frightened man as well as a furious one. Rex refused to accompany me to the studio. Mankiewicz refused to go to the villa. "Tell Rex I've got an Oscar, too," was the message he sent back with me. It went on and on; total deadlock. Eventually Joe, being a gentleman, softened first. The schedule was altered to Rex's satisfaction and, almost as if he'd worked the nervousness out of his system by his entrenched resistance, things got easier. But it was a tense time for all of us.'

'Rex by now suspected everything and everyone,' says Mankiewicz. 'Most stars are quite glad to have days off when they're not needed, but it only made Rex anxious. "What are these people doing behind my back?" That was his first thought. I remember when I was preparing to shoot "The Dance of the Hours", the sequence where Cecil Fox, who's nursed an unrealized ambition to be a ballet dancer, does a *pas seul* around his ornate bedroom. We had a double for Rex, but half an hour before shooting he showed up. *He wasn't being needed*, you see! What were we concealing from him? He followed me around while I took sight lines with a view-finder. "Quite obviously you don't need my help," he said peevishly. "Rex," I said, as patiently as I could, "what I'm doing is trying to find an angle and a bedroom pillar broad enough to cover both you and your double when you pass behind the pillar and he takes over and does the ballet dance across the room. Coping with one of you is tough enough, having two of you is a nightmare." ' Warned off, Rex then kept his dance double under watchful review. The substitution is very cleverly done in the film: no one ever spots it.

Rex's snobbish, agile, duplicitous and physically commanding performance was worth all the pain of the shooting schedule, which went on for five months. It was cruelly diminished, however, when the distributors cut the film's running time after a disastrous box-office when it opened in London in March 1967. 'Life louses up our scripts,' Mankiewicz was fond of saying; it proved true in this case, too, literally so. Rex had particularly regretted losing the Pirandello-type commentary early on in the film's production; it had sent him back to the Italian dramatist's plays – as usual he read far and wide around the current project – and this was to bear fruit in the future.

Home life for Rex and Rachel during this long schedule on the Cinecitta sets, with only a couple of days' location shooting in Venice, was far more painful. Correctly guessing that *The Honey Pot* might not be a pot of gold for anyone, Rex began to worry early and elaborately about losing his new-found popularity and becoming once again a back number as shatteringly as he had done after the superstardom he had acquired on stage in *My Fair Lady* had been succeeded by take-it-or-leave-it roles like that with Rita Hayworth. He was now nearly sixty. Time was running out for him, as it had done for Cecil Fox. And for both men time was money.

In this mood, he grabbed at the chance of another major musical which was offered to him while still shooting *The Honey Pot*. *Doctor Dolittle* was based on Hugh Lofting's children's stories about the kindly country physician whose patients are not people, but animals with whom he can converse. In other words, another Higgins-type role, rooted once more in the magical properties of language to transform relationships, but far less misanthropic since no one would behave to animals with the cavalier callousness that Higgins showed to humans. Rex actually liked animals, or so he believed until he began the film; and the ones he would act with were not likely to top his fee this time, as Audrey Hepburn had done. He was to get well over $500,000. Alan J. Lerner had agreed to do the book and lyrics – that was good protection. Only ... only his old hesitation would not go away. He had genuine grounds for apprehension. A movie like this had a million uncertainties, some of which would be crucial for his career and all of which would give him no rest or peace for many, many months. Moreover, he knew that the worst word one can utter when a movie company couriers a script to your door is 'Yes'.

There was, however, a more basic reason for his hesitation than movie 'politics'. 'I've been a worrier since the age of two,' Rex once admitted to an interviewer. He thought the worrying came from being born under the sign of the vacillating Pisces. 'One of the dangers of Pisces people is seeing too many points of view simultaneously. You get sick of yourself for nagging indecisiveness, and suddenly you force yourself to make an impulsive dive at *something*.'

The agony of indecision was well expressed by Rachel in her journals: 'One minute [Rex] wanted to do [Doctor Dolittle], the next he didn't, so it went to Christopher Plummer. Then Rex wanted it back.' Christopher Plummer had to be paid his $300,000 fee to be bought out:

Days were spent shouting over the phone to Aaron Frosch, Rex's lawyer, or Laurie Evans ... Even Jolie, the little girl with the squint who washed the [household's] clothes, was yelled at. I sacked the Roman servants. The man sneered at me, contemptuously referring to me as 'La Signora'. We dined out that Saturday in Rome with two agents. Rex was in a temper. Abuse flowed. I drank brandy. I came home to emptiness and ice and swallowed Seconal. I came to shouting, 'Alan! Alan! Alan!'[2]

One can imagine the fright Rex had when he discovered Rachel lying, apparently at death's door, though actually breathing gently, on the bathroom floor. 'He had the worst luck with women,' Mankiewicz says. 'They killed themselves, or tried to, in what for him were always foreign countries.' In a panic, Rex called Mankiewicz's villa at 2 am and bawled down the phone, in a mixture of terror and testiness, that Rachel had taken an overdose of tablets and might be dying. Mankiewicz and his assistant, a charming and efficient English girl called Rosemary Matthews, who had seen him through the worst days of *Cleopatra* and who was soon to become his wife, rushed over at once.

'We found Rachel in a bad state,' says Mankiewicz, 'but nothing terminal. We got her to a clinic and a bundle of dollar bills settled things with the doctor and kept the story out of the papers.' A present from Rex was delivered to his director in the New Year: a large silver cigarette box from Asprey's, the London jeweller. On the inside of the lid was inscribed in Rex's handwriting: 'Thank you for Julius Caesar. Thank you for Cecil Fox. Thank you for everything. Rex. January 1966.' All concerned knew what was meant by 'everything'.

With all these strains and stresses telling on him at home and at work, it is no surprise that Rex was in an almost perpetual bad temper. Edith

Jackson, his secretary, usually gave as good as she got, but the breaking point came this time round. She gave in her notice on the spot and went straight upstairs to pack and do her expenses. Soon Rex barged in, continuing to shout at her, while asking if she wanted a reference. Edith declined. 'The trouble with you,' Rex yelled, 'is that you're too much the bloody lady.' Edith riposted: 'Put that down in writing, sign it and I'll take it as my reference.' She went on with her expenses. 'What the hell are you doing? I'm talking to you,' Rex roared. 'My expenses,' Edith said calmly, 'and if you shout at me any more, I'll double them.'[3]

When she went downstairs half an hour later to telephone London and make sure she was met at the airport, she found Rex completely sobered up – no doubt by the thought of all the disturbance in his life a new secretary would involve – and pretending to read the paper. 'By all means, Edith, go ahead ... use the phone,' he said in his sweetest voice.[4] She stayed on, held as so many others were by the man's mercurial nature, without any illusions about him, but curious to see how the old devil would play the next scene ... and the next.

Rex had had to be talked into doing *Doctor Dolittle* by Alan J. Lerner, who had caught the enthusiasm of its producer, Arthur P. Jacobs, and in turn got Rex excited. Then the deal soured on Lerner and his partner, André Previn. They withdrew. Hence Rex's sudden insecurity. To make him 'firm' again, his fee was raised. '[He] was getting more money than God,' Jacobs said.[5] In fact, he received a celestial $750,000 and, as things turned out, never considered it enough. Richard Fleischer was to direct, and Leslie Bricusse, the composer and adapter, was also entrusted with the screenplay. By now ultra-suspicious, overcautious and neurotically self-protective, Rex gave them both 'absolute misery' over the next nine months.[6] 'He queried everything,' said Bricusse.[7] And Jacobs, who was simultaneously producing *Planet of the Apes*, said to an associate, 'You think you got problems? Try apes and animals.'[8]

'And Rex Harrison,' added the associate. Jacobs sighed, 'And Rex.'

First, he made his by now familiar stipulation: his songs must be performed live, not pre-recorded. Then, the lyrics must be specially written for him, which sounds reasonable, but meant that no other artists were likely to want to record them. Thirdly, he wanted to film as little as possible in England. Fleischer scouted Irish locations, but reported back bleakly to the Villa San Genesio that they were 'terribly depressing, faceless places suitable for a Great Potato Famine story.'[9] So Castle Combe, a picturesque English village in the Cotswolds, became the site of Rex's first *parlando* number, the 'Talk to the animals' song.

Then hell began for all concerned. Rex steadfastly objected to anything he considered threatened his pre-eminence in the story. He refused to accept a reference to Dr Dolittle being slightly mad. 'I prefer to set my own character, not to have a preview through another.'[10] He reacted against the introduction of a character called Bumpo, the Doctor's sidekick, who was to be played by Sidney Poitier. Bumpo was struck off. Rex was happy enough to have a bird or beast assist him, but a flesh-and-blood accessory brought out the paranoia. In a letter to Fleischer in May 1955 he wrote: 'It was agreed that no human – now that Poitier is out – should aid my escape [from the asylum].'[11] Fleischer's reply was deemed 'evasive'. 'It was agreed in London – in front of Leslie Bricusse – that the first 40 pages [of the script] would be gone back to *exactly*, not "conform more closely to" what I had accepted.' Rex also repositioned numbers in the story, which meant extensive revisions. No detail was too small to escape notice. 'If it is possible ...' Fleischer wrote in a memo. Against the phrase Rex scribbled petulantly, 'Why shouldn't it be?'[12] He made Bricusse feel like a new pupil in front of a stern and unbending headmaster. Rex objected to Dolittle's being a country doctor; he wanted him to be a Harley Street physician who had *retired* to the country. 'He couldn't see himself – the suave, sophisticated, immaculate Rex – as a country doctor,' Bricusse told David Lewin in an interview.[13] 'I argued that if the audience would accept him talking to animals, they would accept him as anything. But ... I rewrote it [on his lines]. It didn't work and Rex saw it didn't ... [He] said, "I've rolled over on myself," which is his way of apologizing.' It sounded a bit like Homer the basset hound's, too.

These were Rex's working methods, and they deserve recording as such and not entirely as evidence of how difficult he was to accommodate. One tends to forget that Rex's cumulative experience was sound, if tetchily expressed, like that of a monarch who eventually knows more than his prime ministers. He was 'picky', but his instinct was frequently correct. He had learnt wisdom from masters as well as obstinacy from his experience with fools.

This is illustrated in the intense to-ing and fro-ing that went on over the lyric – and the first number in the film – 'Talk to the animals'. Rex objected to the 'simplicity' of the song.[14] Fleischer replied that it was just this simplicity that made it suitable for the doctor's small (human) friend Tommy, who was to sing it. Rex, he said, could chime in occasionally with some more sophisticated comments like, 'Discussing Eastern art and dramas/With intellectual llamas.' Rex was adamant. He remembered what Alan J. Lerner had written: 'The first ten minutes of any musical offering should dictate the style of the entire evening: on what level the work is to be accepted critically and emotionally. Loewe and I wanted Professor Henry Higgins to be the first one to sing.'[15] Rex took Lerner at his word here, too, and why not? That word had been well proven. He insisted that the first solo in the film would have to be about himself and define the Dolittle philosophy of conversing with the animal kingdom. So eventually the lyric was given entirely to Rex.

Rex at this stage did not have too many worries about sharing scenes with the animals. The script that Fleischer was sending him from Hollywood sounded reassuring enough. 'Our animal trainer here is beginning to shape up. The giraffe and the rhino are now being ridden. The chimp carries a tea tray, steals eggs from the chicken and puts them in a pot, and lets the parrot ride upon his head. I understand he's studying direction, too.'[16] Fox insured Rex for $1 million – Audrey Hepburn's fee on *My Fair Lady*, he reflected. So that's what it was worth to be skewered by a rhino. It was only when he started his scenes with the veritable zoo assembled by the studio that he began to realize it was one thing to talk to the animals, quite another to ward off their unpredictable propensity to bite, claw, scratch and spit at him. It was going to be far from a two-way conversation.

Doctor Dolittle, like *Cleopatra*, trapped Rex for almost a year of his life. In the long run, it may have affected his health and customary well-being. Human co-stars frequently invigorated him simply by keeping him on the attack. But no retribution could realistically be taken against animal ones. They inexorably wore him down – and just as unavoidably pushed the budget up, from $12 million to $15 million.

Filming got under way at the end of June 1966 in the Wiltshire village that had been turned into a passable imitation of a Victorian coastal town by damming the stream and building a false waterfront: a move greatly resented by some of the villagers, who formed a local commando unit to try and dynamite it. A bigger enemy was on their side. Out of fifty-six days' shooting, only five were rainless.

Rex quickly discovered that all the well-trained animals whose proficiency in pouring out tea and frying bacon and eggs or simply sitting listening, ears cocked appreciatively, as Dr Dolittle sang to them were having to await his arrival in Hollywood. English quarantine regulations did not allow them to be brought into the country. Instead, a different set of animals took their places and these 'doubles' were not nearly so efficient, obedient or even house-trained. Rex went through agonies doing even a simple scene, such as the one Leslie Bricusse's script described as: 'Dr Dolittle is sitting on a bridge listening to a squirrel talk to a parrot.'

'I didn't have to say anything. They got what was supposed to be a tame squirrel out of its cage and it started to fight like mad. It was no more tame than a lion ... They decided the only thing to do was put little bits of wire around its feet ... and attach it by tacks to the wooden rail of the bridge. They fought with the squirrel during all the rare bursts of sunshine which we'd been awaiting almost the whole of the morning. Then we broke for lunch."[17]

It was proposed giving the squirrel a Valium tablet, but the vet said that giving rodents a sedative had bad effects – they died. A recommended alternative was a slug of gin.

'So after lunch,' said Rex, 'we used one of those fountain-pen reservoir things to drip gin down the squirrel's throat. It went absolutely ape. "Better give it a bit more to quieten it," someone said. So it was fed a bit more through the dropper. We got one shot of it sitting there beside me, looking rather peculiarly at the parrot, which, thank God, was of a more amenable temper. Then it passed out totally – *whump*! – and sprawled on the parapet as flat as a lizard. There was nothing we could do but put one very drunk squirrel back in its cage and hope it didn't have too heavy a hangover when – or if – it woke up the next morning.'

By late August Fox ceded victory to the English climate, as it had done over *Cleopatra*, and moved the unit to Hollywood, where the doctor's house was duplicated on a California ranch. For obvious health and safety reasons, the animals could not be brought on to the sound stages at the studio.

'I was driven half mad with frustration,' Rex recorded.[18]

Concentration, which was all important for Rex, was impossible. Rex had always rated very highly the actors like himself – Gary Cooper, Spencer Tracy among them – who were 'good at looking, thinking and listening'.[19] Animals did not facilitate any of these talents. They broke eye contact with him, lost interest or else came on too strongly and 'overacted': they were very easily distracted.

Health and sanitation were additional nightmares. Sets had to be built at a rake, so that the mess made by animals that urinated or defecated during a take could be flushed away from under Rex's nose. Then the set would have to be disinfected and aired. Rex sometimes reached home reeking of ammoniac fluid. In such conditions he had to reconsider his idea of recording his songs on the spot. At the end of the filming, when the budget had escalated to $18 million, he insisted on lip-synching all his numbers.

Marine location work took place on St Lucia, one of the Windward Islands in the Caribbean, where Dr Dolittle encounters the Great Pink Sea-Snail and hitches a ride back to England on its shell.

Rachel joined Rex there. She had been in New York trying to regain her emotional balance and resume her career – she had now been three years off the screen – by doing an NBC television production of *Blithe*

Spirit. But her instability soon surfaced again. No sooner had Nancy Holmes finally taught her how to swim – such rudimentary skills had up to now eluded her – than she breast-stroked purposefully towards the pen where the trained seals were kept. 'Before we guessed what she was up to, she nearly succeeded in undoing the net and releasing them,' Nancy Holmes recalls. 'Arthur Jacobs almost had a heart attack.' (In fact, he suffered one at the end of shooting.) Jacobs said to Rex, 'We should have taken out an insurance policy against your fucking wife liberating our animals.'[20]

Rachel's prank was not the worst of her madcap exploits. Carey Harrison visited the location and recalls the night she entertained guests at the British Embassy with what she called 'the Dance of the Forty Pussies', a striptease act performed on a table top. 'The ladies retired with incredible speed, leaving only us dinner-jacketed chaps, myself at one end of the table and Dad at the other. I stole a look at him, wondering how he was reacting to this scene. To my amazement, his expression was almost one of gratification. For someone who had always had a reputation as a "bad lad", to have a wife who outdid him in public misbehaviour now seemed to overjoy him. It was as if he was imagining people saying, "Poor Rex, how can he put up with that woman?" It was a moment of great illumination.'

Others besides Carey confirm that Rex had passed beyond the stage of embarrassment at Rachel's conduct. At times helplessness and pity for her were what he felt; at others angry contempt and self-pity were his reactions. There was little he could do, he felt. Worse, there was little he wanted to do. Pamela Mason, former wife of actor James Mason, recalls going over to the house they had rented in North Bedford Drive – one that had belonged to Greta Garbo – and, just as she got there, seeing Rachel come charging out and into a cab. ' "What's happening?" I asked Rex. He said she was going off to kill herself. She was threatening to throw herself off a rock into the sea. "I've done my best, I can do no more," he said.'[21] And indeed that was the limit of it. It was left to Mrs Mason to call the film star Jennifer Jones, who lived adjacent to the rocky promontory where she guessed Rachel was making for, and have Rex's wife intercepted when she arrived by taxi for her suicide attempt. 'They had to talk to her all night before she calmed down and came back. Laurie Evans said to me, "I think she's very seriously ill, mentally." So did Rex, but he was at a total loss to know what to do about it.'[22]

At times, when exhaustion (from the film) and exasperation (with Rachel) overcame Rex, he was quite capable of abetting her misbehaviour to the extent of their seeming like a double act. On one occasion they attended an 'A list' party at The Bistro, then the smartest rendezvous in

Beverly Hills. A lot of Old Hollywood was present including the James Stewarts, Billy Wilders, Fredric Marches, William Wylers, and a sprinkling of new stars and producers like Rock Hudson, Burt Lancaster and Ross Hunter. Rex and Rachel had both been drinking heavily when someone asked Rex to entertain them. He hated performing professionally on a private occasion and usually refused point blank. But as the pianist obligingly struck up 'I've grown accustomed to her face ...', he hoisted himself, heavy-lidded and glowering, on to his feet and went into his *parlando* act, but with words that assuredly had not come from the show. In fact, it emerged he had put a great deal of his own time into writing an alternative version which began 'I've grown accustomed to my prick/ It almost makes the day begin ...' There was a shocked hush; then, as the obscenities tripped crisply off Rex's tongue, the rather conventional set of people decided the best thing to do was appear to enjoy the joke and they joined in the 'fun' with nervous giggles as Rex took his calculated revenge on them. But Rachel was suddenly seized by the idea that she was being overlooked. Not to be outdone by Rex, she ran across the small room and did a series of hand springs in which her mini skirt, falling over her head, revealed she had no undergarments on. She finally balanced against the wall on her head, howling like a dog, while Rex blithely finished his revised version of *My Fair Lady*, which he subsequently entitled *My Big Cock*.

Drink seemed the common bond in these months. 'But the trouble with Rachel was that, when she drank, she didn't eat,' says Pamela Mason. 'Rex drank, but also tucked into his food. Alcoholics die all the time, but it's of malnutrition.'[23] When both went on a binge, the result had a Preston Sturges feel. They were invited to a fund-raising dinner on one of the university campuses honouring George Cukor and fortified themselves against boredom so well in advance that, half way there, they decided to call it off and tried to telephone their apologies. But, failing to discover to whom they should speak, with the logic of the inebriated they drove on to the campus and Rex said to Rachel, 'Go and tell George we can't come.' Pamela Mason takes up the story. 'Rachel sashays into the banqueting room and up to the top table, where Cukor is sitting with two empty spaces right and left, for Rex and Rachel. As she's late and in a ridiculously short skirt, she catches people's eyes – even more when she nears George and goes, "Woof! Woof!" to catch his attention. "George," she says, "Rex and I have come to tell you we can't be here. But before I go" – and she turns to the assembly – "I want to say one big *woof* to all of you.' Then Rex wanders in, forgetting he's already taken his toupée off and it is hanging out of the top pocket of his tuxedo where his handkerchief usually is. He waves at George Cukor sitting there frozen-faced, and then both make their exit. All of which Rex begins dimly to remember next morning, at first puts it down to a bad dream, then wakes up to the horrid reality and lives in terror for the rest of the day in case a picture of his balding face looking the worse for wear will appear in one of the Los Angeles papers.'[24]

More often, though, when they went out together, they would end the evening sparring with rather than supporting each other. Lionel Jeffries was making the film *Camelot* at this time and recalls Rex tearing into the party of Hollywood Brits who had come on to his home for a nightcap from The Daisy, the favourite pub of the Anglo-Saxon colony. 'First of all, he tells Michael Wilding he's never been able to understand a word he says,' says Jeffries. 'Then he berates Margaret Leighton for falling into bed with a nancy boy like Laurence Harvey. Someone else he calls a phoney and says he could never credit how he came to be considered a celebrity ... and so on. In the middle of this tirade, in marches Rachel, takes stock of the scene and announces she's going to put a Welsh curse on Rex. She shuts her eyes, makes a few cabalistic signs, crosses her fingers and directs a string of Welsh words at her husband, which at least shut him up. When we had all sobered up the next day, Rex called. He wanted, he said, to apologize for Rachel. He hoped we'd forgive her!'[25]

At Christmas Rex produced a handful of unwrapped rings from a Beverly Hills jeweller that looked as if they had been picked up on approval as he returned home from the studios and invited her to choose one. They gave a party and Rachel made every effort to behave like a Hollywood hostess. Rex was far from grateful. He turned to Pamela Mason and said, 'What a terrible affair. Whose is it?'[26] Frustration brought out the latent cruelty in each of them. To fill her empty hours, Rachel procured a parakeet from Jungleland and sat at home, while Rex was filming, reading it the dialogue assigned to Polynesia, Dr Dolittle's talking parrot in the movie. Rex told her that, if she was good enough, she could dub the bird's voice in the film.

Symptomatic, perhaps, of her own caged frustration was the act of liberation she performed when they went to the very grand party thrown by Richard Harris, the star of *Camelot*, and his wife Elizabeth. Rachel opened the cage containing the host's pet Chinese mockingbird, not only a prized possession, but one so valuable that, as Nancy Holmes said, 'You wouldn't be surprised to see it kept in a safe.'[27] It hopped out of the window and away into the night. Elizabeth Harris had to try and find a match for it without her Irish-tempered husband knowing.

Rex was being driven mad by the daily frustration of working with the animals, never mind talking to them; Rachel was being tortured by having absolutely nothing to do that absorbed her overdrive. More than their careers were now ruinously out of synch: their natures were finding no meeting point in either marriage or work. 'Rex was a total professional,' says Pamela Mason, 'but he was not a *committed* performer, the way Rachel was. He kept his distance, despite the hard work. She used herself up, whether working or not – consumed herself.'[28] The emptiness of Rachel's days accumulated like a weight on her spirits. She blamed herself for letting it happen to her and agreeing to put her gifts into abeyance in return for the privileged life that Rex had earned. Sterility bred hostility towards him, destructiveness towards herself. One day she had to be brought home from The Bistro drunk. Rex reacted the way he did when he had found Collette and Lilli lying insensible in his bedroom all those years before: coldly accusatory. In the hope that work would burn off her unused energies and 'be a help to our marriage', he agreed to Rachel actively seeking stage or film offers.[29]

An agent, Paul Kohner, was engaged to represent her and *Weekly Variety* in October 1966 carried a full-page picture of Rachel, announcing her 'availability' for offers. Eventually one came. It was from Twentieth Century-Fox to appear in a film of Feydeau's farce *A Flea in Her Ear*, which was going to be shot in Paris the following spring. The star role was already cast. It was her husband.

26: The Gay Life

They came back to Europe early in the summer of 1967 aboard one of the Queens. Rachel made inroads into a case of tequilla a friend had sent her marked 'To be opened on voyage' and jubilantly insulted some of the fur-wrapped women having supper – 'terrible bit of old tat' – before climbing on the piano and belting out the dirtiest of Welsh rugby songs.[1] Rex went to his state room. Plainly his wife was out of control. All he could hope for was that working together on the new film would calm Rachel and give her self-esteem a much needed boost.

He rented a country house at Malmaison, outside Paris, near Jean-Pierre Aumont's estate, and brought over Ruby, the maid they had had in Hollywood, and another servant.

A Flea in Her Ear had been adapted for the stage by John Mortimer and he wrote the screenplay too. As he was preparing to meet Rex in Paris, he took a telephone call. 'That John Mortimer?'[2] – 'Yes.' – 'Rex Harrison here. I want to tell you one thing before we meet, John. Are you listening?' – 'Yes.' – 'Very well,' the reedy, rasping tones went on, 'what I want to tell you is that you are a shit. An absolute shit. You are a shit now and you have always been a shit. Do I make myself clear?' A shaken Mortimer groped for words to answer this unprovoked assault, then a chuckle came down the line and he recognized the voice of David Niven, whose after-dinner party piece was a ribald impersonation of Rex. 'Thought I'd give you a taste of what's ahead of you, old boy,' said Niven.

It would have come as no surprise to Arthur Jacobs, who had had to deal with Rex over the past year's production of *Doctor Dolittle*. He had restrained his temper for a number of reasons: the high budget of nearly $20 million that his star was carrying, his fear of an even more serious heart attack than the one he had suffered in the closing weeks of shooting, and his hope that, despite all this, he could get Rex to star in *Goodbye, Mr Chips*, a musical remake which he was to produce for MGM with Gower Champion directing. Rex had already said no to the script, but then – true to form – changed his mind. Jacobs and Champion flew to Paris to close the deal.

'We drive out to his house in the country,' Jacobs said later, 'and he meets us at the door. "Marvellous day," he says. You know the way he talks ... "Marvellous day. Bloody Mary, anyone? Bloody Mary?" He gets us the Bloody Marys and then he says, "Now let me tell you why I'm not going to do *Mr Chips*." That's the first we heard about it ... It was all set ... Gower looks at me, picks up his attaché case and says, "Sorry, I'm going to the airport, I'm going home." '[3]

Rex derived great satisfaction from giving audiences which ended with his dismissing supplicants with a kick up the ass. The scene was to be repeated frequently in the years ahead.

However, Rachel had given him a fright. He had even consulted Olivier. What does one do with a mad wife? Olivier, divorced from Vivien Leigh, who was to lose her life in December that year by almost wilful neglect of her tubercular condition, replied without much sympathy, 'Soldier on, dear fellow, until hostilities end or you fall in battle.'[4] Instead, Rex was attempting a truce. He had moderated his views about the undesirability of a wife working. Now he was all for it. 'She needs to work', he told Clive Hirschhorn in an interview. 'She's got all this Welsh energy.'[5] Translated, this meant that if she could not be a wife and lead his life, better for him that she should lead her own life and not mess up his. Well, at least it was an adjustment to reality.

In other ways, though, Rex began detaching himself from reality. This was the irony of their respective situations. Rachel might well be unbalanced at times through alcohol or some deeper disturbance, probably to be laid at the door of a childhood which had lacked love or so she believed. But her observation of her condition, as her journals would later reveal, was sharp and truthful: the tragedy was that she could not or would not apply herself to do anything about it. By contrast, Rex's view of himself and life was growing increasingly distorted as he sealed himself unreachably inside his own stardom. John Mortimer noticed this aspect coming more and more to the fore.

'He was obsessionally eager to make himself lovable to audiences, even at the expense of his art. Quite a number of actors are tempted this way. After all, part of being a star is being loved. But Rex used his authority to force everything and everyone to bend to his will over this.'

He was playing dual roles in the film: a debonair French lawyer and a drunken, lower-class porter who was the other man's physical double – a typical ploy of Feydeau farce. 'Oh, no,' he told Mortimer, 'I don't think audiences would like a totally impotent man as the hero. They wouldn't accept me. Couldn't I be made just a little impotent, now and then?'

'He niggled away until he got what he wanted,' says John Mortimer.

Early on, Mortimer realized the film was not succeeding despite being directed by Jacques Charon of the Comédie Française, who had done the London stage version. 'It suited the theatre, not the screen. You needed to see the whole set-up in the ornate brothel that specializes in uniting married couples, though not to each other. You had to take in all the doors that might open at an inopportune moment, the near shaves in avoiding compromising encounters, the cupboard hide-outs and all the amorous cliff-hangers that the comedy of adultery gives rise to. With the film cutting from character to character, you lost this sense of composite comings and goings, concealments and exposures.'

Rex, too, was to blame, Mortimer felt. He could not bring himself to play broad farce. He was predictably excellent as the lawyer, his impotence now scaled down in duration, but he floundered as the porter. His timing remained that of high comedy, not broad farce. It was like watching Higgins playing Doolittle the dustman. The movie was a foreseen disaster. Even at the modest running time of ninety-four minutes, it flagged. Instead of the lightness of clockwork, it moved to the sluggish beat of the ship's engines needed to transport a cargo of illicit goings-on.

In fact, a better, though sadder Feydeau farce was taking place when the day's shooting was over.

Rex kept a close and nervous watch over Rachel. Even one glass of white wine would set her off: she was becoming a 'chemical' alcoholic. Edith Jackson was summoned from her bed early one morning by a phone call from Rex: 'She's gone off her head.'[6] Rachel was lying stark naked on the floor of the suite in the Lancaster Hotel, where they stayed while filming, with Rex trying vainly to subdue her. In a nearby suite ex-King Umberto of Italy and his wife had been awakened by the ruckus, and their equerries and ladies-in-waiting, in night attire and hair-curlers, were clustered in the corridor all adding their voluble Italian to the noise coming from Signor 'Arrison's chamber – 'Ees 'e killing 'er?' Edith probably felt he might like to. They pacified Rachel by forcing a Mogadon tablet down her throat. She went out like a light. The next morning, Rex was informed by the King's equerry: 'His Majesty was not at all pleased by the noise you made last night.' Rex's reply was lengthy and although it contained no word of Italian, it scarcely needed translating. It was not conveyed to His Majesty.

On another occasion Rachel slipped away with Terence Rattigan after Rex had retired. 'Find her,' Edith was commanded and valiantly she dragged herself out of bed, dressed and got the names of a half-dozen lesbian bars from the night porter – she had overheard them discussing a visit – and then made the rounds of them with Rex, asking at each for '*un monsieur anglais*, Terry Rattigan.' Rattigan was found ... Rachel did not return for twenty-four hours.

When she was not drinking, her behaviour was perfectly normal, indeed exemplary. Her part in *A Flea in Her Ear* being comparatively small, she had a dangerous amount of free time on her hands, but she used much of it for self-improvement. She started French language courses at the Berlitz Institute. To her credit, she saw the joke of a fashionably dressed lady arriving daily in her husband's Rolls-Royce and joining the bejeaned teenagers milling around the corridors, flirting or trying to make up their grades before the September term began at their schools. She became quite popular with them – and not only with them.

To Rex's consternation, she did not return one evening and was absent all the next day. When he sat down at the small dinner party which had been arranged for a few select guests that night, there was still no sign of her. But by now he was beyond caring. Half-way though, however, in came Rachel the worse for wear and, sensing a certain embarrassment, she attempted to dispel it by the sort of remark that Kay Kendall might have got away with, just. It was also a creditable effort to speak the language she was learning. '*Excusez moi*,' she announced, '*je suis très tard. Mais j'ai fucké le chauffeur de mon mari.*'[7]

Doctor Dolittle had been tested in front of preview audiences in America with very mixed results. An alarmed Fox exercised its option to make cuts. When Rex saw the film in London, in December 1967, at a gala première in the presence of the Queen, he found it had lost nearly ten minutes. Gone almost entirely was the prologue in which, top-hatted and frock-coated, he rides into the story on a giraffe's back, pulls a molar out of a crocodile with toothache and hitches a ride on a passing rhino. He groaned audibly as he thought of all the tedious (and dangerous) hours he had put in on a sequence in which only he and the giraffe now survived because the rest of it held up the action. Fox took a gloomy view of the film's box-office. It was not going to be a second *Sound of Music*, the studio's biggest post-war money-maker – 'or even *My Fair Lady*', the studio chief, Richard Zanuck, said grimly.[8]

Yet Rex's performance brings a sharp, restorative whiff of Henry Higgins to the animal crackers, not only in the rapture he shows over linguistics – 'Good heavens, I speak *pig*,' he exclaims, triumphantly echoing his cry of triumph in the other film when Eliza learns *not* to speak Cockney – but also in the set bachelor ways of the doctor, which mimic those of the Shavian professor. It takes a shipwreck to soften Rex's studiously maintained air of remoteness where women are concerned and make him confess to his fellow castaway, played by Samantha Eggar, that 'I think I like you/Yes I do.' Higgins might have felt even that was going a bit too far. The film gains immensely from Rex's exceptionally artful and convincingly lovable portrayal of a man who is required to possess the wisdom of Solomon, the patience of Noah and the sympathy of St Francis. For all its whimsy, it carries through it the imprimatur of Rex's presence – a perpendicular authority as eye-catching as an exclamation mark. At the time, it may have seemed like condescension on his part to appear in a children's film, but he condescends to no one in it, animal or human, or to anyone likely to watch it. The tremendous labour it was for him to make scarcely shows. What does come through, in retrospect anyhow, and to those who knew the human risks (quite apart from the financial ones) that were involved in working with a multitude of animals, some fiercely unpredictable despite all possible precautions, is the sheer bravery Rex showed in doing many of the scenes. The last shot of the good Doctor in a huge circle of birds and animals lends him the look of a prophet come to preach. Time has given the film a patina of rarity it did not originally possess.

But Rex smelled box-office failure. He pulled out of most of his première appearances. He adamantly refused to go to Peru – the PushmiPullyu lama in the film had been adopted as the advertising logo in that country – despite being offered the Order of the Golden Condor as publicity bait by a tourism-conscious Government. He did do the Paris première and received a Silver Medal of Honour from the Mayor. The Scandinavian countries offered him no decoration, however, and he insisted that Fox provide him with comfort in lieu of honours, which meant having his Rolls-Royce driven to Sweden through one of the worst snowstorms of the year in order to meet him at Stockholm airport. That piece of prestige transportation cost more than the actual première.

Even in the Swedish capital the spirit of Feydeau created havoc in his life. A delegate to a trades union conference being held in the same grand hotel as Rex and Rachel were inhabiting wandered drunk into their suite, the door of which Rex had forgotten to secure, and lay down on the sofa. Rachel came out of her room completely naked and had hysterics on sighting the intruder. Rex woke up and added his yells to the commotion caused by what he first took to be a drunken Rachel. The innocent Socialist by this time was scared out of his wits by the spectacle of the two Harrisons, one ranting at being disturbed, the other one naked and screaming rape. The publicist accompanying them,

Margaret Gardner, of Rogers and Cowan, which represented Rex, managed to calm things and return everyone to their beds. But she reflected regretfully that it was a pity they were not publicizing *A Flea in Her Ear*.

Even such notorious imbibers and public battlers as the Burtons appear to have been shocked by Rachel's condition. Richard Burton's diaries, first published in Melvyn Bragg's biography *Rich*, give perhaps the most graphic first-hand account of her terrible state at this time:

1 June 1967: We had spent Sunday up at [the villa] and, as usual, it was very liquid. Rachel is still maniacal. We saw [her and Rex] again at La Gritta bar in the port. Fortunately, before Rachel became totally demented, they left for home and dinner about 9.30 pm. On Tuesday evening everyone came aboard [*Kalizma*, the Burtons' yacht] and Rachel became stupendously drunk and was totally uncontrollable ... She insulted Rex sexually, morally, physically and in every way. She lay on the floor in the bar and barked like a dog. At one time she started to masturbate her basset hound – a lovely sloppy old dog called Omar [Homer?]. E[lizabeth Taylor] lectured her. I did. Rex did. All to no avail. She bitterly harangued the memories of Carole Landis and Kay Kendall, hurled imprecations at Lilli Palmer. Christ.

Burton thought Rex 'fantastically tolerant' of Rachel and vowed, 'She wouldn't last forty-eight hours with me.'

Rex, as has already been seen, was seldom a man for the snap decision. But Ned Sherrin, the television satirist turned film producer in the boom-time of the Swinging Sixties, found him even more restless than usual when he turned up at the Villa San Genesio in the hopes of interesting Rachel in a new film, *The Vicar's Wife*, which would star Cary Grant. Rex had read Alan Bennett's screenplay and immediately nosed out its possibilities – for himself.

'Why aren't *I* playing Cary's part in your film?' he rasped.[9]

'He was on edge, I thought,' Sherrin recalls.[10] Rachel was not the trouble this time: it was wig-makers. Two of them were to arrive the next day from London to fit Rex for the film to which he had committed himself in the middle of *A Flea in Her Ear* and was already bitterly regretting.

His indecision over the movie *Staircase* was of a more personal nature than usual. The screenplay by Charles Dyer was based on his play about two ageing homosexual barbers in South London, lonely outsiders, bitching away at each other with sharp tongues that were their only weapons against self-pity and the law's oppressiveness. It was the last kind of film in which Rex could have been imagined. His role was that of the bisexual Charlie, played on the London stage by Paul Scofield.

Even this reassuring precedent did not settle Rex's doubts. Asked by one of his house-guests at Portofino if he had seen Scofield, he snapped, 'Why the hell should I see Paul! Aren't I doing it myself?'¹ Now he devoutly wished he were not.

He had got himself into this fix by succumbing to an offer of a very large sum of money, nearly $1 million, and the assurance that a star of equal eminence would be cast in the role of the other homosexual, Harry, an even more unfortunate specimen of the world's unfair share of afflictions, since he is not only bent, but bald – victim of alopecia or accelerated hair loss. Richard Burton said to Rex, 'I will if you will,' and picked up $1.25 million for doing so. It was still the era when producers believed that anything which Richard Burton and/or Elizabeth Taylor touched turned to gold. This was true, but only of the stars' own fees.

For as long as possible, Rex held on to his options. His hesitation this time, though, reveals more about some of his deeper insecurities than simply an inability to make up his mind. Should he or should he not risk playing a homosexual? He debated it for hours as he, Rachel and Carey walked over the lovely Gower peninsula in rural Wales, where they had been paying a lightning visit to Rachel's ailing mother. 'It impinged on so many insecurities in Rex's nature,' says Carey. 'There was his fear of what the part might force out of him. There was also the fear of how it would look if he turned it down. Would it be more revealing than it would be if he took it on? Then again, if he did take it on, it might refute any rumour that he himself was homosexual. There were so many double and triple possibilities that the more he pondered, the more complicated it got and the steeper and steeper became the moral tail-spin he was in.'

Rex's attitude to homosexuals differed little from that of the average middle-class Edwardian – 'so long as they don't do it in the streets and frighten the horses'. He had to meet and work with 'them' in his profession. He was not homophobic like Jack Buchanan, a contemporary and fellow performer notorious for his refusal to hire any chorus boy with what he thought were effeminate traits. Rex treated 'them' with amused contempt, while respecting any talent they had, especially if it enhanced his own performance. Rumours circulated about him, however, as they did about almost every celebrated English actor of the time, sometimes with justice. Carey Harrison feels that if Rex's nature hid a homosexual side, it was thoroughly sublimated in his art.

An actor who has a feminine side to him acquires many more facets with which to reflect the character he is creating. To say that Olivier benefited from a feminine intuition is not the same as asserting that he had homosexual urges, which has not stopped some writers asserting it anyhow. A few of Rex's acquaintances, and indeed some of his intimates, believe that part of the undeniable pleasure he took in the rows with his wives and mistresses, or in seeing them lose their self-respect as they answered him back in kind, derived from a deep fear and dislike of that gender, which he nevertheless needed in order to feel that his life was complete and 'normal'. If so, it was certainly something he did not wish to recognize in himself, still less to acknowledge. Rattigan, when asked the question, burst into laughter and assured his interviewer, this writer, that Rex was 'as level as Lords cricket ground'.[12] Rex, however, was not unaware of the conjectures about the normality of his sex life, which was certainly a bumpy pitch compared with most people's.

Edith Jackson recalls flying back from Italy with Rachel and the conversation turning to Sir Malcolm Sargent, a notable closet gay of that day, and the man who had given Rex the historic bit of advice to shun *My Fair Lady*. Edith was not long home, when Rex telephoned her and said with some heat, 'What have you and my wife been talking about? What's Malcolm Sargent to do with me?'[13] Edith's reaction was that the master doth protest too much. A guest at Portofino remembers an occasion aboard Rex's cabin cruiser. He had found it necessary to recruit a crew member and had given the job to an Italian boy of striking good looks. On deck one evening Rex fell to musing about wives and marriages, and ended up asking – in a manner that reminded his guest of Henry Higgins – 'What do I want a wife for in any case? All I need is someone to tuck me up at night.'[14] As he spoke, he was looking full at the handsome boy. A second after the words were out of his mouth, he was aware of their possible import and abruptly called it a night. Before he went back to New York, the guest discovered that the cabin boy had been sacked. Rex took no risks, even though the balance of probability is that he had no need to. Not a single homo-erotic liaison has ever turned up in his friends' memories of him, or for that matter in his enemies'.

Rex had not been Stanley Donen's first choice for *Staircase*. He had wanted Paul Scofield to repeat his stage role, but without an audience to feed him intravenously, so to speak, Scofield felt he could be only a pale copy of his stage success. So Donen, in a flash of inspired opportunism, sent the screenplay to Rex and Richard Burton on the same day. Even after netting two of the biggest screen stars of the time, Donen had reservations. '*Staircase* was really a tragedy, a pretty dark one at that, and of limited appeal. It soon became clear that, with Rex and Richard in it, people expected to see a comedy in which gays were mimicked by two famous straights. "We're going to lose our ass," I kept warning Dick

A widower after Kay's death, Rex found comfort – but not remarriage – with Tammy Grimes.

The fatal encounter: Rex and Rachel Roberts in *Platonov* in 1960. In a few days, he had started a romance.

Life at the Villa San Genesio (with the famous Jeep and aboard the cabin cruiser Rex named 'Henry', after his best-known role). For Rachel, it was a taste of Paradise, and the loss of it overshadowed all her later life.

A morning scene on the jetty at Portofino, *circa* 1966: Rex (without toupee) trusts photojournalist Nancy Holmes to take a snap for her personal album while Arthur Barbosa and Rachel Roberts catch up with the news. Robert Bolt (standing) has been brought down to the Villa San Genesio to discuss writing a play for Rex about Charles II.

Cut! Rex is apparently fussed over during a break in the shooting of the opening sequence of *My Fair Lady*. Wilfrid Hyde White, as Colonel Pickering, and Audrey Hepburn, as Eliza, wait for ...

Action! Higgins makes his first acquaintance with the face to which he will grow accustomed. Rex resented that it was being paid five times as much as his own.

Rex and Audrey Hepburn at Ascot, as seen by Hirschfeld.

Looking a little sheep-worn, after nearly a year with the animals, Rex gamely serenades his patient parrot in *Doctor Dolittle*.

Being taught the steps for 'The Dance of the Hours' by Broadway choreographer Lee Theodore for *The Honey Pot*. A double took over, however, for the pirouettes.

With Richard Burton in *Staircase*. The camp joke didn't work out: one star lost interest, the other his nerve. Hollywood lost money.

Happiness is a ready-made family. At least it looks that way with Elizabeth Harris, his fifth wife, and her children. In fact, Rex found the duties of playing father more than he could take.

As Don Quixote (with three cracked ribs): "A wise madness is better than a foolish sanity."

With Julie Harris in *In Praise of Love*. Fifteen years after Kay Kendall's death, he re-lived the benign deception he had practised in the play that Terence Rattigan based on the tragedy.

marvel! lots of love, Mercia [*handwritten inscription*] *Rex 1979*

With Mercia Tinker, his sixth wife, on their wedding day in December 1978.

The last honour: with Mercia outside Buckingham Palace in 1989 shortly after the Queen had made him 'Sir Rex'.

Zanuck, not perhaps the best choice of words. But Dick, too, was into the idea that two notorious cocksmen were going to play queers, as they were called at the time, and he wouldn't listen to what I told him, what Fox was going to get – a small, dark tragedy.'

Rex and Rachel flew to Paris in a private aircraft owned by the banker Loel Guinness at the end of August 1968. Rachel's hope of starring opposite Cary Grant in the Ned Sherrin picture, *The Vicar's Wife*, had fallen though when the film ran into unexpected copyright problems connected with the Sam Goldwyn production of *The Bishop's Wife*. So here she was again, tagging along with Rex, and damn all else to do. Rex had demanded that Fox rent the same manor house at Malmaison for him that he had occupied during *A Flea in Her Ear*. Rachel felt 'stuck like a fly on the flypaper'.[15] It was an unhappy time for everyone. While Burton was appearing in *Staircase* at one Paris studio, Elizabeth Taylor was making *The Only Game in Town* in another part of the city with Warren Beatty as her co-star. Beatty's reputation, deserved or not, made Burton continually uneasy. Making the movies in Paris to facilitate the tax status of their stars meant that exteriors of seedy South London and flashy Las Vegas had to be constructed at enormous expense on alien soil. The pressure was all the greater on Donen to produce not the small, intimate, sad film he had had in mind, but a movie whose scale responded to the salaries of its stars and the costs of its production.

Even before shooting began, he noted with concern the restlessness that Rex was showing and interpreted it, correctly, as a sign that his star had changed his mind about playing a gay. Even so, it was a surprise to him when Rex started looking for a reason to drop out and found it in his hairpiece.

In contrast to the bald character Burton played, whose hairless head was nearly always wrapped in a turbanlike covering of shame, Rex's character sported a luxuriant head of hair. Donen had five or six wigs made in different styles by Wig Creations of London, whose boss, Stanley Hall, personally brought them over to Paris to fit Rex for the make-up test. He was photographed in each with the same lighting every time – 'otherwise we'd never have been able to make up our minds,' says Donen. 'In the projection room the next day, watching the tests, Rex grew angrier and angrier, and finally burst out, "This photography is abominable. It makes me look, well, just *awful*. It's going to destroy the picture if I'm photographed like this." Christopher Challis, who was the lighting photographer, said, "Rex, I'm going to photograph you the way Mr Donen instructs me." Rex whirled round and said to me, "If Challis doesn't apologize immediately, I'm going straight back to Portofino." I said, "This is something between you and me, Rex. In my opinion you have insulted him." Rex snapped, "I'm off." I told Fox immediately. "Very simple," the studio said to me, "fire Challis."

'I said if that was done, it was the end of the movie for me. Fox reconsidered. "Okay, call Rex and stroke him." I said, "No way. If we placate him, he'll become unendurable. The whole movie will be out of control." So what did I recommend? I recommended cabling him, telling him that unless he returned immediately from Portofino, he would be held legally responsible for all expenses incurred, including the possible abandonment of a $5 million movie.'

Rex was back in the studio the day after receiving the cable, behaving as if nothing at all had happened. The same tonic that brought him flying out of his dressing-room when he threatened to abort *My Fair Lady* still packed a kick.

Of course he attempted to get his way in other matters to do with his anxiety over how audiences might react to his playing an 'unlovable' character. 'He'd come out with things like, "I'm not awfully sure about this arty-farty fellow, Stanley. Couldn't I have a scene or two with a woman? I mean, do I need to be queer all the time? Couldn't I just have a lapse or two, now and then?"'

'A lot of light comedy is based on a talent for "camping",' says Robert Flemyng. 'If the comedian is too queer, it can be off-putting. But if you had the luck – as Rex had – to be straight, then you could "camp" it quite wickedly, and people would still laugh. Rex usually got the balance perfectly – until he did *Staircase*. Then it deserted him. The "queerness" was too much "out front", so to speak. He had to confront it, and he didn't like it. Someone said to me at the time, "Rex wants to go to a drag scene and doesn't know where." I said, "Tell Laurie Evans I'll take him down to a pub I've heard about in Camberwell." But I got a message which said, "Sorry, he doesn't want to go, he's changed his mind." He couldn't – he *wouldn't* face it, you see.'

However, once shooting got under way, he was the true professional which his co-star was not. Burton was labouring under great emotional strain at this time. His beloved brother Ifor had been paralysed in a fall at the star's Swiss villa, for which Burton to some extent blamed himself. Then Elizabeth had had a hysterectomy, needed constant drugs to relieve her sciatica and demanded a lot of cosseting by her husband. 'The stars' attitude to the film was very different,' Donen says. 'Rex would rehearse forever, Richard didn't know where he was and didn't care. Rex was totally dedicated, Richard was completely sloppy.'

If Burton lost interest, Rex, to judge from his performance, lost his nerve. Having embarked on playing a gay, he appeared to grow less comfortable with the part as the filming proceeded. There is a feeling of him keeping a distance between himself and the characteristics he is assuming, so that a distasteful flavour of the cabaret lampoon creeps into the performance in a way it never did when Scofield had the part. The critics were quick to spot this. 'One is watching a brilliant high-comedy actor doing something that seems to scare him stiff,' said the *New Yorker*.[6] 'The inevitable result is a turn – a talented piece of slumming with the characteristics of some Night of a Hundred Stars benefit.'

This is not entirely fair. There are moments – though they are only moments – when Rex's dagger-tongued ripostes stutter out at the thought of the serious charge of importuning which the police are bringing against him. Then the actor conveys the authentic horror of an outsider who knows the hostile world is closing in on him. There is no disguising the feeling of a stunt, however. Rex's own nonsexual talents were well deployed, but the gay mask he had assumed only served to discompose him; it was no help in creating a naturalistic figure of comedy pathos.

'Fox thought the movie they were going to get would be something like *The Boys in the Band*,' says Donen. 'Once it opened and they saw what was what, they just walked away from it.'

The world première of *A Flea in Her Ear* took place in Paris that October, during the production of *Staircase*. Donen has cause to recall it. 'There was a gigantic party in a Champs Elysée restaurant which Fox had commandeered for the night. By some insanity, Rex took it on himself to invite the Burtons. We were all in one huge limo when we arrived at the cinema. The *paparazzi* were out in force and all of them made a rush towards Burton and Taylor. They didn't give a damn about Rex and Rachel. They were swept aside – at the première of their own film! As if they didn't exist!

'The same thing happened at the party. Rex and Rachel sat at their table and glowered, while photographers heaved and charged the guards to get through to the Burtons. Eventually Rachel, who had been drinking steadily all night, could take no more. She climbed unsteadily up on to the table and screamed at the top of her voice, "*We are the stars of this fucking film.*" Nobody took any notice of her. Whereupon, she hoisted her skirt up to waist height and bawled, "Here's my pussy. Take some pictures of *it.*" Rex remonstrated with her, but weakly, helplessly. She yelled down to him from her perch. "Don't you talk to me. You can't get it up, you old fart."'

27: The Break-up

That their marriage was breaking down was now obvious to everyone. That Rachel was locked into a severe, long-term mental illness was something that Rex could no longer ignore. He consulted a London psychiatrist about her, who could only advise that she reduce her drinking, take prescribed doses of Seconal to bring her down and find work to keep her steady. Luckily a film offer came along at the end of 1968, starring opposite Nicol Williamson in *The Reckoning*. It was the story of a ruthless, self-made business tycoon who returns to Liverpool to his energizing working-class roots and falls into bed with Rachel's randy housewife. This sort of earthy role had been the making of her eight years ago: it was a return to her roots. But Rex still detested its sleaziness, despite the fact that he himself at that time was playing a painted queen in a seedy London barber's. The double standard never struck Rex. 'Thank God you won't need looks to play a plain duff like that,'[1] was how he greeted *The Reckoning* offer and grumpily agreed to hear her rehearse her lines, both of them locked together without passion in their Plaza-Athénée hotel suite in Paris.

Rachel left for London alone, stayed at the Connaught Hotel, had a one-night stand with a well-known actor and, in desperation and self-disgust, telephoned Rex to tell him about it. He was beyond caring. 'I can't imagine two uglier people together,' was his response.[2] Gamely, she struggled up to Liverpool, confessing to a reporter *en route* that 'I tried to give up work completely, to be a wife to Rex ... But I could not. It's in your blood, and that's that.'[3]

The true magnitude of her error was now rebounding on her with the collapse of her marriage. Filming finished, she threw a huge, frenetic champagne party at the Connaught, behaved wildly and then 'fell into the plane back to Paris and went to Fouquet's with Rex, still sobbing'.[4]

They spent Christmas at Portofino together, but apart in every real sense: 'the house now so dead ... the husband who gave me no nourishment at all. My simple and ordinary needs were never bothered about. No pats on the back at all. I tried to play chess, fixed up the games room with a dart board, intervened if Rex snapped at anyone. I kept on trying. I didn't make a life of my own. I lived entirely through him.'[5]

At the end of February 1969 they both attended that year's Royal Command Film Performance in London. It was *The Prime of Miss Jean Brodie*. Rachel was so emotionally distressed that the doctor had to prescribe Seconal before she had the courage to negotiate the stairs down to their seats in the circle, while the orchestra played music from *Maggie May*. Rex was silent. As soon as the lights went down, she slipped out and spent the evening in the bar drinking gin and sharing her distress with actor Michael Redgrave, a tormented man with his own problems. Then she yielded to Rex's entreaty to go to a clinic for a check-up and 'sleep treatment'. She was given Lithium, the 'truth drug' as it was popularly called, to steady her nerves – 'and the first thing I said was, "I want to fucking well kill him." '[6]

Though each of them recognized they had reached the end, neither could initiate the break. As Joseph L. Mankiewicz said later – about another miserable married couple, the Burtons, but in words that applied to the Harrisons and indeed to the whole tribe to which they belonged – 'Actors don't know how to leave the stage until you give them the lines.'[7] Now Rex could say, with real pain, 'Oh, Joe, why aren't you here writing for me?'

They were in New York in April for Rex to collect a special 'Tony' award for his contribution to the theatre. In public he displayed his customary debonair brio. Alone with Rachel, he was turned in on himself, lost in thought, unresponsive. In tears, she had her hair done at the Carlyle Hotel and heard the hairdresser talking all the time about Kay Kendall. Lindsay Anderson, in town too, begged her to go to an analyst. She rejected the idea; she did not need it, she told him. Really she was telling it to herself. Rex only groaned.

Back in London, she barely got through a television film. While making it, she took a small flat in Eaton Square in her own name. This was enough to start the columnists sniffing for the scent of a separation. But Rex still sat in Portofino, wondering what to do next. Like saying yea or nay to an acting offer, he was gripped by paralysing inertia and almost wished for someone to intervene so that he could see Rachel in the context of another man. Amazingly, someone did.

In the late summer and early autumn of 1969. Rachel went into *Who's Afraid of Virginia Woolf?* with her first husband, Alan Dobie, who had remarried since their divorce and was now enviably settled with a family of three.

Newsmen dropping into Rachel's dressing-room at the Theatre Royal,

Bath, duly noted the silver-framed photograph of Rex inscribed 'To my own dearest Rachel' and the two dozen long-stemmed red roses beside it. But it looked too carefully staged. Rex arrived by train – Rachel had grabbed the Rolls-Royce – to see the play along with Edith Jackson. To Edith, Edward Albee's play about the domestic argy-bargy of George and Martha seemed mild stuff compared to the bitterness she had witnessed over the years between Rex and Rachel. Echoes of it accompanied their departure from Bath the next morning. Rachel stood on the platform bawling at Rex as the train pulled out: 'You'll never get away from me ...'[8] Instead of being angry, Rex was elated by her 'performance': she was humiliating herself.

Strangely, as if the play that ends in the fantasy about a lost child with which Albee finally blesses his sundered couple had reanimated Rachel's own wish to preserve her marriage, she now began to talk again of her and Rex adopting a child. She even visited a Church of England children's home. Significantly, perhaps, she spoke of adopting an Italian child because 'our home is Portofino ... and one thing is certain, it will be a girl. One man is enough for any woman to handle.'[9] Such a child would be an unlikely discovery in a Church of England adoption home, but Rachel's insistence on a Latin infant and a girl at that suggests her need to preserve the Portofino paradise in all its local colour and at the same time temper Rex's chauvinism with an ally, even an immature one, of her own sex. Fantasy, of course. But for someone in her condition – she was now on twelve to fourteen Seconals a day – fantasy can sometimes can be a stronger motivation than reality.

She had fears as well as fantasies. Already the American papers – though not, as yet, the English ones which were more fearful of libel – were printing stories about Rex in the enjoyable company of a beautiful blonde Englishwoman, Elizabeth Harris, the now estranged wife of the actor whose precious Chinese mockingbird Rachel had liberated in Hollywood. Elizabeth and her three boys had been guests at San Genesio that Easter. And in the summer, Rex invited them to join the ninety-foot schooner he had chartered for a Mediterranean cruise. For the first time, Rachel felt that Rex's desertion of her was a possibility.

For Rex, too, 1969 was turning into a crucial year. His recent experiences on three films, each of them draining him emotionally and physically, and all of them box-office disasters, had turned him back towards his first love – the theatre.

He pondered the attractions of Arthur Schnitzler's *Casanova's Home-coming*, an ironic reverie in which the fabled womanizer recalls his early conquests without realizing their emptiness. He even acquired the foreign rights to the work. But either the material proved intractable or, more likely, his interest in it waned. While Rachel was in England, he had plenty of time to read and mostly reject the plays his agents sent him. Then one caught his attention. It offered 'possibilities', that is to say the opportunity to rework its text during production and insert the things he knew would feed *his* talents and amuse *his* audience.

The Lionel Touch was a comedy by a virtually unknown author, George Hulme, a thirty-eight-year-old Canadian, who had even survived a 'test' weekend at San Genesio that summer. 'Very light, very witty,' Rex called the play and added, on scant evidence so far as it concerned his own career, 'It is always satisfying to take on a new playwright's work.'[10] The character which attracted Rex was a raffish, womanizing artist: a chance for him to show temperament and charm. His long-suffering common law wife and children look helplessly on as he tries to elude the bailiffs and avoid arrest: a chance for Rex's outrageous mischievousness and scapegoat forgiveness.

'For once,' said Rex, 'I'm not playing my usual urbane character. Lionel is erratic, temperamental ... it's a bit of a change of image,'[11] – a statement which caused a few eyebrows to rise.

Rex's ruthless reputation for having material altered to fit his own comic talent should have warned everyone in advance. As soon as rehearsals began in London in September 1969 he seized the initiative. He had members of the cast replaced or repositioned on stage so that they did not physically distract from him; one very tall actor was required to sit down as soon as possible after coming on stage. 'It started off,' says Richard Huggett, 'as a bitter, arsenical and uncompromisingly black comedy – a bite in it to the very last line. But when he started rehearsing it – virtually directing it – Rex's enthusiasm waned. Cautiousness took over. Was it perhaps *too* black? Was his character *too* unlovable? It might defeat his hopes of bringing audiences round to sympathizing with a man whose self-centredness formed the substance of the play.' The truth was that the *idea* of playing a monster was attractive to Rex – who *was* one – but not the actual experience of it. He began cutting the text because he feared no one in the audience could actually *love* him. According to Christopher Cazenove, whose West End debut it was to be, 'Rex did a lot of cutting, and mainly the serious stuff.'[12] The effect, Cazenove says, was to leave an attenuated text, mainly witticisms and jokey complications, but without the fibre to produce a well-balanced meal. Rex thus intimidated the cast and devitalized the play.

It was to open in Manchester before the West End. Laurie Evans went up there for the final dress rehearsal on 12 October 1969. 'It was pretty clear it was going to be a disaster. When I went to see Rex in his dressing-room, it was obvious to me that he shared my misgivings. "Not too good, was it?" he said. – "That's understating it, Rex; it was ghastly ... terrible." – "What do I do, Laurie?" – "Well, it looks to me, Rex, your best way out is to become ill. So if I were you I'd start practising lying down." '

The next night the play opened and received what was, in the circumstances, quite a good reception. Well, thought Evans, Manchester first nights are neither here nor there: 'It didn't change my mind about the play.'

The agent went round to Rex's dressing-room and found him in a towering rage. 'See what you've done,' he barked at him. 'You destroyed my confidence last night, you completely undermined me. It's time you quit. You've lost your judgment. You don't know the market any more. You're past it.'

All this was shouted at the top of Rex's voice. Evans recalls, in fairness, that his own replies were fairly voluble too. Outside, a roomful of Manchester worthies listened with shock to the sounds of Rex's bad temper. John Gale, the producer, was hosting a party after the show. There Rex was fulsomely praised. But still in a rage from his confrontation with Laurie Evans, he got to his feet and cried, 'Don't give me that. I don't want compliments from shitty little moneymen like you.'[3] Laurie Evans's wife, Mary, sitting near him and already upset by Rex's vituperative outburst against her husband, uttered a protest. He flew at her. 'Oh, do shut up, you clockwork cunt.'[4]

In retrospect, such rows are part and parcel of the emotionally charged nature of the theatre; most resolve themselves into apologies or green room myth. Laurie Evans waited a few days, but no regrets were expressed, even over the insult to his wife, which weighed far more deeply with him than the villification that Rex, frequently heaped on his associates. 'So I picked up the phone, called Rex and said that I was taking him at his word. Would he please make arrangements to be represented by someone else.' Rex eventually went to Robin Fox, the husband of Angela, whom Rex had known in his touring days and to whose son, Edward, he was godfather.

Rumbles of discontent continued when the play moved to Oxford and the actor Nigel Patrick appeared on the scene, saying he had been hauled in by a management that was at its wits end to know how to save the play. He was there, he announced with some satisfaction, to knock the play into shape and to advise Rex. That was provocation enough. Rex lowered his horns and charged, and another high-pitched row erupted in a public dining-room. Patrick had the pleasure of implanting another *banderilla* in Rex's hide: 'They offered me the play first, you know, and I turned it down.'[5]

The London previews were a nightmare for Rex, who had by this time quarrelled with the author, and yet, when it opened on 5 November 1969, his aura was its compensating grace. Almost ten years had gone by since he had last appeared in the West End. His presence was a rarity for some of the younger critics occupying the aisle seats and the reviews were kinder to him than the play and the circumstances of its production deserved. 'The comedy exists strictly for the sake of Rex Harrison,' said Irving Wardle in *The Times*.[16] And Peter Lewis, in the *Daily Mail*, greeted Rex warmly, though acknowledging that he seemed 'in doubt whether he was playing for real or comic effect'.[17] That Rex could have left any doubt on this score shows how shaken his own judgment must have been by the experience. It was a case of total egotism compounding the errors of an eccentric choice of play and then the attempt to change its nature.

'It wasn't a *bad* performance Rex gave in *The Lionel Touch*,' says Robert Flemyng. 'He was playing a man with lots of children. One of the sons says to him, "Dad, don't you ever think of anything except sex?" There was a pause, then Rex snapped, *"Never!"* With any other actor, you'd have thought, "Well, *that's* quite well timed, it got a good laugh." But when Rex said it, I fell off my seat – almost. There was something about the inflection that was quite unique to him. No other comedian alive could get so much laughter from one word. He does it quite a lot in *My Fair Lady*.'

Just as his earlier wives had rallied to him in a crisis, Rachel stuck closely to him during the débacle, even chartering a light aircraft to take her from London to Manchester for the first night. This was necessary because she was in rehearsals most of the day, playing Milady in *The Three Musketeers Ride Again*, a light-hearted Christmas entertainment being presented by the English Stage Company at the Royal Court.

On 12 December Rex either fell genuinely ill or decided to 'practise lying down'. Suddenly he was out of *The Lionel Touch*, supposedly suffering from fatigue and overwork. He would be out for at least three weeks, the announcement said. Exactly one week later came the news that the gossip columnists had been predicting with increasing confidence. His London lawyer announced that Rex and Rachel were 'living separately and apart'.[18] Rachel was stunned by the bluntness of it. Either unwilling to accept it or emotionally unable to take it in, she said the next day: 'I am sure we are going to be reconciled.'[19] She added to the man from the *Mail*, 'We are just taking a breather, dear.' Then, nearly incoherent, she protested, 'We are adult people ... what is happening is only a little thing, really. The Sixties are over and the Seventies are here – let's all be friends. That's what Rex would want. I love him with all my heart, but I have known the end was near for nearly two months.' From his suite and presumably his sick bed in the Connaught Hotel, Rex merely said: 'I issued a statement ... and I stand by this statement.'[20]

On Christmas Eve Rachel checked into the Royal Court Hotel, next to the theatre in Sloane Square, swallowed fifty aspirin tablets and went to sleep believing and hoping that she would never wake up again. When she did, it was to find herself at St George's Hospital, Knightsbridge, with her stomach being pumped out. 'Jingle Bells' and other carols were ringing in her ears. She thought momentarily that she had died and gone to heaven. She survived. It was the marriage that finally died. When she left St George's, she called Rex and said, 'Let's start married life all over again.'[21] There was a silence. Then he said, 'almost in a whisper', according to Rachel, 'I couldn't. I can't live your life and you can't live mine.' It had come down to that. It was over.

The two of them almost ran into each other before the end of the year. 'Mr Harrison's dining here this evening,' a tactful waiter told her and her friend Eleanor Fazan, when they entered one of London's trendiest restaurants a few days after Rachel came out of hospital. Rachel did not turn tail. She ignored Rex and sat down, but excused herself a few minutes later to go to the loo. When she was a suspiciously long time away, an alarmed Eleanor Fazan went in search of her. Downstairs was a line of pay telephones and Rachel stood in front of them, flinging each receiver in turn against the tiled wall. It was perhaps as well Rex did not meet her.

Through the combination of Christmas and most newspapers not being published, Rex was spared the experience of reading of yet another suicide attempt by one of the women in his life. He returned to the cast of *The Lionel Touch* on 3 January 1970 and struggled on with the play until the run ended three weeks later. It was a fatiguing conclusion to what he considered the worst year of his life. Yet, once again, Rex's innate distaste for looking back with regret or lingering over past misjudgments saw him through. Episodes of his life were like unsuccessful plays: when they closed in tears, temper and pain, well, that was it. He was off looking for something new. Almost as one turns a daily calendar, passing without pause from one date to the next, Rex entered a new existence. On the closing night of *The Lionel Touch*, he drove straight to Luton airport, where a chartered jet was waiting to take him out of the country, away from all theatrical and domestic messes, off to the sun and the freedom of the southern coast of the Mediterranean – to Tangier. As was his preference, he did not travel alone. With him went the Hon. Elizabeth Harris.

Part Six

Elizabeth

28: La Vie en Famille

'Look out for Elizabeth Harris,' Rex had told Laurie Evans a few months earlier, when Evans, then still his agent and friend, had been invited down to Portofino with his wife Mary. 'Bring her with you,' Rex commanded. 'How shall we know her?' Evans asked. 'Slim and blonde and tall, like the rest,' Rex answered.

Elizabeth Harris had been born Elizabeth Rees-Williams in 1936. She was the daughter of a former Labour MP and Government Minister who had crossed over to the Liberal Party and been raised to the Peerage as Baron Ogmore of Bridgend when he lost his Parliamentary seat in the General Election of 1950 which returned the Conservatives to power. Like all the women Rex selected with a serious eye to marriage, she was intelligent as well as beautiful. From a convent school education in Switzerland, she had gone on to the Royal Academy of Dramatic Art, training to be an actress. A fellow student was Peter O'Toole. At twenty, she met and was captivated by an ambitious young Irish actor four years her senior called Richard Harris. Already known for his rebellious and hearty attitude to life, Harris was struggling to make a career for himself in plays and films like *Shake Hands with the Devil* and *The Long and the Short and the Tall*. His prominence increased with the reputation he began to gather as a hell-raiser which, in turn, led to roles that showed him to be a physical and dramatic match for stars like Marlon Brando – as much between the shots of *Mutiny on the Bounty* as in the film.

After that film and the leading role in *This Sporting Life*, as the elemental hero of the Rugby battlefield whose passion smashes itself in frustration against Rachel Roberts's coldly denying landlady, there was no holding him back except, occasionally, by the arms of stronger men than he. By this time Elizabeth and he had married and were living, much like Rachel and Alan Dobie, in a one-bedroom Paddington flat. Elizabeth recalls the party and the end of shooting on *This Sporting Life*, when Rex turned up to keep an eye on Rachel. He made such an unbelievably elegant contrast with her husband, she thought. She had seen Rex on stage in *My Fair Lady*; it had been her father's twenty-first birthday treat for her, and he had had to scrounge tickets for the sold-out show from Rex's brother-in-law, Lord Kilmuir. But it was not until 1950 that they first met and then only briefly, when Rex stopped by the table in a Chelsea restaurant where the Harrises were dining with Laurence Harvey and his then wife Margaret Leighton. Rex ignored the men, talked mainly to Margaret Leighton, but left Elizabeth with an impression of tremendous if rather aloof self-assurance. She felt he was scrutinizing her, even though directing most of his attention elsewhere. 'He was enormously attractive, but inhibiting,' she says today. 'I felt safer saying nothing than making a remark that might draw his sarcasm." He looked to her the opposite of her husband: dangerous, yes, but totally in control of himself.

After only a few years of marriage and with a family already started, Elizabeth had discovered that success only fed the latent proclivities in her husband which gave him the andrenalin to thrive in front of the cameras or behind the footlights, but which made for sometimes sorrier scenes in public and at home, whenever the pressures of alcohol or simply those of celebrity cost him control of his temper. His fits of anger were generally short-lived, but they left wreckage behind them, marital as well as physical. Around the same time as Rex was finding it difficult to cope with Rachel's tantrums, Elizabeth Harris was having to admit to herself that she was scared of the void she felt had opened between her and her husband – and physically scared of the unpredictable moods which occasionally filled it. In her memoirs she recalls that the marriage moved into the background as her husband's then apparently uncontrollable mood swings incited him to bouts of destructive temper and frustration. In Hawaii, for example, when he was making the film of that name in 1965, a gruelling experience for even a seasoned and equable star, he used to run out of the house, according to Elizabeth, into the stream of passing traffic and work off some internal demon by beating with his hands on the windows and bodywork of the automobiles until he had broken and bloodied the skin of his knuckles – much in the same way, one imagines, as he behaved in the scene of a film he made twenty-five years later, playing an obstinate patriarchal Irish farmer who waded into the Atlantic Ocean beating the waves with his stick in an attempt to drive them back from his beloved land. It was frightening, Elizabeth found, though it gave him tremendous power as an actor.

Rex came to one of the huge parties that her husband threw in Hollywood when he was there making *Camelot*. One hundred guests sat down to dinner and 250 more came in later for the drinking and dancing. Like a reformed rake, Rex deplored the excess of it all. 'I did all this years ago. What does Richard think he's doing? Who's he trying to impress? ... It's so *passé* now. This is Old Hollywood and Old Hollywood is dead. You're twenty-five years too late.'²

Rex's words made an impression on Elizabeth. She looked around her and indeed the scene was unreal. If Rex was living his myth, then her own husband was living his fantasy – and a dangerous one at that. She admits to having led a cautious, anxiety-ridden double life 'to get relief'. But she chose another self-destructive individual to comfort her, Robin Douglas Home, younger brother of the playwright, who was later to take his own life. After sensing his disturbed nature and breaking off their relations, Elizabeth found insecurity setting in. She felt fearful of trying to escape from her husband, but was unable to see life with him as anything but living in a gilded jail. 'I longed only to be with a man who was quiet, gentle and whose every thought and word were completely predictable.'³ A breakdown ensued, and that was followed by a legal separation during which she turned for solace and perhaps protection, too, to Christopher Plummer, then estranged from his wife Tammy Grimes. Plummer appeared to bear Rex no resentment for displacing him from *Doctor Dolittle*; quite the opposite, possibly, as he had been paid his fee without having to play with a menagerie of intractable animals for most of a year. On the occasions that she and Plummer went out with the Harrisons, Elizabeth noted how Rachel's conduct, always unpredictable and sometimes amusing, had now become eccentric and akin to a public nightmare for Rex.

One night at the bar of the Connaught Hotel, Rex ordered Rachel to get a move on, drink up and let them go in and have dinner. Rachel's response was to pour an almost full glass of red wine on to the hotel carpet. 'There now,' she said, 'I'm finished. We can go.' 'Christ,' said Rex, to his companions, 'can't *somebody* do something!'⁴

People who share the same sort of miseries, even if they are of different intensity, often find common ground in their need for sympathy. Elizabeth began to see more of Rex between her separation from Richard Harris and her divorce in July 1969, exactly when relations between Rex and Rachel looked like they were going to break down irretrievably.

Elizabeth and her three children – Damian, the eldest boy, and his two brothers – were guests at Portofino and later joined Rex's yachting cruise along with her brother Morgan. During her stay at the villa, she was aware that Rex's interest in her might be something more than a host's. He was remarkably attentive. But then, she told herself, was this not the way he believed he should behave? This was the old charmer making a pass at a beautiful young woman because, well ... because that was what was expected of him. 'It wasn't to be taken seriously, I thought,' she recalls, 'just something in the way of business.'

She first began to suspect it was more serious when Rex dropped in on her unexpectedly in the house she had taken for her family in Bedford Gardens, London, while waiting for her divorce. He was following his custom of turning to an available and sympathetic woman for comfort when his marital affairs had become simply too much even for him to endure or sort out. 'He would sit there and talk for hours about his difficulties,' Elizabeth says. 'Rachel's drinking had defeated him. He told me she had had aversion therapy suggested to her – drinking whisky until she sickened herself of it. Rex said, in all seriousness, "My God, I'd never forgive anyone who turned *me* off whisky for life."'

While Rachel was acting in *Who's Afraid of Virginia Woolf?* in Bath with her ex-husband, Rex was taking advantage of her guaranteed absence from London to pour his heart out to Elizabeth. He even arrived in the middle of a dinner party she was giving, 'forcing me to leave my guests and hear him talk about his sorrows in the next room'. When she went to a restaurant, she could never be quite sure he would not find out where she had gone and turn up there too, joining her and her companion, 'always relying – invariably correctly – on his celebrity smoothing the way into the *tête-à-tête* I might be having with my own man. He'd sit there with us, talking, sipping the wine ... On one occasion, I remember, he tasted a glass of the wine my escort had ordered, made a face and said, "For Christ's sake, don't drink it. It's corked."' Like the Unidentified Guest in T. S. Eliot's *The Cocktail Party*, Rex dominated the social occasion. Only this time, it was clear, it was he who was in search of a guardian – and a home.

Sometimes he would fall asleep downstairs on a sofa in Elizabeth's home while she retired to her bedroom upstairs. At this point he was staying at the Connaught Hotel, but, to be more private, he rented a flat above Colefax & Fowler, the interior decorators, and used to invite Elizabeth over for drinks and more harrowing confessions of his unhappiness. He talked of how he had wanted a family, forgetting, of course, that he already had two sons. Elizabeth soon concluded that what he really wanted was a family *atmosphere*. 'When he visited Bedford Gardens, he seemed to find the family mood created by my three children very much to his liking. Later, of course, it became evident that the *idea* of a family was what appealed to him. The *reality* of one proved a very different matter.'

The growing warmth of their relationship was not without its complications of high and low comedy. When Rachel returned from acting in Bath, she found her suspicions turning very quickly into certainties. Yet neither then nor later did she resent Rex's closeness to Elizabeth Harris with the degree of bitterness that might reasonably have been expected. Knowing Rex's promiscuous nature, she perhaps recognized the inevitability of it. What also helped was Elizabeth's candour, carrying no sense of conquest or triumph over another woman. The blame, if there was any, was on Rex: that is what one expected. He was someone whom both women understood, or thought they did. It was very like the film of *The Constant Husband* which he had made. His promiscuity in it was regarded by the women he met, married and left as a sort of helplessness, to be treated with sympathy like a child that has been naughty, hurt itself and needs comforting. 'This was the strange thing about the power he had,' says Elizabeth. 'One never stopped loving him despite being put through the mangle by him.' Nevertheless, she was disconcerted, not to say alarmed, when she lifted the telephone one day and heard Rachel ask her, point blank, how things stood between her and her husband: 'Are you in love with him, Elizabeth?'[5] Elizabeth told her that, yes, she was sorry, but she was. Not quite the answer Rachel had expected, but the frankness of it seemed to be a relief to her. All she said with resignation in her voice was, 'It happens.'

On another occasion Rachel rang Rex while Elizabeth was there. This time a flaming row erupted between husband and wife, until Elizabeth seized the telephone and spoke to Rachel. 'Then she suddenly became almost collusive in her attitude. It was two women and Rex, a sense of sharing him between us.' This peculiar kind of *ménage à trois*, existing on the emotional plane, though, not the physical one, continued for several months. Not for the first time in Rex's tangled relationships with women, it produced scenes made for the theatre.

One evening, while he was at Bedford Gardens, the doorbell rang. Rachel stood on the mat. Elizabeth poured everyone a drink, while Rex sat uncomfortably between her and his wife, and the Harris boys' pet dog, Dodger, barked excitedly at them and got an answering 'Woof!' from Rachel now and then.

'Finally,' Elizabeth recalls, 'Rachel said that Rex would have to make his mind up there and then. "Which one of us do you want, Rex. Her or me?" Rex gritted his teeth, flashed a look of horror-struck resentment at the women on each side of him, then jerked a thumb at the dog. "I'll take Dodger," he said, and bolted.'

It was like Charles Condomine in *Blithe Spirit* protestingly torn between the wife he was with and the mischievous wraith from the past. Later on, Rex would say to Elizabeth, 'Seen Rachel much these days?' or 'How's Rachel's state of mind?' as if he were speaking of someone he had known once, but put out of mind, even though they might in fact have run into each other in London only a few weeks before. It occurred to Elizabeth that there was so much guilt for Rex to bear that he was mentally burying her, absolving himself of responsibility. It really came as no surprise to her when Rex's health apparently gave way during the run of *The Lionel Touch* at the very time his lawyer was announcing his separation from Rachel. The break, when it came, had proved emotionally devastating.

There was no sexual relationship between Rex and herself, says Elizabeth, until Rex's divorce from Rachel came through. 'He was simply too fatigued. All he wanted was company and comfort.'

After they had landed at Tangier in the chartered jet, they transferred to a yacht, *Calisto*, along with Elizabeth's youngest son, Jamie, and his nanny. Her other sons had returned to their preparatory school after Christmas. Thus began a year in which Rex sought to recuperate from the mess his marriage and career were in simply by the expedient of travel. Keeping on the move, he felt, meant that bad news, of which there was a lot around and probably more on the way, could not reach him or, if it did, distance would have softened the impact and time taken the sting out of it. The *Calisto* put into Lanzarote, an islet in the Canaries several hundreds of miles off the Atlantic coast of Morocco. 'But he didn't like it there,' recalls Edith Jackson, who had been left at the command post back home, 'and cabled me to have a private jet rescue him and take him and the others to Fez.' By this time Jamie and the nanny had flown back to England.

Fez intrigued Rex, fascinated as ever by historical fact he could see and feel. For him, a guide book that was so boring to others was akin to a play script. He liked to mug it up thoroughly before hand; it gave him a feeling of being in command of events. Not entirely, however, as his ever suspicious eye settled on a young Moroccan whom Elizabeth had invited to partner her in one of the night-clubs while Rex sat at the table listening to their guide's account of Fez as the old holy capital of the country. To her surprise, the impulsiveness that had prompted Rex to attack Frank Sinatra when he found Kay Kendall alone with him now caused a punch to be flung at the Moroccan boy, who seemed to Rex to be enjoying the dance too much and too expertly. The lad nimbly sidestepped the fist. It landed on Elizabeth. 'Rex cried, "He made me miss,"' Elizabeth recalls him saying indignantly, as she felt her jaw turning numb from the blow. '"He *ducked*," he went on. He was adept at pinning the blame where it didn't belong.'

While Rex and Elizabeth toured the Moroccan holy places, Rachel flew to Los Angeles in a more shocked condition than she knew. There, over the next few months, she endeavoured to take 'his' cure, by throwing herself energetically into work, accepting whatever was offered. So she opted for a role in a film called *Doctors' Wives*, in which she took the part of a wife who confesses to a lesbian relationship and receives the self-righteous forgiveness of her husband. At the time, this passed for an enlightened, morally daring ending. Unfortunately, it was a case of the sick playing the so-called sick. Rachel could not get over the emotional finality of losing Rex. In Beverly Hills, a place she had always hated, but had gone to because that is where the work was, she now behaved like a refugee desperately trying to create a new identity for herself. She dyed her hair blonde and went on tranquilizers. Rex was supporting her financially while a divorce settlement was worked out. Friends of hers urged her to take him for all he was worth. But a lack of resentment against Elizabeth, plus the pathetic hope that if she behaved 'reasonably' he might come back to her, dissuaded her from seeking vengeance. Despite the physical distance between them, Rex kept a watch on her, never knowing what she might do that would harm him. Her maid kept in touch with his American lawyer, Aaron Frosch, who was working out the divorce terms. Frosch, in turn, reported back to Rex what Rachel was getting up to. It did not make reassuring hearing. One unconventional liaison she formed was with a black hustler who induced her to gamble at Santa Anita race-track using Rex's money and on whom she lavished clothes and liquor, on Rex's money again. Friends warned her this was a dangerous indulgence. Her fear was that Rex might arrive in town in search of her. 'She had this absurd notion that Rex was going to kill her black lover,' says Pamela Mason. '"Nonsense," I said to her, "if anyone's in danger from Rex, it's you. You're going to cost him money." '[6] Nevertheless, the lover faked an attempt on his own life, then tried to make out that Rex had taken out a contract on him. Frosch dealt with the matter privately and apparently successfully.

A more calming and ultimately nourishing influence came into Rachel's distracted existence at this time in the person of a handsome Mexican in his early twenties living in Los Angeles after his divorce from a New York model. Darren Ramirez had few close friends, but a wide range of acquaintances, famous and just social, for he was gregarious by nature and possessed charm, good looks and an easy going disposition. He was at the Beverly Wilshire Hotel when he suddenly caught sight of a woman whom he recognized, despite her newly dyed blonde hair and the mini skirt she wore to draw attention to her long legs and slim waist, as the actress he had admired five or six years earlier when he had seen *This Sporting Life* in a Los Angeles art-house cinema. 'I thought her so wonderful that I returned to see the movie several times. Now here she was in front of me.'[7] Darren Ramirez began a relationship with Rachel that was to last until her death.

Where Rex and Rachel had been naturally combative personalities who spurred each other to greater abuse, Darren was someone with the patient disposition to cushion the blows she sometimes figuratively and physically threw at him. Darren believed that Rex could not feel comfortable hearing about the odd hangers-on collecting around Rachel because of her unattached status. Gradually, he persuaded her to shake them off, see a doctor, enter hospital and undergo a drying out session and the then popular 'sleep cure'.

Thus Rex Harrison, sixty-two, and recuperating in the company of a woman he had come to love and depend on, found his guilty conscience over Rachel being eased by a twenty-three-year-old on the other side of the world.

Rex was impatient to spend the summer of 1970 at his villa in Portofino. Elizabeth was not all that keen. 'The place seemed too full of ghosts' – of other marriages she might have added. Such things, she said, got to her quickly. Just as Rachel had found herself being compared to the memory of Kay Kendall in the cafés, bars and market stalls around the harbour, Elizabeth's arrival ran up against the popularity that Rachel had enjoyed, especially among the younger menfolk of the place. Up at the villa, as she soon discovered, Lilli's way of doing things – the unvarying times for meals, the conventional number of courses, the servants who stood and waited – all contributed to a feeling of trespass familiar to readers of Daphne du Maurier's romantic mystery *Rebecca*. She also realized soon enough how unwelcome any disturbance was. 'I realized that Rex wanted an ordered life quite as much as he needed love. It wasn't all Lilli's doing; he didn't like his set ways altered. I could make do with a sandwich on the terrace for lunch, but not Rex. He insisted on formality – the black tie, the perfectly laid dinner table, the host and hostess at opposite ends of it whether or not there were guests in between us.' Elizabeth would sometimes surprise guests by laying more places than were needed. When questioned, she would say sardonically that they were for 'the other wives' whose 'presence' her own arrival had never dispelled and, she reflected, never would.

Temporary, if unexpected, respite from this haunting sense of the past came when Richard Harris applied for a court order restraining Elizabeth from taking their children to the villa until Rex's divorce from Rachel was through. Rachel was not hurrying over filing a suit in America. She still hoped against hope that he would come back to her. So that Elizabeth and the children could be with him, Rex rented a mansion in the south of France, near Le Lavandou, and the three Harris boys, their cousin and schoolfriends came there for the summer holidays. At first Rex made out that he loved being part of an extended family. It took him back, he said, to the myriad cousins with whom he and his sisters used to spend seaside holidays in Wales as children. But then he quickly grew short-tempered with 'the young devils', as he took to calling the kids. A feeling of fatherhood had never been something he cared much about or knew how to handle when it was presented to him ready-made, so to speak. Relations with his own sons were an off or on affair. What he called absentmindedness where his own boys were concerned reflected his basic lack of interest in children. He once discovered he had written to Carey at his boarding school some months after the boy had left it. Noel, with his interest in the outdoor life and jazz music, was perhaps the easier son for Rex to get along with. Carey had grown up much more politically committed to radical ideas that Rex branded Communism. Rex made little distinction between any parties that wished to dispossess him of income and property. Even Portofino was starting to look a bit dodgy, he thought, as Italy's Communist Party began attacking the *dolce vita* life-style of the previous decade. Now he had to accommodate an invasion of boisterous youngsters.

'I thought at first he was being unreasonable,' Elizabeth says, 'but now I realize he wasn't. We had eleven children coming and going in the house that first summer, all different sizes, ages and temperaments, with the local doctor on call every few days to cope with minor ailments or accidents. I recall his breathing a sigh of satisfaction as he sat in my London home having dinner with me and the boys, the *au pair* girl coping with the youngest child, the lodger popping in and out for coffee, a go-as-you-please, slap-happy atmosphere. ' "Ah, this is what I mean," he'd say, "the informality." But he soon went lukewarm on it.'

At the height of the summer holidays, he did a head count and got to over twenty children in the house. There and then he announced he was off to Portofino. But he was only there for a day or two, after which he could not bear the silence and the loneliness any more, and back he came to France.

For all his sophistication, Elizabeth found Rex very naïve in some of the practical details of life, perhaps because he had always left them to others. 'What about going to the opera?' he asked her on one occasion when they were in Paris and he lifted the phone in their suite in the Hotel Lancaster and called the *concierge*. 'One box at the opera, please,' he ordered. Then he turned quizzically to Elizabeth and said, 'I suppose I did that right?' Opera-going did not figure much in Rex's experience of life, and in the films he had seen people always sat in a box.

After his disastrous experience with *The Lionel Touch* he was excessively wary about any new plays he was offered. As for films, parts for a sixty-two-year-old man were in short supply at the best of times. The early 1970s were the worst of eras for Hollywood, which had begun the decade with inventories overstocked with unreleased films and balance sheets showing only losses on expensive blockbusters of the kind Rex had made, like the Julie Andrews vehicle *Star!* The youth audiences, their appetite whetted by *Easy Rider, Bonnie and Clyde, The Graduate* and *Midnight Cowboy* wanted sexually franker, more explicitly violent movies with young newcomers like Nicholson, Dunaway, Hopper, Hoffman and Fonda, all cast in the liberated life-styles of their audiences. Even the Burtons had suffered box-office humiliation as movies like *Boom!* or *Secret Ceremony* or *The Only Game in Town* were spectacular money-losers. 'Nobody, but *nobody* will pay us a million dollars a picture again for a long time,' Richard Burton entered in his diary.[8] If the curse was on fortune's darlings like the Burtons, could Rex escape it?

In a rare interview at this time, granted to *Esquire* magazine's Jon Bradshaw, Rex spoke of his distaste for contemporary theatre in London and New York. It was offensively vulgar, there was so much nudity in plays and he was revolted by the trendy anti-hero type. 'Today you piss on the rug and you're in.'[9] Though he had once been a notable anti-hero himself, in the days when it was spelled c-a-d, these days one had to be tough, butch, unmannerly – none of which he was. He struck Bradshaw as 'a fashionable man out of fashion [with] nothing but his past to look forward to'.[10]

For a time he thought that producing films might provide his talents with an outlet. He actually acquired the rights to several properties, one an anti-war film, *A Pride of Lions*, to star Henry Fonda and his son Peter; the other, a social comedy, *Nowhere Girl*, in which he saw Shirley MacLaine. 'I may direct it myself,' he announced.[11] However, he was unwilling to finance it himself. And Rex's reputation as a 'difficult' actor, who did not count the cost to others in giving a performance to his own satisfaction, was hardly an encouragement to film companies in hard times.

Still, he valiantly played the role of the family man. He was photographed by Terry O'Neill that Christmas, sitting in his Eaton Square flat, his arm around Elizabeth, with five children at their feet or peeping over their shoulders – two of them his grandchildren from Noel's marriage, three of them Elizabeth's sons. The children wore party hats and were festooned with streamers. 'I've always been a family man,' Rex was quoted as saying, but somehow it did not roll off his tongue as fluently as 'I'm an ordinary man' had done in the *My Fair Lady* score.[12] He looked as comfortable as a reformed Scrooge trying to play Santa Claus. Indeed, he had already suffered through the Harris boys' school play, putting up with small boys in the rows behind him throwing screwed-up toffee papers at his unmistakable head. He had attempted to slip away at the (merciful) intermission, but was intercepted by the school matron, who had found him walking moodily up and down a deserted corridor. Being unwilling to admit that the school production was so awful he could not take another minute of it, Rex feigned an upset stomach. Before he knew what was happening, Matron was preparing to whisk him into the school sanitarium for a check-up and a dose of liver salts. He returned with some speed to the amateur theatricals.

He began to feel trapped again, an impression reinforced when BBC Television prevailed on him to repeat his role in *Platonov*, the play that had brought him and Rachel together. As Rachel was going through with their divorce, she was unavailable. SíAn Phillips took her part.

Some consolation was provided by the divorce settlement which finally came through after Rachel, surrendering to the inevitable, presented it at Santa Monica Superior Court in February 1971 alleging the usual formulaic 'irreconcilable differences'.

Under the settlement, Rachel received a 'farewell present' of $35,000 (worth about £15,000 at the time), $10,000 (£4,200) annual alimony so long as she remained unmarried, falling to half that if she did remarry, and Rex was also ordered to pay up to $100,000 (£42,000) to buy her a house which reverted to him if she predeceased him. One point Rachel did not win: she had asked for custody of the dog, Rex's beloved basset hound Homer. Rex refused to budge. The court exercised its discretion on the dog in favour of the respondent. Homer stayed with his master. Old Hollywood lawyers thought the terms lenient and felt Rex was lucky to have got away with so little in the land of the million-dollar settlement. Richard Harris said he was pleased to know his ex-wife would be remarrying – '15,000 reasons why I'm delighted'.[3] Rachel said, 'I am quite satisfied ... nobody ever promised me a glass slipper.'[4] Rex said, 'Well, I've got my balls back.'[5]

29: Madness in Great Ones

Elizabeth had come to know Rex well enough during the previous year to hesitate now that he was free to marry her, or so one might think. She knew his shortcomings as a surrogate father for her children. She knew his unwillingness or inability to change a life-style that revolved around himself, his creature comforts and desires. And yet she still felt his charm, his authority, his keen appetite for life, even if it were on his terms. Like Rachel and his other wives, she knew of his deep-seated longing for companionship, even more maybe than for sex. Not that he forswore the latter. But the aura of sexiness, though he pretended to detest the word, seemed to satisfy him more than the sometimes troublesome nature of the act itself. 'He needed constant reassurance of his sex appeal,' Elizabeth recalls. 'That was one reason why he didn't like falling out with his ex-wives. To have had no further contact with them would have been an admission that the power he once exercized over them had waned. Remaining on good terms – at least on friendly visiting terms – was proof to Rex that his sexual appeal hadn't run down.'

So where would he and Elizabeth get married? With his memories of the media invasion at Genoa, he was cold on the notion of a register office. On the other hand, a church was hardly appropriate for a fifth marriage. Alan J. Lerner came to the rescue with the offer of his Long Island estate. The ceremony was held there on 26 August 1971. Lerner recalled that the judge who was to unite the couple got lost on the way there. More champagne than even their nerves needed was consumed by Rex and Elizabeth while awaiting him. Added to which, the bride had taken a diuretic pill and was anxious for a quick union so that she could get to the loo.

Rex had leased in the name of Homer Enterprises Ltd, another of his burgeoning service companies, a six-floor house in Wilton Crescent, London, the same elegant section of Belgravia where his boyhood hero Freddy Lonsdale had a home in Wilton Place. This was possibly no coincidence, because over the next few years Rex's behaviour at home seemed to pattern itself more and more on the formalities of life in

Edwardian England, the decade into which he had been born. He found himself increasingly in sympathy with its values and conventions or at least those observed by the moneyed classes of his parents' time. It was an attitude that was to make things even more difficult for Elizabeth. The age gap showed up between them not in any markedly physical difference, for Rex was still his customary debonair, impeccably dressed and, to all appearances, charming man-about-town, a wonderful escort for any young woman, an enviable one for a young wife. But as Rex began to slip back affectionately into the past, in his unshakeable routines and inflexible opinions, Elizabeth perceived herself as someone belonging to another time entirely. What had been quaint or eccentric customs of Rex's soon became infuriating examples of obstinacy and intolerance. It is significant that the two roles he was soon to play on stage and screen both concerned people who made a well-deliberated decision to live in the past, to use it as a refuge from an unpleasant or hostile present.

For the moment, though, once his step-children had gone back to school, he was free to propose a trip round the world with his new bride: London – San Francisco – Honolulu – Hong Kong – Kuala Lumpur – Bangkok – London. The traveller was well pleased by this extended absence from England; the taxman, less so.

Rex proved as pernickety in his choice of furnishings for the Wilton Crescent house as he was in everything to do with a role in the cinema or theatre. Everything about it had to reinforce his idea of himself. He and Elizabeth continued to dress for dinner whether there were guests or not. A butler of such gravity and formality was engaged that the children used to refer to the place as the 'Patagonian Embassy'. Elizabeth, however, being by now a shrewd judge of Rex, concluded that his set ways were also the protection he felt he needed against the unruly ones of his extended family.

'One day in the summer – 1972, I think – the children and myself thought how lovely it would be to lunch outdoors at San Lorenzo' – a nearby fashionable Knightsbridge restaurant – 'since we could sit in the open court. Rex protested vigorously. His chef – all our servants were "his" – had been instructed to prepare lamb cutlets for lunch. He was looking forward to having them at his own dinner table. So the children and I went to the restaurant, while he stayed at home sulking.' At times, Elizabeth noted with amusement, 'Rex would behave with "his" servants as if they were waiters in a restaurant, reproving them for serving him the occasional bottle of wine that didn't please him, ordering them to "take it back" and quite forgetting, or being unwilling to admit, it came from the cellar he had laid down himself. When Rex was in residence, there was a distinct sense of theatre around the place.'

One issue was the new elevator that Rex had had installed in the house. It was supposed to hold three, but, when the young Harrises were back from school with their friends, any number could play – and did, with predictable results. As the fire-brigade summoned from Basil Street, fortunately just round the corner, winched the stalled elevator up to floor level, the children would see Rex's furious face come into view. 'Look at the little buggers,' he'd explode, 'they're *laughing*.'

Homer, too, behaved like someone running interference among the enemy for his master. So frequently did he get in Elizabeth's way that she started believing the dog was a misogynist.

Formality followed Rex wherever he went. During the long school holidays they would all drive into the countryside to have a picnic. But, while Elizabeth and her children spread a cloth on the grass and cracked hard-boiled eggs against their shoe-heels, Rex sat in his Rolls-Royce and drank his chilled wine and had his chauffeur serve him dishes specially prepared for his lunch. Fortunately, those having a *déjeuner sur l'herbe* could see the funny side of it. He had a saving grace of eccentricity about him now.

Nowhere was this more evident than when Elizabeth coaxed him into taking a motoring holiday in the West of Ireland. He dozed fitfully as they passed through 'the Yeats country' and then 'the Synge country', opening an eyelid occasionally to murmur 'another bloody cottage'. They stayed in a stupendous piece of Irish Gothic, Adare Manor, not far from Limerick, and Rex went fishing with the gilly and caught a salmon trout in the local River Magh. By law, he was required to surrender it to the owner of the fishing rights, but Rex treated the fish as if it were a fragment of the true Cross, took it to a little hotel and asked for it to be cooked. When the salmon steaks appeared, however, he tasted them dubiously, declared them to be frozen ones, and could not be convinced that his own fish had not been hijacked. As late as 1991, the story was still being repeated locally, with relish. Unlike most anglers' tales, though, the size of the fish had not grown.

They called on John Huston, the film director, in the imposing grey granite manor of St Cleran's, which he had turned into his Irish home. He had filled it with mementoes of the films he had made all over the world: Toulouse-Lautrec posters (*Moulin Rouge*), a fourteenth-century Christ on a wooden donkey (*A Walk with Love and Death*), Japanese candlesticks taller than a man (*The Barbarian and the Geisha*) and so many glittering ornaments from the pre-Columbian era (*Night of the Iguana*) that the place looked as if the Royal Hunt of the Sun had galloped through it rather than Huston's local foxhounds, the Galway Blazers.

Elizabeth had thought the two men would get on wonderfully well.

Just the opposite. Instead of hobnobbing genially about their careers and the villains they had met and worsted, they were a mismatch from the moment they sat down to supper. Huston had three women friends at the table and obviously enjoyed the haremlike atmosphere created by their worship of him. Rex liked that kind of attention too, but he was fearfully discreet about it, to the point of neurosis. Huston flaunted his power over women, Rex took his for granted and lived for the intrigue. Rex would keep three women on the go at once: the current wife, the ex-wife and the woman he had an eye on as an available prospect. 'Both of them were womanizers, but of entirely different and conflicting styles,' says Elizabeth, whose palms grew sweaty as she realized she had told their driver not to come back for three hours and there was no escape.

Then Huston proposed a visit to his treasures. Here, suddenly, they hit it off. Rex was fascinated by the pre-Columbian art that could summon up history for him with all its sense of theatre. The women were forgotten and the two men parted on better terms than Elizabeth could have predicted.

With more time on his hands than usual, Rex was able to prolong his visits to his villa, plant more shrubs, cultivate his vineyard, oversee the pressing of the olive crop. The children came too on their vacations. Rex's 'den' at San Genesio was a huge room with tall, wide, arched windows, terracotta tiles and ferns growing in the walls; Arthur Barbosa had designed it. In recent years it had acquired a baby grand, Leslie Bricusse's present to Rex, which had required a mule train to drag it up the hill. This was also the room that the Harris boys and their chums liked. They took dinner there while the grown-ups ate, with considerably more formality, in the other wing of the house. 'Rex used to complain, with some justice, that the kids had taken over "his" room,' says Elizabeth. But Portofino, with its hills and harbour, at least diffused the 'invaders' over a larger area. Rex's relationship with the children – unlike 'his' servants, they were never 'his' children – was less edgy there. 'We used to organize film-making competitions with an 8 mm camera,' says Elizabeth. 'The children would shoot and edit their own home movie, then the grown-ups would make theirs. Rex threw himself into the game for once, wrote the script, chose the camera angles, kept track of the continuity, cut the film. It gave him enormous pleasure.' He also liked taking the children out to sea in his boat *Henry*. There they were under captain's orders. No one dared mutiny.

The thing Elizabeth found most daunting in her marriage was the weight of 'history' that Rex brought into it stretching over forty years and four previous wives. She never really felt part of it. The barrier of the things he had done and sometimes suffered in his earlier marriages was maintained by him with a 'No Trespassing' sign: he resisted delving back into it, seldom answered questions about it, did not make her feel a partner in any of it. 'The last thing Rex ever did was hark back. He lived too vitally in the here and now. Others might be crying their eyes out. Rex's attitude was "Sod 'em! I reopen on Monday."'

His worries went deeper than he was prepared to go in recapitulating them even to a sympathetic wife. '"All the success in the world can't bring you self-confidence," was all he was usually prepared to say.'

Elizabeth did her best to repair emotional fences. When Carey got married, she invited Lilli and her husband, Carlos Thompson, to supper so that Rex would not be meeting his ex-wife in church for the first time at the wedding. 'They got on surprisingly well, making Carlos and me feel rather out of it – me certainly.'

However, he was now more unpredictable than ever. His moods changed, particularly when he drank too much. Then the Devil emerged. He still could not take to the idea of what he regarded as a Left-wing son and said to Carey's young wife that, being married to a 'radical', he guessed that made her one too. 'Well, I have news for you all,' he continued, looking round at the other guests. 'You're going to pay your own bill here, I thought you'd be amused to know.' Whereupon, everyone was sent packing down the hill to the hotels in the port. 'You hardly know how to react – to laugh or cry,' says Richard Kershaw, one of those expelled.' 'The next morning, I found an envelope on my breakfast plate – from Rex. It had been left in the hotel at 6.30 am, they said. Rex had brought it down himself. It contained a handsome apology. "I'm having a tough time," it read, "sorry."'

When he was in a mellow mood, the tranquility that settled on him was attractive, though it was always a delicate balance. 'I think I'd like to be buried here,' he mused, while out on the cruiser with Carey and other guests. Carey followed his father's gaze along the peaceful Italian coastline which retained the sense of history that had all vanished from the much more urbanized French Riviera. 'I'll see you are, Dad,' Carey said softly, touched by hearing a rare reference to mortality from his father. Instantly Rex was on guard. Did this boy want him out of the way before his time? 'And I'll do the same for you,' he retorted.

He continued making notes for his memoirs, but the effort it cost him to look back made him nervous and fidgety; the work stalled. Television had beckoned him, but he hesitated. One did not have the control that films gave one, unless it was a television *film* – which is precisely what came along in the new year, 1972.

A cinema version of *Don Quixote*, based on the *Man of La Mancha* musical, was soon to be filmed with Peter O'Toole and Sophia Loren.

But BBC Television, in partnership with Universal Pictures, were planning a straight adaptation of Cervantes's novel to be shot on location in Spain. The budget was £100,000; not a lot now, but in those days a sum of sufficient magnitude to need an international star as a bankable guarantee. Rex was playing a whimsical and chivalrous madman just his own age in a period production of a classic no longer widely read. All this lay outside his usual range. But he yearned to be working again and he was objective enough to recognize a bit of himself in an eccentric nonconformist like the Don, who regarded his own actions as perfectly normal and set out to get what he wanted by disregarding the conventions of his time. Moreover, Rex knew where giants were to be found and had worsted some of them with his own kind of lance – his tongue. Good heavens, it seemed the most natural casting in the world. Why had he not been offered it before now?

As he read everything he could lay his hands on about Cervantes and his hero, he even convinced himself it would introduce him to a new audience. Such a romantic old buffer was surely in tune with the teenage drop-outs of the then bubbling Woodstock generation.

Frank Finlay was cast as his ass-borne manservant Sancho Panza. Alvin Rakoff was signed to direct. All was fixed for a start that summer on the plains of La Mancha – and then Rex fell off a vine terrace at his villa, tumbled down five more levels and crashed on to his right side, cracking three ribs. The armour he had to wear for many scenes caused his injured bones agony. 'He had to mount his horse by step-ladder,' Elizabeth recalls, 'and, once there, stay put in the saddle for hours, as dismounting between takes was too painful. Then there were the horse-flies – La Mancha must have the biggest in Spain – and the sun and no shade except what a big umbrella held over him could provide. God, what a penance he did to get that performance.'

A performance, though, it was and one of Rex's most brilliant and least showy, impeccably maintained at the pitch of a waking dream. Gaunt and Gothic looking, not a spare pound on his seigneurial sticklike figure with a white wisp of beard and whiskers, and brows like curling wavelets, Rex uses a voice that is the key to the role – and to Cervantes. It is precise, but low, part whisper, part reverie, a confidential sharing of the thoughts buzzing round the Don's battered but still erudite brain. It is literary, but colloquial. He speaks his thoughts the way very, very few actors of any generation manage to do, as if not dreaming he is being overheard and, indeed, likely to shoo us away if his monologue were broken by catching sight of us. The film was to be criticized in some places – America mainly – as too slow, too under-dramatized. This misses the point completely. It takes its narrative line from Cervantes's own faithful map of the Don's wanderings – in every sense of the word – and its dramatic engagement from the comic shock that ensues when fantasy runs up against reality. His acts of lunacy are tempered by the mellifluous tribute Rex pays to the language of chivalry. It is a great performance, whose neglect by critics must be set down to the transient nature of the television medium in which he recorded it.

While in Spain, Rex discovered how little some things had changed since his last visit for *Cleopatra*. He tried checking into the Ritz Hotel again in Madrid, this time under the name of Smith. The anti-thespian management penetrated this disguise too. 'The penthouse is no longer available, Mr Smith,' he was told at the front desk. Well, even Don Quixote could not get the better of every windmill.

The manipulation of madness and sanity stimulated other desires which had lain dormant in him since he first conceived them while making *The Honey Pot*. As mentioned already, part of the original script of that film used the Pirandello-like device of having actors comment on their actions, and this had prompted Rex to read his way through the plays of that author, well known on the continent, but neglected in the Anglo-Saxon countries. The result was a determination some day to do Pirandello's play about madness, illusion and what we call reality, *The Emperor Henry IV*.

The role that it offered Rex was, like Don Quixote, spectacularly different from the ones his public had come to expect; therefore, in his present mood and at the age he had reached, it was attractive to him. He needed a challenge; most of all he needed change.

Pirandello's eponymous hero was a rich Italian in the 1920s who suffered a head injury some twenty years earlier during a pageant in which he has played Henry IV, the tyrannical emperor of eleventh-century Germany. Despite his recovery, he decides to feign madness and go on living with all the imperial trappings and courtiers comprising his friends who have adopted the dress and manners of their patron's feudal period, even though they are never quite sure if he recognizes them or if he is really mad. The play ends with a murder and the 'sane' emperor sentenced to live perpetually in the realm of the imagination.

One can easily see the attractions of such a play to a man like Rex, whose own life-style showed how much he preferred the well-ordered conventions of the past to the disorderly world around him. But it went deeper than that.

Madness was the fashionable topic of the early 1970s. The polemicist-psychiatrist R. D. Laing was an influential figure internationally for works like *The Divided Self* and *The Politics of Experience* that subverted the conventional idea of madness and, in Laing's revisionist view, saw it as a rational response to an insane world. Though this had its critics at the time, they were largely drowned out by the rejoicing of the global drop-out movement, which believed it now had a consoling excuse for anti-social conduct. Society was the thing that made you sick. It might well be asked where Rex rubbed shoulders with the theory that would have seemed to him – as indeed it has come to seem to better qualified people – like a ready-made suit to fit the illness of the time. It can be authoritatively stated that he was acquainted with it by Rachel's London psychiatrist: a man who did not himself hold it to be of more than passing interest, and was probably apalled at its media-driven popularity. But Rex, as has been said, was always very susceptible to the ideas current among the company he kept or, in this case, consulted about the woman who was now his ex-wife. The psychiatrist had told him she was unbalanced at times, but quite sane at others. (The line in *Don Quixote* about having 'streaks of lucidity' must have struck a sharp chord.) Rex's wry reply to this was, 'Which was she when she married me?'[2] In later years, he would carry the psychiatrist's letter around with him, describing Rachel's symptoms and giving a prognosis, and fish it out of his pocket whenever the conversation turned to what Rachel was getting up to in America. 'She's mad ... mad,' Rex would snap, waving the letter like an order of commital.[3]

Don Quixote had only reinforced his feelings. The lines that stayed with him years later were: 'The truth lies in a man's dreams ... perhaps in this unhappy world of ours, a wise madness is better than a foolish sanity.'[4] Laing, Cervantes and Pirandello apart, it was a most seductive aphorism for an actor. Rex had noticed that the players he admired most on stage – Ralph Richardson and Wilfrid Lawson were two that sprang to his mind – all had a bit of madness in them. 'I began to long for a touch of madness in my career,' he later wrote.[5] Pirandello's play supplied the means just when the ambition was ripest.

The play had the advantage of being last performed in London in 1927, so dreaded comparisons of *The Cocktail Party* variety were unlikely to be made with his performance. For contractual reasons, though, he had to open it in America first. He commissioned a new, more colloquial translation of it and Clifford Williams was engaged to direct it. Williams had made a masterly job of Anthony Shaffer's *Sleuth* a few years earlier, a play Rex had nosed around, then, fearing there was too much dialogue to remember in a two-hander, had turned it down – and found *The Lionel Touch* instead. Now he hoped Williams would handle *Henry IV* with the same success.

Accompanied by Edith Jackson, he flew to New York early in December 1972, leaving Elizabeth and her sons to follow for Christmas.

The plan was to open in Toronto, tour the States, then come in to Broadway in March 1973 – a gruelling year for a man of nearly sixty-five. To shed the slothful feeling of two years' absence from any stage, he put himself on a strict regime of diet and exercise on moving into the Waldorf Tower: rising at 6.30 am; doing a work-out, studying his part, making notes until breakfast at 8.30; spending from 9.30 am until 6.30 pm at rehearsals; relaxing with Elizabeth until dinner at 8.30 pm; then retiring at 10.30 pm.

Elizabeth happened to be with Rex when Rachel rang him. Rex refused to take it. Then he rang her back. 'Where's the filthy bitch who dumped you?' Elizabeth heard Rachel's strident Welsh voice saying, half-taunting Rex. She grabbed the phone from him and said, 'Hello.' Rachel demanded, 'Who's that?' Elizabeth said, 'The filthy bitch who dumped him.' The voice at the other end of the line broke into an almost audible grin: 'How are you, luv? We must get together.' Of course, the two women, in many ways so different, had one thing in common, as Rex was uncomfortably aware: himself.

It was with reluctance that he took Christmas Day off. Collette, his first wife, called to see him and wish him well. In contrast to her previous style of life, she had become what would now be called a born-again Christian, and was a successful activist in church charities. 'Dotty about the church,' as Rex said to Elizabeth.[6] 'Dottiness' was in his thoughts as he trained for *Henry IV*; he was now going daily to a gym to assist his chest expansion and doing breathing exercises for a performance that he intended to shape in more physical terms than hitherto. It offered opportunities for the kind of bravura acting that Olivier excelled at, but which Rex had seldom tackled.

Rex certainly made an unconventional figure when he appeared in *Henry IV* at the Broadway first night. 'In sackcloth tatters with a great iron cross looped around his neck, petulant beard thrust forward beneath a mouth with a dog's snap to it, [he prostrates] himself before a cowled inquisitor he takes to be a papal emissary, dancing in and out among the archways in arrogant glee, looking at his retinue as though he were Lear before the blow fell.'[7] Thus Walter Kerr in the *Times*. That Lear aspect of it, however, worried other critics. 'Magnificent, but slightly wrong,' said Clive Barnes. 'His madness is tumultuous, rather than introspective, and there is little cunning to it.'[8] Yet most critics agreed on the dramatic effectiveness of one moment. Walter Kerr again: 'After another twenty minutes or so, during which Henry has offered public prayers, perched on a table top, sprinkled his retinue with holy water, cocked his head ogling at the courtiers all too eager to appease him, he is suddenly left alone with his retainers. At once he asks for a cigarette, calls the local chaps by their real names, lets it be known – or assumed – that he is as sane as they. Mr Harrison ... is at his very best in this turnabout.'[9]

Timing was what counted here – the ability to palm the face card that the audience had just seen and replace it with another. When he came to do the play in London, Rex did not ask for a cigarette, but dipped into his own voluminous (yes, Lear-like) robe, fetched forth an anachronistic cigar and lit it in a perfectly co-ordinated movement of his other hand from a concealed matchbox. It was the comic business he relished: the conjurer who used his presence to hold the audience while he performed the trick that triggered the applause.

It was perhaps not as moving a performance as Rex would have wished it to be, but technically it was dazzling. Seldom did critics actually *describe* a performance at such length in their notices or with such emphasis on physicality.

'From emotional displays that are mere posturing,' wrote Walter Kerr, 'he is able to turn to a cackling, quizzical directness, to release the lightly sardonic inflections that go well with the wickedly amused glint in his eye. Playful, he is unusually entertaining; serious as he contemplates the real world to which he may return and asks, "Is it so different out there?", he is genuinely reflective. A mind begins to display its shape behind what has been a busy, a merely busy façade.'[10]

However short he fell on the grandeur and the pathos – and it seems he did not quite scale the bar – Rex had shown his nerve: he had thrown away his customary defences in this essay into naked theatricality. He has reintroduced the play to a new generation. Years later Richard Harris, Elizabeth's ex-husband, was to enjoy a London triumph, thanks to Rex's putting it back into the repertoire of star-actors. As for Rex, a touch of madness was just what he needed at the time to erase the memory of *The Lionel Touch*.

The play had a strictly limited run on Broadway; it ended on 28 April 1973 and Rex rejoined his wife in London. Hardly was he home than he suffered a dramatic interruption from his ex-wife. 'Rachel was a glutton for punishment,' says Darren Ramirez, who was in Paris when he received Rachel's 'hysterical' telephone call. 'She was in London and impulsively called on Rex and Elizabeth. She wanted to see what kind of life they were leading. She'd also had more drink than was good for her. Elizabeth put her and Rex in the library together – Elizabeth always had her head screwed on the right way – and locked both of them in.' Some time elapsed, then there was a furious battering at the door. Rex and Rachel had obviously finished talking. 'He always had a special place in his heart for the outrageous,' Elizabeth says, 'he never really ceased to love her.'

Elizabeth turned the key very quietly, unlocking the door, then shot up to bed as fast as she could. She held her breath. 'He sounded furious, I thought he'll kill me.' She heard someone approaching her bedroom, but it was not Rex, it was Rachel, flushed with drink and the exhilaration of being alone with Rex again, and not offering to tuck Elizabeth in. 'Good night, Liz, it's a funny old world, isn't it?'

Rachel's visit, though, was not so innocent as she made it sound. She knew enough about Rex to realize that however much he loved the wife to whom he was currently married, he hankered after some of the excitements of the one before that. One would think he might have wanted to forget all about it; that was not his way, though. The ex-wife invariably became the recipient of his thoughts about her successor, frequently couched in words that appeared to offer hope of a reconciliation – a loose term that someone like Rachel would have no difficulty in defining more permanently as 'remarriage'. Elizabeth, of course, could not know whether or not Rex had been up to 'his tricks', as she called them, but there were signs, since he was a notoriously careless man as far as concealing his 'little adventures', as he called them, was concerned.

He would grow uncomfortably silent, ignore her, and then, as if smitten by conscience, make it up to her by charm and some token of affection. One by-product of this erratic behaviour was a Cartier watch which he brought home with him in his attaché case – no gift wrapping, just like the handful of rings he had dropped into Rachel's palm on Christmas Eve in Beverly Hills. He then brought home another watch for Elizabeth, having apparently forgotten he had given her the first. This one was much smaller, however. She wondered if the first had been meant for someone else. Then there was the brooch she found which he had recently bought, but hadn't given to her. Over the couple of years they had been married, she had discovered he kept a 'present drawer', the way a bride-to-be keeps a bottom drawer in which to stow away the necessities for married life. Rex bought trinkets and other goodies for women he wanted to impress and kept them at home, so that they would be to hand. Elizabeth taxed him with the brooch. He looked embarrassed and mumbled about its being practically worthless ... some old cheap piece ... means nothing. ' "Right," I said to him, "then I'll get rid of it." So I threw it out of the window into the street.' Rex turned pale, but for once did not dare throw a fit or rush after it. She was sure he was having an affair.

To maintain the secrecy of such infidelities, and thus enhance the thrill of them for him, he occasionally took the sort of precautions that might only occur to characters such as he played on stage or screen.

Before they were married, Elizabeth had gone into the study of his rented apartment to use the telephone and discovered a matchstick, neatly cut in two, had been fixed beneath it, preventing it from settling back on to the cradle and thus stopping it ringing with an incoming call. Anyone calling Rex would have got what sounded like an engaged signal. If Rex wanted to make love in the study, he thus would not need to give the game away in advance by taking the receiver off to ensure their privacy. It also eliminated any need to avoid answering the telephone if it rang, as telephones have a tendency to do at crucial moments, and find himself talking to the husband of the woman he was entertaining or, worse still, to some other woman whom he had hopes of entertaining and to whom he would now have to pretend to be indifferent. The deceptions practised by Rex in love nearly always bordered on farce. A wife or mistress who discovered what he was up to might be surprised; very rarely was she unamused. Elizabeth could allow herself a few chuckles at the rake's stratagems.

30: Expulsion from Eden

Rex had become ever more devious. On his return from America, he received an offer to star in John Mortimer's television film *A Voyage Round My Father*, about the playwright's blind, testy, lawyer parent, which Alvin Rakoff was to direct. It was hoped Rakoff's experience of Rex on *Don Quixote* would make for an easy relationship.

But Rex, who had had to postpone the London production of *Henry IV* until a theatre became available, started rehearsals for the film in the autumn of 1973 without signing a contract. 'Very sly,' says Mortimer. 'Although perfectly friendly to me, save for some curious but rather endearing quirks – the girlfriend I had at the time, he told me, was far too pretty for a chap like me – he made sure he never appeared in an actual shot. If he did that, he knew it might be considered he was contractually bound to appear in the rest of the film, and he was fast losing confidence in the role.'

It was the same old fear of being unloved. People did not want to see plays about blind people, Rex said. Sightlessness was unappealing. Moreover, an actor's own eyes were his most expressive bit of equipment. To be deprived of sight and limited in expression really terrified him. 'The more he rehearsed,' says Mortimer, 'the more he wanted to be able to see. At first, it was only the occasional glimmer of light, then a demand that the character be able to distinguish shapes, then a desire to have eyesight that was only slightly impaired. Really, it got to the point where this crucial aspect of the film was being rendered as insignificant as a bit of grit in the eye that causes the sufferer a little watering.'

'During the time we were trying to make *A Voyage Round My Father*,' says Edward Fox, who was playing the son, 'Rex was sulking. Laurie Evans knew that the money just wasn't there. Rex knew it too. He wasn't going to give anything of himself for free. So he didn't appear for any scenes that required him to be on camera."

Rex was not happy with how Rakoff saw the project. By this time *Don Quixote* had been shown on television. Reviews were mixed, though

Rex got due praise, but he himself felt it had not quite come off. *A Voyage Round My Father* had certain introspective similarities in the protagonist's reveries to *Don Quixote* and Rex felt he needed to carry the audience's attention with him at a livelier tempo than he had done on the Don's gentle cross-country odyssey. Mortimer became aware of this through a curious outburst.

The American law had begun to catch up with the Watergate conspirators in the early autumn of 1973, through courtroom trials and congressional hearings. 'We were discussing the script of my film when Alvin made the remark that, "Perhaps we should investigate the mother's part a little more." Whereupon Rex blew up. "You American shits!" he exploded. Alvin was Canadian, not American, but Rex made no distinction. "You shits! You're never done *investigating*. You always want to investigate everything. That's why you're having this Watergate thing at the moment."'

Anyhow, differences of this kind soon ceased to matter. After a fortnight's location shooting and a few days at the studio, doing all the scenes that could be done without Rex in them, the production finance ran out. The project had to close down. It was not to be reactivated until 1981. Then Laurence Olivier, in the role Rex should have filled, received some of the best notices of his career.

Rex was going through a particularly bad patch, and there were several reasons. His memory was not as good as it had been, and it had always caused him anxiety. Now he was having trouble learning the part, not just remembering it. In addition he had a childish but nagging feeling that the country of his birth was neglecting him. His contemporaries were now appearing in the yearly honours lists – a CBE for this one, a knighthood for that one, men younger than he and of less distinction. It never occurred to him that the omission of his name might be due to his reluctance to live in the land he wanted to honour him and pay its taxes. Or that honours were linked with other and more charitable deeds than appearing in plays and films and earning applause and a fortune. This late menopausal feeling of being unappreciated made for a particularly bad-tempered Rex. He was only partly mollified when the University of Boston made him an honorary Doctor of Humane Letters. All right having a D.Litt. at the end of your name; how much nicer to have a Sir at the start of it.

This desolating feeling that Elizabeth noticed was increased by a threat from an unexpected quarter.

Portofino had changed immensely over the years since he first visited it with Lilli. Not physically: there was little room to expand and building was rigorously controlled, all part of its ostensible charm. But it had evolved politically and socially. When he first built his villa, foreigners were welcomed as an exotic, but profitable addition to the landscape, supporting the small shops and bistros, and employing local labour. Then throughout the 1960s the place became one of the smartest anchorages in the Mediterranean for the yachts of millionaires, film stars and royalty. Sophisticated boutiques and franchises opened to serve them – Fendi, Hermes, Ferragamo, etc. Restaurants like Pitisforo had reservation lists familiar to the *maîtres d'hôtels* at cosmopolitan eating places in the world's capitals. At the same time, Italy was turning ever more sharply Left and a Communist take-over seemed no longer remote, but imminent. Portofino's foreign residents grew anxious, and indeed they had good reason to fear that the neighbourhood might turn against them, even physically.

Anyone dropping down to the little town by the mountain path from Santa Margherita saw the penury or, at least, peasant frugality of the small-holders who farmed the slopes. There was – there still is today – an invisible frontier marking the territory inhabited by generations of blood-related families in dilapidated stone dwellings, scraping a living from a few goats, scrawny olive trees and root crops and, on the crest of the last hill above Portofino, the landscaped grounds, clipped hedges, water-sprinkled lawns and increasingly well-guarded entrance gates of villas like Rex's. Moreover, the townsfolk of Rex's age when he moved there had begun to die off and the locals were more politically conscious, less tolerant of people like Rex, whom they now viewed as decadent capitalists, alien intruders and social parasites. His own peremptory manner towards the locals did not help make him better loved in the community. He easily persuaded himself that he was the special target of the Left-wingers ruling Portofino now and he may well have been right.

This premonitory feeling set him off on a serious search as soon as he returned from Broadway for a second home on the Continent, outside Italy. Not that he had any intention of disposing of San Genesio; he simply sought a politically safer refuge. But it is also true he was starting to feel the strain, not just the frustration of getting up and down the hill and the five-minute hike to where the Jeep was kept in order to finish the journey up to his house. He and Elizabeth found the ideal home, at Beauchamp on Cap Ferrat. It was a mansion built at the turn of the century, Rex's favourite Edwardian period, by the King of the Belgians as a holiday retreat and shooting lodge. It had gardens, a swimming pool and a large amount of greenery that gave it seclusion. Best of all, he could drive his Rolls-Royce straight in through the gates and up to the front door without being forced to change vehicles *en route*. He purchased it in the name of Henry Higgins Enterprises of Vaduz, one of his multiplying service companies and got down to planning the furnishings with Elizabeth. Meanwhile, the Villa San Genesio continued to hold pride of place in his affections. It had been his first real home. It was where his heart was.

However, the servants there had begun giving him trouble. He suspected they had 'Bolshie' sympathies. Perhaps so, but one of them came from Sardinia, from people with tempers as short as his and likely, if roused, to be as brutally obstinate as the master. 'The women were all right,' says Elizabeth. 'It was the gardener who gave us the trouble.' But all of them had become very attached to the things that were Rex's. They lived in the house all year round and, as card-carrying members of the Italian Communist Party, believed in the Marxist maxim that 'property is theft', unless, of course, it belongs to you. 'We arrived in the Jeep,' says Elizabeth, 'and as we got out, Rex spied a large and beautifully ripe orange on one of his trees. He plucked it there and then and was starting to peel it when the irate gardener burst into furious Italian. Rex realized he was being bawled out for enjoying his own fruit. It was a bad omen ...'

Such omens multiplied during the visits they made at the end of 1973 and the following spring. Rex had decided it really was time for a new Jeep. He could not keep 'Scotch taping' the accelerator pedal on to it forever. While doing *Henry IV* on Broadway, he had cabled his man instructions to buy a new vehicle and the money to do so. Looking for the Jeep, Rex eventually located it locked up in a shed belonging to a friend of his gardener several hundred meters up the hillside. He discovered it had been registered in the gardener's name. This did not improve the master – servant relationship.

The master – wife relationship underwent new strains early in 1974 with Rex rehearsing for the London opening of the Pirandello play. Tension became so taut that Elizabeth decided she could not stand the atmosphere at home and took herself off to California. Rex was shutting her and her children out of his life, even answering (and turning down) social invitations sent to them both. 'I realized then why I was seeing so little of my friends.'

It was round about this time that Rex lost the services of Edith Jackson, who had gone through the wars with him, sometimes on opposite sides in the battlefield, for nearly twenty years. The combination of new wife and loyal retainer was at best an uneasy one, and gradually Edith's functions of regulating Rex's expenses and Elizabeth's house-keeping were absorbed, along with all files and records, into the Wilton Crescent house. No longer did Edith have him to hand in her London flat, running the practical, day-to-day parts of his life that he considered to be 'chores' which distracted him from the pleasures of his own irresponsibility. With Edith gone and Elizabeth absent, he became more and more set in his ways.

On returning from California, Elizabeth did not move back to Wilton Crescent, but stayed a short time in a hotel only a step or two across the road while she and her husband tried reconciling the differences of age and temperament that marriage had revealed. 'Rex's main concern was keeping it out of the papers. Odd how any threat of publicity held terror for him. Perhaps it was a throw-back to the "respectability" of his Victorian parents. Or maybe he felt that rumours of a break-up reflected badly on his powers to "hold" a woman. I think, on the whole, *amour-propre* was at the back of it.'

When she did move back into their home, at Rex's pleading that he needed all the support he could get for the play, she found a new butler in residence: a Spaniard, a one-man butler like the one-man dog, and who tended, Elizabeth felt, to come between her and Rex much as Homer did. 'The butler even rebuked me for eating a piece of fruit from a bowl on the table, telling me it was "Mr Harrison's."' Rex, in short, had entered a state of life where he was living like a pampered bachelor, an older, more selfish and much more astute version of the young sprig he had played in the society comedies he had done on tour in the 1920s, with a butler whose severe demeanour equipped him to be a supporting player in any of the mystery melodramas that a stock company might have put on in out-of-season resorts. The pattern and tempo of life was now definitely *his*.

Henry IV was a critical success when it opened in London on 20 February 1974, but its limited season was far from being the sell-out it had been in New York. Rex had played around with the text, restoring cuts made for Americans, who he felt had a short attention span. Maybe the London audiences had too. But the play had also to contend with a massive bout of industrial disruption caused by the Tory Government deciding to challenge the unions – and losing. The new Labour administration, with its punitive taxes on high earners such as he, would have hastened Rex's departure even if the play had not already closed. He reached Portofino at the end of May. Elizabeth joined him in June.

The situation there had deteriorated. Rex had an argument with the gardener that made him feel threatened. There was no alternative: the man had to be let go. Aaron Frosch was fetched over from New York to negotiate his terms: a more menial, yet more edgy deal than the high-powered attorney was in the habit of making. Hollywood had nothing on the local Communist Party, who were acting for Rex's recalcitrant employee. The remaining servants then put in their claims. They wanted one month's salary for each year they had been there, one day's pay for each Sunday they had worked, payments for every fiesta day and every Christmas, and a bonus for every Easter.

Intimidation was used to close the bargaining on their terms. 'One day', says Elizabeth, 'several burly members of the Party arrived on our doorstep to "inspect the servants' quarters", or so they said. They walked through the villa, eyeing the furnishings, kicking doors open, pulling drawers in and out, behaving in a quite frightening way. Rex, thank God, was in his den correcting the galley proofs of the memoirs that at long last he'd got down on paper, and didn't encounter them under his roof. Otherwise, an unholy row would have erupted, perhaps with violence and – who knows? – worse. But he saw these bully-boys "strolling" through the garden and vineyard, and had the wit to stay indoors. I'm convinced that if he'd resisted them, he wouldn't have been long in this world.

'But as far as he was concerned, it was the last straw. His estate had been "invaded". I think this was the moment he made up his mind that his days in San Genesio were over. "There's no question of staying," he said to me afterwards.'

The last months in the villa were unpleasant, nervous ones. Once their demands for back pay had been met, the rest of the servants packed up and left. Gradually, most of the services to the house dropped off or were abruptly terminated. No one came to remove the garbage, drain the cess pit, cleanse the swimming-pool. Telephone calls in and out took ages and were frequently interrupted. The local post office was uncooperative. 'When I'd ring down and ask if there was any mail for us, they couldn't tell us, or wouldn't,' Elizabeth recalls. 'We had to present ourselves in person, which meant a long traipse up and down the hill.' Quite seriously, Rex began to visualize the Red Flag flying from the staff where he had been in the habit of hoisting the red cross of St George.

Disposing of the villa in such a situation was a delicate undertaking. It was to take a long time before a successful deal was negotiated with an Italian industrialist. 'I felt desperately sorry for poor Rex,' Elizabeth says, 'seeing his Eden sold to others.'

The last days at San Genesio were deeply depressing. 'We stayed in the house or near it. So unlike the joys we'd known, walking up to the tiny *albergo* for Pinot Grigio and pasta, taking a carrot or apple to the old black donkey, walking Homer through the pine woods, following the steep goat's path down to San Fruttuoso, lunching at the old abbey, returning on the ferry to Portofino ... all that was slipping away from Rex. And yet he never complained. He was shutting the door on the past and it only remained to turn the key in it.'

Elizabeth had recruited a cousin of hers to help her run the villa until they could move some of the furnishings to Beauchamp and shut the place up. Rex was no great help to the women, and they preferred him not to get involved. He put himself in charge of ice-making, but frequently forgot to shut the refrigerator door and was confronted by a pool of water, and rotting food, when he went to replenish the cubes in the bucket.

When Elizabeth's children came down for the summer holidays, instead of staying at the villa, they all moved into a hotel at Paraggio, about a kilometre along the narrow coast road from Portofino, on a sharp bend where the traffic braked with a screech and the headlamps raked across the bedroom windows making sleep an intermittent business for Rex. Eventually he chartered a yacht, which lay out in the bay, where they would at least be safe from the sinister harassment up at the villa or free of the daily annoyances on the coast.

A final irony occurred, one that Pirandello might have enjoyed, for it lent a mask of illusion to the reality of the final hours at San Genesio.

They were due to move out in September, the same month as Rex's long-delayed memoirs were scheduled for publication in England by Macmillan. He had finished the book in a bleak mood a short time before, wondering if he and Elizabeth would still be together when it appeared. 'He looked in on me one afternoon and asked me what my intentions were,' Elizabeth recalls. ' "What do you mean?" I asked. – "Well, will we be staying together or not? I've got to know. I've the last chapter to finish." He considered playing safe and dedicating the book to Homer.' In the event, though, he could not face reality here, either, and it carried fulsome tributes and a dedication to Elizabeth.

Macmillan had paid him a lot and hoped to recoup their advance by serializing the book in the London *Sunday Express*. Rex demanded to know how the paper would present it and, when he saw the emphasis was, unsurprisingly, on his marriages and divorces, he exploded: 'Christ, I'm not having this! Permission refused.' A worried publisher then persuaded him to let a BBC Television team film a lengthy interview with him in Portofino which would be shown around the publication date. Richard Kershaw, the television and radio commentator, happened to be with Rex when the deal was struck and was immediately canvassed for his opinion on the wisdom of it. ' "What's this chap who's coming to interview me like?" Rex said. "Is he any good?" – "Well," I said, "he's usually very good at getting at money and women." – "Christ, Richard," said Rex, "I wish I were doing the bloody thing with you."' The upshot was that the other team got no nearer San Genesio than the Hotel Splendido. Kershaw and his crew arrived as they departed for home.

The interview was to be shot in two parts, the first in Portofino, the second a few days later in the grounds of the mansion at Beauchamp. By bizarre coincidence of dates, the filming at San Genesio took place on the very day Rex was due to move out. As the crew unloaded their equipment, his personal possessions were being tossed, out of camera range, on to a couple of barrows that two strapping sons of a farmer's widow who lived in the vicinity had volunteered to get down the rough hillside to where the car was parked. Rex's beautifully tailored suits, his books, papers and any other bits and pieces he had not packed were flung into bedsheets, secured with loose knots and wheeled off even as the television crew set up its reflectors and microphones and camera. Nothing of this retreat was filmed. Rex kept his back turned to what must have been a heartbreaking scene of dispossession and kept offering 'wine from my own vineyard' to his visitors and commending the view of the bay to them. It was all quite unreal. It was as if he were totally unaware of what was going on behind him, as if he were still the lord of his domain and preferred to concentrate on the magnificent view, virtually unaltered since he and Lilli had first seen it from this spot twenty-five years before. The vindictiveness of fate could never spoil it for him.

After Kerhsaw had shot Rex walking up to the entrance gate, strolling around the lawn, looking out to sea, behaving as if he were still in residence, they all adjourned to the port for lunch.

There he made an uncharacteristic gesture. He stood the crew their meal, even though he probably thought of them as dangerous Left-wingers. 'Half-way through lunch,' Kershaw recalls, 'two American tourists recognized him, cried out, "Rex!" and made straight for his table. Well, he was with the crew and not surprisingly a bit depressed, so he decided to continue his act and smiled painfully and signed the menu they commandeered and thrust at him. Then I'm blessed if they didn't come back, this time with a tape recorder and home-movie camera and said, "Rex, can you say something?" This was too much, given the state he was in. "Yes," said Rex, putting on his most charming smile, "*Fuck off!*"' Those were probably the last words he uttered in public in Portofino. He left with his head high, tight-lipped, in character, and only the slow, lingering wave he gave his cherished Riva cruiser *Henry* as it set off round the coast to its new berth in the harbour at St Jean-Cap Ferrat betrayed his sadness.

Kershaw accompanied him and Elizabeth in the Rolls-Royce to the new home, and helped him unpack. 'He hadn't had enough suit cases, so he'd pressed a few million lire into Elizabeth's hand and she went and bought a few extra Vuitton valises – she knew his style – from a Portofino boutique. I shall always remember the dozens of shirts spilling out of them as we unpacked at Beauchamp, all of them white, all of them from Turnbull & Asser, his Jermyn Street shirt-makers, many still in the shop wrappings. He'd have gone to the firing squad well tailored.'

Filming the second part of the programme was tougher going. This part of the interview, which was to take place on the lawns of Beauchamp, was to be about his past, present and future. Rex was nervous and irritable for he had much to hide, and he bullied Elizabeth, who was not taking that from him. She gave back as good as she got. It was the intention to continue the interview around a lunch table with Rex and his friends. Elizabeth said sharply: 'We haven't got any friends.' Kershaw diplomatically suggested Rex call Gregory Peck and his French wife, who lived in the vicinity. With the candour that had endeared him to so many of his peers, Rex snapped, 'Good heavens, I can't ask Greg Peck over to take part in some little PR film like this.'

It was Elizabeth who saved the day and salvaged the interview by prevailing on Dirk Bogarde and his manager-companion Tony Forwood to come over from their farmhouse near Grasse. She laid on a large lunch of lobster and the two played up beautifully to Rex's intermittent revelations. The only trouble was, the BBC had not brought any spirit gum to fix his toupée on securely. 'You're a sixty-six-year-old actor,' she said, 'we don't need to see you in a hairpiece to know you're a star.'[2]

But he hated doing it and it was a four-bottle interview: the bald truth in only one sense. 'He knew he wasn't in control of things, and that unsettled him,' says Kershaw. 'Later on, he tried to alter the film when it was going to be shown in the United States – and then to stop it. He moved heaven and earth to try and get Elizabeth cut out of it, for by that time they'd broken up. He claimed the camera angles made him look as if he had a double chin. Somehow, this seemed as important to dear old Rex as suppressing the information that he'd once been married to Lilli Palmer.'

31: Ghosts

The break-up of Rex's marriage to Elizabeth continued; the move to France made little difference. He became even less tolerant of his new family. All of the Harris children loved music, but all of them had different tastes and the house, Elizabeth recalls, would resound with a cacophony of notes from classical to rock. 'Bugger off!' became his customary greeting, no longer pronounced very jocularly. When the doctor was called in now, it was to give Rex vitamin injections for the energy that the holiday household had depleted.

But there was another reason for his tension. The truth was that he had his third wife more often in his thoughts than his present one. The play that Terence Rattigan had postponed writing in the immediate aftermath of Kay Kendall's death had now been written. But it was no longer based on the simple and touching notion that Rex had deliberately behaved badly on occasions to keep Kay from suspecting that her illness was serious enough to warrant an uncharacteristic show of compassion. In the Rattigan version, husband and wife *both* know the illness is fatal, but each conceals the knowledge from the other. As has already been mentioned, this was what some of the closest friends of Rex and Kay had long suspected, though Rex had never admitted it. Now it had been turned into a play that was already being performed on the London stage, the second half of a double bill called *In Praise of Love*. It starred Donald Sinden and Joan Greenwood when it opened in late September 1973. Rex and Elizabeth went to see it, though forewarned by a naturally apprehensive Rattigan that he might not find it to his liking. But Elizabeth said later that if he was upset, he certainly did not show it. And when there was a prospect of the play's being presented on Broadway, Rex made it very clear that he wished to be in it. He did not want it to be the second half of the bill, however, whose first half was a spoof of the opera *Tosca*. The London critics found it fitted rather jarringly with *After Lydia*, which was the title Rattigan had given to the serious side of the evening. So the playwright flew down to Portofino during Rex's last weeks of occupation and

together they lengthened *After Lydia* into a full-length play, which took
for itself the cover-all title *In Praise of Love*. John Dexter was signed to
direct it.

It is quite possible to interpret *In Praise of Love* in ways that do not rely
on its existence as a *pièce à clef*. Rattigan's biographers, Michael Darlow
and Gillian Hodson, make out a plausible case for Rattigan's self-
identification with some of the principal characters. In their opinion, it
represents not aspects of love, but of Terence Rattigan. It has been
suggested, too, that it is a commentary on the extreme reticence of the
English when it comes to expressing their feelings. To this writer, however,
Rattigan himself confirmed that he had been inspired by what he knew
of the 'silent bargain' made by Rex and Kay.[1] And Rex never denied
that he saw himself up there on the stage.

Sebastian Crutwell, the husband in the play, does not at first glance
resemble Rex. He is not a talented actor at the top of his profession,
but an unsuccessful writer, a disillusioned Marxist who has not lived up
to his early promise and now earns a modest living as a literary critic.
In other words, he can be viewed as the failed idealist, an aspect of
Rattigan which he certainly conceded had been killed off by his commercial success in the West End. (Another character in the play is the
'best friend', a best-selling, Hollywood-bound novelist who represents the
Rattigan of acclaim and affluence.) Yet, even before Rex stepped into
the part, Sebastian possessed more of his traits than can be considered
coincidental. For one thing, he has Rex's restlessness; for another, his
limited sympathy for anyone but himself. As Lydia, his wife, says, 'He's
so bad at being bored ... Of course, if I'd told him [I had an incurable
illness] he'd have been quite upset – perhaps even very upset – for a
week or more.'[2] He has also been unfaithful to his wife and, like Rex,
is incompetent at attempting to cover it up. 'He is not a master of
subterfuge,' says his spouse, with weary resignation. Rex's arrogance is
unmistakably present, his extreme annoyance if anyone dares to impute
an unmasculine – ie tender and vulnerable – side to him. When marrying
Lydia, we are told, he is said to have 'roared at some British chaplain
that he'd be buggered if he had to say "Obey".' He thought it was his
line in the marriage service.[3]

'But I imagine he made no objection when he found out it was yours,'
says the best friend.

'Asked for a repetition,' says Lydia, drily; she plainly has no illusions
left about her husband. He fits in exactly with Rex's often stated view
of a wife's naturally inferior position in the marriage set-up. On the
other hand, Rex's tenacity, his refusal to change his mind once it was
made up, however painful the consequences to himself, is part of

Sebastian's better self: 'He sticks to things once he's decided,' says Lydia, approvingly.[4]

Lydia does not resemble Kay Kendall in anything apart from her fatal illness, but she seems closely modelled on Rex's second wife, Lilli Palmer, down to the Lydia-Lilli echo. Like Lilli Palmer, she is foreign born, in this case an Estonian, and although a Roman Catholic in the play, she has a Jewish grandfather, which ties her into Lilli's faith. Moreover, Rex married Lilli with the same consequence, if not quite the same intention, as Sebastian married Lydia: to give her a nationality and to allow her to put her precarious past as a refugee firmly behind her.

There is also a son in the play, Joey, a promising playwright whose Left-wing idealism still angers his father the way that Carey, an established television writer by this time, used to be a source of annoyance to Rex for his radical views.

Rex had never before played a character whose dramatic context bore such a close and detailed resemblance to an episode in his own life. Perhaps he saw the play as a kind of catharsis – or as means of exorcism. The ghosts of the past had been almost palpable to Elizabeth when she lived in the ominous self-containment of Portofino; and her husband's unwillingess or refusal to speak of his other wives appeared to her to be due, in part, to the distance he had deliberately put between himself and them. *In Praise of Love* offered him a way of closing the gap without having to face up to reality. Writing his memoirs had been unwelcome enough; it had taken him the better part of seven years. Now Rattigan presented him with a chapter of his life which proposed a version of the truth between him and Kay, yet still allowed him to maintain his version of the arrangement that she should go to her grave ignorant of her doom.

Even so, humility and gratitude were not much in evidence when he began rehearsals in New York. The possessiveness he had shown in recent plays and films, believing his presence in them entitled him to rework them in order to suit his own gifts or put an ingratiating interpretation on the events in them, began to operate on Rattigan's play, this time with the added temptation of the affinity he felt with Sebastian.

Elizabeth has recalled how Rex kept insisting throughout the rehearsals, which began in October 1974, that the wife's role in the play should be cut back. She protested. He challenged her. 'I said, "Well, it's her tragedy." – "What the hell do you mean?" he said. I said, "Well, she's dying." – "Absolute rubbish. Absolute rubbish."'

The American stage and screen actress Julie Harris had been cast as

Lydia. Like some of Rex's other female co-stars, her initial enthusiasm for working with him was soon diminished by his habit of building up his role at the expense of hers. Rattigan also suffered. Illness and a campaign promise to help the Liberal Party in the autumn General Election, the second that year after a hung Parliament in February, had detained him in England and he did not arrive in New York until a day or two before the play was due to open. What he saw angered him immensely. In addition to cutting his text, Rex was playing the husband's role for what Rattigan considered to be an unwarranted amount of sympathy. He was even hinting to the audience, almost from the start, that he knew about his wife's illness. Again he had been unable to face up to playing a character who might alienate the audience before they were let in on the fact that he was deliberately behaving boorishly to his dying wife. He and Rattigan had a stand-up row. Rex refused to yield. The dispute was continued by letter. But Rattigan knew Rex had the upper hand; he would revert to character – his own, not the playwright's – once Rattigan had gone back home.

Harold French was in New York at the time and witnessed how Rex's tactics extended to the smallest details of his role. Not only did he insist on his own English tailors being used for his wardrobe, but there was a more bizarre display of stubbornness. 'He was determined to bring a bicycle on stage,' French recalls. 'His complaint was that he hadn't got a good exit line. He intended going off stage with the bike and then the audience would hear a loud crash. Rex would reappear, looking aggrieved, perhaps clutching his shin bone, and say something like, "What bloody fool left that bucket there?" It was completely narcissistic, terribly crude. I was asked to have a talk with him.'

' "Tell me the truth," Rex said to me, for openers, "what's the girl like?" He meant Julie Harris. "The girl's marvellous," I said, "but you're fucking awful." He looked very abashed. He knew I was one of the few completely candid friends he had who was not afraid to tell him the truth. "You're playing a hot-tempered writer," I continued, "living three flights up in a London apartment block. Can you imagine anyone carrying a bike up three flights of stairs?" "All right," he said sulkily, "but why doesn't Terry give me a strong exit line?"

' "Rex," I said, "that's a problem for Terry to solve, not you." '

Maybe he was remembering how A. E. Matthews, one of his boyhood heroes whom he had acted with in the Robert Morley play, *Short Story*, had arrived at the theatre on his bicycle and insisted on trundling the machine on stage at rehearsal and propping it surrealistically against the back wall.

Robert Flemyng caught the play in New York and felt the production came a bit too close for Rex's comfort to Kay's death. 'He rather funked the big moment in the last act, when he is supposed to break down and cry. The whole point of the character was to get all those marvellous laughs from the audience – which Rex enjoyed doing – and *then* to shock them by unconcealed grief. Rex simply couldn't manage that.' He had not done it that way when Kay died. There was a block.

Even by opening night Rex knew the play was not right – he would not admit he was not right for it. However, he came off in the first interval in a much better mood. 'It's all right,' he said to an anxious Rattigan, 'Julie didn't get a round of applause when she came on.'⁵ He did.

A few critics, like Clive Barnes, in the *New York Times*, thought it miscast: 'The [wife] is like the Rock of Gibraltar. Why hide from her the knowledge of her impending death?'⁶ And T. E. Kalem in *Time* criticized Rattigan: 'Though famed for his theatrical carpentering, [he] has on this occasion whittled out a theatrical toothpick.'⁷ But on Rex praise descended like love indeed. 'A flicker of an eyelid, an infinitesimal clearing of the throat, and – presto! – a pinch of wit becomes an epigram. The skimpier the play, the more resourceful Mr Harrison.'⁸ Thus Brendan Gill in the *New Yorker*. Technique still carried him through. In a specific sense, he may have shied away at the last minute from facing the past, but, in spite of Rattigan's anxiety and Rex's narcissism, his performance supported the general truth that tragedy can help people bear what they have hitherto found impossible to admit – the depth of feeling they have for each other.

Elizabeth came to New York, but stayed only a few days. He had thanked her lavishly in his memoirs for being 'brave' enough to share his life. It looked increasingly likely now that they would soon be leading separate lives.

Circumstances that, once again, would have made an amusing scene in the sort of comedy Rex excelled at had exposed one of his most secretive eccentricities to her.

'There'd been a small burglary in our house at Cap Ferrat and I came down from London to check what was missing. I was rearranging Rex's things when I came across some old letters of his that had been dumped in the luggage and carried over from Portofino. He hadn't bothered to sort them out before leaving for America to do the play. "Hang on," I said to myself. I thought I had these letters back in London; they were ones that Rex had written me from America, smoothing over some of our differences, or trying to. Then I looked a bit more closely and saw that instead of my name, "My Darling Elizabeth", there was "My Darling Rachel".' They were copies of letters that Rex had sent to his previous wife – and maybe they were copies of letters he'd sent to even earlier wives – all containing the same phrases, thoughts and apologies as the ones in the letters he had sent Elizabeth. His former wives, Elizabeth thought, must have reproached him for the same things as she had done – or else, she reflected, 'Rex knew us so well that he had the excuses written out before the complaints reached him.' It was one of those discoveries about a spouse, small in itself, that helps tilt the balance decisively.

Rachel was in New York while Rex was enjoying success in his play. Despite the turbulent life she had led since their divorce – and at that moment she was having one of her temporary 'splits' from Darren Ramirez and drinking more than ever – Rachel had been working harder than Rex. She had done a play, *Alpha Beta*, with Albert Finney; two plays, *The Visit* and *Chemin de Fer*, on Broadway; a couple of television plays in Wales; the film *Murder on the Orient Express*; and she only drew back from going into a Pirandello play, *The Rules of the Game*, which owed its appearance to Rex's success in making the Italian playwright fashionable again, by being offered a new John Osborne play in London for the end of 1974. She was soon off to Australia to do the film *Picnic at Hanging Rock*.

Not surprisingly, then, she was on a high when she spotted Rex and Elizabeth at the VIP table in '21' shortly before Elizabeth left for London. Rachel was with her new escort, Val Mayer, an actor, and 'we joined them – I bright and smiling with a handsome young man in tow. I didn't want Rex – that's what I was [inwardly] saying.'[9] Rex got the point.

When she returned from her short period of filming in Australia, she called on him at the Regency Hotel in Park Avenue, where he was staying during the run of *In Praise of Love*. Rachel was still elated by travel, stardom and vodka. Rex was fretful and at a loss to know what he was going to do next. They made love, then Rex left for a matinée. Rachel attempted to get out of the hotel, unobserved, by a back door and set off the alarm system, fumbled her excuses and fled down the street. Both of them waited for the tabloids, nervous in case an informant had put two and two together and their indiscretion would be in Liz Smith's column. A silly incident, maybe, but knowing that Rex's marriage was on the brink of break-down added a pinch of hope to the expectation that Rachel had never entirely abandoned – that one day she would make him hers again.

Elizabeth had moved out of the Wilton Crescent house and taken an apartment in nearby Belgrave Place. There was an abortive attempt at a reconciliation in July, when Rex's play ended its run and he returned to France. He still funked the final break; Elizabeth acted. She instructed her lawyer to sue for divorce. It was the first time that Rex had had one of his wives walk out on him – Collette and he had drifted apart, each with their own lover. The blow to his vanity was heavy. He could bear material loss – like the burglary Elizabeth had suffered a month or two before when she discovered some of her jewellery was missing from the London house. 'How much?' Rex asked – 'About £7,000.' – 'Good heavens, I'd no idea I'd given you so much.'[10] But not being able to retain the love of his wife or even to be able to choose the time to rid himself of her – in Rex's view this was unbearable humiliation. While he squirmed and tried to get her to think again, Elizabeth remained dignified but resolute. Rex realized this might be an expensive separation. Elizabeth knew the extent of his wealth better than any of his previous wives.

He was still feeling aggrieved and apprehensive when another blow fell in the shape of Lilli's memoirs. In the German edition she had omitted all references to their 'arrangement' over Kay Kendall. But stung by his book, which practically censored her out of the story, she now revealed in the English translation of her memoirs that she had turned Rex down when he had come to claim his share of the bargain following Kay's death. Rex smarted. It seemed to him that his wives, current and ex, had nothing better to do than tell the public how they had rejected him. It was too humiliating. Lilli's was the cruellest thing anyone had ever done to him. The dispute turned ugly with threats of court proceedings against him by Lilli if Rex persisted in his assertion that she was denigrating him and Kay Kendall 'just to sell her book'.[11]

The issue is one that still divides Lilli's friends from his, though Rex's sister, as mentioned, recalls reading his letters to Lilli and inclines to her interpretation of events.

Down in the dumps and needing company, he moved in with Leslie Bricusse and his wife on their estate near St Paul de Vence in the South of France and then, with Elizabeth's divorce petition due to be heard in December 1975, he gratefully accepted an invitation that would get him out of the country then. It was to be a juror at the Tehran International Film Festival. The Shah's capital seemed as good a refuge as any.

Accompanied by Margaret Gardner, his publicist, he flew to Tehran at the beginning of the month, but no sooner had he been installed in the royal suite at the Intercontinental Hotel than he regretted his hasty acceptance of the invitation. The weather was icy. His jury duties prevented him making the splendid trips he had promised himself to Persepolis, Isfahan and other historic cities. And there were too many journalists around for comfort, all of them no doubt on Lilli's or Elizabeth's side. He needed to communicate almost daily about the divorce with his lawyers in London and was dependent on the good will of the Iranian Minister of Culture for an uninterrupted telephone connection – at their expense, of course. Even the flattering attentions of the Shah and his Empress did not put him in a better mood, especially as the former dropped a heavy hint that, both of them being handsome men, Rex might like to appear as the Shah in an epic about the Pahlavi dynasty that the Iranian state film industry planned to make. 'I played the bloody King of Siam,' Rex confided, 'I'll be damned before I play the bloody Shah of Persia.'[12]

In such a mood, like a desert-island castaway, any company was welcome at his supper table – even this writer.

Rex proceeded to take revenge on his hosts by abusing his *carte blanche* VIP privileges and ordering up the most expensive bottles of wine he could find on the menu of the hotel's new restaurant, a replica of Maxim's of Paris. After tasting it, he would declare it unsatisfactory, send it away and order another expensive vintage. After this had gone on for several nights running, with Rex tasting and turning down dusty bottles costing a fortune, a young Iranian *commis* who had watched him with fascination remarked that 'Milord Harrison' (*sic*) was very like his master. 'Why the hell should I be like the hotel manager?' Rex asked.[13] – 'Oh no, sir, my master the Shah-an-shah,' said the lad with an appropriately reverential gesture. 'He also believes he is going to be poisoned and has a man to taste his food and drink.'

Rex's divorce negotiations went well until the night he attended a huge ball at which Tehran's most celebrated belly-dancers were performing. One wobbled her way across the dance floor towards him, jerked her belly at him in what was no doubt intended as a gesture of respect and possibly arousal, and invited him to dance with her. 'Certainly not,' Rex snapped. 'Go away, you fat cow.'[14] She turned out to be the mistress of the Minister of Culture. From then on Rex's telephonic communications with London became less and less reliable.

He returned to London, humping a Persian carpet for his pains. A week later, on 16 December 1975, in a hearing that lasted barely fifteen minutes, a judge decided that his marriage to Elizabeth had 'irrevocably broken down because of Mr Harrison's conduct'.[15]

Mr Harrison's conduct soon became exemplary, however. He had his Christmas dinner in the Belgrave Place flat of the ex-Mrs Harrison. 'Elizabeth knew he was staying in town for Christmas,' says Richard Kershaw, another of the guests, 'and had moved out of Wilton Crescent into the Berkeley Hotel, which had just opened nearby. "Poor thing," she said, "all on his own. Richard, go round and bring him to lunch."' Rex was physically and emotionally exhausted by all he had recently been through. True to his belief that you should always part from a woman on good terms, he accepted. Patric Walker, the astrologer, was another of the guests and after the meal he offered to read everyone's fortune in the Tarot cards. 'He looked at Elizabeth's cards,' says Kershaw, 'and said, "You're going to be immensely happy and very rich." Then he looked at Rex's and, with a deadpan face, said, "Oh dear, you've got a load of trouble ahead, Rex. It's going to cost *you* a lot of money." Rex managed a smile, a bit uneasily, though.'

The forecast that his divorce would be costly perhaps helped Rex make up his mind to do the commercials he was being offered on American television. The wooing of him had, in fact, begun a year or two earlier. Bryan Forbes, the writer and film director, who had been asked to make one of them, recalls a couple of American executives flying to London to present Rex with a story-board of the shots they visualized. It was the time when media people affected the dress of hippy drop-outs. 'These two arrived at Wilton Crescent looking like prospectors from a gold-mining encampment, in worn jeans, fringed buckskin jackets, neckkerchiefs and Civil War era caps. Rex received them in his Henry Higgins get-up, tweeds and cardigan. They showed him the boards. He didn't waste time, 'Oh dear ... dear, no. You people – you have no taste' – casting a Higginsish eye over the bums in front of him – 'and you look as if you never had any, anyway.' The men found themselves back at London airport an hour or so later, bristling with anger."[6] Said one of them, through gritted teeth, 'I – will – not – be – dictated – to – by – the – talent.' 'But you just have,' said Bryan Forbes, who may have regretted the loss of his fee, but was to relish the tale of Rex's high-handedness.

But, now, humility went with economy. In the new year, 1976, Rex went to Los Angeles and filmed a series of commercials for Dodge automobiles, vaunting the cars' virtues in the *parlando* speech-song tones of *My Fair Lady*. His fee was $1 million. He also sponsored print advertisements for a brand of whisky. Clearly, where fortune was concerned, he was leaving nothing to chance. He had had to sell the Villa San Genesio in circumstances which brought him in only £120,000. As Italy's restrictions on the export of currency were stringent, he reckoned on having to make a visit to Bulgari in Rome or some other jeweller who dealt in handy packets of realizable wealth. He was rich, but he was seventy. Who knew what his needs might be in the coming years or even months?

One immediate need was the old one: the companionship of a woman. In spite of all the pain they had inflicted on each other, he turned to Rachel Roberts. She had returned to Los Angeles after a successful

Broadway run opposite Richard Gere in the Alan Bennett comedy *Habeas Corpus*. Tony Randall had spotted her in it and signed her up for a long-running role in his television situation comedy series, *The Tony Randall Show*, playing the English housekeeper of an eccentric American judge. Segments were being filmed weekly at Studio City in the San Fernando Valley area of Los Angeles. Rachel was well up in the money, so well that Rex asked her if she could lend him $30,000 to tide him over until various accounts of his, on which it may have been imprudent for him to draw while his financial worth was being calculated for the divorce settlement, were again available to him.

Where self-esteem was concerned, however, Rachel was still on a downer. Her drink problem had not diminished, despite going to Alcoholics Anonymous in New York. (Pamela Mason always held she should have gone to AA in Los Angeles: there were more people like herself there, and that was where deals were often done.) But she was strictly teetotal on the set of the television show, which Rex watched being recorded one day, marvelling at the interaction with the audience and the discipline needed to pack it all into what was, by his standards, a frighteningly short recording time. The only signs of Rachel's unstable personality were drawings of all kinds of cats she had made on her dressing-room walls. Tony Randall saw them and recorded in his diary, 'Rachel Roberts is *crazy*.'[17]

Maybe so, but with Rex in town and her lover Darren Ramirez not yet reunited with her, Rachel was everything her ex-husband then desired: motherly, sexy, fun ... 'Rex stayed the night [at the modest apartment she was renting off Sunset Strip]. We went to have a Bloody Mary at the Cock and Bull ... I got drunk with him and walked in floods of tears back to my apartment. I called him [at his hotel] the next morning to apologize and asked him to stay over one night more. He agreed.'[18] But Rex had also seen the cat graffiti on his visit to the set of her television show: his instinct warned him off any longer-term reunion with a woman as lonely as himself and far less stable-minded.

Soon after Rex left for Europe, Rachel and Darren Ramirez got together again and jointly purchased a house on a secluded canyon road called Hutton Drive. Rachel soon fell out of love with *The Tony Randall Show*. She resented its numbing formula content, felt her own role was being under-written and, paradoxically, feared that she might be written out of the show altogether. Rather wildly, as if she might never be offered work again, she flew between Los Angeles and New York and London over the next few months, picking up jobs, actually doing a vast amount of work on stage and television, but increasingly obsessed with Rex ... Rex ... Rex.

Her ex-husband, meanwhile, was still at a loose end. He had put the Wilton Crescent house up for sale on a falling property market: the estimate of £110,000 was far below the £250,000 he had paid for it. But it held too many bad memories now.

He was living in the Beauchamp mansion and was, of necessity, a bit more social than usual. He was seen dining several times with Princess Mary Obelensky, one of the Russian royals who lived in Monaco, a place so full of old people that Rex said it was one of the few spots these days where he actually felt young. The Princess organized the annual backgammon championships in Monte Carlo; she was in her late twenties. Another occasional companion whose literal down-to-earthness Rex came to respect was Pippa Irwin, who had a business as a landscape gardener responsible for some of the great estates on the Cote d'azur. She lived in the Alpes Maritimes, not far from him. She had been in the cast when Rex had starred in the play *Design for Living* in 1938.

No one, however, was to hold Rex's interest so confidently and firmly over the months ahead as a dark-haired woman more than twenty-five years younger than he with fly-away Dietrich-like eyebrows and a firm but placid face whose confident jawline hinted at an iron determination. Her name was Mercia Tinker.

Part Seven

Mercia

32: Lady from Singapore

Mercia Tinker surprised even Rex's closest friends. Very little was known, for sure, about her background apart from the fact that she was born in Singapore of mixed parentage, the daughter of a well-off rubber planter. She was in her late thirties, widely travelled, fluent in several European languages as well as Malay, and had been divorced from a wealthy Swiss industrialist named Schwab, whose interests had been zoology and bird-watching. The dissolution of her marriage had left her an independently wealthy woman. She had a home in New York, but her cosmopolitan outlook coupled to her wealth, sophistication and good looks had given her a taste for life among the expatriates on the Côte d'azur. She was well read, a connoisseur of the arts and obviously had a taste for cultivating the acquaintance of people of talent and position who found her an agreeable if somewhat strong-willed companion.

Where exactly Rex and she met is also a matter of anecdote. One account places it at a dinner party given by Mrs Billy More, the former wife of the late English film star Kenneth More, who had been living near Antibes since she and her husband had separated. When the guests went in to eat, the seating arrangements brought Rex and Mercia together and in a very short time he was being amused by her lively talk and strongly held opinions, and putting on his own brand of apparently effortless charm.

'Mercia had a reputation as a bit of a "culture vulture",' says a friend of both.[1] 'Rex probably was not particularly interested in the things she set store by – opera, ballet, private views at art galleries, and so on. But she is a good conversationalist and can switch from topic to topic until she finds one in tune with the person she's talking to. Since Rex played these elegant, witty and worldly characters, she may also have imagined that he was really like that too. If so, it was the image not the reality, as people who knew him better could have told her. But he obviously had a great appeal for her.' It was reciprocated. A few weeks later, without naming names, Rex remarked to Margaret Gardner, 'I've found someone who'll keep me in order.'[2]

He needed order in his business affairs. They had got badly out of control since he had lost the services of his assistant Edith Jackson and since the tragically premature death from cancer of his agent Robin Fox. Rex was feeling not only sorry for himself, but a bit ashamed as well, a somewhat rarer state for him. Immediately he had heard of Fox's incurable illness, he had left him – 'the very same day,' says Angela Fox. 'When my husband died, Rex wrote to me. He was deeply contrite. "I think I am the one person who behaved very badly to Robin," he said. "I lost my courage. I deserted a great friend. Forgive me." Words like that, most unusual for him.' Soon after Fox's death, Laurie Evans received a call out of the blue. ' "Can we make things up, Laurie?" Well, I'd shown him there were limits to how he could treat people, especially good friends like Mary and me. But I don't harbour animosity. I readily agreed.'

Although Rex had large sums coming in yearly from his recording royalties and tax-free investments, the events of the last few years – the divorce from Elizabeth, the forced sale of his homes in London and Portofino – and his generally lazy attitude to accounting for money once the satisfaction of the high fee had been achieved had all left his finances in a muddle. He did not really know how much he was worth. Mercia Tinker came along most opportunely, speaking the language of banking in several countries, and having a good understanding of figures.

As far as film work went, Rex had now entered the cameo era. If 'stardom' is defined as a name above the title that carries the film, then a 'cameo' connotes an assemblage of names below the title, none of them judged persuasive enough to sell the film alone, but all of them collectively lending it an aura of importance. It was a come down, but then he was nearly seventy, and the money was not bad. At the time, Alexander Salkind and his son Ilya were the principal purveyors of such well-bunched, cameo-laden spectacles, which was how, for £25,000 and a few days' work in England, Rex came to play the Duke of Norfolk in a version of Mark Twain's Tudor period adventure, *The Prince and the Pauper*, co-starring Charlton Heston, Oliver Reed, Ernest Borgnine, Raquel Welch and George C. Scott. The film was registered in Panama, for much the same reasons that many ships are. It was directed by Richard Fleischer, who had weathered such productions of Rex's heyday as *Doctor Dolittle*. Memories of the Harrison–Heston rivalry in *The Agony and the Ecstasy* were still apparent on the page of recent history. 'He was perfectly civil to me,' says Heston, 'but we didn't say much to each other except in front of the camera.' Heston was playing Henry VIII, a role on which Rex may have imagined he held prior rights. According to young Mark Lester, the boy star of *Oliver!*, who was now cast in the dual roles of prince and pauper, Rex said he was only doing the film in order to restock his wine cellar. His five-minute screen appearance was not vintage. He conveyed a concern for Tudor politics on the level of a racegoer anxiously checking the picnic hamper at Ascot to see that nothing important, like the corkscrew, has been left at home. But, considering the distinguished company he was in, he emerged unscathed from the film; and it must have been satisfying to see the Château Latour being laid down in the cellar at Beauchamp. That *was* vintage.

However, something more invigorating was needed to top up the actor in him. He wanted to do a play. He found one by going back to his roots in an out-of-London repertory playhouse. He accepted an invitation to join the company in the season's closing production at the Chichester Theatre Festival. This annual event in the lovely old Sussex town already had a distinguished reputation. 'What can I find that would be a change?' Olivier had asked himself, when he had been invited to become the first director of the spare and graceful hexagon building with its open-plan stage.[3] In much the same mood, needing a tonic, Rex said yes to what, for him, seemed an eccentric vehicle: a French farce by Labiche and Martin entitled *Monsieur Perrichon's Travels*. It was to be directed by Patrick Garland, a youthful talent who had moved successfully between television and theatre, musicals and the classics. Surprise was the initial reaction to the choice of play for Rex; it was almost unknown in England. Rex, however, brought it closer to home when he described the Frenchman of the title as 'immensely conceited, vain and absent-minded'.[4] Type-casting, some said: what more natural?

M. Perrichon, as Irving Wardle reported in his *Times* review, 'is a Sancho Panza who imagines himself Don Quixote, living for private comfort, but believing he lives for national honour', as he takes his wife and family on a grand tour of Switzerland and makes an assault *pour la gloire* on Mont Blanc.[5] It needed, perhaps, an actor better prepared than Rex was to make a fool of himself physically; Peter Sellers, with Inspector Clouseau in mind, might have been the ideal droll. Rex went through the lavish production – German brass bands, yodelling waiters, baggage-toting porters, innumerable sets and even the Alps in back projection – with admirable *élan*. The critics, generally, found him magnetic, but not quite attracting the compass needle of comedy. 'To be funny,' wrote Wardle, '[Perrichon] must appear a man of passion, striking postures of self-intoxicated conviction before collapsing in chagrin and humiliation. As Rex Harrison presents him, a foxy smile playing around the lips and much the most knowing person on the stage, the laughs are pretty sparse.'[6] Garland had given Rex an eye-catching showcase, but the posture he struck was not quite right. It *was* popular though.

Mercia Tinker went to it several times. By now her relationship to Rex was that of a confidante. Like the earlier women in his life, she listened sympathetically to his confession of the loneliness lurking behind the glamorous existence and periodically emerging to drag him down into deep despondency. The constant pessimist, Rex gained relief by unloading his cares on to some woman – very, very seldom a man – prepared to bear them with understanding. The impression that he and Mercia Tinker were attracted to each other in a more than confessional sense was formed by at least one visitor to his dressing-room at Chichester. Gayle Hunnicutt, the American actress whose marriage to David Hemmings had just been dissolved, came round after the show prepared to throw her arms out in the Big Hello of theatreland. It was not to be. 'Mercia was there already and the minute I entered Rex's dressing-room I sensed he was scared that such an extravagant greeting might be misinterpreted by her as evidence of a more intimate relationship between Rex and me, which would have been totally untrue. As it happened, I was wearing a rather elaborate St Laurent gown with an additionally exotic shawl and scarf. Before I could utter any "compromising" words, even a technical "darling", Rex cut in vigorously and said, "My God, I've never seen anyone carrying so many props." '[7] Introductions were then safely effected.

For the run of the play, Rex had rented a large house at Bognor Regis, the Edwardian spa town much frequented by Edward VII, though not much loved by him, to judge from his possibly apocryphal last words, which would have been equally comfortable on Rex's lips – 'Bugger Bognor'. Rex was now trying, unsuccessfully, to get John Mortimer to write a play in which he could star as the monarch. Mercia Tinker could not be with him always and, in her absence, he cautiously entertained Gayle Hunnicutt, enjoying her wit and Texan directness. Over dinner one night, he proposed they both accept the invitation of friends of his to sail across to the Isle of Wight the next day. Mucking about in boats was still Rex's favourite relaxation. Memories of Portofino were apparent in the picture he painted to Gayle Hunnicutt of blue skies, a beautiful English Channel coastline, champagne and a delicately chosen picnic lunch to refresh everyone for the voyage back in the sunset to Chichester harbour. Gayle said yes quickly enough.

Rex's day out turned into an unrehearsed episode from *Monsieur Perrichon's Travels*. There was very little wind when they embarked, but the owner of the yacht chose not to use his motor, perhaps thinking it amateurish in waters frequented by the elite of the sailing fraternity whose social life revolved around the Royal Yacht Squadron club at Cowes on the Isle of Wight. 'The voyage dragged by very slowly,' recalls

Gayle Hunnicutt, 'with grey and watery English skies standing in for azure Mediterranean ones. Rex's face got tighter and tighter. At last we made the Isle of Wight and were greeted with a prospect of utter squalor, litter-strewn shoreline and a scummy jetty, so we decided to lunch on board. The "lunch" was solid English picnic fare, potato salad mainly, and something Rex later called "fucking Spam", tinned ham chopped up and soused in bottled mayonnaise. It did *not* please him one bit.' They made for home, as slowly as they had come. Rex's face grew ever bleaker. Growing nervous, his hosts made the mistake of plying him with drink in the vain hope that it would raise his spirits. He started muttering and gradually his comments grew louder and rougher – 'fucking yacht' ... 'fucking lunch' ... 'fucking people'. The hosts gamely pretended not to hear the gathering storm.

'I was even more anxious than Rex to get back,' Gayle Hunnicutt says, 'for I had a rehearsal the next day in London and there was only one train back to town that evening. As soon as Rex knew this, he turned a disaster into a major crisis. It was as if our very lives depended on not losing a minute. Our hosts must have envied the comparative tolerance enjoyed by galley slaves in Roman times. He also got more and more inebriated. When we landed, he could hardly stand, poor thing, and I had to lead him into the car park. But then I couldn't remember where he'd parked the car and he couldn't remember what it was like.' It grew dark. Suddenly, something in Rex gave way. It was as if the accumulation of annoyances over the last months had deprived him of his customary resilience. He lay down on his back on the ground, raised his arms in supplication to some inattentive deity and, howling like a dog at the moon, he cried, 'Oh God! Oh God! Oh God! Oh God! Will nobody help me?' He then collapsed in total despair – a M. Perrichon with nowhere left for his dignity to retreat to.

His entreaties were answered. A member of the theatre company came by, ran Gayle to the train and Rex back home, leaving him to return the next day and identify his car.

He had sprained one of his vertebrae by having to be hoisted to roof level in a make-believe scene on Mont Blanc. Mercia was an enthusiast for alternative medicine, homeopathic and dietary regimes, and Rex took her advice and gained relief. That brought them closer still.

He was well enough to travel to Vienna in the fall of 1976, after the Chichester production of *Monsieur Perrichon's Travels* closed in September, to make what he described as 'another villa and vineyard' film for the Salkinds: a very free version of Dumas which was released (here and there) three years later under the title *The Fifth Musketeer*. Rex played Colbert, the cunning courtier and Finance Minister. Beau Bridges, Sylvia

Kristel (from *Emmanuelle*), Ursula Andress and Olivia de Havilland were his co-stars, not all of them lucky enough to have as brief a role as he.

What made the experience bearable for him was the company of his ex-wife Elizabeth Harris. As usual, once released from the bonds of matrimony, Rex reverted to a more relaxed and congenial relationship with his ex-wives. For their part, fondness for the old devil had grown as the battle cries of married life receded. It was curious how Rex unfailingly engendered curiosity among his former spouses: they wondered how he was keeping, what he was up to, and relished finding that old habits had not died; and they continued to enjoy the companionship of a man whose public image was still a flattering passport with which to travel.

Elizabeth's own memoirs were just out, under the title *Love, Honour and Dismay*. She was a little apprehensive, knowing the battering he had taken from Lilli's book. 'He told me he wasn't going to read it,' she recalls, 'and, I suppose, didn't, for he behaved as if it didn't exist. Like a bad theatre notice, I suppose. If you didn't read it, it hadn't happened and your performance wasn't affected by it.'

December 1976 found Rex in New York rehearsing Bernard Shaw's *Caesar and Cleopatra*. By now, as he confessed, he felt he had spent 'a good half of my life doing Shaw'.[8] But the dramatist was like an old, reliable friend. Rex enjoyed the feeling of erudition and shrewdness that Shaw's Caesar allowed him to assume. On his way back to his hotel from rehearsals, he had his cab stop in Fifth Avenue and went into Scribner's and asked for all the books they had on Cleopatra. He kept the cab with its meter running while they searched their shelves.

Rachel was also in town, living across Central Park in the flat she had acquired from John Gielgud. Rex's flat-warming present to her had been a crystal ice-bucket with a tiger motif – the nearest thing to her favourite cats he could find. It now cooled the wine that numbed her rational functions after the first glass. In the circumstances, it was a thoughtless gift. They spent Christmas Day together, cooking a turkey, going for walks, chopping up calves' liver for Rachel's cat Rosie. It was like old times, for twenty-four hours.

But when she called him from Los Angeles in the New Year, she heard him say to the hotel switchboard, 'Tell her we're not at home,' and she knew Mercia Tinker had arrived.[9] The operator misunderstood Rex and put her through before he hung up. Cheekily, she reminded him about an invitation he had extended to her to visit him at Beauchamp. The reply she got was icy. 'As I recall it, he said something about there being room in the attic. I told him my days of staying in other people's attics were over. It was understandable, Rex's attitude, I suppose. By then, he'd met the woman who was to become his sixth wife.'[10]

Rehearsals did not go sweetly. He suffered attacks of indigestion which he thought was his ulcer growing back again and he became so obstructive that the English director withdrew and an American, Ellis Raab, took over before the play came into New York on 24 February 1977. The critics panned it. Though lavishly produced (or overproduced), the costumes and scenery alone costing $300,000, it had edited down Shaw's play to fit the attention span – and possibly the understanding, too – of playgoers raised on an undemanding diet of 'prestige' television plays. For the first time, Rex's performance showed signs of age. This was a very weary Caesar, who had forgotten what it was like to be young, and 'though ... suavely entertaining and commanding, [he] has let too many years slip past to give the part full resonance,' as Douglas Watt said in the *Daily News*.[11] Elizabeth Ashley, his Cleopatra, was also judged 'nearer her salad days than her childhood'.[12] The play closed after only twelve performances at a loss of more than $650,000. 'I'm old enough,' said Rex, 'and, after all that's happened to me, wise enough not to care.'[13]

He and Mercia spent the summer in France, leafing through Shaw again – not the plays Rex might do, but Shaw's writings on the ones he had reviewed. It was Rex's idea to conflate his favourite passages from the three volumes of *Our Theatres in the Nineties* into a one-man performance for that year's Edinburgh Festival and to ask Patrick Garland to direct him.

It went well and his spirits rose again during the five matinée performances in which he 'gave voice to the dry, comic assaults [of Shaw], seeming to relish his devastating precision, resonantly wrapping his voice around the words that dissect Henry Irving, Mrs Patrick Campbell or Beerbohm Tree.'[14] He was now much older than most of these heroes of his had been when they tramped the boards, but they seemed nearer to him than they had ever done. Although he did not know it, Rex had begun the journey back to his beginnings. From this time to the end of his life, with the exception of one contemporary play and a revival of *My Fair Lady*, Rex was never again to do a play by a modern author. Shaw, Lonsdale, Barrie, Maugham ... the giants of his youth became the comforters of his old age.

One can pass quickly over the next film he made, a potboiler called *Shalimar*, which he probably undertook so as to have his passage paid to India, where it was filmed in two versions, Hindi and English, and has fortunately remained almost unknown in either. He played an aristocratic English jewel thief who challenges his peers to rob him of an immense ruby. It was shot in Bangalore and, thanks to Mercia's acquaintances among the princely inhabitants of the region, he enjoyed the compensating comforts of palaces and summer residences. As always, he was a good traveller, curious about everything which was foreign to him, peppering his letters to friends with amusing observations of a kind that his conversation didn't often reflect. London in October, then Los Angeles in December, and a few weeks in another Shaw play, *The Devil's Disciple*, a smallish but showy part as General Burgoyne. It allowed him the self-indulgence of teasing the audience's expectations by not appearing until late in the play, until its third and last act, and then taking a gratifying solo curtain as the *de facto* star of the show before shooting off to supper.

Travelling now filled in the days between plays and films. It was often the main reason for accepting the roles. He did a cameo for his old friend Richard Fleischer as a passionate opponent of modern slavery in a Swiss-financed movie, *Ashanti*, which took him to Tel Aviv. When not filming, he joined Mercia in reading their way through the English love poets and romantic writers, and he later published an anthology of his choices. 'Mercia loves learning,' he said, almost apologizing for his own contribution to 'scholarship'.[15] He was not so flattering about Mercia's views on plays and play-acting, and on at least one occasion, when she had left the rehearsal after giving her views to him and the cast, he observed, as if passing on a confidence, 'She doesn't understand – she's one of the audience.'[16]

In the summer of 1978 he signalled the mellow mood he was in by making a recording entitled *Rex Harrison: His Favourite Songs*, a romantic medley from Lerner and Loewe, Burt Bacharach, Irving Berlin and Rodgers and Hart.

He and Mercia enrolled in an art school when they returned to New York in the autumn. Rex discovered, to his secret delight, that he had a better eye than she when it came to painting; his stage concentration carried over naturally into his visual composition. Patrick Garland had introduced them to the vividly coloured scenery of Corsica, where he had a house. Garland, as already mentioned, thought Rex's amateur paintings 'at least as good in technique as Winston Churchill's'.

It was with relief, however, that he found himself on stage again with lines to deliver that had the familiar rhythm he loved, colloquial but pithy, written by one of his chums, William Douglas Home. Home's new play, *The Kingfisher*, had been done in London with Ralph Richardson and Celia Johnson as a venerable couple who had been lovers in their far-off youth and were now resuming their courtship after fifty years, and wondering if the habits acquired in old age would prove an insurmountable barrier. Celia Johnson had declared she did not want to go to Broadway with the play and Richardson was adamant he would not go without her. So it had to be recast. Rex was a natural choice. But when Claudette Colbert was proposed as his co-star, he looked wary. Though seventy-three at the time, Colbert was still one of the toughest-minded and slyest comediennes around. She was likely to play Rex for every point in the game.

'We opened in Philadelphia,' says Lindsay Anderson, who was directing the play. 'Both of them were a bit scared. They had a lot of lines to remember. Rex's nerve went first. Half way through the first act, during rehearsal, he turned towards Claudette and said sharply, "You're not going to talk like that when we do the play, are you? Because if you do, I can't possibly say my lines." He turned to me and snapped, "She's going to ruin it." Claudette didn't rise to this provocation. She just sat there, in her black dress, impassive except for a foot tapping lightly while Rex went on wheezing out complaints. When he eventually ran down, he realized he'd met his match. There was no way of budging her.'

Rex and Claudette Colbert were not made better friends by doing the play together, but they remained the best of enemies. They watched each other keenly and jealously. When Rex was off stage during a performance, relieving himself in the loo, he heard an enormous explosion of applause. Claudette was playing a scene with George Rose, whom both of them had to watch for he, too, playing the butler, was a practised scene-stealer. There was nothing in the play at that point to justify such applause. What on earth had happened? He discovered that Claudette had tripped up when making her entrance and fallen on her face, but she received two rounds of applause: once when she fell, because the audience thought it was part of the play, and again when she made a quick recovery and got up, and they realized it was not. Even applause for an accident stimulated Rex's envy, but he took comfort from the news that she had grazed her chin. 'You couldn't fall flatter than that,' he confided to a friend.[7]

If there was not much generosity on or off stage, there was surprisingly little trouble after the initial clash. According to Lindsay Anderson, 'Rex probably realized that, as the play was virtually a two-hander, for him and Claudette, one of the hands would suffer if the other were noticeably weaker. So he had diminished opportunities for mischief-making.' He continued to keep Claudette under strict surveillance – at one proud moment claiming the bouquet that an admirer had thrown on stage when the playgoer, seeing Claudette move towards it, had yelled out, 'It's not for you, it's for him.' But he knew her worth too. She was briefly indisposed during the run and an understudy stepped in. 'Get Claudette back at once,' Rex snapped. 'I've got to carry this play without help from anyone, and it's killing me."[18] Lindsay Anderson was despatched to Claudette's bedside to see how she was coming along. 'Harrison has never been to see me,' she said, though almost with satisfaction. Elliott Martin, who was presenting the play, ordered, 'Send flowers immediately – from Rex. The production will pay.' Rex graciously consented to attach his card to a huge bouquet of roses. 'Hope you'll get back soon,' he wrote. It sounded more like an ominous order than a message of sympathy.

The play opened in New York on 6 December 1978 and the critcs were generous to it – or, rather, to *them*. 'Harrison [and] Colbert ... lend the static scene a picture-book grace, render fitfully amusing lines as if they had been minted by La Rochefoucauld, and are never so tactless as to reveal that, dramatically speaking, their oxygen supply has been cut off,' T. E. Kalem said in *Time*.[19] Rex's advancing years, impossible to conceal, at least fitted his character perfectly, though he cannot have been delighted to see himself compared (by Richard Eder in the *New York Times*) to 'a petulant and cossetted tortoise'[20] and (by Clive Barnes in the *Daily News*) to 'an ageing leprechaun looking at life with wry annoyance'.[21] He and Claudette had the good fortune to be riding a current trend in venerable stars parading in front of their fans of yesteryear. Henry Fonda, at seventy-three, and Katharine Hepburn, seventy-one, were the leads in the film *On Golden Pond*; Emlyn Williams, also seventy-three, was doing a one-man show based on Saki's writings; and the nonagenarian George Abbott had just made his Broadway directing debut. However near burn-out they were, the light from such stars still reached audiences who were grateful for it.

Though Rex was touchy about his age off stage, he was brilliantly relaxed about it when in character. He could still fill out the part with superb bits of business. Striking a romantic posture, he suddenly allowed an arthritic grimace to register the effort it was costing him. And when Claudette referred to another beau who was courting her, someone even more elderly than Rex's character, her co-star threw himself into a warning imitation of an old chap getting around on two crutches with humped back and spastic limbs. In moments like these, Rex put his own years unflinchingly at the service of his talent.

Mercia had now established herself as an indispensable part of his life. The next step was logical and easily taken. On 17 December 1978 they were married at The Little Church Around the Corner, a rendezvous Rex was getting to know quite well by now.

'I saw that Rex had remarried for the sixth time – to Mercia,'[22] Rachel jotted down in her journals. The 'to Mercia' might have been taken to denote an end to her fantasy of bringing him back to her, but that was not how she saw things. She still felt that only a man with Rex's power could put things right for her, though when and how she had no real idea. She was in London in the summer of 1979 for the première of the film *Yanks*, in which she had a supporting role. Rex was also in town for the publication of his anthology of love poems. Impulsively, screaming inwardly for his support, Rachel called him at his hotel. 'Half of me felt secure and protected talking to him, half of me felt the other side of him,' she recalled.[23] It was the old love-hate relationship. Over the phone, she read him a short story she had written. Entitled *Five Roses*, it was an elegiac evocation of the paradise they had once shared at Portofino and how, when she was expelled from Rex's world, 'every feeling grew cold and curdled'. Rex listened patiently. Then, perhaps not realizing the cruelty implicit in what he was doing, he read her a love poem from his new anthology as well as the book's dedication – 'For Mercia ... my beloved wife from whom I have learnt the art of loving and living at last.' The last two words cut Rachel to the quick. A month later, she was under treatment for alcoholism in a private clinic, sinking 'deeper into despair' and thinking it was '*because Rex had finally remarried happily*'.[24]

Remarried he might be, but Rachel's romance with him was far from over.

33: Another Hollywood Death

When *The Kingfisher* closed in May 1979, Rex and Mercia had their postponed honeymoon, a cruise round the Greek isles, then went back to Beauchamp. Not for long, though. He seized the chance to replenish his wine cellar by making what he called 'a stop-over' appearance in a film being shot in Amsterdam entitled *Mario Puzo's Nine Graves to Rogan.*[1] He appeared in the opening scenes as a high-ranking officer in the German army and in the closing ones as the Allies' nominee for the office of West German chancellor. For topping and tailing this mediocre action-drama, he pocketed £75,000, had five weeks in the attractive Dutch city, all expenses paid – and did not realize it would be his last appearance in a feature film. Retitled *A Time to Die*, the movie dug its own grave. It was an inglorious way to go, but, unsentimental as usual, Rex dismissed it from his mind. He had a bigger project to consider.

Yul Brynner was enjoying a current Broadway success in a revival of the musical *The King and I*, which had made him a star. The show's producers, Mike Merrick and Don Gregory, now approached Rex and proposed that he also recycle his past success in *My Fair Lady*, promising him a most prosperous future if he did so. Their offer had nothing nostalgic about it. He would have full artistic control 'down to the last nail of the scenery', casting approval, a percentage of the gross box-office and of the net profit, and $10,000 [£5,000 approximately] a week.[2] *Variety* called it the most lucrative contract in theatrical history. For signing up for a two-year tour ending on Broadway, Rex would receive something like $2 million a year. 'Astronomical,' he called it.[3] He was asked if he was not a bit long in the tooth now, at seventy-one, to be playing Henry Higgins. 'Shaw would be happy if I were an octogenarian,' he snapped back.[4]

The new production was budgeted at $1.2 million. Rex quickly approved Patrick Garland as director. Rehearsals would have to wait until Rex had taken *The Kingfisher* on tour round America in the first half of 1980; meanwhile, he began knocking his ideas into shape. He wanted to bring Shaw more centrally into the show, he said, putting the emphasis on social reality. So the colours of the production were to be toned down, made more sombre: Edwardian London was a grimy place. He wanted a gaslight feel. Rooms had to look lived in – a bit of dust would not come amiss. He was, in fact, recreating the circumstances, as far as a stage musical allowed, of his own Edwardian childhood. Much of what he called 'the corny business' would also have to go, by which he meant the Cockney pearly kings and queens who had strutted their stuff on stage and screen in the Covent Garden scenes. He wanted a less exuberant, more realistic Doolittle, one who would not play up to the audience as shamelessly as he considered Stanley Holloway had done. He may have been paying off an old score here – he always resented Holloway's rumbustious 'Get me to the church on time' choreography overshadowing Higgins's less showy numbers – but Rex's suggestions were shrewd and they solved the problem of direct comparisons being made with the film and stage versions.

There was self-interest in them too, which was shown in the lengths he went to in selecting an Eliza. He heard a number of American performers attempt to do the double duty of speaking with an East End accent and also the Queen's English. None pleased him. He eventually picked an English actress, Cheryl Kennedy. She could manage the accents all right, but could she sing well enough? She could belt out 'Wouldn't it be luverly . . .', but with other numbers like the trick 'I could have danced all night' some people felt she had to strain for the higher notes. Rex was loyal to her, however. At last he had got *his* Fair Lady, whose acting abilities pleased him and whose singing had the vocal qualities he considered satisfactory beside his own. He even fought the opposition of American Equity to an English Eliza – and won by threatening to withdraw if he did not get his own way, which would have meant the show being cancelled and a large number of Americans losing their jobs in it.

After *The Kingfisher* tour, he tried to build up his strength for a venture that would have stretched a man twenty-five years younger. Could he stand up to the long *My Fair Lady* tour and then Broadway? Mercia took charge of him. She put him on a diet that limited him to Perrier water and one alcoholic drink a day. She located a spa near Beauchamp where mud baths and hot springs relaxed and refreshed him. Mercia herself was a keen nutritionist. She jogged and did a daily work-out. As sometimes happens with a zealous apostle of health, she now and then complained of having 'a back'. Rex was not displeased that even the virtuous experienced a few painful side-effects. But he began rehearsals of *My Fair Lady* in New York that July in a tonic glow of good health.

His two producers were eager to please him in every possible way: a dangerous ambition where Rex was concerned. They flew him by helicopter to the upstate workshops where the scenery for *My Fair Lady* was being manufactured. He inspected it, criticized its brightness, ordered it to be toned down and flew back – an expensive trip. They took him to lunch to discuss the costumes, which he wanted to be more 'everyday' than Cecil Beaton's pattern-plate creations, and handed him the wine list – an expensive meal.

Rachel had seen him in early January, when he was in New York between *The Kingfisher* engagements and the auditions for *My Fair Lady*. She had come with news that she was sure would surprise and impress him. Incredible as it may seem, given her mental unbalance at the time, she had just been offered and had accepted a semester's lectureship at Yale Drama School. It had been the anticipation of seeing Rex which had got her through the interview with the Yale academics, men who would no doubt have been far more cautious if they had encountered her on one of her bad days. She had then called Rex, who at first refused her call, then relented. For the meeting Rachel dressed herself as smartly as she knew, wore her Paris clothes, even had her hair done in a way that would remind him of the Anna Petrovna who had played beside him at the Royal Court twenty years earlier. She arrived at the Drake Hotel with the deliberate intention of reviving his memories of them both in the old days, and, maybe, some stronger emotion too. 'Platonov, my own dear love,' was how she opened the conversation, quoting Chekhov's lines.[5] Rex was wary. Mercia and he were due to fly to Bermuda for a vacation. Yet he convinced himself there was little harm humouring Rachel and seeing how she was bearing up. She mistook his residual affection for reviving interest. Made euphoric by her successful meeting with the Yale people and fortified by champagne, she now told him how 'bereaved' she had been made to feel by his remarriage. It signalled the end of her 'impossible dream' of getting him back again.

Rachel's account of what then transpired has to be treated with reserve: her journals make it clear that, far from fading, her 'dream' took on new life as 'we embraced each other, tearfully. I felt like I felt in the old days: it was a good and well-loved and comfortable feeling.'[6] This is not to say that the encounter developed into anything improper. In the absence of his new wife, Rex would certainly have watched his step. What can be inferred from Rachel's recollection, allowing for her emotional heightening of it, is the concern of a still somewhat guilty ex-husband anxious to reinforce the confidence that, for once, Rachel possessed in herself. He succeeded. 'I left,' she concluded, 'determined to stand on my own two feet and enjoy being me – properly.'[7]

But, in the months ahead, her resolve broke down and she along with it, as loneliness, drink and the age gap between herself and the Yale students derailed her lecture schedule. The adrenalin had started flowing when she saw that 'Rex was impressed by my going to Yale. And I saw again the man behind the myth who, as much as I, wanted to be looked after. The children in Reg and Ray' – Reginald, as she still sometimes called Rex, Ray as Rachel referred to herself – 'met emotionally for a minute.'[8] But she had not been long at Yale before the adrenalin was replaced by alcohol. She made a sorry spectacle of herself. After one particularly appalling bout of drunkenness on campus, she threatened suicide. Athol Fugard, the South African dramatist who was directing one of his own plays at the drama school with Rachel in the cast, had to grapple with a naked woman, flush her barbiturates down the loo and desperately call 'all the numbers we could think of, all round the States, to try and locate Rex Harrison – with no luck'.[9] She fled from the play and the campus, and Yale never heard from her again.

Her subsequent collapse in friends' homes in California only seems to have had the result of strengthening her need for Rex. When she returned to New York in July 1979, he was in the middle of rehearsals for *My Fair Lady*. The role she was playing, in a CBS Television film of John Hershey's *The Wall*, left her with time to look in on the rehearsals. She did more than that, however. 'She attempted to re-enter the show,' says Patrick Garland. 'I was informed by the stage manager that Rachel, who'd been sitting in the circle, was "giving notes" about the acting, singing and so on. Rex wrote the notes, but he was clearly following Rachel's observations. I was very worried. We couldn't have two directors. I had to ask Rex to get her to stop.'

Once or twice Rachel said to Garland that in her opinion Rex's marriage would not last, that it would be like all the rest and it was perhaps over already, bar the announcement. '"Of course it isn't, Rachel," I said, "you're imagining things." It seemed to me that Rex and Mercia were perfectly content together. I put this down to wish fulfilment on Rachel's part.' Soon she flew off to Poland to shoot a scene at Auschwitz for the telefilm she was doing. Rex and Garland went ahead smoothly with the musical.

It had been decided to open the show in New Orleans, though Rex had been apprehensive at first. He feared having to work in the heat of the delta and make his return as Professor Higgins in the city's extravagantly rococo theatre with its Italianate decor, star-twinkling ceiling and fake marble statuary. But his producers had rented a bayou mansion for him and Mercia, and possibly the longest limousine in Louisiana to ferry him in and out of town in air-conditioned comfort; and he took to black-bean soup and Creole salad.

The house was sold out for the first night on 23 September; the reaction was predictable. They came to see Rex and he did not disappoint them. *Variety*'s critic noted a few fluffs in the lyrics due to nerves, but acknowledged the delightful picture he presented of 'irascibility, egotism and sexism'[10] – the last word being the sort of neologism that Professor Higgins might have snorted at, but which was indicative of the changing mores since the evening, twenty-five years earlier, when Rex had petulantly demanded to know why a woman could not be more like a man. Now the *avant garde* of the Women's Movement was throwing up its own opponents of Higgins's sexual chauvinism. Yet Rex's charm was still insidiously effective. Those who had never seen or heard him in person succumbed to him. Those who remembered him in the original musical or the film felt only that he had paid them the ultimate compliment: he had grown older along with them.

Cheryl Kennedy did not fare quite so well, but Rex deemed her excellent. He resisted anew all suggestions that Kate Sullivan, her understudy and the wife of Milo O'Shea, who was playing Doolittle, should be tried out or that another member of the cast, Nancy Ringham, who was in the chorus, should be given a chance. What he did not know was that Nancy Ringham was being coached in the role privately, since it was judged prudent to have someone in reserve in case Cheryl Kennedy had trouble with her voice. Rex judged Higgins the fulcrum on which *My Fair Lady* rested, not Eliza – and *he* was all right.

He had heard that Rachel had suffered another collapse on returning from Poland and had entered the Royal Free Hospital in Hampstead, London. She recorded in her journals that she was not far from the graveyard where Kay Kendall now rested – and she thought she would too, for she felt 'childless, workless and virtually homeless'.[11]

Her only chance, she went on, lay in recovering Rex: 'My Rex, glittering, excitable, high-prancing Rex to whom doors opened. Who is more sybaritic than Rex, who was and is like champagne? Glorious days I loved. Crazy happy days. In-love days. I never noticed the world.'[12] There and then, she sketched out a plan of action and willed herself to be well again in time to carry it out. She knew that *My Fair Lady* was to move on to San Francisco in the middle of October before opening in Los Angeles. Encouraged by at least one friend of hers, who had told her to go out and get what she wanted, Rachel's obsession now determined her to make one last effort to get Rex back. 'Give San Francisco a whirl, Rachel. Otherwise, life is gloomy ... Please God, give me another chance, and give me the strength to love him properly and him love me.'[13]

My Fair Lady was to open in San Francisco on 8 October 1980. Tickets at $27 proved no deterrent; one could not, as the saying went, wedge a toothpick into the sold-out Golden Gate Theater. Bob Dylan and Alistair Cooke were among those standing in line outside Rex's bunkerlike dressing-room in the basement to congratulate him and join him in the one glass of Pouilly Fuissé he was permitted – 'I'd like another,' he said ruefully, 'but *she* wouldn't like it.'[4] Mercia was largely responsible for the stamina he needed, she planned his day for him in detail. It began with yoga – 'marvellous for keeping the figure,' he conceded. Then she saw he took his vitamins and instructed the chauffeur to take him to the gym, where he swam and had his manicure, and, if necessary, a hair trim and a body massage. Then he was returned to the Huntington Hotel for a rest in their two-bedroomed suite. He did not usually take lunch, but a light meal at 4 pm, which Mercia herself prepared, usually of organically grown foodstuffs. She rarely went to the theatre with him, but always awaited his return. Occasionally, with a friend, he would refer to 'Bossy', but the discipline she imposed on Rex maintained his resilience for a longer time than he had any right to expect.

Rachel had discharged herself from the hospital in London and, after staying a few days with friends, she flew back to Los Angeles on 21 October and rang Rex almost as soon as she had settled into her Hutton Drive home with Darren Ramirez. She had willed herself to lay off the red wine long enough to sound sober when she spoke to him. He agreed to her coming to San Francisco to see the show. He had no other motive than a concern with her state of mind and a hope that seeing him again might have a calming effect on her. Perhaps, too, the debt and devotion he owed Mercia would be obvious to her and she would stop making the calls her journals record her putting through to him while she was ill in England. As things turned out, Rex misjudged things fatally, but then so did others who were closer to Rachel than he at this time.

On 29 October, fortified by Valium and a half-bottle of red wine, she somehow got herself on the shuttle aircraft to San Francisco, went to her hotel, ordered champagne and fell asleep, but was up in time to see him in *My Fair Lady*. No one except Rex, she thought, was really first class. 'Wine, genuine enjoyment, emotion and relief all contributed to the tears in my eyes.'[5] She went backstage. They talked. Rex dropped her back at her hotel in his limousine.

The next morning, they took a taxi-ride to the beach and went for a long walk, Rex in his camel-hair jacket and buttercup yellow cashmere sweater and yellow silk Ascot embroidered with delicate flowers: an outfit that might have looked too studied, even effete on a man unable to carry it off as well as his easy authority still permitted him to. They talked about the troubles there had been in their lives. Rex told her of a few he still had, mostly to do with growing old. She saw that his endemic anxieties were still with him, in spite of the security Mercia had attempted to build around him. In a vague way, this comforted Rachel: he was not *so* changed, after all. Peace came, soothing her nerves, but only for a time.

When he accompanied her to the airline office to buy her return ticket, the old terrors associated with loneliness – an absence of Rex – returned. She pulled herself together and went to the show again. 'Rex was a little *piano*. But the urbane curtain call ... the old-world charm ... the life-style. Yes, I saw Rex "properly". I'm admiring, but I'm not adolescently dazzled any more. I see how hard he works, how he can accept prosaic repetition and routine, and quite a lot of unhappiness.'[16]

He promised her financial help with the psychiatric treatment she was undergoing weekly in Los Angeles and the next day she flew back, but not to Hutton Drive. She prevailed on a friend, Carol Scherick, wife of a production executive, to take her under her roof and care for her for a few days at least.

After the visit to Rex in San Francisco, his telephone calls, according to Rachel, became 'guarded, much more guarded'. She suspected that it might have something to do with his anxiety lest Mercia suspected him of harbouring more feelings for Rachel than simply the understandable concern of an ex-husband for a former wife who was mentally ill and physically distressed. But the more 'normal' Rex's calls became, avoiding any risk of emotional involvement by stressing his own daily agenda and concerns, the more keenly Rachel felt the impossibility of regaining him.

As she lay in bed at the Schericks', a hot-water bottle on her stomach, Valium tablets within reach, a vitamin-packed soft drink to hand, she received a call from Rex, who had just been out in a yacht, had had a marvellous time and sounded on top of the world. A deep depression settled on Rachel as she contrasted his condition with hers. Blame replaced love. She lay there, semi-comatose, endlessly calling up the past in her thoughts. She blamed herself and she blamed Rex. She remembered the chance of being a great actress that she had thrown away in order to accommodate herself to her husband's wishes and to enjoy his style and comfort. She became in turns the dependent little girl who had found everything too hard to handle and the vengeful woman whose gifts had been squandered for the sake of an unappreciative man. Neither was, of course, a true account. Rachel Roberts was still a greatly gifted woman who was working harder than many a well-balanced, 'normal' actress and was well able, materially speaking, to enjoy a good life. But she could not see it that way. Her self-esteem was so low that no one – not Rex, not Darren Ramirez, not her friends, not her doctors – could stretch out a hand and raise her confidently back on to the level of sanity and joy.

Rex and Mercia flew down to Los Angeles on 23 November. They were staying in Leslie and Eve Bricusse's Beverly Hills house. His butler accompanied them; Mercia's French maid was joining them later. Rex called Rachel the next day, sounding depressed, saying he did not like the house and he hated Los Angeles. It held bad memories for him. His call triggered Rachel's ambivalence again. 'If only I could still feel my love for him. Could I? Could I unpack and cook as his household does? He was glad I was alive, he said. He is a scamp. Always was. Impossible, I suppose, to live with. Woke up at five o'clock, thinking I was dead. I am very ill.'[7]

Darren Ramirez was now working for I. Magnin, the smart women's wear emporium on Wilshire Boulevard. Carol Scherick called his office there late in the afternoon of 25 November to say that Rex had just come by her home and picked up Rachel. They had gone over to the Hutton Drive house, she thought. It might be better if Darren delayed his return home.

When he did enter 2620 Hutton Drive, a few hours later, he did so hesitantly, hoping Rex and Rachel would have had time to say all they wanted to each other. There was no sound and, when he spotted Rex's Henry Higgins-type hat lying on the sofa, Darren quietly made his way over to Carol Scherick's.

He was there when the phone rang and it was Rachel. Why was he not coming home? Rex had been long gone, she said – he had simply forgotten to take his hat. 'So home I went,' says Darren, 'and found her smashed out of her mind.'[8] She had prepared supper for Rex and herself, and driven drunkenly to the liquor store for some more wine for them – and left her purse there. Rex and she had talked, she said, and then danced gently to a record.

In Rex's arms, Rachel relived the best of what was past. All his fatal charm repossessed her, along with the world it had helped create for them both. 'Yes, I loved Rex, passionately, and all our good larks. Yes, I adored walking up the Champs-Elysées with him. Yes, I adored Joseph's and the Berkeley and ice-cold, perfectly prepared dry Martinis and beautiful wine and brandy and *potage* and brains. Yes, I loved the Rome Express and the adjoining *coupés* and snuggling up to Rex. Yes, I loved our love: it completely tallied with my adolescent fantasies. Yes, I loved the look of Rex's shoulders swaggering down the train corridor. Yes, I loved our walks past the donkey to San Fruttuoso. Yes, I loved the fires, the villa, the books, the cats, Homerino. I loved them passionately.'[9] And then, like sobriety returning, the reality of her present state invaded the brief respite that Rex's visit brought her. '... And for all that,' she told herself, 'I forfeited my birthright ... my voice and my Welsh emotionalism ... my acting. It was all I ever knew or understood.' She should have stayed with her first husband, she said to Rex: 'That's what I needed – something downbeat to balance all my emotionalism and steady me.'

She told him she had wasted her career on him. He had 'upset' her life.[20] Rex, ever the realist, told her in return that she had never been cut out for the awful loneliness that followed the exhilaration of the nightly ordeal on the stage: the nerves in him that screamed in the minutes before he tried to win the audience's attention and hold it; and then the nothingness that was left after the two-hour 'affair' with 'them'. Rachel had to admit it was the truth.

Did this candour of Rex's destroy the last vestige of illusion that, like Blanche DuBois, Rachel was cherishing? Or did it take that final visit to convince her that she never had a hope of winning him back as her own and re-entering his 'magic kingdom'? 'What am I so terribly frightened of?' she asked herself as she wrote up that evening's entry in the secret journals she was keeping unseen even by Darren.[21] And she answered it in the final words she penned: 'Life itself, I think.'

The next day, 26 November 1980, she woke up after Darren had left for work and took in the *Los Angeles Times*. There, on pages one and eleven of the 'Calendar' arts and entertainment supplement, was the interview that Sheila Benson had done with Rex in San Francisco a couple of weeks earlier and held over for the eve of his opening in Los Angeles. There was no mention of Rachel in it, none at all. Of Mercia, yes: she was 'my beloved wife'.[22] Benson asked Rex if he were happy. ' "Who is?" Rex answered. "I don't think that one can honestly say that one is totally happy, no ... I think one has to be a lunatic to be happy. Most lunatics have no lines on their faces at all and no worries." He thinks about it a sobering minute, then brightens momentarily. "I really am *very* happy when I am in the theatre." '

Rachel's body was found at around 3.30 pm that same afternoon by the Mexican gardener who serviced some of the houses on Hutton Drive. She was lying inert on the kitchen floor in a negligée snagged and plucked in a dozen places. Scattered on the floor around her was the debris of what had been a Victorian glass screen used to divide breakfast area from living-room. At first it was thought she had had a heart attack or choked on a piece of muffin later found in her throat. The autopsy told a different story. Police deduced from a rug found amid the bramble bushes on top of the ridge behind the house that she had gone there with the intention of dying from a massive overdose of barbiturates she had secretly hoarded and swallowed. Feeling cold, they surmised, she had returned to the house in a dozy state, tearing her nightdress as she passed by the thorn bushes, and entered the kitchen to make a cup of tea. The kettle had still been steaming when the gardener had found her.

Perhaps she had taken a bite out of the muffin, then washed it down with what she took to be white wine. Only it was not wine: it was household lye, a strong disinfectant that had been kept in a wine bottle. The swig Rachel took from it ended her life almost immediately. She had staggered into the glass screen before collapsing, shattering it into dozens of pieces.

Sybil Christopher, Rachel's best friend and the former wife of Richard Burton who had married Jordan Christopher, rushed over after being telephoned by a neighbour's child on Hutton Drive. Darren Ramirez, summoned from his desk at I. Magnin by a Los Angeles police call, was already there. David Lewin, a leading London show-business journalist who was doing interviews in Los Angeles, had also been called by the police who found the messsage he had left with his Beverly Wilshire number on Rachel's answering machine. It was Lewin who realized Rex must be told at once and left a message at Leslie Bricusse's: 'Rachel has been found dead.'[23]

Patrick Garland takes up the story: 'Rex was absolutely shattered.' He was even more shocked the next day, when it was announced that what had been thought was a death from natural causes had actually been suicide. It was the second time a woman whom Rex had loved had taken her own life in Los Angeles. 'Another man might have been tempted not to open in *My Fair Lady* the day after his ex-wife has committed suicide,' says Garland. 'But Rex was the total professional. He had never welcomed the attention of fans, and luckily we were able to keep the press away from him. So he jumped out of his car and was in through the stage door before anyone could catch him for a "quote". I went and sat with him in his dressing-room at the interval. When he came to the "Grown accustomed to her face" number at the end of the show, I'm as sure as anything that he was singing it with the memory of Rachel in mind. I was standing in the wings, quite close to him, and I saw a tear well over and trickle down his cheek.'

Sybil Christopher had left Rachel's home with a few small mementos of her friend. She had also seen that day's copy of the *Times* in the living-room with Sheila Benson's interview with Rex folded outwards. In the margin Rachel had scribbled a memo to herself – 'Call Syb.'[24]

She also took away a book that had been lying on the coffee table. Called *Unfinished Business* by Maggie Scarf, it bore the subtitle *Pressure*

Points in the Lives of Women. In the chapter entitled 'Diagnosing Despair' appeared the words: 'In a way, the hardest thing *I* had to handle' – the narrator was a woman named Kath – 'was the realization that what I experienced as his coolness or meanness wasn't directed at me personally. He wasn't trying to hurt me, but he couldn't live with it. He couldn't be intimate, not at that point in his life ...' Rachel had added in pencil in the margin '... or ever'.[25]

On the flyleaf Rachel had written: 'I don't want to see Rex. It's not his fault. I just don't want involvement ... I chose Rex over my craft. It happened. Not much of a sin, but I suffer for it dreadfully. I gave away my birthright. Therefore I cannot survive.'[26]

Rex's only recorded comment suggested how his thoughts must have leaped back over the years to his discovery of Carole Landis's body. 'It's a tragedy,' he said. 'Suicide is always a tragedy.'[27]

Pamela Mason blamed Rachel's death on 'Rex's resurrection as a star as he toured in *My Fair Lady*. I think [it] brought it all back [to her – what she had lost]. It was the Third Coming of Rex which fascinated and upset Rachel and called her competitive drive into play again. She loved him, certainly, but her love was combined with her aggression. A bit like Eliza Doolittle's feelings for her mentor in the musical. It was a case of "Just you wait, 'Enry 'Iggins".'[28]

Darren Ramirez reclaimed Rachel's body from the morgue and arranged the cremation. By his own choice, he was the only person present. Rachel made the request in her will that her ashes should not be taken home to her native Wales or be put in any place of remembrance. She preferred to have them scattered over water. Darren pondered and wondered if Malibu would do. Rex called him a few weeks later, did not mention Rachel, but asked if he wanted tickets to see the show. Darren demurred.

'But, after Christmas, I went to see him in his dressing-room and told him about the Malibu idea. He said it sounded wonderful. "Let me look in my diary and see what day next week is free. Oh, no, we've got matinées that day ... and that. By the way," he said to me, suddenly looking a bit anxious, "you don't suppose any of the press will be there, do you?" I suddenly felt very depressed. I said, "Rex, to tell the truth, I haven't quite made up my mind yet. I'll give it some more thought and let you know." "Good idea," he said.'[29]

Eventually, Darren took Rachel's ashes back to England in a small, neatly wrapped box the size of a couple of house bricks, which he carried inside a chic shopping bag from Gianni Versace, for whom he was now working. Somehow the utilitarian box and its contrastingly exotic container seemed to fit the nature of the life within far better than any classical funerary urn. Darren gave the ashes to Lindsay Anderson, who put them on the top shelf in a store cupboard in his flat until Darren and he and Rachel's friends could decide what to do with them. At the date of writing this, Rachel remains there – still in transit.

34: A Chill Wind in Manhattan

Rex attempted to put the memory of Rachel's tragic end behind him as the tour of *My Fair Lady* continued in the early months of 1981. It certainly presented enough problems to be going on with. The critics, and now the producers, were concerned about Cheryl Kennedy's voice and the punishment it was taking from doing eight performances a week. When the Boston engagement approached, there were two previews. The harassed producers decided that there would be three Elizas. The tall and vigorous Nancy Ringham was to do the first preview; Kate Sullivan, the official understudy, the second; and Cheryl Kennedy the opening night. None of this manoeuvring soothed Rex's temper or lulled his suspicions of intrigue behind the scenes, which, in a way, was true. Nancy Ringham had been continuing with her unofficial rehearsals and, in the opinion of those who watched her, was getting better and better.

But the idea of a strong, defiant Eliza did not appeal to Rex one bit. He was used to playing with malleable girls who did not throw him an unexpected verbal punch 'like Jack Dempsey', he said. Besides, he added, he had a loyalty to his first choice, Cheryl Kennedy.

However, the decision was taken out of his hands as the Broadway opening approached in mid-August. Cheryl Kennedy went down with throat trouble. Patrick Garland had to tell the unhappy actress that she was out of the show and would be replaced by Nancy Ringham. The management had to issue an ultimatum to Rex before he accepted this and even then he agreed only if he could personally rehearse the replacement. Some of Nancy Ringham's supporters later felt this had been a fatal mistake. He had toned down her performance, they said, so that she should not be in competition with him for the audience's interest. The reviews following the 18 August opening seemed to agree. They praised her professionalism, but found her performance 'far from electrifying ... her Cockney accent was inconsistent.'' But then even Rex's performance was judged to be that of a septuagenarian whose batteries were running down. He could not match the one and only rival he had to fear – his younger self. He had succumbed to the primary vanity of the old actor-managers he used to admire so much: living on the reputation they had gained in their most popular role, but repeating it too often too long.

Tiredness seemed to infect the show, which had been on tour for the better part of a year. Lacking an Eliza able to stand up to Higgins, it felt even more debilitated in spite of the intelligence that Patrick Garland brought to bear on the reinterpretation of the original. It did respectable business, but did not have the long run predicted for it. It closed in November. Rex was probably glad to see the end of it. The touring, the tragedy of Rachel's death, the in-fighting over Eliza, all had depressed him and reminded him of his age.

Friends of Rex and Mercia remarked how the latter, from around this time, showed increasing concern for his well-being and kept him on a tighter rein than before. Rachel's journals, which had been found after her death and were then being edited by this writer with a view to publication, as she had wished, contained one touching reference to Rex's dread of old age. 'Well,' she said, when he spoke of it, 'don't think you can come back to me when you need looking after.'[2] She meant it flippantly, but he took it seriously and got severely depressed. Now Mercia was undoubtedly 'looking after' him, and making a good job of it.

His eyes had begun to trouble him and she made it a practice to recite the menus to him when they went out. Friends who ate with Rex when Mercia was absent – a rare event, it seemed to them – were '*bouleversé*', as Robert Morley put it, by the difficulty of getting anything to eat. Rex, being too vain to put on his spectacles or to ask the others to read out the dishes available, would engage the *maître d'hôtel* in long, pernickety conversations about what he might have, while his companions had to wait patiently – and hungrily. He continued to drink very little in the way of alcohol, though he sometimes showed his reluctance to fall in with Mercia's regimen. On one stop on the tour, he called room service from his suite and ordered himself four large gin-and-tonics. By mistake, two of them were placed in Mercia's sitting-room. When he retrieved the others from the waiter, he drank one of them thirstily, then unscrewed a shampoo bottle, rinsed it thoroughly and poured in the other gin-and-tonic as a covert stand-by. 'Rex got a bit relaxed, if he'd had too much,' a friend says, 'and Mercia wasn't a girl who cared a lot for relaxation.'[3] Her 'governessy' nature liked to keep things under control. She was well aware of the wild boy Rex had been, although, as he was much older now, she did not have this to bother her like the earlier wives. All the same, she would have been silly not to have recognized the risk from women – from Rachel, even, in her deluded state – who still felt Rex's unextinguished charm. This, together with a genuine concern and love for him, probably made her much more vigilant than she had been.

Rex had sold his home in the south of France and the Harrisons now lived in New York for much of the year. Before she met Rex, Mercia had owned a Fifth Avenue apartment, but her taste ran to contemporary furnishings. Rex had found it too austere for him. He hankered after a touch of the Henry Higgins – masculine and comfortable and antique. They compromised and bought an apartment at 450 East 52nd Street. It was in a slender stone and brick-clad building put up in the mid-1920s, with a tapering tower and an Italianate fusion of New York and Venice in its detailing, an impression assisted by views over the East River. Its residents at one time included Alice Durer Miller, Alexander Woollcott, Henry and Clare Boothe Luce, Jack and Irene Heinz and also Valentina, the *couturière*, her financier husband George Schlee and the latter's mistress Greta Garbo. Privacy in those days was more desirable even than security, and one can see why. Keith Irvine, a student of John Fowler, one half of the fashionable London firm of Colefax & Fowler, undertook to reconcile Rex's and Mercia's preferences. No easy task, but he did it brilliantly. A nineteenth-century lantern illuminated the entrance hall, the walls of which held English Victorian prints; that was Rex's touch. Mercia's was probably evident in the bronze Giacometti chairs paired with a Chinese altar table. The hall could be turned into a small extra dining-room if more space were needed for entertaining.

There was an eighteenth-century pine mantel in the living-room, a Pissarro painting of trees and parkland, a Dunoyer de Segonzac drawing, a Matisse, and a Vlaminck. There were outsize chairs and a sofa covered in oriental chintz with a motif of bamboo and lacquer. Mercia kept the place filled with a variety of potted orchids, adding a delicately exotic touch redolent of her birthplace. Rex had a long, low divan-type bed in his room, which was hung with his own paintings of Corsican and Caribbean scenes. There was one curious note: a chair that looked like a miniature throne, on which Rex sat to preside over dinner parties. A friend sugggests it came from – or was inspired by – a like chair in his Broadway production of the Pirandello play, *The Emperor Henry IV*.

Their library housed a large number of books, Mercia's and his own. Rex's usually had a connection with plays he had done or testified to his love of England and some of its monarchs with whom he obviously felt at least a spiritual kinship: Henry VIII, Charles II and Edward VII. Mercia's books were wider-ranging, more 'literary'. The room also contained a portrait of a plump and stately looking eighteenth-century matron said to have been painted by Sir Joshua Reynolds. It had been suggested to Rex that the picture would look well hanging above the mantelpiece in the living-room. He raised his eyebrows and snapped: 'Certainly not, only one's own ancestors should hang over a fireplace.'[4] In short, it was a comfortable, elegant and cleverly designed apartment – the last home Rex was to know.

Friends who visited him and Mercia were well entertained, usually on caviar and the finest champagne. Most visitors noted the air of serenity Mercia radiated, a cosmopolitan woman with an Oriental cast of mind. 'I suppose they had their differences from time to time,' says a mutual friend, Lady Donaldson, 'but then which of these theatrical people doesn't? The generation I knew, to which Rex belonged, was interested only in the theatre – and themselves. Rex, like most of the men one met then, "acted" all the time – never really off stage. Mercia made a good partner for his type. She was no actress herself, but she reminded me of Gladys Cooper at that age. Very calm, very firm. She kept Rex up to scratch.' It is likely that, as age inexorably crept over him, Rex came to see Mercia as a 'guardian' of *The Cocktail Party* kind. Mercia certainly knew the play; her copy of it was to find its way – by accident? – into the auction of Rex's personal effects. Her own Asian upbringing and careful cultivation of mind and body certainly at times lent a philosophical aspect to her relationship with Rex; it may not have been in the High Catholic tradition of Eliot's redemptive austerity, but, where Rex was concerned, the feeling of someone 'in charge' of him came at the right time in his life.

The extent of Mercia's influence on him is seen in the minor chores she got him to perform – things that, in earlier days, he would have rejected with a blunt expletive had anyone even presumed to propose them. Thus he took part in various low-key ventures in New York on behalf of community charities. One of these was to host a guided tour of The Little Church Around the Corner. Over 150 people attended, drawn by his name. Of course, he knew the place well: he had been twice married there. In a very real sense, he was returning the favour.

He hesitated briefly when Anglia Television proposed he make a film of *The Kingfisher* in England, with Wendy Hiller replacing Claudette Colbert. His momentary delay had nothing to do with his health. He simply thought that one of the minor television franchises might not be able to afford his fee or terms that included a rented house for him and Mercia on location, a chauffeured car and a butler. The costumes for the film were done by the noted English designer Julie Harris, who recalled the time she had seen Rex 'between takes of *Over the Moon* at Denham, prowling around the set like a big silky cat, in evening dress, terribly glamorous'.[5] The glamour began to flake off once she started outfitting him for his television film. 'Without even waiting to hear my view on the suits he should wear, he went to his Savile Row tailor and ordered what he needed for his wardrobe, and blew two-thirds of the budget I had and left me with virtually nothing to put on Wendy Hiller's back.'

Most actors of Rex's eminence and age, seventy-five now, are left facing two alternatives – retirement or Lear. The first was unthinkable; the second was Shakespeare and therefore, he considered, unactable by him. Rex had a third one – Shaw. He would play Shaw's equivalent of Lear, Captain Shotover, the eighty-three-year-old retired captain in *Heartbreak House*, now skippering the allegorical ship of state – pre-World War One Britain – with all its superfluous cargo of hangers-on and ne'er-do-wells, relics of a society that he foresees will dash itself upon the rocks of history. It had been Shaw's testament, a play whose windy eloquence was shot through with lightning bolts of prophecy from the tongue of this elder prophet. For Rex, it recalled the joy of standing in the great windows of the Villa San Genesio amidst the electrical storm and crying, 'Well hit, God!' Shotover, like him, was touched with, but chose to ignore, the signs of his own advancing mortality. Like himself, Shotover is a survivor from a world which he has seen giving place to a new order. Rex felt the world he had known and even helped shape by his style and influence vanishing with the accelerated transience of daily life. Even a small straw showed him how the wind was blowing now – a cold wind too. He was sitting with Mercia one day in the very smartest of New York's restaurants. She complained of the chill in the place caused by excessive air-conditioning. Rex summoned the *maître d'hôtel* and asked – in his usual peremptory manner, no doubt – that it be turned down. In a flat, matter-of-fact tone of voice, all the more vexatious because of the self-assurance with which he now spoke to the man who had once been the most honoured performer on the New York stage, the employee said, 'If you're cold, you can leave.'[6] They stayed. For Rex, *Heartbreak House* had the same premonitory shiver of majesty in terminal decline and no longer granted its due respect. 'A sometimes senile old salt,' John Beaufort wrote in the *Christian Science Monitor*, when he came to do the play on Broadway, 'who nevertheless can suddenly recapture his power to command [and] shuffling absently about, stowing away his dynamite ... can often be as sharp as he is blunt.'[7]

He did the play in London first, just after his seventy-fifth birthday in the spring of 1983. It was directed by John Dexter, who clashed with Rex over the mood. Dexter saw it as primarily Chekhovian, melancholic. Rex wanted it to be Shavian, trenchantly humorous. He perceived that

Dexter's concept exposed him to the risks of ensemble acting which, in his opinion, diminished Shotover's – and Rex's – apocalyptic authority. It was like putting the Captain in the longboat with the crew he had once commanded and giving him an oar like the rest to pull on. Despite the conflict, or maybe because of it, Rex emerged with some of the best notices from the London critics he had ever received.

It was nearly nine years since he had last appeared there. Critics now appreciated the rarity of the event, which might not recur again, as Rex was showing, like Shotover, the signs of senescence as well as fortitude. By happy chance, the character's pithiest commentary on the state of the nation, and his generation in particular, comes at the end of Shaw's didactic polemic and Rex, wearing a patriarchal beard, was able to gather his forces for an eruption of undiminished vigour. 'Sure,' wrote Sheridan Morley,

he is a little fluffy on some of the longer speeches, and there are indeed moments when he appears to be neither coming nor going, but merely hovering like some benign Prospero over a British isle that is still full of noises and somehow no longer very magical. Yet all of this is a perfect role description of Shotover himself, and when Harrison gets into his great speech about England ('The captain is in his bunk, drinking bottled ditchwater, and the crew is gambling in the forecastle. She will strike and sink and split. Do you think the laws of God will be suspended in favour of England because you were born in it?') it is to be reminded with a sudden shock of what an extraordinary talent we have allowed to disappear over the Atlantic in the last forty years.[8]

In New York, where Anthony Page's production opened in December 1983, the tone was wittier, the ripostes were sharper, the mood was more that of the kind of Edwardian country-house party in the era when Rex had been practising and perfecting his tricks. And when the cast recorded the play for American television, Shotover was definitely up front and Rex the acknowledged star, playing the part with artful cajolery of the viewing audience. The measure of attention that Shaw had dispersed over the social landscape was now refocused and concentrated on the largest figure in it.

A new play still eluded him. The problem was not simply his advancing age. It was the material that the age he was living in now regarded as acceptable on stage and screen. 'The only scripts I have been sent recently have been so highly pornographic that I'd like to see the films, but not be in them,' he told a *Time* interviewer.[9] He added: 'One producer said, "Well, if you don't want to do it, leave the script with your porter and we'll pick it up." I said, "I can't leave this with the porter. He might read it." '[10]

As for stage plays, 'The angries have grown old and got their goodies and they don't know what to be angry about any more.'" He had outlived Coward and Rattigan – they died in 1973 and 1977 respectively – and, although both had enjoyed an enormous revival in their last years, their deaths seemed to Rex to separate him even more decisively from the good prose and calculating workmanship on which he himself thrived. Affection for the era of social hypocrisy in which he had grown up and matured his style finally resolved his search. At the age of seventy-six, he at last took the leading role in a play by his beloved Freddy Lonsdale. *Aren't We All?* had been conceived by Lonsdale in 1908, the year Rex was born, and put on in New York in 1923. Lonsdale had always wanted to write a play for Rex, since the actors – Hawtrey, Squire, du Maurier – were all of the generation older than Rex. But now Rex was of an age and temperament when playing a Lonsdale character held a satisfaction akin to going to a country one has always promised oneself to see and only goes to in retirement. It evoked a sense of contentment, which is what Rex needed now, rather than achievement.

Aren't We All? posed a question whose unstated noun was the word 'liars'. In Lonsdale's lexicon, it demanded the smooth assent, 'Of course.' As one reviewer was to remark, the play was not the thing, it was the excuse: the excuse for Rex to play Lord Grenham, a randy peer with a weakness for afternoon assignations with shop girls in the British Museum, who tries to untangle other people's affairs and gets himself entangled in an unlooked-for romance with an old flame. She finally snares him by putting a notice of their engagement in *The Times*. The *fait accompli* secures her man, but to him matrimony sounds like the snap of a dead-lock. The laughter, as frequently happens in Lonsdale, is bitter. As Rex characterized it, 'very funny, very dry and very much of the upper classes'.[12]

The stroke of brilliance was enticing Claudette Colbert over from her Barbados home to play Lord Grenham's old love. The last time she appeared on the West End stage had been in 1928. With the experience of *The Kingfisher* so recently in mind, she and Rex kept a sharp eye on each other. Adding her to the cast provided this play of another era with a contemporary tension derived from the leading players. The mere announcement of the casting caused a premonitory mouthwatering among those who hoped to see Claudette prove more than a match for Rex. As things turned out, she was sometimes his salvation. Rex could conceal or adapt his physical infirmities to the character he was playing, but the deficiencies of his memory were not so easily remedied. In a play where much depended on aphorisms and paradoxes, never mind uttering the right name at the right moment, an attack of forgetfulness could be ruinous. Rex was now prone to these memory blanks. Even having to hesitate a few seconds until he was prompted imperilled his most precious comic possession – his timing. He had no illusions about Lonsdale being easy to play. 'I'd rather have Bernard Shaw any day,' he said. 'Shaw worked for his actors. Lonsdale made them work for him. He gives you practically nothing; he wrote in a weird style all his own.'[13] Sheridan Morley appositely characterized Lonsdale's style as 'essentially the rhythms of his favourite actors and house-party hostesses around World War One'.[14] It was these rhythms that now gave Rex trouble.

The out-of-town opening in Birmingham, in mid-May 1984, sounded a distant early warning signal. After all the trouble he had given at rehearsals, sparing the rest of the cast nothing while he experimented with all manner of variations on the 'reading' of Lonsdale's lines, he now started to forget them. Claudette Colbert, who now knew his part as well as her own (and somewhat better than he did), would feed him a line or two. But on one occasion, unable to put up with such 'condescension' any longer, he advanced to the footlights and addressed the surprised though titillated audience: 'She's given me my lines, but' – note of triumph: how *could* she be so stupid! – 'they're the wrong lines.' The chances are they were not, but vanity compelled him to disown them.

The London previews went well; Rex seemed himself again. Then first-night nerves caused him to stumble once or twice, after which fluffs and missed cues came thick and fast. 'Rex Harrison delivers his lines with a nonchalance which all too often verges on the negligent,' Jack Tinker wrote in the *Daily Mail*.[15] 'During the languid peregrinations around the text,' he continued, 'he occasionally bumps into the odd phrase which even Frederick Lonsdale would recognize as his own.' 'Time after time,' said Kenneth Hurren in the *Mail on Sunday*, 'the cue for a quip hung in the air like a shuttlecock waiting to be hit.'[16] Rex partially recovered his memory in the later stages of the play; and in subsequent performances he and Lonsdale would have had no difficulty recognizing each other. Even when he was not word-perfect, Rex remained pitch-perfect: he preserved the tone, if not the line. But on that first night Claudette was the great stabilizer. She kept her head and, in doing so, kept Rex from losing his nerve.

The New York critics were less niggling than their London *confrères* when *Aren't We All?* opened on Broadway in April 1985 with Rex, as John Simon put it in *New York* magazine, still 'a mite prone to dance around his lines and gradually to sidle up to them'.[17] When he did connect, the old cunning in his voice was irresistible. He could set the house roaring with laughter just by his polysyllabic intonation of a word like 'ab-so-lute-ly'. Gordon Rogoff in the *Village Voice*, by no means a journal sympathetic to such 'two-butler plays' as this one, wrote:

Harrison's face seems to have disappeared into his eye sockets, but that doesn't stop him from demonstrating that even this development can be used by an expert minimalist to show character and intelligence. He shuts out the whites of his eyes no more than three or four times, a signal that he has awakened to something like a decision, or, at least, a resolution of some idea that has been lurking behind his cornea.[18]

Critics on both sides of the Atlantic were touched as well as amused when Lord Grenham reads the announcement of his own engagement which has mysteriously appeared in *The Times*. To someone who says, with slight surprise, 'I thought you were perfectly happy?' he replies with the resigned gravity of a man who feels the far from tender trap of matrimony closing on him: 'Evidently, I wasn't.' At such a moment, when Rex's devilry was checkmated, the old fox looked cornered and almost appealing.

A cross-America tour was begun in September, after a two-month rest. However, Rex had grown a bit tired of Claudette's being an exemplary reproach to him during the London and New York runs. He had never been one to appreciate other people's considerateness if it showed him at a disadvantage. He therefore made discouraging noises about taking Claudette on the tour. Was it not time she had a rest? Would it not be better to get someone who was a bit younger? (She was three years older than he.) Rex ran over the names of a few actresses from back home who would do nicely for the part, but the response was not what he expected. The old Manhattan chill he had experienced in the restaurant with Mercia, hinting at the transience of fame and power, now returned to numb him. But Rex, said his American management, this tour is being sold on Claudette's name, not yours. She is the attraction. They have seen *you* out there, lots of times; they have not seen *her* for years outside New York. A whole generation has grown up and had children without seeing Claudette. And rubbing in the message, no doubt with well-relished asperity, they repeated, 'It's her they want to see, not you.' Rex made some noises which suggested he had forgotten his lines again.

35: Full Circle

When the tour of *Aren't We All?* reached Los Angeles in November 1985, Rex found the city retained its fateful association with the deaths of those he had once loved. Lilli Palmer now lay in hospital there, gravely ill from inoperable cancer and in the last weeks of her life. Rex did not expect her to live through Christmas. He immediately offered to pay for the nursing she needed day and night. Though Lilli had been one of West Germany's best-selling novelists, her wealth had been depleted in recent years by financial reverses. Her marriage had not brought her the happiness she expected. Carlos Thompson had become increasingly restless, his time taken up with the politics of Argentina and his wish to return there and involve himself directly in the struggle against the dictatorship. Lilli died the following January 1986, aged seventy-one. Her husband accompanied her coffin to Forest Lawn burial ground, then set off for South America. Four years later, in Buenos Aires, he killed himself.

Of all the people who had played a role in the Kay Kendall drama, only Rex was left. Over the years he had tended to blame Noël Coward, even more than Lilli. After all, it had been Coward who had crisply advised her against going back to Rex after Kay's death and caused her to change her mind or, as Rex saw it, break her word.

He may have been thinking back to that occasion – and with understandable bitterness – when he had made his notorious attack on Coward in a *Vanity Fair* interview he gave Russell Miller while rehearsing for *Aren't We All?* in New York the previous April. It caused consternation to those who knew both Coward and himself. As the 'Master' was long dead, Rex had nothing to fear and he spoke with what was, even for him, uncommon candour.

'Noël was a terrible cunt in some ways,' he told his interviewer.[1] He went on to say why he hated doing a Coward play – for the reason, already mentioned, that it was hard to avoid sounding like Noël. Then he added that he also thought him 'a lousy actor, personally – he was mannered and unmanly ... Of course, the great thing [today] is to be homosexual. Then no one can say anything about you – it virtually guarantees discreet press coverage. It is too late for me to change my sexual proclivities, however. Far too late.'

'A spectacularly bad thing to say,' Douglas Fairbanks Jr responded.[2] But then that was Rex for you – 'sometimes he lets off steam like that'. Rex's estimation of his peers was usually low, but very, very seldom did he speak for quotation. With old age, one can afford to grow incautious; yet, on this occasion, there was envy too behind the words about Coward. The playwright had been a tax exile like Rex for many of his highest earning years, yet he had been forgiven for his 'disloyalty', if such it was. The nation had eventually recognized what a rare and essentially English talent to amuse Coward possessed. Forgiveness had been sealed not only by the revival of his work but also by a knighthood bestowed on him less than three years before his death, in the begrudging English manner which ensured that those whom the Establishment reluctantly honoured should not have too many years left to enjoy it. Rex had never received a single honour from his country, but was he not unique too? Was he not also regarded the world over as the exemplar of civilized Englishness? Had he not created the immortal character of the great English misogynist Henry Higgins? Robert Flemyng tried to talk sense to him. '"Rex," I said, "it's not just enough to be a marvellous actor, which you are. You've got to do something else too."' He remained resentful and suspicious. Maybe his much-married state had excluded him from the honours list. If so, was there not an insidious double standard at work? Rattigan had been knighted in 1971. He and Coward were both, in the pejorative term of the day, 'closet queens'. Rex had made no secret that he considered it healthier to have a heterosexual appetite, even if he overindulged it. Now it seemed to him he was being penalized. It was not fair! Hence the self-pitying note in his outburst against Coward, disguised as a 'Thank God, I'm normal!' declaration.

It was no coincidence that around this time Rex began referring publicly to his yearning for England and in several interviews made specific reference to his wish to return to England for a longer period than a limited run. He had taken advice from people who knew how the honours system worked. They had assured him that forgiveness, and more, might be on its way if he showed evidence of wanting to settle in Britain. It is extremely unlikely that Rex harboured any such wish or intention. But he played along, greatly heartened by an invitation to lunch with the Prime Minister, Mrs Thatcher, at her official country residence. Another guest had been David Lean, the film director, aged seventy-six and Rex's exact contemporary. Lean was knighted later that same year, 1984. Rex was not. The disappointment was still acute when he gave his ill-advised interview to *Vanity Fair*. What he said about Coward was noted back in England and in Downing Street, where the honours list was drawn up. It was not thought 'the done thing' to attack a countryman like Coward whom the Queen had honoured, especially in the wounding terms Rex had used. It was a costly mistake. That outburst set his own chances of a knighthoood back several years. Notwithstanding the hope of a title he had been encouraged to entertain by political insiders, he was intentionally passed over – and remained so, despite his subsequent protestations that, having lived for years out of forty-two suitcases, he would like nothing better than to 'come home' and find a place with a large kitchen for Mercia and a garden for himself 'in which to potter'.[3] It did not ring true at all. As David Lewin remarked in an interview given by Rex deliberately to foster this impression, 'I cannot visualize Rex Harrison ever pottering.'[4]

He might have stayed longer in England, not to potter, but to act, had things gone better on a new play which very much attracted him in the middle of 1986. *The Far Country* was about an Englishman who has returned from the colonies and finds himself reliving the past. Braham Murray intended to direct it at the Manchester Royal Exchange Theatre. Rex insisted on rewrites, but he found he had not the patience now to sit down with a writer and shape the work to his own specifications. And nor had he the health. He collapsed at the Ritz Hotel in July, though he made a quick recovery in Westminster Hospital. The obituary envelopes were returned to their newspaper libraries. Still, it was an alert. Nothing revived him quicker than work and he was soon in Vienna, playing the Grand Duke Cyril in a two-part 'docu-drama', *Anastasia: The Mystery of Anna*, for American television. Half way through the location filming, a crew member with a long memory reminded him that Lilli had won the Best Actress prize at the Berlin Film Festival almost thirty years before for playing the same character, Anna Anderson, the woman who claimed to be the surviving daughter of Tsar Nicholas. Rex's only response was a groan. Why did people keep opening the door to the past for him?

The idea of a new country which had next to no past appealed to him. He had never been to Australia. He readily agreed when Robert Morley's impresario son, Wilton, suggested a sixteen-week tour there of *Aren't We All?* beginning in October – a good reason, too, for escaping the New York winter, and he looked forward to doing some painting. It was one of those 'good ideas – at the time'. The reality was a nightmare. Never good at press conferences or interviews, Rex found the Australian journalists a sharp-tongued, impertinent tribe who insisted on quizzing him about his propensity to keep on marrying. He was handicapped when he tried to focus on the various occasions this had happened to him by not being able to remember his wives' names. 'How does it feel to be the *doyen* of your profession?' asked a newspaper woman. He may have misheard, but his reply was admirably succinct: 'Fuck off.' He was accounted a great catch in the game of celebrity-baiting, which Australians had brought to a fine art. Even Sinatra had vowed never to return after similar rough handling.

Aren't We All? did not find favour either. Australians were not seduced – though Rex made an exception for Sydney – by an upper-class comedy which condoned a man having two butlers, one for town, the other for the country. No matter that Lonsdale had written it without a thought for egalitarianism in the increasingly republican Antipodes. Rex suffered a fair bit of class-conscious sniping as a result. 'Irksome in the extreme,' was how he summed up the tour to Arthur Barbosa.[5] Only the Aborigines had not struck him as provincial. 'They're a wandering people like me and, like me, they've no way of dealing with alcohol and will lie under a tree until rescued and taken somewhere – which seems pretty perfect. *They* don't have to do a show eight times a week.' Like a child now, Rex delighted in small things. An Aborigine woodcut of a kiwi bird, very primitive, was 'nearly worth the trip'. And how the old days were brought back by his discovery, poking around a junk shop on Sydney waterfront, of a tape of the Mills Brothers singing 'Paper Doll', 'Glow, Worm, Glow', 'Lazy River' and so on. He ordered Arthur a copy for his birthday and hoped that 'old rockin' chair' had not claimed him yet – 'It very nearly got me.'

All told, he would be glad to get back to a civilization which still tolerated a double ration of manservants. Almost defiantly, he decided his next play would be *The Admirable Crichton*, the social comedy in which J. M. Barrie reversed the evolutionary order of Edwardian England and showed the butler to be in every way superior to his aristocratic master.

He returned to London in April 1987 to lay plans for the production, and accompanied Angela Fox and Frances Donaldson to a performance of their father's play *Canaries Sometimes Sing*. To Angela Fox, he seemed to have mellowed. 'It wasn't a very good production of Freddy Lonsdale's play, but Rex didn't savage it, as he might have been expected to do. He never batted an eyelid when Frankie Donaldson said it seemed a poor play. "Well, it's a shame," he said, "it has farcical situations and elements of high comedy, but they didn't know how to knit them together tonight." Someone else in our party said she'd found it a bore – "All that slamming of doors." But Rex wouldn't be drawn. All he said was, "They didn't know how to fit the doors into the comedy." He was still pretty sharp below it all.'

He took them back to the Ritz Hotel, where he and Mercia usually stayed. None of the young waiters appeared to know Rex. They pointed casually to a table. 'Rex rejected it,' Angela Fox recalls, 'and said very quietly, "*That* table – I'll have that one." His days of behaving like a famous actor were over. And yet ... and yet he started with one waiter and, by the time he was into ordering, there were nine standing around us. They knew a star, even if a couple were too young to know the name. Rex handed me the menu. "You read it. I've got one dud eye and another I have to have a cataract operation on." For pudding, he decided he'd like to have some raspberries. There were none, he was told. He repeated his request, again very quietly but insistent and, lo and behold! more raspberries than I'd ever seen appeared.' He signed the bill and, according to Angela Fox, if he left a tip, she did not see him do it. He had had his night at the theatre – in a borrowed Rolls-Royce – and it had been like a treat he was reluctant to say he had not enjoyed. Like many a small boy, he had asked for the unreasonable – the unseasonable raspberries – and been indulged. And now he went off quietly to bed, smacking his lips.

He underwent cataract surgery in New York's Eye and Ear Hospital in September 1987 and made a fair recovery considering he was on the verge of eighty. Many another man, given that the quantity of time left to him was as important as the quality, would have called it a day. Not Rex. There was simply no other way for him to live or, rather, keep alive than work. When he came to London in March, preparing to celebrate his eightieth brithday, Frances Donaldson was amazed to be asked to write a play for him. She was even more astonished when he told her he wanted it to be about J. M. W. Turner, the great English landscape painter and arguably the first Impressionist. The Tate Gallery had been getting ready to open its new Clore Wing devoted to Turner's paintings, and Rex's interest in painting had led him to read the articles appearing in print about the artist's anti-Establishment attitudes and legendary cussedness. He thought it was a role made for him: the creative genius who goes his own way, offends many, but never apologizes, never explains, dies without proper recognition and is then hailed as the greatest innovator of his generation. Lady Donaldson had to disqualify herself. 'I told him I might be the daughter of Freddy Lonsdale, and had written quite a few biographies, but I didn't have it in me to write a stage play.' He looked a bit disappointed, then cheered up. Oh, well, he still had Barrie to do.

The Admirable Crichton, however, was not an ideal choice for Rex. Although he played the Earl of Loam – he was still hankering for a title of his own, but stage titles now seemed the nearest he would get – it was his lordship's butler, Crichton, who was the central character. Edward

Fox had been cast in the part. 'Rex wasn't the star of the show, which displeased him from the start,' he recalls. In any case Rex had a long-standing loathing of 'butler parts', because, as mentioned before, he believed they upstaged the master. Barrie's play proved his instinct right. 'He was quiet at the read-through,' says Fox. He considered that read-throughs were for the other actors. He would decide what to do with his part in his own good time, but things were not so simple. 'Barrie's lines weren't the sort that Rex liked to work with,' says Fox. 'He preferred epigrams and aphorisms. As he spoke his lines, he used to say, "I'm pulling Barrie's balls apart." They gave him few opportunities to do what he wished with them, or even to co-opt a "good line" from a fellow player and insert it into his own dialogue. Barrie's whimsy was proof against Rex's monopolistic practices.'

His infirmities were showing. He looked frail and tottered periodically. On one occasion, a junior member of the cast almost knocked him off his feet as they crowded into the wings for their entrance. Rex turned to the youngster and snapped, 'You cunt!' But it was a push-button response, no feeling behind it. Even with a relatively small part Rex had a hard time remembering his lines. He would come off stage and his dresser would be standing in the wings with his lines written in big letters on an outsize clipboard. Rex would put on his own outsize glasses and the man would shine a torch on the lines while Rex went over them again and again until it was time for him to go back on stage. He paid not the slightest attention to any amused looks he may have attracted. He expected to be deferred to. It seemed to him unthinkable that people were not doing so. On one occasion, at least, he farted loudly and long. The whole house laughed. Rex did not turn a hair ... did not even appear to hear. Aristocrats made up their own rules; polite society might be offended by flatulence, but that was its problem.

He took the same sort of attitude to the rest of the cast where his lines were concerned. Even if he did not get them *quite* right, his fellow players should be able to pick up what he meant and either clarify it for the audience or repair his omissions with lines they had improvised. It did not seem to matter to the audience, he noted, whether he fluffed or not. A few playgoers might even be a wee bit disappointed if he performed impeccably. Needless to say, this lofty attitude, born of anxiety more than arrogance – though that was present too – made for a fair bit of tension on stage some nights, though when Rex was feeling up to the mark (or the text), the very opposite mood prevailed. Just as the elderly *farceur* had done when Rex had appeared in *Charley's Aunt* sixty years before, he would sometimes try to crack up the rest of the cast by 'corpsing' in the middle of their performances.

Either way, he was determined not to give up the theatre, not just yet, not short of physical incapacity, even if it occasionally meant having to have his role played, in part, by proxy.

While he was appearing in *The Admirable Crichton*, Rex was also busy setting up his next play. His determination to keep going had taken on an even more obsessive character, for he looked and moved with painful uncertainty. 'Rex, how are you?' said an acquaintance, running across him in the foyer of the Ritz.[6] 'I'd give anything for a good pee,' he almost whispered, moving into the elevator, barely deigning to see who was speaking to him, hearing the question, but obviously not *wanting* to hear it. 'Mentally, I'm always heading towards the theatre,' he was to write in his posthumously published memoirs.[7] Acting was now the life support machine. Marriage to Mercia kept it in running order.

The play he settled on – the last one he was ever to do – was Somerset Maugham's *The Circle*. It had been first performed in 1921 and now, as one unkind critic was to say, looked older than Rex himself. It seemed a wilful choice: a play that, as written, fully earns ridicule or dismissal by an age that sees it as a museum case of atrophied characters and petrified class-consciousness. But Rex sensed it would play differently. Moreover, a short while before, his own grand-daughter Katherine Harrison, the child of his son Noel, had quite unintentionally caused him some distress by remarking in an interview that, unlike her grand-father, she had ambitions to be a *serious* player. It is quite a common slip to make. Which comedian has not winced when asked why he or she does not do a serious part? Rex, perhaps, was determined to prove that in the last decade of the century, his own 'frivolous' style could still work in a 'trivial' comedy. Yet, in selecting a play like *The Circle* for what was to be his valediction to the stage and a lifetime of acting, he was digging deeper into his past that was perhaps apparent to him.

He consciously modelled the character of Lord Porteus, a once promising politician who wrecked his career by a romantic elopement with his mistress, on the appearance, though certainly not the conduct, of the man so closely linked with the lost paradise of the Villa San Genesio. Max Beerbohm, as mentioned, had even given Rex the name for his villa when they met in Rapallo. Now Rex adopted the walk he remembered went with Max's perambulation through the gardens of the Villino Chiaro, where the Edwardian man of letters had settled after the First World War. Max's immaculate white linen suit now became Rex's costume for part of the play. To his extreme annoyance, though, he could not have it, nor the 1920s style dinner jacket tailored for him in Savile Row. *The Circle* was being presented on Broadway first, then London, and as there were production difficulties which might have involved the theatrical unions, no one wished to increase the risk by having Rex's wardrobe made up overseas. So he was sewn together in rag-trade workshops on the Lower East Side, which did not please him at all. Yet, for all the shortcomings of needle and thread, it was Max the Dandy whom Rex incarnated, the very model of an Edwardian gentleman.

He might also have chosen *The Circle* for its summation of his own philosophy of life, if the hard and sometimes tragic lessons learnt in the course of it can be called a 'philosophy'. Knowing him, it is certain he would have rejected this speculation. He would have pooh-poohed it – possibly used a strong expletive – had anyone suggested that Maugham's drawing-room comedy could be considered relevant to his own adult years. However, the play he chose, out of all the ones available to him from the dramatic canon of, say, Galsworthy, Knoblock or Granville Barker, was about a young couple who repeat the fatal mistakes of their elders by compromising themselves in a romantic escapade. 'It's that very moving and dramatic thing, an echo,' Rex wrote, 'and it raises the whole question, would we do the same again? Would you? What is love? Does love last? Is it worth while breaking up marriages for love?'[8] Eighty-one years old, six times married, once a widower, four times divorced – why, indeed, should Rex *not* be pondering the deeper thoughts behind light comedy?

Again and again in his life he had refused to accept that the dismaying or tragic experience of love was any deterrent to falling in love again. He had continually committed himself to love, marriage, divorce and remarriage, however short-lived each state was, with the inexhaustible drive of a man who never repented of his own mistakes – regretted them, yes, but that was something else, guilt-free and perfunctory – and lamented only the opportunities he had failed to take.

He answered the question that Maugham's play had raised in his own mind – and indeed penned an epitaph for a tumultuous life that was drawing to a close more quickly than he could have foreseen – when he wrote: '... even if you don't think [falling in love] is worth while, you still do it.'[9]

Rehearsals took place in one of New York's most sordid areas, on West 16th Street, and Rex must have rued every one of the steps he had to climb in order to reach the rehearsal hall, for he remembered the exact number, twenty-nine. There was one consolation: he climbed them as Sir Rex Harrison. In July 1989, at Buckingham Palace, while the band played selections from *My Fair Lady*, he had received the first and, as it turned out, only honour his country bestowed on him: a knighthood.

No longer was he 'an ordinary man', as Higgins had put it; but then he never had been.

It had been decided that his co-stars in *The Circle* must be English. No more work for him hearing Americans trying out the accents of his country. Fortunately, Glynis Johns was available to play Rex's wife, Lady Kitty. For the role of the husband she had deserted for Rex, a surprising but imaginative choice was made: Stewart Granger, then seventy-six, the star of many a post-war swashbuckling adventure film. Granger had not been on a stage for forty years and told his agent, when he called, 'I don't do plays.'[10] It was Glynis Johns who told him to stop contemplating his navel and the Pacific from the sundeck of his Malibu home, and take the part. He discovered it was 'a lovely piece for three old fogeys'.[11]

Maybe so, but one of the 'old fogeys' had fangs. 'The producers took me aside and said Rex could be difficult,' Granger recalled.[12] 'They also knew I had a temper, but they asked me to be patient. Rex was a monster, but I controlled myself. [He] didn't like swashbuckling, romantic, Hollywood leading men. The first thing he said to me was, "Why don't you go back to Los Angeles?" He always called me Granger.'

Throughout rehearsals, Rex played his sly game of seeking the advantage by unsettling his co-stars, but he was dealing with tough old material like himself. The upstaging continued, however, when they opened at the campus theatre of Duke University in North Carolina. 'One night,' Granger said, '[Rex] pulled out a handkerchief and let out the biggest sneeze you've ever heard over one of my best jokes. That was it. When we got off stage, while the play was still going on, I put my face in his and said: "If you ever do that again, you motherfucker, I'll break your fucking leg." And I meant it.'[13] He later saw the funny-pathetic side of one old chap well into his seventies, missing half a lung, threatening grievous bodily harm to another in his eighties, who could scarcely see.

Rex's bodily afflictions had continued with an eye haemorrhage which compelled him to break off rehearsing and lie in bed, very still, for five days until the blood layer that had built up was dispersed. He suffered agonizing bouts of toothache. His teeth had always been troublesome. While eating dinner once at '21' he had been an entranced observer of a brand new set of dentures that Noël Coward had just had fitted and was commending to his fellow sufferer by placing them on his bread plate and pointing out their workmanship. 'Why didn't I have all mine out, too?' Rex was heard to lament.[14] He did not fail to note that the peer he played in *The Circle* also had trouble with his 'damn new teeth'. Perhaps empathy was responsible for his sufferings as much as dental decay. But he was in such pain that when they got to Baltimore, Mercia rushed him in to a dentist in a convenient mall for immediate attention.

The effects of the anaesthetic and drops he was taking for the developing glaucoma in his eye had a comic-catastrophic effect on him later in the day. He was unable to go on stage and returned to his hotel where, as it happened, Duncan Wheldon, the London theatrical impresario, had just arrived in order to complete the plans for transferring the play to the West End in the spring of 1990. To his surprise and alarm, he found Rex lying on his bed, and a concerned Mercia calling a doctor in the belief that her husband might have suffered a slight stroke. Wheldon was asked to sit with him until the physician arrived. He engaged Rex in small talk about the play and mentioned Glynis Johns, hoping to himself that Rex would not make difficulties about her coming with the play to London. Rex at first said nothing, then murmured 'Glynis?' Wheldon, a little baffled and fearing the worst, repeated, 'Yes, Rex ... Glynis ... Glynis Johns.' Rex's brow, knitted in thought, relaxed. 'Oh, yes, Glynis ... Such a nice girl. Such a good actress. What's become of Glynis Johns?' His absentmindedness was put down to the combination of dental anaesthetic and eye opiates.[15]

The ages of the three principals in *The Circle* totalled 223 years, but Broadway can be merciless to those whose time is obviously spent. Grey hairs do not draw a more lenient sentence. So one has to accept as genuine the admiration which greeted the play and its stars. Rex was the usual, if now excusable, mass of nerves before opening night and adopted a defensive stance in advance when he replied to an interviewer's tactfully phrased question about his 'approach to the text'. 'It may not be Maugham precisely, but it's near enough. And it's good Harrison.'[16]

Even the most justifiably feared of the critics, John Simon of *New York* magazine, allowed that 'we should all be so endearingly sly, spry and spiffy as Rex Harrison at eighty-one. He still moves like the most debonair of *bon vivants*, flashes that sweet-and-sour smile of his (equally good for seduction and sarcasm) and utters his lines as trippingly as a skilled child skipping rope. Only the walk is a bit slower, but is a leisurely stroll worse than a brisk constitutional?'[17] Howard Kissel in the *Daily News* wrote: 'Rex Harrison has raised crotchetiness to a great art. Much of his role consists of being peevish. He does it, however, with rascally exuberance.'[18] And even Rex's compatriot, the British-born Clive Barnes of the *New York Post*, found only praise for him: 'eyes hooded, voice malicious with honeyed contempt ... splendidly shambling ... proud in disappointment, unbowed by the triviality of his life'.[19] What they and other critics were celebrating was not simply a performance. It was indeed a life and, unlike Lord Porteus's, not a trivial one either. Even in his infirm state, Rex was visibly and audibly the product, perhaps the end product, of a great acting tradition. The critic of the *Village Voice*,

Michael Feingold, who said that in *The Circle* he afforded one 'tiny glimpses of what he must have been like in this sort of play circa 1939', was underestimating the longevity of Rex's artistic pedigree.[20] Nearer the mark was Edith Oliver's comment in the *New Yorker*: '[Rex Harrison] is so at home in his role that one would think he was invented by Maugham.'[21]

Just as Tennyson's mythic hero Ulysses at the end of his voyaging could say:

I will drink
Life to the lees: all times I have enjoy'd
Greatly, have suffer'd greatly, both with those
That loved me, and alone...
I am become a name;
For always roaming with a hungry heart ...
I am a part of all that I have met

so, only months away from his last appearance on the stage, in a role that for all its 'triviality' had brought him touchingly full circle, Rex appeared to those who judged and enjoyed him to have become a part of all that he had played.

Epilogue

36: The Death of an Englishman

'Mercia's got everything arranged for when I die.'¹ Rex's remark to Elizabeth Harris is one of the few references to his own mortality that friends can recall him making. Of course he recognized it was not an option, something one accepted or turned down like a social invitation, always subject to a superior offer, but he left this sort of thing to his wife nowadays, so why not death?

Rex, naturally enough at his age, had to have a lot of check-ups for insurance purposes, yet, until his last years, he always enjoyed excellent health. Apart from the peripheral ailments that come with growing old – toothache, eye troubles, tiredness in his legs – his main organs appeared robust enough. His heart was strong. He had given up smoking thirty-five years earlier and now deplored the addiction among the young. As for drink: a whisky and soda, maybe, though since marrying Mercia he had reverted to the Guinness he used to knock back with Arthur Barbosa and 'the troops' in the back bar of the Adelphi Hotel, Liverpool, sixty years before. In his cups, as in other things, Rex was returning to the past. There was an air of acceptance about his domestic life nowadays. Frances Donaldson reports that he said to Mercia, 'I don't know what I've done to deserve you.' Mercia replied, 'It's taken you fourteen years to find that out?' His son Carey recalls hearing him quote T. S. Eliot in moments when the air was empty of conversation. It was a passage which had given him great trouble to learn when he was preparing the role of Sir Henry Harcourt-Reilly in *The Cocktail Party*, casting a dispassionate eye over the way most marriages are held together by the quiet stoicism of the spirit. Now the words came to his tongue without any difficulty at all:

> They do not repine;
> Are contented with the morning that separates
> And with the evening that brings together
> For casual talk before the fire
> Two people who know they do not understand each other,
> Breeding children whom they do not understand

And who will never understand them ...
It is a good life ...

He had survived so much, Rex said, he would likely go on for ever. But early in the new year, 1990, he began to feel stomach pains that were sharper than any he remembered. He went to his doctor and said to the man, 'I don't want to know the results. Send them to Mercia.'[2]

'His reaction makes one wonder whether he sensed his time was coming,' says Carey. 'Most people agree that Rex wouldn't have wished to know he was dying. He didn't enjoy drawing up wills and having to consider how he should dispose of his worldly goods. Making decisions in everyday life was hard enough, God knows. Having to think further ahead would be agony.' So only Mercia read the report. It told her that Rex was suffering from cancer of the pancreas, and that it was in an advanced state. He could only expect to live a few more months. For the most benign reasons, knowing his impatience with any disease that intruded into his carefully guarded existence, Mercia decided that the only way she could protect her husband was deliberately to mislead him. In fact, she did exactly what Rex is reputed to have done for the dying Kay Kendall. Mercia pretended Rex's indisposition was minor – an inflamed gall bladder – and concealed the real gravity of his condition from him and everyone else, including his immediate family.

Of course he felt tired, she told him, he would have to take more rest and regain his strength before they could do the gall bladder operation. Meantime, he really should consider giving up the idea of going with *The Circle* to London later in the year. 'I'm getting a divorce [if you do it],' she said, 'because I'm sick of being alone all the time in a hotel.'[3] No doubt she *was* tired of impersonal hotel suites however comfortable, room service however punctual and the empty evenings of a 'stage widow' until her husband came home for an absurdly late meal and then bed. But if Rex had gone to London, she would have gone too. She put it brutally in order to allay any anxiety he might feel that she was not telling him the truth about his illness. It was the way Rex had behaved to Kay Kendall, and it appears to have satisfied Rex. In his last interview he said, 'I've reached a stage of life where I would really like a good six months off from having to do anything. And that's only because I'm tired.'[4] But again one cannot be sure that Rex, like Kay, did not guess he was near his end and found it more compelling to play the role he had been allocated, rather than the huge unknown scenario that acknowledgement of imminent death would have imposed on him.

It was a difficult call for Mercia. She had to judge when it was best to have Carey and Noel Harrison arrive in New York without risk of tipping off their father to the fact that death was drawing near. 'Fortunately,' says Carey, 'he didn't keep close enough track of his sons' movements to be totally alarmed or instantly suspicious if we turned up together in New York. Yet he had a lot of cunning beneath his apparent vagueness, so we had to be careful. If you tried to smuggle something past Rex, he was likely to spot it at once. But Mercia played it cleverly.'

Despite his intestinal pains, Rex had been continuing to perform in *The Circle* eight times a week – six evenings, two matinées – as if the process of acting was itself a pain-killer. But by mid-May he had to give up and the play closed in preparation for its London season. A little over a week later, Mercia sent for the boys. 'Noel and I arrived in New York at more or less the same time, but our alibis appeared to hold up,' says Carey. Noel Harrison is not so sure Rex was taken in by the arrival of his two sons. 'As soon as he saw us, he said, "Oh, my God!"' Noel recalls. 'But as he made no other comment, it remained an open question whether it was simply the surprise of seeing the two of us there, for his welcomes were always a bit problematical, or whether he sensed it was a portent of his own demise. We were content to leave it at that.'

Rex had been stuffed full of sedatives and other drugs to reduce his discomfort. He could easily have believed that all he was suffering from was an inflamed gall bladder. For the same reason – that removal to a hospital would certainly have given the game away – it had been decided to nurse him at home. So a rather heavy hospital cot was squeezed into his bedroom. 'There he lay, poor darling,' says Carey, 'in semi-darkness and a fairly dozy state. Sometimes he'd be asleep and quite peaceful-looking, which struck me as totally unnatural. At other times, he'd be his old bullying self, being rude to the nurses and swearing at the man who came to shave him and trim his hair. He'd always reacted against people fussing and fretting over him. To see him in a bad temper was really very reassuring. There were times when I said to myself, "No, he's not dying, he'll see us off first."'

His sons stayed close to Rex's bedside for about a week to ten days. His condition did not alter much. They went out and bought him recordings of the traditional American jazz he had always loved and this music played softly on the tape deck as he lay there. They took it in turns to swap places, one at the head of the bed near Rex, the other at the foot. It was not a large room and now quite cramped by the substitution of the hospital cot for Rex's low, modern divan bed.

'On this afternoon,' says Carey, 'we'd been keeping vigil and Noel whispered to me, "Are you uncomfortable?" I had the hard upright chair. It was maybe time to change over. We had thought Rex was asleep. But he clearly wasn't. For on hearing Noel, his voice suddenly came out of the darkness next to us, like some disturbed spirit, and rasped out, "Yes, I am, *bloody* uncomfortable." I knew then Noel and I were absolutely in the lion's den. It was beyond me not to react, yet I knew that to respond to Rex in a solicitous manner was the surest way of provoking him. But like a sentimental idiot, I said, "Is there anything I can do for you, Dad?" We heard him turn his head. I don't think he could actually make me out, but he recognized my voice, and he said, "I'll tell you what you can do. You can drop dead." They were the last words he ever spoke to me.'

Part of Carey, the filial side of him, was profoundly shocked, but the other part of him, the creative writer, was also elated. It was such a wonderful exit line coming from a man who had always kicked up hell over getting off stage with a good bit of dialogue. Totally in keeping!

'What then happened was that Noel and I shuffled round the cot, squeezed between it and the walls, until we'd changed places. Noel had always been braver than I in tackling Rex. Dad remained suspicious of me throughout life, and I had to do a lot of ducking and covering because of my politics and my writing. But now Noel – foolishly! – started a conversation with Rex, saying things like, "Do you like the music, Dad? It's not too loud, is it?" For his pains, he got roundly sworn at and called "a cunt" – to my enormous relief. As we were bundled out of the room by the nurse at the end of our vigil, I hugged Noel and said, "Thank Christ, I wasn't the only one to be cursed by Dad on his deathbed." The whole episode had been like something out of Ben Jonson's *Volpone*.' Noel recalls that, 'We stood there half laughing, half crying, remembering some of the great rows we'd each of us had with Dad in the past.'

Neither Carey nor Noel was present when the time came for Rex to leave the turbulent life he had shaped for himself over eighty-two years. Noel had had to return home to Los Angeles and Carey had left the bedside for the day. The end came in the early hours of 2 June 1990. Shortly before 5 am, just as the curtained room was letting in light from sunrise over the East River, Rex passed away in unaccustomed silence.

When Mercia telephoned Laurie Evans in London not many minutes later, Rex's long-time agent and old friend (give or take a rowdy parting and chastened return) asked if she wanted him to help with the arrangements. He was told it was all done. 'I gathered his body was already out of the apartment.' What Rex had said was true: Mercia had it all arranged. A short time before, she had been along to the funeral directors' and prepared in detail for the cremation of her husband. Since

New York state law does not permit cremations, it was to take place in New Jersey.

'I'd been very anxious to sit a little with my father after he'd died,' Carey recalls. 'It's my belief that the spirit takes some time to leave the body finally. I hadn't had the chance to do so with my mother, who'd died in Los Angeles. But to my surprise, Rex's body had already been whisked away and I had to chase it, so to speak. Happily, they laid Dad out for me in the mortuary in New York and I was able to spend a little time sitting beside him, although he was in a rather beastly pine coffin and a lady was being laid out behind a curtain nearby, getting a lot of the attention and stealing a small part of what was positively my father's last appearance. He would have hated being upstaged that way.

'I must admit there were other moments of black comedy very appropriate to Rex. I didn't understand the cremation procedure and was particularly anxious to be reassured that I'd be collecting Rex's ashes, and his alone, and not part of the day's takings, so to speak. They very patiently explained the whole process to me and left me in no doubt I'd be getting his remains, unpolluted by anyone else's. But when I went up afterwards to collect them, they couldn't release them to me without a fax from his lawyers. "Yes, Dad," I thought, "you're still in charge." When I did get clearance, the man came into the waiting-room carrying the urn I'd chosen – the least hideous of the ones available – but also holding something behind his back. I thought he looked a bit apologetic. "I'm terribly sorry," he said, "but we've found your father won't all fit into one container" – and he brought forth what he was holding – "so we've put the rest of him in another box." Really rather considerate of them, but so bizarre at the time. So off I went with the two containers and eventually united the contents and made Rex a whole man again.'

Carey took the ashes with him when he returned to London. Mercia had nursed Rex magnificently and made all the other arrangements impeccably. But it was thought she had been slightly unnerved by the death itself, possibly the first time she had had to deal with such an event, and she seemed glad for others to take over.

Carey was surprised and touched to discover that Rex had remembered his son's wishes to have his own ashes scattered near Portofino, for in his will he asked that he end up there too, on that beautiful coast where once he had stood and said, 'I shall build my house here.'

'I felt,' says Carey, 'that in a vague way it was not only a tribute to the precious part of his life he'd spent at San Genesio, but also one of those embarrassed gestures of fatherliness he had made from time to time. Rex was able to show affection for Noel and me, but it took a sideways move for him to do so, if I can speak of death like that. I sought a piece of the coast as virgin and lush as it must have looked when he first visited it.'

He selected a spot on the familiar old walk to San Fruttuoso, where the volcanic rock projected a couple of hundred feet out over the Mediterranean and the air was pungent with the odour of umbrella pines and herbs. On a calm and sunny day in 1991, Carey and Noel and some of their children walked up what had been the old mule track above the Hotel Splendido which Rex had bumped over in many a hair-raising drive home in the Jeep, only now it had been widened and was well enough paved for the small three-wheel delivery trucks which Italians love to whizz up and down it like a mini-motorway. They passsed the Villa San Genesio, now renamed, its terrace rooms glassed in, a helicopter pad adjacent to it, a television monitor camera mounted in a cypress tree picking out any stranger at the gate. On they went, out along the mountain top with the dazzling *pointilliste* sea far below them. And there they mixed Rex's ashes with the native elements of the place and, it was hoped, its sympathetic spirits.

'I kept a little of them back,' says Carey, 'in order to scatter on my mother's grave at Forest Lawn, in California. Aunt Sylvia encouraged me to do so. Likewise, I've retained a pinch for when my time comes and I can join Rex. That's why I brought my children, so they can see it as a sort of family rite and not be dismayed when they do it for me.'

Rather to the surprise of both sons, Rex's will made provision for them. 'I wouldn't call it extravagant, but in view of what he'd threatened to do at various times − that he'd leave it all to wildlife and we wouldn't get a penny − it was pleasantly unexpected. I think I may owe it to Mercia's persuasiveness. Lilli had disinherited me as completely as possible under Swiss law, which was almost totally. The house, the furnishings, the valuables, any money, even her paintings all went to Carlos Thompson. So I was relieved that Dad remembered me. Not just for the sake of the legacy, though that was welcome, but I'd have hated to be disinherited by *both* parents! It alarmed me that Lilli set so little store by blood ties. I felt that in spite of all the ways Rex cut himself off from his family, he wasn't entirely indifferent to the call of the blood. Mercia got him to come to church with her, not always unwillingly. He was never a religious man in any organized sense, but he wasn't deaf to spirituality. There was something deep in Rex that he occasionally heard, if he listened hard enough.'

Rex had died on a Saturday. It was mid-morning, dangerously near the deadline for their Sunday editions, when the English papers received the newsflash. The next day's obituaries were extensive, everything considered, but testified to the utility of facts rather than judgments when space has to be filled against the clock. In the main, they were conventional and noncommittal. 'Stamina', 'irascibility', 'charm' and, again and again, the word 'gentlemanly' were the commonest epithets. The headline writers had some trouble reconciling the two sides of Rex's nature, the randy and the exemplary, the sexy and the gentlemanly, in the same banner. 'Rex – the very model of a rakish English gentleman', said one broadsheet, compounding its difficulties by trying to work in a touch of Gilbert and Sullivan as well.[5] 'His ability to look calm in a crisis contributed to the genial air of a well-bred, cultivated Englishman who was susceptible to girls, but not to social conventions,' was another summing up, true as far as it went, yet almost comical in its reticence.[6] Hugo Vickers managed the task best in a full-page obituary in the *Independent*: 'A man who was guilty of the most ungentlemanly behaviour to colleagues and to ladies in everyday life came to represent on stage the most virtuous and courageous of Englishmen.'[7]

Fellow actors who had known Rex well or worked with him were hard to reach on a weekend or perhaps declined to comment. A profession which customarily smothers its great ones with praise when they are taken from the stage kept unusually mum. Edward Fox was an exception. He spoke of 'the accumulated glory of [Rex's] past career – a field-marshal among thespians weighed down with honours of past campaigns'.[8] And Patrick Garland, reached at Chichester, corrected an error that cropped up lamentably every now and then in the obituaries: 'He was always the acknowledged master of high comedy and not light comedy, as too many imitators falsely imagined.'[9]

Maggie Smith was a principal speaker at a memorial service held on 17 June 1990 in The Little Church Around the Corner in New York. She located in Rex a loyalty – the word probably puzzled many of the fellow performers packing the church, until she explained that 'he was loyal to his authors. I suppose it *is* sad that we never saw him in Molière or Shakespeare – he would have been a superb Tartuffe – and, surely, a marvellously testy Prospero or an arrogant, dangerous Lear. But even more than sixty years in the theatre is not long enough to accomplish *everything*.'[10]

There was a difference of opinion between Rex's widow and her advisers about the form that a thanksgiving service for his life should take in London. Duncan Wheldon offered to let it be held in one of his theatres. 'But I thought Rex would have preferred a service in the traditional English way,' Laurie Evans says. He decided on the parish church of St Martin-in-the-Fields, Trafalgar Square, a place which has given thanks for the life and gifts of many of the greatest names in theatre. Mercia, it seemed to him, was not too impressed. However, Rex's New York lawyer, Harold Schiff, authorized him to go ahead and book the church, and defray the cost by charging it to Rex's account at International Creative Management, where Evans was chairman. He asked Patrick Garland to arrange the service and contributions with Carey Harrison's assistance. 'I thought even Rex would have been proud of what they did.'

The service was held on 12 September 1990. Sir John Mills read from John Donne's *Devotions*; Edward Fox from a Max Beerbohm essay on actors; Carey Harrison from Hugh Whitemore's *Don Quixote* screenplay; Patrick Garland gave the address; and Rex's love of jazz, the music that had literally played him out of this world, was commemorated in a blues number performed by the Guildhall Jazz Quartet. But the moment that hushed the assembly was contributed by the man they were all remembering. Crackling and crisp, performing, as Carey Harrison says, 'the most amazing vocal arabesques', Rex's voice filled the great church from the readings he had recorded of *Much Ado About Nothing* in 1962. This had been Carey's idea. 'It was always my frustration, as a fan of my father's, that he would never tackle Shakespeare on the stage.' Maybe Rex himself would have preferred to 'go out' speaking Shaw; but, here at least, the son got his own way.

Lady Harrison sat in the front row of the pews. Not far from her was Rex's sister. Since the death of her first husband, the Earl of Kilmuir, in 1967, Sylvia had remarried and been widowed again: she was now the Dowager Countess De La Warr, an attractive woman in her mid-eighties, with the slim figure of a girl and an outgoing, welcoming disposition very unlike her brother's. Rex's first wife, Collette, was still living, but in poor health and no longer able to care for herself. After some years at a convent hospital in Chelsea, she was moved to a Plymouth nursing home. She died there in May 1991, well loved by those who had nursed her and who found her, as her sister Jane, Duchess of Somerset, says, 'rather exciting and different'." The Dowager Duchess of Somerset was present at the service. So, too, besides Carey and Noel, were Elizabeth Harris, now running a successful consultancy business; Harold French, in his nineties, but still active in Garrick Club circles; Richard Kershaw; and the Barbosas, Arthur and Isabel, who had come up from their country cottage near Tunbridge Wells to take final leave of the friend who, in his last years, used to sneak off from the Ritz Hotel and become 'Reggie' again, eating cold beef with beer with them in a Kent pub. It was not as large a turn-out as had been hoped for; but then the holiday season had not quite ended and anyway Rex was a man who did not conceal his views about people. An outspoken life is sometimes reflected in what he would have called, without it troubling him, a poor house.

'Afterwards,' says Laurie Evans, 'we had drinks and sandwiches in a nearby restaurant.' Mercia did not seem very involved. It was difficult for her, perhaps, since so many of those present had known Rex far longer than she: a fact she generously acknowledged when answering letters of condolence by intimating to those who had written that it was she who should be offering condolences to *them*. On this occasion, too, the task of organizing things, at which she excelled, had been done by others. She left Laurie Evans in no doubt who, in future, would be taking care of Rex's affairs.

Mercia was the principal beneficiary of Rex's estate. The value of it has not been disclosed, but with the investments made from largely tax-free earnings over many years, plus the recurring royalties from his *My Fair Lady* recordings (film and stage versions), it is undoubtedly substantial. Mercia, already a rich woman in her own right, became a much richer woman.

Those who knew Rex intimately, and even the much larger number aware of how private he tried to keep his life, were taken aback to hear that his widow planned to auction off his personal effects in New York before the end of the year. Some felt it was inappropriate to let strangers get their hands on his personal goods and chattels. But perhaps the tokens and icons of his long career did not have the same sentimental attachment to Mercia as they did for many of his friends who might have welcomed some mementos of him, something Rex's will omitted to provide. Mercia's motives, however, were clearly not inspired by gain. The money raised, after the auctioneers' deductions, would go to funding an acting scholarship at the University of Boston, which had given Rex an honorary degree and would be the custodian of his papers. To get a scholarship in Rex's name, Mercia needed to raise $125,000; if she succeeded, the university would match it.

Thus many of the things he had owned, prized, used, worn, created or lived with over most of sixty years were put up for public bids on 13 December 1990 at the William Doyle Galleries on the Upper East Side. Bidding was brisk, many prices well above estimate. A first edition of *The Cocktail Party*, inscribed to Rex by T. S. Eliot, fetched $1,300; a framed cover of *Time* magazine for 23 July 1956, featuring Rex in *My Fair Lady*, $100; a box lot of Henry Higgins's cardigans, $4,000; a group of Higgins-style tweed hats, $375; Rex's antique make-up chair, $3,100; Rex's make-up box and hairpiece, $125. His bed and bed linen were not sold. The sum total raised was $91,050, subject to the deduction of expenses, taxes, etc. If the owner's charisma was not reflected in the prices to the same exaggerated extent as at other celebrity auctions, it was nevertheless a respectable sum for recessionary times, though it did not appease those who still feel it was an inappropriate way to help commemorate Rex. The shortfall between the sum raised at the auction and that needed to gain matching funds from the university was quickly made up by donations from Rex's friends. Dr Howard Gotlieb, curator of special collections, also disclosed that many small gifts of money were received from hundreds of ordinary members of the public who had enjoyed Rex's performances over the years. The first Rex Harrison Acting Scholarship was being awarded in the fall of 1992.

Like him or hate him, Rex was a phenomenon. As all stars do, he turned his needs into obsessional strengths. Without formal training, he invented a character for himself out of the roles he played and refined it until it was native to him. Only his oldest friends, those who had known him as Reggie, wondered at the existence of Rex Harrison. Angela Fox puts it simply and shrewdly when she says that, running into him again years after their first encounter, she discovered that 'the boy I loved had become the man he admired'.

It was unsurprising that the Professor Higgins image of Rex as the perfect English gentleman should have dominated people's feelings when they heard of his death. Even Rex had not been able to live down the myth, however much the more scandalous side of him tried. Stage and film transmuted his human failings into entertaining virtues the minute the curtain went up on him or he presented his profile – left side, please – to the camera.

Rex's life and career confirmed that one does not need to be greatly loved by one's peers to be a great actor. Just as he left no heir to the tradition of naturalism he represented, so he made sure there would be no usurper while he was alive. Rex dominated, rather than commanded. He would never have made a good man for the troops to serve under; more than likely, they would have shot him under cover of battle. Audiences gave him the love that his own profession often denied him. Because he remained an insecure man – for if one lost the audience, what was left? – he could also be a dangerous one. He had, to borrow Abel Gance's phrase, the charm of dynamite. No one felt safe handling him, and he encouraged that feeling of trepidation. But what compensation his gifts brought those who did not have to suffer them. What skill he employed to release himself from the deep loneliness inside him and project a romantic personality which posed its own teasing enigma. Rex raised the voice of the spoilt child to the pitch of irresistible seductiveness. No one bettered him at playing the arrogant charmer, the forgivable rake, the personable rascal, the self-enraptured heartbreaker who could be wilfully cruel, who deserved punishment and yet constantly got off with a free pardon, not even bound over to be of good conduct.

In real life, of course, the comedy of a man who personified elegance and sexiness could turn – and often did – into the tragedy of a man whose charm was fatal.

The same obsessions that turned Rex into such a great actor were omissions in the tally of things that more prudent people bear in mind. He was almost totally lacking in a sense of consequence. He seldom paused to connect cause with effect. It is not an unusual trait among performers. Often it is what cuts them out of the crowd of people who hang back, restrained by mundane things like responsibility. It contributed largely to Rex's charm. Not to be inhibited, not to give a damn; the recurrent triumph of instinct over experience. He never learned from his mistakes and never lacked the boldness to repeat them. The destructive result was sometimes fatal when the people he took as wives or mistresses did not fit into the make-believe which had formed him. Life was an extension of art. If living it to the full yielded victims, even bodies, that was too bad; but they would vanish in the intervals between the scenes.

The world treated Rex generously. No more than he deserved, he would have thought; and he would have been right. Yet the longer he lived – and even by today's standards of longevity, he lived a considerable time – the more he discovered the world was not nearly as amusing a place as some of the plays or films he did make it out to be. A more timorous man would have adapted, made his peace with things. Not he. He gave the impression on the days when his spirits were arrogantly high, and he had a play on the go, or a new romance he must keep from the wife, that he rather expected better of the world and would do his damnedest to make sure it lived up to his expectations this time ... next time ... the time after that.

'The thing about Rex,' says Elizabeth Harris, 'is that it wasn't a life he had – nothing as simple as that. It was a history.' True, and he lived it with the single-mindedness of an absolute monarch.

Chronology

1908
5 March: born in Huyton, near Liverpool, to William and Edith Harrison, youngest of three children and only son.

1913
September (*circa*): Begins attending local kindergarten mainly for girls.

1915
June (*circa*): Moves with family to Sheffield for father's war work. Attends Birkdale preparatory school as day boy.

1918
June (*circa*): Moves back with family to Sefton Park, Liverpool. Enrolled in Liverpool College.

1922
May: Makes first appearances on public stage in school productions of *A Midsummer Night's Dream* and *The Blue Bird*.

1925
30 May: Attends first rehearsal at Liverpool Repertory Company. Appears in *Thirty Minutes in a Street*.

1926
Takes succession of small parts in (*inter alia*) *Old English, Links, Doctor Knock, Gold, A Kiss for Cinderella*.

1927
Milestones, Abraham Lincoln.
June: Quits Liverpool Repertory Company to try luck in London.
September: Starts touring experience in *Charley's Aunt*.

1928
Potiphar's Wife (tour).

1929
Continues touring in *Alibi, The Chinese Bungalow*.

1930
Makes first appearances in films *The Great Game, The School for Scandal*.
Tours in *A Cup of Kindness*. Appears on West End stage in *Richard III,
Getting George Married*.

1931
Continues West End appearances in *The Ninth Man*.
May to September: Joins Cardiff Repertory Company and appears in
(*inter alia*) *Square Crooks, The Berg, The Joan Danvers, Meet the Wife, Other
Men's Wives, After All*.

1932
Resumes touring in *For the Love of Mike*.

1933
Appears in West End in *Another Language*. Resumes touring in (*inter alia*)
Road House, Mother of Pearl.

1934
January (*circa*): Marries Collette Thomas.
Begins to establish himself on West End stage in *No Way Back, Death at
Court, Divisions, Our Mutual Father, Anthony and Anna*.
Films *Get Your Man, Leave It to Blanche*.

1935
29 January: First son, Noel, born.
Man of Yesterday, The Wicked Flee (tour). Films *All at Sea*. First important
West End role in *Short Story*.
Marriage beginning to break down due to incompatibility of
temperaments.

1936
Charity Begins (one-night performance only).
February: Goes to New York, with Collette, for *Sweet Aloes* (4 March).
9 March: Makes unsuccessful screen test for Warner Bros. in New York.
March/April: Returns to England, appears in *Heroes Don't Care* (10 June).
July: Signs film contract with Alexander Korda.
6 November: Achieves West End stardom in *French Without Tears*.
14 December: First Korda film, *Men Are Not Gods*, premiered.

1937
7 June: *Storm in a Teacup* premiered.
26 December: *School for Husbands* premiered.

1938
19 October: *St Martin's Lane* (US title: *Sidewalks of London*) premiered.
28 October: *The Citadel* premiered.

1939
25 January: *Design for Living.*
14 April: *The Silent Battle* (US title: *Continental Express*) premiered.
14 November: *Over the Moon* premiered.
20 November: Having failed to enlist in army, resumes touring in *Design for Living.* Encounters Lilli Palmer in Birmingham and begins affair.

1940
17 April: *Ten Days in Paris* (US title: *Missing Ten Days*) premiered.
25 July: *Night Train to Munich* (US title: *Night Train*) premiered.
June/July: Joins Chelsea Home Guard for short and unsatisfying spell of duty.
July: Accepts role in *Major Barbara.*
Autumn: Separated from first wife, Collette Thomas, now serving with Red Cross, sets up home with Lilli Palmer.

1941
27 March: *No Time for Comedy.*
7 April: *Major Barbara* premiered.

1942
January: Enlists in Royal Air Force and serves as flying control liaison officer at numerous air bases in south-east England.
Summer: Divorced from Collette Thomas.

1943
25 January: Marries Lilli Palmer.

1944
19 February: Second son, Carey, born.
March: Released from RAF duties to return to entertainment sphere.
Films *Blithe Spirit* and *I Live in Grosvenor Square.*

1945
5 April: *Blithe Spirit* premiered.
May: Begins filming *The Rake's Progress.*
19 July: *I Live in Grosvenor Square* (US title: *A Yank in London*) premiered.
Summer: Tours liberated Europe with Anna Neagle in revival of *French Without Tears.*

November: Leaves with Lilli Palmer for United States to take up Hollywood contract with Twentieth Century–Fox.

7 December: *The Rake's Progress* (US title: *Notorious Gentleman*) premiered.

1946
20 June: *Anna and the King of Siam* premiered.

1947
26 June: *The Ghost and Mrs Muir* premiered.

Summer: Begins affair with Carole Landis.

September: Returns to England to make *Escape* and be near Carole Landis who is filming there.

20 September: *The Foxes of Harrow* premiered.

1948
January: Returns to Hollywood to begin filming *Unfaithfully Yours* and resume affair with Carole Landis.

28 March: *Escape* has London premiere.

June/July: Following press disclosure of Landis affair, Lilli Palmer leaves for New York, RH continues to see mistress.

4/5 July: Carole Landis takes fatal overdose.

5–9 July: Suffers 'trial by press' for presumed role in Landis suicide and is called to testify at inquest. Lilli Palmer returns to stand by him. Shortly afterwards, both leave Hollywood for Europe, prior to RH appearing in *Anne of the Thousand Days* on Broadway.

Summer: Recovers from Landis suicide in Paris and, while Lilli films in Marseilles, begins affair with Martine Carol before returning to United States.

6 November: *Unfaithfully Yours* premiered to disastrous box-office.

8 December: Achieves tremendous success in *Anne of the Thousand Days*.

1949
July: Holidays with Lilli at Santa Margherita, Italy, visists Portofino for first time and decides to build villa on mountainside there.

1950
3 May: Returns to the West End in *The Cocktail Party*.

14 November: Stars with Lilli in *Bell, Book and Candle* on Broadway.

1951
9 February: *The Long Dark Hall* premiered.

September: Returns to Hollywood with Lilli to film *The Four-Poster*.

1952
13 February: Opens in *Venus Observed* on Broadway.

15 October: *The Four-Poster* premiered.

9 November: TV film of *Trial of Anne Boleyn* transmitted.

1953
15 January: *The Love of Four Colonels* followed by a tour in US and Canada.

November: Filming *King Richard and the Crusaders*.

1954
Spring: Filming *The Constant Husband* in England, meets Kay Kendall and begins affair.

Summer: Surprised by Kay Kendall's turning up at Portofino. Discloses affair to Lilli and leaves with Kay for brief holiday. Lilli Palmer leaves for London where she and Rex are to appear in English production of *Bell, Book and Candle*.

6 August: *King Richard and the Crusaders* premiered.

5 October: Opens in West End in *Bell, Book and Candle* with Lilli Palmer. Continues romance with Kay Kendall. Separates from Lilli, but both are compelled by contract to continue playing together.

1955
January: Approached by Lerner and Loewe to commit to appearing in *My Fair Lady* (then called *Lady Liza*). Hesitates, but finally agrees. Prepares himself for role during rest of year.

22 April: *The Constant Husband* premiered.

1956
15 March: Achieves success of his career in *My Fair Lady* on Broadway.

Late December: Told by physician about Kay Kendall's mortal illness. Sends for Lilli.

1957
January: Agrees with Lilli to get divorce and marry Kay. Lilli agrees to remarry him upon Kay's death.

4 February: Lilli Palmer files for Mexican divorce.

23 June: Marries Kay Kendall.

1958
Winter: Filming *The Reluctant Debutante* with Kay Kendall in Paris, simultaneously concealing her illness from her.

30 April: Repeats *My Fair Lady* triumph on London stage.

14 August: *The Reluctant Debutante* premiered in New York.

10 December: Kay Kendall opens in *The Bright One*, directed by Rex, quickly closes.

1959
Summer: Sustains Kay Kendall in Portofino following collapse in her health after filming *Once More, With Feeling*.
6 September: Kay Kendall dies of leukemia in London, buried 9 September in Hampstead. Lilli refuses to dissolve her own marriage to remarry Rex.
8 December: Opens on Broadway in *The Fighting Cock*.

1960
April: Films *Midnight Lace* in Hollywood and starts affair with Tammy Grimes to whom he makes unsuccessful marriage proposal.
13 October: Opens in *Platonov* in London opposite Rachel Roberts and begins affair with her.

1961
February: Accompanied by Rachel, arrives in Madrid to film *The Happy Thieves* with Rita Hayworth.
July: Agrees to appear in *August for the People*, then accepts offer to star in *Cleopatra* from Twentieth Century–Fox.
4 September: *August for the People* and quickly closes on Rex's departure for Rome.
20 December: *The Happy Thieves* premiered in Chicago.

1962
Winter: Filming *Cleopatra* in Rome.
21 March: Marries Rachel Roberts in Genoa.
25 October: Wins role in film of *My Fair Lady*.

1963
February: Re-shooting *Cleopatra* battle scenes in Spain.
May: Begins filming *My Fair Lady*.
12 June: *Cleopatra* premiered.
Summer–Winter: Marriage difficulties begin to show incompatibilities.

1964
April: Filming *The Yellow Rolls-Royce* in London.
June: Filming *The Agony and the Ecstasy* in Rome.
22 October: *My Fair Lady* premiered.
31 December: *The Yellow Rolls-Royce* premiered.

1965
5 April: Wins 'Best Actor' Academy Award for role of Professor Higgins in *My Fair Lady*.
May: Serves on jury of Cannes Film Festival.
July: Attends premiere of *My Fair Lady* in Moscow.

September: Filming *The Honey Pot* in Rome. Marital relationship with Rachel worsens after her second suicide attempt.
7 October: *The Agony and the Ecstasy* premiered.

1966
June: Filming *Doctor Dolittle*. Marriage now in dire straits owing to Rachel's drinking, Rex's absorption in work, etc.

1967
21 March: *The Honey Pot* premiered in London.
June: Filming *A Flea in Her Ear* in Paris with Rachel in last attempt to save marriage.
12 December: *Doctor Dolittle* premiered in London.

1968
September: Filming *Staircase* in Paris with Richard Burton.

1969
20 August: *Staircase* premiered in New York.
5 November: Opens in West End in disastrous production of *The Lionel Touch*.
19 December: Announces separation from Rachel Roberts who attempts suicide.

1970
January: Leaves for vacation abroad with Elizabeth Harris. Spends most of the year travelling and seeking new projects.

1971
20 February: Divorced from Rachel Roberts.
March: Films *Platonov* for BBC TV.
26 August: Marries Elizabeth Harris. Marriage soon under strain from new-found family responsibilities.

1972
May: Filming *The Adventures of Don Quixote* in Spain despite cracked ribs after fall.

1973
7 January: *The Adventures of Don Quixote* transmitted on BBC TV.
18 March: Opens in *The Emperor Henry IV* on Broadway.
Summer: Acquires additional home, Villa Beauchamp, Cap Ferrat, France.
November: Given honorary degree of Doctor of Humane Letters, University of Boston.

1974
20 February: *The Emperor Henry IV* on West End stage.
Summer: Quits Villa San Genesio, Portofino, following local antagonism.
Settles in new home in south of France. Relations with Elizabeth Harris
deteriorating.
10 December: Opens on Broadway in *In Praise of Love.*

1975
July: Breakdown of marriage and separation.
December: Serves on jury of Tehran Film Festival.
16 December: Divorced from Elizabeth Harris.

1976
May: Filming *The Prince and the Pauper.*
3 August: Opens in *Monsieur Perrichon's Travels* at Chichester.
October: Filming *The Fifth Musketeer* in Vienna.

1977
24 February: Opens in *Caesar and Cleopatra* on Broadway.
Spring: Frequently seen in the company of Mercia Tinker, Anglo-Asian
acquaintance made in south of France.
2 June: *The Prince and the Pauper* premiered in London.
30 August: Gives readings from Shaw in *Our Theatre in the Nineties* at
Edinburgh Film Festival.
September: Filming *Shalimar* in India, accompanied by Mercia Tinker.
16 December: Appears in *The Devil's Disciple* in Los Angeles.

1978
Spring: Filming *Ashanti* in Israel.
8 December: Opens in *The Kingfisher* on Broadway with Claudette
Colbert.
17 December: Marries Mercia Tinker in New York.
December: *Shalimar* premiered in India.

1979
Spring/Summer: Filming *A Time to Die* in Amsterdam.
April: *Ashanti* on general release in United States.
September: *The Fifth Musketeer* on general release in United States.

1980
July: Begins rehearsals in New York for new production of *My Fair Lady.*
29 October: Reunion with ex-wife Rachel Roberts in San Francisco
where he is playing in *My Fair Lady.*
26 November: Rachel Roberts takes fatal overdose in Los Angeles on
eve of Rex's opening in *My Fair Lady.*

1981
18 August: Opens in *My Fair Lady* on Broadway.

1982
Summer: Filming *The Kingfisher* in England for Anglia Television.
23 December: *The Kingfisher* transmitted on ITV.

1983
10 March: Opens in *Heartbreak House* in West End.
September (*circa*): *A Time to Die* on general release in United States.
7 December: Opens in *Heartbreak House* in New York.

1984
20 June: Opens in *Aren't We All?* in West End.

1985
29 April: Opens in *Aren't We All?* on Broadway and later tours.
Winter: Health problems – cataracts, etc. – accumulating.

1986
28 January: Lilli Palmer dies of cancer in Los Angeles.

1987
Year spent in treatment of cataracts, preparations for new play.

1988
8 July: Opens in *The Admirable Crichton* in West End.

1989
25 July: Knighted by the Queen at Buckingham Palace.
20 November: Opens in *The Circle* on Broadway.

1990
11 May: Quits play because of illness, whose terminal nature is compassionately concealed from him by Mercia.
2 June: Dies in New York, aged 82. Ashes later scattered by sons Noel and Carey over the sea near Portofino.

Source Notes

1: The Property of a Gentleman

1 'Garbo sells ...' New York *Post*, 23 November 1990.
2 *Time*, 22 April 1985.
3 Patrick Garland to author, 3 January 1992.
4 'It annoys me ...' RH to Jon Bradshaw, *Esquire*, July 1972.
5 'Among the greatest bits ...' Robert Morley to author, 31 August 1990.
6 'Is it very hard ...' *A Damned Serious Business* by Rex Harrison (Bantam, 1989), p. 239.
7 'As a civilian ...' *Ibid.*, p. 223.

2: Applause, Please

1 'Reggie dear ...' Sylvia, Countess De La Warr DBE, interviewed Liphook, 19 July, 20 September 1991.
2 'Terror ...' RH to Richard Kershaw, BBC TV interview out-takes, Portofino, 14, 30 September 1974.
3 'I've always liked ...' RH to author, Tehran, 4 December 1975.
4 'I play lords ...' *Ibid.*
5 'Alone in my imagination ...' RH to Kershaw.
6 'My first romantic urge ...' *Rex* by Rex Harrison (Macmillan, 1974), p. 11.
7 'For some reason ...' RH to Kershaw.
8 'As so often happens ...' RH to author, Tehran, 4 December 1975.
9 'JOHNS together ...' Poem, December 1917, by unnamed Birkdale prep. school teacher, communicated to author by Edward Hutchins, former member of staff.
10 'Like having treacle ...' RH to author, London, July 1982.
11 'A hugely and hideously ...' RH to Philip Key, Liverpool *Post*, 9 February 1983.
12 'I suppose the only real ...' RH to Kershaw.
13 'A sort of basin ...' *Ibid.*

3: 'That Noisy Harrison Boy'

1 'Natty suit ...' RH to Kershaw, *op. cit.*
2 'Took a small curtain call ...' *Rex*, p. 19.
3 'Please attend ...' *Ibid.*, p. 19. (RH gets the date wrong in his account, citing 1924, instead of 1925).
4 'Degraded and debased ...' RH to Kershaw, *op. cit.*
5 'What he thought ...' *Rex*, p. 20.
6 'The most fearful shock ...' RH to Kershaw, *op. cit.*
7 'The loincloth ...' Twentieth Century-Fox press release, 1945.
8 '"Harrison, are you ..."' RH to Kershaw, *op. cit.*
9 'There was still ...' Arthur Barbosa interviewed Tunbridge Wells, 22 February 1991.
10 'Putting a lowering ...' *Life Is a Four-Letter Word* by Nicholas Monsarrat (Cassell, 1966), p. 4.
11 'A ferocious draught ...' *Ibid.*, p. 7.
12 'My own lovely ...' RH to Kershaw, *op. cit.*
13 'Since we were here ...' Monsarrat, *op. cit.*, p. 389.
14 'Perhaps six ...' *Rex*, p. 25.
15 It was the dawn ...' *Gerald* by Daphne du Maurier
16 'The development ...' *The Actor-Managers* by Frances Donaldson (Weidenfeld, 1970), p. 175.
17 'A lot of people ...' Edith Evans quoted by Frances Donaldson, *ibid.*, p. 176.
18 '[It] was personal ...' *ibid.*, p. 175.
19 'Personality players ...' *A Damned Serious Business*, p. 19.

4: Chasing Girls and Jobs

1 'I do beg you ...' RH to Kershaw, *op. cit.*
2 'None of them ...' *Rex*, p. 22.
3 'High comedy is a form ...' *A Damned Serious Business*, p. 27.
4 'Great fun ...' RH to Kershaw, *op. cit.*
5 'I still had no ...' RH to author, Tehran, 4 December 1975.
6 'He told me ...' Sir Anthony Havelock-Allan Bt, interviewed London, 25 July 1991.
7 'A complete phoney ...' Angela Fox, interviewed London, 18 October 1991.
8 'Christine ...' *Slightly Foxed* by Angela Fox (Fontana, 1987), p. 114.
9 'Chelly brossom accent ...' *Rex*, p. 37.
10 'Rex learned ...' Robert Morley, interviewed Wargrave, 31 August 1990.
11 'A damned serious ...' RH to author, Tehran, 5 December 1975.
12 'As unintelligible ...' *Ibid.*
13 'Make a gesture ...' *Ibid.*

14 'I'd vaguely heard . . .' Robert Flemyng, interviewed London, 9 January 1991.
15 'He was a great one . . .' Tom Macaulay quoted in *Rex Harrison* by Roy Moseley with Philip and Martin Masheter (New English Library, 1987), p. 24.

5: Breakdown on Broadway

1 'Can't you get a job? . . .' Private information.
2 'Glib impudence . . .' *The Stage* quoted by Moseley *et al.*, *op. cit.*, p. 27.
3 'Amid the petrol . . .' *Rex*, p. 40.
4 'A touch of madness . . .' *A Damned Serious Business*, p. 41.
5 'Terrible American accent . . .' *Ibid.*, p. 51.
6 'A rather bad actor . . .' Private information.
7 'The American epilogue . . .' Brooks Atkinson, the *New York Times*, 5 March 1936.
8 'The play could not . . .' Arthur Pollock, Brooklyn *Daily Eagle*, 5 March 1936.
9 'He has the most . . .' Brooks Atkinson, *op. cit.*
10 'A newcomer . . .' Jack Anderson, New York *Evening Journal*, 5 March 1936.
11 'The ebullient . . .' John Mason Brown, New York *Evening Post*, 5 March 1936.
12 'The inestimable . . .' Ardis Smith, New York *World Telegram*, 5 March 1936.
13 'And now a word . . .' Robert Coleman, New York *Daily Mirror*, 5 March 1936.
14 'Running around . . .' Quoted correspondence from Stuart Aarons to Jacob Wilk, Warner Bros, Burbank, 3 March 1936.
15 'Was weazled out . . .' *Ibid.*
16 'One dollar . . .' Contact (undated, but signed by RH) between Warner Bros and RH.
17 'She returned . . .' Private information.
18 'Working in a hat shop . . .' *Rex*, p. 47.
19 'Imagine poking . . .' *Ibid.*, p. 48.
20 'The great discovery . . .' *Freddy Lonsdale* by Frances Donaldson (Heinemann, 1958), p. 128.
21 'Rex Harrison proves . . .' *Theatre World* quoted by Moseley *et al.*, *op. cit.*, p. 31.

6: Breakthrough in London

1 'I gabbled . . .' RH to Freda Bruce Lockhart, *Film Weekly*, 25 December 1937.
2 'I took Kay Hammond . . .' Harold French, interviewed London, 12 August 1990.

3 'Trevor Howard "dried" ...' *I Never Thought I Could* by Harold French (Secker & Warburg, 1973), p. 75.

4 'Roland Culver ...' *Ibid*, p. 76.

5 'In a hundred years ...' *French Without Tears* by Terence Rattigan. *Collected Plays* (Hamish Hamilton, 1953) p. 50.

6 'You can't judge women ...' *Ibid.*, p. 17.

7 'You'd like anything ...' *Ibid.*, p. 61.

8 'First of all ...' *Ibid.*, p. 64.

9 'It isn't funny ...' *Ibid.*, p. 69.

10 'And with Vivien ...' *Rex*, p. 52.

11 'Not only booted ...' Frank S.Nugent, *New York Times*, 7 February 1939.

12 'Then it was like ...' Diana Churchill, interviewed London, 27 September 1991.

13 'Trying to do ...' RH to Freda Bruce Lockhart, *op. cit.*

14 '"Rex, you worry ..."' RH to author, Tehran, 5 December 1975.

15 'I used to hear them ...' Noel Harrison interviewed in Los Angeles, 4 May 1992.

7: Casualty of War

1 'Not, in my opinion ...' *Rex*, p. 59.

2 'Rex Harrison is outstandingly ...' *Monthly Film Bulletin*, April 1939, pp. 67–9.

3 'We don't care ...' Theodore Strauss, *New York Times*, 21 April 1941.

4 'Oh, *mon brave* ...' RH quoted in Liverpool *Post*, 3 November 1978.

5 'Convinced this was the end ...' RH to author, Tehran, 3 December 1975.

6 'Some ass ...' *Ibid.*

7 'Rex, where have ...' *Ibid.*

8 'Kissing my old self ...' *Ibid.*

8: Assignations and Alarms

1 'He was that rare ...' *Change Lobsters and Dance* by Lilli Palmer (Macmillan, New York, 1975), p. 110.

2 'This unchallengeable man ...' *Ibid.*, p. 19.

3 'Serious, sometimes threatening ...' *Ibid.*, p. 19.

4 'You'll need a ...' *Ibid.*, p. 56.

5 'Oh, I wouldn't have ...' *Ibid.*, p. 6.

6 'Work on every single ...' *Ibid.*, p. 101.

7 'War as a *force majeure* ...' *Ibid.*, p. 101.

8 'Everything one did ...' *Ibid.*, p. 101.

9 'Self-invited actor fellow ...' RH to Arthur Barbosa.

10 'If she'd been free ...' Joan Buckmaster, interviewed Wargrave, 31 August 1990.
11 'Rex just loved ...' Sidney Gilliat, interviewed London, 25 October 1990.
12 'I really did enjoy ...' RH to author, Tehran, 3 December 1975.
13 'Rex has the face ...' Robert Morley to author.
14 '[Rex Harrison] thinks ...' Shaw to Pascal, quoted in *The Disciple and His Devil* by Valerie Pascal (Michael Joseph, 1971), p. 96.
15 'Fumbled and mumbled ...' *Rex*, p. 71.
16 'But he may never ...' *Ibid.*, p. 71.
17 'Oh, the endless ...' Ronald Neame, interviewed London, 28 April 1991.

9: Rex's War

1 'Rex was furious ...' Elisabeth Welch interviewed London, 25 October 1990.
2 'It was all slightly ...' RH to Kershaw.
3 'Long-limbed and magnetic ...' Ivor Brown, *Observer*, 30 March 1941.
4 'To call [Major Barbara] ...' Bosley Crowther, *New York Times*, 15 May 1941.
5 'I'd rather not be, sir ...' *A Damned Serious Business*, p. 74.
6 'The police said ...' 18 February 1942, unsourced news clipping.
7 'A descendant of ...' *Lilliput*, January 1942.
8 'My beautiful tweeds ...' *Ibid.*
9 'She quite expected ...' *Ibid.*
10 'Rather pompous ...' *Ibid.*
11 'You don't think ...' Private source to author.
12 'Er, I'm in rather ...' *Ibid.*
13 'The thing costs ...' *Ibid.*
14 'Rex sat down ...' Lilli Palmer, *op. cit.*, p. 118.

10: Wraiths and Rakes

1 'That doesn't sound ...' David Lean quoted in *David Lean* by Steven Silverman (Deutsch, 1989), p. 55.
2 'My dear you've just ...' *Ibid.*, p. 56.
3 'Just a fraction fatter ...' RH to author, Tehran, 3 December 1975.
4 'By no means ...' Sidney Gilliat in letter to author, 1 October 1991.
5 'It gave me an odd feeling ...' *Bugles and a Tiger* by John Masters (Michael Joseph, 1956) p. 55.
6 'Putting a generation ...' C. A. Lejeune, *Observer*, 9 December 1945.
7 'One of those irresistibly ...' James Agate, *Tatler*, 12 December 1945.
8 'Well, anyone can see ...' Sidney Gilliat to author.
9 'But she was a calculator ...' Private source to author.
10 'A very determined ...' Private source to author.

11 'What about our deal? ...' *Twenty-Five Thousand Sunsets* by Herbert Wilcox (Bodley Head, 1967), p. 65.

11: **Royal Bloomers**

1 'As soon as Rex ...' Dame Anna Neagle to author, September 1983.
2 'If I may say so ...' *Not Quite a Gentleman* by Roland Culver (Kimber, 1979), p. 107.
3 'They were courting me ...' RH to author, Tehran, 3 December 1975.
4 'It was a very big decision ...' *Ibid.*
5 'If anyone ever suggests ...' RH quoted by Barbosa to author.
6 'Gee, you're just ...' *Rex*, p. 86.
7 'In importing Harrison ...' Pete Martin, *Saturday Evening Post*, 15 May 1948.
8 'If you're a bobby-soxer ...' *Photoplay*, March 1946.
9 'Seduced by its ease ...' *Rex*, p. 85.
10 '... as if he had been set down ...' Pete Martin, *op. cit.*
11 'Miss Palmer ...' Louella Parsons, Los Angeles *Examiner*, 9 March 1946.
12 'Relax ...' Lilli Palmer, *op. cit.*, p. 131.
13 'Staccato and high-pitched ...' *Ibid.*, p. 132.
14 'He looked at me ...' *Photoplay*, March 1946.
15 'Handed him ...' Hedda Hopper, Los Angeles *Times*, 3 March 1946.
16 'What in the world ...' Lilli Palmer, *op. cit.*, p. 133.
17 'Even when he stoops ...' *New Yorker*, 24 June 1946.
18 'A Fisherman ...' Thomas M.Pryor, *New York Times*, 23 June 1946.
19 'Intellectual insularity ...' *Ibid.*
20 'With his crisp accent ...' Hedda Hopper, Los Angeles *Times*, 3 March 1946.
21 'Taxes ...' RH to Thomas M. Pryor, *New York Times*, 23 June 1946.
22 'My Stradivarius ...' Joseph L. Mankiewicz quoted in *People Will Talk* by Kenneth L. Geist (Scribner's, 1978), p. 133.
23 'English actors ...' Joseph L. Mankiewicz interviewed Bedford, NY., 25 April 1991.
24 'A bit of ectoplasm ...' *Time*, 23 June 1947.
25 'Beating about ...' RH to Hedda Hopper, Los Angeles *Times*, 20 May 1947.
26 'Impatient and desperate ...' *Rex*, p. 94.

12: **The Fatal Affair**

1 'When you've got a Scotch ...' RH quoted by Lilli Palmer, *op. cit.*, p. 159.
2 'Mustn't be stuffy ... *Ibid.*, p. 160.
3 'Women ... always leave ...' RH quoted in *Rita Hayworth: A Memoir* by James Hill (Simon & Schuster, 1973), p. 223.
4 'If Cagney ...' *Rex*, p. 93.

5 'Very simple ...' RH quoted in *Photoplay*, September 1947.

6 'It was not passion ...' Private source to author.

7 'Dull ... pompous ...' Bosley Crowther, *New York Times*, 25 September 1947.

8 'Illegitimate son ...' C. A. Lejeune, *Observer*, 17 October 1948.

9 'These two endless ...' RH quoted by Barbosa to author.

10 'Louella feels ...' Bebe Daniels, script of *The Louella Parsons Show*, broadcast 20 June 1948. Transcript in University of Southern California Cinema-TV Library.

11 'Extremely interesting ...' RH quoted by Barbosa to author.

13: Unfaithfully Hers

1 'Try to give us ...' RH quoted by Barbosa to author.

2 'Grimness and a sense ...' *The Times*, 29 February 1948.

3 'Part better ...' RH material, University of Southern California archives.

4 'Which actors ...' RH material, *ibid.*, unsourced reference.

5 'I don't say ...' *Rex*, p. 101.

6 'She was absolutely ...' Roy Moseley *et al.*, *op. cit.*, p. 105.

7 'His sound stage ...' Los Angeles *Times*, 23 March 1948.

8 'Carole Landis's ...' Walter Winchell quoted by Schmidlapp, Los Angeles *Examiner*, 8 July 1948.

9 'Had been screwing ...' RH quoted by Barbosa to author.

10 'Hair-raising ...' *Ibid.*

11 'What is called ...' *Ibid.*

12 'What do I do? ...' Private source to author.

13 'Booked continuously ...' Private source to author.

14 'In a bugger's muddle ...' RH quoted by Barbosa to author.

15 'Probably with the odd ...' *Ibid.*

16 'Lilli and I ...' RH quoted by Barbosa to author.

17 'She's flat ...' RH quoted by Barbosa to author.

18 'It's impossible ...' Carole Landis quoted by Barbosa to author.

19 'I read this play ...' *Rex*, p. 104.

20 'A marvellous change ...' *Ibid.*

21 'Marry a rich man ...' Los Angeles *Examiner*, 7 July 1948.

22 'Well ... I think she's dead ...' RH quoted Los Angeles *Examiner*, 6 July 1948.

14: A Hollywood Death

1 'Oh, no, my darling ...' Los Angeles *Examiner*, 6 July 1948.

2 'Dearest Mommie ...' *Ibid.*

3 'I felt her pulse ...' Los Angeles *Examiner*, 7 July 1948.

4 'By looking from A to Z . . .' *Rex*, p. 206.

5 'The idea hadn't . . .' Los Angeles *Examiner*, 6 July 1948.

6 'Someone calling . . .' *Ibid.*

7 'A male voice . . .' *Ibid.*

8 'I asked the police . . .' *Ibid.*

9 'Something terrible . . .' RH quoted by Emlyn Williams to author, *circa* December 1983.

10 'I love Rex . . .' Los Angeles *Examiner*, 7 July 1948.

11 'I had dinner . . .' *Ibid.*, 6 July 1948.

12 'They say the shocking . . .' Dorothy Manners, *Ibid.*

13 'And she had been . . .' *Ibid.*

14 'As one of the best scouts . . .' *Ibid.*

15 'Where's my tea? . . .' Private source to author.

16 'As well as feeling . . .' Carey Harrison, interviewed Dublin, 2 November 1991.

17 'We talked . . .' Los Angeles *Examiner*, 7 July 1948.

18 'Is that *all* . . .' *Ibid.*

19 'Did Carole Landis . . .' *Ibid.*, 8 July 1948.

20 'After the police . . .' *Ibid.*

21 'Does Harrison know . . .' *Ibid.*

22 'She [Mrs Wasson] didn't know . . .' *Ibid.*, 9 July 1948.

23 '[He looked] pale . . .' *Ibid.*

24 'All the questions . . .' *Ibid.*

25 'Taking that deposition . . .' *Ibid.*

26 '[He] was nervous . . .' *Ibid.*

27 'I think she'd have . . .' *Ibid.*

28 'I don't think . . .' *Ibid.*

29 'Sorry, I can't . . .' *Ibid.*

30 'Harrison nimbly stepped . . .' *Ibid.*

31 'It contained . . .' Lilli Palmer, *op. cit.*, pp 179–80.

32 'A former Los Angeles policeman . . .' Private source to author.

15: The Comeback

1 'I think the change . . .' Roland Culver, *op. cit.*, p. 00?

2 'Impending separation . . .' Los Angeles *Examiner*, 13 August 1948.

3 'Making allowance . . .' *Daily Express*, 28 July 1948.

4 'Gloriously alien . . .' RH to author, Tehran, 3 December 1975.

5 'I remember Rex asking me . . .' David Tomlinson, interviewed London, 29 April 1992.

6 'It's going to be tough . . .' RH quoted by Barbosa to author.

7 'As more a little boy ...' *Sun and Shadow* by Jean-Pierre Aumont (Norton, 1976), p. 174.

8 'I don't believe ...' Louella Parsons, Los Angeles *Examiner*, 22 October, 1948.

9 'There is only ...' RH quoted by Barbosa to author.

10 'So life's an absolute hell ...' *Ibid.*

11 'They're all ...' RH quoted by Barbosa to author.

12 'God help me ...' *Ibid.*

13 'God is wonderful ...' *Ibid.*

14 'In terms of theatre ...' Terence Rattigan to author, *circa* March 1963.

15 'Interesting ...' *Rex*, p. 124.

16 'Sitting for several hours ...' *Ibid.*, p. 123.

17 'If we were all judged ...' *The Cocktail Party* by T. S. Eliot (Faber, 1950), p. 165.

16: Up at the Villa, Down in the City

1 'Man-of-the-world ...' Harold Hobson, *Sunday Times*, 16 May 1950.

2 'Has formed certain ...' *Daily Telegraph*, 4 May 1950.

3 '[Eliot] points up ...' *Rex*, p. 123.

4 'Very abstract ...' RH to Henry Hewes, *Saturday Review*, 10 May 1952.

5 'Smart ...' T. C. Worsley, *New Statesman*, 12 May 1950.

6 'And avoid ...' T. S. Eliot in letter to E.Martin Browne quoted in *The Making of T. S. Eliot's Plays* by E. Martin Browne (Cambridge University Press, 1969), p. 248.

7 'Brings me ...' *Ibid.*, p. 249.

8 'It's going to get ...' *A Private View* by Irene Mayer Selznick (Weidenfeld, 1983), p. 330.

9 '[He] groped around ...' *Ibid.*, p. 331.

10 'Ticked over ...' *Ibid.*, p. 331.

11 'The junior Lunts ...' *Variety*, 21 November 1950.

12 'Such meat-and-potatoes ...' John Chapman, *Daily News*, 15 November 1950.

13 'What in God's name ...' Lilli Palmer, *op. cit.*, p. 137.

14 'Magnificent ...' RH to author, Tehran, 3 December 1975.

15 'A kind of negligent ...' *Freddy Lonsdale* by Frances Donaldson, p. xxii.

16 '[He[knew that ...' *Ibid.*, p. 227.

17 'The disciplined ...' *Ibid.*, p. 250.

18 'Place the four fingers ...' *Ibid.*, p. xv.

19 'I don't see ...' Hedda Hopper, Los Angeles *Times*, 21 May 1951.

20 'To everyone's amazement ...' Jones Harris interviewed London, 22 October 1990.

21 'One adjusts ...' Lilli Palmer, *op. cit.*, p. 248.

22 'I suppose it's too late ...' RH to Henry Hewes, *Saturday Review*, 10 May 1952.
23 'I played him ...' *Ibid.*
24 'It's always ...' *Ibid.*
25 'The language course ...' RH quoted by Barbosa to author.
26 'The little twerp ...' Private source to author.
27 'Very depressed ...' RH to author, Tehran, 4 December 1975.
28 'No intention ...' *A Damned Serious Business*, p. 109.
29 'Fairly riotous ...' *Ibid.*
30 'Only peasants ...' *Ibid.*
31 'It would have been ...' Peter Ustinov interviewed London, 19 September 1991.
32 'As he airily ...' *The Times*, 18 October 1954.
33 'A character who appears ...' Dilys Powell, *Sunday Times*, 17 October 1954.
34 'Harrison plays ...' Philip Hamburger, *New Yorker*, 28 August 1954.
35 'A greased ...' Howard Thompson, *New York Times*, 23 August 1954.
36 'The husband's career ...' RH quoted in *New York Times*, undated reference, probably August 1954.

17: 'Ravished over Cold Beef'

1 'A freak ...' Donald Zec, *Daily Mirror*, 3 June 1954.
2 'One husband ...' Sally Staples, *Sunday Express*, 5 February 1949.
3 'Kay made ...' *Snakes and Ladders* by Dirk Bogarde (Chatto & Windus, 1978), p. 147.
4 'I left the table ...' Private source to author.
5 'It was frightening ...' *Rex*, p. 137.
6 'Total ...' *Ibid.* p. 139.
7 'Er, er ... the press fellows ...' Private source to author.
8 '[It was] in the open ...' Lilli Palmer, *op. cit.*, p. 266.
9 'Lilli's got ...' Private source to author.
10 'Rex Harrison ...' *The Noël Coward Diaries*, ed. Graham Payn & Sheridan Morley (Weidenfeld, 1982), p. 241.
11 'I was with Rex ...' Lawrence Evans interviewed London, 18 December 1990, 21 February 1991, 27 November 1991.
12 'Take a lover ...' Lilli Palmer, *op. cit.*, p. 268.
13 'Oh, for God's sake ...' *For Adults Only* by Diana Dors (W.H.Allen, 1978), p. 134.

18: Tyrannosaurus Rex

1 'But he couldn't face up ...' Sheridan Morley interviewed London, 24 February 1991.

2 'Were covered ...' Alan J. Lerner quoted Roy Mosley *et al.*, *op. cit.*, p. 158.

3 'I hate them ...' *A Damned Serious Business*, p. 117.

4 'If you do ...' Edith Jackson interviewed London, *circa* November 1984.

5 'She had grown up ...' *Rex*, p. 138.

6 'I don't know why ...' *On the Street Where I Live* by Alan J. Lerner (Norton, 1978), p. 63.

7 'Well, what do you ...' *The Moon's a Balloon* by David Niven (Hamish Hamilton, 1971), p. 264.

8 'Binkie made possible ...' *Binkie Beaumont* by Richard Huggett (Hodder & Stoughton, 1989), p. 462.

9 '[It] isn't how much ...' Alan J. Lerner, *op. cit.*, p. 59.

10 'The commitment to marriage ...' *Ibid.*, p. 57.

11 'It's a melancholy ...' *Ibid.*, p. 92.

12 'No, I don't ...' *Ibid.*, p. 57.

13 'Very tiresome ...' *Cecil Beaton* by Hugo Vickers (Weidenfeld, 1985), p. 391.

14 'You'll look ...' Alan J. Lerner, *op. cit.*, p. 101.

15 'What did you say? ...' Robert Morley to author.

16 'Out from behind ...' *Time*, 23 July 1956.

17 'I thought it ...' P. G. Wodehouse *cit. P. G. Wodehouse: A Biography* by Frances Donaldson (Weidenfeld, 1982), pp. 345–6.

18 'Dedicated and priestlike ...' *Rex*, p. 150.

19 'Sometimes in the hurry ...' Dirk Bogarde, *op. cit.*, p. 159.

19: The Masquerade

1 'You are both ...' Lilli Palmer, *op. cit.*, p. 275.

2 'I would marry ...' *Rex*, p. 152.

3 'A fairy tale ...' Lilli Palmer quoted by Lawrence Evans to author.

4 'I could marry ...' Lilli Palmer, *op. cit.*, p. 276.

5 'Let's face it ...' *Daily Mail*, 15 February 1957.

6 'Harrisburg ... the youngest blimp ...' *Ibid.*

7 'Come home ... sort of yellow.' RH quoted by Jones Harris to author.

8 'What rubbish ...' RH to author, Tehran, 3 December 1975.

9 'Is it possible ...' *Ibid.*

10 'Charlie's brilliant ...' *Ibid.*

11 'Good God ...' *Daily Express*, 16 January 1958.

12 'We wouldn't play ...' RH quoted by Lawrence Evans to author.

13 'He took exception ...' The Hon. William Douglas Home interviewed Kilmeston, 4 November 1990.

14 'I assure you ...' *I Remember It Well* by Vincente Minnelli (Doubleday, 1974), p. 320.

15 'She garbles ...' A. H. Weiler, *New York Times*, 15 August 1958.
16 'Although they last ...' *Ibid.*

20: Circle of Deception

1 'You won't be needing ...' Richard Huggett, *op. cit.*, p. 464.
2 'But I do need ...' *Ibid.*, p. 464.
3 'Well, you won't ...' *Ibid.*, p. 465.
4 'Rex, my dear ...' *Ibid.*, p. 465.
5 'Rex, please don't ...' *Ibid.*, p. 466.
6 'It's like a housewife ...' RH to David Lewin, *Daily Mail*, 2 March 1959.
7 'And Miss Kendall ...' Roy Moseley *et al.*, *op. cit.*, p. 187.
8 'The poor dear ...' Graham Payn and Sheridan Morley, *op. cit.*, p. 385.
9 'I shall let ...' Lilli Palmer, *op. cit.*, p. 279.
10 'Reeked of deceit ...' *Ibid.*, p. 278.
11 'You know what ...' *Sunday Express*, 29 March 1959.
12 'Kay and I ...' Stanley Donen, interviewed Beverly Hills, 17 April 1991.
13 'A death watch ...' RH quoted by Barbosa to author.
14 'I'm only here ...' *Daily Mail*, 31 August 1959.
15 'To that church ...' Private source to author.

21: The Reluctant Widower

1 'Be kind ...' Dirk Bogarde, *op. cit.*, p. 157.
2 'How long do you ...' Jon Bradshaw, *Esquire*, July 1972.
3 '[Rattigan] put out ...' Michael Darlow and Gillian Hodson, *op. cit.*, p. 252.
4 'There was ...' Lilli Palmer, *op. cit.*, p. 280.
5 'You did well ...' *Ibid.*, p. 280.
6 'It's nice to know ...' *Daily Mail*, 9 May 1958.
7 'Rex did brilliantly ...' Peter Brook interviewed Paris, 27 February 1992.
8 'It has been ...' *Doris Day: Her Own Story* by A. E. Hotchner (W. H. Allen, 1976), p. 217.
9 'God is ...' *Rex*, p. 182.
10 'We are still friends ...' *Sunday Express*, 27 March 1960.
11 'So I've been told ...' Tammy Grimes interviewed New York, 12 December 1991.
12 'I was instantly ...' *Confessions of an Actor* by Laurence Olivier (Weidenfeld, 1982), p. 180.

22: The Enchanter's Castle

1 'Outrage ...' *No Bells on Sunday*, ed. Alexander Walker (Pavilion, 1984) p. 43.
2 'Rex crackled ...' *Ibid.*, pp. 43–44.

3 'A guarded look ...' *Ibid.*, p. 44.

4 'Being a Celt ...' Lindsay Anderson, interviewed London, 24 March 1991.

5 'Cut a dash ...' *Ibid.*, p. 44.

6 'He looked at me ...' *Ibid.*, p. 47.

7 'Rachel, has it ever ...' Karel Reisz to author, *circa* May 1983.

8 'And *de luxe* it was ...' Rachel Roberts, *op. cit.*, p. 47.

9 'Why should I go ...?' RH quoted by Tammy Grimes to author.

10 'A word of advice ...' James Hill, *op. cit.*, p. 222.

11 'I would not be surprised ...' *Daily Telegraph*, 8 July 1961.

12 'The new one ...' Rachel Roberts, *op. cit.*, p. 51.

13 'Squandered it ...' *Almost a Gentleman* by John Osborne (Faber, 1991), p. 196.

14 'I wrapped a sock ...' Rachel Roberts, *op. cit.*, p. 51.

15 'Gleam again ...' *Ibid.*, p. 51.

16 'The cupidity of rich actors ...' John Osborne, *op. cit.*, p. 187.

17 'I don't think ...' Rachel Roberts, unpublished diaries.

18 'You did what anyone ...' *Ibid.*

19 'For God's sake ...' *Ibid.*

20 'The world was not ...' Rachel Roberts, *op. cit.*, p. 58.

21 'A stop-gap ...' *Rex*, p. 198.

22 'Made it plain ...' Karel Reisz to author, *circa* May 1983.

23 'Puffed up ...' Rachel Roberts, *op. cit.*, p. 58.

24 'We both drank ...' Rachel Roberts, unpublished diaries.

23: 'By George, I've Got It!'

1 'Before I married ...' Clive Hirschhorn, *Sunday Express*, 23 September 1978.

2 'Want a vodka?' Jean Marsh to author, *circa* September 1983.

3 'Both of us ...' *Ibid.*

4 'When *My Fair Lady* ...' Los Angeles *Times*, 8 May 1960.

5 'Not only will I not ...' Cary Grant, anecdotal evidence from many sources.

6 'Sorry, *signora* ...' Rachel Roberts, *op. cit.*, p. 88.

7 'I hope O'Toole ...' Letter from George Cukor to Steve Trilling, 24 September 1962, USC archives.

8 'To take pictures *à la playboy* ...' Rachel Roberts, unpublished diaries.

9 'A few silly snaps ...' Rachel Roberts, *op. cit.*, p. 62.

10 'By George ...' Nancy Holmes to author, *circa* August 1983.

11 'You know ...' Stanley Donen to author.

12 'It seemed like ...' Rachel Roberts, unpublished diaries.

13 'I was looking ...' Rachel Roberts, *op. cit.*, p. 62.

14 'Hell, he looks ...' *Daily News*, 23 April 1963.

15 'Elegant and guarded ...' Rachel Roberts, *op. cit.*, p. 65.

16 'A terrible little faggot ...' *Ibid.*, p. 64.

17 'Car from Portofino ...' Invoice in USC Archives.
18 'Rex is surprisingly ...' Hugo Vickers, *op. cit.*, letter from Beaton to Eileen Hose, 27 August 1963, p. 471.
19 'Six years later ...' Hugo Vickers, *Ibid.*, p. 464.
20 'I imagined ...' Rachel Roberts, unpublished diaries.
21 'And he deemed it ...' Cecil Beaton, USC Archives.
22 'The footwear ...' Invoice note, *ibid.*

24: Agony and a Little Ecstasy

1 'Wept and woke up ...' Rachel Roberts, *op. cit.*, p. 65.
2 'Rex would leap up ...' *Ibid.*, p. 65.
3 'I ignored it loftily ...' *Ibid.*, p. 65.
4 'Bright and breezy ...' *Ibid.*, p. 65.
5 'Reverend ...' Rachel Roberts, unpublished diaries.
6 'Your pope opera ...' *Ibid.*,
7 'The Lunts ...' *Ibid.*
8 'Aloof and disdainful ...' Richard Huggett, interviewed London, 22 August 1991.
9 'Anyhow, where ...' Anthony Asquith quoted by Huggett to author.
10 'Didn't want to play ...' Lionel Bart to author, *circa* July 1983.
11 'Here an actor ...' Jack Hamilton, *Look*, 18 June 1963.
12 'He was very, very anxious ...' Charlton Heston, interviewed Beverly Hills, 15 April 1991.
13 'Rex has the temperament ...' *The Actor's Life* by Charlton Heston (Dutton, 1976), p. 203.
14 'Thinks the world ...' *Rex*, p. 215.
15 'An air of evil ...' *Ibid.*, p. 217.
16 'Fish murderer ...' Rachel Roberts quoted by Nancy Holmes to author, *circa* July 1983.
17 'Rachel was lowering ...' *Ibid.*
18 'Of course, the sticky ...' *Ibid.*
19 'Was good but difficult ...' Lionel Bart to author, *circa* August 1983.
20 'Rachel got pissed ...' *Ibid.*
21 'As a proper ...' *Daily Mail*, 15 May 1964.
22 'What I need ...' *Daily Mail*, 3 March 1965.
23 'Noisier than ever ...' Graham Payn and Sheridan Morley, *op. cit.*, 16 May 1965, p. 599.
24 'Pull you down ...' Rachel Roberts, unpublished diaries.
25 'The fit was on her ...' RH to author, London, *circa* November 1982.
26 'How dare you ...' Nancy Holmes to author *circa* August 1983.
27 'Rachel, this is Russia ...' *Ibid.*

28 'Nancy, I've found . . .' *Ibid.*
29 'I'll put you . . .' *Ibid.*
30 'Is that you, Rachel? . . .' *Ibid.*

25: Animal Crackers

1 'Far less relaxed . . .' *People will Talk* by Kenneth L. Geist (Scribner's, 1978), p. 350.
2 'One minute [Rex] . . .' Rachel Roberts, *op. cit.*, p. 73.
3 'The trouble with you . . .' Edith Jackson to author *circa* October 1984.
4 'By all means, Edith . . .' *Ibid.*
5 '[He] was getting . . .' *The Studio* by John Gregory Dunne (Farrar Straus and Giroux, 1968) p. 35.
6 'Absolute misery . . .' Roy Mosley *et al., op. cit.*, p. 233.
7 'He queried . . .' *Ibid.*, p. 234.
8 'You think . . .' John Gregory Dunne, *op. cit.*, p. 95.
9 'Terribly depressing . . .' Letter from Richard Fleischer to RH, 2 November 1965, USC Archives.
10 'I prefer to set . . .' Letter from RH to Richard Fleischer, 19 May 1966, USC Archives.
11 'It was agreed . . .' Letter from RH to Richard Fleischer, 10 May 1966, USC Archives.
12 'If it is possible . . . why shouldn't it be?' Richard Fleischer memo, 30 May 1966, USC Archives.
13 'He couldn't see himself . . .' David Lewin, *Daily Mail*, 2 May 1967.
14 'Simplicity . . .' Richard Fleischer memo, undated, USC Archives.
15 'The first ten minutes . . .' *The Alpha* RHO Journal, Vol. 1, No 2, 'Creation of a Lady' by Alan J. Lerner, p. 5, USC Archives.
16 'Our animal trainer here . . .' Letter from Richard Fleischer to RH, 30 March 1966, USC Archives.
17 'I didn't have to say . . .' RH to Kershaw.
18 'I was driven . . .' *A Damned Serious Business*, p. 198.
19 'Good at looking . . .' *Time*, 22 April 1985.
20 'Before we guessed . . .' Nancy Holmes to author, *circa* August 1983.
21 'What's happening . . .' Pamela Mason to author, *circa* September 1983.
22 'They had to talk . . .' *Ibid.*
23 'But the trouble . . .' *Ibid.*
24 'Rachel sashays . . .' *Ibid.*
25 'First of all . . .' Lionel Jeffries to author, *circa* September 1983.
26 'What a terrible affair . . .' Rachel Roberts, unpublished diaries.
27 'You wouldn't be surprised . . .' Nancy Holmes to author *circa* August 1983.

28 'Rex was a total ...' Pamela Mason to author, *circa* September 1983.

29 'Be a help ...' *Rex*, p. 229.

26: The Gay Life

1 'Terrible bit ...' Lionel Jeffries to author, *circa* September 1983.

2 'That John Mortimer?' John Mortimer interviewed London, 28 November, 2 December 1990.

3 'We drive out ...' John Gregory Dunne, *op. cit.*, p. 190.

4 'Soldier on ...' Rachel Roberts, unpublished diaries.

5 'She needs to work ...' Clive Hirschhorn, *Sunday Express*, 30 August 1977.

6 'She's gone off ...' Edith Jackson to author, *circa* October 1983.

7 '*Excusez-moi* ...' John Mortimer *et al* to author.

8 'Or even *My Fair Lady* ...' John Gregory Dunne, *op. cit.*, p. 197.

9 'Why aren't I playing ...' Ned Sherrin to author, *circa* July 1983.

10 'He was on edge ...' *Ibid.*

11 'Why the hell ...' *Ibid.*

12 'As level as Lords ...' Terence Rattigan to author, *circa* March 1963.

13 'What have you ...' Edith Jackson to author, *circa* October 1983.

14 'What do I want ...' Private source to author.

15 'Stuck like a fly ...' Rachel Roberts, unpublished diaries.

16 'One is watching ...' *New Yorker*, 30 August 1969.

27: The Break-up

1 'Thank God you won't ...' Rachel Roberts, unpublished diaries.

2 'I can't imagine ...' Rachel Roberts, *op. cit.*, p. 84.

3 'I tried to give up ...' *Evening Standard*, 20 November 1968.

4 'Fell into the plane ...' *Ibid.*, p. 84.

5 'The house now so dead ...' *Ibid.*, p. 85.

6 'And the first thing ...' *ibid.*, p. 84.

7 'Actors don't know ...' Joseph L. Mankiewicz to author, 9 April 1988,

8 'You'll never get away ...' Rachel Roberts, unpublished diaries.

9 'Our home in Portofino ...' *Daily Sketch*, 1 September 1959.

10 'It is always satisfying ...' *Daily Mail*, 4 October 1969.

11 'For once ...' *Ibid.*

12 'Rex did a lot ...' Roy Moseley *et al.*, *op. cit.*, p. 243.

13 'Don't give me that ...' RH quoted by Angela Fox to author.

14 'Oh, do shut up ...' Private information to author.

15 'They offered me ...' Nigel Patrick quoted by Richard Huggett to author.

16 'They comedy exists ...' Irving Wardle, *The Times*, 6 November 1969.

17 'In doubt ...' Peter Lewis, *Daily Mail*, 6 November 1969.

18 'Living separately . . .' *Evening Standard*, 19 December 1969.
19 'I am sure . . .' *Daily Mail*, 20 December 1969.
20 'I issued a statement . . .' *Evening Standard*, 20 December 1969.
21 'Let's start married life . . .' Rachel Roberts, *op. cit.*, p. 142.

28: La Vie en Famille

1 'He was enormously attractive . . .' The Hon. Elizabeth Harris interviewed London, 3 May 1991.
2 'I did all this . . .' *Love, Honour and Dismay* by Elizabeth Harris (Weidenfeld, 1976), pp 102–3.
3 'I longed only to be . . .' *Ibid.*, p. 93.
4 'There now . . .' Private source to author.
5 'Are you in love . . .' Rachel Roberts, unpublished diaries.
6 'She had this absurd . . .' Pamela Mason to author, *circa* September 1983.
7 'I thought her so wonderful . . .' Darren Ramirez to author, *circa* July 1983.
8 'Nobody, but *nobody* . . .' Melvyn Bragg and Sally Burton, *op. cit.*, p. 324.
9 'Today you piss . . .' Jon Bradshaw, *Esquire*, July 1972.
10 'A fashionable man . . .' *Ibid.*
11 'I may direct it . . .' *Daily Mail*, 26 July 1970.
12 'I've always been . . .' *Daily Mail*, 23 December 1970.
13 '15,000 reasons . . .' *Daily Mail*, 20 November 1970.
14 'I'm quite satisfied . . .' Rachel Roberts, *op. cit.*, p. 93.
15 'Well, I've got my balls . . .' RH quoted by Robert Flemyng to author.

29: Madness in Great Ones

1 'Well, I have news . . .' RH quoted by Richard Kershaw to author.
2 'Which was she . . .?' RH to author, *circa* November 1982.
3 'She's mad . . . mad . . .' *Ibid.*
4 'The truth lies . . .' Hugh Whitemore, scenario for *The Adventures of Don Quixote*, BBC Television, 1973.
5 'I began to long . . .' *A Damned Serious Business*, p. 205.
6 'Dotty about the church . . .' RH quoted by Elizabeth Harris to author.
7 'In sackcloth tatters . . .' Walter Kerr, *New York Times*, 8 April 1973.
8 'Magnificent, but . . .' Clive Barnes, *New York Times*, 29 March 1973.
9 'After another twenty . . .' Walter Kerr, *New York Times*, 8 April 1973.
10 'From emotional displays . . .' *Ibid.*

30: Expulsion from Eden

1 'During the time . . .' Edward Fox interviewed London, 29 June 1991.
2 'You're a sixty-six-year-old . . .' Elizabeth Harris to author.

31: Ghosts

1 'Silent bargain ...' Terence Rattigan to author, *circa* March 1963.
2 'He's so bad ...' *After Lydia* by Terence Rattigan, *Collected Plays*, Vol. 2 (Methuen, 1985), p. 187.
3 'Roared at some British ...' *Ibid.*, p. 198.
4 'He sticks to things ...' *Ibid.*, p. 198.
5 'It's all right ...' RH quoted by Elizabeth Harris to author.
6 'The [wife] is like ...' Clive Barnes, *New York Times*, 11 December 1974.
7 'Though famed for ...' T. E. Kalem, *Time*, 29 December 1974.
8 'A flicker of an eyelid ...' Brendan Gill, *New Yorker*, 23 December 1974.
9 'We joined them ...' Rachel Roberts, *op. cit.*, p. 121.
10 'How much ...' *Daily Mail*, 10 June 1975.
11 'Just to sell ...' *Daily Mail*, 10 October 1975.
12 'I played the bloody ...' RH to author, Tehran, 5 December 1975.
13 'Why the hell ...' *Ibid.*
14 'Certainly not ...' *Ibid.*, 6 December 1975.
15 'Irrevocably broken down ...' *Daily Mail*, 17 December 1975.
16 'These two arrived ...' Bryan Forbes interviewed Wentworth, 11 October 1990.
17 'Rachel Roberts is crazy ...' Tony Randall to author, *circa* February 1984.
18 'Rex stayed the night ...' Rachel Roberts, *op. cit.*, p. 130.

32: Lady from Singapore

1 'Mercia had a reputation ...' Private source to author.
2 'I've found someone ...' RH quoted by Margaret Gardner to author.
3 'What can I find ...' Laurence Oliver, *op. cit.*, p. 197.
4 'Immensely conceited ...' *Daily Telegraph*, 20 July 1976.
5 '[M. Perrichon] is a Sancho Panza ...' Irving Wardle, *The Times*, 4 August 1976.
6 'To be funny ...' *Ibid.*
7 'Mercia was there ...' Gayle Hunnicutt interviewed London, 21 May 1991.
8 'A good half ...' *Daily News*, 15 December 1976.
9 'Tell her we're not at home ...' Rachel Roberts, *op. cit.*, p. 130.
10 'As I recall it ...' *Ibid.*
11 'Though suavely entertaining ...' Douglas Watt, *Daily News*, 25 February 1977.
12 'Nearer her salad days ...' *Ibid.*
13 'I'm old enough ...' *Daily Mail*, 24 March 1977.
14 'Gave voice to the dry ...' Ned Chaillet, *The Times*, 1 September 1977.
15 'Mercia loves learning ...' Private source to author.
16 'She doesn't understand ...' *Ibid.*

17 'You couldn't fall flatter ...' *Ibid.*
18 'Get Claudette ...' RH quoted by Lindsay Anderson to author.
19 'Harrison [and] Colbert ...' T. E. Kalem, *Time*, 18 December 1978.
20 'A petulant ...' Richard Eder, *New York Times*, 7 December 1978.
21 'An ageing leprechaun ...' Clive Barnes, *Daily News*, 7 December 1978.
22 'I saw that Rex ...' Rachel Roberts, *op. cit.*, p. 140.
23 'Half of me ...' *Ibid.*, p. 160.
24 'Because Rex ...' *Ibid.*, p. 165.

33: Another Hollywood Death

1 'A stop-over ...' RH quoted in Los Angeles *Times*, 18 January 1980.
2 'Down to the last nail ...' RH quoted in *Daily Express*, 23 May 1979.
3 'Astronomical ...' *Ibid.*
4 'Shaw would've been happy ...' *Ibid.*
5 'Platonov, my own ...' Rachel Roberts, *op. cit.*, p. 175.
6 'We embraced ...' *Ibid.*
7 'I left ...' *Ibid.*, p. 174.
8 'Rex was ...' *Ibid.*, p. 175.
9 'All the numbers ...' Athol Fugard to author, *circa* 1983.
10 'Irascibility ...' *Variety*, 30 September 1980.
11 'Childless ...' Rachel Roberts, *op. cit.*, p. 197.
12 'My Rex ...' *Ibid.*, p. 217.
13 'Give San Francisco ...' *Ibid.*
14 'I'd like another ...' Private source to author.
15 'Wine, genuine enjoyment ...' Rachel Roberts, *op. cit.*, p. 223.
16 'Rex was a little ...' *Ibid.*
17 'If only I could ...' *Ibid.*, p. 235.
18 'So home I went ...' Darren Ramirez to author, *circa* July 1983.
19 'Yes, I loved Rex ...' Rachel Roberts, *op. cit.*, p. 233.
20 'Upset ...' *Ibid.*, p. 235.
21 'What am I ...' *Ibid.*
22 'My beloved ...' RH to Sheila Benson, Los Angeles *Times*, 26 November 1980.
23 'Rachel has been found ...' David Lewin to author, *circa* August 1983.
24 'Call Syb ...' Sybil Christopher to author, *circa* September 1983.
25 '... or ever.' *Ibid.*
26 'I don't want ...' Rachel Roberts, unknown date.
27 'It's a tragedy ...' RH quoted in *Daily Express*, 28 November 1980.
28 'Rex's resurrection ...' Pamela Mason to author, *circa* September 1983.
29 'But after Christmas ...' Darren Ramirez to author, *circa* July 1983.

34: A Chill Wind in Manhattan

1 'Far from electrifying ...' Howard Kissel, *Daily News*, 19 August 1981.
2 'Well, don't think ...' Rachel Roberts, unpublished journals.
3 'Rex got a bit ...' Private source to author.
4 'Certainly not ...' RH quoted in *Architectural Digest*, December 1985.
5 'Between takes of ...' Julie Harris interviewed London, 18 October 1990.
6 'If you're cold ...' Private source to author.
7 'A sometimes senile ...' John Beaufort, *Christian Science Monitor*, 8 December 1983.
8 'Sure he is a little fluffy ...' *Our Theatres in the Eighties* by Sheridan Morley (Hodder & Stoughton, 1990), p. 56.
9 'The only scripts ...' RH quoted in *Time*, 22 April 1985.
10 'One producer ...' *Ibid.*
11 'The angries ...' *Ibid.*
12 'Very funny ...' RH quoted by Arthur Barbosa to author.
13 'I'd rather have ...' RH to Sheridan Morley, *The Times*, 16 May 1984.
14 'Essentially the rhythms ...' Sheridan Morley, *op. cit.*, p. 87.
15 'Rex Harrison delivers ...' Jack Tinker, *Daily Mail*, 22 June 1984.
16 'Time after time ...' Kenneth Hurren, *Mail on Sunday*, 24 June 1984.
17 'A mite prone ...' John Simon, *New York* Magazine, 13 May 1985.
18 'Harrison's face ...' Gordon Rogoff, *Village Voice*, 7 May 1985.

35: Full Circle

1 'Noel was a terrible ..' RH to Russell Miller, *Vanity Fair*, April 1985.
2 'A spectacularly bad ...' Douglas Fairbanks Jr, *Daily Telegraph*, 3 April 1985.
3 'Come home ...' RH to David Lewin, *Daily Mail*, 19 August 1986.
4 'I cannot visualize ...' David Lewin, *Ibid.*
5 'Irksome in the extreme ...' RH quoted by Arthur Barbosa to author.
6 'Rex, how are you? ...' Private source to author.
7 'Mentally, I'm always heading ...' *A Damned Serious Business*, p. 231.
8 'It's that very moving ...' *Ibid.*, p. 225.
9 'Even if you don't ...' *Ibid.*
10 'I don't do ...' Stewart Granger to Michael Owen, *Evening Standard*, 17 August 1990.
11 'A lovely piece ...' *Ibid.*
12 'The producers ...' *Ibid.*
13 'One night ...' *Ibid.*
14 'Why didn't ...' RH quoted by Rachel Roberts to author, *circa* 1976.
15 'Glynis ...' Duncan Wheldon, *Loose Ends*, BBC Radio 4, 28 March 1992.
16 'It may not be Maugham ...' RH quoted in *Daily Mail*, 26 December 1989.
17 'We should all be ...' John Simon, *New York* Magazine, 4 December 1989.

18 'Rex Harrison has raised ...' Howard Kissel, *Daily News*, 21 November 1989.
19 'Eyes hooded ...' Clive Barnes, New York *Post*, 21 November 1989.
20 'Tiny glimpses ...' Michael Feingold, *Village Voice*, 5 December 1989.
21 '[Rex Harrison] is so at home ...' Edith Oliver, *New Yorker*, 4 December 1989.

36: The Death of an Englishman

1 'Mercia's got ...' RH quoted by Elizabeth Harris to author.
2 'I don't want to know ...' RH quoted by Carey Harrison to author.
3 'I'm getting a divorce ...' Lady Harrison, *Evening Standard*, 12 June 1990.
4 'I've reached a stage ...' RH, *Evening Standard*, 10 May 1990.
5 'Rex – the very model ...' *Sunday Telegraph*, 3 June 1990.
6 'His ability ...' *Sunday Times*, 3 June 1990.
7 'A man who was ...' Hugo Vickers, *Independent*, 4 June 1990.
8 'The accumulated glory ...' Edward Fox, *Sunday Telegraph*, 3 June 1990.
9 'He was always ...' Patrick Garland, *Sunday Telegraph*, 3 June 1990.
10 'He was loyal ...' Dame Maggie Smith, memorial service for RH, The Little Church Around the Corner, New York, 17 June 1990.
11 'Rather exciting ...' Jane, Duchess of Somerset, to author, 30 April 1992.

Bibliography

I wish to express my indebtedness to the authors and publishers of the following works, from which 'fair usage' quotation appears in the text of this book.

Aumont, Jean-Pierre: *Sun and Shadow* (Norton, 1976)

Bogarde, Dirk: *Snakes and Ladders* (Chatto & Windus, 1978)

Bragg, Melvyn: *Rich, The Life of Richard Burton* (Hodder & Stoughton, 1988)

Browne, E.Martin: *The Making of T.S.Eliot's Plays* (Cambridge University Press, 1969)

Culver, Roland: *Not Quite a Gentleman* (Kimber, 1979)

Donaldson, Frances: *The Actor-Manager* (Weidenfeld, 1970)

Donaldson, Frances: *Freddy Lonsdale* (Heinemann, 1958)

Donaldson, Frances: *P. G. Wodehouse: A Biography* (Weidenfeld, 1982)

Dors, Diana: *For Adults Only* (W.H.Allen, 1978)

du Maurier, Daphne: *Gerald*

Dunne, John Gregory: *The Studio* (Farrar, Straus & Giroux, 1968)

Eliot, T.S.: *The Cocktail Party* (Faber, 1950)

Fox, Angela: *Slightly Foxed* (Fontana, 1987)

French, Harold: *I Never Thought I Could* (Secker & Warburg, 1973)

Geist, Kenneth L.: *People Will Talk* (Scribner's, 1978)

Harris, Elizabeth: *Love, Honour and Dismay* (Weidenfeld, 1976)

Harrison, Rex: *A Damned Serious Business* (Bantam, 1989)

Harrison, Rex: *Rex* (Macmillan, 1975)

Hill, James: *Rita Hayworth: A Memoir* (Simon & Schuster, 1973)

Hotchner, A.E.: *Doris Day: Her Own Story* (W.H.Allen, 1976)

Huggett, Richard: *Binkie Beaumont* (Hodder & Stoughton, 1989)

Lerner, Alan J.: *On the Street Where I Live* (Norton, 1978)

Masters, John: *Bugles and a Tiger* (Michael Joseph, 1956)

Minnelli, Vincente: *I Remember It Well* (Doubleday, 1974)

Monsarrat, Nicholas: *Life Is a Four-Letter Word* (Cassell, 1966)

Morley, Sheridan: *Our Theatres in the Eighties* (Hodder & Stoughton, 1990)

Moseley, Roy with Philip and Martin Macheter: *Rex Harrison* (New English Library, 1987)

Niven, David: *The Moon's a Balloon* (Hamish Hamilton, 1971)

Olivier, Laurence: *Confessions of an Actor* (Weidenfeld, 1982)

Osborne, John: *Almost a Gentleman* (Faber, 1991)

Palmer, Lilli: *Change Lobsters and Dance* (Macmillan, NY, 1976)

Pascal, Valerie: *The Disciple and His Devil* (Michael Joseph, 1971)

Payn, Graham and Morley, Sheridan ed: *The Noël Coward Diaries* (Weidenfeld, 1982)

Rattigan, Terence: *Collected Plays* (Hamish Hamilton, 1953)

Selznick, Irene Mayer: *A Private View* (Weidenfeld, 1983)

Silverman, Steven: *David Lean* (Andre Deutsch, 1989)

Vickers, Hugo: *Cecil Beaton* (Weidenfeld, 1985)

Walker, Alexander, ed.: *No Bells on Sunday: The Journals of Rachel Roberts* (Pavilion, 1984)

Wilcox, Herbert; *Twenty-Five Thousand Sunsets* (The Bodley Head, 1967)

Thanks are expressed to the following newspapers and journals from which quotations appear in the text in this order:

New York Post, Timer, Esquire, The New York Times, Brooklyn Daily Eagle, New York Evening Journal, New York Daily Mirror, Film Weekly, Theatre World, The Observer, Lilliput, The Tatler, Los Angeles Times, Photoplay, The Times, Los Angeles Examiner, Daily Express, The Sunday Times, The Daily Telegraph, The New Statesman, Variety, The New Yorker, Daily Mirror, New York Magazine, Sunday Express, Daily Sketch, Evening Standard, Architectural Digest, Christian Science Monitor, The Mail on Sunday, Village Voice, Vanity Fair, The Sunday Telegraph.

Index